Lecture Notes in Artificial Intelligence 992

Subseries of Lecture Notes in Computer Science
Edited by J. G. Carbonell and J. Siekmann

Lecture Notes in Computer Science

Edited by G. Goos, J. Hartmanis and J. van Leeuwen

D1649129

Springer
Berlin
Heidelberg
New York
Barcelona
Budapest
Hong Kong
London
Milan
Paris
Santa Clara
Singapore
Tokyo

Marco Gori Giovanni Soda (Eds.)

Topics in
Artificial Intelligence

4th Congress of the Italian Association
for Artificial Intelligence AI*IA '95
Florence, Italy, October 11-13, 1995
Proceedings

 Springer

Series Editors

Jaime G. Carbonell, Carnegie Mellon University, USA

Jörg Siekmann, University of Saarland, DFKI, Germany

Volume Editors

Marco Gori
Giovanni Soda
Universitá di Firenze, Dipartimento di Sistemi e Informatica
Via S. Marta, 3, I-50139 Firenze, Italy

Cataloging-in-Publication Data applied for

Die Deutsche Bibliothek - CIP-Einheitsaufnahme

Topics in artificial intelligence : Florence, Italy, October 11 -
13, 1995 ; proceedings / Marco Gori ; Giovanni Soda (ed.). -
Berlin ; Heidelberg ; New York ; Barcelona ; Budapest ; Hong
Kong ; London ; Milan ; Paris ; Tokyo : Springer, 1995
  (Lecture notes in computer science ; Vol. 992 : Lecture notes in
  artificial intelligence) (... conference of the Italian Association for
  Artificial Intelligence, AIIA ; 4)
  ISBN 3-540-60437-5
NE: Gori, Marco [Hrsg.]; 1. GT; Italian Association for Artificial
  Intelligence: ... congress of ...

CR Subject Classification (1991): I.2

ISBN 3-540-60437-5 Springer-Verlag Berlin Heidelberg New York

© Springer-Verlag Berlin Heidelberg 1995
Printed in Germany

Typesetting: Camera ready by author
SPIN 10485804   06/3142 – 5 4 3 2 1 0   Printed on acid-free paper

Preface

This book collects the 43 (31 long and 12 short) papers that have been selected for the scientific track of the Fourth Congress of the Italian Association for Artificial Intelligence. In the selection of the papers, the Program Committee has selected long papers from contributions presenting more complete work and short papers from those reporting ongoing research or results whose presentation could be kept short.

The papers have been distributed into 10 specific topics and report significant research, with a truly international character, in the most attractive fields of artificial intelligence.

Besides consolidated and traditional topics, with a well-established tradition in Italy, such as knowledge representation, automated reasoning, natural language processing, machine learning, and robotics and planning, there are papers on cognitive models, distributed artificial intelligence, connectionist models, model based reasoning, and fuzzy systems. We warmly encourage a rich and profitable interaction among these areas, and we welcome the presence of new approaches as a sign of liveliness in the research on artificial intelligence. Although the presence of papers on apparently loosely related topics requires different formalisms and theoretical background, we are confident that many intriguing aspects involving artificial intelligence lie in these differences.

Inspecting the book we can see significant interest in natural language processing, machine learning, knowledge representation, robotics and planning, which are all topics for which two sessions are reserved in the congress. The highest number of papers is in machine learning, an area that has been receiving growing attention, and that is also likely to interact strongly with emerging models based on neural networks and fuzzy systems.

Although far from representing a comprehensive volume on artificial intelligence research, we believe that this book gives a clear picture of most interesting active areas and most promising directions in the field.

Finally, we warmly acknowledge the financial support of the Consiglio Nazionale delle Ricerche (Comitato Scienze d'ingegneria e Architettura e Comitato Scienze e Tecnologia dell'informazione) for having partially covered the publication of this book.

Florence, July 1995   Marco Gori and Giovanni Soda

Foreword

The Congress of the Italian Association for Artificial Intelligence is a traditional calendar event in the field of artificial intelligence for both researchers interested in methodological aspects and practitioners involved in applications. The congress is the most relevant Italian event in the field of artificial antelligence and receives the attention of many researchers from different countries.

The fourth meeting, this year, is held in Florence and is organized into 14 scientific tracks with 43 papers and one application track with 5 papers.

In addition to the contributed papers collected in this book, the program includes invited talks and tutorials covering advanced topics. Invited speakers are Robert Milne of the Intelligent Applications Ltd (Scotland) and Jude Shavlik of the University of Wisconsin (USA), who give talks on building intelligent applications and on the integration of symbolic and connectionist models, respectively.

Two additional workshops are scheduled with the purpose of illustrating significant applications in the field of artificial intelligence. The first one deals with the role of knowledge-based technologies in management, while the second one covers the application of artificial intelligence to public administration. These workshops have been mainly conceived for potential users of artificial intelligence technologies so as to stimulate active interactions with them. I am confident that such interactions are fundamental to building significant applications, and that they are also likely to provide a useful feedback to theoretical investigations.

Many people have contributed in different ways to the success of the congress. First of all, the members of the Program Committee who efficiently handled the reviewing of the 101 submitted papers for the scientific track. They provided three in-depth reviews for each manuscript by relying on the support of valuable reviewers. The Organizing Committee worked hard to solve all typical problems related to local arrangements. I thank them all very much for their support.

Special thanks go to Piero Torasso, who chaired the last edition of the congress, for his valuable support in solving of a number of different problems arising during the organization.

The last word is for Marco Gori and Elisabetta Grazzini who have shared with me all the problems related to the arrangement of the events of the congress.

Florence, July 1995   Giovanni Soda, AI*IA95 Program Chairman

Program Chairman
Giovanni SODA (Università di Firenze)

Program Committee - Scientific Track
Stefania BANDINI (Università di Milano)
Amedeo CAPPELLI (CNR - Pisa)
Amedeo CESTA (CNR - Roma)
Marco COLOMBETTI (Politecnico di Milano)
Mauro DI MANZO (Università di Genova)
Floriana ESPOSITO (Università di Bari)
Massimo GALLANTI (CISE - Milano)
Fausto GIUNCHIGLIA (IRST e Università di Trento)
Marco GORI (Università di Firenze)
Leonardo LESMO (Università di Torino)
Daniele NARDI (Università di Roma)
Enrico PAGELLO (Università di Padova)
Vito ROBERTO (Università di Udine)
Oliviero STOCK (IRST - Trento)
Giuseppe TRAUTTEUR (Università di Napoli)
Franco TURINI (Università di Pisa)

Program Committee - Application Track
Franco CANEPA (Imit - Novara)
Giannetto LEVIZZARI (Centro Ricerche FIAT - Orbassano (TO))
Fabio MALABOCCHIA (Cselt - Torino)
Fulvio MARCOZ (Alenia - Roma)
Renato PETRIOLI (Fondazione Bordoni - Roma)
Roberto SERRA (Ferruzzi Finanziaria - Ravenna)
Lorenzo TOMADA (Agip - Milano)

Organizing Commitee
Carlo BIAGIOLI (IDG - CNR Firenze)
Francesca CESARINI (Università di Firenze)
Marco GORI (Università di Firenze)
Elisabetta GRAZZINI (Università di Firenze)
Fabio PIPPOLINI (IAMI - CNR - Firenze)

Referees

Amati G.
Apolloni B.
Apt K.R.
Armando A.
Artale A.
Attardi G.
Badaloni S.
Bandini S.
Barbuti R.
Bison P.
Boldrin L.
Bonarini A.
Bonatti P.
Bouquet P.
Bresciani
Cadoli M.
Caglioti V.
Campadelli P.
Cappelli A.
Carlucci Aiello L.
Carpineto C.
Castelfranchi C.
Catarsi M.N.
Cattoni R.
Cesta A.
Chella A.
Cialdea M.
Ciapessoni E.
Cimatti A.
Ciravegna F.
Coiawiz T.
Colombetti M.
Console L.
Conte R.
Contiero S.
Crippa G.

D'Aloisi D.
De Giacomo G.
Di Manzo M.
Dondossoia G.
Donini F.M.
Dorigo M.
Dragoni A. F.
Errico B.
Fabiano A.
Ferrara A.
Ferrari C.
Ferrari G.
Franconi E.
Frasconi P.
Frixione M.
Gallanti M.
Gambardella L.M.
Gaspari M.
Gerevini A.
Ghidini C.
Gini G.
Giordana A.
Giordano L.
Giretti A.
Giunchiglia E.
Giunchiglia F.
Gola E.
Gori M.
Guarino N.
Gunetti D.
Landi L.
Lanzarone G.
Lavelli A.
Lesmo L.
Liberatore P.
Lombardo V.

Maggini M.
Magnini B.
Malerba D.
Mancarella P.
Manco G.
Maniezzo V.
Martelli A.
Massacci F.
Masulli F.
Mauri G.
Mazzeranghi D.
Miceli M.
Milani A.
Moretti L.
Nolfi S.
Not E.
Oboe R.
Oddi A.
Pagello E.
Pecchiari P.
Perini A.
Perona P.
Pianesi F.
Pirrelli V.
Pogliano P.
Portinale L.
Posenato R.
Prodanof I.
Raffaetà A.
Renso C.
Roberto V.
Romano G.
Rosati R.
Ruggieri S.
Rumolo G.
Saitta L.

Salis R.
Santucci G.
Sbattella L.
Schaerf A.
Schaerf M.
Sossai C.
Scutellà M.G.
Sebag M.
Sebastiani R.
Sebastiani F.
Semeraro G.
Serafini L.
Shavlik J.
Simone C.
Spalazzi L.
Sperduti A.
Stock O.
Strapparava C.
Temperini M.
Terenziani P.
Theseider Dupré D.
Torasso P.
Tornielli G.
Trautteur G.
Traverso P.
Turini F.
Valigi P.
Varzi A.C.
Villafiorita A.
Walsh T.
Zaccaria R.
Zanaboni A.M.
Zanardo A.

Table of Contents

Automated Reasoning

Knowledge Representation 2

Cognitive Models

Machine Learning 2

Distributed Artificial Intelligence

Natural Language Generation as Constraint-Based Configuration

Nils Lenke

Universität Duisburg
FB 3 - Computerlinguistik
47048 Duisburg

Tel.: +49-203-379-2007
E-Mail: he233le@unidui.uni-duisburg.de

Abstract: In this paper we propose to view Natural Language Generation as a constraint-based configuration process. Starting from the notion of paraphrases it is shown that an NLG system must be able to explain the existence of free paraphrases and of different styles which are related to interdependent choices during the generation process. It is then shown that traditional systems are not up to this because of their static generation strategies. As an alternative, constraint-based configuration is proposed. With the help of an example it is shown that a typical configuration system, PLAKON, can be used to generate natural language sentences.

1. Introduction

It is a triviality of linguistics that any language may be used to produce an unlimited set of utterances. Of course, only a limited set of utterances can sensibly be uttered in a certain situation. Such a set can be called a paraphrastic set [Hiz 1964] which means that all utterances are believed to "say the same thing in different words". That such a definition is problematic has been shown elsewhere [Lenke 1994]. The problem becomes obvious if different views on the number of such paraphrases are compared. On the one hand, the approach of Meaning Text Theory [Mel'cuk & Zolkovskij 1970], [Mel'cuk 1981] claims that for one semantic expression more than a hundred thousand paraphrases may exist [Mel'cuk 1981, p. 31f.]. On the other hand, Chafe [1971] claims that (nearly) no paraphrases exist in English, because there are always certain differences between two utterances which may be meaningful to the speaker. He concludes:

> "What I am saying is that the notion that language is full of paraphrases, in the sense of different surface structures which reflect the same semantic structure, is mistaken." [Chafe 1971, S. 11]

Despite the apparent conflict between these two positions, they have both found proponents in the field of computational linguistics. Systems have been proposed that can produce a more or less large paraphrastic set from an expression in a meaning representation formalism. One typical example is the system BABEL [Goldmann 1975]. This approach has been heavily criticised by Hovy [1988] because BABEL produced *free* paraphrases, that is, did not make a motivated choice between them. In Hovy's system, only one formulation is generated as *the* appropriate formulation under pragmatic constraints:

> "Since different realizations of a topic convey different pragmatic effects, the pragmatic aspects of communication must help to control the choices facing the generator." [Hovy 1988, S. 13]

If one wants to follow Hovy, it is clear that the naive position of linguistics which claims that there are many free paraphrases is mistaken. But, on the other hand, are Chafe and Hovy absolutely correct in claiming that there are no free paraphrases and that each choice can be motivated?

2. Free Choice vs. Pragmatic Constraints

Maybe, a look into the human generation process might give an answer to this question. Since this process itself is difficult to look into, we have taken a look at the products of this process, i.e. naturally occuring texts. To be more concrete, we have compared two different translations of the same text ("A Tale of Two Cities" by Charles Dickens), especially with respect to the translation of discourse markers signalling concession. The idea was that in a translation setting the content to be verbalized and the pragmatic parameters guiding the generation process should roughly be the same because they are given by the source text, which serves as the common basis for both translators. A more detailed account of the results has been given elsewhere [Lenke, Grote & Stede 1995]; here, only one typical example can be given:

> (1a) "Though the earth was cold and wet, the sky was clear, and the sun rose bright, placid, and beautiful." [Charles Dickens, "A Tale of Two Cities, electronic version = original]

> (1b) "Obgleich der Erdboden kalt und feucht war, war doch der Himmel heiter, und die Sonne ging hell, ruhig und schön auf." [translation 1]

> (1c) "Die Erde war kalt und feucht, der Himmel aber klar, und die Sonne erhob sich in ruhiger Pracht." [translation 2]

From examples like this, some observation can be made:

- Despite the common basis there are certain differences between the two translations, pointing to a certain amount of free choice between formulation variants.
- Which translation is better depends on the criteria one has. Translation 1 is nearer to the original whereas translation 2 may be better stylistically (e.g. it avoids the double "war" of translation 1).
- Choices in one part of the translation constrain the choices in another part: Choosing "obgleich" as the translation of "though" at the same time chooses a hypotactic construction (translation 1), whereas the choice of a paratactic construction requires the use of a paratactic conjunction like "aber" (translation 2). This point is central to the argumentation of this paper and will be elaborated below.
- If the whole text is examined, certain translation patterns emerge, which are typical for a certain translator. These patterns amount to different *styles* of these translators (and, similarly, of authors in general).

To conclude, one can say that a model of the text generation process has to allow for the following:

- It must be able to produce an appropriate formulation considering pragmatic constraints.

- It must account for different formulations if the priorities of the constraints are changed.
- It must also allow for a certain amount of free variation.
- It must account for the interdependencies between different choices.
- It must be able to explain the existence of different styles.

Generation systems and architectures that have been proposed so far do not fulfill these requirements as will be shown below. We will therefore propose a new framework which seems promising in this respect. As a preparation for the introduction of this framework, we will here describe as an analogy a situation in which requirements similar to those given above are valid: the construction of car. A look at the cars in our streets shows that:

- Certain features of a car are firmly required by the function of a car: transportation. So, a car needs some wheels and an engine.
- Different priorities produce different cars: cheap cars differ from fast cars and from cars which are able to carry a heavy load.
- There is a certain amount of free choice which cannot easily been explained away. There are e.g. cars in different colours and cars with front wheel and back wheel drive.
- There are interdependencies between the choices to be made. For example, if you choose to make a car with four doors it has to be longer or the front doors have to be narrower.
- Different brands of cars show a certain style: Ferraris are nearly always red, Audis always front wheel driven (if not 4wd).

As the construction is seen as a typical *configuration* task it will be proposed here to regard language generations as a configuration task as well. This will be explained in more detail below. First, it will be shown that architectures proposed so far are inadequate.

3. The Architecture of NLG Systems
A well known modularization of the text generation process is the distinction between content selection and form planning, or strategic and tactical generation. It is a topic of active discussion how the interaction between these phases should look like. We will not contribute to this discussion here but concentrate on the form planning aspect. Another distinction can be drawn between schema-based [McKeown 1985] and plan-based approaches [Appelt 1988] to the generation of coherent discourses. What is involved here is the macro-planning of a text, that is, its segmentation into paragraphs and sentences and relations among them.
We are here more concerned with the micro planning aspect, that is the planning of a single sentence. This includes the selection between syntactic features and the selection of words or lexicalisation. Many early systems simplified this task by assuming a 1:1 mapping between concepts and words. Then, a real choice between words simply is not necessary. Obviously, such an approach is not adequate for the generation of high quality texts. But, if a real lexicalisation takes place, then the question arises how it is related to the syntactic choice processes, i.e. the choices paratactic vs. hypotactic clause complex, active vs. passive and the like. In principle, three answers have been given to this question: lexicalisation first, lexicalisation last and lexicalisation and syntax intertwined [Matthiesen 1991: 277ff.].

4

Lexicalisation first. Many systems take this approach because of the following: The syntactic nature of a sentence is highly dependent on the verb[1], on its semantic and syntactic case frame. It is therefore a plausible strategy to select the verb first and organize the syntactic structure accordingly.

Lexicalisation last. On the other hand, in many cases the syntactic nature of a sentence is given in advance, for example, because a certain phrase has to be thematic (i.e. fronted), or the sentence is to be built in parallel to its predecessor. In such a case, the words have to be inserted into a syntactic structure and have to be selected accordingly.

Lexicalisation and syntax intertwined. This is the solution propagated in Systemic Functional Grammar [Matthiesen 1991: 278]. Here, a lexico-grammatical stratum is assumed which combines syntactic and lexical choices. This is the obvious consequence from the observation that both argumentations given above are valid. If one takes a closer look at this approach some problems emerge. First of all, proponents admit that lexicalisation choices take place at the most delicate systems of the lexico-grammatical stratum:

> "Lexis and grammar together constitute one unified resource, called *lexicogrammar* in systemic linguistics. Lexis is thus one part of lexicogrammar; more specifically, if we model lexicogrammar as large networks of inter-related grammatical and lexical choices, these choices are ordered taxonomically from very general ones to more specific ones and lexical choices are more specific than grammatical ones. [...] The taxonomic ordering is called delicacy and lexical choices are thus more delicate than grammatical ones." [Matthiesen 1991: 253]

Consequently, the systemic approach is quite similar to the "lexicalisation last"-approach. Indeed, regarding the overall architecture of a systemic generation system, it is hard to see how the selection of a certain word could have consequences for syntactic choices which normally already have been made at that point in time.

As a second problem, the *static order* of the choices may be mentioned. Even if the beforementioned problem could be solved by a subtle arrangement of lexical and syntactical choices in the network, this would still be static, that is, always the same for all sentences to be generated. As will be shown in the next section this is not appropriate. **Rather, we need an architecture which can change the order of choices to be made from sentence to sentence.** This certainly cannot be done by one of the approaches cited above without leading to quite unnatural solutions, e.g. extensive backtracking and revision.

4. Interdependencies Between Choices

As we have seen above, there are interdependencies between the choices which have to be made during the generation of a sentence. In example 1, there is a connection between the choice of a discourse marker for the concession relation ("aber" vs. "obgleich") and the choice between a hypotactic or paratactic construction. Obviously, the two translators made different decisions during one of these choices, leading to a different decision in the other choice, and finally to different translations. But it cannot be said a posteriori in which *direction* the dependency worked. We can only guess that translator 1 decided to stick to the original, chose a near translation of "though" and had therefore to realize a hypotactic construction which lead to the ugly

---

[1] Or vice versa! See below.

"war, war". It could equally well be that he chose the syntagmatic construction to copy the original and had therefore to select an appropriate marker (i.e. "obgleich" , "obwohl" or the like and not "aber", "trotzdem" or the like). That this question cannot be solved here is not so important. What is important is that obviously both directions are plausible and may occur during the generation of a text. In other words: These interdependencies have to be represented as direction independent rules in a generation system and the direction in which use is made of them depends on the specific circumstances of the generation of a specific sentence.

In other areas of AI, such direction independent regularities are modelled as constraints [Güsgen 1989]. Constraints can be used in both directions during processes of constraint propagation which may be used to test a certain configuration or generate a configuration. Constraints are also the central mechanism used in configuration systems. We will argue here that constraints and configuration are an appropriate approach to sentence generation as well.

Constraints have been proposed recently for use in natural language processing. Menzel [1992] uses constraints to analyse mistakes in the context of a computer aided foreign language teaching system. He models congruency relations e.g. between nouns, adjectives and determiners in a noun phrase as constraints. Parsing is shown to be suitable for a solution with constraints in [Blache 1992]. [Saint-Dizier 1992] deals with the modelling of precedence relations in Constraint Logic Programming (CLP). C. Lehner [1993] stresses the similarities between CLP and modern linguistic formalisms like HPSG, CUG and the like. [Emele et al 1992] show how their formalism of Typed Feature Structures (TFS) can deal with the interaction of constraints from multiple linguistic levels, following an argumentation quite similar to the one proposed here. A similar approach has also been followed in COMET [McKeown et al. 1990]. [Ward 1988] has proposed a system using an activation-spreading mechanism to let constraints stemming from different linguistic levels interact.

The rest of the paper will show in some detail that and how constraints can be used in this domain and, more generally, how natural language generation can be understood as a *configuration* problem. This approach has got two advantages over the use of constraints alone: First, configuration systems usually offer a much greater range of strategies for solving the configuration task than the simple constraint-satisfaction strategies of CLP systems or the unification-based strategies of systems like TFS. Second, viewing the generation of natural language as a configuration task offers a new perspective on NLG.

5. Configuration as a Task for Expert Systems

Biundo et al [1994] define a configuration task as the construction of a system that fulfills certain constraints and realizes certain requirements given in advance. AI systems for configuration tasks normally deal with technical domains. Biundo et al [1994] give as a typical example the assembly of a bicycle from second hand parts which is directed by individual demands of a client. They give a list of 6 aspects of a configuration task, these will be exemplified by the corresponding aspects of the bicycle domain and of the natural language domain:

Configuration Objects: This can be abstract classes of objects of which an indefinite number is available or a limited set of concrete objects. In the bicycle domain, these would be the available parts (wheels, frames, screws etc.) and the partial constructions constructed from them. In the NLG domain, these would be the words which are available in the lexicon and phrases which are constructed from them.

Parameters or Features: These are the attributes of the objects. In the bicycle domain, these could be the length of screws, the diameter of the wheels, colour of the parts etc. In the NLG domain, these could be all the usual syntactic (case, gender, number), semantic (human / not human, abstract / concrete), or stylistic (colloquial, negative connotation) features which can be attributed to words and phrases.

Configuration restrictions: These are the constraints which represent the knowledge about what a correct configuration is. In the bicycle domain, these would be the fact that two wheels are necessary, the knowledge that these have to be of equal diameter etc. In the NLG domain, it would be all the syntactic, semantic and pragmatic knowledge needed for the generation of a sentence. All these things, from the knowledge that there has to be a verb and a subject, that a congruency exists between noun and adjective, that the selection of "obgleich" triggers a hypotactic sentence construction (and vice versa) can be represented in a uniform formalism, the constraint formalism.

Demanded parameters: These form the vocabulary for the formulation of the task which is to be solved. In the bicycle domain, it would be the description of the functionality of the bicycle including information about priorities of some features over others in case that a conflict arises. In the NLG domain it would be the description of the sentence to be generated, as it would be generated by the content selection phase. It would include the semantic content to be verbalized, stylistic parameters, words which must be used, and also priorities of some features over others.

Associations of demands with solutions: These encode expert knowledge about how to proceed from demands to solutions and how to evaluate a possible solution in respect of the demands.

Configuration strategies and heuristics: These encode the knowledge about the configuration process itself. They have to decide on the the serialization of choices to be made and on how to resolve conflicts which may arise. Possible strategies are depth-first with backtracking, breadth-first or an intelligent combinations of these. In the NLG domain, this is one of the main advantages over traditional approaches and over CLP based systems because more flexible strategies are possible.

6. A Concrete Example

To make all this a bit more concrete, we will show how an example[2] can be modelled in the framework of a concrete configuration system, i.e. PLAKON[3] [Cunis et al 1991; Cunis & Günter 1990]. PLAKON is a toolbox from which expert systems for configuration tasks in different domains can be constructed. Its modules offer formalisms and algorithms for the six aspects introduced above.

As an example, we will deal with a micro-micro-grammer which is able of generating sentences like the following:

---

[2] To make it feasible for presentation here, the example is *very* tiny and some definitions used in it may seem idiosyncratic from a pure linguistic viewpoint.

[3] I would like to thank Michael Sprenger who invited me to GMD, St. Augustin and helped me transforming vague ideas into a running example.

(2a)   A boy comes despite the rain.
(2b)   Some tiny boys come despite the thunderstorm.
(2c)   Smart nice boys come although it rains.

Besides the obvious syntactic constraints (e.g. the number congruency between subject and verb) there is an interdependency between two choices which is modelled on example 1 and which is of special interest here. It is the interdependency between the choice of the concession marker ("although" or "despite") and the form of the conceded circumstance (clause or nominal group). For example, if "although" is chosen, the weather can only be described with "rain" because no verbal form of "thunderstorm" exists[4]. On the other hand, if "thunderstorm" is chosen, "despite" must be chosen as the concession marker.

Configuration Objects.
These can be modelled in PLAKON with the help of a formalism of the KL-ONE-type [Cunis 1991]. As said above words and phrases have to be represented as configuration objects. It is quite easy to design a word / phrase class hierarchy in KL-ONE, an approach which is not far away from approaches of a hierarchical lexicon, cf. [Daelemans et al. 1992]. For our example, we need 16 classes. The definitions of all 16 classes cannot be given here, the inheritance hierarchy can be seen in figure 1, below. A Nominal Group can be defined as follows:

```
(ist!   (ein NominalGroup2)
        (ein Phrase
               (Number {'Singular 'Plural})
               (part-of
               (:OR     (EIN Clause)
                        (EIN Sentence)))
               (has-parts #{#[(EIN Konstruktionsobjekt) 0 6] ':=
                                 #[(EIN Det) 0 1]
                                 #[(EIN Adjective) 0 4]
                                 #[(EIN Noun) 0 1]})))
```

That is, a Nominal Group is a kind of *Phrase* and has got the syntactic feature *Number*.
Beside the inheritance information there is also information on the has-parts / part-of hierarchy of the construction objects. It is the backbone of any construction process as the constituency (ID-rules) is the backbone of NLG. As can be seen, a Nominal Group may be part of a clause or a sentence and consists of an optional determiner, an optional noun and up to four adjectives. The aim of the configuration process is to obtain a complete specification of one complex construction object. In our domain this is a sentence. Of course, also the linear precedence (LP) of constituents would have to be modelled in a more complete system. This is omitted here, but could be done with PLAKON's *sequences*.
PLAKON allows to model other objects in addition which are no construction objects but so-called *world objects*. These are not changed during the construction process and form the world, into which the unit under construction is to be embedded. In our domain, these could be used to model the semantics of the sentence, i.e. a t-box of concepts describing the meaning of the words and an a-box containing instances of

---

[4] Of course, forms like "a thunderstorm occurs" exist, but cf. the footnote 2 again.

these concepts which together form the content to be verbalized. This has not been done in our example, though.

Parameters and features
Some of these have already been used in the last section for the definition of the configuration parts, e.g. *Number*.

Configuration restrictions
Here, constraints have their natural place. PLAKON allows for different types of constraints [Syska & Cunis 1991]. As has been said above, constraints can be used to model congruency relations, e.g. between a Nominal Group and its parts:

```
(CONSTRAIN ((#?N1 (ein NominalGroup1))
            (#?DET1 (ein Det (part-of #?N1))))
 (EQUAL (#?N1 Number) (#?DET1 Number))
 :NAME NG1NUMBERCONG1)
```

This constraint - as all constraints in PLAKON - consists of two parts: 1) the domain pattern describing when the application of a constraint is appropriate. Here it is the test if we have got a Nominal Group and a Determiner which is part of this group. 2) Then the constraint restriction must hold: the number of the nominal group must be equal to the number of the Determiner. Similar constraints hold for the other parts of a Nominal Group. (The definitons of all 14 constraints used for our example cannot be given here.)
The set of all potential constraints is evaluated after each step of the construction process. If a constraint the domain pattern of which is fulfilled is detected it is instantiated and added to the constraint network of the construction under development. In it, information could - similar to unification in modern linguistic formalisms - flow in all directions. If the number of the NG was known, it could flow downwards to its parts; if the number of one of the words was known from the lexicon it could flow upwards to the group and downwards again to its sisters, and it could flow in more than one way, potentially resulting in a conflict which would have to be resolved.
Constraints can be used to formalize linguistic knowledge of all types. It can e.g. also be used to model the subject-verb congruency and the interdependency of our tiny example mentioned above:

```
(CONSTRAIN ((#?S1 (ein Sentence))
            (#?N1 (ein NominalGroup2 (part-of #?S1)))
            (#?V1 (ein Verb (part-of #?S1))))
 (EQUAL (#?N1 Number) (#?V1 Number)) :NAME SUBVERBCONGS)

(CONSTRAIN ((#?S1 (ein Sentence))
            (#?M1 (ein Marker (part-of #?S1)))
            (#?C1 (ein Circumstance (part-of #?S1))))
 (EQUAL (#?M1 Demands) (#?C1 Type)) :NAME INTERDEP)
```

The second constraint relates the type of the circumstance, clause (e.g. "it rains") or group (e.g. "the rain"), and the type which is demanded by the concession marker ("although" demands a clause and "despite" a group).

Certainly, this could be modelled more elegantly, e.g. with the help of PLAKON's existence-claiming constraints which can introduce new components into the construction. Also PLAKON's (not yet implemented) classification of constraints into hard constraints which must hold and soft constraints which may be relaxed might be helpful. Syntactic restrictions could be modelled as hard constraints, stylistic preferences as soft constraints. The latter ones could then be relaxed to resolve a potential conflict (remember examples (1b) and (1c) in which the translators obviously relaxed different constraints).

What might be surprising at first is that also the lexicon of our tiny example is modelled with constraints. One has to consider that a word in our example is a tupel consisting of a string, the identifier of a concept and the values of the words syntactic features. So the lexicon is a relation which can be modelled as a set of tuples. Cf. the following constraint definition, which describes the lexical entries for verbs of our example.

```
(CONSTRAIN ((#?V1 (ein Verb)))
    (tupel ((#?V1 Number) (#?V1 TERMINALSTR) (#?V1 SCONCEPT))
        (singular COME KOMMEN)
        (plural COMES KOMMEN)
        (singular VRAIN REGEN)
        (plural RAINS REGEN)))
```

The advantage of this type of definition is that it is direction independent once again.

Demanded parameters
These have to be used for the interface between the early phases of the generation process and our configuration-based generator for sentences. With their help, the content of the sentence to be generated and potential restrictions (e.g. of stylistic nature) have to be fixed here.

Associations of demands with solutions
Only one of the aspects mentioned above will be regarded here, namely the evaluation of the sentence under construction against the demanded parameters. PLAKON has got a special feature for that, an interface to external simulation modules [Strecker 1991]. In technical domains, it can be used to add technical simulations of the future performance of the device under construction. In our domain, one could for example add a module which works with a spreading-activation mechanism and is used to test if potential lexical and structural ambiguities can be resolved by the context [Mehl 1993, 1995]. This could not easily be tested by local constraints because more than one sentence may be involved.

Configuration strategies and heuristics
PLAKON's construction process leads from an initial partial construction to the complete solution. The basic mechanism consists of a cycle of 4 steps [Cunis & Günter 1991]:

10

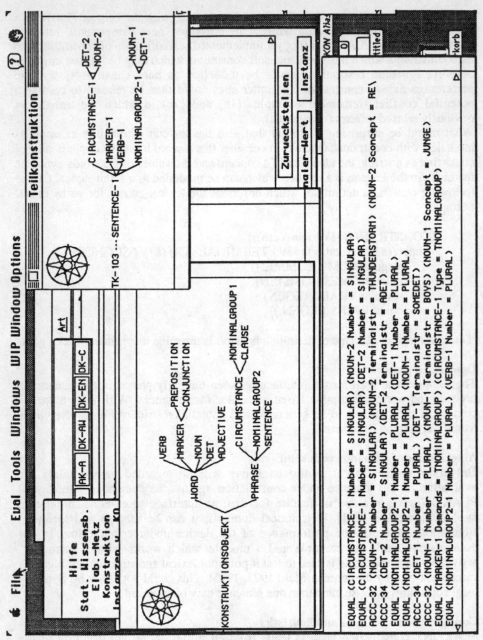

Figure 1: Screenshot of a successfull configuration session with PLAKON.

1. The actual partial construction is fixed.
2a. A set of potential construction steps which could be done next is collected. These could be:
   • decomposing an object along the has-parts-hierarchy.
   • specializing an object along an is-a-relation.
   • integrating a component from already constructed parts along the has-parts-hierarchy.
   • fixing or constraining feature values, e.g. by constraint propagation.
2b. Guided by selection criteria one of the steps is chosen.
3. The selected step is executed.
4. The constraint net is propagated e.g. to test for conflicts which have to be resolved.

It is one of the strengths of PLAKON that the process can be controlled by user definable strategies [Cunis & Günter 1990]. The whole process can be divided into phases, for each phase a separate strategy may be defined. Sets of rules can be defined which test when a change of strategy is needed and which strategy should be used next. Each strategy controls several aspects of the basic cycle, e.g. the selection among the construction steps on the agenda, the fixing of foci describing which parts of the construction should be worked on first, how conflicts should be resolved and many more.

This flexibility of strategies is a major advantage of the configuration paradigm over existing generation systems. It can also be used to explain different styles. Different strategies will lead to different constructions, i.e. sentences, (if more than one is possible). And the same strategy will lead to similar solutions in many sentences. In our example, a simple default strategy was used, which on many occasions interacts with the user and lets him / her choose between alternatives. Figure 1 shows the result of a successful configuration of the sentence "Some boys come despite a thunderstorm".

7. Summary & Conclusion

Starting from the amount of free choice inherent in the task of natural language generation we have put up some requirements that a NLG system must fulfil. It was then shown that traditional architectures are not up to this requirements, especially because of their limited and static strategies. As an alternative, we have put forward the configuration paradigm as a potentially framework for NLG. It was shown with the help of an example how the NLG task can be mapped onto the features of a typical configuration system.

Such a solution would indeed be up to the requirements mentioned above because of its making use of direction-independent constraints and flexible construction strategies. Further research should show how much the AI sub-fields of NLG and Configuration could learn from each other.

8. Bibliography

Appelt, D. E.: "Planning Natural-Language Referring Expressions", in: D. D. McDonald & L. Bolc (eds.): "Natural Language Generation Systems", Berlin: Springer, 1988, pp. 69 - 97.

Biundo, S.; A. Günter, J. Herzberg, J. Schneeberger & W. Tank: "Planen und Konfigurieren", in: G. Görz (ed.): "Einführung in die Künstliche Intelligenz", Bonn: Addison Wesley, 1994.

Blache, P.: "Using Active Constraints to Parse GPSGs", in: Proc. of COLING 92, Nantes, 1992.

Chafe, W. L.: "Directionality and Paraphrase", in *Language*, Volume 47, Number 1, 1971, pp. 1 - 26.

Cunis, R. & A. Günter: "PLAKON. Vorläufiges Handbuch für Version 1.0", 1990.

Cunis, R.; A. Günter & H. Strecker (eds.): "Das PLAKON-Buch", Springer, 1991.

Cunis, R.: "Modellierung technischer Systeme in der Begriffshierarchie", in: [Cunis et al. 1991], pp. 58-76.

Daelemans, W., K. De Smedt, G. Gazdar: "Inheritance in Natural Language Processing", in: *Computational Linguistics*, Vol. 18, 1992, No. 2, pp. 205-218.

Emele, M.; U. Heid, St. Momma & R. Zajac: "Interactions between Linguistic Constraints: Procedural vs. Declarative Approaches", in: Machine Translation 7: 61 - 98, 1992.

Goldman, N. M.: "Conceptual Generation", in: R. C. Schank (ed): Conceptual Information Processing, Amsterdam, 1975, pp. 289 - 374.

Güsgen, H.W. : "CONSAT: A System for Constraint Satisfaction", Pitman, 1989.

Hiz, H. "The Role of Paraphrase in Grammar", in: *Report on the 15th Round Table Meeting on Linguistics and Language Studies*, Washington, 1964.

Hovy, E.H.: "Generating Natural Language under Pragmatic Constraints", Hillsdale: Lawrence Erlbaum, 1988.

Lehner, C.: "Grammatikentwicklung mit Constraint-Logik-Programmierung", St. Augustin: infix, 1993.

Lenke, N.: "Anticipating the Reader's Problems and the Generation of Paraphrases", in: *Proceedings of COLING 94*, Kyoto, 1994.

Lenke, N.; B. Grote & M. Stede: "What is a concession relation and when should you utter one?", paper presented at ICCS-95, San Sebastian, 1995.

Matthiesen, C.: "Lexico(Grammatical) choice in text generation", in: C.L. Paris, W.R. Swartout & W.C. Mann (eds.): "Natural Language Generation in Artificial Intelligence and Computational Linguistics", Boston: Kluwer, 1991.

McKeown, K. R.: "Discourse Strategies for Generating Natural Language Text", in: *Artificial Intelligence* 27, 1985, pp. 1 - 42.

McKeown, K.; M. Elhadad, Y. Fukumoto, J. Lim, C. Lombardi, J. Robin & F. Smadja: "Natural Language Generation in COMET", in: R. Dale et al. (eds.): "Current Research in Natural Language Generation", Academic Press, 1990.

Mehl, St.: "Dynamische semantische Netze. Zur Kontextabhängigkeit von Wortbedeutungen", Sank Augustin: infix, 1993.

Mehl, St.: "Interaction between syntax and semantics: The case of gerund translation", Proc. of the 5th European Workshop on NLG, Leiden, 1995.

Mel'cuk, I. A.: "Meaning-Text Models: A Recent Trend in Soviet Linguistics", in *Ann. Rev. Anthropology 1981*, 10:27 - 62.

Mel'cuk, I.A. & A. K. Zolkovskij: "Towards a functioning 'Meaning-Text' Model of Language", in *Linguistics*, Vol. 5-7, 1970, pp. 10-47.

Menzel, W.: "Modellbasierte Fehlerdiagnose in Sprachlehrsystemen.", Tübingen: Niemeyer,1992.

Saint-Dizier, P.: "A Constraint Logic Programming Treatment of Syntactic Choice in Natural Language Generation", in: R Dale et al. (eds.): "Aspects of Automated Natural Language Generation", Berlin: Springer, 1992.

Strecker 1991, H.: "Simulation in PLAKON", in: [Cunis et al. 1991], pp. 145 - 154.

Syska, I. & R. Cunis: "Constraints in PLAKON", [Cunis et al. 1991], pp. 111 - 130.

Ward, N.: "Issues in Word Choice", in: Proc. of COLING '88, Budapest, 1988, pp. 726 - 731.

Issues of Multilinguality in the Automatic Generation of Administrative Instructional Texts

Elena Not, Emanuele Pianta

IRST - Istituto per la Ricerca Scientifica e Tecnologica
Loc. Pantè di Povo - 38050 Trento (Italy)
tel. +39-461-314444
{not ; pianta}@irst.itc.it

Abstract: In this paper we address the development of a system for the multilingual automatic generation of instructions in the administrative field. English, Italian and German have been taken as target languages and pension forms as target domain. We describe the knowledge resources required to produce coherent and cohesive instructional texts, taking into account the distinction between knowledge about how to communicate in a specific domain and general communication knowledge. To represent domain dependent communication knowledge we introduce the notion of communication schemata as a variant of schemata taking into account the central role of intentions in human communication. We illustrate some types of language dependent variations that a multilingual generation system should be able to cope with.

1. Introduction

Application forms represent one of the main communication channels between the citizens and the Public Administration. Whenever a citizen wants to apply for a document or a benefit, he/she is required to fill out a form, specifying various kinds of information, from personal details to income data. The requested information reflects the current status of the legislation and may be quite complex. For this reason forms very often include instructions that help the applicant to fill them out.

Producing clear and effective application forms, is a major and permanent effort for large public institutions. Every time some changes are introduced in the current legislation about the services offered to citizens or the obligations expected from them, new application forms need to be created or old ones need to be revised. The problem is even more complex in multilingual areas, where public documentation must appear in all the official languages. Administrative agreements between different countries (for example in the pension domain) are another source of multilingual forms, and so could be in the future massive immigration.

A possible solution to the problem of producing and maintaining multilingual versions of forms is the use of automatic tools, such as machine translation or multilingual generation systems. The Gist project (LRE 062-09)[1] explores the latter

---

[1] The GIST consortium includes academic and industrial partners [IRST (Trento, Italy), ITRI (University of Brighton, England), ÖFAI (Vienna, Austria), Quinary (Milano, Italy), Universidade Complutense de Madrid (Spain)] as well as two user groups collaborating actively to the specification and evaluation of the system [INPS - the Italian National Security Service - and the Autonome Province of Bolzano].

solution, addressing the development of a system for the automatic generation of pension forms in three different languages: English, Italian and German.

1.1 Generating Multilingual Administrative Instructions

The major distinguishing feature of a multilingual generation system -as opposed to machine translation- is the fact that the input is an abstract representation of the content from which the generation process starts in parallel for all the different output languages. The advantage is that we avoid all the ambiguity and inconsistency problems posed by the comprehension of a natural language text. Furthermore the representation of the content is not biased by the structure of the source text. This allows the system to plan more flexibly the final texts, choosing, right from the beginning of the planning process, the discourse structures and the cohesive devices that are more natural and effective in each language.

We took the production of bilingual documents (Italian and German) for the Italian bilingual province of Bolzano (PAB) as the reference applicative scenario for the GIST project. Currently, all the public documentation circulating inside the province has to be produced in both languages. For documents with national validity, like laws or forms for benefit claims, the original Italian version of texts is first produced in Rome and then sent to Bolzano for translation. By law, the translation has to guarantee that the texts in the two languages have the same content and the same presentational structure to offer equal opportunities to the Italian and German linguistic groups. We focused our attention on bilingual forms related to pensions issued by the Italian national social security service (INPS). To add more generality to this scenario, in view of the growing needs for multilinguality in the E.U., we also considered English forms produced by the British national social security department (DSS).

The Gist system will re-use and integrate some existing tools and deliver new components on the basis of theoretical and empirical research. The final prototype is expected to provide good quality drafts, to be post-edited by professional writers and/or translators.

2. The Gist Architecture

An overall sketch of the GIST architecture is shown in fig. 1. The system is made up of four main components: the User Interface, allowing the user to input in the content of the message and some global parameters constraining the text generation; the Strategical Planner, building Text Plans for the three languages; three distinct Tactical Generators, responsible for the linguistic realization of the text plans; the Knowledge Base where domain dependent (Domain Model) and general linguistic (Upper Model) concepts are defined.

Some of the components are build re-using or adapting existing tools. The Knowledge Base is implemented[2] using the LOOM representation language [MacGregor and Bates, 1987]. A Generalized Upper Model is used, which is build starting from existing Upper Models for English/German [Henschel, 1993] and Italian (partly developed within the project [Bateman et al, 1994]). All Tactical Generators are

---

[2] See [Fabris et al., 1994] for more information on the implementation of the domain knowledge of GIST.

adaptations of existing systems. For English, the KPML system, developed at IPSI-GMD as an extension of PENMAN [Penman, 1989], is used. The generator for Italian has been developed at IRST and is based on a GB-style unification grammar [Pianesi, 1991]. The generator for German, instead, has been developed at ÖFAI and is based on a HPSG grammar implemented in the FUF formalism [Elhadad, 1991]. The language used to describe the input text plan (ESPL) is an extended version, developed in the project, of the Sentence Plan Language [Kasper, 1989] which has already been used successfully in a number of generation systems. The language ESPL includes features and keywords necessary to describe the semantic content and the structure of the text to be produced in all the three languages.

Other modules have been specifically developed for the project needs. A graphical interface based on the form layout helps the author to specify the instructional content of the form. A menu-based on-line help is provided to inform the author about the alternative items of knowledge available to compose the message. Major research emphasis in the project is put in the development of the strategical component that builds the communicative and the rhetorical structures and selects some cohesive devices. In this paper we will mainly focus on the description of this component.

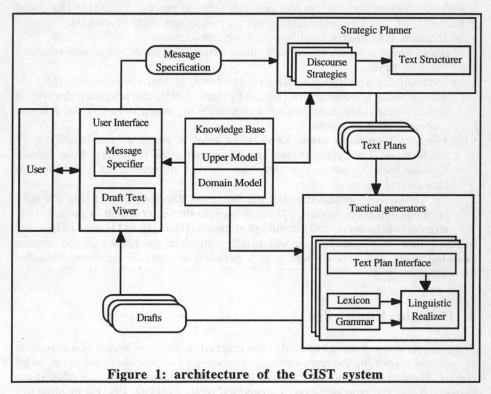

Figure 1: architecture of the GIST system

3. Strategical Planner: the Adopted Approach

Most current approaches to strategical planning agree on the use of some form of schema-like structure to represent precompiled information about how to communicate effectively some information. However the solutions proposed may differ in the importance given to an explicit and detailed representation of the communicative intentions underlying the production of the text. On one extreme, in McKeown's seminal work [1985] -which has inspired the schema-based approach- the connection between intentions and discourse structure is made only at a very high level. On the other side, [Hovy, 1988] and more clearly [Moore and Paris,1993] showed the opportunity of a much more fine-grained representation of intentions, first of all in dialogue systems where user's follow up questions can occur based on the failure of the system's communicative intentions.

In the GIST application domain we found it useful to distinguish -with respect to intentions- between the corpus analysis phase and the system design and implementation phase. During the corpus analysis we examined intentions at a fine-grained level to identify communicatively meaningful textual structures. But for the system design/implementation, considering that in our domain no natural language dialogue occurs between the user and the system, we decided to support only a simplified representation of intentional information.

As first step in designing the Text Structurer we pursued a clear definition of the knowledge sources coming into play in the generation process. Following [Kittredge et al., 1991] we consider as relevant for our purposes three levels of analysis:
- the **Domain Knowledge** level, at which we can identity
  - the *Content representation*, describing objects of the message and relations between them;
- the **Domain Communication Knowledge** level, at which we can identify
  - the *Communicative structure* [Not and Pianta, 1995], characterizing the way in which a domain specific content is textually organised to satisfy the relevant communicative intentions;
- the **General Communication Knowledge** level, at which we can identify
  - the *Rhetorical structure* [Mann and Thompson, 1987], showing how domain specific communicative structures are realized through domain independent rhetorical relations;
  - the *Cohesive structure* showing the linguistic expressions realizing the RST relations and other linguistic phenomena introducing cohesion in the text (e.g. anaphoric expressions and thematic progression) [Halliday and Hasan, 1976].
In the following paragraphs we will briefly introduce the results of the domain knowledge analysis and we will give a detailed account of the communicative knowledge analysis.

4. Domain Knowledge

The analysis of the domain knowledge has resulted in the specification of a collection of concepts supporting the representation of procedures commonly found in our target corpus. These concepts include types of actions, states, objects and a set of relations between them. The representation of procedural relations [ITRI, 1994] is inspired to a plan formalism which is an extension of the STRIPS-style operators developed by Fikes [1971] and expanded in the NOAH system [Sacerdoti, 1977].

As an example of how the instructional content of a text can be represented in terms of concepts and relations, let's consider the following sentences that represent the English translation of an excerpt taken from the INPS form ANF/dip, used to claim family benefits.

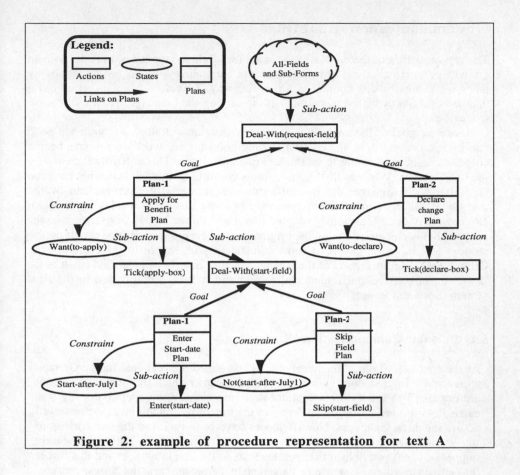

Figure 2: example of procedure representation for text A

Text A:
Tick the appropriate box to indicate whether you are applying for Family Benefit or if you are declaring a change of family situation.
If you are applying for Family Benefit, remember that the benefit runs from the 1st of July of the current year and the 30th of June of the following year. If your entitlement to Family Benefit began after the 1st of July, you must give the date on which it began.

To represent the information contained in this excerpt, a set of entities must be present in the knowledge base (e.g. box, family, family benefit, date). Instances are created for the specific objects occurring in the form. The procedure is represented through plans, actions and constraining states, as sketched in fig. 2.
This procedural representation is automatically build from the message abstract specifications inserted by the user through the input interface.

5. Communication Knowledge

The representation of the content is the same for all three languages, thus the domain knowledge works as a sort of *interlingua*. On the contrary, it is expected that every language expresses this content in a peculiar way. To verify this we carried out a detailed analysis of the corpus aiming at identifying the language specific discourse strategies.

Since the goal of the analysis is to identify discourse strategies to generate good quality instructional text, the optimal starting point for our work would have been a corpus of texts conforming to established quality criteria. This is hardly the case for the GIST corpus. Whereas the English forms conform to English standards for good administrative language, the Italian/German forms are still characterized by the traditional Italian administrative style; only in some cases recent rules for a clearer language have been consciously adopted [Scott and Power, 1994]. For this reason the analysis has been carried out on the original texts, keeping in mind that the discourse strategies to be used may need some adjustment with regard to the current texts. Criteria for the improvement of the language quality have been identified (such as the limitation of passive and impersonal forms) and will be incorporated in the final system [Scott and Power, 1994].

5.1 Domain Communication Knowledge

As the first step of our corpus analysis, we examined the bilingual Italian/German texts and the English ones with respect to the order in which the chunks of content are organised to satisfy the communicative intentions. A comparative study was carried out to verify whether differences in content presentation can be observed across the three languages. No differences have been found in the comparison of Italian and German forms. This is due to the fact that the Italian legislation imposes content parallelism between the texts in the two languages and this forces the German translators to respect a paragraph by paragraph meaning correspondence. On the contrary, substantial differences have been detected when comparing INPS and DSS forms dealing with the same type of information.

The Italian/German forms are divided in two distinguished parts: a graphical part which is a collection of fields to be filled in and a textual part, usually presented on another page, that contains help notes to be read for a correct filling in of the form. In English forms, instead, requests for data and instructions are mixed together. The applicant is told the relevant information right before or after a field or a choice point. Also information is often repeated or restated to make sure that the reader understands correctly.

Another difference comes out in the way in which relevant concept definitions are introduced. In English, legal or complex definitions are often avoided if it is possible to express the same concept in a more intuitive and simple way. See the following example taken from a bilingual Italian/English form (claim for benefit under the Social Security Agreement between Italy and Australia):

Italian: Dispone unitamente al proprio coniuge o separatamente, di somme investite presso consorzi finanziari, grandi o piccoli, oppure di somme giacenti presso istituti finanziari fruttanti interessi oppure di somme prestate a interesse, o di qualsiasi altra somma in qualche modo investita?

Do you (and/or your spouse) own money invested in (big or small) financial consortia, or interests bearing sums deposited in financial institutions or sums lent with interest, or any other sum somehow invested?

English: Do you (and/or your spouse) have any other investments not already disclosed on this form?

More generally speaking, we have identified content presentational patterns that typically occur in the different languages. The exploitation of these patterns by an automatic generation tool is important because if the hearer is told things the way he/she is accustomed to, the understanding effort will be lower and the relevance of the text higher[3].

To represent how these patterns are related to the underlying hierarchy of communicative intentions, we have defined the formalism of *communication schemata* [Not and Pianta, 1995], partially inspired by [Moore and Paris, 1993] . A communication schema is a variant of a rhetorical schema [McKeown, 1985] integrated with the intentions that the presentational pattern is meant to satisfy. A communication schema has the following structure:

HEAD: a descriptor of the type *predicate(arg1,..argn)* that identifies a plan to achieve a set of intentions.
INTENTIONS: a gloss specifying informally the set of intentions that motivate the use of the schema.
EFFECT: a structure describing formally the main intention of the schema (intention to affect the mental state of the hearer).
BODY: a set of sub-schemata that articulate the schema.
CONSTRAINTS: KB related constraints on the applicability of the schema
ORDER: constraints on the order of presentation of the sub-schemata introduced in the body.

We assume that each text in our domain can be described by a *communicative plan* that is produced by the application of one or more communication schemata. Here follows a sample communication schema:

HEAD: procedure(Action,Type,Actor)
INTENTIONS: "to get from the applicant some information and possibly to make him/her to do some related action"
EFFECT: goal(Actor, give-info(Actor,Action))
BODY: optional(context(Action,Actor))
        instructions(Actor,Type,FirstInstruction)
        optional(comment(Action,Actor))
CONSTRAINTS: first_instruction(Type,Action,FirstInstruction)
ORDER: before(context, instructions), before(instructions, comment)

This schema tells that if we want the reader to give some information, the most effective text should contain a sequence of instructions describing the actions he/she has to perform, possibly preceded by some information that help in executing the instructions (e.g. the definition of a relevant concept) and followed by motivations or

---

[3]See [Not and Pianta, 1995] for a more detailed argumentation on this point.

comments on the answer modality.

When a text has to be produced with the communicative goal of having the reader fill out a form, the planning process of the generator is activated with the head "procedure(fill_out_form_X, fill-out, reader)". Then the text structurer chooses a schema in its library that matches the head and recursively expands the heads in the body of the schema. The choice of the suitable schema also depends on the information available in the KB. Figure 3 shows a portion of the communicative plan for text A above.

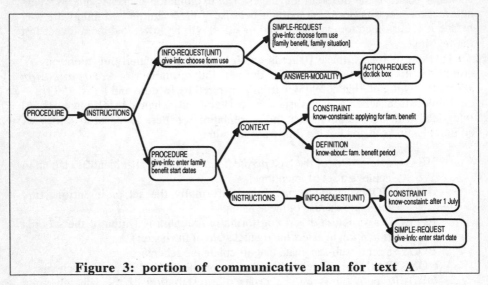

Figure 3: portion of communicative plan for text A

5.2 General Communication Knowledge

To analyze the domain independent links occurring between text chunks we took as theoretical reference the Rhetorical Structure Theory (RST) [Mann and Thompson, 1987]. We observed that, in the various languages, the same content can be structured by different rhetorical relations. For example sometimes in Italian a subordinate clause is introduced in the text whereas in German and in English a coordinate construction is preferred, as in the example in fig. 4, taken from the Italian/German bilingual INPS form *ANF/dip*.

For a multilingual generation system to be able to choose correctly the most effective presentation of the content of the text, it is necessary to identify in each language the discourse context that fires the application of the various rhetorical relations. We defined choice rules that depend on the communicative structure and on the semantic relations between the entities in the domain model. The structure of a rule is as follows:

C-PLAN-ROOT: root of communicative plan to be mapped
C-PLAN-DAUGHTERS: daughters of the above root
SEM-CONSTRAINTS: semantic constraints to satisfy
R-TREE: applicable RST relation

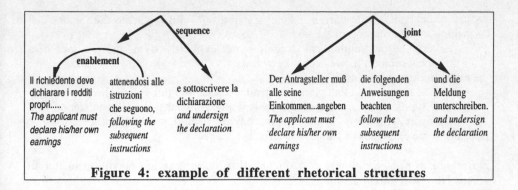

Figure 4: example of different rhetorical structures

Example of rhetorical choice rule:

```
C-PLAN-ROOT:    instructions(Plan,Actor)
C-PLAN-DAUGHTERS:  [request(_,_,Action1,Actor),
                    request(_,_,Action2,Actor)]
SEM-CONSTRAINTS: temporal-sequence(Action1,Action2)
R-TREE: circumstance + [satellite,nucleus]
```

The rules are used to decorate the communicative plan with rhetorical information and may vary across different languages.

For example, we have observed that when a description of how an action can be performed has to be produced, in Italian the emphasis is put on the main action and an *enablement* relation is used (as in figure 4). In English, on the contrary, emphasis is put on the way the action can be performed and a *purpose* relation is preferred (as in "Follow the subsequent instructions to declare your earnings"). See fig.5 for an example of a communicative plan decorated with rhetorical information.

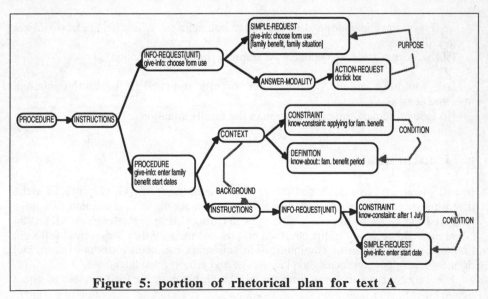

Figure 5: portion of rhetorical plan for text A

A further analysis of the corpus is being carried out with regard to the factors that contribute to the cohesion of the text:

- markers and/or grammatical structures that explicitly signal the presence of a rhetorical relation between chunks of text;
- anaphoric expressions;
- thematic progression that guides the reader's attention through the text;
- other types of grammatical and lexical phenomena, like ellipsis, repetition, synonymy, antonymy, hyponymy, meronymy [Halliday and Hasan, 1985].

Here are some examples of variations across languages:

Difference in the explicitness of a rhetorical relation (explicit condition in Italian versus NP restriction in German):

Sono inabili, se maggiorenni, coloro che ...
[Are unable-to-work, if come-of-age, those who ...]

Volljährige Arbeitsunfähige sind jene ...
[Come-of-age unable-to-work are those who ...]

Difference in thematization:

Il lavoratore - dopo aver indicato i propri dati anagrafici - deve dichiarare ...
[The worker - after having declared his/her own personal details - must declare ...]

Nachdem der Arbeitnehmer seine Personalien eingetragen hat, muss er melden ...
[After the worker has declared his own personal details, he must declare ...]

Different syntactic construction (explicit if-clause in Italian versus nominalization in German):

Se il lavoratore intende segnalare la variazione nella situazione del nucleo familiare gia` dichiarata ...
[If the worker wants to declare a variation in the family situation ...]

Bei Meldung einer Änderung der bereits dem NISF bekanntgegebenen Familiensituation ...
[In case of declaration of a variation in the family situation ...]

6. Conclusion

In this paper we have described the approach adopted in the GIST project for the multilingual generation of instructional texts in the administrative domain. We have analysed the types of discourse strategies and linguistic phenomena that affect the coherence and cohesion of the observed corpus and the way they vary across different languages. The notion of communication schemata has been introduced to model domain-dependent communication knowledge and precompiled intentions.

It is expected that the project results will be highly reusable for a number of direct extensions:

- adaptation of the GIST results to other multilingual administrative environments (i.e. other bilingual areas, European Community).
- extension of the knowledge resources to deal with other domains with strong procedural emphasis.
- interfacing of the system with other automatic tools that build the initial message representation. For example, the GIST generator could be activated by an expert system that reasons on citizens' data to check their social security position.
- integration of the system with a reader model that describes the reader's social security situation and his/her level of expertise with regard to the bureaucratic language. The model could guide the generator to build *reader customized* forms and instructions containing only the relevant information and the options applicable to the specific reader.
- exploitation of tools developed by other projects to increase the flexibility of the output interface of the system. These tools could include, for example, more sophisticated post-editing tools or dictionaries to help revise the text.

References

[Bateman et al., 1990] J.A. Bateman, R.T. Kasper, J. Moore, R. Whitney. *A general organization of knowledge for natural language processing: the PENMAN Upper Model.* Technical Report, USC/Information Sciences Institute, Marina del Rey, California, 1990

[Bateman et al., 1994] J.A. Bateman, Bernardo Magnini, Fabio Rinaldi. "The Generalized {Italian, German, English} Upper Model.", in *Proceedings of the ECAI-94 Workshop on Implemented Ontologies*, Amsterdam, 1994

[Delin et al., 1994] Judy Delin, Anthony Hartley, Donia Scott, Keith Vander Linden. "Expressing Procedural Relationships in Multilingual Instructions", in *Proceedings of the VII International Natural Language Generation Workshop*, Kennebunkport, Maine, 21-24 June 1994

[Elhadad, 1991] Michael Elhadad, *The Universal Unifier User Manual, version 5.0.* Technical report, Dept. of Computer Science, Columbia University, 1991

[Fabris et at., 1994] Giovanni Fabris, Keith Vander Linden and Richard Power. "Implementation of the Upper and Domain Models", GIST deliverable TSP-1b, LRE project 062-09, November 1994

[Fikes and Nilsson, 1971] R. E. Fikes and N. Nilsson. "STRIPS: a new approach to the application of theorem proving to problem solving", *Artificial Intelligence*, 2: 189-208, 1971

[Halliday and Hasan, 1976] M. Halliday and R. Hasan, *Cohesion in English*, Longman, 1976

[Halliday and Hasan, 1985] M. Halliday and R. Hasan, *Language, context and text: Aspects of language in a social-semiotic perspective.* Deakin University Press

[Henschel, 1993] Renate Henschel. "Merging the English and German Upper Model.", IPSI-GMD Report, 1993

[Hovy, 1988] Eduard H. Hovy, "Planning coherent multisentential text", in Proceedings of the ACL, 1988

[ITRI, 1994] ITRI, "Requirements and Architecture Specification", GIST deliverable RA1, LRE project 062-09, May 1994

[Kasper, 1989] R. T. Kasper. "A flexible interface for linking applications to Penman's sentence generator.", in *Proceedings of the DARPA Speech and Natural Language Workshop*, Philadelphia, 1989

[Kittredge et al., 1991] Richard Kittredge, Tanya Korelski and Owen Rambow. "On the need for domain communication knowledge", in *Computational Intelligence*, 7(4), 305-314, 1991

[Mann and Thompson, 1987] W.C. Mann, S.A. Thompson. "Rhetorical Structure Theory: A Theory of Text Organization", in L.Polanyi (ed.), *The Structure of Discourse*, Ablex Publishing Corporation, 1987

[McGregor, 1991] R. McGregor. "The evolving Technology of Classification-based Knowledge Representation Systems", in J.F. Sowa (ed.), *Principles of Semantic Networks. Explorations in the representation of knowledge*, Morgan Kaufmann Publishers, Inc., 1991

[McKeown, 1985] Kathleen R. McKeown, "Discourse strategies for generating natural-language text", in *Artificial Intelligence*, 27(1), 1-41, 1985

[Not and Pianta, 1995] Elena Not and Emanuele Pianta, "Specifications for the Text Structurer", GIST Deliverable TST-2, LRE project 062-09, April 1995

[Moore and Paris, 1993] Johanna D. Moore and Cecil L. Paris, "Planning text for advisory dialogues: Capturing intentional and rhetorical information". Computational Linguistics, 19(4), 651-694, 1993

[Paris and Scott, 1994] Cecile Paris, Donia Scott. "Intentions, structure and expression in multi-lingual instructions", in *Proceedings of the VII International Natural Language Generation Workshop*, Kennebunkport, Maine, 21-24 June 1994

[Penman, 1989]*The Penman User Guide*. Information Sciences Institute, Marina del Rey, California, 1989

[Pianesi, 1991] Fabio Pianesi. "Head Driven Bottom Up Generation and Government and Binding: A Unified Perspective", in *Proceedings of the 3rd European Workshop on Natural Language Generation*, Innsbruck, 1991

[Sacerdoti, 1977] E.D. Sacerdoti. *A Structure for Plans and Behaviour*. Elsevier, New York, 1977

[Scott and Power, 1994] Donia Scott and Richard Power (editors), "Characteristicts of Administrative Forms in English, German and Italian", GIST deliverable EV-1, LRE project 062-09, November 1994

[Sperber and Wilson. 1986] Dan Sperber and Deirdre Wilson, *Relevance: Communication and Cognition*, Basil Blackwell, Oxford, 1986.

Extending Q-learning to Fuzzy Classifier Systems

Andrea Bonarini

Politecnico di Milano Artificial Intelligence and Robotics Project
Dipartimento di Elettronica e Informazione - Politecnico di Milano
Piazza Leonardo da Vinci, 32 - 20133 Milano - Italy
Phone: +39 2 2399 3525 - Fax: +39 2 2399 3587
E-mail: bonarini@elet.polimi.it

Abstract

In this paper, we present how a reinforcement learning approach (ELF - Evolutionary Learning of Fuzzy rules) implements an extension of the popular Q-Learning algorithm to Fuzzy Classifier Systems. We discuss how chains of fuzzy rules may be identified by an evolutionary learning system that provides delayed reinforcement.

We mention other recent proposals for Fuzzy Q-Learning, and we point out how ELF is more efficient, and more suitable to learn behaviors for autonomous agents in unstructured, real environments.

We conclude the paper with an example of the application of the Fuzzy Q-Learning features of ELF to learning a fuzzy system that implements a behavior for an autonomous agent.

1. Introduction

The main goal of the research presented in this paper is to investigate the possibility of using techniques borrowed from *Genetic Algorithms* (*GA*) and *Learning Classifier Systems* (*LCS*) to learn *Fuzzy Logic Controllers* (*FLC*) for *autonomous agents*.

The focus of this paper is on some features of a new, evolutionary learning algorithm (*ELF - Evolutionary Learning of Fuzzy rules*)[3][6], that we have successfully applied to learn FLC for real robots. In particular, we discuss the possibility of applying ELF to learn chains of rules that bring to desired states, where reinforcement is given (*delayed reinforcement*). This problem has been faced by many researchers [7][13] in the last years, mostly using a popular technique: *Q-Learning* [12]. With the increasing interest about Fuzzy Logic applications, some researchers have investigated the possibility of extending Q-Learning with some Fuzzy Logic features [1][8]. Independently, we have implemented ELF [2], where a simple mechanism is oriented to achieve results analogous to those provided by *Fuzzy Q-Learning*. Recently, we have introduced new features bringing this capability of ELF even closer to the basic mechanisms of Q-Learning.

This paper is organized as follows. In Section 2, we provide a background about Q-Learning and the so-far proposed fuzzy extensions of it. In Section 3, we summarize ELF with particular reference to those of its features that are related with Q-Learning. In Section 4 we present the application of ELF to the synthesis of a FLC that implements a behavior for an autonomous agent.

2. Q-Learning and Fuzzy Logic

The aim of Q-Learning is to find a control rule that maximizes at each control cycle the expected discounted sum of future reward. It is based on the estimation of the real-valued function $Q(x, a)$ that gives the expected discounted sum of future rewards for performing action a_k in state x_k, and performing optimally thereafter. At each step $k+1$, the value of the estimate $\hat{Q}(x_k, a_k)$ is updated using the formula:

$$\hat{Q}(x_k, a_k) = \hat{Q}(x_k, a_k) + \beta \left[r_k + \gamma \max_b \hat{Q}(x_{k+1}, b) - \hat{Q}(x_k, a_k) \right] \qquad [1]$$

where b is an action done from state x_{k+1} (reached by performing action a_k in state x_k), r_k is the reward given at time k, β and γ are discount factors, weighting, respectively, the increment with respect to the present Q value, and the contribution to the future states.

In his proposal, Glorennec [8] considers a whole set of fuzzy rules as an *agent* that produces an action a. There is a one-to-one relationship between an agent and the action it produces. Therefore, the performance of each agent is evaluated independently from that of each other. He introduces a rule quality q, that makes it possible to compute $\hat{Q}(x_k, a_k)$, by the formula:

$$\hat{Q}(x_k, a_k) = \frac{1}{2^n} \sum_{i \in H(x_k)} q(i, a_k) \qquad [2]$$

where $H(x_k)$ is the set of fuzzy rules that fire in the state x_k, and n is the number of input variables. Due to introduction of rule quality, the reinforcement can be dispatched to the rules that fire in a state by applying the formula

$$\Delta q(i, a_k) = 2^n act(i) \Delta Q \qquad [3]$$

where $act(i)$ is the mean relative activity of rule i during the time spent by the process in the state x_k. In other terms, in this proposal, several possible combinations of fuzzy rules (that is, FLCs, here called *agents*) are evaluated one at a time. Two problems may arise when applying this approach to learn a FLC for an autonomous agent. First of all, the FLC contains all the possible rules, thus it may be very large and it may be difficult to ensure its correct evaluation [4][6]. Second, a lot of time is required to evaluate all the possible FLCs in a real environment.

Glorennec has also proposed a dynamic version of his Fuzzy Q-Learning [8], where reinforcement is given to agents when they perform better than what they did in the past. This evaluation is done basing on the computation of the error among the current and the desired state. This is an application of the proposed mechanism to a problem different from delayed reinforcement, since at each time step we should evaluate the local performance, and estimate the above-cited error. In the next section we will present how ELF dynamically generates reinforcement for intermediate states, with the only information available in the original delayed reinforcement problem definition.

Berenji [1] proposes another Fuzzy Logic extension of Q-Learning. In this case, we do not have fuzzy rules, but "fuzzy constraints" among the actions that can be done in a given state. The updating formula becomes:

$$\hat{Q}(x_k, a_k) = \hat{Q}(x_k, a_k) + \beta \left[\left(r_k + \gamma \max_b \hat{Q}(x_{k+1}, b) \right) \wedge \mu_C(x_k, a_k) - \hat{Q}(x_k, a_k) \right] \qquad [4]$$

where $\mu_C(x_k, a_k)$ is the degree of satisfaction of the fuzzy constraint C, obtained by the application of C to the state x_k and action a_k. The operator $\wedge$ is a fuzzy *AND* operator, (that is, the "minimum", as the author states). At each step, the action with the maximum Q value is selected, and brings the system in a new state. In this case, actions are not *combined*, as in traditional fuzzy systems, but only *selected*. Thus, the fuzzy extension concerns only the constraints that influence the selection of the action. Since it is not trivial to extend this approach such that it could compare with Glorennec's and ours, we no longer discuss it, although it has been called "Fuzzy Q-Learning".

3. ELF and Fuzzy Q-Learning

In this section, we summarize the main features of ELF, focusing on those related to the evolution of chains of rules, through delayed reinforcement. A more detailed description of ELF can be found in [6].

3.1. Overview of the algorithm

ELF is a Fuzzy Classifier System [11] that works on a population of fuzzy rules. We associate with each rule information about how good it has been judged in its life (its *strength*), and how much it contributed to past actions (its *past_activity*).

We have introduced the concept of *fuzzy* state as a state described by a vector of values of fuzzy variables. A fuzzy state may be visited only partially. This feature is very interesting for the implementation of autonomous agents, where it is important to evaluate also partial achievements of states. Moreover, since more than one fuzzy state may be visited at the same time, possibly with different degrees, we have a smooth transition between a state and its neighbors. This is also a desired property for many behaviors of autonomous agents.

In ELF, the population of rules is partitioned into sub-populations, whose members share the same values for the antecedent variables (i.e., they fire in the same fuzzy state). Therefore, in each sub-population we have rules with the same antecedents, and different consequents, competing to propose the best consequent for the state described by the antecedent.

Since the rules are fuzzy, the same state may be matched by different antecedents. Therefore, the sub-populations cooperate to produce the control action, while the members of a sub-population compete with each other. This is a way to have both the most interesting feature of FLC (*cooperation* among rules), and the feature needed by evolutionary learning systems (*competition* among the members of a population).

The dimension of each sub-population is dynamically adapted according to the current performance of the autonomous agent in the corresponding state. At the beginning, the sub-populations can grow to explore a large search space. As the performance of the agent improves in a state, the maximum number of rules belonging to the sub-population corresponding to that state is decreased, and the worst rule is killed. The goal is to obtain the minimum number of rules with a satisfactory performance.

When the agent is in a state not sufficiently covered with by any rule, a *cover detector* [9] operator generates a new rule. ELF may either build a rule base from scratch, or work with an initial rule base. The agent designer may also define constraints on the shape of the rules, as proposed by Grefenstette [10].

We call a sequence of control cycles ending with a state evaluation an *episode*. Each episode either lasts for a givpn number of control cycles, or ends when a given state is reached. During an episode, only one rule per sub-population (randomly selected among the rules of a matching sub-population) can trigger. At the end of each episode, ELF evaluates the current state, and translates the evaluation into a reinforcement for the rules that have contributed to reach the state, taking into account the learnt limitations of the agent. For a discussion about this feature, see [4] and [6]. ELF distributes reinforcement to the rules that fired during an episode, proportionally to a rule's contribution to the obtained result.

When a FLC has a good performance and does not change for a given number of evaluation steps, it is saved, mutation is applied to the worst rule, and the learning process continues.

At the end of the experimental trial, ELF may have saved many sub-optimal populations. The best one may be selected. For some of the covered states (i.e., for some sub-populations), it may contain more than one rule, each one proposing a different action. For each state the best rule is selected. The so-obtained FLC is the best performing obtained by ELF.

3.2. Reinforcement distribution and Fuzzy Q-Learning

In this section we discuss more in detail the reinforcement distribution aspects, since these are relevant to understand the relationship between ELF and Q-Learning.

The strength of a rule (s_r, in the formula below) is updated by the function:

$$s_r(t) = s_r(t-1) + \left(reinf(t) - s_r(t-1)\right) * \frac{cc_r(t)}{pc_r(t)} \qquad [5]$$

In other terms, the rule strength is incremented by a quantity proportional to the difference between the present reinforcement (*reinf*) and the past strength, multiplied by the contribution of the rule to the actions performed in the current episode (cc_r), weighted by the parameter pc_r. The current contribution (cc_r) is a number in $[0..1]$ stating how much the actions proposed by this rule have contributed to the actions actually done in the episode. For instance, if we have an episode where two actions should be performed, and rule r_1 matches both the states that occurs during the episode, respectively with degrees 0.5 and 0.7, and another rule r_2 matches both the states respectively with degrees 0.5 and 0.3, then $cc_{r1} = (0.5+0.7) / (0.5+0.7+0.5+0.3)$. More formally:

$$cc_{\hat{r}} = \frac{\displaystyle\sum_{s\in S(e)}\mu_s(\hat{r})}{\displaystyle\sum_{\substack{s\in S(e)\\ r in R}}\mu_s(r)} \qquad [6]$$

where $\hat{r}$ is the rule under examination, s is a state belonging to the set of states S that occur during an episode e, $\mu_s(r)$ is the degree of firing of rule r in the state s, and R is the set of firing rules. This mechanism is needed to take into account the nature of the fuzzy inferential algorithm. Because of it, a rule contributes to the global action proportionally to its degree of firing, in turn proportional to the degree of matching with the current state. For what concerns pc_r, it is updated at each rule activation by adding the current contribution (cc_r) to the old value of pc_r, until a given maximum, named *EnoughTested*, is reached; a typical value for *EnoughTested* is in [10..20]. This means that the formula that updates the rule strength changes during the rule life. It is a weighted average until the rule is tested enough, then becoming similar to an ARMA formula, where the weight of each increment is constant, apart the cc_r factor.

ELF may also reinforce rules triggered during past episodes. The agent designer may state that there is some *correlation* (represented as a value in [0..1]) between an episode and the previous ones. He or she may consider that for a given behavior, a state depends not only on what happened during the current episode, but also on the actions done till then. The rules triggered in a past episode e_{t-j} receive a reinforcement at time t, given by:

$$s_r(t) = s_r(t-1) + \left(reinf(t) - s_r(t-1)\right)*\frac{cc_r(t-j)}{pc_r(t-j)}*decay \qquad [7]$$

where *reinf* is the reinforcement obtained at the end of the current episode, $\frac{cc_r(t-j)}{pc_r(t-j)}$ is computed with respect to episode e_{t-j} (occurred j time steps before the current episode e_t), and *decay* is a value given by:

$$decay = correlation^n \qquad [8]$$

where n is the number of episodes from episode e and the current one. This mechanism tends to evolve rules that bring the agent through a chain of states to a goal state.

We call a goal state defined by a fuzzy description a *fuzzy goal state*. This is a straightforward extension to a fuzzy representation of the concept of goal state defined for Q-Learning. The main difference is that a fuzzy goal state may be reached only in part, whereas a goal state is either reached or not.

If we consider x_k as a fuzzy state, and a_k as a fuzzy action (i.e., the output of a fuzzy rule), since in ELF there is only one rule that fires in a given fuzzy state and proposing a given fuzzy action, we may write:

$$\hat{Q}_r(x_k, a_k) = s_r(t) \qquad [9]$$

where $\hat{Q}_r(x_k, a_k)$ is the estimate of the expected discounted sum of reward, given that in the state x_k the rule r proposes the action a_k. Thus, we may re-write the more general formula for s_r with terms that make it possible to compare it with the standard Q-Learning updating formula [1]:

$$\hat{Q}_r(x_k, a_k) = \hat{Q}_r(x_k, a_k) + \frac{cc_r(x_k)}{pc_r(x_k)} \left[r_k + fr_r - \hat{Q}_r(x_k, a_k) \right] \qquad [10]$$

where fr_r, for the rules in the final rulebase, is:

$$fr_r = \sum_{i=1,n} correlation^i * \max_{b_i \in H(\tilde{x}_{k+i})} \hat{Q}_{r_i}(\tilde{x}_{k+i}, b_i) \qquad [11]$$

In other terms, fr_r is the weighted sum of the $\hat{Q}_{r_i}(\tilde{x}_{k+i}, b_i)$, where $\tilde{x}_{k+i}$ is the state reached from the state $\tilde{x}_{k+i-1}$ by applying action b_{i-1}. The sum is done for all the steps from 1 to n, where n is the number of steps for which $correlation^{n+1} < \varepsilon$.

The factor $\dfrac{cc_r(x_k)}{pc_r(x_k)}$ in formula [10] can be assimilated to the factor β in formula [1], since, as this last, it weights the importance of the increment, with respect to the old value. The main differences between β and $\dfrac{cc_r(x_k)}{pc_r(x_k)}$ are that this last factor:

1. changes (due to pc_r) during the evolution of the system; this speeds up the first evolutionary steps, since it gives higher relevance to the events occurring at the beginning;
2. is proportional to the relative importance of the current rule, due to cc_r, thus changing with the degree of activity of the rule under examination.

The other main difference between formulae [10] and [1] is the part concerning the contribution from future actions, fr_r (formula [11]). The parameter *correlation* corresponds straightforwardly to γ. Thus, with respect to the standard Q-learning formula, we consider contributions from more than one step ahead.

As a final comment, we would like to remark as the approach we have described for fuzzy states and actions, automatically generalizes to real-valued states and actions, since a state described by real-valued variables is covered by more that one fuzzy state, i.e., it is matched by fuzzy rules belonging to different sub-populations. These rules, combined by a fuzzy inferential mechanism, produce a real-valued action to be sent to the actuators. In other terms, ELF implements a sort of Q-Learning where states and actions are not discrete, but belong to continuous domains.

3.3. ELF and Dynamic Fuzzy Q-Learning

In ELF, we may have an initial set of fuzzy goal states, for each of which a desirability is defined. Reinforcement obtained by rules bringing to a fuzzy goal state is propagated with the above mentioned mechanism. Once another state becomes *strong* enough (i.e., it has been visited enough times, and the rules that cover it have a high strength), it enters in the set of fuzzy goal states and begins to contribute to future reinforcement. Therefore, the set of states that produces reinforcement is dynamically augmented. This solves the problems that arise when only relatively few fuzzy goal states are available at the beginning of the learning trial. For instance, with a typical discount factor (*correlation*) in the interval [0.6, 0.9], without the dynamic generation of fuzzy goal states we cannot propagate significant contributions to actions done more than few episodes preceding the reinforced one; thus, it would be impossible to learn long rule chains.

Comparing this approach with the Dynamic Fuzzy Q-Learning proposed by Glorennec [8], we may notice that we do not need any measure of the error between the current state and the desired one, thus facing the original delayed reinforcement problem. Moreover, a fuzzy goal state may become desirable because it may bring to more than one of the original fuzzy goal states. This may help to evolve a population of rules that achieve a multi-objective result, by chaining in long structures.

4. Experimental results

In this section, we present some experimental results obtained by applying the presented approach to the robot CAT, both to learn basic behaviors, and how to coordinate them.

4.1 CAT, the agent

We have implemented CAT as a modular, low-cost, versatile, autonomous, mobile robot. It is based on a toy car, 40 cm. long, and 25 cm. wide (Figure 1).

Figure 1 - CAT

CAT can move forward and backward at a maximum speed of 0.3 m/s, and it has a steering radius of 1.2 meters.

The hardware architecture is functionally layered. A small microcomputer (Siemens 8535) supports the exchange of information among the cards that control sensors, actuators and communication ports connected with external computers or other agents.

CAT has a 60 cm. high, rotating turret moved by a step motor. The turret holds four, Polaroid, ultrasonic sensors. The rotating turret also holds an infrared receiver that can detect the distance from infrared beacons positioned from 30 cm. to 6 meters from the sensor. Combining the information that comes from this sensor with the information about the absolute rotation of the turret it is also possible to detect the direction of the beacons with a precision of 3.5 degrees.

Sensors on the turret can be used with high flexibility: for instance we may cover 360 degrees with the 4 sonars by rotating twice the turret by 30 degrees, but we may also decide to have more reliable data taking more measurements, or to consider only obstacles in front.

ELF runs on an on-board, 80486-based card.

The mechanical features of this agent make its use particularly challenging. We mention here only the major sources of possible problems: the car-like kinematics requires particular attention in narrow environments, the limited number of sensors, their unreliability, their precision, and their configuration requires smart elaboration. Finally, the imperfect actuators produce imprecise actions.

We have applied ELF both to the actual CAT and to its simulated model.

4.2. Learning a basic behavior

We present in this section an experiment where ELF has learnt a *Follow_wall_on_a_side* behavior for CAT: the robot should go to a given distance from a wall and continue, maintaining the wall always on a side. When CAT is controlled by an FLC, we call it *Fuzzy CAT*.

In this case the antecedents are the direction of the closer wall (*Wall_Dir*) and its distance (*Dist*) (Figure 2). The consequents are *Speed* and *Steering*.

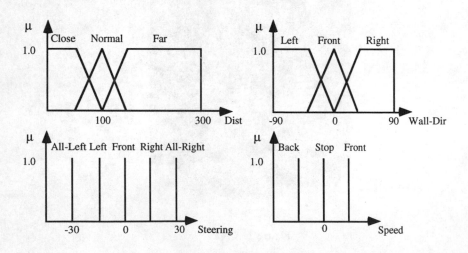

Figure 2 - The variables used in the experiment

Episodes have a length of 5 control cycles, and the *correlation* factor is 0.8. The fuzzy goal states are {(*Wall_Dir* IS Left)∧(*Dist* IS Normal)} and {(*Wall_Dir* IS Right)∧(*Dist* IS Normal)}. They are given an evaluation of 1.0 over 1.0.

Usually, after an average of about 3000 control cycles a rule base showing the desired behavior emerges: Fuzzy CAT follows a wall on a side also in presence of obstacles, starting from random initial positions (Figure 3).

In [4] we have discussed how it is difficult to give some *objective performance evaluation* for tasks to be performed by autonomous agents in a real environment. In particular, for the task of following a wall also in presence of obstacles, the performance can be heavily affected by several aspects, including: agent's characteristics -- such as maximum steering radius, speed, length of the control cycle, type and quantity of sensorial data -- environment characteristics, -- in this case the width of the corridor, the dimension and the relative position of the obstacles -- and the initial position of the agent. Therefore, we have adopted the criterion of testing the identified FLCs in a set of randomly generated situations, considering that CAT has the above mentioned characteristics that cannot be modified.

We have tried each FLC on 4 different corridors, generating in each from 1 to 5 obstacles, and starting from 12 different initial conditions. In these conditions Fuzzy CAT arrives at the end of the corridor in about 92% of the trials. Some of the situations that it has not been able to tackle with this simple behavior concerned particular placements of the obstacles, as discussed in the next section.

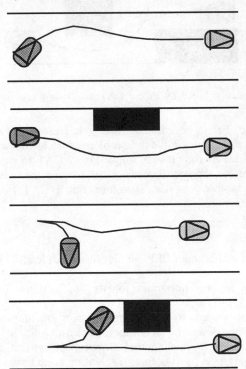

Figure 3 - Some of the situations faced by Fuzzy CAT applying the
Follow_wall_on_a_side **behavior**

We have applied ELF also to learning the same task, but giving a reinforcement at the end of each episode. In this case the reinforcement was $r = 1 - |e|$, where $|e|$ is the absolute position error with respect to the reference (the desired distance from the closer wall). In this case, we have continuous reinforcement instead of delayed reinforcement. In less than 1,000 control cycles a stable FLC generally emerges, but it has problems to face situations that require maneuvering, such as the last two in Figure 3. Therefore, delayed reinforcement has shown to be a valid approach for those situations where the desired task (such as the achievement of a fuzzy goal state) cannot be always described in terms of some error function.

4.2. Learning a complex behavior

To face situations as the one shown in Figure 4, we have applied ELF to learning different basic behaviors, including the above cited, and then to learning a behavior coordinator [5] that can decide the relative importance of the basic behaviors it coordinates. The coordinated behaviors propose an action each, and the coordinator weights the proposals considering a description of the state. Details about this application of ELF and some preliminary results are given in [5], and cannot be reported here.

Figure 4 - A situation faced by Fuzzy CAT applying a coordinated behavior.

In this case, the fuzzy coordinator can recognize that the basic behavior *Follow_wall_on_a_side* cannot solve the problems such as the one shown in figure 4, where the two obstacles are too close to allow Fuzzy CAT to pass through, given its steering radius. Therefore, the coordinator decides to give the maximum weight to the action proposed by another behavior. Therefore, Fuzzy CAT maneuvers and escapes from the blocking situation.

5. Conclusion

We have presented in this paper ELF, an algorithm that learns FLCs and extends Q-Learning.

ELF shows many features important for its application to the development of autonomous agents [3][6]:

- it is robust with respect to the typical imprecision of the learning parameters which occurs when designing an autonomous agent ;
- it learns Fuzzy Logic Controllers that show robustness and smoothness;
- it is robust with respect to ill-defined evaluation programs;
- it can accept a priori knowledge in terms of fuzzy rules and constraints on their shape;
- it can be applied to a wide range of learning tasks, including continuous reinforcement learning, delayed reinforcement learning, and constrained learning.

We have mentioned the other so-far proposed approaches for Fuzzy Q-learning, and we have discussed how ELF is more general than one of them [1], and in principle more effective than the other one [8] to learn FLCs in real environments. A direct comparison between ELF and the Fuzzy Q-Learning approach proposed by Glorennec [8] is not possible, at the state of the art, since we have faced different problems. A common effort between our two research teams is planned in the next future, to define benchmarks and compare our and other similar approaches that may be proposed in the next years.

Moreover, it is quite difficult to compare the performance we have obtained with ELF and that obtained by other non-fuzzy, Q-Learning proposals. Almost all the applications presented in the field refer to ideal environments where a state corresponds to a box in a grid. What it is learnt there are strategic behaviors, whereas we learn also how to face problems in a real environment, with non-ideal sensors.

Some applications of Q-Learning algorithms have been done in a real environment [7], but they face a problem different from ours, whose definition is not clear enough to make it possible an experimental comparison. An interesting point is the design effort described in [7] to limit the search space, by selecting a small number of discrete values for input and output variables. The similar problem is faced in ELF by adopting a fuzzy representation of values. This make it possible to exploit the full range of values, and at the same time to have a relatively small search space.

As a last remark, we recall that Fuzzy Q-Learning extends the principles of Q-Learning to continuous descriptions of states and actions. A deeper inquiry about the potential impact of this is also planned.

Acknowledgments

We would like to thank all the students who implemented the versions of ELF, and the Fuzzy CAT: they contributed substantially also to the theoretical and methodological aspects here reported.

This work has been partially supported by the MURST Project 60% "Development of autonomous agents through Machine Learning".

References

[1] H. R. Berenji, Fuzzy Q-Learning: a new approach for fuzzy dynamic programming. *Proc. Third IEEE Int. Conf. on Fuzzy Systems*. IEEE Computer Press, Piscataway, NJ, pp. 486-491, 1994.

[2] A Bonarini, ELF: learning incomplete fuzzy rule sets for an autonomous robot, *Proc. of EUFIT '93*, ELITE Foundation, Aachen, Germany, pp. 69-75, 1993.

[3] Bonarini A., Evolutionary learning of general fuzzy rules with biased evaluation functions: competition and cooperation. In *Proc. of IEEE WCCI - Evolutionary Computation* IEEE Computer Press, Piscataway NJ, pp. 51-56,1994,

[4] A. Bonarini, Some methodological issues about designing autonomous agents which learn their behaviors: the ELF experience. In R. Trappl (Ed.) *Cybernetics and Systems Research '94*,World Scientific Publishing, Singapore, pp. 1435-1442, 1994.

[5] A. Bonarini, Learning to coordinate fuzzy behaviors for autonomous agents. *Proc. EUFIT '94* ELITE Foundation, Aachen, Germany, pp. 475-479, 1994.

[6] A. Bonarini, Evolutionary learning of fuzzy rules: competition and cooperation. To appear in W. Pedrycz (Ed.) *Fuzzy modeling: paradigms and practice*, Kluwer Academic Publishers, Norwell, MA, 1995.

[7] J. H. Connell, S. Mahadevan, Automatic programming of behavior-based robots using reinforcement learning, *Artificial Intelligence*, Vol. 55, no.2, pp. 311-365, 1992.

[8] P. Y. Glorennec, Fuzzy Q-learning and Evolutionary Strategy for adaptive fuzzy control, *Proc. EUFIT '94* ELITE Foundation, Aachen, Germany, pp. 35-40, 1994.

[9] J. J. Grefenstette, Lamarckian learning in multi-agent environmemts, *Proc. of the Fourth Int. Conf. on Genetic Algorithms*, Morgan Kaufmann, San Mateo, CA, pp. 346–353, 1991.

[10] J. J. Grefenstette, The evolution of strategies for multiagent environments. *Adaptive Behavior*, Vol.1, no.1, pp. 65-91, 1992.

[11] M. Valenzuela-Rendón, The fuzzy classifier system: a classifier system for continuously varying variables. *Proc. of the 4th Int. Conf. on Genetic Algorithms*, Morgan Kaufmann, San Mateo, CA,pp. 346–353, 1991.

[12] C. Watkins, P. Dayan, Q-Learning, *Machine Learning*, Vol. 8, pp. 279-292, 1992.

[13] S. W. Wilson, ZCS, a zeroeth level Classifier System, *Evolutionary Computation*, Vol. 2, no.1, pp. 1-18, 1994

Fuzzy Cognitive Maps in Multi-Agent Environments

Paulo Camargo Silva

University of Erlangen-Nuernberg
Am Weichselgarten 9
D-91058 Erlangen
Tel.: (+49 9131) 85-9913
Fax : (+49 9131) 85-9905
camargo@immd8.informatik.uni-erlangen.de
Germany

Abstract. In the last years we have seen a large development about fuzzy cognitive maps (FCMs). The theoretical base of FCM is connected with the neural networks theory (differential hebbian learning) and fuzzy sets and systems theory. There are applications of the FCM in the following fields of research: adaptive network cognitive processor, analyze and extend graph theoretical behavior, plant control, information requirement analysis, analysis electrical circuit, model gastric-appetite behavior and popular political development. Our interest in this work is to show the importance of combination of FCM with the multi-agent modal logic of knowledge and belief to model structures of complex design in multi-agent environments. We make an application to plant control. The model that we introduce can be used to model popular political development, social systems, and military strategy, and others. In Goto and Yamaguchi [1991] is shown as FCMs can model plant control. In our point of view an ideal model of plant control must not involve the opinion of an expert about a plant control, but the opinion of a group of experts. If each expert of a group makes a FCM on a plant control, it is interesting to investigate what signifies the common knowledge of group about this plant control. Moreover is interesting to know what each agent of group knows about the FCM made by others agents. This can be much important in the design of plant control and to build political model, social systems, and military strategy. With reference to multi-agent modal logic of knowledge and belief, we make a generalization of work of Friedman and Halpern [1994a], Friedman and Halpern [1994b], by using of fuzzy measures. The multi-agent modal logic of knowledge and belief with fuzzy measures allows interpret fuzzy statements with linguistic fuzzy quantifiers such as developed in FCM.

1 THEORETICAL BASE

Contemporaneous researches have shown the possibility of introduce plausibility measures in the semantics structures of multi-agent modal logic of knowledge and belief, Friedman and Halpern [1994a], Friedman and Halpern [1994b], Friedman and Halpern [1994c]. The researches make possible that this logic interprets statements such as:

"It *typically* does not rain in

San Francisco in the summer" (1)

The introduction of plausibility measures in the semantic structure of multi-agent modal logic of knowledge and belief creates a large field of research, because a large set of fuzzy measures can be introduced in the semantic structure of multi-agent modal logic of knowledge and belief. In others words, plausibility measures are a particular case of fuzzy measures, Sugeno [1977] and Dubois and Prade [1982]. Fuzzy measures can be introduced in the semantics structures of multi-agent modal logic of knowledge and belief. This fact produces a generalization of semantics structures of the multi-agent modal logic of knowledge and belief with plausibility measures. The introduction of fuzzy measures in the multi-agent modal logic of knowledge and belief make possibles interpret statements such as:

$$\text{Bad weather} \xrightarrow{ALWAYS} \text{Freeway congestion} \qquad (2)$$

This is:

$$\text{Bad weather } always \text{ increases freeway congestion} \qquad (3)$$

This type of fuzzy statements are used in FCM, Kosko [1992]. Details of this type of fuzzy statements with linguistic fuzzy quantifiers can be seen in Zadeh [1978]. In fact, this type of statement is the particular case of a family of statements that can be interpret by multi-agent modal logic of knowledge and belief with fuzzy measures.

In this article we introduce the multi-agent modal logic of knowledge and belief. This logic is composed of n agents, a propositional reality, the operator $K_i p$, that signifies "the agent i knows p" and the fuzzy operator $\leadsto_i$. This logic interprets statements such as:

$$K_i(p \leadsto_i q) \qquad (4)$$

In others words, the agent i knows that $p \leadsto_i q$ is true. This is a theoretical base to affirm that the agent i can know a fuzzy statement of type shown above (2). This is:

$$K_i(\text{Bad weather} \xrightarrow{ALWAYS} \text{Freeway congestion}) \qquad (5)$$

This signifies to say that the multi-agent modal logic of knowledge and belief with fuzzy measures introduced in its semantic structure is able to interpret the situation where the set of agents (experts) make a FCM about a phenomenon. This interpretation make possible extract different levels of knowledge of group altogether about the phenomenon.

2 FUZZY COGNITIVE MAPS

In neural networks theory, FCM can be considered as supervised learning (hard-wired learning) and unsupervised learning (differential Hebbian learning). The FCM is a signed directed graph with feedback that represents causal relations between concepts. The nodes of graph represent the concepts and the edges represent causal relations between concepts. The positive edge represents excitatory causal relation between the nodes and negative edge represents inhibitory causal relation between the nodes. Moreover the edges have weights that can be: (1) linguistic fuzzy quantifiers; (2) { +1, 0, -1 }; (3) [0, 1]. In others words, given two concepts C_i and C_j, the edge l_{ij} has a positive value or negative value and a weight. To simplify, in this article, we consider the case most simple of FCM that has the weights in set { +1, 0, -1 }. The edge $l_{ij} = 0$ indicates that there is no causal relation between the concepts. The edge $l_{ij} = -1$ indicates that the causal relation between C_i and C_j is negative. This signifies that C_i decreases as C_j increases and C_i increases as C_j decreases. The edge $l_{ij} = 1$ indicates that the causal relation between C_i and C_j is positive. This signifies that C_i increases as C_j increases and C_i decreases as C_j decreases (see Kosko [1992]). For applications, see Edson et. al. [1988], Myers et. al. [1988], Goto et. al. [1989], Mentazeni et. al. [1986], Styblinski et. al. [1991, 1988], Taber[1987, 1991].

3 MULTI-AGENT MODAL LOGIC OF KNOWLEDGE AND BELIEF

Now we introduce the multi-agent modal logic of knowledge and belief, Halpern and Moses [1992]. We consider a world constituted of n agents and a propositional reality. Given a nonempty set $\aleph$ of primitive propositions $p, q, r, \ldots$. One defines $\mathcal{P}_n(\aleph)$ as a set of formula closing off under conjunction, negation, and the modal operators K_i and fuzzy operator $\leadsto_i$. We read the modal operator $K_i p$ as "the agent i knows p". The fuzzy operator $\leadsto_i$ is a generalization of the operator $\to_i$ defined in Friedman and Halpern [1994a]. Below we present details.

A semantic for this language is given by the Kripke structure:

$$\langle W, v, R_1, \ldots R_n, \mathcal{P} \rangle \tag{6}$$

where W is a set of possible worlds, v is a truth assignment for each possible world and R_i are fuzzy relations of accessibility. $\mathcal{P}$ is a fuzzy space that each agent make on each possible world such that:

$$\mathcal{P}(w, i) = (\Omega(w, i), X(w, i), \Pi(w, i), \preceq (w, i)) \tag{7}$$

where $\mathcal{P}(w, i)$ defines the fuzzy space of agent i in possible world w, $\Omega(w, i)$ is a subset of W, $X(w, i)$ is a σ-algebra on $\Omega(w, i)$, $\Pi(w, i)$ is a set of fuzzy measures designated by agent i for all elements of set $X(w, i)$ and $\preceq (w, i)$ is a pre-order on the elements of set $X(w, i)$ that is based on its fuzzy measures $\Pi(w, i)$.

The structure $\mathcal{P}(w, i)$ can produce a set of structures with the specific type of fuzzy measure that is used in $\Pi(w, i)$, for example:

One can suppose the structure:

$$\mathcal{P}^{Pl}(w, i) = (\Omega(w, i), X(w, i), \Pi^{Pl}(w, i), \preceq (w, i)) \tag{8}$$

where $\Pi^{Pl}(w, i)$ is a plausibility measure that designates for each subset of $\Omega(w, i)$, elements of σ-algebra $X(w, i)$. Let A be as an element of $X(w, i)$. Then:

$$\Pi^{Pl}(w, i)(A) \in [0, 1] \tag{9}$$

If we denote by $\Pi^{Bel}(w, i)$ a belief measure on the elements of $X(w, i)$, we have:

$$1 - \Pi^{Bel}(w, i)(\overline{A}) = \Pi^{Pl}(w, i)(A) \tag{10}$$

This makes possible to create the structure:

$$\mathcal{P}^{Bel} = (\Omega(w, i), X(w, i), \Pi^{Bel}(w, i), \preceq (w, i)) \tag{11}$$

Likewise one can suppose the structure:

$$\mathcal{P}^{POSS}(w, i) = (\Omega(w, i), X(w, i), \Pi^{POSS}(w, i), \\ \preceq (w, i)) \tag{12}$$

where $\Pi^{POSS}(w, i)$ is the possibility measure that is designated for each element of the σ-algebra $X(w, i)$. If A is an element of $X(w, i)$, then:

$$\Pi^{POSS}(w, i)(A) \in [0, 1] \tag{13}$$

This makes possible create the structure:

$$\mathcal{P}^{NEC}(w, i) = (\Omega(w, i), X(w, i), \Pi^{NEC}(w, i), \\ \preceq (w, i)) \tag{14}$$

We have now the Kripke structure defined. The semantics is similar to standard Kripke structure, the only difference is the introduction of formulas of type:

$$\varphi \rightsquigarrow_i \psi \tag{15}$$

As we said, formerly, our objective is that fuzzy measures can be seen as a plausibility measures as defined in Friedman and Halpern[1994a], Friedman and Halpern [1994b]. In works Friedman and Halpern [1994a], Friedman and Halpern [1994b] a proposition such as:

$$\varphi \rightarrow_i \psi \tag{16}$$

is true in a possible world w if ψ is true in the most plausible $\varphi - worlds$ in $\Omega(w, i)$. In our structure we say that $\varphi \rightsquigarrow_i \psi$ is true in a possible world w

if ψ is true in the most compatibles $\varphi - worlds$ in $\Omega(w,i)$. This means that if we refer to necessity measure (or possibility measure), we say that $\varphi \rightsquigarrow_i \psi$ is true in a possible world w if ψ is true in the most possible $\varphi - worlds$ in $\Omega(w,i)$. (In this case one must not confuse most possible $\varphi - worlds$, possible here connected with possibility measures, with possible worlds connected with relation of accessibility.)

We require that the following relations are respected in our theory as in Friedman and Halpern[1994a], Friedman and Halpern[1994b]

1. CONS: For all worlds w, $\Omega \subseteq R_i(w)$.
2. NORM: For all worlds w, $\Omega \neq \emptyset$.
3. REF: For all worlds w, $w \in \Omega(w,i)$
4. SDP: For all w and w' if $(w,w') \in R_i$ then $\mathcal{P}(w,i) = \mathcal{P}(w',i)$.
5. UNIF: For all w, if $w' \in \Omega(w,i)$ then $\mathcal{P}(w,i) = \mathcal{P}(w',i)$.
6. RANK: For all w and i, $\mathcal{P}(w,i)$ is ranked.

Note that as we have defined the relation of accessibility through fuzzy relations, the values in this relation of accessibility are in internal $[0,1]$. This fact does not obstruct that the properties above respect Friedman and Halpern[1994a], Friedman and Halpern[1994b].

If we consider the Kripke structure as defined before. We can define $\mathcal{M}$ as a class of all Kripke structures as defined above and $\mathcal{M}_{CONS}$ a class of Kripke structures that respect the CONS and $\mathcal{M}_{CONS,NORM}$ the class of Kripke structure that respect the CONS and NORM.

4   OPERATORS OF KNOWLEDGE

The relations CONS, NORM, REF, SDP, UNIF, RANK, above correspond an axiomatic structure (see Friedman and Halpern [1994a]). For our purpose is useful the axiom correspondent with the relation SDP:

$$p \rightsquigarrow_i q \Rightarrow K_i(p \rightsquigarrow_i q) \tag{17}$$

Our aim in this section is to introduce operators of knowledge. In the language introduced in the last section, we include the operators of group, such as:

$S_G(p \rightsquigarrow_i q)$ - Some group know $p \rightsquigarrow_i q$

$$S_G(p \rightsquigarrow_i q) \equiv \bigvee_{i \in G} K_i(p \rightsquigarrow_i q) \tag{18}$$

$E_G(p \rightsquigarrow_i q)$ - All in group know $p \rightsquigarrow_i q$

$$E_G(p \rightsquigarrow_i q) \equiv \bigwedge_{i \in G} K_i(p \rightsquigarrow_i q) \tag{19}$$

$E_G^K(p \rightsquigarrow_i q)$, $K \geq 1$ - This operator is called $E_G^K - knowledge$, is an extension of $E_G(p \rightsquigarrow_i q)$:

$$E_G^1(p \leadsto_i q) \equiv E_G(p \leadsto_i q) \tag{20}$$

$$E_G^{K+1}(p \leadsto_i q) \equiv E_G E_G^K(p \leadsto_i q), K \geq 1 \tag{21}$$

$C_G(p \leadsto_i q)$, common knowledge, the statement $p \leadsto_i q$ is a common knowledge in group G, if $p \leadsto q$ is $E_G^K - knowledge$ for all $K \geq 1$, in others words:

$$C_G(p \leadsto_i q) \equiv E_G(p \leadsto_i q) \wedge E_G^2(p \leadsto_i q)$$
$$\wedge \ldots \wedge E_G^m(p \leadsto_i q) \wedge \ldots \tag{22}$$

An important property of operators is given by:

$$C(p \leadsto_i q) \Rightarrow \ldots \Rightarrow E^K(p \leadsto_i q) \Rightarrow \ldots$$
$$\Rightarrow E(p \leadsto_i q) \Rightarrow S(p \leadsto q) \Rightarrow p \leadsto_i q \tag{23}$$

As seen above, the multi-agent modal logic of knowledge and belief that we present in this article generalize the logic presented in Friedman and Halpern[1994a]. This generalization is possible because plausibility measures are a particular case of fuzzy measures. These measures are a generalization for several measures such as: necessity measures, plausibility measures, possibility measures, belief measures, and others. The structure developed by Friedman and Halpern [1994a], Friedman and Halpern [1994b] uses plausibility measures. And is able to interpret statement such as $\rightarrow_i$. Since the structure introduced in this article presents a generalization of structure developed by Friedman and Halpern [1994a], we present a family of statements that can be interpreted by our structure. So that the statement of form $\rightarrow_i$ are a particular type of statements of form $\leadsto_i$. The operators of knowledge presented above are not contrary to intuition, and have the same effect that statements of type $\rightarrow_i$.

5 CONCLUSION

In this article we present FCMs in multi-agent environments. We make a successful application of this theory in a model of plant control. However we don't present this application in this article. We present in this article a theoretical framework that permits an application of FCMs in a multi-agent environment.

6 REFERENCES

HALPERN, J., & MOSES, Y. [1992] - A Guide to Completeness and Complexity for for Modal Logic of Knowledge and Belief, Artificial Intelligence Vol.54, No. 3, april 319-379.

TABER, W. R. [1991] - Knowledge Processing with Fuzzy Cognitive Maps, Expert Systems with Applications, Vol. 2, 83-87.

EDSON, B., TURNER, C., MEYERS, M., & SIMPSON, P.[1988] - The Adaptive Networks Cognitive Processor, Proceedings of the 1988 Aerospace Applications of Artificial Intelligence (AAAIC 88), Vol.II.

MYERS, M., TURNER, C., KUCZEWSKI, R., & SIMPSON, P. [1988] - ANCP Adaptive Network Cognitive Processor: Vols I & II, TRW MEAD, Final Report Prepared for Air Force Wright Aeronautical Laboratories

STYBLINSKI, M. & MEYER, B. [1988] - Fuzzy Cognitive Map, Signal Flow Graphs, and Qualitative Circuit Analysis, Proceedings of the IEEE International Conference on Neural Network: Vol. II, (pp. 549-556). San Diego: IEEE.

MENTAZENI, A. & CONRATH, D. [1986] - The Use of Cognitive Mapping for Information Requirement Analysis, Management Information Systems Quarterly.

SUGENO, M.[1977] - Fuzzy Measures and Fuzzy Integrals - a survey, in Gupta, M.M., Saridis, G.N., and Gaines, B.R.[1977].

GUPTA, M.M., et. al.[1977] - Fuzzy Automata and Decision Processes, North-Holland, New York.

DUBOIS, H. & PRADE, D. [1982] - A Class of Fuzzy Measures based on Triangular Norms, International, J. of General Systems, 8.

KOSKO, B. [1992] - Neural Networks and Fuzzy Systems: A Dynamical Systems Approach to Machine Intelligence, Prentice Hall, New York.

STYBLINSKI, M. & MEYER, B. [1991] - Signal Flow Graphs vs Fuzzy Cognitive in Application to Qualitative Circuit Analysis, International Journal of Man-Machine Studies, 35, 175-186.

GOTO, K., & MURAKAMI, J., YAMAGUCHI, T., & YAMANAKA, Y., [1989] - Application of Fuzzy Cognitive Maps to Supporting for Plant Control, (in Japanese) 10th Knowledge Engineering Symposium, 99-104.

GOTO, K., & YAMAGUCH. T.[1991] - Fuzzy Associative Memory Application to a Plant Modeling, in Kohonen, K., Makisara, O. Simula, O., and Kangas, J. [1991]

KOHONEN, K., MAKISARA, O. SIMULA, O., & KANGAS, J. [1991] - Artificial Neural Networks, Vol.2, North-Holland.

ZHANG, W., & CHEN, S. [1988] - A Logical Architecture for Cognitive Maps, Proceedings of the 2nd IEEE International Conference on Neural Network, Vol. I, 231-238, july.

FRIEDMAN, N. & HALPERN, J.[1994a] - A knowledge-Based Framework For Belief Change Part I: Foundations, Proceedings of Theoretical Aspects of Reasoning about Knowledge, Morgan Kaufman.

FRIEDMAN, N. & HALPERN, J.[1994b] - A Knowledge-Based Framework For Belief Change Part II: Revision and Update, Principles of Knowledge Representation and Reasoning: Proc. Fourth International Conference (KR'94)

FRIEDMAN, N. & HALPERN, J.[1994c] - On the Complexity of Conditional Logics, in Principles of Knowledge Representation and Reasoning: Proc. Fourth International Conference (KR'94).

ZADEH, L.A.[1978] - Fuzzy sets as a Basis for a Theory of Possibility, Fuzzy Sets and Systems , Vol.1, No. 1, pp.3-28.

Multiple Predicate Learning with RTL

Cristina Baroglio and **Marco Botta**

Dipartimento di Informatica - Universita` di Torino

Corso Svizzera 185 - 10149 Torino - ITALY

e-mail: {baroglio,botta}@di.unito.it

Abstract. RTL is an algorithm designed to learn any number of simple, mutually dependent relations, producing recursive programs that are stratified in the sense given by Apt. In this paper, we present a revised algorithm and its implementation based on previous theoretical works that establish properties and limits of the learning framework. The algorithm is described both in abstract form and through an example. Emphasis is put on the way RTL uses induction and domain knowledge to guide the search towards specific kinds of hypothesis. The algorithm has been tested on three different domains obtaining encouraging results, as reported in the discussion. Finally, it is shown experimentally that the control strategy realized is somewhat independent of the order in which concepts are learned.

1. Introduction

Multiple predicate learning is a very difficult task that only recently has been explicitly addressed in the machine learning literature (Baroglio et al., 1992; Giordana et al., 1993; De Raedt et al., 1993b). Earlier induction programs, were based on the strong assumption that concepts are independent one another and therefore, they could not adequately handle the problem, even in the simple case of a set of dependent relations where recursion do not occur. Even if in many applications such an assumption is reasonable, this is not generally true: for instance, labelling problems in scene analysis, speech recognition, fault diagnosis and game theory are some examples in which the independence assumption does not hold.

The main problem with these approaches is that they are affected by excessive complexity, due to the number of extensional checks to be performed. As an example, let us consider the following clauses defining a recursive relation:

$$c_1 : \psi(x,y) \rightarrow p(x) \qquad\qquad c_2 : p(y) \wedge \varphi(x,y) \rightarrow p(x)$$

Clause c_1 should be learned first, and then c_2 can be induced. Now, suppose that a third clause $c_3 : \eta(x,y) \rightarrow p(x)$ still needs to be learned because c_1 and c_2 do not cover all positive examples. After c_3 is added to the theory, it is necessary to check theory consistency, as clause c_2 now also depends on c_3. Complexity grows combinatorially when more than one concept has to be learned.

Furthermore, the classical ILP approaches (strong and weak setting, as classified by De Raedt et al. (1993a)), have other limitations. For instance, many classical ILP systems (such as FOIL (Quinlan, 1990), GOLEM (Muggleton & Feng, 1990) and LINUS (Lavrač et al., 1991)) are not designed to learn more than one concept at a time. Thus, under the strong setting, the order of learning clauses may affect the results of the learning task, and sometimes even the existence of a solution (De Raedt et al., 1993a). Also incremental systems, such as CIGOL (Muggleton & Buntine, 1988), CLINT (De Raedt, 1992), MIS (Shapiro, 1983) and MOBAL (Kietz & Wrobel, 1992), present the same problem.

On the other hand, some theory revision systems (e.g. FORTE (Richards & Mooney, 1991) and AUDREY (Wogulis, 1991)) can learn multiple concepts, though different orderings of the learning examples lead to different results, and some of them (e.g., AUDREY) cannot handle recursion.

A solution to overcome these drawbacks is that of explicitly representing dependency information, by using dependency hierarchies and exploiting it to guide the learning process (see for instance (Esposito et al., 1993)).

A different solution is that of designing specific algorithms to address a multiple predicate learning task, such as MPL (De Raedt et al., 1993b) and RTL (Baroglio et al., 1992; Giordana et al., 1993). MPL proposes a method to avoid the ordering dependence of the learning process that dynamically associates head and body of a learning clause, but, as a side effect, complexity is dramatically increased. RTL, on the other hand, aims at reducing the complexity of the induction process by implementing a control strategy that makes each inductive step simpler and automatically discovers a correct learning order. In order to do that, it restricts the class of programs it can learn to a subset of stratified programs, allowing recursive cycles only if they depend upon the immediately preceding step (i.e. a program for generating Fibonacci's number sequence cannot be learned). Therefore, RTL's major concern is to reduce the complexity arising from the interaction among clauses involved in recursive loops. As pointed out in (Baroglio et al., 1992) and (De Raedt & Lavrač, 1993a), adding or deleting a clause involved in a recursive loop requires the model of the program to be recomputed. Nevertheless, in many cases, such an expensive step can be avoided if program changes are appropriately restricted and if a proper policy is followed during the induction process (see (Giordana et al., 1993) for a formal dissertation).

This paper pursues three main goals: a new algorithm that solves some technical flaws and extends to a larger class of programs the abstract RTL algorithm reported in (Giordana et al., 1993) is presented; a full and sound implementation of the new algorithm is described; a set of experiments aimed at testing the current potentialities of the algorithm is finally discussed.

2. The methodology

RTL is an algorithm developed to learn a set of interdependent, (possibly) mutually recursive concepts that can be represented by a stratified theory. To this aim it adopts a *context switching* strategy: the set of concepts to be learnt is organized in a circular queue from which a concept is removed only when all of its positive instances have been covered. In this way, RTL learns a first (possibly recursive) partial definition for a concept, then it switches its attention and learns a first partial definition the next concept, and so on. When it gets back on the first concept, it can learn a second partial definition that may also depend upon the previously learnt ones. Suppose, for instance, that RTL has to learn the following clauses defining concepts p and q (Greek letters denote a conjunction of literals):

$$\alpha(x,y) \rightarrow p(x,y) \qquad\qquad \beta(x,y) \rightarrow q(x,y)$$
$$\gamma(x,y,z) \wedge q(z,y) \rightarrow p(x,y) \qquad \delta(x,y,z) \wedge p(z,y) \rightarrow q(x,y)$$

By learning a concept at a time, it is not possible to come up with the desired clauses. On the other hand, since RTL learns partial definitions, it will learn the first two clauses and then it will search for the mutually recursive ones. As a side effect, this strategy makes RTL almost independent of the initial concept ordering.

RTL starts from a set F of learning instances and, taking into account that a logic program terminates only if it has an acyclic ground graph (Apt et al., 1988), it first builds a non recursive program G, that has an isomorphic ground graph covering the whole F. Then, it transforms G into a recursive program T, that has the same ground graph on F. The construction of G is fundamentally a monotonic process without backtracking. Moreover, the recursive program T can be built without any extensional checks, provided that specific properties hold for G (Giordana et al., 1993).

RTL control strategy interleaves inductive steps and theory driven steps in order to facilitate the discovery of recursive structures. G is induced starting from the *golden points*, i.e. the base clauses of the recursive program T. Then, definitions depending on them are sought, and the process is repeated until all instances are covered.

RTL uses theory based heuristics to simplify the discovery of recursive structures. Let us suppose that $\varphi(x,y) \rightarrow h_0(x)$ is a base clause defining concept h learnt at some point. First, RTL looks for a formula $\psi(x,y)$ such that $\psi(x,y) \wedge h_0(y) \rightarrow h_1(x)$ is also a partial definition for concept h. Then, before anything else, it tries $\psi(x,y) \wedge h_1(y) \rightarrow h_2(x)$. If also this is a correct definition, it is added to G and this step is repeated. It is evident that if the models of F have a recursive structure, this will be captured in G by a set of structurally identical clauses, chained through the corresponding predicate names h_0, h_1, h_2, etc. Such chains will then be generalized into recursive clauses in T. It should be noticed that recursive generalizations that need extensional checks (such as those leading to recursion through negated literals) are prevented by creating strata (Apt et al., 1988).

3. Basic Notions and Definitions

In the following we will adopt standard ILP terminology and introduce some basic definitions to allow a better understanding of RTL. Concepts are represented by a set of program clauses (a *theory*) expressed in a function-free FOPL augmented with negation. A theory, in order to be tractable by the system, must be *stratified* (Apt et al., 1988). Stratification determines priority levels (strata) of a set of predicates and guarantees that a predicate is not dependent on its negation, thus generating an acyclic ground graph over the learning set.

Definition 3.1 Given two predicates r and s having the same arity and corresponding to database relations R and S, respectively, R is said a *subrelation* of S iff the clause $r \rightarrow s$ is true. This also implies that $R \subseteq S$. ♦

Definition 3.2 Two clauses c_1 and c_2 are said *correspondent clauses* w.r.t. a relation R if they can be made identical by renaming predicates corresponding to subrelations of R. ♦

47

For instance, clauses c_1: $\varphi(x, y) \wedge r_1(x) \rightarrow k(x)$ and c_2: $\varphi(x, y) \wedge r_2(x) \rightarrow k(x)$, where r_1 and r_2 are predicates denoting subrelations of R, are correspondent clauses.

Definition 3.3 A set of clauses having the following structure:

c_0: $\alpha(\bar{x}, \bar{y}) \rightarrow h_0(\bar{x})$

c_i: $h_{i-1}(\bar{y}) \wedge \varphi(\bar{x}, \bar{y}, \bar{z}) \rightarrow h_i(\bar{x})$, $\forall i \in [1,n]$

where $\bar{x}$, $\bar{y}$, $\bar{z}$ are lists of variables, and the h_is denote subrelations of the same relation H, is a *simply recurrent theory* G. Clause c_i is said to be *recurrent*, because subrelations of H are present both in the body and in the head of c_i. Clause c_0 is said a *golden point* of relation H if $\alpha(\bar{x}, \bar{y})$ does not contain any occurrence of subrelations of H. A golden point represents the base case of a recursive definition. ◆
A simply recurrent theory is a non recursive program that partially defines a concept h and has an isomorphic ground graph covering only positive instances of h.

Definition 3.4 Let G be a simply recurrent theory. The theory T that results by renaming all subrelations h_i of the same relation H occurring in G to a unique name h, is a *simply recursive theory*. The operation performed is called *recursive generalization*. ◆
As an example, let G be the set $\{\alpha(x) \rightarrow h_0(x), h_0(y) \wedge \varphi(x,y) \rightarrow h_1(x), h_1(y) \wedge \varphi(x,y) \rightarrow h_2(x)\}$, where h_0, h_1, and h_2 denote subrelations of H; T = $\{\alpha(x) \rightarrow h(x), h(y) \wedge \varphi(x,y) \rightarrow h(x)\}$ is a recursive generalization of G. The recursive generalization process is not just a renaming operation but a further induction step: in fact, having seen that G is true on the learning instances, it is induced that also its recursive generalization T is true in general. The recursive generalization process is sound under specific conditions as formally stated in (Giordana et al., 1993).

Definition 3.5 A *simply recursive network* is a set of simply recursive theories with no dependency loops[1]. A simply recursive network SRN is *complete* iff adding to it any correspondent of a clause $c \in$ SRN its extension on the learning set F do not change. ◆
The simply recursive theories that belong to a complete simply recursive network are partial definitions of the concepts to be learned that can be further generalized by applying a stratification process without the need of extensional checks, as proved in (Giordana et al., 1993).

4. The Actual Algorithm

RTL repeats three main phases: (1) inducing a simply recurrent theory, (2) generalizing to a simply recursive theory, (3) generalizing a set of complete simply recursive networks to close a stratum. In doing so, RTL generates programs which are stratified in the sense given by Apt (Apt et al., 1988) avoiding the combinatorial explosion of extensional checks. Fig. 1 reports a high level description of the main algorithm.

---

[1] A simply recursive theory T1 is said to *depend directly* upon a simply recursive theory T2 if it contains at least one subrelation h1 that is defined by means of a subrelation h2, that belongs to T2. It is said to *depend* on T2 if it depends directly on T2 or if it depends on a theory T3 that depends on T2.

queue = list of concepts to be learned
repeat
    concept_to_learn = next in queue
- Phase (1): inducing a simply recurrent theory
  - Induce a golden point
  - Induce a recurrent definition from the golden point
  - Iterate the recurrent definition in order to find the fixed point of the recursion
- Phase (2): generalizing to a simply recursive theory
  - Apply the recursive generalization step by renaming predicates to a unique name
- Phase (3): generalizing a set of complete simply recursive networks
  - **If** the found simply recursive theories form a complete simply recursive network **then** Apply Stratification
- Add the new definitions to the set of features usable for learning at next step
- **If** there are instances of concept concept_to_learn not yet covered **then**
      append concept_to_learn to the end of queue

until all instances are covered

Fig. 1 - RTL main algorithm.

The first step builds a simply recurrent theory: this is the most critical point in RTL, since the structure of the learned theory depends on the selection of *good* golden points and recurrent clauses, a problem inherent to the task and not related to the method itself. MPL (De Raedt et al., 1993b) tries to solve the problem by adopting a strategy that dynamically allows to add and retract clauses until the program reaches a maximum of an assigned evaluation function. Also in RTL the non-recursive theory G can be dynamically modified if we accept an increase in the complexity of the process. However, in the current version of the algorithm, powerful heuristics to guide the selection of golden points and recurrents take precedence over refinements of the theory.

The induction procedure RTL uses is that of KBI (Botta, 1994), a system that is able to learn first order clauses from theory and data. Basically, this procedure differs from the one of FOIL and similar systems in the search structure adopted, which allows the system to learn non-operational clauses by using both operational and non-operational predicates defined in a theory. The inductive search is guided by a heuristic criterion that accounts for completeness and consistency, similar to the information gain heuristic used in FOIL. Moreover, this criterion has been extended to account also for simplicity.

A simplicity criterion has been used more or less explicitly in many inductive systems starting from INDUCE (Michalski, 1983). Here, it is particularly relevant to privilege the discovery of recursive structures. In fact, being every model in F finite, it is always possible to find a non recursive theory covering all the training events if no limit is put on the complexity of the clauses. On the other hand, if a problem has a recursive nature, simple definitions for golden points and recurrent clauses should be easy to find. In RTL simplicity does not depend on the number of literals, as it is usually done, but on the number of variables occurring in the body of an inductive hypothesis. By limiting this number, KBI learns clauses of an upper-bounded complexity. For example, if we want to find a golden point for the concept *male ancestor* (m-a(x,y) means x is a male ancestor of y), KBI is first configured to learn a clause with two variables (x and y); if it finds a consistent definition, this is used as a golden point; if not, the limit on the number of variables is raised by one and the induction process repeated, until either a consistent definition is found or a maximum has been reached. Note that this is not a failing case (no solution exists): the definition we are looking for cannot be found now because it might depend on one that has not been learned yet.

A recurrent definition is learned from a template that describes the structure of the clause body, in a such a way that, if a concept can be described by a recursive definition, RTL is biased to learn such a definition. Templates are extremely simple and only contain a reference to a golden point definition. This way, they can be generated in an automatic way by the algorithm. The number of different templates only depends on the arity of the goal concept. For instance, given a golden point definition for a predicate $h_0(x)$, the following template is generated:

$$\text{diff}(x,y) \wedge h_0(y) \rightarrow h_1(x)$$

Starting from it, the inductive system can only learn a clause of the following form:

$$\psi(x,y) \wedge h_0(y) \rightarrow h_1(x)$$

ensuring that a recursive definition, if exists, is found by RTL. Moreover, since, in general, different recursive definitions can have the same base, RTL can reuse previously generated golden points to learn new recurrent clauses.

Once a recurrent definition has been found, it is iterated to find the fixed point. Let us consider the following example: let c_1: $\text{anc}_1(x,z) \wedge \text{father}(z,y) \rightarrow \text{anc}_2(x,y)$ be a recurrent clause; the iteration step on c_1 generates a correspondent clause c_2: $\text{anc}_2(x,z) \wedge \text{father}(z,y) \rightarrow \text{anc}_3(x,y)$ by introducing a new predicate anc_3, whose truth is proved on the learning instances. If it covers some new instance and no couterexamples, the iteration process is repeated on c_2. The process stops when a correspondent clause covers counterexamples or no instances at all. If it is consistent, the recursive generalization step is performed, otherwise all found definitions are added to the theory as linked clauses with no recursion.

When no new definitions can be found in the preceding steps, a complete simply recursive network has been built up; *stratification* can now be applied in order to define a borderline between definitions belonging to a stratum and definitions that will be obtained later on, in such a way that no generalizations can be made across the borderline. Moreover, stratification is applied if one of the following conditions holds:

- when a negative definition is generated, to avoid loops through negation
- when iteration covers counterexamples, to avoid recursive generalizations leading to inconsistencies (this happens for example when the system has to learn two concepts and one is a subconcept of the other)
- when all instances have been covered, to generalize among simply recursive theories heading to the same concept

RTL first identifies the set of simply recursive networks involved, and then tries a higher level generalization within them, by renaming to a unique name all subrelations h_i of the same relation H. Then, the topmost generated predicates are exported from the stratum and declared operational, so that future generalizations will not take them into account.

The use of negation needs some more comment. In order to prevent recursion through negated literals, RTL can use negation at any step only on literals corresponding to operational predicates. Predicates corresponding to target concepts can be used as negated literals only in the specific case that they belong to a closed stratum.

5. An Example

To better explain the crucial steps of RTL, let us trace how it deals with a simple example: the problem is that of learning two mutually recursive concepts, *female* and *male ancestors*, from a family tree consisting of 20 instances per concept, in terms of operational predicates like *father*, *mother*, *male* and *female*. It should be noted that this simple example cannot be solved by classical learning systems because complete definitions depend on one another. Choosing which concept to learn first is not a problem in this case (neither in general, see next section), since concepts descriptions are symmetrical.

The first phase consists in forming a simply recurrent theory: one of the following golden points is induced by KBI (depending on the distribution of instances):

$$father(x,y) \rightarrow m\text{-}a_0(x,y)$$
$$male(x) \wedge father(x,y) \rightarrow m\text{-}a_0(x,y)$$
$$female(y) \wedge father(x,y) \rightarrow m\text{-}a_0(x,y)$$

Notice that they are all correct even though two of them contain redundant literals. Then, a recurrent clause is learned from a template automatically generated by RTL: in particular, given a binary predicate like m-a(x,y), the following set of templates is produced:

$$m\text{-}a_0(x,z) \wedge diff(z,y) \rightarrow m\text{-}a_1(x,y) \quad m\text{-}a_0(z,y) \wedge diff(z,x) \rightarrow m\text{-}a_1(x,y)$$
$$m\text{-}a_0(y,z) \wedge diff(z,x) \rightarrow m\text{-}a_1(x,y) \quad m\text{-}a_0(z,x) \wedge diff(z,y) \rightarrow m\text{-}a_1(x,y)$$

The last two clauses would not be generated if the predicate is commutative. The inductive process is then repeated as before until a consistent clause is found or there is no template left. Again, depending on the distribution of instances, one of the following recurrent clauses is learned at this step:

$$m\text{-}a_0(x,z) \wedge diff(z,y) \wedge father(z,y) \rightarrow m\text{-}a_1(x,y)$$
$$m\text{-}a_0(x,z) \wedge diff(z,x) \wedge mother(z,y) \rightarrow m\text{-}a_1(x,y)$$

The iteration phase can now be performed and ends when a correspondent clause does not cover new instances, i.e. when a fixed point of the iteration process has been reached.

By applying recursive generalization to the simply recurrent theory so obtained, the following definition, m-a'(x,y), is added to the background theory:

$$father(x,y) \rightarrow m\text{-}a'(x,y) \qquad m\text{-}a'(x,z) \wedge diff(z,y) \wedge father(z,y) \rightarrow m\text{-}a'(x,y)$$

Since there are instances of male ancestor not covered by this definition, the concept is appended to the queue of concepts to be learned. The focus is then switched to the next concept, f-a(x,y), and the following recursive definition that uses m-a' is built up:

$$\text{mother}(x,y) \rightarrow \text{f-a'}(x,y) \qquad \text{f-a'}(x,z) \wedge \text{diff}(z,y) \wedge \text{m-a'}(z,y) \rightarrow \text{f-a'}(x,y)$$

In this case, too, there are instances of female ancestor not covered, so the concept is appended to the queue of concepts to be learned.

In the next iteration, RTL concentrates again on male ancestors. As mentioned in Section 4, before inducing a new golden point, RTL looks for a new recurrent clause using the previously learned golden points. The following recursive generalization comes out:

$$\text{father}(x,y) \rightarrow \text{m-a''}(x,y) \qquad \text{m-a''}(x,z) \wedge \text{diff}(z,y) \wedge \text{f-a'}(z,y) \rightarrow \text{m-a''}(x,y)$$

Repeating this process a number of times, RTL builds up a set of simply recursive theories which form a complete simply recursive network that can be further generalized by applying stratification. The final theory contains the following six clauses, that are complete, consistent and correct w.r.t. the instances provided:

$$\text{father}(x,y) \rightarrow \text{m-a}(x,y) \qquad\qquad \text{mother}(x,y) \rightarrow \text{f-a}(x,y)$$

$$\text{m-a}(x,z) \wedge \text{diff}(z,y) \wedge \text{father}(z,y) \rightarrow \text{m-a}(x,y)\text{f-a}(x,z \wedge \text{diff}(z,y) \wedge \text{m-a}(z,y) \rightarrow \text{f-a}(x,y)$$

$$\text{m-a}(x,z) \wedge \text{diff}(z,y) \wedge \text{f-a}(z,y) \rightarrow \text{m-a}(x,y)\text{f-a}(x,z) \wedge \text{diff}(z,y) \wedge \text{f-a}(z,y) \rightarrow \text{f-a}(x,y)$$

6. Experiments

RTL was run on three different problems: the first is the example introduced in the previous section, in which the aim was to show that the learning strategy implemented makes RTL really able to build mutually recursive definitions. In this experiment, we used several randomly generated family trees with different distributions of female and male components, different predicate sets each including irrelevant predicates, such as *sister* and *brother*, or redundant predicates, such as *son* and *daughter*. In all cases, RTL found a correct mutually recursive theory. By only using predicates such as *male*, *female*, *father* and *mother*, it tested ~1250 literals and learned the following clauses (where *diff* has been removed for simplicity, and *male* and *female* can also be removed because subsumed):

$$\text{male}(x) \wedge \text{father}(x,y) \rightarrow \text{m-a}(x,y) \qquad \text{female}(x) \wedge \text{mother}(x,y) \rightarrow \text{f-a}(x,y)$$

$$\text{m-a}(x,z) \wedge \text{m-a}(z,y) \rightarrow \text{m-a}(x,y) \qquad \text{f-a}(x,z) \wedge \text{m-a}(z,y) \rightarrow \text{f-a}(x,y)$$

$$\text{m-a}(x,z) \wedge \text{f-a}(z,y) \rightarrow \text{m-a}(x,y) \qquad \text{f-a}(x,z) \wedge \text{f-a}(z,y) \rightarrow \text{f-a}(x,y)$$

Adding redundant predicates (*son* and *daughter*) to the set of features RTL can use, it tested 1600 literals (~25% more), obtaining equivalent definitions:

$$\text{male}(x) \wedge \text{son}(y,x) \rightarrow \text{m-a}(x,y) \qquad \text{female}(x) \wedge \text{mother}(x,y) \rightarrow \text{f-a}(x,y)$$

$$\text{m-a}(x,z) \wedge \text{m-a}(z,y) \rightarrow \text{m-a}(x,y) \qquad \text{f-a}(x,z) \wedge \text{m-a}(z,y) \rightarrow \text{f-a}(x,y)$$

$$\text{m-a}(x,z) \wedge \text{f-a}(z,y) \rightarrow \text{m-a}(x,y) \qquad \text{f-a}(x,z) \wedge \text{f-a}(z,y) \rightarrow \text{f-a}(x,y)$$

It is interesting to notice that, since we did not use any kind of additional knowledge about "importance" or "significance" of predicates, RTL can use *son* and *father* interchangeably, and so the choice between the two is just a matter of which is tested first. On the other hand, irrelevant predicates (*sister*, *brother*, *uncle* and *aunt*, all defined in terms of the operational predicates *male*, *female*, *father* and *mother*) did not influence the result but increased the number of tested literals by another 20% (1830 tested literals).

The aim of the second experiment is to show RTL independence of the initial concept learning order. We considered a document understanding problem, in which concepts are dependent according to a predefined hierarchy (see (Esposito et al., 1993) for a complete description of the application). There are five concepts to be learned, namely *sender* of the letter, *receiver*, *logotype*, *reference number* and *date*, in terms of operational predicates such as *height*, *width*, *position*, *type*, *relative position* and *relative alignment* of objects in a document. The learning set consists of 20 documents composed of 261 objects, 23 of which are instances of concept *sender*, 29 are instances of *receiver*, 20 of *logotype*, 26 of *reference number* and 26 of *date*. The test set consists of 10 documents composed of 133 objects, 12 of which are instances of concept *sender*, 10 are instances of *receiver*, 10 of *logotype*, 19 of *reference number* and 11 of *date*. The concept dependencies hierarchy as defined in (Esposito et al., 1993) is shown in Fig. 2.

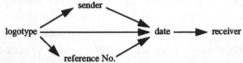

Fig. 2 - The hierarchy of concept dependencies.

RTL has been run 120 times, once for each possible ordering of concepts, recording the learned concept dependencies, the number of tested literals and the corresponding performances on the test set. In all cases, RTL found a dependency among *reference number*, *date* and *receiver*, see Fig. 3, but no dependencies among *logotype*, *sender* and the other concepts.

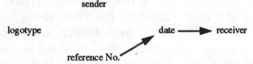

Fig. 3 - The concept dependencies found by RTL.

Table I - RTL results on the document understanding problem.

	Frequency	Sender	Receiver	Logo	Reference No.	Date	Error Rate %	Ambiguity Rate %	Tested Literals
Case A	40	1/0	1/4	0/0	2/0	0/1	3.23	8.06	11030
Case B	20	1/0	1/0	0/0	2/0	1/0	0.0	8.07	11460
Case C	20	1/0	1/5	0/0	2/0	0/1	3.23	9.68	10633
Case D	20	1/0	1/0	0/0	2/0	0/1	1.62	4.84	9028
Case E	20	1/0	1/4	0/0	2/0	0/1	3.23	8.06	10613

All possible orderings can be grouped into five clusters according to their performances on the test set (the five rows in Table I). In particular, the relative frequency of appearance is reported in the first column; columns from 2 to 6 report the number of omission/commission errors made by the clauses learned for each concept. The overall performances are reported in the error rate and ambiguity rate columns (these values are computed w.r.t. the total number of instances). Omission errors contribute to the ambiguity rate, because in these cases RTL was not able to assign a label to the instances giving an ambigous answer, whereas commission errors contribute to the error rate. The last column reports the average number of tested literals.

As it can be noticed, in 80 out of 120 initial orderings (rows 1, 3 and 5) the performances are almost identical as well as the number of tested literals. In 20 cases (row 2), the performances are better, but at the highest cost. In other 20 cases (row 4), RTL found good definitions (1.62% error rate) at the lowest cost. It should be pointed out that the ordering corresponding to the concept hierarchy outlined in Fig. 2, is included in case C and does not correspond to the best results. This is somewhat counter-intuitive, since that ordering enlightens the correct dependencies, but this information is useful only when concepts are learned one after the other. Instead, at each step, RTL learns a partial concept definition, that exploits only partial dependencies among concepts. Anyway, as the obtained results are comparable one another, we can conclude that RTL is experimentally independent of the initial concept order.

The third problem has been designed to test the effectiveness of RTL control strategy: we selected a subset of the Pascal grammar, by considering only if-then, while-do and assignment statements, and generated examples and counterexamples of Pascal programs. The goal of RTL is to learn the subset of Pascal grammar used to generate the instances. The problem is interesting for two reasons: the recursive structure of Pascal instructions is a natural application for a system that claims to learn recursive definitions; secondly, learning a grammar is a significant problem in a large class of applications. In particular, the relationship between golden points and recurrent clauses in the Pascal statements is very interesting: in fact, the same golden point (for instance, an assignment statement) can be used for building up many recurrent clauses. Originally, RTL algorithm (Baroglio et al., 1992) made the strong assumption that two recursive definitions of the same concept are based on different golden points; this assumption has been removed in the current version and the algorithm redesigned to explicitly take into account this situation.

RTL has been configured to learn only one concept, namely the Pascal statement: each statement is represented by a set of tokens, as reported in Fig. 4; the concept description language contains *type* predicates, like *ifthen*, *cond*, *while*, *assign*, etc., and binary relationships, like *before* (x is immediately before y), *part-of* (x is part of y), etc., all of which are mandatory for a consistent and complete definition.

if a<5 then while b>a do b := b-1;	**ifthen cond while cond assign**
(a)	(b)

Fig. 4 - (a) A Pascal statement and (b) its representation.

Different learning sets, in which the number of positive and negative instances vary, have been tried. For each statement considered there is at least one positive and one negative instance in the learning set. In all cases, RTL found the following consistent definitions (st stands for statement):

$$st'(x) \leftarrow assign(x)$$
$$st'(x) \leftarrow ifthen(x) \wedge st'(y) \wedge part\text{-}of(y,x) \wedge part\text{-}of(z,x) \wedge cond(z) \wedge before(z,y)$$
$$st''(x) \leftarrow assign(x)$$
$$st''(x) \leftarrow while(x) \wedge st''(y) \wedge part\text{-}of(y,x) \wedge part\text{-}of(z,x) \wedge cond(z) \wedge before(z,y)$$

Fig. 5 - Definition found by RTL for the Pascal statements problem.

As a matter of fact, RTL did not find the following definitions, that would complete the concept description:

$$st'''(x) \leftarrow while(x) \land st'(y) \land part\text{-}of(y,x) \land part\text{-}of(z,x) \land cond(z) \land before(z,y)$$
$$st'''(x) \leftarrow while(x) \land st''(y) \land part\text{-}of(y,x) \land part\text{-}of(z,x) \land cond(z) \land before(z,y)$$
$$st^{iv}(x) \leftarrow while(x) \land st'(y) \land part\text{-}of(y,x) \land part\text{-}of(z,x) \land cond(z) \land before(z,y)$$
$$st^{iv}(x) \leftarrow while(x) \land st^{iv}(y) \land part\text{-}of(y,x) \land part\text{-}of(z,x) \land cond(z) \land before(z,y)$$

this is probably because the golden points are too complex, and the inductive procedure is misled by the information gain measure used to evaluate hypotheses. Two possible solutions are currently under study: the first, that still needs an extensive theoretical study, consists in enhancing the stratification process in such a way that definitions as the ones in Fig. 5 can be *merged* to define a unique predicate. The second solution is more practical and concerns the way in which RTL generates the templates for learning recurrent clauses: actually, a template is generated only from golden point definitions, but it might also be possible to build a template from a previously learned recursive definition. For instance, after the definitions in Fig. 5 have been learned, RTL considers again assign(x) $\rightarrow$ st'''(x) as a golden point and build up the following template: st'''(y) $\land$ diff(x,y) $\rightarrow$ st^{iv}(x). It might also build up templates like the following:

$$st'(y) \land diff(x,y) \rightarrow st^{iv}(x) \qquad\qquad st''(y) \land diff(x,y) \rightarrow st^{iv}(x)$$

by explicitly inserting st' and st'' (the previously learned partial definitions) in the body of the clause.

7. Conclusions and Future Work

In this paper, an algorithm for inducing function-free, recursive programs defining multiple concepts has been presented. The main goal of the algorithm (the reduction of the complexity of a task that in many cases is intractable) has been achieved by selecting a proper inductive strategy and restricting the class of learnable programs. Even so, practical applications are still interesting. In particular, RTL proved to be effective to infer the recursive structure of multi-dimensional, interconnected sequences of objects, such as ancestors in family trees and Pascal statement grammar. Problems of this type are frequently encountered in robotics applications and image interpretation. Anyway, extending the class of learnable programs RTL can deal with is one of the main enhancement under study.

Acknowledgements
We would like to thank Attilio Giordana for many useful suggestions in reviewing a draft of this paper, and Lorenza Saitta for her helpful comments on previous work.

References
K.R. Apt, H.A. Blair, and A. Walker: "Towards a Theory of Declarative Knowledge", in *Foundations of Deductive Databases and Logic Programming*, J. Minker (Ed), Morgan Kaufmann, Los Altos, CA, 89-148, 1988.

55

C. Baroglio, A. Giordana, and L. Saitta: "Learning Mutually Dependent Relations", *Journal of Intelligent Information Systems, 1*, Kluwer Academic Publishers, 159-176, 1992.

M. Botta: "Learning First Order Theories", *Proc of the ISMIS-94, LNAI 869*, Charlotte, NC, 356-365, 1994.

M. Botta, and A. Giordana: "SMART+: A Multi-Strategy Learning Tool", *Proc. of the 13th International Joint Conference on Artificial Intelligence, IJCAI-93*, Chambery, France, 937-943, 1993.

L. De Raedt: *Interactive Theory Revision*, Academic Press, 1992.

L. De Raedt, and N. Lavrač: "The Many Faces of Inductive Logic Programming", *Proc. of the 7th International Symposium on Methodologies for Intelligent Systems, ISMIS-93*, Trondheim, Norway, 435-449, 1993a.

L. De Raedt, N. Lavrač, and S. Džeroski: "Multiple Predicate Learning", *Proc. of the 13th International Joint Conference on Artificial Intelligence, IJCAI-93*, Chambery, France, 1037-1042, 1993b.

F. Esposito, D. Malerba, G. Semeraro, and M. Pazzani: "A Machine Learning Approach to Document Understanding", *Proc. of the 2nd Intenational Workshop on Multistrategy Learning*, Harpers Ferry, WV, 276-292, 1993.

A. Giordana, L. Saitta, and C. Baroglio: "Learning Simple Recursive Theories", *Proc. of the 7th International Symposium on Methodologies for Intelligent Systems, ISMIS-93*, Trondheim, Norway, 425-434, 1993.

J.U. Kietz, and S. Wrobel: "Controlling the Complexity of Learning in Logic though Syntactic and Task-Oriented Models", in *Inductive Logic Programming*, S. Muggleton (Ed)., Academinc Pres, 1992.

N. Lavrač, S. Džeroski, and M. Grobelnik: "Learning Non Recursive Definitions of Relations with LINUS", *Proc. of the 5th European Working Session on Learning, LNAI 482*, Springer-Verlag, 1991.

R.S. Michalski: "A Theory and Methodology of Inductive Learning", *Artificial Intelligence, 20*, 111-161, 1983.

S. Muggleton, and W. Buntine: "Machine Invention of First-order Predicates by Inverting Resolution", *Proc. of the 5th International Conference on Machine Learning*, Ann Arbor, MI, 339-352, 1988.

S. Muggleton, and C. Feng: "Efficient Induction of Logic Programs", *Proc. of the 1st Conference on Algorithmic Learning Theory*, Ohmsha, Tokio, Japn, 1990.

R. Quinlan: "Learning Logical Definitions from Relations", *Machine Learning, 5*, 239-266, 1990.

B.L. Richards, and R.J. Mooney: "First Order Theory Revision", *Proc. of the 8th International Workshop on Machine Learning*, Morgan Kaufmann, 447-451, 1991.

H. Shapiro: *Algorithmic Program Debugging*, MIT Press, 1983.

J. Wogulis: "Revising Relational Theories", *Proc. of the 8th International Workshop on Machine Learning*, Morgan Kaufmann, 462-466, 1991.

Learning While -Solving Problems in Single Agent Search: Preliminary Results

Tim Humphrey

Lexis-Nexis

Dayton, OH USA

Anna Bramanti-Gregor*

Department of Computer Science & Engineering

Wright State University, Dayton, OH 45435 USA

Henry W. Davis

Abstract: A traditional problem with best first search on hard problems is that space requirements are too large. However, space saving approaches require excessive time. We describe an approach which uses best first search, so as to keep time complexity low; it keeps space needs small because, through a statistical learning process, it builds accurate heuristics while solving problems. Unlike other search paradigms, solutions returned are accompanied with a statistical error assessment. In experiments solution quality is found high and time complexity is several orders of magnitude lower than competing techniques. The approach does not build a single heuristic for the whole domain. Instead, a new heuristic is built for each problem encountered: the learning time for constructing such "problem relevant" heuristics is low.

1. Introduction

Search is an important component of problem solving in artificial intelligence. Some of the areas in which search algorithms play a key role are combinatorial optimization, game playing, learning, planning, robotics, and theorem proving. Problem solving in these areas often involves searching a large space of alternatives. To reduce the size of the search space it is critical to use effective heuristic functions, or "heuristics".

We are interested in "best first search", the most commonly used form of heuristic search in single agent state space problems. A problem with best first search is that, while effective on problems of medium difficulty, its space requirements have proven too large for hard problems. For example, in the sliding tile domain, A*, a common best first search algorithm, easily solves 8-puzzle problems optimally with the Manhattan distance heuristic. In the 15-puzzle, however, it builds search trees too large for current computing resources. In the TSP, maps with 25 or more cities have over 10^{23} solution paths competing for consideration. Search trees built by A* to solve such problems are too large to be computationally practical when optimal solutions are demanded. A consequence of this is that space saving algorithms such as IDA*, or depth first branch and bound, are used on such problems. See for example [9]. But now time complexity becomes very large.

----

* Deceased

We describe a problem solving paradigm called searching with accurately constructed heuristics (SACH). SACH is designed to use best first search techniques on hard problems so as to keep time complexity low. Space needs are small because, through a statistical learning process, SACH generates accurate heuristics; solutions are found even though severe constraints are placed on search tree sizes.

SACH is intended to produce high quality, but not necessarilly optimal, solutions. It also produces, with each solution, a statistical error assessment. This important information is not provided in any other search paradigm of which we are aware. Real-world problems are often NP-hard and resources often limited, while optimal solutions are not usually required. We believe that this kind of trade in return for computational tractability is realistic.

Experimental work is ongoing in sliding tiles and TSP domains. In the 15-puzzle SACH solutions have 2% error on average and require several orders of magnitude less time to obtain than when competing methods are used. The TSP maps on which SACH has been tried have city counts of 20, 33, 42, and 57. Space needs normally preclude A* techniques on maps of these sizes. Only the 57-city problem was solved non-optimally (3% error). Error assessment is in line with experimental observation and search trees are small in both domains (under 20,000 nodes).

The overall structure of SACH is described in Section 2. Experimental results are in Section 3. SACH builds heuristics by combining user-provided features. The basic strategy is that multiple search attempts are made on each problem; from the search tree of an unsuccessful effort, statistics are taken and linear regression is performed to build a new heuristic for still another endeavor to solve the problem. The process begins anew with each problem; ie., no effort is made to build a single strong heuristic for all problems. Our method is fundamentally different from other approaches to building heuristic functions statistically, as is discussed in Section 5.

A significant question this raises is "can one obtain useful statistical information about state space graph structure near the goal by studying incomplete search trees rooted at start?" We have found that, in many important cases, one can (Section 4). Section 6 concludes.

Notation

G	Locally finite directed graph.
problem	An element (s,t) of GxG; s is the start, t the goal.
C*	Optimal length of solution to some problem.
C	Solution length to a problem returned by a search algorithm.
solution quality	C/C*
h(n)	Heuristic function evaluated at state, or node, n.

g(n)   Shortest distance yet found by A* from s to n.

A*(h)   A* algorithm using g+h as evaluator.

2. Overview of SACH structure

Heuristic Functions and Control

By a *feature* is meant a function which measures some difference between a problem state and a goal state[a]. It is a real-valued function on GxG. For example, in the sliding tile domain "number of tiles out of place", Manhattan distance, and "reversal count" are all features.

A heuristic function built by humans is not part of the input to SACH. It is replaced by a set of features. These are assessed by statistical routines for combination into a heuristic. The burden of building a heuristic is removed from the human user and placed on the system because statistical routines make better and more prompt use of performance information than can a human.

SACH builds several new heuristics with each problem it encounters, as opposed to building a general-purpose heuristic for the whole domain: we say its heuristic functions are *problem relevant*, rather than *domain relevant*. There are two reasons for this design.

(1) In difficult search domains one cannot easily acquire for statistical sampling a large number of perfect solutions to random problems. Either the time or the space requirements are too large. Therefore, building an effective domain relevant heuristic is ruled out.

(2) The features known to humans may be quite adequate for generating high quality solutions to individual problems. However, they may be too weak for combination into a powerful domain relevant heuristic.

The input feature list is enlarged by humans who add to it certain cross products and powers (viz., square roots and squares) of its original terms. The augmented list, now used by SACH, is called an "extended feature" list. The technique for obtaining extended features from features follows that commonly used by statisticians in "model building" [10]. Extended feature examples are in [2, 11].

SACH heuristics are linear combinations of extended features and are built by linear regression. The solution process is in stages. During each stage the given problem is solved or partially solved by A*. The search tree built in one stage provides data needed by the statistical routines that build the heuristic used in the next stage. In SACH's linear regression the response (dependent) variable is optimum distance between two nodes. The independent variables are extended features corresponding to the same two nodes. By taking measurements between expanded nodes and their ancestors on a search tree, an abundance of useful information is obtained for linear regression even when the search tree represents an unsuccessful effort to solve the problem. Heuristics so built by SACH are called *fitted heuristics*.

....

A (Initialize) h := initial heuristic; DATA, SOLNS :=
    empty set.
B (Generate fitted heuristics; attempt to solve problem)
    Do ENOUGH times:
  (i) Apply A*(h) to (s,t) but allow no more than
       MAX_SPACE nodes to be expanded. DATA := sample
       data from search tree for use in linear
       regression. If a solution is found, then add it
       to SOLNS.
  (ii) If more fitted heuristics are desired, then use
       DATA to build a new fitted heuristic, h.
C (Multiply step; performed only if no solutions are
    found in step B)
    - z := 1
    - Do ENOUGH2 times or until SOLNS is not empty:
    - z := z + INCREMENT
    - For each fitted heuristic h produced in step B do:
      - Apply A*(zh) to (s,t) but allow no more than
        MAX_SPACE nodes to be expanded.
      - If a solution is found, then add it to SOLNS.
D If SOLNS not empty, then return the best solution with
    error assessment; otherwise report failure.

Figure 2.1. SACH control structure for solving a single problem, (s,t). The user provides features which are extended. In B(i) problem solving is attempted. From the search tree created, data is collected so that in B(ii) another fitted heuristic may be built. Extended features are used in B(ii). If, after ENOUGH tries, no solution has been found, then SACH tries to obtain solutions by using A* with multiplied versions of the fitted heuristics it has built (step C).

....

The initial heuristic used is a given admissible one (possibly zero), which, by Mero's technique [6], may be assumed consistent. As a result, the initial search tree has the optimal possible distances between expanded nodes; sampled data for the response variable for the first fitted heuristic is therefore correct, promoting accuracy for this heuristic. We have found that within the sequence of fitted heuristics built, there is a tendency for the accuracy to be maintained while the ranges of the heuristics increase.

The basic SACH control structure is shown in Figure 2.1. Fitted heuristics are generated and used in step B where the space allowed for search trees is constrained by MAX_SPACE. This parameter is determined by space/time considerations of the problem solving environment. For example, in 15-puzzle experiments, we have set it to 10,000; this has caused our maximum space needs (nodes generated) to be under 20,000. Similarly, ENOUGH is a parameter which controls the number of fitted heuristics generated; it also is determined by the problem solving environment. For the 15-puzzle we set it to 20.

Often, when A*(h) uses excessive time without finding a olution, employing the "multiplied heuristic", zh, where z > 1, causes a solution to be found: however, solution quality may degrade. Discussions of the reasons are in [1,3]. Step C uses this mechanism. For example, in the 15-puzzle we set INCREMENT to 0.1 and ENOUGH2 to 3.

SACH may fail to find a solution. So far we have found that, with reasonable space allotment and standard features, this has not been a problem in the 15-puzzle or TSP (less or equal 57 cities).

Error Assessment

In the standard linear regression model, error in the regression equation is assumed independent, normally distributed and of constant variance. This enables a prediction interval to be stated for values of the response variable. Using this, SACH is able to provide probabilistic estimates of upper bounds for solutions it returns. We have proven the following:

Theorem (Upper bound for solution error). Suppose the SACH heuristic, h, is built from extended features $h_1,...,h_k$ and that it returns a solution of length C. Then, given $0 < ß < 0.5$, the probability is at least $1 - ß$ that

$$(2.1) \quad C - C^* \leq \sup\{t(ß)STDI(h_1(n),...,h_k(n)) : n \text{ belongs to } G\}.$$

Here t references the t-distribution and STDI is the standard error of (individual) prediction.

We call the right side of (2.1) a $100(1 - ß)\%$ *certainty bound for actual error*; it is estimated from the sample set used to build h and the result is called an *estimated certainty bound*.

The main idea of the proof is that one applies the prediction interval theorem of linear regression to the value of h on the shallowest open node of an optimal solution path during the last iteration of A*. The error term of the linear regression equation absorbs, (a), inaccuracies in response variable sampling and, (b), the natural variability of the response variable with respect to extended features.

3. Performance Overview

Experiments with SACH are preliminary and ongoing. They have been conducted in the TSP and 15-puzzle domains. In both domains constraints on the search tree size have kept space needs modest - under 20,000 nodes. It is relevant to know the time spent learning since learning is part of the problem solving process. It is under 3%, by far the majority being spent gathering data for linear regression.

Korf Number	C*	C	C/C*	SACH GEN	IDA* GEN
3	59	59	1.00	787,796	565,994,203
10	59	59	1.00	1,226,791	198,758,703
14	59	59	1.00	392,644	1,369 596,778
15	62	64	1.03	388,167	543,598,067
17	66	74	1.12	358,151	607,399,560
22	59	61	1.03	782,553	750,746,755
32	59	59	1.00	1,122,748	661,041,936
33	60	60	1.00	1,159,346	480,637,867
43	64	64	1.00	360,754	41,124,767
49	59	63	1.07	380,870	1,809,933,698
53	64	64	1.00	376,711	465,225,698
60	66	66	1.00	1,180,773	3,337,690,331
66	61	61	1.00	1,179,826	1,957,191,378
82	62	62	1.00	812,415	5,506,801,123
88	65	69	1.06	350,942	6,009,130,748
AVG			1.02	724,032	1,620,321,441

Table 3.1. Performance of SACH and IDA* on the 15 hardest of 100 random 15-puzzles problems. GEN denotes number of nodes generated; for SACH it is summed over all search efforts. Solution quality (C/C*) is 1 for IDA* because it is admissible with the Manhattan distance heuristic, which was used. The average ratio of GEN(IDA*) to GEN(SACH) is 2,238

In the 15-puzzle A* has not been used to obtain optimal solutions because its space needs are too large[b]. However IDA* has. To get some performance comparisons, SACH has been run on the hardest 15 (i.e., largest C* value) of the 100 random 15-puzzle problems in [4]; see Table 3.1. SACH generates several orders of magnitude fewer nodes, indicating substantial speed improvement. The tradeoff for this is only 2% reduction in average solution quality.

In Table 3.2 we show typical results when the error bound theorem of Section 2 is applied to the 15 puzzle. We consider 95% and

84% certainty bounds. We have found the observations in line with theoretical predictions. An upper bound on solution quality is implicit in the theorem by applying the formula: solution quality bound = C/(C - error bound). It is shown in the table.

Korf #	C*	estimated certainty bounds on actual error		observed error	estimated certainty bounds on actual SQ		observed SQ
		95%	84%		95%	84%	
16	42	3.211	1.952	0	1.083	1.049	1.000
13	46	4.738	2.880	4	1.105	1.061	1.087
15	62	3.731	2.268	2	1.062	1.037	1.032

Table 3.2. Estimated certainty bounds for actual errors and solution qualities (SQ) are compared with observed values for 15 puzzle problems in easy, medium and hard categories (C* = 42, 46 and 62, respectively). The 95% bounds are correct. One of the 84% bounds is too low; the others are correct and tight.

In the TSP SACH has been tested on Euclidean maps with 33, 42, and 57 cities, all taken from the literature.[£] In addition, it has been tested on 20 random 20-city problems. (We view the latter as being of only medium difficulty.) All except the 57-city problem were solved optimally. Solution quality in the 57-city was 1.03. As in the 15-puzzle, error assessment has been in agreement with experiments.

The input features for the sliding tile domain consist mainly of historical heuristics such as number of tiles-out-of-place, Manhattan distance, and reversal count. For the TSP they are based on minimum spanning tree, nearest neighbor, cheapest insertion, and related ideas.

4. Enhancing the learning mechanism

The iterations in step B of Figure 2.1 may be viewed as learning phases. The sample data used to build a fitted heuristic is thrown away after the heuristic is built. Only the fitted heuristic is passed to the next learning phase. This heuristic is an abstraction of the search experience of this phase and is the vehicle for communicating such experience to the next phase. We have found that these heuristics are not domain relevant. Even those which successfully solve the problem for which they are designed are of little use in solving other problems.

Is it possible to sample the search tree so as to enhence accuracy of the fitted heuristic relative to the current problem? In a large number of cases, yes.

In many situations the goal is known in advance. Sliding tiles are an example. In sampling the tree, the end point of the path being sampled which simulates a goal should be near the tree root. In the following search phase, start and goal are interchanged. The effect is that at any time A* is seeking a goal for which its heuristic has been especially sensitized. This was done in the runs which produced the data in Table 3.1. By comparison, when the goals are not interchanged, average GEN is 31% larger and solution quality is 1.07 instead of 1.02. In the 15-puzzle the cost of traversing an edge is the same in both directions, namely, one. However, the technique just described works even if this is not the case.

In the TSP a similar phenomenon occurs without any "interchanging of start and goal". Since the path being sought returns to the start node, heuristics built while learning accuracy relative to the state space region near start contain information relevant to the search's end. This is true for asymmetric TSPs as well as symmetric ones.

In some scheduling problems, the TSP situation described above may be simulated. For example, suppose we want the best schedule for a traveler who visits all cities once but we have no constraint on where the journey starts and ends. By adding a virtual city whose distance to all others is zero and requesting that the traveler start and end at the virtual city, we obtain an equivalent problem and the same environment for learning fitted heuristics as in the TSP. An analogous line of thought applies to job shop scheduling.

5. Other approaches and comparisons with SACH

The idea of representing heuristic information as a linear combination of features goes back to Samuel's work in checkers. It is common in game playing programs to use as a heuristic function some linear combination of features whose coefficients have been learned from experience in previous games. The most conspicuous difference between game playing heuristics and those built by SACH is that the former are domain relevant, whereas SACH heuristics are problem relevant.

In single agent search it is usual for the heuristic function to be an ad hoc linear combination of features. Two single agent systems which provide alternatives to ad hoc linear combination have been detailed in the literature. MULTIPLE [8] and PLS [7] both use sample data taken from a training set, and linear regression, to build heuristics which are linear combinations of features. In each case a domain relevant heuristic is constructed prior to problem solving time. We overview these systems briefly and compare them with SACH^c.

MULTIPLE searches implicit AND/OR trees using resolution to find proofs of predicate calculus theorems. The learning program is given a list of features which are real-valued functions of subgoals in the search tree. They reflect syntactic properties of the subgoal statement. These features are combined linearly into two heuristic functions by solving training problems, and using data so obtained in linear regression. The heuristics are now used in problem solving with best first search.

The main version of PLS works with OR-graphs (like SACH), rather than AND/OR graphs. It learns a domain relevant heuristic, h, to be used in best first search from a list of features and a training set of domain problems. For each node n, h(n) is viewed as an approximation of the probability that n lies on an optimal solution path. In Rendell's variation of best first search, the evaluator is h alone, not the more traditional g+h.

The main structural differences between statistical learning in MULTIPLE and PLS versus SACH are as follows.

(1) Both MULTIPLE and PLS build a domain relevant heuristic from a training set before problem solving. SACH heuristics are problem relevant and built during problem solving.

(2) All three systems learn in stages, or phases. In MULTIPLE and PLS communication between the stages is by sample data. Sample data is augmented by more data in each stage and the accumulation is passed to the next stage. In SACH the only item passed between stages is the fitted heuristic (which may be viewed as an abstraction of sample data).

(3) The response variables of MULTIPLE, likelihood that a subgoal is provable and its merit, and the probabilistic one, described earlier, for PLS are hard to sample accurately. Such sampling is needed by the statistical routines. The SACH response variable is easily sampled from a search tree.

The domains of MULTIPLE and SACH are so different that it is impossible to compare performances. However, PLS has been run in the 15-puzzle domain. On random problems Rendell reports low average node expansion but not such good solution quality: 353 and 2.13, respectively[a,e]. To obtain high quality solutions, as does SACH, it would appear that many more nodes need be expanded, at least when standard features are used.

6. Conclusions

We have focused on single agent search problems which are too hard for best first search because of their space requirements; however alternative control structures (depth first branch and bound, or IDA*) use excessive time. By adding a statistical learning component to the A* algorithm, we are able to build accurate heuristics from user supplied features while problem solving. The resulting strategy, called SACH, has low space needs and is significantly faster than competing methods even when learning time is taken into account. For example, in the 15-puzzle (in which best first search has heretofore not produced high quality solutions) SACH averages only 2% error and runs several orders of magnitude faster than the classical competing admissible approach, IDA*.

65

A unique aspect of SACH is that its heuristics are built anew with each problem encountered. This eliminates the need for accurate and hard-to-get statistical information before problem solving. It also allows that features known to humans may not support a strong global heuristic, but may be excellent for solving individual problems.

SACH is designed to meet a practical need for computational tractability in real-world problems. Its use assumes that guaranteed completeness and perfection in solution quality may, to some extent, be traded for lower use of computing resources and statistical assessment of solution errors. We believe this is an attractive trade.

References

1   Bramanti-Gregor A., Davis H.W. and Ganschow F.G., Strengthening heuristics for lower cost optimal and near optimal solutions in A* search, Proceedings of the 10th European Conference on Artificial Intelligence (1992) 6-10.
2   Bramanti-Gregor A. and Davis H.W., The statistical learning or accurate heuristics, Proceedings of the 13th International Joint Conference on Artificial Intelligence (1993) 1079-1085.
3   Davis H.W. and Chenoweth S., The mathematical modeling of heuristics, Annals Of Mathematics and Artificial Intelligence 5 (1992) 191-228.
4   Korf R.E., Depth-first iterative-deepening: an optimal admissible tree search, Artificial Intelligence 27 (1985) 97-109.
5   Korf R.E., Linear-space best-first search: summary of results, Proceedings of the National Conference on Artificial Intelligence (1992).
6   Mero L., A heuristic search algorithm with modifiable estimate, Artificial Intelligence 23 (1984) 13-27.
7   Rendell L., Conceptual knowledge acquisition in search, in Computational Models of Learning, L. Bolc ed., Springer-Verlag (1987) 89- 159.
8   Slagle J.E. and Farrel C.D., Experiments in automatic learning for a multipurpose heuristic program, Communications of the ACM 14 (1971) 91-99.
9   Vempaty N.R., Kumar V. and Korf R.E., Depth-first vs best-first search, Proceedings of the 9th National Conference on Artificial Intelligence (1991) 434-440.
10 Weisberg S., Applied Linear Regression, John Wiley & Sons, 1985.
11 Gregor A., Strengthening heuristic knowledge in A* search, Ph.D Dissertation, Dept. of Computer Science, Wright State University, Dayton, Ohio, USA (1993).

Endnotes

Notes reference superscripts in text.

a The formal definition we use of a feature requires only that it be a real-valued function defined on pairs of problem states. Features may take on negative values. A feature whose values have no correlation to the true distance between its arguments will not be chosen for use by the linear regression routines.

A heuristic function may be viewed as a feature . The notion of "feature" depends on context. For example, in sliding tile problems the Manhattan distance is often used as a "heuristic" with A*; alternatively, it may be only one component of a more sophisticated heuristic. In the latter case we view it as a "feature".

b The highest quality solutions of which we know, obtained by A*, have on average 50% error. Multiplied Manhattan distance is used as the heuristic and approximately 100,000 nodes are generated [5].

c In [2] "early learning" also precompiles a domain relevant heuristic using linear regression. It is designed for problems of medium difficulty, whereas SACH is designed to solve hard problems. The SACH approach evolved from "early learning" studies and we do not discuss its precursor here.

d In the 15-puzzle 353 nodes expanded implies that approximately 700 nodes are generated.

e Rendell reports average solution length to be 113. Solution quality of 2.13 follows from the fact that average optimal solution length for 15-puzzle problems is known to be 53 [4].

f The peculiar city count numbers are because we used TSP's with published optimum solution lengths (or best known in the 57-city case).

Automatic Construction of Navigable Concept Networks Characterizing Text Databases

Claudio Carpineto and Giovanni Romano
Fondazione Ugo Bordoni
Via Baldassarre Castiglione 59, 00142, Rome, Italy
{carpinet, romano}@fub.it

Abstract

In this paper we present a comprehensive approach to conceptual structuring and intelligent navigation of text databases. Given any collection of texts, we first automatically extract a set of index terms describing each text. Next, we use a particular lattice conceptual clustering method to build a network of clustered texts whose nodes are described using the index terms. We argue that the resulting network supports an hybrid navigational approach to text retrieval - implemented into an actual user interface - that combines browsing potentials with good retrieval performance. We present the results of an experiment on subject searching where this approach outperformed a conventional Boolean retrieval system.

1. Introduction

Especially after the advent of Internet, the amount of available information represented as text databases has rapidly grown. This is the case for bibliographic collections, news and message files, software libraries, multimedia repositories with text captions, etc. Most usually, these databases are accessed to retrieve items of interest or to explore their content, therefore it is useful to organize the information into some sort of structure and then let the user navigate through it. In fact, the organizing/navigating paradigm is becoming very popular (Thompson and Croft, 1989; Maarek et al, 1991; Lucarella et al, 1993; Bowman et al, 1994). One main problem of this approach is creating the atomic pieces of information and linking them, which usually requires subjective and time-consuming decisions. We argue that conceptual clustering techniques (Michalski, 1983) may be helpful to automate this process.

In an abstract browsing retrieval setting there is a collection of documents described by a set of index terms and the user wants to find elements of interest by navigating through a network of clustered documents. Conceptual clustering presents three basic features for supporting this task, in that the clusters are (a) automatically generated from the document-term relation, (b) described by a conceptual description, (c) organized into a hierarchy showing their generality/specificity. In this paper we present an approach to organizing a collection of documents that is based on a particular lattice conceptual clustering method (Carpineto and Romano, 1993). It turns out that the resulting clustering structure presents many useful advantages for supporting browsing retrieval from the document collection, but in order to build a practical system two more questions need be addressed. The first concerns the set of index terms used in the clustering process. While in most conceptual clustering task it is assumed that the set of properties describing the objects to be clustered is given, this assumption is often unrealistic for textual objects, which are usually available unindexed. To solve this problem we have developed a module for automatic indexing that combines linguistic and statistical concepts. The second issue to address is the construction of an actual interface to enable the interaction between the user and the support network. We have realized a visual interface to the concept lattice that provides a hybrid navigational strategy integrating two conventional retrieval techniques - link-based and query-based navigation - and a novel one - user-bounded navigation.

A major part of this paper is an empirical evaluation of the retrieval effectiveness of the overall system. It is often remarked that, at least for sizable databases and typical retrieval tasks such as subject searching, the structure-based approaches to information retrieval have not yet proven to be an effective alternative to more conventional query-based methods. We address this issue, and present the results of an experiment on subject searching in a standard reasonably-sized database, where the lattice method performed significantly better than a conventional Boolean system.

The rest of the paper is organized in the following way. In section 2 we present the automatic indexing method. In section 3 we introduce the lattice conceptual clustering method, while in section 4 we characterize its utility for browsing retrieval. Section 5 contains a description of the visual retrieval interface. In section 6 we describe the experimental evaluation. Finally, we offer some conclusion and directions for future work in section 7.

2. Automatic Indexing

The first task for building a conceptual representation of a text database is to identify the content of each text. Basically, there are two kinds of approaches. In the AI-based approach, natural language processing techniques (Sowa, 1984; Srihari and Burhans, 1994) or machine learning techniques (Barletta and Mark, 1988; Baudin et al, 1994) can be used to build or refine an internal representation of each text. Although most of these methods can produce deep conceptual indices, they can only work in restricted environments and usually require extensive knowledge about the semantics of the application domain. An alternative approach for content extraction that is domain-independent, knowledge-free, and efficient is adopted in most information retrieval systems. Our indexing procedure is inspired by the latter approach. It consists of the following steps.

1. Text segmentation

Our system first identifies the individual words occurring in a text collection, ignoring punctuation and case.

2. Word stemming

We reduce each word to word-stem form. This is done by using a very large morphological lexicon for English (Karp et al, 1992) that contains the standard inflections for nouns (singular, plural, singular genitive, plural genitive), verbs (infinitive, third person singular, past tense, past participle, progressive form), adjectives (base, comparative, superlative). The lexicon can handle more than 317,000 inflected forms derived from over 90,000 roots.

3. Stop wording

We use a stop list to delete from the texts the (root) words that are insufficiently specific to represent content. Our stop list has been obtained by unioning two stop lists, a "pragmatic" one and a "grammatical" one. The former is a typical stop list in use in information retrieval, included in the CACM dataset; it contains 428 common function words, such as *the*, *of*, *this*, *on*, etc. and some verbs, e.g., *have*, *can*, *indicate*, etc. The latter, consisting of 403 words, was built by extracting from the lexicon mentioned above all the entries labeled as either pronouns, or conjunctions, or prepositions, or determiners. The final stop list contains 638 words.

4. Word weighting

For each remaining word we derive a measure of its usefulness for indexing purposes. The goal is to identify words that characterize the documents to which they are assigned, while also discriminating them from the remainder of the collection. In fact, most of the weigthing functions that have been proposed tend to favor terms occurring with relatively high frequencies in some individual documents, but with a relatively low overall collection frequency (Salton, 1989). We use the *Signal-Noise Ratio* method, which has an information theory basis; the signal of term k for a collection of n documents is defined as follows

$$SIGNAL_k = \log_2(TOTFREQ_k) - NOISE_k \text{ , where}$$

$$NOISE_k = \sum_{i=1}^{n} \frac{FREQ_{ik}}{TOTFREQ_k} \log_2 \frac{TOTFREQ_k}{FREQ_{ik}}$$

5. Index word selection

Each document is indexed by the set of words relative to the document whose signal-noise ratio is greater than a fixed threshold; if some document remains unindexed, it is assigned a minimum fixed number of words with the highest scores. By varying these two parameters we can choose an informative but restricted set of indexes which is suitable for the subsequent processes of cluster formation and visualization.

This basic indexing method could be improved in a variety of ways, without hurting its generality and efficiency. For instance, we could use vocabulary normalization tools such as synonym list and thesarus associations, or using adjacent words to form term-phrases (Maarek et al, 1991; Chen et al, 1994). We have to emphasize, however, that it has been often reported that in many practical situations the use of more elaborated systems than single-word term extraction did not result in significant performance improvement (Salton, 1989).

Computationally, the indexing module works fairly well. We organized the lexicon into a digital search tree, or trie, and represented all other information (stop-words, weights, etc.) into the same stucture. The memory requirement is still quite demanding (about 10 M-bytes, approximately as much as that of the original unstructured lexicon) but the whole indexing process is fast.

We tested the system on the data set CISI, a widely used bibliographical collection of 1460 information science abstracts. The data set initially contained 184,584 words, 9706 of which were distinct. After stemming and stop wording the data set contained 90154 words, with 7598 distinct words. We next computed the signal-noise ratio and selected all words whose weight was greater than or equal to 1.00, the minimum number of indices per document being set to 4. With this choice each document was indexed by an average of 5.2 terms. To illustrate this application, in table 1 we show a small CISI sample consisting of 6 documents. The table also shows the set of indices associated with each document, with their signal-noise ratio values.

Table 1. An automatically indexed subset of the CISI collection

Doc. 1
Vocabulary Building and Control Techniques, Wall, Eugene
The rationale is given for creation and maintainance by an information center of a controlled indexing and retrieval vocabulary.. Basic vocabulary principles are (1) use of natural language, (2) development of hospitality to new concepts, (3) provision of adequate cross-referencing, and (4) formatting for easy use.. Terminalogical conventions necessary for development and control of a useful vocabulary are summarized, and the techniques for applying these conventions to construct a thesaurus are described.. Computerized editing techniques and updating techniques are briefly set forth..
(INDEX 1.85) (INFORMATION 1.64) (CROSS-REFERENCE 1.63) (LANGUAGE 1.44) (THESAURUS 1.43) (VOCABULARY 1.26) (RETRIEVAL 1.26) (CENTER 1.03)

Doc. 2
Word-Word Associations in Document Retrieval Systems, Lesk, M. E.
The SMART automatic document retrieval system is used to study association procedures for automatic content analysis.. The effect of word frequency and other parameters on the association process is investigated through examination of related pairs and through retrieval experiments.. Associated pairs of words usually reflect localized word meanings, and true synonyms cannot readily be found from first or second order relationships in our document collections.. There is little overlap between word relationships found through associations and those used in thesaurus construction, and the effects of word associations and a thesaurus in retrieval are independent.. The use of associations in retrieval experiments improves not only recall, by permitting new matches between requests and documents, but also precision, by reinforcing existing matches.. In our experiments, the precision effect is responsible for most of the improvement possible with associations.. A properly constructed thesaurus, however, offers better performance than statistical association methods..
(SYSTEM 1.63) (DOCUMENT 1.60) (THESAURUS 1.43) (WORD 1.38) (REQUEST 1.34) (RETRIEVAL 1.26) (SMART 1.25) (PRECISION 1.18) (AUTOMATIC 1.16)

Doc. 3
A Comparison Between Manual and Automatic Indexing Methods, Salton, Gerard
The effectiveness of conventional document indexing is compared with that achievable by fully automatic text processing methods.. Evaluation results are given for a comparison between the MEDLARS search system used at the National Library of Medicine and the experimental SMART system, and conclusions are reached concerning the design of future automatic information systems..
(LIBRARY 2.12) (INDEX 1.85) (MEDLAR 1.81) (INFORMATION 1.64) (SYSTEM 1.63) (DOCUMENT 1.60) (SEARCH 1.38) (SMART 1.25) (TEXT 1.24) (AUTOMATIC 1.16)

Doc. 4
Automated Keyword Classification for Information Retrieval, Sparck-Jones, K.
This book is primarily a research monograph, in which the discussion of the main topics has been broadened so that they are related to their surrounding context in information retrieval as a whole; it is not a textbook, and no attempt has therefore been made to justify the choice of topic, or account for the use of certain concepts, or to provide an elementary description of either. For instance in Chapter 1, it is assumed that the reader is familiar with the idea of using keywords in information retrieval: I have not considered the relation between this kind of retrieval device and a controlled thesaurus or descriptor set, or that between the use of simple class lists as document descriptions and the use of descriptions with a syntactic structure, for example. Equally, in Chapter 2, I have made use of recall/precision ratios as a means of characterising retrieval performance, without justification or argument; but this does not mean that I am unaware of the difficulties of doing this, or of the attention which has been devoted to, and controversy which has raged round, this subject; it is simply that from the point of view of my main purpose it is reasonable to use these ratios.
(CLASSIFICATION 1.74) (INFORMATION 1.64) (DOCUMENT 1.60) (THESAURUS 1.43) (RETRIEVAL 1.26) (DESCRIPTOR 1.26) (CHAPTER 1.24) (BOOK 1.20) (PRECISION 1.18) (SUBJECT 1.02)

Doc. 5
Classification and Indexing in Science, Vickery, B.C.
The preface to the first edition of this book - which is reproduced following this - shows that in 1958 the classification ideas in it were felt to be controversial, needing to be championed. A few years before, the Classification Research Group had issued a memorandum proclaiming 'the need for a faceted classification as the basis of all methods of information retrieval.' As part-author of this memorandum, I must now judge the claim to have been too bold, even brash. But it has been vindicated to an extent, for both in theory and practice the value of facet analysis, in the organization of subject vocabularies for indexing and search, has been widely accepted - whether these vocabularies are classified or alphabetical, and whether used in pre- or post-coordinate fashion.
(INDEX 1.85) (CLASSIFICATION 1.74) (INFORMATION 1.64) (SEARCH 1.38) (VOCABULARY 1.26) (SCIENCE 1.26) (RETRIEVAL 1.26) (BOOK 1.20) (THEORY 1.15) (SUBJECT 1.02)

Doc. 6
Factors Determining the Performance of Indexing Systems, Cleverdon, C.W.
The test results are presented for a number of different index languages using various devices which affect recall or precision. Within the environment of this test, it is shown that the best performance was obtained with the group of eight index languages which used single terms. The group of fifteen index languages which were based on concepts gave the worst performance, while a group of six index languages based on the Thesaurus of Engineering Terms of the Engineers Joint Council were intermediary. Of the single term index languages, the only method of improving performance was to group synonyms and word forms, and any broader groupings of terms depressed performance. The use of precision devices such as links gave no advantage as compared to the basic device of simple coordination.
(INDEX 1.85) (SYSTEM 1.63) (LANGUAGE 1.44) (THESAURUS 1.43) (TERM 1.40) (WORD 1.38) (PRECISION 1.18)

3. Lattice Conceptual Clustering

The second stage of our system exploits the index terms determined in the earlier stage to build a concept network characterizing the whole database. The approach is based on a particular clustering structure, called Galois lattice. Given a binary relation between a set of documents and a set of terms, the Galois lattice is a set of clusters, in which each cluster is a couple, composed of a subset of documents (D), called extent, and a subset of terms (T), called intent. Each couple (D,T) must be a complete couple, meaning that T must contain just those terms shared by all the documents in D, and, similarly, the documents in D must be precisely those sharing all the terms in T. The set of couples can then be ordered by applying the standard set inclusion relation to the set of terms (or, dually, to the set of documents) that describe each couple. The resulting ordered set, which is usually represented by a Hasse diagram, turns out to be a lattice.

We explain the structure by an example. Consider again the simple database shown in table 1 but, for the sake of illustration, assume that each document is described only by the terms whose score is > 1.4. The corresponding Galois lattice is shown in figure 1. The ascending paths represent the subclass/superclass relation; the bottom class is defined by the set of all terms and contains no documents, the top class contain all documents and is defined by their common terms (none, in this case). Note that, due to the completeness requirement, the lattice usually contains only a small subset of the set of classes that can be (theoretically) generated combining the terms in all possible ways.

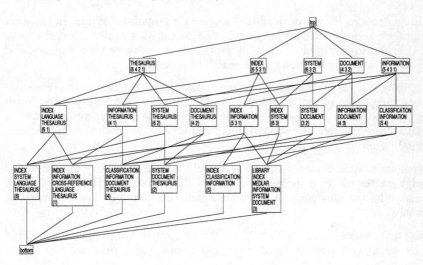

Figure 1. The Galois lattice of the database in table 1.

Given the definition of Galois lattices, we addressed the problem of their automatic determination. We implemented in a system named GALOIS an algorithm that builds the lattice incrementally, where each update takes time proportional to the number of documents to be clustered. We also studied the space complexity of Galois lattice, and found empirical and theoretical evidence that the size of the lattice grows linearly with respect to the number of documents. A detailed explanation of

Galois lattices, of their complexity and of the construction algorithm is contained in (Carpineto and Romano, 1994a).

Galois lattices have many applications, including prediction of unknown attributes and discovery of implications between database attribute values (Carpineto and Romano, 1993). In this paper we are interested in their utilization for supporting information retrieval. This issue is addressed in the next section.

4. Concept Lattices as Retrieval Support Structures

The potentials of clustering for information retrieval have long been known, the main justification for this being what van Rijsbergen termed the cluster hypothesis, namely the fact that documents associated in the same clusters tend to be relevant to the same questions. However, the statistical clustering methods that have predominately been used in information retrieval (e.g., Willet, 1988; Crouch et al, 1989; Maarek et al, 1991) are affected by their inability of producing a conceptual description of the classes generated. By contrast, conceptual clustering techniques usually provide an intensional description of the clusters generated, which may improve both the effectiveness of hierarchy navigation, for interactive searches, and the efficiency of the query-cluster matching process, for automatic searches. This seems to be indeed one key feature for supporting browsing retrieval, but the task in question suggests other desirable properties of the cluster structure.

• Graph navigation is more flexible than tree navigation. While in a strict hierarchical clustering each class has exactly one parent, in a lattice clustering there are many paths to a particular class. This facilitates recovery from bad decision making while traversing the hierarchy in search of documents.

• It is usually the case that a same document is relevant to two or more queries which happen to have incomparable descriptions. Therefore the ability to deal with non-disjoint classes is an important feature of browsing retrieval systems; lattice conceptual clustering naturally supports this functionality, as opposed to hierarchical conceptual clustering.

• In information retrieval domains there is usually an available body of background knowledge expressed as a thesaurus of terms. The ability to incorporate such knowledge into the clustering of documents may considerably improve retrieval performance[1]

• Because text databases may be very large, the computational complexity involved in cluster hierarchy formation is of great importance. $O(n^2)$ time and $O(n)$ space

---

[1] The basic Galois lattice is a purely syntactic structure, in which the order over the classes is independent of possible semantic relationships between terms; however, in presence of auxiliary information expressed as a subconcept/superconcept relationship between the terms, the lattice can be adapted so that more general attributes index more general classes. The essence of this generalization is that when we compute the terms shared by sets of documents we have to take into account also the terms that are implicitly possessed by each document according to the auxiliary information. Indeed, GALOIS can build a thesaurus-enriched lattice (see Carpineto and Romano, 1994a).

clustering algorithms are generally considered to be efficient for retrieval purposes (Willet, 1988).

• In dynamic databases the structure underlying navigation may change as new items are added. Incremental conceptual clustering techniques may therefore be important to reduce the response time of the browser.

Most (conceptual) clustering systems can handle some of these issues but not all of them, GALOIS meets all these general requirements; in addition, a Galois lattice enjoys other useful properties, which make it suitable for supporting a hybrid navigational paradigm involving multiple and integrated retrieval strategies. The first is that in addition to supporting browsing, a concept lattice of documents also allows an easy form of direct query specification. In fact, each node in the lattice can be seen as a query formed of a conjunction of terms (the intent) with the retrieved documents (the extent). The second is that the lattice allows gradual enlargement or refinement of a query. More precisely, following edges departing upward (downward) from a query produces all minimal conjunctive enlargements (refinements) of the query with respect to that particular database. Third, the lattice supports a useful and simple form of incremental pruning of the search space driven by user-specified term-based constraints. In the next section we describe a visual retrieval interface based on these principles.

5. Hybrid Navigation of Concept Lattices

To enable the interaction between the user and the lattice we have realized a prototype interface on top of GALOIS, named ULYSSES[2]. The first problem in the design of the interface is the visualization of the search space. We adopted an approach similar to generalized fish-eye view (Furnas, 1986), in which there is a current focus of interest and the adjacent nodes are displayed with decreasing level of detail as we move away from the focus. As the lattice is typically too large to fit on a screen, we defined some parameters controlling the size and the topology of the region to be displayed. The advantage of this approach is that of selectively maximizing the amount of information that can be displayed, without sacrificing local detail around the focus. In figure 2 we show an example screen of ULYSSES relative to the lattice in figure 1, where the current focus is the highlighted node. The lattice is re-displayed whenever some action taken by the user has the effect of modifying the current focus or some of its neighboroughing nodes in the current screen.

The first way for the user to retrieve items of interst is browsing through the network. ULYSSES allows selection of any node on the current screen by graphical direct manipulation, i.e. by pointing and clicking with the mouse on the desired node, and display of the documents associated with it. The second search strategy is querying. A query can be formulated in two manners: either the user specifies the new terms from scratch, or the user modifies the current query (i.e., the intent of the current focus). In the latter case the user can remove some terms, or add new terms,

---

[2] ULYSSES, like the indexing module and GALOIS, has been implemented in Common Lisp, and runs on a Symbolics Lisp Machine. We are currently porting the whole system, which consists of about 300 K-bytes of code, to PowerMac.

or generalise/specialize some current terms using the information contained in the thesaurus. The result of a query is the class of the lattice that exactly matches the query, if there is any, or one or more classes which best partially match the query according to some heuristic criteria. As a third interaction mode, ULYSSES allows the user to restrict the retrieval space from which she is retrieving information, rather than just accessing it in various ways. We called this bounding, because the user may specify constraints that the sought documents have to satisfy, and the search space is bounded accordingly using a representation similar to version spaces. The constraint are expressed as inequality relations between the description of any admissible class c and some conjunction of terms c1. In our framework, which is logically similar to that proposed in (Mellish, 1991), there are four types of constraints (i.e., $c \geq c1$, $c \leq c1$, $c \neg\geq c1$, $c \neg\leq c1$); each constraint produces a simple graphical partition of the search space, and possesses a meaningful interpretation from an information retrieval point of view. As more and more constraints are seen the search space shrinks and may eventually converge to the target class; if the constraints are too strong the space becomes empty and the user is given the possibility of retracting some of the previously asserted constraints.

One of the most interesting features of ULYSSES is that these interaction modes can be naturally combined to produce a hybrid retrieval strategy that best reflects the user's goal and domain knowledge. For instance, the user may first query the system to locate the region of interest, and then browse through it; bounding may occur at any time, based on the knowledge that the user has or learns by the feedback from the structure. The bound facility is best described in (Carpineto and Romano, 1994b), while a thorough discussion of the whole interface and of the increased retrieval capabilities of hybrid approaches is contained in (Carpineto and Romano, 1995).

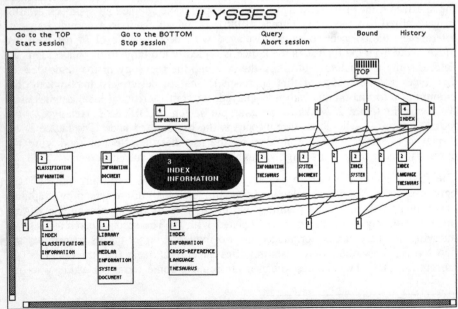

Figure 2. Display screen of ULYSSES, relative to the lattice in figure 1, focusing on the node INDEX, INFORMATION

6. Evaluation of the System's Retrieval Effectiveness

We evaluated the effectiveness of our system on subject searching; this is a familiar task where a user is to retrieve a set of documents relevant to a given question expressed in natural language. We compared the performance of our system with that of a Boolean retrieval system, which is known to perform well on this task and is easy to implement. The experiment was conducted on the CISI collection, that was first automatically indexed as specified in section 2. The same indexing relation was next used to generate the Boolean and the lattice databases. The lattice contained 4707 nodes described on average by 3.61 terms, with an average of 3.45 parents per node and a depth ranging from 2 to 11 edges.

The experimental protocol was as follows. The two retrieval methods were evaluated by two external subjects on 10 queries randomly selected among the 35 questions that are associated with the CISI data set[3]. Each question had its set of relevant documents associated with it, the average number of relevant documents per question being 39. For assigning questions to the two methods a repeated-measures design was used, in which each user searched each question using each method; also, to minimize sequence effects the experimentation of one method was did only a few days after the experimentation of the other, and the order of searching was varied over the question set. During each search the user, who was not asked to finish within a certain time period, could see the abstract of the documents returned in response to boolean queries - in the Boolean method - or associated to the nodes visited - in the lattice method. The documents judged to be relevant by the user, as well as those scanned during the search, were noted as retrieved documents. For each search we considered four measures: recall, precision,[4] number of queries formulated, search time (i.e., the time taken by the user to perform his task). The results are displayed in table 2.

Table 2. Average values of retrieval performance measures

Method	recall	precision	number of queries	search time (sec)
Boolean retrieval	0.32 (s = 0.16)	0.42 (s = 0.15)	5.87 (s = 1.35)	1787 (s = 561)
Lattice-based retrieval	0.45 (s = 0.18)	0.58 (s = 0.10)	2.00 (s = 0.75)	1677 (s = 796)

The table shows that the lattice-based method obtained better evaluation scores for

---

[3] An example of question is the following: What possibilities are there for automatic grammatical and contextual analysis of articles for inclusion in an information retrieval system?

[4] Recall is defined as the ratio of number of items retrieved and relevant to number of items relevant; precision is the ratio of number of items retrieved and relevant to number of items retrieved. Recall measures the ability to retrieve all relevant documents, while precision measures the ability to retrieve only relevant documents.

each measure. A paired t-test revealed no effect of the method on search time ($p = 0.19$), but it did reveal the superiority of the lattice method with respect to recall ($p = 0.003$) and precision ($p = 0.07$). Thus, these results show that the conceptual structuring of the database helped the user focus the search on relevant regions of the retrieval space, which resulted in an improvement of both recall and precision. More specifically, we observed that in the Boolean method it was often difficult to formulate queries returning document lists of reasonable size; consequently, the user was often engaged in time-consuming scannings of the vocabulary window in an attempt to refine overly general queries. By contrast, in the lattice-based method the user exploited the feedback obtained from the structure for refining direct queries, thus reducing the need for other direct queries. This phenomenon is also witnessed by the statistics on the number of queries, which are markedly different in the two methods. Before closing this section, we have to emphasize that this experiment was not designed to measure browsing capabilities, for which our approach has a clear advantage over the Boolean method.

7. Conclusion

The major contribution of this work consists of bringing artificial intelligence, information retrieval, and user interface techniques to bear to build intelligent and robust text retrieval systems. We first presented a method for automatically constructing concept networks characterizing unindexed text databases. We next discussed the potentials of this kind of structure for supporting text retrieval, and presented an actual interface for navigating through the network. The system described here is applicable to collections of texts that vary in subject matter, scope and extent, and does not require domain-specific preconstructed knowledge structures. We compared the performance of this approach on subject searching with that of a Boolean retrieval system. The results were quite encouraging, in that the lattice method showed significantly better recall and precision compared to the Boolean method.

The next step of this research will be aimed at expanding the applicability of the system by making it available on the Internet. The idea is that of using the powerful tools available in World Wide Web for searching networked information such as Netscape or Lycos, as a pre-processing step, and then applying our system to the set of elements retrieved in this way, specified in some fixed format. In this view, our system will act as a conceptual browser of the information retrieved after a Web search, for improving its presentation and facilitating its access.

Acknowledgments

This work has been carried out within the framework of the agreement between the Italian PT Administration and the Fondazione Ugo Bordoni.

References

Barletta, R., Mark, W. (1988). Explanation-Based Indexing of Cases. *Proceedings of AAAI-88*, St. Paul, Minnesota, Morgan Kaufmann.

Baudin, C., Pell, B., Kedar, S. (1994). Incremental Acquisition of Conceptual Indices for Multimedia Design Documentation. *Proceedings of the AAAI-94 Workshop on Indexing and Reuse in Multimedia Systems*, Seattle, Washington.

Bowman, M., Danzig, P., Manber, U., & Schwartz, F. (1994). Scalable Internet Resource Discovery: Research Problems and Approaches. *Communications of the ACM*, 37, 8, pp. 98-114.

Carpineto, C., & Romano, G. (1993). GALOIS: An order-theoretic approach to conceptual clustering. *Proceedings of the 10th International Conference on Machine Learning* (pp. 33-40), Amherst, MA:Morgan Kaufmann.

Carpineto, C., & Romano, G. (1994a). A lattice conceptual clustering system and its application to browsing retrieval. Submitted to Machine Learning.

Carpineto, C., & Romano, G. (1994b). Dynamically bounding browsable retrieval spaces: an application to Galois lattices. In *Proceedings of RIAO 94: Intelligent Multimedia Information Retrieval Systems and Management*(pp. 520-533), New York.

Carpineto, C., & Romano, G. (1995). ULYSSES: A lattice-based multiple interaction strategy retrieval interface. To appear in *Proceedings of EWHCI'95: 5th East-West Human Computer Interaction Conference*, Moscow .

Chen, H., Hsu, P., Orwig, R., Hoopes, L., Nunamaker, J. (1994). Automatic concept classification of text from electronic meeting. *Communications of the ACM*, 37, 10, pp. 57-73.

Crouch, D., Crouch, C., & Andreas, G. (1989). The use of cluster hierarchies in hypertext information retrieval. *Proceedings of the ACM Hypertext '89 Conference* (pp. 225-237), Pittsburgh, PA: ACM.

Furnas, G. (1986). Generalized fisheye views. *Proceedings of the Human Factors in Computing Systems* (pp.16-23). North Holland.

Karp, D., Schabes, Y., Zaidel, M., Egedi, D. (1992). A freely available wide coverage morphological analyzer for English. *Proceedings of the 14th International Conference on Computational Linguistics (COLING '92)*, Nantes, France.

Lucarella, D., Parisotto, S., Zanzi, A. (1993). MORE: Multimedia Object Retrieval Environment. *Proceedings of the Fifth ACM Conference on Hypertext* (pp. 39-50). Seattle, WA.

Maarek, Y., Berry, D., & Kaiser, G. (1991). An Information Retrieval Approach For Automatically Constructing Software Libraries. *IEEE Transactions on Software Engineering*, 17, 8, 800-813.

Mellish, C. (1991). The description identification problem. *Artificial Intelligence*, 52, 2, 151-168.

Michalski, R., Stepp, R. (1983). Learning from observation: Conceptual clustering. In R. Michalski, J. Carbonell, T. Mitchell (Eds.), *Machine Learning: An Artificial Intelligence Approach (Vol. 1)*. Palo Alto, CA: Tioga Publishing.

Salton, G. (1989). *Automatic Text Processing: The transformation, Analysis and Retrieval of Information by Computer*. Addison Wesley.

Sowa, J. (1984). *Conceptual Structures: Information Processing in Mind and Machine*, Addison-Wesley, 1984.

Srihari, R., Burhans, D. (1994). Visual Semantics: Extracting Visual Information from Text Accompanying Pictures. *Proceedings of AAAI-94*, Seattle, Washington, AAAI Press.

Thompson, R., & Croft, B. (1989). Support for browsing in an intelligent text retrieval system. *International Journal of Man-machine Studies*, 30, 639-668.

Willet, P. (1988). Recent trends in hierarchic document clustering: a critical review. *Information Processing & Management*, 24, 5, 577-597.

Temporal Prediction:
Dealing with Change and Interactions within a Causal Framework

Marco Gazza, Pietro Torasso

Dipartimento di Informatica - Universita' di Torino
C.so Svizzera 185 - 10149 Torino (Italy)

Abstract. This paper represents a first step in extending previous work on causation to deal with highly interacting patterns of change. A causal-temporal ontology is devised that is able to distinguish between different types of causation depending on the action-type of the entities involved in the causal rules and on persistence features of the phenomenon to be modeled. We introduce a discrete time structure and we associate appropriate temporal metric parameters to each causal rule in order to model delay and persistence. Moreover, several criteria have been developed for handling cases where different causal rules interact by predicting opposites effects on the same feature of the world. In the present paper we focus our attention on the task of temporal prediction and on the game between *Ego* and *Nature*.

1 Introduction

Reasoning about change plays a central role in describing situations that evolve over time and the AI community has devoted significant amount of research efforts in dealing with such a problem [13]. The problem of change and persistency has been mainly investigated in the context of planning, but other relevant contributions to a in-depth analysis of the relation between time, change, persistency and causality have been obtained by investigating qualitative reasoning [6] and diagnostic problem solving for systems evolving over time [4].

In the classical approaches to planning, the problem of change is dealt with by assuming that an agent acts on the world performing some kind of action for modifying part (of the properties) of the world itself, while the world does not change by itself. Moreover, in many cases, the temporal aspects are limited to the temporal ordering of actions, without taking into consideration metric aspects. Sandewall [11] has proposed a framework where most of the previous work on change and action can be analyzed and compared. Moreover, Sandewall has introduced the notion of game between agents, namely a rational one, called *Ego*, and the *World*, i.e. the environment *Ego* acts on. In the proposal by Sandewall, *Ego* plays a prevailing role in developing the universe: it executes actions and causes changes to occur, while the *World* can only comply with the orders of *Ego*, making the changes effective and moving the time forward.

In the present paper we aim at analyzing situations where the *World* evolves by itself with or without the presence of *Ego*, who can perform actions in order to modify the overall evolution. We believe this is a more realistic setting, in particular if one is interested in the monitoring, diagnosis and repair of physical systems. In the common-sense analysis of time, change and persistency many researchers have recognized that causality plays a major role. For example, Shoham [12] requires that every variation in a certain situation is motivated by a cause. More recently Stein and Morgenstern [14] have proposed a new way of using causation as preference criterion between models of a theory by introducing the notion of *motivation*.

In our analysis we consider causality as the central mechanism for explaining change and evolution. However, various aspects strongly interrelated have to be addressed:
- the need (or the opportunity) of introducing different kinds of causation
- the relation between "action type", time and persistency
- the need (or the opportunity) of dealing with metric temporal constraints.

Temporal aspects play a major role in the analysis of causation: Rieger and Grinberg [10] have subdivided causation into *one − shot* causation and *continuous* causation; they assert that a relation is continuous if the presence of the cause is continuously required in order to sustain the effect, while a relation is one-shot if the presence of the cause is only momentarily required in order to produce the effect. Even if this distinction is very relevant, there is the need to take into consideration the action-type ontology, so that one can deal with processes, states or events and can describe actions with duration, instead of considering only instantaneous ones.

The problem of introducing several types of causation, deepending on action-types of the causes and on persistence criteria for the effect has been addressed in [15] and a causal-temporal ontology has been devised to describe mutual inferences between action types and causal relations. The analysis in [15] is limited to qualitative temporal constraints and the analysis of persistence is restricted to the case when a single agent is present. Quite recently some approaches have been proposed which aim at dealing with complex forms of patterns of change; for example the work in [9] allows one to reason about situation involving multiple agents where events can occur in parallel, but there are severe constraints on the type of events which can interact. However, scenarios where different causes concern the same effect in different ways are quite common in the real world, and we need a way to express such interactions if we want to move beyond toy examples. A notable work addressing such problems is the one by Allen [2]: events are exploited as basic tools for expressing interacting patterns of change.

In the present paper, we aim to extend the analysis reported in [15]i by considering metric temporal constraints and taking into consideration the game between *Ego* and the *World* with the final goal of capturing common-sense description of a changing environment.

In the following, some examples (related to a mechanical domain) are reported in order to show the main characteristics and problems arising in making temporal prediction when quantitative temporal constraints are taken into account and causal relations highly interact.

Example 1. Let us consider the follwing pair of causal relations:

    R1   *eng_ovrh* cause *coolant_ovrh*

    R2   *turn_key_cw* cause *engine_on*

R1 is a typical example of what Rieger and Grinberg [10] call *continuous* causation since the presence of effect *coolant_ovrh* (i.e.coolant liquid overheating) lasts as long as the cause *eng_ovrh* (i.e. engine overheating) sustains it. However, the causal relation can be made more precise by introducing quantitative time delays: if we assume that *coolant_ovrh* starts five minutes after the onset of *eng_ovrh* (and ceases two minutes after that *eng_ovrh* decays) we can predict that *coolant_ovrh* holds in the interval [15,112] if we know that *eng_ovrh* holds in the interval [10,100]. On the contrary, R2 is an example of what Rieger and Grinberg call *one − shot* causation, since the effect can persist even if the cause has been terminated long time ago. In fact, in our example, some time after the ignition key is turned clockwise (*turn_key_cw*), the engine starts and continues to be on indefinitely (at least theoretically, abstracting from considerations like fuel consumption and mechanical wear and tear).

Example 2. For analyzing interactions among causal relations let us consider rule R2 and the following rule:

    R3   *fuel_lack* cause not *engine_on*

First of all, it is worth noting that both R2 and R3 refer actually to the same feature as effect, namely *engine_on*, but R2 with a positive occurence while R3 with a negative one. The two rules R2 and R3 interact over the effect and potentially can provide conflicting predictions. From *turn_key_cw* it is possible to guess that, for example, *engine_on* starts to hold at time $t_1=100$ (and continues to hold later on) and from the fact that *fuel_lack* starts to hold (let us say from $t_2=145$) one could predict that not *engine_on* will start to hold shortly after (let us suppose from $t_3=150$). In order to resolve conflicting predictions, we have to assume, for example, that the causal relation R3 has greater strength than R2. If this is the case, we can predict that *engine_on* holds in the interval [100,149], while *engine_on* does not hold starting from $t_3=150$.

Example 3. Causal connections might interact in very complex ways. Let us consider:

    R4   *oil_loss* cause not *lubrification_ok*

    R5   *adding_oil* cause *lubrification_ok*

From a common-sense point of view, it is obvious that, if *oil_loss* is present, sooner or later the situation of not *lubrification_ok* will be reached. It is also obvious that the action of *adding_oil* to the engine resets the lubrification system to the nominal behaviour (i.e. *lubrification_ok*) but does not guarantee that *lubrification_ok* will persist over a long period. In fact, if *oil_loss* persists after the execution of action of *adding − oil*, sooner or later the situation of not *lubrification_ok* will appear again. In order to model complex interactions the mechanism of assigning different strengths to the rules is not sufficient: it is necessary to devise methods for dealing with sequences of changes and in particular for re-evaluating predictions at appropriate time points.

2 Causal-Temporal ontology

In this section we give a formal description of the notions introduced so far. In order to reason about change, we must provide a way for representing knowledge about the world, i.e. to construct a model of the domain of interest. From this standpoint, we refer to descriptions like *eng_overh* in R1 as entities of the model, so an entity represents a propositional description of a relevant aspect of the domain (entities can be compared to propositional fluents usually used in Situation Calculus [8]). Since we are dealing with change, the truth value of an entity may vary over time: we associate a history to each entity, namely the chronicle of the values that the entity assumes over time (we assume a discrete time structure). To be more precise, a history is a list of fragments, where a fragment is a pair [interval,value] and an interval is defined as a pair of two time points $[t_1,t_2]$ such that $t_1 \leq t_2$. A history must be maximal with respect to the extension and the value, that is there are no overlapping fragments and two fragments with the same value cannot meet.

In order to model the world, we subdivide entities into *exogenous* entities and *endogenous* entities. The exogenous ones are not explained in the causal model, that is there is no causal link involving such entities as an effect; their history is an input datum to the predictive process. On the contrary, endogenous entities always play the role of effect in some causal connection, and the task of prediction actually has the purpose of computing their history. As concerns action-type ontology, we have adopted a minimalistic approach where we partition situations (namely all the entities, from this standpoint) into *homogeneous* situations, for which the subinterval property holds [1], often referred to states and processes in the literature and *culminating* situations, for which the subinterval property does not hold, commonly referred to as events.

By taking into account the game between *Ego* and *Nature*, we can make another distinction (orthogonal with respect the one concerning homogeneous and culminating situations): we consider an exogenous entity (either a homogeneous or culminating situation) as an *action* if this exogenous entity is under the control of *Ego*, whereas an exogenous entity under the control of *Nature* is called *initial cause*. All endogenous entities are referred to as *partial states*, since they describe a local view on the status of the modeled system.

The general form of a causal rule is:

$E_1 \wedge \ldots \wedge E_n$ in_context $E_{n+1} \wedge \ldots \wedge E_m$ cause E (Temporal Param.)

Entities $E_1, E_2, \ldots, E_n$ play the role of causes, while $E_{n+1}, E_{n+2}, \ldots, E_m$ play the role of contexts since they describe optional contextual conditions that enable the causes to produce the effect. The set of all the causes and the contexts is named *premise* of the causal relation. The effect E of any causal relation is unique: if the same set of causes and contexts produces many effects, we may write down several causal rules with the same premise. In the formalism, effects and contexts are restricted to be homogeneous entities, while no restriction is imposed to causes with respect to the action-type ontology presented above (that is, causes can be either homogeneous situations or culminating situations). It is worth noting that each E_i mentioned in the causal rules can occur either in positive or in negative form (i.e., it is possible that E_i=not E_i', where E_i' is the symbol referring to an entity in the model) just in case E_i refers to an homogeneous situation. Temporal parameters, described in the following, capture the temporal features of the causal connection, like delays between cause and effect.

2.1 Synchronization of situations

Since the premise of a causal rule involves a set of entities (causes and contexts) it is clear that conditions stated by causes and contexts must hold simultaneously over a non empty time interval in order to produce the effect. The notion of synchronization introduced in [5] has been revised in order to take into account the action-type of the entities occurring in the premise. When the premise of a rule involves only entities which are homogeneous situations, the synchronization can be easily defined as the set of time intervals where all the conditions expressed in the premise of the rule hold. Consequently, the history of the premise can be evaluated: it contains only true-valued fragments, since every fragment belonging to it refers to an episode where all the conditions (both positive and negative) on causes and contexts hold. As an example, let us consider a refined version of R1 where a contextual condition has been added (*irreg_flow* represents the fact that the coolant flow in the sealed circuit is not regular):

R1'   *eng_ovrh* in context not *irreg_flow* cause *coolant_ovrh*

Let us suppose to have the following histories: history(*eng_ovrh*)= $\{[[0,10],f],$ $[[11,100],t],[[101,\infty],f]\}$ and history(*irreg_flow*) $= \{[[0,\infty],f]\}$, where t stands for true and f for false. First we have to evaluate the history of the contextual condition: since *irreg_flow* does not hold over any time interval, then not *irreg_flow* holds over the entire time line, namely history(not *irreg_flow*) $= \{[[0,\infty],t]\}$. Since in R1' both the cause and the context are homogeneous situations the synchronization is evaluated according the criterion defined above and produces as history of the premise the set containing just the fragment $[[11,100],t]$. When the premise involves as cause an entity which is a culminating situation, the notion of synchronization has to be revised: synchronization collapses to a single time point, that is the culmination point of the cause provided that it belongs to a time interval where all contextual conditions hold. Let us consider as an example the refined version of R2

R2'   *turn_key_cw* in context *battery_ok* cause *engine_on*

If we suppose that history(*turn_key_cw*)=$\{[[0,5],f], [[6,8],t], [[9,\infty],f]\}$ (i.e. this culminating situation happens in the interval [6,8] and reaches the culmination at time t=8), and that the battery works correctly, that is history(*battery_ok*) $= \{[[0,\infty],t]\}$, the synchronization of the conditions forming the premise of this rule is the set containing the fragment $[[8,8],t]$.

2.2 Different types of causal relations

The causal-temporal ontology we have devised includes five different types of causal relation, depending on the action-type of the causes and on persistence criteria for the effect. The first one, which models continuous causation and is denoted as type A, has the following form

$$E_1 \wedge ... \wedge E_n \text{ in\_context } E_{n+1} \wedge ... \wedge E_m \text{ A-cause } E \ (MP, OT, DT)$$

In causal relations of type A, causes, contexts and the effect are constrained to be homogeneous situations. As concerns temporal parameters, type-A causation involves three of them. *Minimal persistence* time (MP) indicates how long should last (at minimum) a fragment of the history of the premise in order to have an occurrence of the effect E. Therefore, MP acts as a threshold on the duration of the fragments of the premise: if the duration of the fragment does not exceed MP, the rule cannot cause the effect to occur. If MP is zero, this means it is sufficient that the premise is true in a single time point in order to produce the effect. The *onset* time (OT) denotes how many time units after reaching MP the effect actually appears. The *decay* time (DT) indicates how many time units after the end of the fragment of the premise the effect ends.

The causal rule R1' reported above can be seen as an example of type A causation; if we specify the temporal parameters as $MP=5, OT=0, DT=2$ (basic time units are minutes) we have that in order to have the effect, the situation where both *eng_ovrh* and not *irreg_flow* hold should last for at least 5 minutes (the threshold given by MP). Moreover, as soon as the duration of a fragment in the history of the premise situation exceeds MP, *coolant_ovrh* starts to hold (since $OT=0$). *Coolant_ovrh* turns to false two minutes after the last time point when the premise holds (the premise turns to false when *eng_ovrh* ceases to be true or coolant flow turns to irregular).

Formally, let $f_p = [[b_p, e_p], t]$ be a fragment from the history of the premise of the causal rule of type A. If $e_p - b_p \geq MP$ then $f_E = [[b_E, e_E], val]$ will be the corresponding fragment from the history of the effect and the following relations between the temporal entities hold:

$$(i) \ b_E = b_p + MP + OT \qquad\qquad (ii) \ e_E = max\{b_E, e_p + DT\}$$

Since the focus of the work is on temporal prediction, the equation (i) and (ii) can be viewed as assignement statements that allows one to infer F_E on the basis of f_p by means of forward propagation in time. Rule (ii) deserves some comment since it enforces the fact that, if the condition $e_p - b_p \geq MP$ is verified, the effect must occur, at least over a single time point. This is not guaranteed by the simpler relation $e_E = e_p + DT$; in fact, if OT is much larger than DT we could have situations where $e_E < b_E$ (which is clearly inconsistent with the definition of time interval). The value val of f_E depends on the literal E representing the effect: if E is a positive literal, then val is true, if E is a negative literal then val is false.

The second type of causation we discuss here is denoted as type C causation and is aimed at capturing one-shot causation. The general form of this kind of causal rule is:

$$E_1 \text{ in\_context } E_2 \wedge ... \wedge E_m \text{ C-cause } E \ (OT).$$

Such a rule involves a single cause E_1 which is restricted to be a culminating situation, while contexts and the effect are to be homogeneous ones. The only temporal parameter is OT which specifies the onset of the effect starting from

type	persistence	action-type	parameters	propagation rule
A	Continuous	Homogeneous	MP, OT, DT	if $e_p - b_p \geq MP$ holds, then $b_E = b_p + MP + OT$, $e_E = max\{bE, ep + DT\}$
B	One-Shot	Culminating	OT, D	$b_E = e_p + OT$, $e_E = b_E + D$
C	One-Shot	Culminating	OT	$b_E = e_p + OT$, $e_E = \infty$
D	One-Shot	Homogeneous	MP, OT, D	if $e_p - b_p \geq MP$ holds, then $b_E = b_p + MP + OT$, $e_E = b_E + D$
E	One-Shot	Homogeneous	MP, OT	if $e_p - b_p \geq MP$ holds, then $b_E = b_p + MP + OT$, $e_E = \infty$

Table 1. Summary of the main properties of different types of causal rules

the culmination instant of the cause E_1. In type C causation the persistence of the effect is independent from persistence of the premise, therefore nothing can be said about the end of the effect. The propagation rules governing type C causation are:

$$(i)\ b_E = e_p + OT \qquad (ii)\ e_E = \infty$$

Let us reconsider causal rule R2' and let us specify the temporal parameter ($OT=3$). We have that the effect of turning the key (i.e. *engine_on*) starts to hold three seconds after that the key is completely turned (i.e. after the culmination) and lasts indefinitely. Obviously, the causal relation reaches the effect just in case the contextual condition *battery_ok* holds in the time instant when the cause reaches the culmination.

For lack of space we cannot describe in detail the other types of causation we have devised to deal with change. Table 1 summarizes the main characteristics and propagation rules for the five types of causation. It is worth noting that in type B causation (where the action type of the cause is a culminating situation) and in type D (where the causes are homogeneous situation) we have introduced another temporal parameter (D for *duration*) which is a finite quantity and specifies how long will last the effect from the instant the effect starts to hold. Such kind of causal rule can be used, for example, to model the scenario where a traffic light turns to green some time after a pedestrian has pushed the button and the traffic light remains green for a predefined amount of time.

3 Dealing with Interactions

Since we are interested in modeling the game between *Ego* and *Nature*, we have to face the problem of interactions. With this term we indicate the situation when we have two opposite predictions for the same endogenous entity E over the same interval. We have already introduced such a situation in example 2 and we have shown that a possible way for dealing with conflicting predictions is the introduction of priorities among causal rules. In case two causal rules (let us say T_1 with priority p_1 and T_2 with priority p_2) interact on entity E and predict opposite values for E, the conflict is solved by retaining the prediction made by causal rule T_1 if $p_1 > p_2$. Priorities can be seen as a form of meta-knowledge which can solve some of the interactions, but it is not always possible to specify priorities, as pointed out in the following example. Let us consider the two rules

R2' *turn_key_cw* in_context *battery_ok* C-cause *engine_on* (OT=3)

R2" *turn_key_ccw* C-cause not *engine_on* (OT=1)

where *turn_key_ccw* means turning the ignition key counterclockwise. There is no reason to assign more strength to a rule with respect to the other (that is, there is no basis for assigning different levels of priority). In similar cases we have to resort to the criterion of *Most Recent Change* which states that in presence of opposite predictions on entity E, the one to be retained concerns the change that has occurred latest in time. Let us suppose that initially engine is off, history(*turn_key_cw*)={[[0, 5], f], [[6, 8], t], [[9, ∞], f]} and history(*battery_ok*) = {[[0, ∞], t]}. On the sole basis of R2' it is possible to predict *engine_on* starting from t=11. However, if history(*turn_key_ccw*)={[[0, 49], f], [[50, 50], t], [[51, ∞], f]} we have also the prediction, obtained via R2", that *engine_on* starts to be false from time t=51. Since the two rules have the same priority, the criterion of Most Recent Change is applied: therefore the prediction to be retained for the entity *engine_on* in the interval [51, ∞] is the one given by R2" since involves the change which occurred latest in time. Obviously, *engine_on* is true in the interval [11,50] by taking into consideration the portion of prediction obtained via R2' not conflicting with any other prediction.

The Most Recent Change criterion and priorities are not mutually exclusive: for modeling real-world problems these two mechanisms have to be integrated. In our framework it is possible to specify for each endogenous entity E a priority list $PRIORITY(E) = P_1, \ldots, P_n$ where each P_i is a (not empty) set of causal relations. Inside a given P_i all the rules have the same priority and if some conflicting prediction occur, the Most Recent Change criterion is used to solve the conflict. If conflicting predictions occur because of causal rules belonging to different priority sets, the history of the entity E is evaluated by considering that P_j has a greater strength than P_i, if P_i precedes P_j in $PRIORITY(E)$.

Re-evaluation of predictions. As shown in example 3, there are cases of very subtle interactions among causal rules. When we have rules in the same level of priority, Most Recent Change is the basic mechanism for evaluating the history of entities, but for some type of causal rules is not sufficient. Let us consider that at time t_1 entity E starts to hold and last until time t_4 because of a rule S_1 involving type A causation (that is a form of continuos causation) whose premise holds from t_0 until t_3. However if there is a prediction of not E starting at time t_2 ($t_1 < t_2 < t_4$) because of a rule S_2 of Type C (a one-shot rule), the prediction of not E will be retained because this change is the last in time, according to the Most Recent Change criterion. If at time t_2 the premise of rule S_1 is still true we will have that after some time rule S_1 will cause again the presence of E. Therefore we can consider t_2 as a starting point of a new episode of the premise of S_1 which will last until t_3 and we have to re-evaluate the prediction on E by taking into account that the premise of S_1 hold from t_2 till t_3. This new forward temporal propagation will predict that E will start to hold from time t_5 and, since $t_5 > t_2$, according to the Most recent change criterion this prediction will be maintained and the opposite prediction of not E will be limited to the interval $[t_2, t_5 - 1]$. This mechanism is not an ad-hoc solution valid just for specific cases. This mechanism has to be used also when we have a type-E rule interacting with type-C rule as in example 3. In [7] we have reported an in-depth analysis of the possible kinds of interaction among different types of causation and a formalization of the predictive process based on an algebraic approach.

The Inertia Assumption and the default value. In most cases, causal relations does not provide a complete history for a certain entity, that is an history including a temporal prediction for each time point t. In order to have complete histories for each endogenous entity we require the specification of a *default value* for each of them; this default value represents the value that the entity assumes in absence of explicit predictions. The introduction of a default value corresponds to make an explicit assumption of inertia: an entity persists in its default value unless some change happens to modify it. In order to deal with default vaule in our framework it is sufficient to introduce the notion of default prediction for entity E containing just a single fragment $[[0, \infty], def]$ where def is the default value of E and to assume that all causal rules in $PRIORITY(E)$ have greater strength than the default prediction. In this way any time there is a prediction coming from a causal rule the history of E includes such a prediction whereas the default prediction is used just to complete the history for the time interval no prediction exists. In [7] we discuss how the introduction of a default value for the endogenous entities and the explicit prediction of persistence for the effect in the causal relations allow us to address the frame problem.

4 An Overall Example

In this section a more complex example concerning a mechanical domain is reported in order to sketch the complex game between *Ego* and the *Nature*. The domain model is characterized by the following causal-temporal relations (some of them have been introduced in previous sections):

r1: *wrn_pist_rings* A-cause *oil_loss* (MP=0,OT=0,DT=0)
r2: *adt_add* in_context RPM_lt_1500 C-cause not *oil_loss* (OT=1)
r3: *adt_add* in_context RPM_lt_1500 C-cause not *insuff_lubrif* (OT=1)
r4: *oil_loss* E-cause *insuff_lubrif* (MP=6000, OT=0)
r5: *oil_add* in_context RPM_lt_1500 C-cause not *insuff_lubrif* (OT=1)
r6: *speed_up* A-cause not RPM_lt_1500 (MP=0,OT=0,DT=0)
r7: *insuff_lubrif* E-cause *eng_melt* (MP=15,OT=0)
r8: *insuff_lubrif* A-cause *eng_ovrh* (MP=10,OT=0,DT=5)
r9: *eng_ovrh* in_context not *irreg_flow* A-cause *coolant_ovrh*(MP=5,OT=0,DT=2)

entity	priority(entity)	default value
oil_loss	[[r1],[r2]]	*f*
RPM_lt_1500	[[r6]]	*t*
insuff_lubrif	[[r4,r5],[r3]]	*f*
eng_melt	[[r7]]	*f*
eng_ovrh	[[r8]]	*f*
coolant_ovrh	[[r9]]	*f*

Table 2. Summary of priority lists and default values of entities

In such a model we take minutes as basic time unit; given this time granularity, some temporal parameters are put equal to zero. The entities *wrn_pist_rings* (worn- out piston rings) and *irreg_flow* play the role of initial causes under the control of *Nature*, whereas *adt_add* (addition of additive), *oil_add* and *speed_up* are actions under the control of *Ego*. The entities *oil_loss*, *RPM_lt_1500* (rounds per minute less than 1500), *insuff_lubrif*, *eng_melt* (engine melting), *eng_ovrh* (engine overheating), *coolant_ovrh* (coolant liquid overheating) are endogenous entities playing the role of partial states. The default value and the *PRIORITY* set list for each endogenous entity are given in table 2. Let us imagine a scenario where history(*wrn_pist_rings*)={[[0, 9], *f*], [[10, ∞], *t*]}, i.e. piston rings become consumpt at time 10, and no action is executed. According to the causal relations r1-r9, we have the following predictions on the endogenous entities *oil_loss*, *insuff_lubrif* and *eng_melt*:

history(*oil_loss*)={[[0, 9], *f*], [[10, ∞], *t*]},
history(*insuff_lubrif*)={[[0, 6009], *f*], [[6010, ∞], *t*]},
history(*eng_melt*)={[[0, 6024], *f*], [[6025, ∞], *t*]}.

Let us consider a slightly different scenario where *Ego* adds oil at time $t=6500$. Since we are not aware of any *speed_up* action, there is no specific prediction for *RPM_lt_1500* and therefore history(*RPM_lt_1500*)={[[0, ∞], *f*]} because of the default prediction. The synchronization of the premise of r5 has success and via r5 the hystory fragment [[6501, ∞], *f*] is predicted for the entity *insuff_lubrif*. Since r4 and r5 provide conflicting predictions on such entity and they have the same priority, the Most Recent Change criterium is invoked and the prediction given by r5 is maintained. However, since r4 is of type E and r5 is of type C also the mechanism of prediction re-evaluation on rule 4 is invoked at time $t=6501$. The resulting hystory is history(*insuff_lubrif*) = {[[0, 6009], *f*], [[6010, 6500], *t*], [[6501, 12501], *f*], [[12502, ∞], *t*]} while the histories of *oil_loss* and *eng_melt* do not change. By considering the game between *Ego* and *Nature*, it is easy to see that the action of *add_oil* performed by *Ego* at time 6500 does not prevent engine from melting and the problem of *insuff_lubrif* is not definetively solved. On the contrary, if *Ego* performs the same action at time $t=6015$ there is a significant delay in the onset of engine melting as shown by the following histories: history(*insuff_lubrif*) = {[[0, 6009], *f*], [[6010, 6015], *t*], [[6016, 12016], *f*], [[12017, ∞], *t*]}, history(*eng_melt*) = {[[0, 12031], *f*], [[12032, ∞], *t*]}. The significant change in the history of *eng_melt* is due to the fact the r7 cannot be applied on the fragment $[[6010, 6015], t]$ of *insuff_lubrif* because the duration of this fragment is lower than the MP value specified for r7 ($MP=15$). Let us consider now the case where *Ego*, at $t=6015$, performs the action of adding additive instead of the one of adding oil. The predictions are quite different from the ones of the previous scenario since *Ego* is able not only to find a remedy for *oil_loss* and *lubrif_insuff*, but also to prevent the occurrence of engine melting:

history(oil_loss)=$\{[[0, 9], f], [[10, 6015], t], [[6016, \infty], f]\}$
history($insuff\_lubrif$)=$\{[[0, 6009], f], [[6010, 6015], t], [[6016, \infty], f]\}$
history(eng_melt)=$\{[[0, \infty], f]\}$.

Action *adt_add* at $t=6015$ activates both r2 and r3; since r2 has higher priority than r1 wrt to *oil_loss* the conflict between the predictions of r1 and r2 is solved by preferring the prediction provided by r2 (the same occurs for r3 and r4 wrt *insuff_lubrif*).

5 Discussion

The work presented in the paper is a first step in analyzing the problem of temporal prediction when two agents, i.e. *Ego* and *Nature*, interact on the same physical system. Following the approach taken in [15], the introduction of a causal-temporal ontology provides a way for taking separate the knowledge specific for a domain (encoded by the causal rules) from the knowledge about interaction. In fact, each single causal rule represents a *local* point of view which captures the causal-temporal relations just for the entities involved in the rule itself and no reference is made to other entities which can possibly interfere with the causal process modelled by the single rule. However, the assignment of a rule to one of the types of causation specified by the causal-temporal ontology is a high level specification of the mechanisms governing temporal prediction and interactions. In fact, the causal-temporal ontology specifies the propagation rules valid for each type of causation and the invocation of the prediction re-evaluation mechanism when appropriate. General criteria are not always sufficient for modeling in the correct way complex interactions and therefore our framework provides the designer of the knowledge base with the facility of specifying a priority list for each entity. Priorities can be seen as an explicit *global* meta-knowledge which specifies domain-dependent interactions among causal rules.

In order to test the generality of the causal-temporal ontology several tests have been performed by modeling both mechanical domains and medical domains. A prototype (written in Prolog) has been developed which is able to simulate the game between *Ego* and the *Nature*. This prototype can be considered the core module for a larger system aimed at supporting a user in the activity of temporal planning. The example reported in section 4 shows how critical can be the choice of the actions to be performed by *Ego* (and their location in time) for the temporal evolution of the modeled system.

Further work is needed to fully evaluate the kind of phenomena that can be modeled within our framework. For example, so far we have restricted our attention to causal models where no feedback exists (in other words, if we consider entities as nodes and causal connections as arcs of a graph, the resulting causal network must be acyclic).

Another limit of the current version of the prototype concerns the fact that temporal parameters are restricted to be crisp values and no uncertainty is allowed. In previous work [3][5] we have already attached this problem by expressing temporal parameters as range of admissible values rather than a single value. Unfortunately, the introduction of uncertainty about temporal location and temporal parameters considerably increases the computational efforts in making temporal predictions since a large number of alternatives scenarios have to be considered. Moreover, in case of very vague information, the prediction task becomes almost useless since almost nothing can be predicted.

References

1. J. Allen. Towards a general theory of action and time. *Artificial Intelligence*, 23:123–154, 1984.
2. J. Allen and G. Ferguson. Actions and events in interval temporal logic. *J. of Logic and Computation*, 4:531–579, 1994.
3. L. Console, A. Janin Rivolin, and P. Torasso. Fuzzy temporal reasoning on causal models. *International Journal of Intelligent Systems*, 6:107–133, 1991.
4. L. Console and P. Torasso. On the co-operation between abductive and temporal reasoning in medical diagnosis. *Artificial Intelligence in Medicine*, 3(6):291–311, 1991.
5. L. Console and P. Torasso. Temporal constraint satisfaction on causal models. *Information Sciences*, 68(1):1–32, 1993.
6. K. Forbus. Qualitative physics: past, present and future. In H.E. Shrobe, editor, *Exploring Artificial Intelligence*, pages 239–295. Morgan Kaufman, 1988.
7. M. Gazza and P. Torasso. Temporal prediction: Dealing with change and interaction within a causal framework. Technical report, Dip. Informatica, Universita' di Torino, 1995.
8. J. McCarthy and P.J. Hayes. Some philosophical problems from the standpoint of artificial intelligence. In B. Meltzer and D. Michie, editors, *Machine Intelligence, 4*, pages 463–502. Edinburgh U.P., 1969.
9. D. Morley, M. Georgeff, and A.Rao. A monotonic formalism for events and systems of events. *J. Logic and Computation*, 4:701–720, 1994.
10. C. Rieger and M. Grinberg. The declarative representation and simulation of causality in physical mechanisms. In *Proc. IJCAI 77*, pages 250–256, 1977.
11. E. Sandewall. The range of applicability of some non-monotonic logics for strict inertia. *J. Logic and Computation*, 4:581–615, 1994.
12. Y. Shoham. Nonmonotonic reasoning and causation. *Cognitive Science*, 14:213–252, 1990.
13. Y. Shoham and E. Sandewall. Nonmonotonic temporal reasoning. In *Handbook of artificial intelligence and logic programming*. Stanford University, 1994.
14. L.A. Stein and L. Morgenstern. Motivated action theory: a formal theory of causal reasoning. *Artificial Intelligence*, 71:1–42, 1994.
15. P. Terenziani and P. Torasso. Time, action-type and causation: An integrated analysis. *Computational Intelligence*, 11(3), 1995.

Non-first-order features
in concept languages

Francesco M. Donini, Daniele Nardi and Riccardo Rosati*

Dipartimento di Informatica e Sistemistica,
Università di Roma "La Sapienza",
Via Salaria 113, I-00198 Roma, Italy
email: {donini,nardi,rosati}@dis.uniroma1.it

Abstract. In this paper we propose an epistemic concept language, where the epistemic operator is interpreted in terms of minimal knowledge. We show that the proposed formalism provides an adequate characterization of many non-first-order aspects of frame-based knowledge representation systems, by admitting in the knowledge base various forms of epistemic sentences. In particular, we address the formalization of defaults and role closure.
We argue that the minimization of knowledge captures intuitive and natural forms of reasoning that arise by restricting the attention to the individuals that are known to the knowledge base. Many of these forms of reasoning are actually provided by several knowledge representation systems, whose implementation is object centered.

1 Introduction

Concept languages (also called terminological logics, description languages) have been studied in the past years to provide a formal characterization of frame-based system. However, while the fragment of first-order logic which characterizes the most popular constructs of these languages has been clearly identified (see for example [25]), there is not yet consensus on the practical aspects of frame systems that cannot be formalized in a classical first-order setting. In fact, frame-based systems, as well as systems based on concept languages [3, 13], admit both forms of nonmonotonic reasoning, such as defaults and closed world reasoning, and procedural features, e.g. rules. These issues have been addressed in the recent literature (see for example [1, 5, 16, 17, 22]), but the proposals typically capture one of the above mentioned aspects.

In this paper we propose a concept language with an epistemic operator, with the aim of providing a unified framework to capture the following features: defaults, procedural rules, weak definitions, role and concept closures. The framework proposed here is a generalization of the one described in [5] to a family of epistemic languages, which is parametric with respect to the accessibility relation between possible world structures. The nonmonotonic character of the

---

* Work partially supported by Italian MURST 60% "Tecniche di Ragionamento non Monotono".

formalism is enforced by a preference criterion for selecting models based on the notion of minimal knowledge [8, 11], as in the case of the ground nonmonotonic modal logics [6, 9, 15, 20, 23].

Different forms of non-first-order reasoning can be captured in a modal epistemic language by identifying classes of epistemic sentences. In particular, for epistemic concept language, the modal operator has been first introduced in the query language to express queries to a first-order concept knowledge base [4]. In this case one can express a form of closed-world reasoning, as well as integrity constraints in the style of [19]. In [5], the knowledge base admits a simple form of epistemic sentences and is therefore is constituted by a pair $(\mathcal{R}, \mathcal{A})$, where $\mathcal{A}$ is a concept knowledge base and $\mathcal{R}$ is a set of epistemic sentences of the form $\mathbf{K}C \sqsubseteq D$, where C, D are concept expressions. In this setting it is possible to formalize procedural rules in the style of CLASSIC [3], and weak definitions that arise by treating the definition $A \doteq D$ as the two weaker inclusions $\{\mathbf{K}A \sqsubseteq D, \mathbf{K}D \sqsubseteq A\}$.

In the present paper we address two additional kinds of epistemic sentences in the knowledge base:

1. Sentences representing defaults based on the translation given in [24]; the epistemic sentences used in [5] to represent rules can be viewed as a special case of defaults, however, we show that defaults can not be adequately represented in that framework.
2. Sentences admitting the knowledge operator in role expressions; in this case it is possible to capture the notion of role closure as it is provided in actual systems [3, 13]; in addition, by generalizing the use of the epistemic operators in concept expressions, it is possible to express the idea of concept closure, which has often been considered as a desirable extension of these systems.

The intuitive reason that makes the proposed approach suitable for a precise characterization of the behaviour of implemented systems is that the minimization of knowledge on possible world structures carries the idea of restricting reasoning on individuals that are known to the knowledge base (i.e. individuals that have an explicit name). In fact, most implementations are object centered, which enables them to perform efficient reasoning on the properties of individuals. However, the resulting behaviour is not only justified by implementation considerations, but carries an intuitive and natural restriction of the reasoning that the system is required to perform. Since in our setting different forms of reasoning are allowed, the expressivity of the formalism is substantially enriched, giving the knowledge base designer the option to choose between standard logical reasoning and reasoning which is restricted to the individuals known to the system. We provide an example of this enriched expressivity by extending the idea of closure to concepts.

The paper is organized as follows. We first introduce the epistemic language $\mathcal{ALCK}$. We then address the representation of defaults in the epistemic concept language. We finally consider other uses of the epistemic operator discussing both role and concept closure.

2 An Epistemic Concept Language

In this section we briefly introduce an epistemic concept language, which is an extension of the concept language $\mathcal{ALC}$ with an epistemic operator. Generally speaking, we use $\mathbf{K}C$ to denote the set of individuals *known* to be instances of the concept C in every model for the knowledge base. The syntax of $\mathcal{ALCK}$, as in [5], admits the epistemic operator before any concept and role expression of the language $\mathcal{ALC}$.

The syntactic definition of $\mathcal{ALCK}$ is as follows (C, D denote concepts, R denotes a role, A denotes a primitive concept and P a primitive role):

$$
\begin{aligned}
C, D \longrightarrow \quad & A \mid & & \text{(primitive concept)} \\
& \top \mid & & \text{(top)} \\
& \bot \mid & & \text{(bottom)} \\
& C \sqcap D \mid & & \text{(intersection)} \\
& C \sqcup D \mid & & \text{(union)} \\
& \neg C \mid & & \text{(complement)} \\
& \forall R.C \mid & & \text{(universal quantification)} \\
& \exists R.C \mid & & \text{(existential quantification)} \\
& \mathbf{K}C & & \text{(epistemic concept)} \\
R \longrightarrow \quad & P \mid & & \text{(primitive role)} \\
& \mathbf{K}P & & \text{(epistemic role).}
\end{aligned}
$$

The semantics of $\mathcal{ALCK}$ is based on the Common Domain Assumption (i.e. every interpretation is defined over a fixed domain, called Δ) and on the Rigid Term Assumption (i.e. for every interpretation the mapping from the individuals into the domain elements, called γ, is fixed).

An *epistemic interpretation* is a four-tuple $(\mathcal{I}, \mathcal{W}, \mathcal{R}, \mathcal{V})$ where $\mathcal{W}$ a set of possible worlds, $\mathcal{I}$ is a possible world such that $\mathcal{I} \in \mathcal{W}$, $\mathcal{R}$ is a binary relation on $\mathcal{W}$, and $\mathcal{V}$ is a function mapping each world belonging to $\mathcal{W}$ into an $\mathcal{ALC}$ interpretation, such that the following equations are satisfied:

$$\top^{\mathcal{I},\mathcal{W},\mathcal{R},\mathcal{V}} = \Delta$$

$$\bot^{\mathcal{I},\mathcal{W},\mathcal{R},\mathcal{V}} = \emptyset$$

$$A^{\mathcal{I},\mathcal{W},\mathcal{R},\mathcal{V}} = A^{\mathcal{V}(\mathcal{I})} \subseteq \Delta$$

$$P^{\mathcal{I},\mathcal{W},\mathcal{R},\mathcal{V}} = P^{\mathcal{V}(\mathcal{I})} \subseteq \Delta \times \Delta$$

$$(C \sqcap D)^{\mathcal{I},\mathcal{W},\mathcal{R},\mathcal{V}} = C^{\mathcal{I},\mathcal{W},\mathcal{R},\mathcal{V}} \cap D^{\mathcal{I},\mathcal{W},\mathcal{R},\mathcal{V}}$$

$$(C \sqcup D)^{\mathcal{I},\mathcal{W},\mathcal{R},\mathcal{V}} = C^{\mathcal{I},\mathcal{W},\mathcal{R},\mathcal{V}} \cup D^{\mathcal{I},\mathcal{W},\mathcal{R},\mathcal{V}}$$

$$(\neg C)^{\mathcal{I},\mathcal{W},\mathcal{R},\mathcal{V}} = \Delta \setminus C^{\mathcal{I},\mathcal{W},\mathcal{R},\mathcal{V}}$$

$$(\forall R.C)^{\mathcal{I},\mathcal{W},\mathcal{R},\mathcal{V}} = \{d_1 \in \Delta \mid \forall d_2. (d_1, d_2) \in R^{\mathcal{I},\mathcal{W},\mathcal{R},\mathcal{V}} \rightarrow d_2 \in C^{\mathcal{I},\mathcal{W},\mathcal{R},\mathcal{V}}\}$$

$$(\exists R.C)^{\mathcal{I},\mathcal{W},\mathcal{R},\mathcal{V}} = \{d_1 \in \Delta \mid \exists d_2. (d_1, d_2) \in R^{\mathcal{I},\mathcal{W},\mathcal{R},\mathcal{V}} \wedge d_2 \in C^{\mathcal{I},\mathcal{W},\mathcal{R},\mathcal{V}}\}$$

$$(\mathbf{K}C)^{\mathcal{I},\mathcal{W},\mathcal{R},\mathcal{V}} = \bigcap_{(\mathcal{I},\mathcal{J}) \in \mathcal{R}} (C^{\mathcal{J},\mathcal{W},\mathcal{R},\mathcal{V}})$$

$$(\mathbf{K}P)^{\mathcal{I},\mathcal{W},\mathcal{R},\mathcal{V}} = \bigcap_{(\mathcal{I},\mathcal{J}) \in \mathcal{R}} (P^{\mathcal{J},\mathcal{W},\mathcal{R},\mathcal{V}}).$$

An $\mathcal{ALCK}$-knowledge base Ψ is a pair $\Psi = \langle \mathcal{T}, \mathcal{A} \rangle$, where $\mathcal{T}$, called the *TBox*, is a set of inclusion statements of the form

$$C \sqsubseteq D$$

with $C, D \in \mathcal{ALCK}$, and $\mathcal{A}$ (the *ABox*) of is a set of membership assertions, of the forms

$$C(a), R(a, b)$$

with $C, R \in \mathcal{ALCK}$ and a, b are names of individuals. The truth of inclusion statements and membership assertions in an epistemic interpretation is defined as set inclusion and set membership, respectively.

An *epistemic model* for an $\mathcal{ALCK}$-knowledge base Ψ is a triple $(\mathcal{W}, \mathcal{R}, \mathcal{V})$ such that for each world $\mathcal{I} \in \mathcal{W}$, every sentence (inclusion or membership assertion) of Ψ is true in the epistemic interpretation $(\mathcal{I}, \mathcal{W}, \mathcal{R}, \mathcal{V})$.

A *preferred model* for Ψ is an epistemic model which is minimal with respect to a partial order among epistemic models.

An $\mathcal{ALCK}$-knowledge base Ψ is said to be *satisfiable* if there exists a preferred model for Ψ, *unsatisfiable* otherwise. Ψ logically implies an assertion σ, written $\Psi \models \sigma$, if σ is true in every preferred model for Ψ.

The above definitions are parametric with respect to both the accessibility relation and the preference criterion used to select among the epistemic models. The first parameter is actually used to characterize a family of epistemic concept languages, while the preference criterion is defined according to the idea of minimal knowledge.

Let us first consider the special case corresponding to the semantics adopted in [5]. We choose an accessibility relation such that $\mathcal{R} = \mathcal{W} \times \mathcal{W}$, thus obtaining to the so-called universal S5 structures. In this case worlds and interpretation coincide and one can avoid the introduction of $\mathcal{V}$. This gives an easy way of expressing the preference criterion: a preferred model for Ψ is a triple $(\mathcal{W}, \mathcal{W} \times \mathcal{W}, \mathcal{V})$, where $\mathcal{W}$ is any maximal set of worlds such that for each $\mathcal{J} \in \mathcal{W}$, every sentence (inclusion or membership assertion) of Ψ is true in $(\mathcal{J}, \mathcal{W}, \mathcal{W} \times \mathcal{W}, \mathcal{V})$.

The idea of minimal knowledge is expressed by this criterion as maximizing ignorance, since including in the epistemic model all the possible worlds restricts the set of sentences that are known. More generally, the idea of minimal knowledge can be explained as the minimization of the objective (i.e. non-modal sentences) and is expressed by the following fixpoint equation.

Given a normal modal logic $\mathcal{S}$, a consistent set of formulas T is an $\mathcal{S}_G$-*expansion* for a set $I \subseteq \mathcal{L}_K$ if

$$T = Cn_{\mathcal{S}}(I \cup \{\neg K\varphi \mid \varphi \in \mathcal{L} \setminus T\}). \tag{1}$$

where $Cn_{\mathcal{S}}$ is the consequence operator of modal logic $\mathcal{S}$, $\mathcal{L}$ is the propositional language and $\mathcal{L}_K$ is the propositional language augmented by the modal operator K. The resulting (nonmonotonic) consequence operator is defined as the intersection of all $\mathcal{S}_G$-expansions for I.

The above equation defines a family of nonmonotonic modal logics, called ground logics [6, 9, 20, 23]: for every normal modal logic $\mathcal{S}$, the corresponding *ground* nonmonotonic modal logic $\mathcal{S}_G$ is obtained by means of the above fixpoint equation.

Ground nonmonotonic modal logics have also been given a semantic characterization in terms of a preference criterion among possible worlds described in [15], that we can adopt also in the framework of $\mathcal{ALCK}$.

Therefore, by varying the class of possible world structures taken into consideration, one can obtain, as for ground logics, the family $\mathcal{ALCK}(\mathcal{S}_G)$. In the following we shall refer mostly to the case $\mathcal{ALCK}(\mathcal{S}5_G)$ and simply call it $\mathcal{ALCK}$ when there is no ambiguity.

3 Defaults as epistemic sentences

In this section we discuss whether defaults are representable as epistemic sentences in $\mathcal{ALCK}$. Recall that the interpretation of the modal operator in $\mathcal{ALCK}$ corresponds to the first-order extension of the propositional ground nonmonotonic logic $\mathcal{S}5_G$. We show that this particular logic does not admit any modular translation for default theories, while such a translation is possible in the case of ground logics built from modal systems different from $\mathcal{S}5$.

We first briefly recall default logic [18], then present some properties of propositional ground modal logics logics with respect to their ability to capture rules and defaults, and finally turn our attention to concept languages by defining a modal concept language which admits a modular translation for default theories.

We recall that a propositional default theory is a pair (D, W), such that D is a set of defaults, i.e. inference rules of the form

$$\frac{\alpha : M\beta_1, \ldots, M\beta_n}{\gamma}$$

where $\alpha, \beta_i, \gamma \in \mathcal{L}$, W is a theory in $\mathcal{L}$ and $M\beta$ is interpreted as: "it is consistent to assume β". A *justification-free default* is a default where the justification part is empty, i.e. of the form

$$\frac{\alpha :}{\gamma}$$

We are interested in the translation of a default theory into a modal theory. Therefore we give the following definitions (taken from [7]).

Definition 1. A *faithful* translation from default logic to a ground nonmonotonic logic $\mathcal{S}_G$ is a mapping *tr* which transforms each default theory $\mathcal{D}$ into a modal theory $tr(\mathcal{D})$ such that the objective (i.e. non-modal) parts of the $\mathcal{S}_G$-expansions of $tr(\mathcal{D})$ are exactly the default extensions of $\mathcal{D}$.

As pointed out by Gottlob [7], not every translation that is faithful is useful in practice. In particular, we would like to be able to turn each default into a modal sentence, independently of other defaults and of the theory. Such translations are called modular.

Definition 2. A translation tr from default logic to a ground nonmonotonic logic S is *modular* iff for each default set D and each $W \subseteq \mathcal{L}$ it holds that $tr(D, W) = tr(D, \emptyset) \cup W$.

We shall use the modular translation emb introduced in [24].

$$emb(d) = K\alpha \wedge K\neg K\neg\beta_1 \wedge \ldots \wedge K\neg K\neg\beta_n \supset \gamma$$

$$emb(D, W) = W \cup \{emb(d) \mid d \in D\}$$

where d is a default. We now show some properties of ground logics with respect to their ability to capture defaults.

A first interesting result concerns the existence of modular translations for *justification-free* defaults. In particular, we have that $emb(D, W)$ provides the desired result for *any* ground nonmonotonic logic.

Theorem 3. *There exists a faithful modular translation from justification-free default theories to any ground nonmonotonic logic.*

Proof. Let (D, W) be a default theory such that D is a collection of justification-free defaults. Then (D, W) has exactly one default extension S. The theory $emb(D, W)$ has $ST(S)$, i.e. the unique stable theory[2] T such that $T \cap \mathcal{L} = Cn(S)$, where Cn is the propositional consequence operator, as its only K_G-expansion[3] (see Theorem 5 below). Moreover, it can be shown that every $S5$-model $\mathcal{M}$ for $emb(D, W)$ is such that $Th(\mathcal{M}) \cap \mathcal{L} \subseteq S$, where $Th(\mathcal{M}) = \{\varphi \in \mathcal{L}_K \mid \mathcal{M} \models \varphi\}$. This implies that $ST(S)$ is the only $S5_G$-expansion for $emb(D, W)$. Thus, for every logic S such that $K \subseteq S \subseteq S5$, theory $emb(D, W)$ admits exactly one S_G-expansion $ST(S)$. Therefore for such logics emb is a faithful translation for justification-free defaults. $\square$

With respect to defaults we start with a negative result on the logic $S5_G$. Notice that this result also holds for logic $\mathcal{ALCK}$, which corresponds to a first-order extension of $S5_G$.

Theorem 4. *There exists no faithful modular translation from default logic to $S5_G$.*

Proof. Consider the default theory (D, W_0) such that $D = \{\frac{:a}{a}\}$, $W_0 = \emptyset$, and suppose tr is a faithful modular translation from DL to $S5_G$. Faithfulness of tr implies that $tr(D, W_0)$ has only one $S5_G$-expansion $T = ST(a)$. Therefore, in every (monotonic) $S5$-model $\mathcal{M}$ for $tr(D, W_0)$ it holds that $\mathcal{M} \models a$. Now, given $W_1 = \{\neg a\}$, by the hypothesis of modularity of tr it follows that $tr(D, W_1) = tr(D, W_0) \cup W_1$. Consequently, $tr(D, W_1)$ is an $S5$-inconsistent theory, and hence it has no $S5_G$-expansions, while on the other hand the default theory (D, W_1) has

---

[2] We recall that a theory $T \subseteq \mathcal{L}_K$ is *stable* if T is closed under propositional consequence, for every $\varphi \in \mathcal{L}_K$, if $\varphi \in T$ then $K\varphi \in T$, and for every $\varphi \in \mathcal{L}_K$, if $\varphi \notin T$ then $\neg K\varphi \in T$.

[3] K_G denotes the ground logic obtained from the modal logic K, not to be confused with the symbol used for the epistemic operator.

the default extension $Cn(\{\neg a\})$, thus contradicting the hypothesis of faithfulness of tr.   □

The impossibility of a faithful modular translation from default theories to $S5_G$ originates from the monotonicity of this particular logic with respect to objective formulae, in the sense that for each $I, \varphi \in \mathcal{L}_K$ and for each $\psi \in \mathcal{L}$, if $I \models_{S5_G} \psi$ then $I \cup \varphi \models_{S5_G} \psi$. Therefore in $S5_G$ only modal formulae can change their validity when new information is added. Since no other ground logic shares this characteristic with $S5_G$, this negative behaviour seems to be restricted to the logic $S5_G$ only. On the other hand, for a wide class of ground logics we obtain the following positive result (which is analogous to that obtained for McDermott and Doyle's logics in [24]).

Theorem 5. *Given a modal logic S such that $K \subseteq S \subseteq S4F$, there exists a faithful modular translation from default logic to the ground nonmonotonic logic S_G.*

Sketch of the proof. (For the detailed proof see [15]) First, it is shown that if S is a default extension for the default theory (D, W), then $ST(S)$ is an S_G-expansion for $emb(D, W)$ for any modal logic S such that $K \subseteq S \subseteq S5$. Then, we prove that if $ST(S)$ is a $S4F_G$-expansion for $emb(D, W)$, then S is a default extension for (D, W). This is obtained by exploiting a correspondence between minimal expansions in McDermott and Doyle logics and ground expansions. The two above results imply that, for each modal logic S such that $K \subseteq S \subseteq S4F$, emb is a faithful translation for S; since emb is modular, this concludes the proof.   □

We now turn our attention to the problem of expressing defaults in concept languages. In this framework one has to deal with the issue of giving a semantics to open defaults, i.e. defaults in which free variables occur. The semantics of open defaults is still debated [2, 12]; we adopt the semantics proposed by Baader and Hollunder [1], which restricts the application of defaults only to the individuals explicitly mentioned in the ABox. Notice that this semantics can be viewed as the natural extension of the semantics of rules given in [5], where rules apply only to the known individuals in the knowledge base. Such formalization of rules is in fact the same obtained by applying emb to justification-free defaults. As shown below, this translation is faithful for every logic $\mathcal{ALCK}(S_G)$.

The following theorem shows that, under this semantics, default theories are expressible in a large subset of the family $\mathcal{ALCK}(S_G)$.

Theorem 6. *Given a modal logic S such that $K \subseteq S \subseteq S4F$, there exists a faithful modular translation from default logic to the concept language $\mathcal{ALCK}(S_G)$.*

Proof. We show that the following modular translation τ is faithful:

$$\tau(\frac{\alpha : M\beta_1 \dots M\beta_n}{\gamma}) = K(O \wedge \alpha) \wedge K\neg K\neg\beta_1 \wedge \dots \wedge K\neg K\neg\beta_n \supset \gamma \quad (2)$$

where O is a concept whose extension comprises all the individuals explicitly mentioned in the ABox, namely we assume that for each individual a there exists an assertion $O(a)$ in the ABox. Now, adding formula $K(O \wedge \alpha) \wedge K \neg K \neg \beta_1 \wedge \ldots \wedge K \neg K \neg \beta_n \supset \gamma$ in the TBox exactly corresponds to adding in the ABox the set of its instances on all individuals (both known and unknown), i.e. two sets of closed formulae, one on known individuals and the other one on unknown individuals, which we call respectively KD and UD. These formulae correspond to propositional defaults according to the translation emb. Now, Theorem 5 guarantees that the set of formulae KD exactly corresponds to the instances of the default rule on known individuals. On the other hand, none of the propositional defaults corresponding to the set UD can be applied, because of the presence of the conjunct O in the prerequisite: consequently, τ is a faithful translation for default theories under the semantics of Baader and Hollunder. □

Since a preferred model (see [15]) is always an $S5$-model (given that every S_G-expansion is a stable expansion), the use of a different accessibility relation affects the epistemic models of the knowledge base, but does not change the interpretation of the epistemic operator in the queries. Therefore, we can define a decision procedure for $\mathcal{ALC}$-knowledge bases containing defaults, and allowing epistemic queries. Such a procedure employs the calculus for $\mathcal{ALCK}(S5_G)$ defined in [4] and separately treats defaults, for example using the method of Schwind and Risch [21] instanciating each default on all the known individuals. Consequently, instance checking for this kind of knowledge bases is a decidable problem.

4 Role and concept closure

In this section, we first show that role closure can be nicely formalized in our setting by using epistemic roles, then we discuss a new form of concept closure obtained by using epistemic concept expressions. We develop the discussion by presenting a few examples and checking the corresponding behaviour of implementations. Examples are explained by referring to the (more intuitive) logic $\mathcal{ALCK}(S5_G)$. However, the same epistemic models arise if one interprets sentences in $\mathcal{ALCK}(S4F_G)$.

Closure on roles is available both in CLASSIC(see [3]) and in LOOM (see [13]). The idea is to restrict universal role quantifications to the known individuals filling the role in the knowledge base. E.g., consider the following knowledge base, which has been developed in the system CLASSIC.

$$\texttt{vegetarian} \doteq \forall \texttt{EATS.plant} \qquad \texttt{EATS(Bob, Celery)} \qquad \texttt{plant(Celery)}$$

If one applies the closure operator to the role EATS, then CLASSIC infers vegetarian(Bob). We can formalize the above sequence of operations by introducing the epistemic operator in the knowledge base. In particular, the definition vegetarian $\doteq$ $\forall$EATS.plant plus the closure of EATS can be represented by **vegetarian** $\doteq$ $\forall$**KEATS.plant**. The difference with CLASSIC is that a subsequent assertion **EATS(Bob,Hamburger)** would cause a system warning in CLASSIC, while in our epistemic setting would simply mean that **vegetarian(Bob)** no longer holds.

Another interesting example points out the procedural nature of the closure operator. Let us consider the following knowledge base, which includes two rules expressed as epistemic sentences, and the closure operator is again expressed in epistemic terms:

$$\mathbf{K}(\forall KR.A) \sqsubseteq (FILLS\,Q\,c) \quad R(a,b) \quad A(b)$$
$$\mathbf{K}(\forall KQ.B) \sqsubseteq (FILLS\,R\,c) \quad Q(a,b) \quad B(b)$$

Note that when the two above rules are applied to the individual a, the consequent of each rule makes the antecedent of the other rule false. E.g., adding $(FILLS\,Q\,c)(a)$ (that is, adding $Q(a,c)$) makes $(\forall KQ.B)(a)$ false, since $\mathbf{K}B(c)$ is false. Hence, this knowledge base admits two epistemic models, one in which $Q(a,c)$ holds by effect of the first rule, and another one in which $R(a,c)$ holds because the second rule is applied. The situation is reproducible in CLASSIC, which selects one extension or the other, based on the order in which the closure operations are executed. In other words, if R is closed first, then the first rule is applied, and this inhibits the application of the second one, and vice versa when Q is closed first.

Finally, we turn our attention to other uses of the epistemic operator that become possible in our setting. In particular, we can state complete knowledge about a concept. Consider for example a university, whose professors have offices inside buldings. Let Σ be the following knowledge base:

$$
\begin{array}{ll}
\texttt{university(ULS)} & \texttt{has-office(Bob, room2)} \\
\texttt{professor(George)} & \texttt{has-office(George, room1)} \\
\texttt{professor(Bob)} & \texttt{is-in(room1, MainBuilding)} \\
\texttt{building(MainBuilding)} & \texttt{is-in(room2, MainBuilding)}
\end{array}
$$

and consider the (informal) assertion $\mathcal{A}$ = "the university has a rector, who is a professor". One may express the assertion as $\exists$**has-rector.professor(ULS)**. Consider the question to the knowledge base "Do you know the building where the rector's office is?", which can be expressed as the following query:

$$Q = \mathbf{K}\exists\texttt{has-rector.}\exists\texttt{has-office.}\exists\texttt{is-in.}\mathbf{K}\texttt{building(ULS)}$$

Of course the answer is No, since the rector can be any (unknown) professor whose office we don't know about. This is captured by the fact that

$$\Sigma \cup \{\exists\texttt{has-rector.professor(ULS)}\} \models \neg Q$$

In fact, since the knowledge base $\Sigma \cup \{\exists\texttt{has-rector.professor(ULS)}\}$ is modal-free, it has one epistemic model, whose set of worlds coincides with the set of all first-order models of the knowledge base. Since in different worlds there can be a different (known or unknown) rector, with the office in any building, the knowledge base cannot know which is the building of the rector's office.

Suppose now that we know who the professors are, that is, we have complete knowledge about professors of the university. In this case, the assertion A should be expressed as ∃has-rector.Kprofessor(ULS) and its reading becomes "the university has a rector, which is *one of* the (known) professors". Now we have that

$$\Sigma \cup \{\exists\text{has-rector.\textbf{K}professor(ULS)}\} \models Q$$

which correctly captures the fact that the knowledge base knows where the rector's office is, namely, in the main building. In fact, in each epistemic model satisfying ∃has-rector.Kprofessor(ULS) the rector is a known professor, the same in every world of the model. Since there are two known professors, there are two epistemic models of $\Sigma \cup \{\exists\text{has-rector.\textbf{K}professor(ULS)}\}$. In one model, George is the rector, while in the other Bob is. In both models, every world contains the fact that the rector's office is in the main building.

Notice that the kind of closure on roles that we have just described is not available in implemented systems, although it seems to be both useful and natural. We expect that other uses of the epistemic operator can be found and we are currently investigating this possibility.

5   Conclusions

In this paper we have proposed a nonmonotonic modal formalism based on the idea of minimization of knowledge, that captures the intuition of restricting certain forms of reasoning to the individuals known to the knowledge base. The result is a language that is parametric with respect to the class of epistemic models, as in the case of ground nonmonotonic modal logics.

We have shown that a number of non-first-order features that are common in knowledge representation systems based on concept languages can be nicely formalized by allowing various forms of epistemic statements in the knowledge bases. In particular, the formalism allows for the representation of defaults, by adopting a translation that generalizes the one previously proposed for the treatment of procedural rules and weak inclusions. In addition, we have addressed the mechanism of role closure, arguing that it can be represented by using the epistemic operator on role expressions. Finally we have presented an example based on the idea of concept closure, that is considered a desirable extension of knowledge representation systems based on concept languages.

Therefore, we believe that the proposed formalism contributes to fill in the gap between theory and practice by providing forms of reasoning that both have a natural interpretation and correspond to some of the features implemented in the systems. However, a number of issues remain to be invistigated. In particular, we expect to identify other patterns of sentences corresponding to practically interesting forms of reasoning, both to explain system behaviours and to propose system extensions. In addition, we aim at devising reasoning methods that are appropriate for the different classes of epistemic sentences to be included in the knowledge base.

Acknowledgements

We would like to thank Marco Cadoli and one anonymous referee for their careful reading of the paper, their comments and suggestions for the improvement of the presentation.

References

1. F. Baader and R. Hollunder. Embedding defaults into terminological knowledge representation formalisms. In *Proceedings of KR-92*, pages 306–317, Morgan Kaufmann, 1992.
2. F. Baader and K. Schlechta. A semantics for open normal defaults via a modified preferential approach. DFKI research report RR-93-13, 1993.
3. R. J. Brachman, D. McGuinness, P. F. Patel-Schneider, L. A. Resnick. Living with CLASSIC: When and How to Use a KL-ONE-Like Language. In *Principles of Semantic Networks*, J. Sowa ed., Morgan Kaufmann, 1990.
4. Francesco M. Donini, Maurizio Lenzerini, Daniele Nardi, Werner Nutt, Andrea Schaerf. Adding epistemic operators to concept languages. In *Proceedings of KR-92*, pages 342–353, Morgan Kaufmann, 1992.
5. Francesco M. Donini, Maurizio Lenzerini, Daniele Nardi, Werner Nutt, Andrea Schaerf. Queries, Rules and Definitions as Epistemic Sentences in Concept Languages. In *Theoretical Foundations of Knowledge Representation and Reasoning*, Gerhard Lakemeyer and Bernhard Nebel eds., LNAI 810, Springer-Verlag, 1994.
6. F. M. Donini, D. Nardi and R. Rosati. Ground Nonmonotonic Modal Logics for Knowledge Representation. To appear in *Proceedings of WOCFAI-95*.
7. Georg Gottlob. The Power of Beliefs - or - Translating Default Logic into Standard Autoepistemic Logic. In *Proc. of the 13th Int. Joint Conf. on Artificial Intelligence IJCAI-93*, Chambery, France, 1993.
8. J. Halpern and Y. Moses. Towards a theory of knowledge and ignorance: preliminary report. In K. Apt editor, *Logics and models of concurrent systems*, pages 459–476, Springer-Verlag, 1985.
9. M. Kaminski. Embedding a default system into nonmonotonic logic. *Fundamenta Informaticae*, 14:345–354, 1991.
10. Hector J. Levesque. Foundations of a functional approach to knowledge representation. *Artificial Intelligence Journal*, 23:155–212, 1984.
11. Vladimir Lifschitz. Nonmonotonic databases and epistemic queries. In *Proc. of the 12th Int. Joint Conf. on Artificial Intelligence IJCAI-91*, Sydney, 1991.
12. Vladimir Lifschitz. On open defaults. In *Proc. of the Symposium on Computational Logics*, Brüssel, Belgium, 1990.
13. Robert MacGregor. A deductive pattern matcher. In *Proc. of the 7th Nat. Conf. on Artificial Intelligence (AAAI-88)*, pages 403–408, 1988.
14. V.W. Marek and M. Truszczyński. Nonmonotonic logic. Context-dependent reasoning. Springer-Verlag, 1993.
15. D. Nardi and R. Rosati. A preference semantics for ground nonmonotonic modal logics. To appear in *Proc. of EPIA-95*.
16. Lin Padgham and Tingting Zhang. A terminological logic with defaults: a definition and an application. In *Proc. of the 13th Int. Joint Conf. on Artificial Intelligence IJCAI-93*, pages 662–668, Chambery, France, 1993.

17. J. Quantz and V. Royer. A preference semantics for defaults in terminological logics. In *Proceedings of KR-92*, pages 294–305, Morgan Kaufmann, 1992.
18. R. Reiter, A Logic for Default Reasoning. *Artificial Intelligence Journal*, 13:81–132, 1980.
19. R. Reiter. On asking what a database knows. In J. W. Lloyd, editor, *Symposium on Computational Logics*, pages 96–113. Springer-Verlag, ESPRIT Basic Research Action Series, 1990.
20. G. Schwarz. Bounding introspection in nonmonotonic logics. In *Proceedings of the 3rd international conference on principles of knowledge representation and reasoning (KR-92)*, pages 581–590, Morgan Kaufmann, 1992.
21. C. Schwind and V. Risch. A tableau-based characterisation for default logic. In *Proceedings of the First European Conference on Symbolic and Quantitative Approaches for Uncertainty*, pages 310–317, Marseilles, France, 1991.
22. Umberto Straccia. Default inheritance reasoning in hybrid KL-ONE-style logics. In *Proc. of the 13th Int. Joint Conf. on Artificial Intelligence IJCAI-93*, pages 676–681, Chambery, France, 1993.
23. M. Tiomkin and M. Kaminski. Nonmonotonic default modal logics. In *Proceedings of the Third Conference on Theoretical Aspects of Reasoning about Knowledge (TARK-90)*, pages 73–84, 1990.
24. M. Truszczyński. Modal interpretations of default logic. In *Proc. of the 12th Int. Joint Conf. on Artificial Intelligence IJCAI-91*, Sydney, 1991.
25. William A. Woods and James G. Schmolze. The KL-ONE Family. *Semantic Networks in Artificial Intelligence*. Published as a special issue of *Computers & Mathematics with Applications*, Volume 23, Number 2–9, 1992, pages 133–178.

PDL-based framework for reasoning about actions

Giuseppe De Giacomo and Maurizio Lenzerini

Dipartimento di Informatica e Sistemistica
Università di Roma "La Sapienza"
Via Salaria 113, 00198 Roma, Italia
{degiacomo,lenzerini}@assi.dis.uniroma1.it

Abstract. Propositional Dynamic Logics (PDL's) provide a suitable formal framework for modeling actions and reasoning about them. However, the basic language of PDL's lack several features that are important for a sophisticated treatment of actions. In this paper, we present a new logic that is obtained by enriching the basic PDL with powerful modeling constructs that allow us to represent determinism and non-determinisms, concurrency, hierarchies, mutual exclusion, backward execution, and non-execution of actions. We demonstrate, by means of examples, the expressive power of the formalism. In particular, we show that although nonmonotonicity is not generally captured by PDL's, our logic is perfectly suited for exploiting monotonic solutions to the frame problem. Finally, we establish that the proposed formalism is decidable, and that the basic reasoning problems are EXPTIME-complete.

1 Introduction

Propositional Dynamic Logics (PDL's) are modal logics for describing and reasoning about system dynamics in terms of states and actions (or events) modeled as relations between states (see [19, 15, 23] for surveys on PDL's, see also [31] for a somewhat different account). The basic language of PDL includes atomic propositions, that are interpreted as simple properties of states, plus the construct $[R]\phi$, where ϕ is a formula and R is an action, whose meaning is that all executions of the action R terminate in a state where ϕ is true. The action R can be either atomic or complex, i.e. constituted by sequential composition, nondeterministic choice, iteration, or test.

PDL's have been originally developed in Theoretical Computer Science to reason about program schemas [9], and their variants have been adopted to specify and verify properties of reactive processes (e.g., Hennessy Milner Logic [16, 22], modal mu-calculus [18, 20, 31]). In Artificial Intelligence, PDL's have been extensively used in establishing decidability and computational complexity results of many formalisms: for example they have been used in investigating Common Knowledge [14], Conditional Logics [10], Description Logics [29, 6, 7], Features Logics [1].

Though PDL's have been only sparingly adopted for reasoning about actions (main exceptions being [28, 17], but also [4]) there are two significant arguments that make them attractive.

1. Transition systems are the semantics adopted by an increasing number of proposal in reasoning about actions (see for example [3]). Transition systems are exactly the semantics underling PDL's.
2. Reiter's work on cognitive robotics [24, 26, 27, 21] has somewhat diverged the interest from nonmonotonic solutions to the frame problem, by illustrating that monotonic solutions are often very succinct. Now, while PDL's generally do not capture nonmonotonicity, they allow for exploiting the epistemological insight of the monotonic solutions to the frame problem, as shown later (see also [8]).

The general advantages PDL's offer in reasoning about actions are, on the one hand, the ability of expressing nondeterministic and complex actions, and, on the other hand, the availability of sophisticated tools for studying their computational aspects such as decidability, complexity, and reasoning algorithms.

In this paper we propose a very powerful Propositional Dynamic Logic, $\mathcal{DIFR}$, which offers an effective framework to model and reason about actions. The logic extends the previous formalisms in many ways. It allows for boolean expressions of atomic actions by which we can denote both the concurrent execution and the nonexecution of actions. It allows for expressing interdependencies between atomic actions such as specialization or mutual exclusion. It also includes constructs to impose the determinism of boolean combinations of atomic actions and their inverse. Notably, the logic is decidable and its computational complexity is EXPTIME (tight bound) as for the simplest PDL [9].

The rest of the paper is organized as follows: In Section 2 we introduce the logic $\mathcal{DIFR}$ both formally and intuitively; In Section 3 we illustrate, by means of examples, the use of $\mathcal{DIFR}$ in modeling and reasoning about actions; In Section 4 we discuss $\mathcal{DIFR}$ main features individually and we draw some conclusions.

2   The logic $\mathcal{DIFR}$

Formulae in the logic $\mathcal{DIFR}$ are of two sorts: *action formulae* and *state formulae*.

Action Formulae describe properties, by means of boolean operators, of *atomic actions* -i.e., actions that cannot be broken in sequences of smaller actions. The abstract syntax of action formulae is as follows:

$$\rho ::= P \mid \mathbf{any} \mid \rho_1 \wedge \rho_2 \mid \rho_1 \vee \rho_2 \mid \neg\rho$$

where P denotes a primitive action, and **any** denotes a special atomic action that can be thought of as "the most general atomic action". Observe that an atomic action denoted by an action formulae is composed, in general, by a set of primitive actions intended to be executed in parallel.

State Formulae describe properties of states in terms of propositions and complex actions. The abstract syntax for state formulae is as follows:

$$\phi ::= A \mid \top \mid \bot \mid \phi_1 \wedge \phi_2 \mid \phi_1 \vee \phi_2 \mid \neg\phi \mid$$
$$[R]\phi \mid \langle R \rangle \phi \mid (\mathbf{fun}\ r)$$
$$r ::= \rho \mid \rho^-$$
$$R ::= r \mid R_1 \vee R_2 \mid R_1; R_2 \mid R^* \mid \phi? \mid R^-$$

where A denotes a primitive proposition, $\top$ denotes "true", $\bot$ denotes "false", ϕ (possibly with subscript) denotes a state formula, r denotes a *simple action* which is either an atomic action or the inverse of an atomic action (i.e, set of primitive actions or of inverse of primitive actions), and finally R (possibly with subscript) denotes a complex action composing simple actions by nondeterministic choice, sequential composition, reflexive transitive closure, test, and inverse.

Let us explain the intuitive meaning of some formulae: the action formula $P_1 \wedge P_2$ means "perform P_1 and P_2 in parallel"; $\neg P$ means "don't perform P". In general an atomic formula ρ denotes a set of primitive actions that are performed in parallel and a set that are not performed at all (note that primitive actions that are not in these sets could be performed as well -i.e., we are adopting an open semantics for action formulae).

By forcing the validity of action formulae we can represent *hierarchies* of atomic actions, for example by $climb\_stairs \Rightarrow climb$ [1] we can represent that the action $climb\_stairs$ is a specialization of the action $climb$. In the same way we can represent *mutual exclusion*, for example by $\neg(open\_window \wedge close\_window)$ we can represent that the actions $open\_window$ and $close\_window$ cannot be performed together.

From atomic actions we build complex actions by means of constructors that are intuitively interpreted as follows: $R_1 \vee R_2$ means "nondeterministically perform R_1 or perform R_2"; $R_1; R_2$ means "perform R_1 and then R_2"; R^* means "repeat R a nondeterministically chosen number of times"; $\phi?$ means "test ϕ and proceed only if true"; R^- means "perform R in reverse". By using these constructs we can build complex action such as **if** ϕ **then** R_1 **else** R_2, which is represented by $(\phi?; R_2) \vee (\neg\phi?; R_2)$, or **while** ϕ **do** R which is represented by $(\phi?; R)^*; \neg\phi?$.

Turning to state formulae: $[R]\phi$ expresses that after *every performance* of the action R the property ϕ is satisfied; $\langle R \rangle \phi$ expresses that after *some performance* of the action R the property ϕ is satisfied -i.e. the execution of R *can* lead to a state where ϕ holds (recall that actions are nondeterministic in general).

The formula $\langle R \rangle \top$ expresses the *capability* of performing R; $[R]\bot$ expresses the *inability* of performing R; $[\neg r]\bot$ expresses the *inability* of performing any atomic actions *other than* those denoted by r; $[\neg \mathbf{any}]\bot$ expresses the inability of performing any atomic actions at all; $\langle \mathbf{any} \rangle \top \wedge [\neg r]\bot$ expresses the *necessity* or *inevitability* to perform some of the atomic actions denoted by r.

---

[1] As usual we will use $a \Rightarrow b$ an abbreviation of $\neg a \vee b$.

The construct $(\mathbf{fun}\, r)$ called *functional restriction* allows us to impose that the performance of a simple action r (i.e., an atomic action or the inverse of an atomic action) is deterministic. Hence $[r]\phi \wedge (\mathbf{fun}\, r)$ expresses that *if* the atomic action r is performed, then it *deterministically* leads to a state where ϕ holds. Note that this does not implies that the action r can be performed. The formula $\langle r \rangle \phi \wedge (\mathbf{fun}\, r)$ expresses that atomic action r *can* be performed and deterministically leads to a state where ϕ holds.

Propositional Dynamic Logics are subsets of Second Order Logic, or, more precisely, of First Order Logic plus Fixpoints. Typical properties that are not first order definable are: $\langle R^* \rangle \phi$, which expresses the *capability* for performing R *until* ϕ holds, and is equivalent to the least fixpoint of the operator $\lambda X.(\phi \vee \langle R \rangle X)$; $[R^*]\phi$, which expresses that ϕ holds in any state reachable from the current one by performing R any number of times, and is equivalent to the greatest fixpoint of the operator $\lambda X.(\phi \wedge [R]X)$. Interesting special cases of the last formula are: $[\mathbf{any}^*]\phi$, which expresses that ϕ holds *from now on* -i.e., no matter how the world evolves from the current state ϕ will be true; and $[(\mathbf{any} \vee \mathbf{any}^-)^*]\phi$, which expresses that ϕ holds in the whole connected component containing the current state (the state in which the formula holds).

The formal semantics of $\mathcal{DIFR}$ is based on the notion of *Kripke structure* or *transition system*, which is defined as a triple $M = (\mathcal{S}, \{\mathcal{R}_R\}, \mathcal{V})$, where $\mathcal{S}$ denotes a set of states, $\{\mathcal{R}_R\}$ is a family of binary relations over $\mathcal{S}$, such that each action R is given a meaning through $\mathcal{R}_R$, and $\mathcal{V}$ is a mapping from atomic propositions to subsets of $\mathcal{S}$ such that $\mathcal{V}(A)$ determines the states where the proposition A is true. The family $\{\mathcal{R}_R\}$ is systematically defined as follows:

$$\mathcal{R}\mathbf{any} \subseteq \mathcal{S} \times \mathcal{S},$$
$$\mathcal{R}_P \subseteq \mathcal{R}\mathbf{any},$$
$$\mathcal{R}_{\rho_1 \wedge \rho_2} = \mathcal{R}_{\rho_1} \cap \mathcal{R}_{\rho_2},$$
$$\mathcal{R}_{\rho_1 \vee \rho_2} = \mathcal{R}_{\rho_1} \cup \mathcal{R}_{\rho_2},$$
$$\mathcal{R}_{\neg \rho} = \mathcal{R}\mathbf{any} - \mathcal{R}_\rho,$$
$$\mathcal{R}_{\rho^-} = \{(s_1, s_2) \in \mathcal{S} \times \mathcal{S} \mid (s_2, s_1) \in \mathcal{R}_\rho\},$$
$$\mathcal{R}_r = \mathcal{R}_\rho \quad \text{if } r = \rho,$$
$$\mathcal{R}_r = \mathcal{R}_{\rho^-} \quad \text{if } r = \rho^-,$$
$$\mathcal{R}_{R_1 \vee R_2} = \mathcal{R}_{R_1} \cup \mathcal{R}_{R_2},$$
$$\mathcal{R}_{R_1 ; R_2} = \mathcal{R}_{R_1} \circ \mathcal{R}_{R_2} \quad \text{(seq. comp. of } \mathcal{R}_{R_1} \text{ and } \mathcal{R}_{R_2}),$$
$$\mathcal{R}_{R^*} = (\mathcal{R}_R)^* \quad \text{(refl. trans. closure of } \mathcal{R}_R),$$
$$\mathcal{R}_{R^-} = \{(s_1, s_2) \in \mathcal{S} \times \mathcal{S} \mid (s_2, s_1) \in \mathcal{R}_R\},$$
$$\mathcal{R}_{\phi?} = \{(s, s) \in \mathcal{S} \times \mathcal{S} \mid M, s \models \phi\}.$$

Note that actions (even primitive actions) are nondeterministic in general.

The conditions for a state formula ϕ to hold at a state s of a structure M, written $M, s \models \phi$, are:

$$M, s \models A \text{ iff } s \in \mathcal{V}(A)$$
$$M, s \models \top \quad always,$$
$$M, s \models \bot \quad never,$$
$$M, s \models \phi_1 \wedge \phi_2 \text{ iff } M, s \models \phi_1 \text{ and } M, s \models \phi_2,$$
$$M, s \models \phi_1 \vee \phi_2 \text{ iff } M, s \models \phi_1 \text{ or } M, s \models \phi_2,$$
$$M, s \models \neg\phi \text{ iff } M, s \not\models \phi,$$
$$M, s \models \langle R \rangle \phi \text{ iff } \exists s'.(s, s') \in \mathcal{R}_R \text{ and } M, s' \models \phi,$$
$$M, s \models [R]\phi \text{ iff } \forall s'.(s, s') \in \mathcal{R}_R \text{ implies } M, s' \models \phi,$$
$$M, s \models (\mathbf{fun}\, r) \text{ iff exists } at \ most \ one \ s'.(s, s') \in \mathcal{R}_r.$$

A structure M is a model of an action formula ρ if $\mathcal{R}_\rho = \mathcal{R}_{\mathbf{any}}$. A structure M is a model of a state formula ϕ if for all s in M, $M, s \models \phi$. Let Γ be a finite set of both state and action formulae, a structure is a model of Γ if is a model of every formula in Γ. A set of formulae Γ *logically implies* a (state or action) formula ψ, written

$$\Gamma \models \psi$$

if all the models of Γ are models of ψ as well.

A crucial question to be answered is: Is logical implication decidable in $\mathcal{DIFR}$? If yes, which is its computational complexity? Note that known results in PDL's do not help directly. It is possible to prove (see [5]) that this problem is indeed decidable and its computational complexity can be precisely characterized, by providing a reduction to the PDL $\mathcal{DIF}$ presented in [6].

Theorem 1. *Logical implication for* $\mathcal{DIFR}$ *is an EXPTIME-complete problem.*

Observe that logical implication is already EXPTIME-complete for the basic modal logic $\mathcal{K}$ (which corresponds to a Propositional Dynamic Logic including just one primitive action, no functional restrictions, and no action constructor at all).

3 Examples

Below we show the power of $\mathcal{DIFR}$ in modeling a dynamically changing world by means of two examples. We remark that those examples do not aim at providing the definitive $\mathcal{DIFR}$-based formalizations of the scenarios they describe, nor they exhaust the possibility of using $\mathcal{DIFR}$ in representing and reasoning about actions[2]. They are intended to give a taste of what can be done with such a logic. In the examples we refer to situation calculus as it is presented in [24, 26, 27, 21].

Example: Lifting both sides of a table A vase is on top of a table, and if just one side is lifted then it slides down and falls on the floor. However if both

---

[2] In addition these examples do not make use of many features of the logic such as axioms on atomic actions.

sides are simultaneously lifted this doesn't happen [12]. We formalize the scenario as follows. We consider the following primitive propositions (corresponding to "propositional" fluents in situation calculus): *vase_on_table*, *down_left_side*, *down_right_side*; and the following primitive actions (corresponding to actions in situation calculus[3]): *vase_slides_down*, *lift_left*, *lift_right*. The intended meaning of these propositions and actions is the natural one (sometimes we use initials as abbreviations):

As usual actions have *preconditions* which are conditions that must be satisfied in order to be able to perform the action[4].

$$\langle lift\_left \rangle \top \equiv down\_left\_side$$
$$\langle lift\_right \rangle \top \equiv down\_right\_side$$
$$\langle vsd \rangle \top \equiv (vot \wedge ((dls \wedge \neg drs) \vee (\neg dls \wedge drs)))$$

Actually the if part of the last axioms must be strengthened: If the vase is on the table and one of the side of the table is not on the floor, then it is *inevitable* (not just possible) that the vase slides towards the floor. This can be enforced by:

$$(vot \wedge ((dls \wedge \neg drs) \vee (\neg dls \wedge drs))) \Rightarrow \langle \mathbf{any} \rangle \top \wedge [\neg vsd] \bot.$$

We also need to specify when the actions *lift_left* and *lift_right* can be performed simultaneously. With the next axiom we assert that they can be performed simultaneously simply if they both can be performed individually:

$$\langle lift\_left \wedge lift\_right \rangle \top \equiv \langle lift\_left \rangle \top \wedge \langle lift\_right \rangle \top.$$

Actions have *effects* if they can be performed[5]:

$$[lift\_left] \neg down\_left\_side$$
$$[lift\_right] \neg down\_right\_side$$
$$[vase\_slides\_down] \neg vase\_on\_table$$

As usual we need to cope with the frame problem. We do it by adopting a monotonic solution as in [13, 30, 24]. We enforce the following *frame axioms* saying that if the vase is on the table then all atomic actions not including *vase_slides_down* leave the vase on the table; if the vase is not on the table then no atomic action will change its position; etc.:

$$vase\_on\_table \Rightarrow [\neg vase\_slides\_down] vase\_on\_table$$
$$down\_left\_side \Rightarrow [\neg lift\_left] down\_left\_side$$
$$down\_right\_side \Rightarrow [\neg lift\_right] down\_right\_side$$

$$\neg vase\_on\_table \Rightarrow [\mathbf{any}] \neg vase\_on\_table$$
$$\neg down\_left\_side \Rightarrow [\mathbf{any}] \neg down\_left\_side$$
$$\neg down\_right\_side \Rightarrow [\mathbf{any}] \neg down\_right\_side$$

---

[3] Note that (contrary to what is usually assumed in situation calculus) actions are not necessarily deterministic in $\mathcal{DIFR}$.

[4] Note that $\langle r \rangle \top$ have the same role as $Poss(a, s)$ in Reiter's situation calculus.

[5] Note that state formulae of the form $[a]\phi$ have the same role as $Poss(a, s) \Rightarrow \phi(do(a, s))$ which is a common formula configuration in Reiter's situation calculus [24, 27].

We adopted the last three axioms for sake of brevity.

Let us call Γ the set of the axioms above and let the starting situation be described by

$$S \doteq vase\_on\_table \wedge down\_left\_side \wedge down\_right\_side.$$

Then we can make the following two inferences. On the one hand:

$$\Gamma \models S \Rightarrow [ll \wedge lr][vase\_slides\_down]\bot$$

that is if the vase is on the table and both the sides of the table are on the floor, then lifting the two sides concurrently does not make the vase falling. On the other hand:

$$\Gamma \models S \Rightarrow [ll \wedge \neg lr][lr]\neg vase\_on\_table$$

that is if the vase is on the table and both the sides of the table are on the floor, then lifting first the left side without lifting the right side and then the right side, has as a result that the vase is fallen. Notice that the above inferences don't say anything about the possibility of performing the actions described, however this possibility is guaranteed by $\Gamma \models S \Rightarrow \langle lift\_left \wedge lift\_right \rangle \top$ and $\Gamma \models S \Rightarrow \langle (lift\_left \wedge \neg lift\_right); lift\_right) \rangle \top$ respectively.

Example: Making the heating operative We want to make our (gas) heating operative. To do so we need to strike a match, to turn its gas handle on and to ignite the security flame spot. To strike a match we need to concurrently press the match against the match box and rub it until it fires.

We make the following intuitive assumption: the past is *backward linear* that is from any state there is only one accessible (immediately) previous state. This can be easily imposed by means of the following axiom:

$$\textbf{(fun any}^-\textbf{)}.$$

We assume the following preconditions and effects of actions.
Preconditions:

$$\langle turn\_on\_gas \rangle \top \equiv \neg gas\_open$$
$$\langle turn\_off\_gas \rangle \top \equiv gas\_open$$
$$\langle ignite\_flame\_spot \rangle \top \equiv match\_lit$$
$$\langle press \rangle \top \Rightarrow \neg match\_lit$$
$$\langle rub \rangle \top \Rightarrow \neg match\_lit$$
$$\langle \textbf{while} \neg match\_lit \textbf{ do } (press \wedge rub) \rangle \top$$

Effects:

$$match\_lit \wedge gas\_open \Rightarrow$$
$$[ignite\_flame\_spot]heating\_operative$$
$$[turn\_on\_gas]gas\_open$$
$$[turn\_off\_gas]\neg gas\_open$$

In this example we model frame axioms more systematically starting from *explanation closure axioms* [30] in line with [24, 27]. There are two main difficulty in following this approach in PDL: the first is that, as in any modal logic, we can directly refer to just one state the "current one", the second is that we cannot quantify on atomic actions. In $\mathcal{DIFR}$ we can overcome these difficulties. By assuming (**fun any**$^-$) from the current state we can univocally refer back to *the* previous state through the action **any**$^-$. On the other hand by using the action **any** we can simulate the universal quantification on atomic actions. Hence we proceed as follows from the current state we make a step forward and then we model the various condition backward. This leads to the following frame axioms:

$$[\textbf{any}]\neg gas\_open \Rightarrow$$
$$\langle \textbf{any}^- \rangle \neg gas\_open \vee \langle turn\_off\_gas^- \rangle \top$$
$$[\textbf{any}]\neg match\_lit \Rightarrow$$
$$\langle \textbf{any}^- \rangle \neg match\_lit$$
$$[\textbf{any}]\neg heating\_operative \Rightarrow$$
$$\langle \textbf{any}^- \rangle \neg heating\_operative$$

$$[\textbf{any}]gas\_open \Rightarrow$$
$$\langle \textbf{any}^- \rangle gas\_open \vee \langle turn\_on\_gas^- \rangle \top$$
$$[\textbf{any}]match\_lit \Rightarrow$$
$$\langle \textbf{any}^- \rangle match\_lit \vee \langle (press \wedge rub)^- \rangle \top$$
$$[\textbf{any}]heating\_operative \Rightarrow$$
$$\langle \textbf{any}^- \rangle heating\_operative \vee$$
$$\langle ignite\_flame\_spot^- \rangle gas\_open$$

For example the last axiom says: "consider any successor state (such a state has exactly one previous state which is the current state), if the heating is operative in such a state then either it was operative in the previous state or the action *ignite_flame_spot* was just performed and the gas was open in the previous state".[6]

Let us call Γ the set of all these axioms, and let the starting situation be described by

$$S \doteq \neg open\_gas \wedge \neg match\_lit \wedge \neg heating\_operative$$

---

[6] The frame axioms can be proved to be equivalent to the following ones (respecting the order):

$$gas\_open \Rightarrow [\neg turn\_off\_gas]gas\_open$$
$$match\_lit \Rightarrow [\textbf{any}]match\_lit$$
$$heating\_operative \Rightarrow [\textbf{any}]heating\_operative$$

$$\neg gas\_open \Rightarrow [\neg turn\_on\_gas]\neg gas\_open$$
$$\neg match\_lit \Rightarrow [\neg (press \wedge rub)]\neg match\_lit$$
$$\neg heating\_operative \Rightarrow$$
$$[\neg ignite\_flame\_spot \vee$$
$$\neg gas\_open?; \textbf{any}]\neg heating\_operative.$$

The last axiom says: "if the heating is not operative then every performance of an atomic action not including *ignite_flame_spot* and every performance of any action starting from a state in which the gas is not open, leads to a state where the heating is still not operative".

The first inference we are interested in is the following:

$$\Gamma \models S \Rightarrow \langle \textbf{any}^* \rangle heating\_operative$$

i.e., there is a sequence of action (a plan) starting from a situation described by S resulting in making the heating operative. Assuming all primitive actions to be deterministic, inferences of the form

$$\Gamma \models S \Rightarrow \langle \textbf{any}^* \rangle G$$

are the typical starting point in planning synthesis [11]: if the answer is yes then from the proof we can generate a working plan to achieve the goal G starting from an initial situation described by S. The dual of the above inference

$$\Gamma \models S \Rightarrow [\textbf{any}^*]\neg G$$

is of interest as well: it establishes that there are no plan at all achieving a given goal G starting from a situation described be S.

Next inference says that the complex action "strike a match turn on the gas, ignite the control flame spot" results in making the heating operative:

$$\Gamma \models \langle \textbf{while } \neg match\_lit \textbf{ do } (press \wedge push);$$
$$turn\_on\_gas;$$
$$ignite\_flame\_spot$$
$$\rangle heating\_operative$$

Note that the similar action "turn on the gas, strike a match, ignite the control flame spot" is not guaranteed to make the heating operative.

$$\Gamma \not\models \langle turn\_on\_gas;$$
$$\textbf{while } \neg match\_lit \textbf{ do } (press \wedge push);$$
$$ignite\_flame\_spot$$
$$\rangle heating\_operative$$

The reason why above the complex action may fail is because the gas could be turned off while we are trying to strike the match.

The problem of checking inferences as the two above is known as *projection problem* (see e.g. [26]). A typical projection problem as the form: Does G hold in the state reachable from initial situation described by S by executing the (complex) action α? This corresponds to checking the inference below:

$$\Gamma \models S \Rightarrow \langle \alpha \rangle G.$$

We have seen that executing the complex action "turn on the gas, strike a match, ignite the control flame spot" may fail to make the heating operative. If this is the case, the following inference tells us that the gas has been turned off before striking the match succeeded:

$$\Gamma \models \langle turn\_on\_gas;$$
$$\textbf{while } \neg match\_lit \textbf{ do } (press \wedge push);$$
$$ignite\_flame\_spot$$
$$\rangle(\neg heating\_operative \Rightarrow$$
$$\langle (\textbf{any}^-; \textbf{any}^-)^*; turn\_off\_gas \rangle \top)$$

Inferences as the one above are answers to "historical queries" [26, 25] -i.e., queries of the form: if from the initial state described by S we execute the complex action α getting ϕ, then does this implies that before the termination of α, a given formula ϕ' is true in some state, or that a given action a has been executed? These questions can be answered by checking the inferences[7]:

$$\Gamma \models S \Rightarrow \langle\alpha\rangle(\phi \Rightarrow \langle(\mathbf{any}^-)^*\rangle\phi')$$

$$\Gamma \models S \Rightarrow \langle\alpha\rangle(\phi \Rightarrow \langle(\mathbf{any}^-)^*; a^-\rangle\top).$$

4 Discussion

It is our opinion that Propositional Dynamic Logics offer a elegant framework with a well understood semantics and precise computational characterization, that makes them a kind of Principled Monotonic Propositional Situation Calculus extended to deal with complex actions.

According to this perspective, $\mathcal{DIFR}$ has been designed to address issues that are important in modeling actions but are not satisfactorily dealt with by traditional PDL's. Here, we briefly discuss the most relevant features of $\mathcal{DIFR}$ in modeling actions.

• The ability of specifying the performance of different atomic actions concurrently. This characteristic, illustrated in the examples of Section 3, is one of the most original aspects of $\mathcal{DIFR}$. Indeed, the attention to reason about concurrent actions has emerged only recently. $\mathcal{DIFR}$ takes into account concurrency of actions that cannot be interrupted (atomic actions in our terminology). Obviously further work has to be done for capturing more general forms of concurrency. In this context, we argue that it is relevant for the AI community to look at the vast computer science literature on modeling concurrent processes.

• The ability of specifying the "non-execution" of atomic actions. This feature called for a careful definition of the notion of "non-executing an action". In our approach, this notion has been formulated by interpreting it as "the execution of some action other than a given one". Observe that it is essentially this feature that allows us to provide a compact representation of the frame axioms, as illustrated in the examples above.

• The ability of structuring atomic actions. In particular, $\mathcal{DIFR}$ allow the designer to organize actions in hierarchies, where actions are related by means of two basic mechanisms: one for stating that an action is a specialization of another one, and the other for representing mutual exclusion between actions.

---

[7] Observe that ϕ' (a) could be true (executed) before the starting of α in the formulation above. To avoid this we need to distinguish the initial state, for example by assuming that the initial situation does not have a past, which can be done by including in S the state formula $[\mathbf{any}^-]\bot$.

• The ability of distinguishing deterministic and nondeterministic atomic actions. Note that in $\mathcal{DIFR}$ the determinism or nondeterminism of an atomic action may be modeled on a state-to-state basis. This ability provides the designer with more expressive power with respect to the case where actions are assumed to be always deterministic. Indeed in this last case there is no distinction between nondeterminism and incomplete knowledge about the situation resulting from executing an action (see for example [2]).

• The ability of expressing properties of both future and past states. In particular, the usual linearity of the past can be asserted. This ability makes our logic capable to reason about not only projection problems but also historical queries. Some examples of these have been provided in Section 3.

The result on the computational properties of $\mathcal{DIFR}$ shows that the logic is decidable, which means that reasoning procedure that are sound, complete, and terminating are available. Space limitations prevented us to elaborate more on this issue, the interested reader is referred to [5] for a deep investigation.

References

1. P. Blackburn and E. Spaan. A modal perspective on computational complexity of attribute value grammar. *Journal of Logic, Language and Computation*, 2:129–169, 1993.
2. C. Boutilier and N. Friedman. Nondeterministic actions and the frame problem. In [3], 39–44, 1995.
3. C. Boutilier, M. Goldszmidt, T. Dean, S. Hanks, D. Heckerman, and R. Reiter, editors. *Working notes of the AAAI 1995 Spring Symposium on Extending Theories of Action: Formal and Practical Applications*, Stanford, CA, USA, 1995.
4. P. Cohen and H. Levesque. Intention is choice with communication. *Artificial Intelligence*, 42:213–261, 1990.
5. G. De Giacomo. *Decidability of Class-Based Knowledge Representation Formalisms and their Application to Medical Terminology Servers*. PhD thesis, Dipartimento di Informatica e Sistemistica, Università di Roma "La Sapienza", 1995.
6. G. De Giacomo and M. Lenzerini. Boosting the correspondence between description logics and propositional dynamic logics. In *Proceedings of the 12th National Conference on Artificial Intelligence*, pages 205–212, 1994.
7. G. De Giacomo and M. Lenzerini. Description logics with inverse roles, functional restrictions, and n-ary relations. In *Proceedings of the 4th European Workshop on Logics in Artificial Intelligence*, LNAI 838, pages 332–346. Springer-Verlag, 1994.
8. G. De Giacomo and M. Lenzerini. Enhanced propositional dynamic logic for reasoning about concurrent actions (extended abstract). In [3], pages 62–67, 1995.
9. N. J. Fisher and R. E. Ladner. Propositional dynamic logic of regular programs. *Journal of Computer and System Sciences*, 18:194–211, 1979.
10. N. Friedman and J. Halpern. On the complexity of conditional logics. In *Proc. of the 4th Int. Conf. on Principles of Knowledge Representation and Reasoning*, 1994.
11. C. Green. Theorem proving by resolution as basis for question-answering systems. In *Machine Intelligence*, volume 4, pages 183–205. American Elsevier, 1969.

12. G. Grosse. Propositional state event logic. In *Proceedings of the 4th European Workshop on Logics in Artificial Intelligence*, LNAI 838, pages 316–331. Springer-Verlag, 1994.

13. A. Haas. The case for domain-specific frame axioms. In *Proc. of the Workshop on the Frame Problem*, pages 343–348. Morgan Kaufmann Publishers, 1987.

14. J. Halpern and Y. Moses. A guide to completeness and complexity for modal logics of knowledge and belief. *Artificial Intelligence*, 54:319–379, 1992.

15. D. Harel. Dynamic logic. In D. M. Gabbay and F. Guenthner, editors, *Handbook of Philosophical Logic*, pages 497–603. D. Reidel Publishing Company, Oxford, 1984.

16. M. Hennessy and R. Milner. Algebraic laws for nondetrminism and concurrency. *Journal of Association for Computing Machinery*, 32:137–162, 1985.

17. H. Kautz. A first order dynamic logic for planning. Master's thesis, Department of Computer Science, University of Toronto, Toronto, Ontario, Canada, 1980.

18. D. Kozen. Results on the propositional mu-calculus. *Theoretical Computer Science*, 27:333–355, 1983.

19. D. Kozen and J. Tiuryn. Logics of programs. In J. van Leeuwen, editor, *Handbook of Theoretical Computer Science*, pages 790–840. Elsevier Science Publishers, 1990.

20. K. J. Larsen. Proof systems for satisfiability in Hennessy-Milner logic with recursion. *Theoretical Computer Science*, 72:265–288, 1990.

21. F. Lin and R. Reiter. State constraints revisited. *Journal of Logic and Computation, Special Issue on Action and Processes*, 4(5):655–678, 1994.

22. M. Milner. *Communication and Concurrency*. Prentice-Hall, 1989.

23. R. Parikh. Propositional dynamic logic of programs: A survey. In *Proceedings of the 1st Workshop on Logic of Programs*, LNCS 125, pages 102–144. Springer-Verlag, 1981.

24. R. Reiter. The frame problem in the situation calculus: A simple solution (sometimes) and a completeness result for goal regression. In *Artificial Intelligence and Mathematical Theory of Computation: Papers in Honor of John McCarthy*, pages 359–380. Academic Press, 1991.

25. R. Reiter. Formalizing database evolution in the situation calculus. In *Proc. Int. Conf. on Fifth Generation Computer Systems*, pages 600–609, 1992.

26. R. Reiter. The projection problem in the situation calculus: a soundness and completeness result, with an application to database updates. In *Proc. First Int. Conf. on AI Planning Systems*, pages 198–203, 1992.

27. R. Reiter. Proving properties of states in the situation calculus. *Artificial Intelligence*, 64:337–351, 1993.

28. S. Rosenschein. Plan synthesis: a logical approach. In *Proc. of the 8th Int. Joint Conf. on Artificial Intelligence*, 1981.

29. K. Schild. A correspondence theory for terminological logics: Preliminary report. In *Proc. of the 12th Int. Joint Conf. on Artificial Intelligence*, 1991.

30. L. Schubert. Monotonic solution of the frame problem in the situation calculus: an efficient method for worlds with fully specified actions. In *Knowledge representation and Defeasible Reasoning*, pages 23–67. Kluwer Academic Press, 1990.

31. C. Stirling. Modal and temporal logic. In S. Abramsky, D. M. Gabbay, and T. S. E. Maibaum, editors, *Handbook of Logic in Computer Science*, pages 477–563. Clarendon Press, Oxford, 1992.

Dependency graphs in natural language processing

Cristina Barbero and Vincenzo Lombardo

Dipartimento di Informatica - Universita` di Torino
c.so Svizzera 185 - 10149 Torino - Italy

Centro di Scienze Cognitive - Universita` e Politecnico di Torino
via Lagrange 3 - 10123 Torino - Italy

e-mail: cris, vincenzo@di.unito.it

Abstract. The paper illustrates the suitability of the dependency approach in practical applications of NLP. We introduce a compact representation called dependency graph, produced by an all-path left-to-right parser for a dependency grammar. The dependency graph keeps all the syntactic trees of a sentence in a single structure, thus allowing an economy of representation and an easier comparison between the alternative paths for the semantic processor.

1 Introduction

In NLP systems, practical parsers have to face two common difficulties that are caused by syntactic ambiguities. The first difficulty concerns the efficiency of the syntactic representation: the parses of a sentence may grow exponentially [Church, Patil 82] and a parsing algorithm would take an exponential time only to enumerate the possible parses; the second difficulty concerns the interface between the parser and the semantic interpreter. In order to overcome these difficulties, two major approaches have been proposed in the computational linguistics literature: chart parsing and parse forest representations.

Chart parsing [Kay 80] [Wiren 87] builds a concise but implicit representation of the syntactic trees: the step of building a chart is polynomial but the extraction of the individual structures is exponential. This approach to build a chart structure with a fast parsing process has revealed a greater efficiency when the functional and semantic constraints are applied to all the possible combinations of the chart edges at the end of parsing, while trying to keep a compact disjunctive format as far as possible [Maxwell, Kaplan 93].

Parse forests [Tomita 87] [Seo, Simmons 89] [Lombardo, Lesmo 94] represent the set of syntactic trees by sharing the common substructures and packing into a single node the constituents that span the same input fragment. The parsing process deals explicitly with the individual parses and offers various forms of interleaving with the functional and the semantic components, while benefiting from these contributions in the evaluation of the best local structure for the fragment of the sentence that raised an ambiguity.

The *dependency graph* [Lombardo, Lesmo 94] is a parse forest that is the result of an all-path parsing algorithm based on a dependency grammar [Tesniere 59]: the syntactic structure is expressed in terms of *head-modifier* (also called *dependency*) *relations* between pairs of words, a head and a modifier. This relation defines a *dependency tree*, whose root is a word that does not depend on any other word. Figure 1 illustrates the difference between the dependency and the more usual constituency approaches via an example of the tree structures associated with the sentence "The chef cooked a fish".

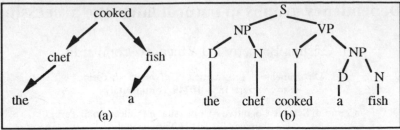

Figure 1. Syntactic structures for the sentence "The chef cooked a fish".

Notice that the leftward or rightward orientation of arrows in the dependency tree of fig. 1a represents the ordering constraints: the modifiers that precede the head stand on its left, the modifiers that follow the head stand on its right.

In spite of the little attention received in the past, a number of formalisms, born both in the linguistics and the computational linguistics communities, witness the fertility of the dependency approach and the variety of possible applications in NLP. Dependency-based syntax is at the core of implemented systems in areas like speech recognition [Giachin, Rullent 89] [Baggia et al. 92], machine translation [Johnson et al. 85] [Maruyama 90], text generation [Kittredge, Polguere 91] [Rambow, Korelsky 92]. The dependency-based approaches seem to be well suited to handle the real language constructs, as revealed by interesting aspects of current research: the treatment of free word order constructs, the relation between the traditional approaches and the emerging methods of shallow parsing, the handling of multiple structures originated by the syntactic ambiguities and the consequent emphasis on a close interaction with semantics in real parsing.

This paper proposes the dependency graph as a useful syntactic representation in practical NLP applications. The next section describes the structure of the dependency graph and how it represents several parse trees. The section 3 reviews the parsing algorithm. Then we will discuss how to use the dependency graph in practical NLP applications.

2 Structure of the dependency graph

A dependency tree expresses the dominance relations that exist for pairs of words in the sentence, according to the constraints given by the dependency rules. A *dependency rule* has the form $X(Y_1\ Y_2\ ...\ Y_{i-1}\ \#\ Y_{i+1}\ ...\ Y_m)$, where $X, Y_1, ..., Y_m$ are syntactic categories (preterminals, in constituency terms) and $\#$ is a special symbol that gives the position of the head. The rule enumerates the categories $Y_1, ..., Y_m$ that depend upon X in the order given by the rule, where X occupies the position of $\#$ (see fig. 2). The root of a dependency tree is a word that belongs to a *root category*.

A *dependency graph* is a compact representation of the dependency trees that are associated with a sentence. Compactness results from the application two well-known techniques: subtree sharing, that allows multiple attachments of a single subtree, and local packing, that associates multiple words with a single node (featuring several *slots*).

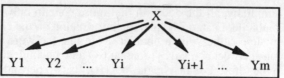

Figure 2. A dependency rule

A node *n* is a triple $<c, j, P>$, where *c* is the category of the node, *j* is the position of the leftmost word in the subtree rooted by *n*, and *P* is a set of slots, each containing the lexical information on a word in the sentence. The various parses in the dependency graph are kept distinct via a mechanism that assigns numerical indices to the substructures that are *not* unanimously shared by all the parses. An index consists of a pair of numbers: the first is a progressive number associated with each ambiguity point, the second identifies one alternative solution for that ambiguity. In other words, an index *i.j* labels the *j*-th alternative of the *i*-th ambiguity. *A parse cannot contain indices that have the same first element but differ for the second.*

In fig. 3 we report the dependency graph that represents the nine parses (fig. 4) associated with the sentence

(1)   Internet e` un giornale aperto al pubblico dove ognuno puo` dire la sua.

"Internet is a journal open at/to-the public where everyone can say the her/his."

Internet is a journal open to the public where everyone can have her/his say. appeared on an Italian newspaper.

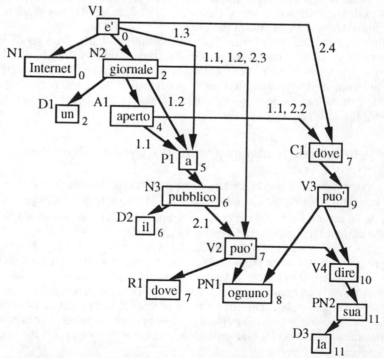

Figure 3. Dependency graph of "Internet e` un giornale aperto al pubblico dove ognuno puo` dire la sua" (*Internet is a journal open to the public where everyone can have her/his say*)

For the sake of simplicity, all the nodes in the figure contain only one slot (no local packing - see [Lombardo, Lesmo 94]) and the information on the category appears in the name of the node together with a number. Note that the word "dove" (*where*) is lexically ambiguous between a relative pronoun (R) and a complementizer (C). There is a single root in the forest, i.e. the copula "e`" (*is*). Its two dependents are "Internet" and the nominal "un giornale aperto" (*a journal open*). Note that the adjective "aperto" (*open*) can only be attached to "giornale", because the copula is already saturated with its arguments. "Al pubblico" (*to the public*), as a prepositional phrase, has three attachment points: "aperto" (*open to the public*), "giornale" (*a journal to the public*), "e`" (*is at the public*). This ambiguity point is marked with the index 1 and the three solutions for it are marked 1, 2 and 3 respectively, resulting in the three indices 1.1, 1.2 and 1.3 from the lowest to the highest attachment point (see fig. 3). The three edges cannot appear in the same parse, and this is stated by their mutual exclusion because of the index marking. The parsing of the clause "dove ognuno puo` dire la sua" (*where everyone can have her/his say*) faces two types of ambiguities: the category of "dove" determines whether the clause is a locative clause (C) that depends on the main clause, or a locative relative clause (R) that depends on a noun. In the first case there are two attachment points, the adjective "aperto" (*a journal open where everyone can have her/his say*) and the copula "e`" (*Internet is where ...*); in the second case there are again two attachment points, the nouns "pubblico" (*the public where ...*) and "giornale" (*a journal where ...*). As far as the first set of indices is concerned, the attachment points "pubblico" and "e`" are licensed by all the indices (1.1, 1.2, 1.3), while "aperto" is licensed by 1.1 and "giornale" is licensed by 1.1 and 1.2. The reasons of this will be clear in the next section. The four attachments are kept mutually exclusive with a new set of indices, {2.1, 2.2, 2.3, 2.4}, that mark the four arcs that link the clause to the rest of the graph.

Fig. 4 illustrates the individual parses of the example sentence. The set of indices associated with each parse represents the combination of indices that allows to single it out of the dependency graph. The enumeration of all the possible parses from the graph is accomplished by visiting the graph in depth-first order and collecting all the compatible indices (i.e. the indices that are not mutually exclusive) (see [Lombardo, Barbero 94] for details).

3 How to build a dependency graph: the parsing algorithm

The parsing algorithm combines top-down predictions and bottom-up filtering. It features two basic operations: CrLink(Cat), that CReates a node of category Cat and LINKs it to an open node in the dependency graph[1]; Fill(N), that associates the node N with the current input word. The compatibility of the category of Node and of the current input word is tested by the applicability conditions of Fill. The operation CrLink provides the top-down predictions of the algorithm, while a precomputation of the left corner information for each category provides the bottom-up filtering. A node created by CrLink is an empty structure, that does not contain any word and that does not govern any modifier, but states that a word of that category must be inserted there sometimes in the following and that this word must govern some modifiers according to the constraints provided by one dependency rule for that category; the operation

---

[1] An *open* node is a node that has not been saturated yet, i.e. such that further dependents can be still attached to it.

119

Fill satisfies this expectation if the sentential order meets its applicability conditions.

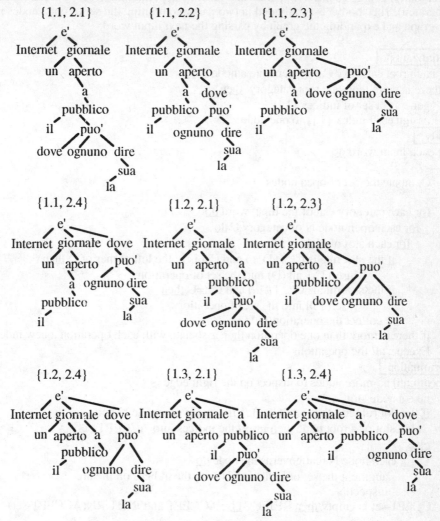

Figure 4. The individual parses of the graph in fig. 3.

Once a node of category C has been created, it evolves according to the set of dependency rules that have C as head category. Each dependency rule marks a different path in the analysis; therefore each slot of the node is associated with a rule $C(D_1 D_2 ... D_i \# D_{i+1} ... D_n)$. The algorithm parses first the left modifiers, then the word, and, finally, the right modifiers. The rule is augmented with a marker (I), that signals the portion of rule that has been analyzed. So, after the first modifier has been parsed, the rule has the form $C(D_1 | D_2 ... D_i \# D_{i+1} ... D_n)$. The parsing of a modifier of category D is accomplished by an operation CrLink(D), followed by the completion of the corresponding subtree; to parse a word is accomplished by a Fill of a slot with the current input word.

The parsing algorithm is outlined in fig. 5. The algorithm begins by creating the possible root nodes and specifying that they are the open nodes. The various roots will (eventually) belong to different parses and must be kept distinct (a set of indices 1.j is generated). The "body" is subdivided in two parts: computing the set of open nodes in the graph and expanding the graph by parsing the next input word.

Initialization

<u>for</u> each root category Cat <u>do</u> generate a node
<u>If</u> there is more than one root category <u>then</u>
     generate a set of indices {1.j}
     assign each index {1.j} to one node

Body

<u>for</u> each input word <u>do</u>
1 ----
     Compute the set of open nodes
2 ----
     <u>for</u> each category Cat of the input word <u>do</u>
       <u>for</u> each open node N of category C <u>do</u>
         <u>for</u> each slot of N <u>do</u>
           <u>if</u> the slot rule is C(... | D ...) and Cat is in the left corner of D <u>then</u>
               insert CrLink(D) into the set of operation
           <u>if</u> the slot rule is C(... | # ...) and Cat=C <u>then</u>
               insert Fill into the set of operations
           /* collect the operation(s) */
     <u>if</u> there is more than one operation <u>then</u> associate with each operation a new index
     Execute all the operations

Termination

<u>repeat until</u> no more nodes to inspect on the right edge
     take a node slot
     <u>if</u> the slot rule has the form C(...|) /* the slot is complete */ and
       is a slot of a root node <u>then</u> insert the indices into ACCEPT-set
     <u>else</u>
       <u>for</u> each node N that governs the node <u>do</u>
         augment the set of indices of N with the indices on the arc
         inspect N
<u>if</u> ACCEPT-set is empty <u>then</u> REJECT <u>else</u> ACCEPT and RETURN(ACCEPT-set)

Figure 5. The parsing algorithm

1)   The set of open nodes (more precisely node-slots) is gathered by climbing the dependency graph from the nodes that were filled in the last step of the "for-each-input-word" loop. A movement upward is allowed only when a node under examination is complete, i.e. all the modifiers and the head predicted by a dependency rule associated with it have been found. The arcs that are traversed while moving upward can be labelled with indices. Encountering an index implies that (a) the parser must select the node-slot of the governor which is compatible with it; (b) any new extension of the graph from higher nodes must be labelled with such an index. The search for open nodes continues until the first non-complete node is found.
2)   All the operations (CrLink and Fill) that are licensed by the dependency rules associated with the open nodes on the input word are collected to be executed. If the

121

set of operations has a cardinality greater than 1, we are at an ambiguity point (say the i-th) and a new set of indices which share the first component (i) is generated, in order to mark the different paths. The operations are executed and the set of indices associated with them (i.e. the indices just generated + the indices collected in the previous phase) is assigned to the new arcs (in case of CRLINK) and node-slots (in case of FILL).

In the "termination" phase, the algorithm climbs from the nodes that were filled with the last input word to the roots of the dependency graph, by traversing only complete nodes. All the indices found in the paths that reached the roots form the ACCEPTset, that contains all the pairs <root, set-of-indices>, each identifying one syntactic tree in the graph.

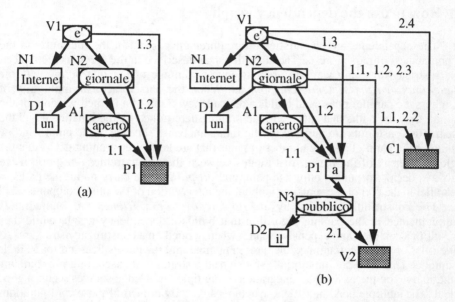

Figure 6. Two snapshots in the analysis of "Internet e' un giornale aperto al pubblico dove ognuno puo' dire la sua"

In order to illustrate how the algorithm works, let us trace two meaningful steps of the parsing algorithm on the example sentence (1). When the input word is the preposition "a" (*in/at*), the open nodes are V1, N2 and A1 (see fig. 6a), gathered by climbing the graph from the node A1, filled with the previous input word ("aperto" - *open*). There are three operations licensed: CrLink(Prep) to A1, CrLink(Prep) to N2 and CrLink(Prep) to V1. The node created, P1, is shared by the three links. Three indices, 1.1, 1.2 and 1.3, are necessary to keep the three paths distinct: the same substructure, rooted by P1, participates in three parses (fig. 6a). The next ambiguity point comes after the analysis of the word "pubblico" (*public*), when the parser faces the task of accomodating the word "dove", relativizer and complementizer, in the graph. Starting from N3, the algorithm computes the set of open nodes: (a) N3 is still open, since a noun can have right modifiers; (b) A1 is open with the index 1.1, encountered on the arc to P1; (c) N2 is open with two indices, 1.1 and 1.2, because of the two possible paths followed in climbing; (d) V1 is open with all of the three indices. The set of operations contains four CrLinks: (a) CrLink(Verb) to N3 with no indices (the category Verb is the head of the relative clause); (b)

CrLink(Complementizer) to A1 with an index 1.1; (c) CrLink(Verb) to N2 with two indices 1.1 and 1.2; (d) CrLink(Complementizer) to V1 with no indices (because all of the indices 1.j have been encountered). There are two possible shares: a verb node and a complementizer node (fig.6b). Besides, four further indices are necessary to keep the new arcs distinct (2.1, 2.2, 2.3, 2.4).

In the termination phase the right edge of the dependency graph in fig. 3 is traversed, starting from the node PN2, filled with the last input word. Nine paths take to the root, exactly those that are singled out in fig. 4. The ACCEPTset returned is $\{<V1, \{1.1, 2.1\}>, <V1, \{1.1, 2.2\}>, <V1, \{1.1, 2.3\}>, <V1, \{1.1, 2.4\}>, <V1, \{1.2, 2.1\}>, <V1, \{1.2, 2.3\}>, <V1, \{1.2, 2.4\}>, <V1, \{1.3, 2.1\}>, <V1, \{1.3, 2.4\}>\}$.

4 How to use the dependency graph

The dependency graph satisfies the requirements posed in the literature on the compactness of parse forests. The all-path parser described in the previous section can be restricted in many ways in order to take advantage of the *interaction with the functional and the semantic components*. When the parser faces an ambiguity, it triggers the parallel phase and builds a dependency graph of a limited window of the input: only the paths that survive to the pruning determined by the functional and the semantic constraints are pursued for the future analysis. The size of the input window analyzed in parallel and the number of paths that are kept after pruning determine the global strategy of the parser, that ranges between the two extremes *one-path*, if we always decide to pursue only one path, and *all-path*, if we carry on all the paths in parallel to the end of the sentence without the intervention of the other components.

The constraints provided by the *subcategorization frames* are immediately implemented in the parsing algorithm that builds a dependency graph, while they result in a complex and expensive search when applied on a constituency structure. As the rules of realistic grammars increase in number and the parses licensed for a single sentence tend to a combinatorial explosion, the strategy of discarding unpromising alternatives on the basis of an integration of multiple knowledge sources seems a good deal. The multiple head-modifiers structures are easily pruned of those configurations that are not mapped on a subcategorization frame. Also the *interface with the semantic component* is smoother than the constituency counterpart, because of a direct translation of the head-modifiers structures into the predicate-arguments relations contained in a knowledge base. Note that most interpreters in NLP do little more than applying selectional restrictions to predicate-arguments configurations, in today's semantically unsophisticated systems.

The dependency approach also offers a perspicuous *treatment of free-word order constructs* in natural languages. Free ordered languages, like Slavonic languages [Sgall et al. 86] [Mel'cuk 88], have been the traditional area of dependency syntax for decades; but all natural languages exhibit free word order to a certain extent: topicalizations and extractions are very common in real texts even in configurational languages. For partially configurational languages, like Italian, where constituents order is highly free [Matthews 81] [MacWhinney et al. 84], the structural properties offered by head-modifiers representations are very advantageous. The impact of this characteristic on the assignment of grammatical relations and the consequent case analysis in NLP is particularly relevant: SVO is only the most common order, but all the other five permutations are admissible, also in written language [Stock 89], as the following examples show [Renzi 88].

SOV: *Gli amici di Piero solo la giacca a quadri hanno notato*
         "Piero's friends have noted only the jacket with squares"
OVS: *Una proposta analoga ha fatto Mario*
         "Mario has made an analogous proposal"
VOS: *A questo libro ha dato un importante contributo il professor Piga*
         "Professor Piga has given an important contribution to this book"
OSV: *Una pipa sempre diversa il maestro di violino regala ogni anno a Luigi*
         "The teacher of violin gives an always different pipe to Luigi every
         year"
VSO: *Ho portato io il libro che avevate ordinato*
         "I have brought the book that you had ordered"

These constituents distributions, which are even less restricted in subordinate clauses[2], are all immediately represented as one-level dependency structures, thus reducing the number of alternative parses in the compact representation. The task of assigning grammatical functions to constituents relies on the semantic information [Lesmo, Lombardo 92].

This trend toward a stronger contribution from the semantic component also emerges in the area of the "shallow parsing techniques" for tasks of information extraction from real texts [Church et al. 89] [Jacobs 92], that have produced interesting results in the last years. Some of these methods stem from knowledge of linguistic and semantic relations between words in a restricted domain. Dependency-based approaches assign relation-based representations to a sentence: the *integration of a weak method with a dependency parser* is much more immediate than with a constituency parser, which must necessarily be followed by a phase of relation extraction, that navigates in an intricate forest of alternative constituent aggregations.

5 A possible application in real text analysis

One of the possible applications of the dependency graph and the parsing above described is in real text analysis. We are working at the moment on the definition of a flexible environment for real text analysis, in which it is possible to test different strategies in sentence processing. In particular, we want to define a general framework in which we can apply several heuristics provided by the psycholinguistic research and based on the observations on the human sentence parsing mechanism, and test their validity in free text analysis. In fact we claim that the computational models of the human parsing mechanism can be useful in efficient parsing of free texts.

The requirements posed by a flexible environment of this kind are:

---

[2] Consider, for example, the relative clauses in
   L'altalena che vide il bambino nel parco e` sempre piena di gente.
   The swing that saw the baby in the park is always full of people.
   "The swing that the baby saw in the park is always full of people."
and
   La signora che vide il bambino per strada aveva gli occhi azzurri.
ambiguous between the two readings
   The lady who saw the baby in (the) street had blue eyes.
   The lady whom the baby saw in (the) street had blue eyes.
where the assignment of grammatical relations is an exclusive semantic and pragmatic competence, respectively.

1)   the combination of top-down predictions and bottom-up filtering.

2)   the possibility of applying the preferences to select a specific path after a limited phase of parallelism.

3)   the possibility of interleaving syntax and semantics at any degree.

Let us see how the dependency graph and the parser described in section 3 satisfy these requirements:

1)   the parser combines top-down predictions and bottom-up filtering. The top-down character of the parser is realized by the operation *crlink(Cat)*. This operation makes a guess on the existence of a node of category Cat and the related subtree. But the parse table licenses the application of *crlink* only in the specific contexts given by the input words belonging to the categories of the set First(Cat), that represent the possible left corners for the category Cat.

This requirement (combination of top-down predictions and bottom-up filtering) has emerged both in the psycholinguistic and the computational approaches. Top-down predictions introduce expectations on the parse structure. But the predictions must be checked on the actual input string, to avoid an explosion of useless paths; this check is carried out by a data-driven or bottom-up component.

2)   the parser is basically all-path. In case of ambiguity it can explore the several paths with a pseudoparallel strategy, for a given portion of the input (by varying the length of this portion, several intermediate processing strategies are defined): after this limited phase of parallelism, a specific path can be selected. The compact representation allows to focus the substructures that are alternative to one another and to select one path on the basis of the local context. In case one path reveals to be wrong, we must be able to identify the portions of the representation that belong to that path. The index mechanism allows to focus on the alternative parses for the same fragment, and to retrieve the portions of the dependency graph belonging to a specific path at each moment during the parsing process.

3)   the parser supports an incremental interpretation at a fine grain of interaction. By "incremental interpretation" we mean that the semantic representation is extended as soon as the syntactic structure is extended. But the degree of interleaving depends on the specific strategy at hand. It can range from the clause level, to the phrase level, to the word level. Even finer interactions can be defined if the atomic operations of the parser go deeper than the word level. The dependency structure produced is always connected: hence the semantic interpreter can be invoked after any extension, provided by both a *crlink* and a *fill*.

An environment with these characteristics needs a recovery mechanism that is able to revise the abandoned paths when we pursue a strategy one-path. The recovery mechanism is fully described in [Lombardo 95]. The index mechanism provides the communication medium between the parser and the recovery mechanism. The path that is active at the moment of the breakdown represents the choices that were made in the past history of the parsing process. The recovery mechanism searches for structures that are labelled with indices that are incompatible with the active path and by means of heuristics switches to a new active path. It works selectively on the parts of the structure that depended on the wrong choice, instead of a blind revision. This allows to gain much time and to save some work made previously that is still valid in the new path.

6 Conclusion

The paper has presented a compact representation for the set of the dependency trees that are associated with a sentence. This structure, called dependency graph, is the syntactic structure that results from an incremental parsing algorithm possibly interleaved with the functional and the semantic constraints. The dependency structures are more easily interpreted by the semantic component, since the configuration "head-thematic roles" is immediately mirrored by the dependency relations.

The paper also showed how an environment based on the parser and the dependency graph described can be used in real text analysis, exploiting the principles indicated by the psycholinguistic research.

However, discontinuous constituents frequently appear in many real language constructs [Disco 90]. The dependency formalism proposed in this paper is fully projective and exhibits many difficulties in dealing with such constructs. If we relax the projective constraint, we are able to exploit the full power of a dependency approach, as revealed by the theoretical studies conducted by many researchers in linguistics [Mel'cuk 88].

References

[Baggia et al. 92] Baggia P., Gerbino E., Giachin E., Rullent C., *Real-time linguistic analysis for continuous speech understanding*, Proceedings of ANLP 92, Trento (Italy), 1992, pp. 33-39.

[Church, Patil 82] Church K., Patil R., *Coping with Syntactic Ambiguity or How to Put the Block in the Box on the Table*, **Computational Linguistics 8/3-4**, 1982, pp.139-149.

[Church et al. 89] Church K., Gale W., Hanks P., Hindle D., *Parsing, word associations, and predicate-argument relations,* Proceedings of the International Workshop on Parsing Technology, CMU, 1989.

[Disco 90] Proceedings of the Symposium on Discontinuous Constituency, Institute for Language Technology and Artificial Intelligence, Tilburg University, Tilburg, The Netherlands, January 25-27, 1990.

[Gaifman 65] Gaifman H., *Dependency Systems and Phrase Structure Systems*, **Information and Control 8**, 1965, pp. 304-337.

[Giachin, Rullent 89] Giachin E., Rullent C., *Real-time linguistic analysis for continuous speech understarding*, Proceedings of IJCAI 89, Detroit, 1989.

[Jacobs 92] Jacobs P. S., *Parsing Run Amok: Relation-Driven Control for Text Analysis*, Proceedings of AAAI 92, San Jose' (CA), 1992, pp. 315-321.

[Jacobs, Rau 93] Jacobs P. S., Rau L.F., *Innovations in Text Interpretation*, **Artificial Intelligence 63**, 1993, pp.143-192.

[Johnson et al. 85] Johnson R., King M., des Tombe L., *EUROTRA: a Multilingual System under Development*, **Computational Linguistics 11/2-3**, 1985, pp. 155-169.

[Kay 80] Kay M., *Algorithm schemata and data structures in syntactic processing*, in **Readings in Natural Language Processing**, edited by B. J. Grosz, K. Sparck-Jones, and B. L. Webber, pp. 35-70, 1995. Morgan Kaufmann.

[Kittredge, Polguere 91] Kittredge R., Polguere A., *Dependency Grammars for Bilingual Text Generation: Inside FoG's Stratificational Models*, Proc. of the Int. Conf. on Current Issues in Comp. Linguistics, 1991, pp. 318-330.

[Lesmo, Lombardo 92] Lesmo L., Lombardo V., *The assignment of grammatical relations in natural language processing*, Proceedings of COLING 92, Nantes, 1992, pp. 1090-1094.

[Lombardo 95] Lombardo V., *Parsing and Recovery*, to appear in Proc. 17th Annual Meeting of the Cognitive Science Society, Pittsburgh, July 1995.

[Lombardo, Barbero 94] Lombardo V., Barbero C., *Syntactic Trees and Compact Representations in Natural Language Processing*, Proceedings of the 6th International Conference on AI: Methodology, Systems, Applications, Sofia, Bulgaria, 1994, pp. 333-342.

[Lombardo, Lesmo 94] Lombardo V., Lesmo L., *A Compact Syntactic Representation*, in Martin-Vide C. (editor), **Current Issues in Mathematical Linguistics**, Elsevier Science B.V., 1994, pp. 191-200.

[MacWhinney et al. 84] MacWhinney B., Bates E., Kliegl R., *Cue validity and sentence interpretation in English, German and Italian*, **Journal of Verbal Learning and Verbal Behavior 23**, 1984, pp. 127-150.

[Maruyama 90] Maruyama H., *Structural Disambiguation with Constraint Propagation*, Proceedings of ACL 90, 1990, pp. 31-38.

[Matthews 81] Matthews P. H., **Syntax**, Cambridge University Press, 1981.

[Maxwell, Kaplan 93] Maxwell J.T., Kaplan R.M., *The Interface between Phrasal and Functional Constraints*, **Computational Linguistics** , December 1993.

[Mel'cuk 88] Mel'cuk I., *Dependency Syntax: Theory and Practice*, NYSU Press, New York, 1988.

[Rambow, Korelsky 92] Rambow O., Korelsky T., *Applied Text Generation*, Proceedings of ANLP 92, Trento (Italy), 1992, pp. 40-47.

[Renzi 88] Renzi L., **Grande Grammatica Italiana di Consultazione**, Bologna:Il Mulino, 1988.

[Seo, Simmons 89] Seo J., Simmons R. F., *Syntactic Graphs: A representation for the Union of All Ambiguous Parse Trees*, **Computational Linguistics 15/1**, 1989, pp. 19-32.

[Sgall et al. 86] Sgall P., Haijcova E., Panevova J., *The Meaning of the Sentence in its Semantic and Pragmatic Aspects*, D. Reidel Publishing Company, 1986.

[Stock 89] Stock O., *Parsing with Flexibility, Dynamic Strategies, and Idioms in Mind*, **Computational Linguistics 15**, 1989, pp. 1-18.

[Tesniere 59] Tesniere L., *Elements de syntaxe structurale*, Klincksieck, Paris, 1959.

[Tomita 87] Tomita M., *An Efficient Augmented-Context-Free Parsing Algorithm*, **Computational Linguistics 13**, 1987, pp. 31-46.

[Wiren 87] Wiren M., *A Comparison of Rule-Invocation Strategies in Context-free Chart Parsing*, Proceedings of EACL 87, 1987, pp. 226-233.

Integrating Shallow and Linguistic Techniques for Information Extraction from Text

Fabio Ciravegna
Nicola Cancedda*

Istituto per la Ricerca Scientifica e Tecnologica
I-38050 Loc. Pantè di Povo, Trento, Italy
e-mail: cirave@irst.itc.it

Abstract. Many experiments have shown that traditional approaches to bothNatural Language Processing (NLP) and Information Retrieval (IR) are not effective enough to extract information from text; as a matter of fact shallow techniques (such as statistics, keyword analysis, etc.) tend to be imprecise, although efficient and transportable, whereas linguistic approaches tend to be very precise but not robust and efficient. Integrating NLP and IR is the challenge for the evolution of text processing systems for the next few years. In this paper an architecture that integrates shallow and linguistic processing is presented. Shallow techniques are used to limit the linguistic analysis to the interesting sections, and to help the parser reduce the overhead. The linguistic analyzer carefully extracts the information, controlling the combinatorics of parsing and any misdirected parsing efforts. Some preliminary results show that the architecture has considerable advantages with respect to traditional approaches to information extraction from text.

1 Introduction

As in AI in general, scale-up is the forcing function behind many developments in NLP techniques in the last few years. Extensive data collections require sound interfaces to locate the needed information efficiently and correctly. Availability of funding for task driven applications (e.g. within Linguistic Engineering in the EEC or Tipster in the USA) has shifted research focus towards scale-up compatible approaches since the end of the 80s. This is particularly evident for fields such as text processing, in which scale-up is mandatory to make text repositories or news-wires really usable. In 1992 Paul Jacobs set out the following research directions for the use of Natural Language Processing in text understanding [13]:

- from peer evaluation to performance evaluation: techniques are to be tested in task-oriented evaluations, validating theoretical motivation with quantitative results; new theories have to arise from application demands;

---

* Current address: Dipartimento di Informatica e Sistemistica, Università di Roma "La Sapienza"; e-mail:cancedda@assi.dis.uniroma1.it

- from stories to news stories: in depth understanding of stories will be out of reach of the technology for a long time; nevertheless extracting facts from short news stories is definitely at hand;

- from sentence to text: from now on NLP systems will have to process millions of words and be tested according to performance metrics related to the global texts, whereas until recently they were tested mostly on carefully selected or invented sentences;

- from full parsing to partial parsing: until parsers will be robust enough to cope with extended texts, more effort has to go into obtaining partial results rather than producing complex parses and broad coverage.

Since then, experience has shown that traditional models of language analysis as used in interfaces are not suitable, because the information extraction task is so difficult, that systems that do relatively little parsing often appear to do as well as programs that can parse using well-developed grammars and models of language [1]. Broad coverage parsers, for example, "run amok" (i.e. go mad) when confronted with extended input without sufficient information to control the interpretation process. Nevertheless both the parsing and the no-parsing approaches (e.g.. Information Retrieval techniques), are not effective enough to provide the correct solution for text handling; as a matter of fact shallow techniques (such as statistics, keyword analysis, etc.) tend to be imprecise, although efficient and transportable, whereas the linguistic approaches tend to be very precise but not robust and efficient. An evolution towards a progressive convergence between NLP and Information Retrieval technologies was then the obvious follow-up: control mechanisms were introduced to reduce the combinatorics of parsing [7], [11] [4]; partial parsing was preferred to complete parsing; finite state models of language developed consistently [1]; pattern matching techniques were coupled with adequate Knowledge Bases to get generality [6] and statistics to obtain scalability [18]. The message of the last years of research is that programs that combine sound partial parsing with other strategies seem to outperform both the traditional parsing and the no-parsing approaches.

---

1. A DUE MILIARDI L'UTILE LORDO DI DHL ITALIA

La Dhl International, filiale italiana del network Dhl, ha conseguito un utile lordo, prima delle imposte, superiore ai due miliardi; un risultato raggiunto dopo un incremento del 30% degli ammortamenti per. investimenti. Il fatturato e' cresciuto del 20% a quota 221 miliardi.

2. RINCARI DA PRIMATO PER I SUINI NEGLI USA

I prezzi dei suini sui mercati statunitensi spot hanno raggiunto ieri valori da record assoluto, con 68 dollari per cwt (hundredweight, unita' pari a 50,8 kg). La scarsa offerta e la richiesta dell'industria salsamentaria hanno provocato l'impennata, che pero' non si e' trasferita se non parzialmente sul mercato a termine di Chicago, dove livelli da primato erano stati registrati il giorno precedente.

3. ELECTROLUX PUNTA A UNITA' WHIRLPOOL

Il gruppo svedese Electrolux ha lanciato un'offerta d'acquisto per la divisione aspirapolveri della statunitense Whirlpool. La Electrolux concorre con altre societa', e il risultato dell'offerta sara' reso noto tra qualche mese. La somma offerta non e' stata rivelata, ma la stampa svedese ha parlato di 500 milioni di corone (circa 100 miliardi di lire).

Fig. 1. Some examples taken from the corpus

In the following sections, after a short introduction to the text corpus, an architecture for extracting information from short news items will be outlined; it is based on a multilevel approach that captures the current issues in text processing towards an integration of linguistic and shallow technologies. Some preliminary results seem to show considerable advantages in respect to traditional approaches to information extraction from text.

2 The Corpus

The corpus is composed of short on-line news (*"brevi"*) taken from the Italian financial newspaper "IL SOLE 24 Ore". The average length of each *breve* is about 70 words. Some examples are illustrated in Figure 1. The main information carried by such news items is generally summarizable in rigid structures such as templates, being simple factual information on economical aspects of financial entities (e.g. budgets, production rates, market situations, take-overs, and so on). Some additional information can be present in the text: for example a drought can be pointed out as responsible for causing a rise in a crops' price; such additional information is generally loosely related to the economical topic and is often outside the focus of the reader. From a linguistic point of view, standard language together with some sub-language specific forms are used in the texts. Unknown proper names or acronyms are expected to be found (e.g. company names, locations, etc.). A restricted number of classes of text are identifiable in the corpus: Text1 is classifiable as final balance information, whereas Text2 is information on price change, and Text3 is an attempted company take over.

The aim of the information extraction task in these texts is to extract the main information, skipping the rest of the text, and to rout the message and the extracted information to the interested users. The kind of task and text is more or less comparable with those adopted for exercises such as MUC conferences [21]. Experiments were recently carried out on a small set of about 200 news items derived from the 1990 electronic collection. The next sections focus on system architecture.

3 The System Architecture

The overall architecture of the information extraction system is outlined in Figure 2. It is based on four main modules: the text zoner, the preparser, the linguistic analyzer and the template generator [2].

The *Text Zoner* recognises superficial text formats (e.g. SGML), separating the text body from the text title and/or some structured fields; it also recognises sentence boundaries.

The *Preparser* is a multi-level processor based on shallow techniques, mainly pattern matching and statistics; it classifies the messages, filters out any irrelevant parts of the text, and provides some hints on how to control the linguistic

---

[2] These terms are used following [9].

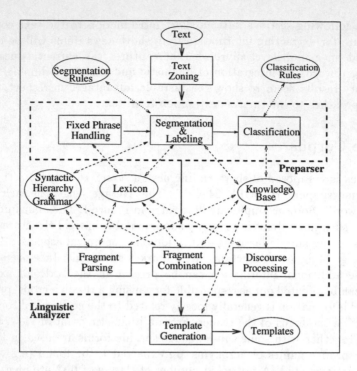

Fig. 2. The System Architecture

analyzer. It is composed of three main modules: the segmenter, the labeller and the classifier. The segmenter splits each sentence into constituents (such as simple nominal, verbal, prepositional phrases, etc.). After the text is segmented, a labeller assigns a set of semantic labels to each segment; those labels are names of concepts in the knowledge base and are used as a representation of text for classification purposes. Through classification, every text is then assigned to one or more classes in a pre-defined set. The final result of the preparser is a segmented text coupled with a list of pairs *(CLASS Estimated-Probability)* in which *CLASS* is the identifier for a (set of) templates and *Estimated-Probability* is used to check for the reliability of the assignment to such class. In Figure 3 the results of the preparser for Text1 are shown. The preparser results can be used for two purposes: to help the linguistic analyzer in the information extraction task and to rout the message to an interest group defined for a given message class. Concerning the first purpose: the segments constitute the text sections analyzed by the parser during the "fragment recognition" phase of linguistic analysis (see below); the results of text labelling are used to filter out any portion of text not providing interesting information; finally text classification determines the particular template to be filled in by the linguistic analyzer.

The *Linguistic Analyzer* extracts information from the text using Natural Language Processing. It is based on a general syntax-driven approach based on a chart parser coupled with semantic and pragmatic modules. The parser actions are strictly controlled by a module that uses the results of the preparser to prevent combinatorics and misdirected parsing efforts. The analyzer strategy is based on a preliminary parsing of fragments of input carrying elementary information, to create more complete analysis the second time around. During fragment parsing the segments detected by the preparser are analyzed, producing basic constituents such as simple NPs, PPs, and so on. During fragment combination different strategies are available: a syntax driven strategy controlled by general and domain-specific heuristics, a task-driven strategy controlled by the template-filling needs, etc. The parser is able to focus on the most promising solutions, pruning those with low reliability or likelihood. The result of the linguistic analyzer is a set of weighted (partial) parses coupled with their (weighted) semantic interpretation.

Title: A DUE MILIARDI L'UTILE LORDO DI DHL ITALIA	
Body: [La Dhl International <Soc> ,] [filiale italiana <SubSoc>] [del network Dhl <Soc> ,] [ha conseguito <Conseg>] [un utile lordo <GrandEcon> ,] [prima delle imposte <Tax> ,] [superiore a due miliardi <RelQuant> ;] [un risultato <Result>] [raggiunto <Conseg>] [dopo un incremento <Rise>] [del 30% <Percent>] [degli ammortamenti <GrandEco>] [per investimenti <GrandEco> .][Il fatturato <GrandEco> [e' cresciuto <Rise>] {del 20% <Percent>] [a quota 221 milardi <Quantity>]	
Classes: (SOC 0.9)	

Fig. 3. The Preparser's Result for Text1

Finally, the *Template Generator* normalises the extracted information in a form suitable to be inserted into an information system such as a data base; the templates are filled using the (partial) results provided by the linguistic analyzer. The final results for Text1 are shown in Figure 4.

The rest of the paper discusses some of the modules mentioned above.

3.1 Preparser

The contribution of shallow techniques to text analysis is located in the preparser. The preparser is composed of: a fixed phrase handler (for objects such as dates, numbers and so on), a proper name recognizer, a segmenter, a labeller for segments and a classifier. The resources needed by the preparser are: a lexicon, a hierarchy of syntactic types and a knowledge base.

The lexicon is composed of an application specific dictionary and a more generic lexical knowledge-base [16]. The fixed phrase handler is defined by a context-free grammar for recognizing dates and numbers, whereas the proper name handler is mainly a semantic active chart parser.

Segmentation The role of the segmenter is to split the different sentences of the text into constituents such as simple nominal, verbal, prepositional phrases, etc.

In the past McDonald suggested segmenting the text on the basis of closed-class words [17], while others relied on the detection of template activators and role fillers [11]. The closed-class word approach has the advantage of being domain independent, whereas domain driven segmentation tends to be more effective. A combination of the two methods (with more weight on closed-class word segmentation) seems to be the best solution. In our approach the boundaries of the constituents are detected mainly on the basis of closed-class word occurrences, with a domain dependent filter. The rules have the following form:

<RULE> ::= IF {option?} <TEST> THEN <ACTION> ;

where <ACTION> is a segmentation action, <TEST> is a set of conditions of segmentation, and the options are related to some (optional) conditions on the look-ahead window. The test conditions use the syntactic hierarchy defined in the linguistic analyzer grammar. There follows an example of a closed-class word based rule segmenting before a pronoun if it is not introduced by a preposition:

```
IF (AND  (pronoun x2)
         (NOT (prep x1)))
     THEN x1|x2
```

Classification Most of the work in text classification was concerned with the use of classical Information Retrieval techniques such as statistical and keyword analysis, or pattern matching [18]. In the last few years pattern matching was enhanced with the use of knowledge bases [8]; a linguistic parser was provided to improve the results of hierarchical pattern matching [6]. The advantages of joint use of statistical and knowledge-based techniques were pointed out in [12]. In our approach, the classifier is organized as a hierarchical pattern matcher integrated with statistical information. Patterns are both generated manually by a user and automatically by means of corpus analysis. The classifier is able to provide accuracy evaluation of its own results, so that it is possible to use sophisticated training techniques. The classifier is "thesaurus-based", but in contrast with traditional approaches there is no need to define a thesaurus specifically for the classification task: some of the resources developed for the linguistic analyzer (the lexicon and the knowledge base) can be exploited instead.

The classification task is performed by applying a set of classification rules to a segmented and labelled text. Each rule has a left hand side (*condition*) and a right hand side (*classification action*), in which *condition* is a combination of tests to be matched against sequences of (adjacent) segments, and *classification action* is a sequence of assignment of the text to some classes. Each element of the condition specifies a test on semantic labels (i.e. names of concepts in the knowledge base) of segments; each test is a (boolean combination of) subsumption test(s)[3]. If the condition of a rule is true on a sequence of segments, then

---

[3] Given the name of a concept C in the rule, the subsumption test is satisfied if there is at least one label assigned to the text segment corresponding to a concept equal to or more specific than C in the knowledge base.

the classification actions are performed. Each action is a pair *(CLASS estimated-probability)*, where *CLASS* stands for the name of a class the text can be assigned to and *estimated-probability* is a numeric value between 0 and 1 interpreted as the probability that the text belongs to the *CLASS*, known that CONDITION is true. For example, a classification rule could be:

```
IF AND (organization x1)
        (achievement x2)
        OR (production x3)
          (economic-result x3)
 THEN ((SOC 0.72)(PROD 0.56))
```

The left hand side of this rule would match successfully against a sequence of three segments labelled as "(<society>) (<achievement>) (<profit>)" provided that <society> is subsumed by <organization> and <profit> is subsumed by <economic-result> in the knowledge base.

A rule can be applied more than once in a text: the estimated probabilities for each class are derived combining the scores of the different applications using the formula for statistically independent events:

$$prob^*_{CLASS,i} = 1 - (1 - prob_{CLASS,i})^k$$

where i is an index in the rule-set, k is the number of times the i_{th} rule was applied successfully in the text and $prob_{CLASS,i}$ is the rule estimated probability associated to *CLASS* in the right hand side of the i_{th} rule.

As different rules can point to the same class, the same kind of combination is performed on the results obtained by all the different rules:

$$prob_{(CLASS)} = 1 - \prod_{i=1}^{n}(1 - prob^*_{CLASS,i})$$

The final result of the application of the whole rule-set is then again a list of pairs, with the same intended meaning of the ones in the right hand sides of rules.

The procedure followed to determine the composition of the rule set is semi-automatic and is done in two steps: first, a set of simple rules is found that exploit the results of the statistical analysis of a corpus of pre-classified texts. In the second step, the rule-set is enriched by a human expert to reduce the incidence of classification errors. The estimated probabilities for the hand-made rules are determined automatically, relying on the statistical analysis of the corpus.

The decision on wether to assign a text to a class or not is eventually made comparing the obtained estimated probability with a category dependent threshold[4]. When a text is assigned to a class, it is coupled with the class-specific templates, to be filled by the linguistic analyzer.

---

[4] As a side effect, the (absolute value of the) difference between the estimated probability and the threshold can be interpreted as a measure of the confidence the classifier has in its own decision.

3.2 Linguistic Analysis

As mentioned, linguistic approaches tend to be unreliable and inefficient when coping with extended input such as text, so that in the past some of the most complex ones had to be abandoned [1]. Pattern matching, statistics, semantic, statistical and syntactic heuristics were coupled with the linguistic analyzer to avoid combinatorics and crashes [11], [7], [4]. In our approach a general linguistic analyzer is used: it is the same analyzer used within other IRST projects, such as for multimedia interfaces; the only difference is located within a module that controls parsing to avoid combinatorics, misdirected effort and gaps in the coverage; it mainly relies on the information provided by the preparser's results: the topics of the text (i.e. the target templates), the interesting sections and a partition of the text into small units (segments). Linguistic analysis is performed in two steps: segment parsing and combination. During *segment parsing* the segments produced by the preparser are analyzed in a syntax-driven manner, producing basic constituents such as simple NPs, PPs, and so on. During *segment combination* different strategies are available. Syntactic and semantic analyses are interleaved. The result of the linguistic analyzer is a set of weighted partial parses coupled with their (weighted) semantic interpretation. The lin-

Company:	DHL-Italia	Company:	DHL-Italia
Mother Company:	DHL	Mother Company:	DHL
Kind-of-Result:	Utile lordo	Kind-of-Result:	Fatturato
Result:	+ > 2.000.000.000	Result:	+ 221.000.000.000
Currency:	LIT	Currency:	LIT
		Percentage:	+ 20%

Company:	DHL-Italia
Mother Company:	DHL
Kind-of-Result:	Ammortamenti per Investimenti
Percentage:	+ 30%

Fig. 4. The Final Results for Text1

guistic analyzer is composed of: a bidirectional chart parser, a lexical semantic module and a reference resolution module; the available resources are a Typed Features Structure Based Grammar, a linguistically motivated Knowledge Base and a domain-specific fixed phrase dictionary. A bidirectional chart parser is a chart parser [14] that adopts a bidirectional strategy in analyzing the input. It means that parsing starts from several triggering elements of the sentence and proceeds outward from them [19]. The choice of the triggering elements is made following the indication of the preparser (island-driven strategy) or using linguistically motivated elements (head-driven strategy). Bidirectionality improves flexibility at the cost of a certain computational overhead [19]. The parser is coupled with an agenda, i.e. a structure in which the tasks to be performed are stored. A task is, for example, a combination of two edges in the chart. The parser unification grammar is based on Typed Feature Structure Logics; the analyzer is coupled with an environment for the development and debugging of grammars and lexica. The semantic module uses a Knowledge Base written in LOOM, a KL-ONE-like language [15]. The upper part of the ontology is based on the Generalized Upper Model [2], an abstract representation layer that allows the organization of the non-linguistically oriented domain knowledge in a linguistically motivated way.

As efficiency is a strict constraint in text processing, a special parsing control module was developed to focus the parsing process on the most promising solutions. The controller operates on the agenda mechanism, sorting the tasks in the agenda through a set of scores representing general and domain-specific heuristics. Periodic agenda pruning removes the lower score tasks. The agenda controller allows leaving some attachments unresolved to avoid combinatorics or misdirected actions[5]. Four heuristics are currently integrated: segmentation observance, grammar rule score, template filling and coverage. There follows a short description of the strategies; for details on their composition and on the agenda control, see [5].

Segmentation Observance. The tasks generated by edges spanning a whole segment are given an extra score during segment combination, whereas they are delayed during segment parsing. Edges not observing the segmentation (i.e. spanning across segment boundaries) are always given a low score. This criterion introduces some kind of top-down control on the parser and prevents a kind of phenomenon similar to garden paths that uncontrolled parsers tend to show [5].

Rule Score. In a grammar the rules do not have the same likelihood to be applied; some of them are very common, but others can be very unlikely, although possible; the number of grammar rules rarely applied tends to be very high especially in a free word order language like Italian. This criterion allows focus to be put on the most probable solutions.

Template Filling The ability of a solution to fill some parts of the templates is another sorting criteria for tasks, as it favors the most interesting solutions from an applicative point of view, contributing in avoiding misdirected parsing efforts. The templates relevant for the current text were determined by the classifier during preprocessing.

Coverage. It seems obvious that a task generating an edge spanning a wider part of the input is to be preferred to a shorter one.

4 Discussion

The aim of the approach presented in this paper is to integrate efficient and general but shallow methods (such as statistics and pattern matching) with linguistic analysis that, although precise, can not actually provide the necessary

---

[5] As a matter of fact the attachment of some constituents such as PPs, although heavily contributing in determining the combinatorics of parsing, does not always contribute very much to the result of the analysis; even worse, an otherwise inconsequential attachment decision can actually interfere with getting the correct semantic interpretation, as reported in [13].

efficiency and robustness. Shallow techniques are used to classify the text, to filter out uninteresting information, and to help the linguistic analyzer in controlling the parsing action. Linguistic analysis is performed to extract the information from text, maintaining robustness and efficiency. The two levels are independent, making it possible to define applications using only one of the two.

The approach has considerable advantages over the classical NLP-based ones to information extraction (such as [10]), as it preserves the precision of the linguistic techniques, avoiding many of their disadvantages, mainly the inefficiency. The score mechanism to sort the agenda introduces a sort of top-down control on the parser action, which allows focus to be put on the most promising solutions. It both avoids the use of determinism (that often can prevent the analyzer from finding the correct solution) and a blind search in an enormous search space. It also allows the parser's search space to be pruned when an appropriate solution is found [5].

The two level parsing schema was inspired by that used in some case-frame based architectures such as [4]. In such an approach the analyzer processes the text using a deterministic syntax-driven strategy to recognize fragments of text representing semantic objects (i.e. case-frames). Afterwards a semantic-driven strategy combines the segments. In our approach the segment boundaries are determined without using the parser; that method is more application independent and allows determinism to be avoided, although it can introduce some errors to be corrected by the linguistic analyzer. The use of the syntax-driven strategy in the segment combination phase allows the generality of the grammar to be preserved, avoiding duplication of syntactic information in the semantic-driven analyzer, which is common in many case-frame based techniques.

From a theoretical point of view, our strategy outperforms finite-state model approaches [1] as it tends to be more reliable in the analysis; its main drawback with respect to finite-state models is the resource development time (although part of grammar and lexicon, and the upper model in the KB, are transportable across the applications).

5   Preliminary Results and Conclusion

A system to extract information from on-line news-stories based on the architecture mentioned above is currently under development. Both the Text Zoner and the Preparser were implemented and tested. The main parts of the linguistic analyzer have been implemented and are under test. The current *lexicon* is composed of only the domain specific dictionary (about 1,000 forms); a project for the development of the generic lexical knowledge-base mentioned in the architecture started in March 1995. The *segmenter* mainly relies on the closed-class word approach with a slight domain-dependent correction. It was tested on about 120 texts with more than 99% success rate. The grammar is expressed in a simple declarative formalism so that a new rule may be easily added. The closed class check is based on the syntactic hierarchy used by the grammatical analyzer so as to simplify the work of writing a segmentation grammar. The *classifier* is based on statistical pattern matching in which the rules can be automatically or manually acquired; it was tested on the same small corpus by means of different techniques; in a leaving-one-out test on the 120 news items the classifier scored 0,71 in terms of precision and 0,80 in recall. These results seem to be comparable with those obtained with more complex approaches[3]. The chart *parser* is currently working in a head driven way; fragment combination is done by adopting weighted syntax-driven strategies. Some preliminary results seem to show that the parsing approach guarantees both precision and efficiency; in particular the agenda control strategy allows a reduction of up to 40% in the number of edges produced, always following the most promising solution [5]. *Reference resolution* is the less developed part of the architecture; currently a simple economy criterion based on the reference to discourse concepts is used to cope with the linguistic analyzer's partial results. The approach is currently insufficient, as discourse processing was demonstrated to be a very difficult task in text processing [20]. The *template filler* uses the results provided by the linguistic analyzer to fill the templates, gently overcoming gaps in the analysis.

Future development will concentrate on evolution of parsing control and on a more effective approach in discourse processing.

Acknowledgment

Alberto Lavelli developed the bidirectional chart parser and contributed in the definition and implementation of the agenda control mechanism; he also provided lots of suggestions about this paper.

References

1. Douglas E. Appelt, Jerry R. Hobbs, John Bear, David Israel, and Mabry Tyson. Fastus: A finite-state processor for information extraction from real-world text. In *Proceedings of the Thirteenth International Joint Conference on Artificial Intelligence*, Chambery, France, 1993.
2. John A. Bateman, Bernardo Magnini, and Fabio Rinaldi. The generalized {Italian,German,English} Upper Model. In *Proceedings of the ECAI-94 workshop on Implemented Ontologies*, Amsterdam, The Netherlands, 1994.
3. Nicola Cancedda. Segmentazione e classificazione in un sistema per l'estrazione di conoscenza da testi. Tesi di Laurea; Universita' degli Studi di Roma "La Sapienza", December 1994.
4. Fabio Ciravegna. Understanding messages in a diagnostic domain. *Information Processing and Management*, 1995. (to appear in the Special Issue on Summarizing Texts).
5. Fabio Ciravegna and Alberto Lavelli. Controlling bidirectional parsing for efficient text analysis. In *Fourth International Workshop on Parsing Technologies (IWPT'95)*, Prague, September 1995.
6. Luca Gilardoni, Paola Prunotto, and Gianluigi Rocca. Hierarchical pattern matching for knowledge based news categorization. In *Proceedings of the RIAO '94*, New York, October 1994.

7. The PLUM System Group. BBN: Description of the PLUM system as used for MUC-5. In Beth M. Sundheim, editor, *Fifth Message Understanding Conference (MUC5)*, Baltimore, Maryland, August 1993. Morgan Kaufmann Publishers, Inc. (San Francisco, CA).

8. Philip J. Hayes, Laura E. Knecht, and Monica J. Cellio. A news story categorization system. In *Proceedings of the Second Conference on Applied Natural Language Processing*, Austin, Texas, 1988.

9. Jerry R. Hobbs. The generic information extraction system. In B. Sundheim, editor, *Fifth Message Understanding Conference (MUC-5)*, San Francisco, CA, August 1993. Morgan Kaufmann Publishers, Inc.

10. Jerry R. Hobbs, Douglas E. Appelt, and Mabry Tyson. Robust processing of real-world natural-language texts. In *Proceedings of the Second Conference on Applied Natural Language Processing*, Trento, Italy, March 1992.

11. Paul S. Jacobs. To parse or not to parse: Relation-driven text skimming. In *Proceedings of the Thirteenth International Conference on Computational Linguistics*, Helsinki, Finland, 1990.

12. Paul S. Jacobs. Joining statistics with nlp for text categorization. In *Proceedings of the Third Conference on Applied Natural Language Processing*, Trento, Italy, 1992.

13. Paul S. Jacobs. Parsing run amok: Relation-driven control for text analysis. In *Proceedings of the Tenth National Conference on Artificial Intelligence*, San Jose, California, July 1992. AAAI.

14. Martin Kay. Algorithm schemata and data structures in syntactic processing. Technical report, Xerox Palo Alto Research Center, Palo Alto CA, 1980.

15. R. M. MacGregor and R. Bates. The LOOM knowledge representation language. Technical Report ISI/RS-87-188, USC/ISI, 1987.

16. Bernardo Magnini, Carlo Strapparava, Fabio Ciravegna, and Emanuele Pianta. A project for the construction of an italian lexical knowledge base in the framework of wordnet. In *International Workshop on the "Future of the Dictionary"*, Grenoble, October 1994.

17. David D. McDonald. Robust partial-parsing through incremental, multi-algorithm processing. In Paul S. Jacobs, editor, *Text-Based Intelligent Systems*. Lawrence Erlbaum Associates, 1992.

18. Ellen Riloff and Wendy Lehnert. Classifying texts using relevancy signatures. In *Proceedings of the Tenth National Conference on Artificial Intelligence*, San Jose, California, July 1992.

19. Giorgio Satta and Oliviero Stock. Bi-directional context free grammar parsing for natural language processing. *Artificial Intelligence*, September 1994.

20. Beth M. Sundheim, editor. *Third Message Understanding Conference (MUC-3)*. Morgan Kaufmann Publishers, Inc., San Diego, CA, May 1991. San Mateo, CA.

21. Beth M. Sundheim, editor. *Fifth Message Understanding Conference (MUC5)*. Morgan Kaufmann Publishers, Inc., San Francisco CA, August 1993.

Recognizing preliminary sentences in dialogue interpretation *

Liliana Ardissono, Guido Boella and Dario Sestero

Dip. di Informatica - Università di Torino Cso Svizzera 185, 10149 Torino, Italy

Abstract. In traditional plan-based dialogue interpretation systems, speech-acts are directly used for identifying the speaker's domain plans and little analysis is performed of the role of sentences in dialogue. This may lead to the activation of a large number of hypotheses on an agent's domain plans. In this paper, we describe how to interpret background sentences occurring in a dialogue by using knowledge coming from the linguistic and domain levels, and from a model of the user. We consider two kinds of utterances: the first one justifies the performance of subsequent speech-acts; the second represents information to be used for constraining the interpretation process of the other speech-act.

1 Introduction

People often open dialogues with some background information. Sometimes, this information is given to make the interpretation of the other utterances easier for their interlocutors; other times, background information is used to justify the subsequent speech acts, or to check whether the preconditions of the actions which should be performed next are met (pre-sequences). Many plan recognition systems interpret input sentences without performing a discourse analysis ([5, 1]); others (e.g. [8]) perform a basic one, but they still don't pay attention enough to the communicative role of sentences; in general, all of them use speech-acts for identifying the speaker's domain plans, without considering the fact that, sometimes, utterances are too general to address particular actions in the domain. This may cause an explosion of alternatives in the hypothesis space, which is then handled by the application of focusing techniques [5], for reducing the number of hypotheses to the coherent ones. However, this explosion could be prevented by recognizing a priori the relation among the sentences within a chunk of dialogue. Consider the following examples:

[a] *"Sono uno studente lavoratore. Mi può dare il modulo per pagare le tasse annuali di iscrizione?"* [I'm a working student. Can you give me the module for paying the annual tuition fee?]

[b] *"Voglio prendere un libro in biblioteca. Puoi darmi le chiavi?"* [I want to take a book from the the library. Can you give me the keys?]

---

* This work was partially supported by MURST 60%, by the Italian National Research Council (CNR), project "Pianificazione Automatica"

[c] *"La biblioteca e' chiusa. Puoi darmi le chiavi?"* [The library is closed. Can you give me the keys?]

An application of action identification techniques to examples like [a] would produce a large set of alternative actions, which should be matched with the previous context of the dialogue. On the other hand, a local domain analysis of the chunks of dialogue should be performed, before linking the identified plans with the previous context. In particular, the first sentence of example [a] is uttered to provide a general information about the user, useful for disambiguating the alternative interpretations for the second utterance (so that the proper domain action is chosen). In [b], the first sentence addresses the user's plan, so that the next utterance is motivated. Example [c] is similar, but the first sentence is more indirect than in case [b].

In this paper, we analyze background sentences, focusing on sentences which support subsequent speech acts by motivating them, or by constraining their possible interpretations. For space reasons, we will not deal with pre-sequences.[2] We use a communicative level of interpretation for executing a first domain analysis within the single turns in the dialogues, and for linking only the resulting plans to the hypotheses on the speaker's domain plans built in the previous part of the dialogue.

2   The general interpretation framework

In our framework, dialogues are interpreted as a form of collective behavior involving two agents, who negotiate some common intentions [6]. In particular, we deal with the recognition of direct and indirect speech-acts [2], linguistic strategies, problem solving activities and domain level plans identified by the input utterances [4]. Communicative acts are used for representing linguistic strategies and consist of plans composed of sequences of speech-acts referring to domain-related actions. Problem solving actions represent the private reasoning activity performed by an agent who wants to obtain some goal, and take into account the aspects of cooperation in dialogues. Domain actions represent the activities which the user is asking information about. The knowledge about the four types of actions is represented hierarchically in three separate libraries. The system [3] accepts (Italian) NL sentences and performs a syntactic and semantic analysis. Then it performs the speech-act analysis, which leads to the identification of the domain actions involved by the utterances (e.g. given a request, the requested action is identified). The analysis of background statements is performed after the speech-acts interpretation: given the speech-acts and the domain actions associated with the input sentences, communicative acts are considered,

---

[2] Since pre-sequences refer to the control of the preconditions of (linguistic or domain) actions which are planned next, they can be interpreted by analyzing the speaker's problem-solving activity. As an example of pre-sequence, consider the question *"Do you have a pen?"* If the interlocutor reacts promptly by providing the first speaker with the pen, the interaction stops; otherwise, the speaker could continue the dialogue with the explicit request "Can you give it to me?" [9].

to see whether the speech-acts may be locally related with each other by using the domain knowledge. This analysis makes it possible to identify background statements (on the basis of the relation existing between the identified domain actions) and to filter out the interpretations of the input sentences which don't relate to each other. In this way, a reduced number of domain plans is selected, to be then linked to the previous context of the dialogue. During the interpretation, the system applies user modeling acquisition rules to the recognized speech-acts, to build a model of the user (UM), where individual preferences, beliefs, properties and other specific information are kept. Also stereotypical knowledge about users is used for enhancing the predictive power of the system and building the UM more quickly.

3   The communicative acts

We introduce the *Grounded* and *Supported* communicative acts to interpret chunks of dialogues where some sentences (which we will call *satellites* [11]) support a subsequent speech-act (*nucleus*), by constraining its possible interpretations (e.g. [a] in section 1), or by addressing the motivations for uttering it ([b], [c]). While Maybury [10] introduces communicative acts as hierarchical plans for describing strategies of generation of coherent discourse (e.g. argumentation), we use communicative acts at a finer level, for characterizing the relation among the single sentences in a chunk of dialogue. In particular, communicative acts are used for influencing the hearer's interpretation process or, in general, to support the coherence of the dialogue.

In the description of communicative acts, we will focus on the relation between background information and main speech-acts. So, we will restrict our description to cases where background information is given in a single speech-act (if several sentences occur, coherence relations among them must be considered, too). For an analysis of coherence relations between utterances, see [7].

The *Grounded* communicative act represents the chunks of dialogue where a sentence makes explicit the reasons for the occurrence of a speech-act. The background utterance (which can occur before or after the nucleus) could be either the expression of the intention of executing a certain action, as in [b], or the expression of a condition which justifies the performance of the main speech-act, by giving a motivation for addressing the domain action involved by it, as in [c]. The only acceptable sequences of utterances are those for which, using domain knowledge, it is possible to identify an inferential chain (based on enablement relations among actions) which links the information expressed by the satellite to the action inferred from the nucleus. E.g. in [c], the 'give-keys' action enables the 'open(SP,Library)' action, which in turn makes false the expressed 'closed(Library)' condition. This inference explicits that the speaker has the goal 'open(Library)' and, at the same time, it explains why s/he asks for the keys. In general, the link between the utterances composing a communicative act might be weaker. For example, in [b] the speaker expresses the intention of executing the 'Borrow-book(SP,Library)' action, which has the substep of going

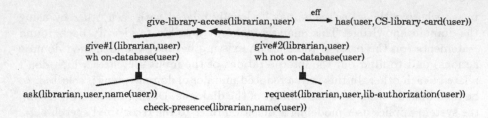

Fig. 1. The apply-for-library-access plan

to the library, and this step has the 'open(Library)' precondition. In similar examples, the search for the relation among actions in the domain plan library is performed by means of focusing heuristics [5], which identify all the possible linking paths through the generalization and decomposition hierarchies. More precisely, actions are identified from the speech-acts, by inspecting the domain level plan library (actions are identified because mentioned directly, or starting from a condition, by means of action identification heuristics [5]); then, the paths which link the selected actions through decomposition and generalization links are identified by navigating the library.

Also in traditional plan recognition systems, the relations among sentences are identified by applying action identification procedures to speech-acts, and then trying to apply focusing procedures to the identified actions, so discarding the unrelated ones. However, the speaker's communicative plans are not explicit. So, sentences are analyzed separately, without keeping into account that they are intentionally stated together, and that the role of a satellite is to motivate the action involved by the nucleus. Considering this fact may be very important when a context has already been introduced by the previous part of the dialogue. In fact, several alternative plans might be built, by linking each of the activated actions to the hypotheses on the user's plans identified from the previous utterances. On the contrary, if communicative acts are recognized, they can be used for filtering the number of hypotheses locally, so that only the selected ones are related to the previous context.

The *Supported* communicative act represents the chunks of dialogue where a background utterance provides a context for restricting the possible interpretations of the main speech-act, and for choosing the proper domain action identified by it (e.g. suppose that there are two different procedures for enrolling in university either as a full-time, or working student; they differ for some substeps, but both of them have a subaction of getting the modules for enrolling. Since different types of module exist for full-time and working students, different constraints on the module type appear in the decomposition of the enrolling actions. Therefore, in example [a], the speaker's status is important to identify the right plan having "give-module" as a step). Different supporting relations may link the speech-acts: 1) In the simplest case, the background sentence refers to some preconditions or constraints of the actions addressed in the nucleus (e.g. in "I'm a CS student. I'd like to access the computer labs", where being CS students is a constraint of 'access-lab'). 2) As a second case, the provided information might not address directly the main action involved in the chunks of dialogue; so, focusing heuristics must be used for checking whether the involved actions are related in the plan library (see the discussion on example [a]). 3) Sometimes, the relation among the background sentence and the nucleus is indirect, and the knowledge contained in the plan library is not enough to identify it. This corresponds to a violation of Grice's relation maxim; however, under the hypothesis that the speaker is anyway cooperative, another type of coherence link among the speech-acts must be found. In order to do that, we also use the information about the user acquired during the interaction (and contained in the UM). Information inferred by stereotypes activation is particularly relevant to this task, because it may not be directly related to the specific sentences formulated in the dialogue (stereotypes contain general properties of a category of agents, and their activation enables to predict the characteristics of a user in a broader spectrum of the domain than that relative to the actions addressed explicitly during the dialogue). The idea is then to look for the coherence relation among sentences in a dialogue using the contents of the UM, as well as those of the plan library. Before describing in more detail this interpretation process, it must be noted that, being the three cases ordered on the basis of their indirectness, they must be considered in sequence. So, the plan library is inspected first and, if no path can be found which connects the actions identified by a satellite to those activated by the nucleus, the contents of the UM are considered for applying the focusing heuristics to the actions which can be identified by them. Only the most recently introduced information is used for finding the relation among the speech-acts (the contents of the UM are marked so that it is possible to know which utterance caused their introduction). Moreover, the various kinds of information about the user have a different impact on the determination of the coherence relations among actions (e.g. properties and goals are more relevant than knowledge on the domain). So, the contents to be used are further ordered by preference heuristics.

In order to show this situation with an example, consider the action of giving the library access to an agent, shown in Figure 1, which librarians execute for providing somebody with a library card. This action has two more specific cases ("give#1" and "give#2"), according to the fact that the agent's name is recorded on the library database or not. In the first case, the librarian asks the agent's name, and checks that it is present in the database; in the second, the librarian must request an authorization to use the library, signed by a faculty. Suppose that the agent says *"Sono uno studente di Informatica. Vorrei avere la tessera della biblioteca."* [I'm a CS student; I would like to have the library card]. While the second utterance identifies immediately the "give-library-access(Librarian, SP)" action, the "CS-student(SP)" condition does not appear in the plan. The information added into the UM after the interpretation of the first utterance must be used for establishing the coherence relation between the two sentences. In particular, the first sentence makes it possible to activate the CS-student stereotype, which contains the property "on-database(agt)" (CS students' names are recorded in the library database). Since the "give#1" action has this condition as a restriction, focusing procedures can be used for finding a path in the plan library which leads to the "give-library-access" action, which has been identified by the condition addressed in the second sentence.

4 Conclusions

In this paper, we analyzed two kinds of background utterances (in the 'grounded' and 'supported' communicative acts), which may occur in chunks of dialogues to motivate the subsequent speech-acts, or restrict the number of their possible interpretations. We pointed out that sequences of sentences corresponding to these communicative acts should be first analyzed locally, with respect to the rest of the dialogue, in order to identify the coherence relations existing among the involved actions, and only after that they should be integrated into the context of the global dialogue. Moreover, especially for supported speech-acts, the relationship between the utterances should be analyzed by considering knowledge about domain actions, and information about the user (collected in the User Model): in fact, the link between the sentences could be found by analyzing information about the user which has not been stated explicitly in the previous part of the dialogue, but has to be inferred from the given information (her/his properties, goals, etc).

References

1. J.F. Allen. Recognizing intentions from natural language utterances. In M. Brady and R.C. Berwick, editors, *Computational models of discourse*, pages 107–166. MIT Press, 1983.
2. L. Ardissono, G. Boella, and L. Lesmo. A computational approach to speech acts recognition. In *Proc. 17th Cognitive Science Conference*, Pittsburgh, 1995.
3. L. Ardissono, L. Lesmo, P. Pogliano, and P. Terenziani. Representation of determiners in natural language. In *Proc. 12th IJCAI*, pages 997–1002, Sydney, 1991.
4. L. Ardissono, A. Lombardo, and D. Sestero. A flexible approach to cooperative response generation in information-seeking dialogues. In *Proc. 31st Annual Meeting ACL*, pages 274–276, Columbus, 1993.
5. S. Carberry. *Plan Recognition in Natural Language Dialogue*. MIT Press, 1990.
6. P. R. Cohen and H. J. Levesque. Confirmation and joint action. In *Proc. 12th IJCAI*, pages 951–957, Sydney, 1991.
7. N. Green and S. Carberry. a hybrid reasoning model for indirect answers. In *Proc. 32nd Annual Meeting of ACL*, pages 58–65, Las Cruces, New Mexico, 1994.
8. L. Lambert. *Recognizing Complex Discourse Acts: A Tripartite Plan-Based Model of Dialogue*. PhD thesis, University of Delaware, 1993.
9. S. C. Levinson. *Pragmatics*. Cambridge University Press, Cambridge, 1983.
10. M.T. Maybury. Communicative acts for generating natural language arguments. In *Proc. 11th Conf. AAAI*, pages 357–364, Washington DC, 1993.
11. J.D. Moore and C.L. Paris. Constructing coherent text using rethorical relations. In *Proc. 10th Annual Conf. Cognitive Science Society*, 1988.

Contextuality and Non-extensional Identity: the Inescapable Symbiosis in NLP

Ioannis Kanellos and Victor Hugo Zaldivar-Carrillo*

École Nationale Supérieure des Télécommunications de Bretagne
BP 832
29285 Brest Cedex FRANCE

Abstract. In this paper we examine two kernel traits that a KR approach has to share in order to capture traditional structuralist analysis of semantics: non-extensionality and semantic identification/differentiation. We set up the formal requisites for a non-extensional definition of representational entities. The notion of identity is re-evaluated supporting modularity. Its partial forms, seen as particular effects of interpretational strategies, are investigated.

KEYWORDS: Extensionality and non-extensionality in knowledge representation; non-extensional identity; partial identity forms.

1 Introduction

In the area of NLP the limits of the *representational locality* of traditional KR systems are quite plain: one can hardly find entities with the same semantic clarity of KR units. In recent years, the interest for context grew up significantly. The invested hope is that of the possibility to capture some semantic characteristics that traditional KR paradigms seem unable to model. First of all, the notion of semantic identity is actually not locally given but continuously constructed by global interpretational strategies. From a classical structuralist point of view, such strategies select (and/or annihilate) semic traits for a given unit; different interpretational strategies may give different semantic identities to the same unit. On the other hand, semic traits may be given under semantically equivalent descriptions [7]. Such a conception give birth to a general formal pogramme for a KRS aiming at truthfully modelling the notion of semantic identity. Such a system has to be set up on non-extensional structural criteria and recognize a large variety of locally instituted semantic identities.

We give a first glimpse of such a system.

---

* The authors are grateful to Ms. Janet Ormrod for the final revision of the paper.

2 Basic Representational Units: "Concepts" and "Theories"

Let us assume the existence of a non-empty set C and call concepts its elements. In a (representational) level just above it let us introduce the notion of "theory", a term used here in a technical manner (for a detailed discussion and the motivations of such terminology see [6, 4]). A theory represents a property of (or a relation between) concepts. These representational entities are articulated in a hierarchy.

The first level (called T_0) is somehow a "receptacle" which contains finite tuples of concepts *i.e.*:

$$T_0 =_{df} \bigcup_{i=1}^{n} C^i; \quad \text{where every } C^i \text{ is given by} \tag{1}$$
$$C^i =_{df} \prod_{j=1}^{i} C_j \quad \text{and } C_j =_{df} C \text{ for every } 1 \le j \le i \ .$$

The entities in T_0, of the form $c_{(n)i} =_{df} (c_{i1}, c_{i2} \ldots, c_{in})$, are called "vector-concepts".

Axiom 1: T_0 is extensional.

We ought to understand this axiom as follows: any two vector-concepts $c_{(n)i}$ and $c_{(n)j}$ are equal if and only if, for every k, $1 \le k \le n$, $c_{ik} = c_{jk}$; and, furthermore, that any two classes of vector-concepts P_1 and P_2 are equal if and only if, for any c, $c \in P_1 \Leftrightarrow c \in P_2$.

The level T_1 (theories of rank 1) gives T_0 its structured status.

$$T_1 =_{df} \{t \mid t \text{ expresses a relation over } C^i \, (1 \le i \le n)\} \ . \tag{2}$$

An element of T_1 is generally designated by $t_{j(n)i}$; j specifies the level of the theory (here equal to 1), n represents its arity and i its name; whenever no confusion is possible, we can omit some of these indices.

Levels 0 and 1 are not independent; they are linked together by the notion of *extension of a theory*:

$$ext\,(t_{(n)i}) =_{df} \{c \mid c \in T_0 \text{ and } c \text{ satisfies the relation } t_{(n)i}\} \ . \tag{3}$$

Obviously, theories in T_1 can be structured by a partial order relation, noted $\le_{ext}$, based on the inclusion of theories' extensions:

$$t_{(n)i} \le_{ext} t_{(n)j} \quad \text{iff} \quad ext\,(t_{(n)i}) \subseteq ext\,(t_{(n)j}) \ . \tag{4}$$

Furthermore:

$$t_{(n)i} =_{ext} t_{(n)j} \quad \text{iff} \quad ext\,(t_{(n)i}) = ext\,(t_{(n)j}) \ . \tag{5}$$

The discernibility in T_1 of two such theories is ensured by axiomatic means:

Axiom 2: T_1 is non-extensional.

This axiom implies that given a theory t of T_1 there are, generally, $t_1, \ldots, t_n$ in T_1, for a natural n, such that $t_1 =_{ext} t_2 =_{ext} \cdots =_{ext} t_n =_{ext} t$.

A more organic link between the levels T_0 and T_1 is necessary. This is done by virtue of the next axiom. It may be understood as a "structural adequacy axiom" of T_0 and T_1:

Axiom 3 : Let $E \subset T_0$ such that $\forall x,y \in E$, x and y are vector-concepts of the same arity; then there is a natural $n \geq 1$ et $t_1,\ldots,t_n \in T_1$ such that $\forall i = 1,\ldots,n$ $ext(t_i) = E$.

Obviously $|T_1|>|T_0|$. The non-extensionality of T_1 is illustrated in figure 1.

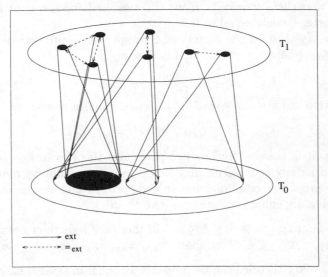

Fig. 1. Non-extensionality of T_1

3   Non-Extensionality, Polysemy and Identity

The immediate implication is that the notion of identity (of a theory) is seriously affected: it takes a more "collective" form. The investigation of the problem of identity is here inescapable. From a structuralist point of view, what essentially operates a context in NLP is the constitution of "isotopies" [3, 7]. An isotopy may be seen as the constitution of an equivalence class constructed by recurrent semic traits of textual inputs. As an equivalence class, an isotopy induces a certain indiscernibility between linguistic items sharing these semic traits. Such an indiscernibility is, of course, intelligible within interpretative objectives. Its investigation results from a systematic exploration of the analytic character of the notion of theory.

3.1 Projections of a Theory

Consider $t_{(n)i}$, an n-ary theory in T_1; we define its j-projection, $1 \leq j \leq n$ (noted $P_j(t_{(n)i})$), as a unary theory in T_1, noted $\hat{t}_{ij}$, such that:

$$ext\left(\hat{t}_{ij}\right) =_{df} \left\{ c \mid \begin{array}{l} \text{where c is such that there is a } c \in ext\left(t_{(n)i}\right) \\ \text{whose j-component is } c \end{array} \right\} . \qquad (6)$$

Axiom 3 ensures that such a definition is not vacuous. On the other hand, Axiom 2 states that there are maybe many theories verifying the same definitional conditions (extensionally equal to $\hat{t}_{ij}$).

Clearly, n-ary theories can be related through their j-projections via a relation (noted $\leq_{ext}$) based on extensional inclusion:

$$t_{(n)i} \leq_{P-j} t_{(n)k} \quad \text{iff} \quad \hat{t}_{ij} \leq_{ext} \hat{t}_{kj} . \qquad (7)$$

This relation induces the so-called *projective equality*, noted $=_{P-j}$:

$$t_{(n)i} =_{P-j} t_{(n)k} \quad \text{iff} \quad \hat{t}_{ij} =_{ext} \hat{t}_{kj} . \qquad (8)$$

Of course, it is possible for any two particular theories to find several projections extensionally equal. This may be taken into account by a quantitative criterion: the *projective equality degree* (noted "*ped*") which represents the number of extensionally equal projections of two theories:

$$ped\left(t_{(n)i}, t_{(n)j}\right) = k, 0 \leq k \leq n, \quad \text{iff there are k distinct naturals} \atop 1 \leq m_1, ..., m_k \leq n \quad \text{such that} \quad \hat{t}_{m_h i} =_{ext} \hat{t}_{m_h j}, \ 1 \leq h \leq k . \qquad (9)$$

Thus, two n-ary theories can be projectively equal in several different ways, *i.e.*, there are several ways in which one may construct partial isotopies from a given textual input. The *ped* establishes a hierarchy of different ways to consider two theories as more or less projectively equal.

However, if $ped\left(t_{(n)j}, t_{(n)j}\right) = n$ we do not necessarily have $t_{(n)i} =_{ext} t_{(n)j}$; the converse is clearly true. This means that the extensional indiscernibility between two theories of the same arity is more subtle than the (partial) indiscernibility of their respective unary projections. The notion of *ped* has interesting interpretations; one may understand partial identity forms as indicating (unary) formal dimensions in which two NLP inputs are "sense-indiscernible" *i.e.*, semantically inter-exchangeable although not generally identical.

This interpretation may be generalized.

3.2 P-o/k and Pgen Projective Identity Orders

Indiscernibility schemata required by semantic isotopies are not necessarily subordinated by the input order; thus one may allow cross-comparisons between two n-ary theories *i.e.*, one may compare the o-projection of $t_{(n)i}$ with the k-projection of $t_{(n)j}$. This *non-ordered projective relation*, noted $\leq_{P-o/k}$, is defined as follows: for $t_{(n)i}, t_{(n)j} \in T_1$

$$t_{(n)i} \leq_{P-o/k} t_{(n)j} \quad \text{iff} \quad \hat{t}_{io} \leq_{ext} \hat{t}_{jk} . \qquad (10)$$

149

The implied *non-ordered projective equality*, noted $=_{P-o/k}$, is, thus, defined:

$$t_{(n)i} =_{P-o/k} t_{(n)j} \quad \text{iff} \quad \hat{t}_{io} =_{ext} \hat{t}_{jk} . \tag{11}$$

We have, then, several ways to compare two theories of the same arity; but we can furthermore proceed to a more extended generalization removing the restriction over the arity of the theories compared. This general projective relation, noted $\leq_{Pgen}$, is defined as follows: for $t_{(n)i}, t_{(m)j} \in T_1$, and $m \neq n$ naturals:

$$t_{(n)i} \leq_{Pgen} t_{(m)j} \quad \text{iff} \quad \hat{t}_{io} \leq_{ext} \hat{t}_{jk} . \tag{12}$$

And this relation leads to the introduction of a weaker notion of indiscernibility between two theories in T_1, the *general projective equality*, noted $=_{Pgen}$:

$$t_{(n)i} =_{Pgen} t_{(m)j} \quad \text{iff} \quad \hat{t}_{io} =_{ext} \hat{t}_{jk} . \tag{13}$$

One may similarly generalize the notion of *ped* obtaining $ped_{P-i/j}$ and ped_{Pgen} respectively. Such definitions modalize the notion of identity in a non-extensional framework; indeed, two theories may be considered as more or less indistinguishable from the point of view of the KR structural impact insofar as:

$$(t_1 =_{ext} t_2) \Rightarrow (t_1 =_{P-j} t_2) \Rightarrow (t_1 =_{P-o/k} t_2) \tag{14}$$

and even

$$(t_1 =_{P-j} t_2) \Rightarrow (t_1 =_{P-o/k} t_2) \Rightarrow (t_1 =_{Pgen} t_2) \tag{15}$$

if one defines $=_{P-j}$ and $=_{P-o/k}$ also standing for theories of different arity.

In a quite similar way, one can complete this program on projective identity orders by generalizing the notion of a theory projection. The aim is uniformly the same: to model all relational incidences of partial indiscernibility. So, for a theory $t_{(n)i}$ and for every natural $1 \leq k < n$ one may define k-ary projections, respective orders and forms of equalities corresponding to $=_{P-j}$, $=_{P-o/k}$ and $=_{Pgen}$.

We shall limit ourselves to the generalization of the $=_{P-j}$ relation for different types of k-ary projections of a theory.

3.3 *K*-ary Projective Indiscernibility between Theories

There are actually several ways to build up k-ary projections; two of them seem to be more relevant in NL semantics. The first one is the *adjacent k-ary projection of a theory from its j-component*. Consider an n-ary theory $t_{(n)i}$ in T_1; its adjacent k-ary projection from its j-component (noted $P_{o(k)-j}(t_{(n)i})$) is a k-ary theory $\hat{t}_{(k)ij}$ in T_1 such that:

$$ext\left(\hat{t}_{(k)ij}\right) =_{df} \left\{ (c_{m_1}, c_{m_2}, \ldots, c_{m_k}) \mid \begin{array}{l} \exists c \in ext\left(t_{(n)i}\right) \quad \text{such that} \\ c_{m_1} \text{ is its j-component} \\ c_{m_2} \text{ is its j+1-component} \\ \vdots \\ c_{m_k} \text{ is its j+(k-1)-component} \end{array} \right\} . \tag{16}$$

The extension of an adjacent k-ary projection is built up by taking the k adjacent components of the elements in the extension of $t_{(n)i}$ beginning from the j-component ($j + k \leq n$). The other way to build a k-ary projection is in a non-adjacent manner. The *non-adjacent k-ary projection* of an n-ary theory $t_{(n)i}$ (noted $P_{(k)-\{\mathcal{H}\}}\left(t_{(n)i}\right)$) is a k-ary theory $\hat{t}_{(k)i\{\mathcal{H}\}}$ such that:

$$ ext\left(\hat{t}_{(k)i\{\mathcal{H}\}}\right) =_{df} \left\{ (c_{g_1}, c_{g_2}, \ldots, c_{g_k}) \ \middle| \ \begin{array}{l} \exists c \in ext\left(t_{(n)i}\right) \quad \text{such that} \\ c_{g_1} \text{ is its } \mathcal{H}_1\text{-component} \\ c_{g_2} \text{ is its } \mathcal{H}_2\text{-component} \\ \vdots \\ c_{g_k} \text{ is its } \mathcal{H}_k\text{-component} \end{array} \right\} . \tag{17}$$

where $\mathcal{H}$ is an injection from $\{1, \ldots, k\}$ to $\{1, \ldots, n\}$.

We can introduce some equality notions based on these new kinds of projections. For instance, the *ordered adjacent k-ary projective equality* between two n-ary theories $t_{(n)i}$ and $t_{(n)p}$ in T_1 (noted $=_{Po(k)-j}$):

$$t_{(n)i} =_{Po(k)-j} t_{(n)p} \quad \text{iff} \quad \hat{t}_{(k)ij} =_{ext} \hat{t}_{(k)pj} \tag{18}$$

and the related *ordered non-adjacent k-ary projective equality* (noted $=_{P(k)-\{\mathcal{H}\}}$):

$$t_{(n)i} =_{P(k)-\{\mathcal{H}\}} t_{(n)p} \quad \text{iff} \quad \hat{t}_{(k)i\{\mathcal{H}\}} =_{ext} \hat{t}_{(k)p\{\mathcal{H}\}} . \tag{19}$$

And, of course, we can introduce two new degrees of semantic indiscernibility between two theories (the *adjacent k-ary projective equality degree*, noted $ped_{o(k)}$, and the *non-adjacent* one noted $ped_{(k)}$) both of them defined in a straightforward manner. For the second one:

$$\begin{array}{c} ped_{(k)}\left(t_{(n)i}, t_{(n)p}\right) = m \quad \text{iff} \\ \exists m \quad \text{functions} \quad \mathcal{H}_1, \cdots, \mathcal{H}_m \quad \text{such that} \\ \forall s, 1 \leq s \leq m \\ P_{(k)-\{\mathcal{H}_s\}}\left(t_{(n)i}\right) =_{ext} P_{(k)-\{\mathcal{H}_s\}}\left(t_{(n)p}\right) \end{array} . \tag{20}$$

It can be shown that: if $t_{(n)i}$ and $t_{(n)p}$ are two n-ary ($n \neq 2$) theories in T_1 and for every k, $1 \leq k < n$ we have the maximum values for $ped_{o(k)}\left(t_{(n)i}, t_{(n)p}\right)$ and $ped_{(k)}\left(t_{(n)i}, t_{(n)p}\right)$ then $t_{(n)i} =_{ext} t_{(n)p}$.

The last two forms of projective equality may be understood as characterizing the full range of partial semic neutralizations. In semantics, neutralization processes annihilate oppositions between semantic units; as such, they may be seen as "indiscernibility operators" over semantic features. What they actually do is to organize the semantic material into original local structures. In such structures only partial comparison criteria are relevant. Thus, two NL inputs may be semantically the "same" or "different" depending on what oppositions or identities between semantic features have been locally activated.

4 Perspectives

Drastically limited in space, we can only describe basic perspectives for this model.

At first, it is possible to consider a third level, T_2, in which one may "internalize" most of the notions already developed ("extension of a theory", "extensionally equal", "projection of a theory", etc.). T_2 contains "complex theories" (*i.e.*, theories which express relations between theories of rank 1 and concepts); it is also non-extensional in the same sense.

And secondly, one may give a formal definition of the notion of semantic identity of a concept c in non-extensional terms; it is a subset $SI_k(c)$ of $int_g(c)$ where:

$$int_g(c_i) =_{df} \left\{ t_{(m)k} \mid \exists \hat{t}_{jk}, 1 \leq j \leq m, \quad \text{such that} \quad c_i \in ext\left(\hat{t}_{jk}\right) \right\} . \qquad (21)$$

Thus, a concept c has many semantic identities corresponding to contextually instituted semic descriptions. And two such identities may be "more or less" indiscernible depending on local (projective) indiscernibility criteria operating on the theories they contain.

References

1. R. Carnap. *Introduction to semantics*. Harvard University Press, 1942.
2. F. Giunchiglia. Contextual reasoning. In *Proc. of the IJCAI-93 workshop on "Using Knowledge in its Context"*, pages 39–49, 1993.
3. A.-J. Greimas. *Sémantique Structurale*. Presses Universitaires de France, Paris, réédition, 1986.
4. D. L. Medin. Concepts and Conceptual Structures. *American Psychologist*, 44(12):1469–1481, 1989.
5. R. Montague. *Formal Philosophy. Selected Papers from R. Montague*. New Haven, London, New York, 1979.
6. G. L. Murphy and D. L. Medin. The Role of Theories in Conceptual Coherence. *Psychological Review*, 92(3):286–316, 1985.
7. F. Rastier. *Sémantique Interprétative*. Formes sémiotiques. Presses Universitaires de France, Paris, 1987.
8. E. N. Zalta. *Abstract Objects*, volume 160 of *Synthese library*. D. Reidel Publishing Company, 1983.
9. E. N. Zalta. *Intensional Logic and the Metaphysics of Intentionality*. Bradford Book. MIT Press, Cambridge, MA, 1988.

Priorities in Default Logic Revisited

Grigoris Antoniou

Dept. of Management, The University of Newcastle,
Callaghan, NSW 2308, Australia,
mgga@alinga.newcastle.edu.au

Abstract. One of the drawbacks of Reiter's original presentation of Default Logic is the difficulty of expressing priorities among defaults. Recently, Brewka proposed an expansion of Default Logic which allows for explicit reasoning about priorities in Default Logic. In this paper we give an alternative, operational characterization of extensions; it is also technically simpler and therefore more easily applicable. Further we investigate some properties of the logic paying special attention to the existence of extensions. We present some sufficient conditions for a default theory with priorities to have at least one extension.

1   Introduction

Default Logic [12] is one of the main approaches of nonmonotonic reasoning, and seems to be promising to find its way to practical applications, since the concept of a default is occurring in many problem domains and is thus easily explained to users.

Defaults may conflict each other; in this case, there may be several extensions, each one representing one possibility of resolving inconsistency. But there are many situations, especially in applications like diagnosis, design or legal reasoning, where some of these possibilities should be disregarded for being less plausible. Technically speaking, we would like to give some defaults higher priority.

One of the major shortcomings of Reiter's original presentation of Default Logic is that it does not provide any means of expressing priorities among defaults other than putting additional information into the justifications of defaults. This approach has two disadvantages: firstly, it leads to poorly understandable and maintainable theories. And secondly, the default theories are required to go beyond normal theories that have many desirable features [12].

According to Brewka [4], the classical approaches taken to resolve these difficulties may be classified into two categories:

- approaches which handle implicit priority information that has to be specified by the user and is not part of the logical language [2,6,8,9]
- approaches that handle implicit priority information based on specificity of defaults [5,10,14,15].

The second type of approaches suffers from the drawback that specificity may not be the appropriate criterion for preferring a default to another. In legal reasoning, for example, a law may be preferred to another because it is older or because it has a higher authorization (see [7,11]).

The first type of approaches, on the other hand, is often too rigid, in that it expects from the user to give a priority ordering which is global and may not be changed over time (for example when additional information becomes available).

In a recent paper [4], Brewka has proposed an alternative approach which overcomes these difficulties. Informally speaking, he allows statements about priorities among defaults as part of the logical language, and also reasoning on priorities by default. This means that statements like

If A is true, default 1 should be usually preferred to default 2

may be expressed in the logic and treated as usual defaults would. This idea is natural and simple on one side, and extremely flexible on the other side. We believe that its expressive power is sufficient to model priorities among defaults in any application domain.

Informally speaking, the semantics definition of the logic presented in [4] takes the following approach: compute the extensions in the sense of classical default logic, and eliminate those extensions E that cannot be reconstructed as PDL extensions using an ordering which is compatible with the priority information contained in E. PDL is hereby another variant of default logic [3] based on partial orderings of defaults. This definition of the semantics can be criticized in various aspects:

- it refers to two different logics (Default Logic and PDL)
- it uses two distinct steps
- it is not constructive in the sense that after a default extension E is determined, a total ordering of defaults must be guessed which is then used in the subsequent PDL "test".

In this paper, we address the first two problems by giving a simple, operational characterization of priority extensions; the third one is replaced by a search through the space of default sequences (*processes*). It is a slight modification of a similar model for classical default logic [1]. It avoids use of PDL and of a two-step-approach by collecting the information needed while trying to establish that E is a default logic extension (in the classical sense).

Then we turn our attention to some theoretical properties of the logic. Unfortunately, our results are of a negative nature (even though not deep or surprising): by adding priority reasoning to normal default logic, the usual desirable properties of normal default theories like existence of extensions, semi-monotonicity, or goal-driven query evaluation are lost.

Finally, we look closer at the existence of extensions. Since it is not guaranteed, we give some simple sufficient conditions for default theories to possess at least one extension. Throughout the paper we assume that the reader is familiar with basic notions and notation of predicate logic, as found, e.g., in [13].

2   Basics of Default Logic

A *default* δ is a string $\frac{\varphi:\psi_1,\ldots,\psi_n}{\chi}$ with closed first-order formulae φ, $\psi_1,\ldots,\psi_n$, χ ($n > 0$). φ is the *prerequisite*, $\psi_1,\ldots,\psi_n$ the *justifications*, and χ the *consequent* of δ (which is sometimes denoted by $cons(\delta)$). A *default schema* is a string of the form $\frac{\varphi:\psi_1,\ldots,\psi_n}{\chi}$ with arbitrary formulae. Such a schema defines a set of defaults, namely the set of all ground instances $\frac{\varphi\sigma:\psi_1\sigma,\ldots,\psi_n\sigma}{\chi\sigma}$, where σ is an arbitrary ground substitution assigning terms to all free variables of $\varphi, \psi_1,\ldots,\psi_n,\chi$ ($n > 0$). δ is called a *normal default* if it has the form $\frac{\varphi:\psi}{\psi}$.

A *default theory* T is a pair (W,D) consisting of a set of closed formulae W (the set of truths) and a denumerable set of defaults D. The default set D may be defined using default schemata. T is called *normal* if all defaults in D are normal. In this paper we shall only consider finite sets of defaults D (although the concepts of this section are applicable to infinite theories, too).

Let $\delta = \frac{\varphi:\psi_1,\ldots,\psi_n}{\chi}$ be a default, and E and F sets of formulae. We say that δ *is applicable to F with respect to belief set E* iff φ is included in F, and $\neg\psi_1,\ldots,\neg\psi_n$ are not included in E. For a set D of defaults, we say that F *is closed under D with respect to E* iff, for every default δ in D that is applicable to F with respect to belief set E, its consequent χ is also contained in F.

Given a default theory $T = (W,D)$ and a set of closed formulas E, let $\Lambda_T(E)$ be the least set of closed formulas that contains W, is closed under logical conclusion and closed under D with respect to E. A set of closed formulas E is called an *extension* of T iff $\Lambda_T(E) = E$.

The above standard definition of extension is based on fixed-points. In the following, we give an alternative characterization of extensions presented in [1], because its ideas will be central for the model in section 4.

Let $T = (W,D)$ be a default theory and $\Pi = (\delta_0, \delta_1, \delta_2,\ldots)$ a finite or infinite sequence of defaults from D not containing any repetitions (modelling an application order of defaults from D). We denote by $\Pi[k]$ the initial segment of Π of length k, provided the length of Π is at least k.

(a) $In(\Pi)$ is $Th(M)$ (the first-order deductive closure of M), where M is the set of formulas of W united with all consequents of defaults occurring in Π.

(b) $Out(\Pi)$ is the set of the negations of justifications of defaults in Π.

(c) Π is called a *process of T* iff δ_k is applicable to $In(\Pi[k])$ w.r.t. belief set $In(\Pi[k])$, for every k such that δ_k occurs in Π.

(d) Π is called *successful* iff $In(\Pi) \cap Out(\Pi) = \emptyset$, otherwise it is called *failed*.

(e) Π is *closed* iff every $\delta \in D$ which is applicable to $In(\Pi)$ with respect to belief set $In(\Pi)$ already occurs in Π.

$In(\Pi)$ collects all formulae in which we believe after application of the defaults in Π, while $Out(\Pi)$ contains formulae which we should avoid to believe for the sake of consistency. The following theorem states the relationship between the extensions of a default theory T and the closed successful processes of T.

Theorem 1. *Let $T = (W, D)$ be a default theory. If Π is a closed successful process of T, then $In(\Pi)$ is an extension of T. Conversely, for every extension E of T there exists a closed, successful process Π of T with $E = In(\Pi)$.*

It is possible to get an overview of all extensions of a theory T by a systematic test of all possible processes, comprised in a so-called *process tree*. Instead of giving a formal definition, which is straightforward, we illustrate the idea by the following example. Let $T = (\emptyset, \{\frac{true:p}{p}, \frac{true:q}{\neg p}\})$. The process tree of T shows that T has exactly one extension, namely $Th(\neg p)$.

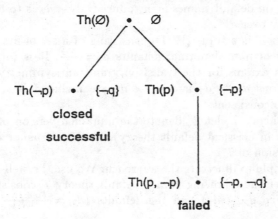

3 A system for reasoning about priorities

First we introduce a variant of default logic called PDL [3]. Theories in PDL are normal default theories $T = (W, D)$ augmented by a strict partial order $<$ on the set of defaults D. Restriction to normal default theories is justified by arguing that their expressive power is sufficient provided that means for representing priorities are available.

Definition 2. Let E be a set of formulae, and $\delta = \frac{\varphi:\psi}{\psi}$ a normal default. We say that δ is *active in E* iff $\varphi \in E$, $\psi \notin E$ and $\neg\psi \notin E$.

Definition 3. Let $T = (W, D, <)$ be a (prioritized) default theory, and $\ll$ a strict total order on D containing $<$. We say that E is the *PDL-extension of T generated by* $\ll$ iff $E = \cup E_i$, whereby E_i are defined as follows:

- $E_0 = Th(W)$
- $E_{i+1} = E_i$ if there is no default in D active in E_i.
- $E_{i+1} = Th(E_i \cup \{\psi\})$ where ψ is the consequent of the $\ll$-minimal default in D active in E_i.

Definition 4. Let $T = (W, D, <)$ be a (prioritized) default theory. E is a *PDL-extension of T* iff there is a strict total order on D which contains $<$ and generates E.

Note that *PDL* allows the user to specify priorities among defaults, but only in a rigid, predefined form. In contrast to this, the logic we shall present next (introduced in [4]) allows for far greater flexibility in specifying and reasoning about priorities. We call the logic *PRDL* for "Priority Reasoning in Default Logic". Brewka's original presentation of *PRDL* is based on *PDL*.

To be able to reason about default priorities, defaults are augmented by a (unique) name; so, named defaults have the form $d = \frac{\varphi:\psi}{\psi}$. Whenever no confusion arises, we shall assume that d_i is the name of δ_i, and that δ_i is the default with name d_i. Apart from naming defaults, a special symbol $\prec$ representing default priorities and acting on default names is introduced. $d_1 \prec d_2$ is to be read as "give default d_1 priority over d_2".

A *named default theory* T is a tuple (W, D) consisting of a set of first order formulae W and a set D of named normal defaults $d = \frac{\phi:\psi}{\psi}$. It is implicitly assumed that W contains axioms for the transitivity and antisymmetry of $\prec$. Therefore, if both assertions $d_1 \prec d_2$ and $d_2 \prec d_1$ are included in a set E containing W, E will be inconsistent.

For a named default theory T, let T' denote the unnamed version of T (in which the defaults are as in classical default theory). A *DL-extension of* T is defined as a (usual) extension of T'.

Let us look at an example to illustrate the approach. We use the well-known birds domain, and consider the following named default theory T consisting of the formulae $\{penguin, bird, d_2 \prec d_1\}$ and the defaults $\{d_1 = \frac{bird:flies}{flies}, d_2 = \frac{penguin:\neg flies}{\neg flies}\}$.

The unnamed default theory T' has two extensions: $E_1 = Th(\{penguin, bird, flies, d_2 \prec d_1\})$, and $E_2 = Th(\{penguin, bird, d_2 \prec d_1, \neg flies\})$. Intuitively, only E_2 should be a priority extension of T, since the way E_1 is derived (d_1 is preferred over d_2) is not consistent with the priority information in W, and thus in E_1. The following definitions that introduce the semantics of *PRDL* are aiming at achieving exactly this effect.

Definition 5. Let $T = (D, W)$ be a named default theory, E a a set of formulae including W, and $\ll$ a strict total order on D'. Then, $\ll$ is *compatible with* E iff

$$E \cup \{d_i \prec d_j \mid d_i = \delta_i \in D, d_j = \delta_j \in D, \delta_i \ll \delta_j\}$$

is consistent.

Definition 6. Let $T = (W, D)$ be a named default theory. E is a *priority extension* of T iff E is a DL extension of T, and E is a PDL-extension of $(W, D, \ll)$ for some total order $\ll$ that is compatible with E.

We leave it to the reader to verify that in the example above, E_2 is the only priority extension of T. The problem with the definition we have just given is first that it refers to two different variants of default logic, uses two steps, and is nonconstructive in the sense that the total order $\ll$ compatible with E has to be guessed.

In the following section we show that these difficulties are unnecessary complications of a simple intuitive idea. Indeed, the method we shall present is only a slight variation of the process tree model for the classical default logic given in section 2. We shall show that it is unnecessary to use two steps: a total order $\ll$ is not needed, and the necessary information to establish that E is a priority extension of T will be gathered along the way while trying to show that E is a DL extension of T. One consequence of the approach will be that no reference to PDL is required.

4 An operational interpretation

The interpretation of $PRDL$ we shall propose in the following is very similar to that presented in section 2 for classical default logic. In fact, the only thing we must additionally take care of is the priority information. If a default δ has been just applied instead of some others, it should not turn out that δ should not have been applied at that stage. Stated another way: when a default is applied, we decide to give it higher priority to all other defaults that are applicable at the time. This decision should remain consistent even after application of further defaults.

Since we restrict attention to *normal* defaults augmented by priority information, the Out-set is unnecessary (all processes of a normal default theory are successful). Instead, in the following we shall associate with "prioritized processes" (for a formal definition see below) a set Pri which will be used to check whether the priority decisions made are compatible with the current knowledge base (the In-set). The following figure shows the modified process tree for the example from the previous section. The left-hand branch leads to a failed situation because $In \cup Pri$ is inconsistent (it includes both $d_1 \prec d_2$ and $d_2 \prec d_1$).

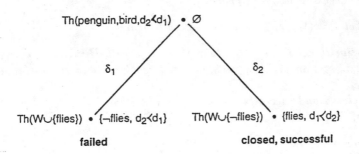

Already at this stage, the advantages of our approach should have become apparent. We do not have to use another logic; the process model is essentially the same as for default logic; the information needed to establish that E is a priority extension is gathered along the way while establishing that E is a DL extension of E. A second run w.r.t. a total order to be guessed is not needed. Finally, our method is operational, and thus easily applied.

In the following we shall give the formal definition of a (modified) process tree and prove the equivalence of our approach to Brewka's presentation. The definition here concerns the entire process tree and not one process as in section 2. The reason is clear: whereas in default logic we may analyze a process stand alone, in $PRDL$ we must take alternative defaults into consideration. This means that at each node, we have to determine all applicable defaults before proceeding along one choice.

Given a named default theory $T = (W, D)$, the *process tree proc(T)* of T consists of nodes n and edges e. With each node n, we associate sets of formulae $In(n)$ and $Pri(n)$. Also, with each edge e we associate a default $def(e)$. The root of $proc(T)$ is the node n_0 with $In(n_0) = Th(W)$ and $Pri(n_0) = \emptyset$.

Let n be any node that has already been constructed. The tree can be expanded at n in the following way: let $\delta_1, \ldots, \delta_k$ be the unnamed defaults that are applicable to $In(n)$ w.r.t. $In(n)$, and that have not been used as labels of edges on the path connecting n with the root. Then, the process tree is expanded by inserting child nodes n_i corresponding to the application of $\delta_i \in \{\delta_1, \ldots, \delta_k\}$. For each of the nodes n_i we define the In and Pri-set as follows:

$$In(n_i) = Th(In(n) \cup \{cons(\delta_i)\})$$
$$Pri(n_i) = Pri(n) \cup \{d_i \prec d_j \mid j \in \{1, \ldots, k\}, j \neq i\}.$$

n is *closed* if it is a leaf, i.e. if $k = 0$. n is *successful* iff $In(n) \cup Pri(n)$ is consistent. Finally, one notational convention: we denote the path within $proc(T)$ from the root to a node n_m by $\Pi = (n_0, < \delta_1, n_1 >, \ldots, < \delta_m, n_m >)$, whereby δ_i is $def(e_i)$ for the edge e_i connecting n_{i-1} with n_i. Note that all paths are finite since in this paper (like in [4]) we only consider finite sets D of defaults. The following theorem states the equivalence between priority extensions of T and closed and successful nodes of $proc(T)$.

Theorem 7. *Let $T = (W, D)$ be a named default theory.*

(a) *If E is a priority extension of T, then there is a path $\Pi = (n_0, < \delta_1, n_1 > , \ldots, < \delta_m, n_m >)$ in $proc(T)$ such that n_m is closed and successful, and $In(n_m) = E$.*

(b) *If n_m is a closed and successful node in $proc(T)$, then $In(n_m)$ is a priority extension of T.*

Proof. (b) :
Let n be a closed and successful node in $proc(T)$, and $\Pi = (n_0, < \delta_1, n_1 >, \ldots, < \delta_m, n_m >)$ the associated path. First note that $In(n)$ is a DL-extension of T; this is a direct implication of the fact that the In-set is defined as for default logic, and that all defaults are normal.

Consider the set $M = \{d_i \prec d_j \mid In(n) \cup Pri(n) \models d_i \prec d_j\} \cup IRREF \cup TRANS$, where $IRREF$ and $TRANS$ are the irreflexivity and transitivity axiom for $\prec$ respectively. Since n is successful, M is consistent. Therefore, there is a total ordering $\ll$ on unnamed defaults which is consistent with M. Taking such a total ordering, we show that $In(n_m)$ is the PDL-extension generated by $\ll$; then we are finished.

δ_1 is the $\ll$-minimal default applicable to $Th(W)$ w.r.t. $Th(W)$. To see this, suppose that $\delta^1,\ldots,\delta^k$ are the other applicable defaults. Then, $\delta_1 \ll \delta^i$, since $d_1 \prec d^i \in Pri(n_1)$, and therefore $d_1 \prec d^i \in M$. The same argument shows that δ_2 is the next applicable default etc.

(a):
Let E be a priority extension of T. Then, E is a DL-extension of T, and also a PDL extension of T w.r.t. a total order $\ll$ compatible with E. Let $(\delta_1,\ldots,\delta_m)$ be the defaults applied in this order to establish that E is a PDL-extension of T w.r.t. $\ll$ (according to definition 3). Then, there is a path $(n_0, <\delta_1, n_1>,\ldots, < \delta_m, n_m >)$ in $proc(T)$. Further, $In(n_m) = E$.

Now, n_m is closed since E is a DL-extension of T. Finally, n_m is also successful. Otherwise, $In(n_m) \cup Pri(n_m)$ would include some information stating that some default δ'_k should have been preferred to δ_k for a $k \in \{1,\ldots,m\}$. But δ_k was defined as the $\ll$-minimal default applicable to $In(n_{k-1})$ w.r.t. $In(n_{k-1})$. This means that $\ll$ is inconsistent with $In(n_m) = E$ which is a contradiction. □

We conclude this section with another example that demonstrates our model. Let $T = (\emptyset, \{d_1 = \frac{true:d_2 \prec d_1}{d_2 \prec d_1}, d_2 = \frac{true:d_1 \prec d_2}{d_1 \prec d_2}\})$. The following process tree shows that T has no priority extension.

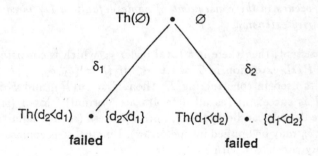

5 Discussion of properties

In classical default logic, normal default theories have some very desirable properties. These include existence of extensions, semi-monotonicity, and goal-driven query evaluation. Unfortunately, none of these properties is preserved when reasoning about priorities is added. The last example in the previous section (borrowed from [4]) shows that a named default theory may possess no priority extension.

Here is an example which shows that $PRDL$ is not semi-monotonic. Consider the theory $T = (W, D)$ with $W = \emptyset$ and $D = \{d_1 = \frac{true:a}{a}, d_2 = \frac{true:\neg a}{\neg a}\}$. T has two priority extensions, $E_1 = Th(\neg a)$ and $E_2 = Th(a)$. Now expand D as follows: $D' = D \cup \{d_3 = \frac{true:d_1 \prec d_2}{d_1 \prec d_2}\}$. The named default theory (W, D') has only the extension $E = Th(\{a, d_1 \prec d_2\})$. The priority extension E_1 of (W, D) is not included in a priority extension of (W, D').

The theory $T' = (W, D')$ of the last example also shows that a goal-driven query evaluation known from normal default theories is not possible here: the query ?- $\neg a$ fails, although we would be tempted to give a positive answer if we thought in a goal-driven way. Naturally, $PRDL$ also violates abstract properties like cumulativity, since already normal default theories do.

6 Existence of extensions

In this section we give some simple sufficient conditions for the existence of extensions of a named default theory $T = (W, D)$. In the following, we shall consider named default theories with the following restriction: for each default δ, its consequent either contains no occurrence of $\prec$, or it is an atomic formula of the form $d_i \prec d_j$. We call such theories *restricted*. If additonally the only occurrences of $d_i \prec d_j$ in W are as elements of W, then T is called *strongly restricted*.

Lemma 8. *Let T be a restricted named default theory. Suppose that $M = W \cup \{d_i \prec d_j \mid d_i \prec d_j$ occurs in the consequent of some default in $D\}$ is consistent. Then T has a priority extension.*

Proof. If M is consistent, then there is a total order $\ll$ which is consistent with M. Let E be the PDL-extension of T w.r.t. $\ll$. If $\Pi = (\delta_1, \delta_2, \ldots, \delta_n)$ is the sequence of defaults used in constructing E, then $E = In(\Pi)$, and E is a DL extension of T: Π is successful (as all defaults are normal), closed (since, by definition, no more default can be applied), and a process (as, by definition, the defaults $\delta_1, \delta_2, \ldots, \delta_n$ may be applied in this order). Finally, $\ll$ is consistent with E since it is already consistent with M. □

Lemma 9. *Let T be a strongly restricted named default theory. If no atomic formula $d_i \prec d_j$ is included in any default sequent in D, then T has always an extension.*

Proof. Suppose W is inconsistent. Then T has as (the only) extension the set of all formulae. So, suppose that W is consistent. Then, the set of formulae $d_i \prec d_j$ included in $Th(W)$ is also consistent. This means that there is some total ordering $\ll$ on the unnamed defaults of D such that

$$W \cup \{d_i \prec d_j \mid d_i = \delta_i \in D, d_j = \delta_j \in D, \delta_i \ll \delta_j\}$$

is consistent. Define E as the PDL extension generated by $\ll$. E is a DL-extension of T. It remains to show that $\ll$ is compatible with E. Because of the imposed restrictions on T, the information on $\prec$ contained in E is the same as in W. By construction, $\ll$ is compatible with E. □

We must be very careful about the sufficient conditions. For example, the above lemma is not even true for restricted default theories. To see this, consider the restricted named default theory $T = (W, D)$ with $W = \{a \to d_1 \prec d_2, \neg a \to d_2 \prec d_1\}$ and $D = \{d_1 = \frac{true:\neg a}{\neg a}, d_2 = \frac{true:a}{a}\}$. T has no priority extension, although it satisfies the other condition of Lemma 9.

Lemma 10. *Let T be a restricted named default theory such that $\prec$ does not occur in W. Let $E = In(\delta_1, \ldots, \delta_k)$ be a DL extension of T. If no formula $d \prec d_i$ and $i \in \{1, \ldots, k\}$) is a consequent of a default δ_j ($j \in \{1, \ldots, k\}$), then E is also a priority extension of T.*

Proof. On the corresponding path in $proc(T)$, the Pri-set collects formulae of the form $d_i \prec d$ while defaults $\delta_1, \ldots, \delta_k$ are being applied. If E were not a priority extension of T, then $In(n_k) \cup Pri(n_k)$ would be inconsistent for the leaf node n_k of the path in $proc(T)$. By the restrictions imposed on T, this can only happen if $d \prec d_i \in In(n_k)$ for some $d_i \prec d \in Pri(n_k)$. Now, where could this $d_i \prec d \in Out(n_k)$ come from? By the restrictions imposed on T, it can only be a member of W, a consequent of some default δ_j for $j \in \{1, \ldots, k\}$, or be derived using the transitivity of $\prec$. The first two cases are impossible (due to the conditions of the lemma); a simple inductive argument shows then that $d_i \prec d \in Out(n_k)$ could not have been introduced through transitivity. Therefore, we are finished. □

Also, if $\prec$ occurs in W, the conclusion of Lemma 10 may be wrong. Consider the strongly restricted named theory $T = (W, D)$ with $W = \{d_2 \prec d_1\}$ and $D = \{d_1 = \frac{true:a}{a}, d_2 = \frac{true:\neg a}{\neg a}\}$. $E = Th(a)$ fulfills the other conditions on E and T, but is not a priority extension of T.

7 Conclusion

We gave an alternative, operational characterization of priority extensions for Brewka's logic [4]. We think that our method of determining extensions is simpler and clearer. Therefore, we hope to contribute to making Default Logic more useable in practical applications. Also, we investigated some properties of the logic and gave some sufficient conditions for the existence of extensions.

Future work includes finding weaker sufficient conditions for the existence of extensions, and implementation of the priority reasoning method. Our operational model will be the starting point for implementation work within the CIN Project (Cchange and Information processing in Newcastle).

References

1. G. Antoniou and V. Sperschneider. Operational Interpretation of Nonmonotonic Logics - Part 1: Default Logic. *Artificial Intelligence Review*, 1994
2. G. Brewka. Preferred subtheories - an extended logical framework for default reasoning. In *Proc. IJCAI-89*, 1989
3. G. Brewka. Adding priorities and specificity to default logic. *Technical report GMD*, 1993
4. G. Brewka. Reasoning About Priorities in Default Logic. In *Proc. AAAI-94*, 1994
5. H. Geffner and J. Pearl. Conditional entailment: Bridging two approaches to default reasoning. *Artificial Intelligence* 53, 1992
6. B. Grsohof. Generalizing prioritization. In *Proc. 1st Knowledge Representation and Reasoning*, 1991
7. T. Gordon. *The Pleadings Game: An Artificial Intelligence Model for Procedural Justice*. Ph.D. Dissertation, Darmstadt 1993
8. K. Konolige. Hierarchical autoepistemic theories for nonmonotonic reasoning. In *Proc. AAAI-88*, 1988
9. V. Lifschitz. Computing circumscription. In *Proc. IJCAI-85*, 1985
10. J. Pearl. System Z: A natural ordering of defaults with tractable applications to nonmonotonic reasoning. In *Proc. Third Conference on Theoretical Aspects of Reasoning about Knowledge*, 1990
11. H. Prakken. *Logical Tools for Modelling Legal Argument*. Ph.D. Dissertation, VU Amsterdam 1993
12. R. Reiter. A logic for default reasoning. *Artificial Intelligence* 13, 1980
13. V. Sperschneider and G. Antoniou. *Logic: A Foundation for Computer Science*. Addison-Wesley 1991
14. D.S. Touretzky. *The Mathematics of Inheritance*. Pitman 1986
15. D.S. Touretzky, J.F. Horty, and R.H. Thomason. A clash of intuitions: The current state of nonmonotonic multiple inheritance systems. In *Proc. IJCAI-87*, 1987

Boolean approach for representing and solving constraint-satisfaction problems

Hachemi Bennaceur *

Abstract

In this paper, we propose a new way for representing and solving constraint-satisfaction problems (CSPs). We first show that a CSP can be modelized by a single pseudo-Boolean function. Then some theoretical results establishing the links between a CSP and its associated pseudo-Boolean function are described. We propose a Branch and Bound method exploiting this representation for solving CSPs. This method follows the same scheme developed by the Forward-Checking procedure. The main difference between the Branch and bound method and the Forward-Checking method lies in the computation performed at every node of the search tree. The Branch and Bound method uses the constraints in an active way to infer a knowledge about the problem. Then a solution or failure may be detected quickly.

1 Introduction

The constraint-satisfaction problem consists to assign values to variables which are subject to a set of constraints. This problem has many applications in artificial intelligence.

Classically, a binary constraint-satisfaction problem (CSP) is represented by a constraint graph. This representation is used both in the pre-processing phase and the search phase for solving CSPs. Some filtering concepts of CSPs are defined using the constraint graph representation such as : arc consistency, path consistency [4, 10], circuit consistency [3]. The constraint graph is also used to define an order of variables instantiation during the search. It allows the characterization of polynomial classes of CSPs instances [6].

In this paper, we propose another way for representing and solving the constraint-satisfaction problems. We first show that a constraint-satisfaction problem can be modelized as a quadratic unconstrained 0-1 minimization problem (Q) (it consists of minimizing a quadratic pseudo-Boolean function without constraints). We also show that a CSP has a solution if and only if the value of the corresponding quadratic unconstrained 0-1 minimization problem (Q) is null. This result is used to guide the search and to prune the search space.

A Branch and Bound method exploiting this representation is developed. It follows the same scheme described in the Forward-Checking procedure. The main difference between the proposed method and the Forward-Checking method lies in the computation performed at every node of the search tree. The proposed method uses the constraints in an active way to infer a knowledge about the problem. Then a solution or failure may be detected quickly. In fact, it is possible to evaluate in linear time a lower bound for the problem (Q). Then each node of the search tree is evaluated. And this evaluation can detect a failure or a solution. The functioning of this method is as follows : after the instantiation of some variables of a given CSP P, the propagation process leads naturally to filter the CSP (like in the procedure Forward-Checking); we eliminate all values directly inconsistent with the value of the last variable instantiated. Values of

---

* LIPN, CNRS URA 1507, Institut Galilée, Université Paris-Nord, avenue J.B.Clément - 93430 Villetaneuse - France. email:bennaceur@ura1507.univ-paris13.fr

some binary variables of the problem (Q) can be deduced; then either the domains of some variables of the CSP are reduced, or values are deduced for some variables of the CSP. In the last case the filtering process is repeated. The advantage of this method is the exploitation in a judicious way of the propagation process for computing an evaluation of the problem (Q). The representation (problem (Q)) used by this method co-operates with the propagation process by exchanging information in order to deduce a knowledge about the problem (reduction, detection of a failure or a solution).

The second section introduces some preliminaries about CSPs, while the following section describes the modelization process of a CSP by a pseudo-Boolean function. The fourth section presents some results for establishing the links between a CSP and its associated pseudo-Boolean function. This is followed in section 5 by a backtrack algorithm using these results. Section 6 compares the Forward-Checking procedure with our algorithm on a sample example.

2 Preliminaries

In this section, we present the formalism of CSPs introduced by Montanari[11] and some notions about CSPs. A binary CSP P is defined by (X, D, C, R), where:
-X is a set of n variables $\{X_1, X_2,...,X_n\}$;
-D is a set of n domains $\{D_1,D_2,...,D_n\}$ where each D_i is the set of the possible values for X_i;
-C is a set of m constraints where each constraint C_{ij} between the variables X_i and X_j is defined by its relation R_{ij}.
-R is a set of m relations R_{ij}, where R_{ij} is a subset of the Cartesian product $D_i \times D_j$ specifying the compatible values between X_i and X_j.
Given a CSP, the question can be to find all solutions or one solution, or to know whether there exists a solution; this problem is known to be NP-complete.
The constraint graph represents variables and constraints of the CSP in the form of a network, where each variable is represented by a vertex and each constraint by an edge.
For any constraint C_{ij}, the predicate $R_{ij}(v_i,v_j)$ holds if and only if (v_i,v_j) belongs to the relation R_{ij}.
The predicate $C(X_i, X_j)$ holds if there exists a constraint between the variables X_i and X_j.

3 A CSP as a Pseudo-Boolean Function

In this section we show that a constraint-satisfaction problem can be modelized by a quadratic pseudo-Boolean function. We recall that a pseudo-Boolean function is a function defined from $\{0, 1\}^n$ to $\mathbb{R}$. ·

3.1 Modelization

The Modelization process of a CSP as a pseudo-Boolean function leads to a complex formula with a lot of indices on variables, which can seem very hard to understand. We prefer to describe this process by an example.
Example: Given a CSP P=(X, D, C, R), with X={X_1, X_2, X_3} and D={D_1, D_2, D_3} where D_1={v_1, v_2, v_3, v_4}, D_2={v_1, v_2}, and D_3={v_1, v_2, v_3}, and the constraints C_i i=1,2,3 defined by the relations

R_{12}	
X_1	X_2
v_1	v_2
v_2	v_1
v_3	v_1
v_4	v_1
v_4	v_2

R_{13}	
X_1	X_3
v_1	v_2
v_2	v_1
v_3	v_3
v_4	v_1
v_4	v_3

R_{23}	
X_2	X_3
v_1	v_2
v_2	v_1
v_2	v_3

we associate to each variable X_i of the CSP d_i binary variables x_{ij} $j=1,...,d_i$ (where d_i is the size of D_i), such that $\qquad x_{ij}=1$ if $X_i=v_j$ $v_j \in D_i$,

$\qquad\qquad\qquad\qquad\qquad x_{ij}=0$ otherwise.

Then to X_1 is associated the set of binary variables $\{ x_{11}, x_{12}, x_{13} , x_{14}\}$, to X_2 the set $\{x_{21}, x_{22}\}$ and to X_3 the set $\{x_{31}, x_{32}, x_{33}\}$.

If C_k is a constraint between two variables X_i and X_j of the CSP, for each couple (v_r, v_s) such that $\neg R_{ij}(v_r, v_s)$ we generate a constraint

$$x_{ir} x_{js} = 0 . \qquad (1)$$

Thus for each constraint between the variables X_i and X_j of the CSP we generate at most $d_i \times d_j - 1$ constraints of type (1). Since the product $x_{ir} x_{js}$ is nonnegative, these constraints can be aggregated in a single constraint:

$$x_{11}x_{21} + x_{12}x_{22} + x_{13}x_{22} + x_{11}x_{31} + x_{11}x_{33} + x_{12}x_{32} + x_{12}x_{33} + x_{13}x_{31}$$
$$+ x_{13}x_{32} + x_{14}x_{32} + x_{21}x_{31} + x_{21}x_{33} + x_{22}x_{32} = 0 \qquad (2)$$

The following constraints express the fact that the variables X_i $i=1,...,n$ of the CSP take only one value in a solution :
$$\begin{aligned} x_{11} + x_{12} + x_{13} + x_{14} &= 1 \\ x_{21} + x_{22} &= 1 \qquad (3) \\ x_{31} + x_{32} + x_{33} &= 1 \end{aligned}$$

At this point, we can claim that the CSP has a solution if and only if the system of constraints (2) and (3) has one.

Now we can refine this system for building an equivalent pseudo-Boolean function as follows :

we use the equations of the system (3) to express some variables in function of the others. For instance
$$\begin{aligned} x_{11} &= 1 - x_{12} - x_{13} - x_{14} \\ x_{21} &= 1 - x_{22} \\ x_{31} &= 1 - x_{32} - x_{33} . \end{aligned}$$

By substitution in the system (2), we obtain a new system of constraints equivalent to (2) and (3):
$$3 - 2x_{12} - x_{13} - 2x_{14} - 2x_{22} - 2x_{32} + 2x_{12}x_{22} + 2x_{12}x_{32} + x_{12}x_{33}$$
$$+ x_{14}x_{22} + 2x_{14}x_{32} + 2x_{13}x_{22} - x_{13}x_{33} + x_{13}x_{32} + 2x_{22}x_{32} = 0 ; \qquad (4)$$
$$x_{12} + x_{13} + x_{14} \le 1; \quad x_{32} + x_{33} \le 1.$$

The constraints
$$x_{12} + x_{13} + x_{14} \le 1; \quad x_{32} + x_{33} \le 1$$
can be rewritten respectively as follows :
$$x_{12}x_{13} = 0, \quad x_{12}x_{14} = 0 \quad x_{13}x_{14} = 0;$$
$$x_{32}x_{33} = 0.$$

Since the quadratic terms are nonnegative, the system (4) is equivalent to the quadratic pseudo-Boolean equation :
$$q(x) = 3 - 2x_{12} - x_{13} - 2x_{14} - 2x_{22} - 2x_{32} + 2x_{12}x_{22} + 2x_{12}x_{32} + x_{12}x_{33}$$
$$+ x_{14}x_{22} + 2x_{14}x_{32} + 2x_{13}x_{22} - x_{13}x_{33} + x_{13}x_{32} + 2x_{22}x_{32} + x_{12}x_{13}$$
$$+ x_{12}x_{14} + x_{13}x_{14} + x_{32}x_{33} = 0.$$

We deduce that the CSP has a solution if and only if the quadratic pseudo-Boolean equation $q(x) = 0$ has one.

We consider now, the following quadratic unconstrained 0-1 minimization problem:
$$(Q) : \min q(x) .$$

Theorem 1.
The value of the problem (Q) is positive (value (Q) ≥ 0), and it is equal to 0 if and only if the CSP has a solution.
Proof.
By construction of the quadratic pseudo-Boolean equation the value of the problem (Q) is positive. And the value of (Q) is equal to 0 if and only if there exists a solution to the equation $q(x)=0$. Hence, if and only if the CSP has a solution. ◆

Obviously, the theorem is valid for any binary CSP and the equivalent quadratic pseudo-Boolean function $q(x)$ can be obtained easily following the above modelization. Moreover the problem (Q) has this form :

$$minq(x) = min\ (const + \sum_{j=1}^{N} q_j x_j + \sum_{\substack{i=1 \\ i<j}}^{N}\sum_{j=1}^{N} q_{ij} x_i x_j), \quad where\ const,\ q_j\ and\ q_{ij}\ are$$

integer constants and N is the number of binary variables of the function $q(x)$.
Notice that N is bounded by nd, where n is the number of variables of the CSP and d is the size of the largest domain of its variables.
<u>**Remark.**</u>
More generally a n-ary CSP can be modelized by a pseudo-Boolean function by following the same process.

4 Resolution of the Problem (Q)

The quadratic unconstrained 0-1 minimization problem has received several studies in the mathematical programming area. Many methods have been developed for solving this problem [2, 5, 7, 8]. Some of them identify certain polynomial classes of this problem [5]. These works can naturally be exploited for improving the solving of CSPs, and for characterizing polynomial classes of these problems.
Classically, the problem (Q) is solved by the Branch and Bound method. It is well known that this method uses two bounds (a lower and an upper bound) of the problem (Q) for pruning the search space. The size of the search tree depends on the quality of these bounds.
<u>Lower bound</u> : This bound is generally evaluated by defining a relaxation of the problem (Q). Many methods have been developed for building and solving a relaxation of a quadratic unconstrained 0-1 minimization problem[2, 7]. Unfortunately, in our case, these methods cannot be adapted or are inefficient because of the high complexity of solving these relaxations. But in our case the propagation process itself used for solving CSPs may contribute to compute a good lower bound for the problem (Q).
Then, we propose to define an adequate relaxation for the problem (Q), which can be solved in linear time. This bound is first used to see whether a CSP has a solution (corollaries 1 and 2), and in addition to filter the CSP (propositions 1 and 2).
<u>Upper bound</u> : This bound is classically computed by finding a feasible solution to the problem. For our problem (Q), the upper bound is fixed to 0, since by theorem (1) when the value of (Q) exceeds 0 the associated CSP has no solution. Then, during the searching of a solution, we prune away all subprolems[1] of (Q) whose the lower bound greater than 0.

---

[1]A subproblem of (Q) is obtained by instantiating some variables of (Q).

4.1 Relaxation of the Problem (Q)

Every quadratic pseudo-Boolean function $q(x)$ has a unique polynomial expression in its variables $x_1,...,x_N$ [8]. However, allowing the use of complemented and uncomplemented variables, denoted $\overline{x}$ and x, one can always obtain from q an expression $p(x,\overline{x})$ such that : $q(x) = p(x,\overline{x}) + q_0$

where q_0 is a constant and $p = p_1T_1 + p_2T_2 +...+ p_mT_m$,

where all p_i are positive constants (i=1,...,m) and T_i's are literals or products of two literals, (a literal being a complemented or an uncomplemented variable). p is called a posiform associated to the function q, and in general it is not unique (e. g. $x_1+ \overline{x}_1 x_2 = x_2+ x_1 \overline{x}_2$). A posiform can be supposed normal, i.e. $T_i \ne T_j$ for $i \ne j$ and $T_i= c_ix_k$ C implies that for all $j \ne i$, $T_j \ne c_j \overline{x}_kC$, where C is the constant 1 or a literal.

The quadratic Boolean function $\widehat{p} = T_1 \vee T_2 \vee ... \vee T_m$ is called the Boolean span of p (i.e. $\widehat{p}$ is a 2-SAT problem in a disjunctive form).

4.2. Construction of a Posiform of a Quadratic Pseudo-Boolean Function

Given a CSP P and its associated quadratic pseudo-Boolean function with N variables

$$q(x) = const + \sum_{j=1}^{N} q_j x_j + \sum_{i=1}^{N} \sum_{\substack{j=1 \\ i<j}}^{N} q_{ij} x_i x_j \, ,$$

the following rules can be applied to compute a posiform p^2 (the rules are applied while it is possible) :

rule 1 : - if $q_j < 0$ then replace x_j by $1- \overline{x}_j$.

rule 2 : - if $q_{ij} < 0$ then replace $-x_ix_j$ by

$$x_i \overline{x}_j + \overline{x}_i - 1 \text{ if } q_i \ne 0;$$
$$\overline{x}_ix_j + \overline{x}_j - 1 \text{ otherwise.}$$

rule 3 : let $\overline{q}_i$ and $\overline{q}_j$ be the coefficients of $\overline{x}_i$ and $\overline{x}_j$
- if $\overline{q}_i>0$, $\overline{q}_j>0$ and $q_{ij}>0$ then let $v=\min \{ \overline{q}_i , \overline{q}_j, q_{ij} \}$;

$$\text{replace } v(\overline{x}_i + x_ix_j) \text{ by } v(x_j + \overline{x}_i \overline{x}_j),$$

rule 4 : - replace $vx_i + v' \overline{x}_i$ by

$$v + (v' - v) \overline{x}_i \text{ if } v' > v$$
$$v' + (v - v')x_i \text{ otherwise.}$$

Obviously, the obtained constant q_0 is a lower bound of $q(x)$, since by definition the posiform is positive then $q(x) \ge q_0$ for all $x \in \{0,1\}^N$.

A posiform of the CSP of the previous example is :

$p(x, \overline{x}) = 2\overline{x}_{13} + x_{13}\overline{x}_{33} + 2\overline{x}_{12}\overline{x}_{22} + 2\overline{x}_{14}\overline{x}_{32} + 2x_{12}x_{32} + x_{12}x_{33} + x_{14}x_{22} + 2x_{13}x_{22} +$

$x_{13}x_{32} + 2x_{22}x_{32} + x_{12}x_{13} + x_{12}x_{14} + x_{13}x_{14} + x_{32}x_{33}$

---

[2]Neither the posiform nor its associated constant q_0 are uniquely determined by the rules.

and q_0 is equal to -3. The quadratic pseudo-Boolean function of this CSP can be rewritten as follows : $q(x)= -3 + p(x, \overline{x})$, (p defined above).

If δ is the number of the quadratic terms of the pseudo-Boolean function $q(x)$ associated to a given CSP, the complexity of computing a posiform is in $O(\delta)$. Notice that δ is bounded by md^2, where m is the number of constraints of the CSP and d the largest domain of its variables.

Corollary 1. The CSP P has no solution if the constant q_0 is strictly greater than 0.
Proof.
Let (Q) : min $q(x)$ be the quadratic unconstrained minimization problem associated to the CSP P, and q_0 the constant obtained after applying the above rules to $q(x)$.
Since $q_0 \leq$ value(Q), if $q_0 > 0$ then the value of (Q) is greater than 0. Hence by theorem (1), the CSP P has no solution.   ◆

Corollary 2. If the constant q_0 is equal to 0, then the CSP has a solution if and only if $\widehat{p}$ (the Span of p) is consistent.
Proof.
Let p be a posiform obtained after applying the above rules to q(x), and $\widehat{p}$ its span. If the Boolean equation $\widehat{p}\,(x, \overline{x})=0$ is consistent and $q_0=0$ then there exists an affectation of values in $\{0, 1\}$ for x_i i=1,...,N such that $q(x)=0$ and the value of (Q) is equal to 0. Hence, by theorem (1) the CSP P has a solution. Else (i.e. the Span is inconsistent) $p(x, \overline{x}) > 0$, then by theorem (1) the CSP P has no solution.   ◆
Checking consistency of a quadratic Boolean equation requires $O(\delta)$ time [1], where δ is the number of quadratic terms.

4.3 Reduction of the CSP.
We use the previous results for fixing definitively some variables of the CSP. The following propositions allow either the fixation of a variable X_i of a CSP to a value v_r $\in D_i$ if $x_{ir}=1$, or the elimination of a value v_r from D_i if $x_{ir}=0$.
Proposition 1.
If, after assigning the value $\theta \in \{0,1\}$ to x_j, either the constant q_0 becomes strictly greater than 0, or becomes equal to 0 and the span $\widehat{p}$ of the posiform p is not consistent, then x_j must be fixed definitively to $1-\theta$.
Proof.
As is shown below the associated quadratic pseudo-Boolean equation to the CSP P can be rewritten as follows : $q(x) = q_0 + p(x, \overline{x})$.
Setting x_j to θ in $q(x)$, the quadratic pseudo-Boolean equation becomes
$$q(x) = q'_0 + p'(x, \overline{x}).$$
It is clear that $p'(x, \overline{x})$ is a posiform, and if q'_0 is greater than 0 then we deduce from corollary (2) that the CSP P with $x_j=\theta$ hypothesis has no solution, then x_j must take the value $1-\theta$ in all solutions. In the same way, if $q'_0 =0$ and the span $\widehat{p}$ is not consistent the variable x_j must take the value $1-\theta$ in all solutions.   ◆

Proposition 2 [5].

Let x* be an optimal solution of (Q), if there exists k such that :

$$q_k + \sum_{j=1\,j\neq k}^{n} min(0, q_{jk} + q_{kj}) > 0 \quad (resp.\, q_k + \sum_{j=1\,j\neq k}^{n} max(0, q_{jk} + q_{kj}) < 0)$$

then, in x*, x_k must take the value 0 (resp. the value 1).

Notice that, by definition of $q(x)$, q_{jk} is null if j>k; since j≠k then either q_{jk} or q_{kj} is null.

The application of the proposition (2) leads to reduce considerably the search space. Using this proposition, we can eliminate some values of the domains of certain variables which can belonging to a solution of the CSP, then some solutions of the CSP, if it has, can be not considered. But we are sure that we do not eliminate all solutions.

5 Search

The search of a solution to a CSP exploits simultaneously the data of the CSP (the domains of variables and the relations) and its associated modelization with a pseudo-Boolean function in complementary way. The theoretical results presented above are used at every node of the search tree for filtering the associated subproblem and for detecting quickly a failure or a solution.

In fact, After the instantiation of some variables of a given CSP P, naturally the propagation process leads to filter the CSP (like in the procedure Forward-Checking). The knowledge deduced is also propagated over the quadratic pseudo-Boolean function, then the above results are applied to the problem (Q), to infer other knowledge about the problem. So, this propagation process is repeated while a new knowledge about the problem is inferred.

Let $q(x) = q_0 + p(x, \overline{x})$ be the associated pseudo-Boolean function of the CSP P. In the following section, we present the treatment performed at the node k of the search tree.

5.1 Treatment Performed at the Node k of the Search Tree

Let us assume that some variables of the CSP P are instantiated, then some binary variables of the problem (Q) will be assigned to 0 or 1. Let I_0, I_1 be the sets of variables assigned respectively to 0 and 1, and I_2 the set of variables non-assigned.

The pseudo-Boolean function of the subproblem associated to the node k is

$$q(x^{(k)}) = q'_0 + p'(x^{(k)}, \overline{x}^{(k)}) \text{ where } q'_0 = q_0 + v,$$

where v is a nonnegative constant and p' is a posiform depending on the variables of I_2 (notice that the quadratic pseudo-Boolean function of a CSP is computed only once, $q(x^{(k)})$ is obtained by the propagation of values of the instantiated variables on $q(x)$ and the application of the two last rules described above).

5.1.1 Reduction of the Subproblem ($P^{(k)}$)

We first apply the classical filtering like in the Forward-Checking procedure; we eliminate all directly inconsistent values with the value of the last variable instantiated. Then, some binary variables of the problem (Q) will be assigned to 0 or 1. The values are reported on the pseudo-Boolean equation. Using the above results (proposition (1) and (2)), values of some binary variables of the problem (Q) can be deduced, then either the domains of some variables of the CSP are reduced, or values are deduced for some variables of the CSP. In the last case the filtering process is repeated.

The filtering process consists in :

- eliminating all directly inconsistent values with the value of the last variable instantiated.
- applying the propositions (1) and (2) to the subproblem $P^{(k)}$ for inferring the values of certain variables.

5.1.2 Backtracking cases
A backtracking is performed if one of these conditions is verified :

(i) there exists an empty domain D_i, where i belongs to the set of non-instantiated variables of the CSP; or there exists an empty relation R_{kj} between two non-instantiated variables X_k and X_j.

(ii) the constant q'_0 of $q(x^{(k)})$ is strictly greater than 0 (in this case, it is not necessary to solve the associated subproblem because the value of the problem (Q) will be greater than 0 (corollary 1)), the node does not lead to a solution.

(iii) the constant q'_0 is equal to 0, then
- either the associated *Span* is consistent, then there exists a solution such that the value of the problem (Q) is equal to 0, and the corresponding CSP has a solution. Hence, the search is stopped,
- or, the associated *Span* is inconsistent, then the value of the subproblem $P^{(k)}$ is greater than 0 and the node does not lead to a solution.

5.2 Algorithms
An algorithm for solving constraint-satisfaction problems is provided in fig. 1. This algorithm explores the search space of solutions following the depth first search strategy. At each node of the search tree, a variable and a value are chosen using one of the classical heuristics. Then, the procedure of filtering is solicited.

SEARCH (D, k, q_0, p, q^3)
$(D=\{D_1, D_2,..., D_n\})$
if k=n then a solution is found

else $D' \leftarrow D, p' \leftarrow p, q' \leftarrow q, q'_0 \leftarrow q_0$
         choose a variable X_i from X (X is the set of non-instantiated variables)
         choose a value v_r from D_i
         instantiate X_i to v_r
         delete v_r from D_i

         backtrack $\leftarrow$ FILTER $(D, k, i, v_r, q_0, p, q)$
         if backtrack then
         While D_i is not empty do
                 SEARCH(D', k, q'_0, p', q')
         else
                 SEARCH$(D, k+1, q_0, p, q)$

Fig. 1. A backtracking algorithm.

---

[3] q is the quadratic pseudo-Boolean function obtained by the modelization process.

A procedure for filtering CSPs during the search is provided in Fig. 2. It is essentially a translation of the classical propagation process (elimination of inconsistent values with the value of the last instantiated variable) using the criteria of existence of a solution given in the above corollaries.

FILTER (D, k, i, v_r, q_0, **p**, q)
$I_0 \leftarrow$ empty, $I_1 \leftarrow \{ir\}$
(I_0, I_1 are the sets of binary variables assigned respectively to 0 and 1)
consistency $\leftarrow$ true
while consistency **do**
    for each X_j : $C(X_i, X_j)$ **do**
        for each value v_c in D_j **do**
            if $\neg R_{ij}(v_r, v_c)$ **then**
            delete v_c from D_j
            $I_0 \leftarrow I_0 \cup \{jc\}$ (i.e. $X_j \neq v_c$ then $x_{jc}=0$)
            if D_j is empty **then** return(true)
        COMPUTE(I_0, I_1, q_0, **p**)
        if $q_0 > 0$ **then** return(true) (corollary 1)
        if $q_0 = 0$ **then**
        if the span of **p** is consistent
            then exit, the CSP has a solution (corollary 2),
            else return(true) (corollary 2)
        consistency $\leftarrow$ REDUCE(D, k, I_0, I_1, q_0, **p**, q)
return(false)

Fig. 2. A filtering procedure.

The procedure REDUCE translates the reduction tests of the propositions 1 and 2. It can be applied if a backtrack is not generated in the procedure FILTER.

REDUCE(D, k, I_0, I_1, q_0, **p**, q)
for each linear term $q_{jc} x_{jc}$ of **p** **do**
    COMPUTE($\{\}$, $\{jc\}$, q_0, **p**)
    if $q_0 > 0$ or ($q_0 =0$ and the span of **p** is not consistent)
        then delete v_{jc} from D_j (proposition 1)
        $I_0 \leftarrow I_0 \cup \{jc\}$
for each linear term $\overline{q}_{jc} \overline{x}_{jc}$ of **p** **do**
    COMPUTE($\{jc\}$, $\{\}$, q_0, **p**)
    if $q_0 > 0$ or ($q_0 =0$ and the span of **p** is not consistent)
        then k $\leftarrow$ k+1 (the variable X_j must take the value v_c, proposition 1)
        $I_1 \leftarrow \{jc\}$
        return(true)
for each linear term $q_{jc} x_{jc}$ of $q(x)$ such that $q_{jc} \geq 0$ **do**
    if $q_{j_c} + \sum_{i_r=1, j_c \neq i_r}^{n} min(0, q_{j_c i_r} + q_{i_r j_c}) > 0$

then $I_0 \leftarrow I_0 \cup \{jc\}$
delete v_c from D_j (proposition 2)
update $q(x)$ $(x_{jc} \leftarrow 0)$
for each linear term $q_{jc}x_{jc}$ of $q(x)$ such that $q_{jc} \leq 0$ do

$$\text{if } q_{j_c} + \sum_{i_r = 1 j_c \neq i_r}^{n} max(0, q_{j_c i_r} + q_{i_r j_c}) < 0$$

then $k \leftarrow k+1$ (the variable X_j must take the value v_c, proposition 2)
$I_1 \leftarrow \{jc\}$
update $q(x)$ $(x_{jc} \leftarrow 1)$
return(true)

return(false).

Fig 3. A reduction procedure

The following procedure computes the value of q_0 when some binary variables of the posiform **p** are known.

COMPUTE(I_0, I_1, q_0, **p**)
(I_0, I_1 are the sets of binary variables of **p** assigned respectively to 0 and 1)
$v \leftarrow 0$
for each index jc in I_0 do

replace x_{jc} by 0 and $\overline{x}_{jc}$ by 1 in **p**

$v \leftarrow v +$ constant terms of **p**

apply the rules (3) and (4) on **p**

for each index ir in I_1 do

replace x_{ir} by 1 and $\overline{x}_{ir}$ by 0 in **p**

$v \leftarrow v +$ constant terms of **p**

apply the rules (3) and (4) on **p**

$q_0 \leftarrow q_0 + v$

Fig. 4. A procedure for computing the constant q_0 of the posiform **p**.

6 Analysis

6.1 Complexity Analysis
In this section we evaluate the complexity of reduction and backtracking tests used in the method.
Given a CSP P with n variables, and let d be the size of the largest domains of its variables. The complexity of the reduction and backtracking tests (except the third backtracking test, (iii) of 5.1.2.) are linear in $O(|I_2|)$, where I_2 is the set of non-instantiated variables, $|I_2|$ is bounded by nd.

Concerning the third backtracking test, the complexity of checking consistency of the *Span* is linear in the number of its quadratic terms, it is bounded by md^2, where m is the number of constraints of P.

Notice that, when the last backtracking case is applied, either a solution is found, or a backtracking is effected.

6.2 Comparison with Forward-Checking

The difference between the Branch and Bound method and the Forward-Checking method is situated in the computation performed at every node of the search tree. The method uses the constraints in an active way to infer a knowledge about the problem.

In fact, when considering a value v for a variable X_i of a given CSP, Forward-Checking prunes away all the values inconsistent with v. As we have seen, the proposed method will in addition perform some tests for pruning away other values and detecting a failure or a solution quickly. The evaluation of nodes of the search tree integrated in the propagation process allows the deduction of an important knowledge about the CSP during the search.

Reconsider the CSP of the previous example. Its associated pseudo-Boolean function is

$q(x) = -3 + p(x, \bar{x})$ (where $p(x, \bar{x})$ is the posiform computed in section 4.2.).

When we instantiate x_{12} to 1 (X_1 to v_2), the propagation process implies $x_{22} = x_{33} = x_{32} = x_{13} = x_{14} = 0$, and the value of (Q) will be equal to 1. Then by theorem (1) a backtracking will be generated. In the same way the Forward-Checking method deduces that $D_2 = \{v_1\}$ and $D_3 = \{v_1\}$. The instantiation of X_2 to v_1 leads to an inconsistency since D_3 becomes empty; then a backtracking is generated. So, another value is assigned to X_1. Let v_4 be this value ($x_{14} = 1$), the propagation process leads to $x_{12} = x_{13} = x_{32} = 0$, this information is propagated in the posiform of the quadratic pseudo-Boolean equation. Then $q(x)$ becomes equal to $\bar{x}_{22}$. q_0 is equal to 0 and the Span $\bar{x}_{22}$ is consistent ($x_{22} = 1$). Hence, by corollary (2) the CSP has a solution. Let see now what happens when we use the Forward-Checking method. When X_1 is instantiated to v_4, the value v_2 is eliminated from D_3 ($D_2 = \{v_1, v_2\}$, $D_3 = \{v_1, v_3\}$). The instantiation of X_2 to v_1 leads to a failure. Then, when X_2 is instantiated to the value v_2 we instantiate X_3, for example, to v_1, (v_3 would be convenient), a solution is found for this CSP.

We observe on this simple example that the propagation of the knowledge between the data of the CSP and its pseudo-Boolean function reduces the number of explored nodes of the search space.

The fig. 5.a and 5.b summarize the solving of the problem by the Forward-Checking procedure and our method.

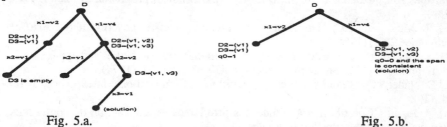

Fig. 5.a.   Fig. 5.b.

7 Conclusion

We have proposed a backtrack algorithm for solving a constraint-satisfaction problem. It follows the same scheme described in the Forward-Checking procedure. The main difference between the proposed method and the Forward-Checking method lies in the computation performed at every node of the search tree.

The representation of a CSP by a pseudo-Boolean function allows the evaluation in linear time of each node of the search tree. Then a solution or a failure may be detected prematurely. This representation is also used to define some filtering tests (proposition 1 and 2). The advantage of our method is the use of the constraints of the problem in an active way to infer a knowledge. In fact, the representation puts in interaction all constraints of the problem, and then the problem can be considered globally during the search, and the quantity of knowledge inferred can be more important than if it were considered partially.

In the Forward-Checking procedure, the propagation process is not substantially exploited. The Branch and Bound method can be seen as a way to improve this propagation. As shown in section 6, the classical filtering used in the Forward-Checking procedure (elimination of values inconsistent with the value of the last instantiated variable) can be exploited by the pseudo-Boolean function for obtaining a good evaluation of the nodes during the search. Hence, this leads to reduce considerably the search space.

References

[1] B. Aspvall, M.F. Plass and R.E. Tarjan, "A linear algorithm for testing the truth of certain quantified Boolean formulas", Information Processing Letters 8, 121-123, (1979).
[2] F. Barahona, M. Jüngler and G. Reinelt, "Experiments in quadratic 0-1 programming", Mathematical Programming 44, 127-137 (1989).
[3] H. Bennaceur, "Partial consistency for constraint-satisfaction problems", Proceedings of the 11th European Conference on Artificial Intelligence, 120-125, (1994).
[4] C. Bessière, "Arc-consistency and arc-consistency again", Research Note, Vol. 65, 1, 179-190, (1994).
[5] Y. Crama, "Recognition problems for special classes of polynomials in 0-1 variables", Mathematical Programming 44, 127-137, (1989).
[6] E.C.Freuder, "A sufficient condition for backtrack-free search", Journal of the ACM, vol. 29 n° 1, 24-32, (1982).
[7] V.P. Gulti, S.K. Gupta and A.K. Mittal, "Unconstrained quadratic bivalent programming problem", European Journal of Operational Research 15, 121-125, (1994).
[8] P.L. Hammer and P. Hansen, "Logical relations in quadratic 0-1 optimization", Revue roumaine de mathématiques pures et appliqués, tome XXVI, n° 3, 421-429, (1981).
[9] P.L. Hammer, P. Hansen and B. Simeoné, "Roof Duality, complementation and persistency in quadratic 0-1 optimization", Mathematical programming, 28, 121-155, (1984).
[10] R. Mohr and T.C. Hendeson, "Arc and path consistency revisited", Artificial Intelligence 28-2, (1986).
[11] U. Montanari, "Networks of constraints: Fundamental properties and applications to picture processing", Information Sciences, vol. 7 n°2, 95-132, (1974).
[12] B. Nadel, "Constraint satisfaction algorithms", Computational Intelligence, 5, 188-224, (1986).
[13] P. Jegou, "Contribution à l'étude des problèmes de satisfaction de contraintes", Thèse de Doctorat, Montpellier II, France, (1991).
[14] A. Sutter, "Programmation non linéaire en variables 0-1", Thèse de doctorat du CNAM (Paris), (1989).

Composing decision procedures: the approach and a case study*

Mauro Di Manzo
Paolo Pecchiari

Mechanized Reasoning Group
DIST – University of Genova, 16145 Genova, Italy
{mauro,peck}@dist.unige.it

Keywords: interactive theorem proving, decision procedures

Abstract. In this paper we address the problem of strengthening the inferential capabilities of an interactive theorem prover with complex and reusable proof procedures. We focus on the construction of proof procedures built out of decision procedures for (decidable) quantifier-free theories. The idea is to build proof procedures in a structured way. A set of deciders provides the low-level reasoning capabilities, while the high-level (*i.e.* strategical) reasoning procedures are to be synthesized on top of it. The main goal of the paper is to show that this approach has many advantages and is of wide applicability. As a case study we consider the synthesis of a proof procedure for the existential fragment of first order logic built on top of a propositional decider. This procedure is particularly well suited for describing our approach, since in it there is a neat separation between the propositional and the first order reasoning components.

1 Introduction

In this paper we consider the problem of strengthening the inferential capabilities of an interactive theorem prover with complex and reusable proof procedures. So far, the most noticeable works concerned with the integration of decision procedures inside theorem proving systems have been developed in the setting of completely automated theorem proving. For example:

- Nelson and Oppen [NO78] face the problem of integrating decision procedures for disjoint theories (namely the theory of reals under addition, a theory of list structure, and a theory of arrays);
- Boyer and Moore [BM88] study the problem of integrating a decision procedure for linear arithmetic within their prover;

* The authors want to thank Alessandro Armando, Enrico Giunchiglia, and Fausto Giunchiglia for the many invaluable suggestions and comments. This work has been supported by the Italian National Research Council (CNR), Progetto Finalizzato Sistemi Informatici e Calcolo Parallelo (Special Project on Information Systems and Parallel Computing).

– Stickel [Sti85] shows how resolution can be enhanced by exploiting a set of
  deciders for disjoint theories (namely the theory of partial ordering and a
  taxonomic theory).

All these works are concerned with building and integrating procedures specialized to deal with particular subproblems w.r.t. a given general and uniform proof
strategy. Their main goal is to increment the efficiency and/or the applicability
of the theorem prover.

The situation is quite different for interactive theorem proving systems. In
fact in such systems the heuristic strategy is not fixed. Their main feature is that
of providing the means for expressing and executing user-defined proof strategies. Unfortunately, due to the simplicity of the basic inference steps typically
provided by an interactive prover, the activity of designing and implementing
complex proof strategies may turn out to be a laborious and hard task. Enriching the system with a set of predefined proof procedures is a way to overcome
this difficulty. Hence in this setting decision procedures are not only regarded as
tools for speeding up the system, but as *building blocks* to be used for facilitating
the synthesis of higher level proof strategies. The idea underlying the approach
we propose in this paper is to build proof procedures in a structured way. A
set of decision procedures for (decidable) quantifier-free theories provides the
low-level reasoning capabilities, while the high-level (*i.e.* strategical) reasoning
procedures are to be synthesized on top of it.

We think that this approach has many advantages and is of wide applicability.
First of all, deciders for quantifier-free theories provide the right building blocks
for designing and implementing complex and higher level proof procedures. In
fact, most of the proof procedures are composed by steps of propositional reasoning intermixed with steps carrying out higher level strategical functionalities
(*e.g.* the expansion of (part of) the formula, the unfolding of definitions, or the
choice of the inductive argument). Second, this approach guarantees that decidability and efficiency are retained on important (decidable) subclasses, while
uniform proof strategies often sacrifice them for the sake of generality. As shown
in [Joy76], resolution is not a decision procedure for most solvable classes; even
the refinements proposed in [Joy76], while succeeding in turning resolution into
a decider for several solvable classes, are still unable to achieve the same result
for the Bernays-Schönfinkel class (*i.e.* the class of prenex universal-existential
formulas without function symbols). Finally, the modularity of the procedures
assures that any modification in the implementation can be accomplished locally
(which is a desirable property from a software engineering standpoint).

In this paper we consider as a case study the synthesis of a proof procedure (called FOLTAUT) for the existential fragment of first order logic (prenex
existential formulas without function symbols). The particular proof strategy
adopted for FOLTAUT (based on the *partial instantiation technique* first introduced in [Jer88]) is particularly well suited for describing our approach, since
in it there is a sharp separation between the following two activities: generation
of instances of the formula to be proven and propositional analysis to establish
whether the disjunction of the instances so far generated is a tautology. Being

already provided with deciders for quantifier-free theories, the realization of the proof procedure has been limited to the implementation of the generation step and of the high level strategy supervising the interplay of the two main steps.

The work presented in this paper (and in the companion paper [AG93]) is part of a wider project aiming at enriching interactive theorem provers with complex proof procedures.

Outline: In order to give the flavor of the whole project and to make the paper self-contained, we present in section 2 the set of deciders presented in [AG93] (and implemented in the GETFOL system [Giu92]) and give in section 3 some hints on how complex proof procedures can be built out of them. The FOLTAUT procedure is presented and discussed in section 4. Section 5 contains some final remarks.

2 The System of Deciders

In the GETFOL system we have implemented a hierarchical and modular structure of procedures which can be either invoked individually or jointly with the others. At the bottom of the hierarchy there are deciders (namely PTAUT and PTAUTEQ) working on a quantifier-free first order language (hereon by abuse of language we call them propositional deciders). PTAUT decides the set of first order formulas provable using only the propositional deductive machinery (moreover it returns a falsifying assignment whenever the input formula is not a tautology). For instance, the formula $(P(x) \wedge R(x,b)) \rightarrow (P(x) \vee R(x,b))$ can be easily inferred by a single application of PTAUT. PTAUT is a generalization of the Davis-Putnam-Loveland procedure (hereon DPL)[DP60] to non clausal formulas. The core of PTAUT is a procedure capable of partially evaluating the input formula w.r.t. a partial assignment of truth-values to the atomic subformulas.

PTAUTEQ is the result of adapting PTAUT to take into account the properties of equality. The main difference is that, before a formula is simplified w.r.t. some (partial) assignment, the assignment is tested to check whether it is model of the quantifier-free theory of equality. The formula $(P(x) \wedge x = y) \rightarrow (P(y) \wedge y = x)$ can be easily inferred by a single application of PTAUTEQ.

On top of the propositional deciders there are two rewriting procedures (namely tautren and phexp), mapping the first-order formula in input into a quantifier-free formula. The mappings are such that the decision problem of the input (first-order) formula is related to the decision problem of the returned (quantifier-free) formula in a useful way. In particular, tautren atomizes equal (modulo renaming of bound variables) quantified subformulas into newly introduced propositional letters. For instance the formula

$$(\exists x.F(x) \wedge \exists x.G(x)) \rightarrow ((\forall x.(F(x) \rightarrow H(x)) \wedge \forall x.(G(x) \rightarrow J(x))) \leftrightarrow \\ ((\exists y.G(y) \rightarrow \forall x.(F(x) \rightarrow H(x))) \wedge \\ (\exists x.F(x) \rightarrow \forall y.(G(y) \rightarrow J(y))))) \tag{1}$$

is mapped into the propositional formula

$$(A \wedge B) \rightarrow ((C \wedge D) \leftrightarrow ((B \rightarrow C) \wedge (A \rightarrow D))) \qquad (2)$$

The relation between the decision problems of the input formula (say α) and of the output formula (say α') is that $\vdash \alpha'$ only if $\vdash \alpha$.

A more careful reduction to the quantifier-free fragment is performed by **phexp**. **phexp** maps an existential formula α into a quantifier-free formula α' such that $\vdash \alpha'$ if and only if $\vdash \alpha$. The formula α' is an improved version of the Herbrand's expansion of α [DG79]. An application of **phexp** to the following formula:

$$(((P(x) \wedge \neg Q(y)) \vee ((Q(a) \vee R(a)) \wedge (\neg Q(b) \vee \neg S(b)))) \vee$$
$$((F(z) \wedge \neg G(z)) \wedge S(v))) \vee ((\neg P(c) \vee \neg F(c)) \vee G(c)) \qquad (3)$$

yields

$$((((P(a) \vee P(b) \vee P(c)) \wedge (\neg Q(a) \vee \neg Q(b) \vee \neg Q(c))) \vee$$
$$((Q(a) \vee R(a)) \wedge (\neg Q(b) \vee \neg S(b)))) \vee$$
$$(((F(a) \wedge \neg G(a)) \vee (F(b) \wedge \neg G(b)) \vee (F(c) \wedge \neg G(c))) \wedge$$
$$(S(a) \vee S(b) \vee S(c)))) \vee ((\neg P(c) \vee \neg F(c)) \vee G(c)) \qquad (4)$$

In [AG93] it is shown that, the size of (4) is 44 times smaller than the size of the standard Herbrand's expansion of (3).

At the top of the hierarchy there is the **reduce** rewriting procedure. **reduce** tries a set of truthful preserving rewriting rules on the input formula aiming at rewriting it into a logically equivalent formula that can be easily turned into an existential one via skolemization. The rewriting rules employed by **reduce** are the usual rules expressing the distributivity of quantifiers through propositional connectives and the commutativity and associativity of propositional connectives. For instance, a single application of **reduce** turns the formula

$$(\exists x. F(x) \wedge \exists x. G(x)) \rightarrow ((\forall x. (F(x) \rightarrow H(x)) \wedge \forall x. (G(x) \rightarrow J(x))) \leftrightarrow$$
$$(\forall x. \forall y. ((F(x) \wedge G(y)) \rightarrow (H(x) \wedge J(y))))) \qquad (5)$$

into (1). **reduce** considerably enlarges the set of formulas which can be solved by using the system of deciders (e.g. the *monadic calculus* can be reduced to the existential fragment by means of **reduce**).

3 Building Complex Proof Procedures

New powerful proof procedures can be easily built by exploiting the functionalities provided by the predefined procedures presented in the previous section. For instance, a decider for the existential fragment can be assembled by combining **phexp** with a propositional decider (*e.g.* either **PTAUT** or **PTAUTEQ**). The resulting decider can easily solve the formula (3) by applying **PTAUT** to the result of the application of **phexp** (*i.e.* the formula (4)). Extending such a procedure with an application to **reduce** (*i.e.* the proof strategy invoking **reduce**, **phexp** and **PTAUT** in sequence) we obtain a decider for the monadic calculus.

However, even if such procedures considerably enrich the inferential capabilities of the prover, they suffer of intrinsic limitations. In particular, even if smaller in size than the standard Herbrand's expansion, the formula generated by `phexp` may still have (in the worst case) exponential dimension in the number of existential variables occurring in the input formula. This severely limits the applicability of procedures defined in terms of `phexp`. More effective proof strategies can be synthesized by observing that Herbrand's theorem suggests an algorithmic schema characterized by the iteration of two distinguished phases: generation of sets of instances of the initial formula and propositional testing to establish whether the disjunction of the instances so far generated is a tautology.

The proof procedures proposed in the past differ in the degree of interplay between the two steps. Gilmore's procedure [Gil60] is a straightforward realization of the previous schema. It builds an enumeration $S_1, S_2, \ldots$ of sets of ground instances and at each step applies a tautology checker. The major drawback of the approach resides in the fact that the invocation of the tautology checker does not exploit the computation carried out in previous calls. Prawitz (in [Pra60]) is apparently the first to recognize that a significant gain in effectiveness could be achieved by making the instances generation phase be driven by the propositional analysis. A further step is then accomplished by Robinson who collapses the two steps into a unique and uniform inference rule, *i.e. resolution.* However resolution is inherently a *local* inference rule. The major drawback of this fact is that even trivial theorems require several applications of the rule. The latest generation of procedures [And81, Bib82] have rediscovered the separation between the two steps of instance generation and propositional analysis (which - adopting Andrews' terminology - are called *amplification* and search over the set of *vertical paths* respectively).

The key characteristic of `FOLTAUT` is a neat separation between such two activities which can be naturally implemented in a modular way. Roughly speaking the procedure implements the following strategy:

1. a decider for a quantifier-free theory (*e.g.* `PTAUT`) is applied to the input formula[2] in order to determine whether it is a tautologous formula;
2. if the previous step yields a positive answer, then the procedure halts reporting that the initial formula is valid; otherwise,
3. given a falsifying assignment, the procedure searches for a set of instances whose disjunction is true on all the possible extensions of the falsifying assignment. If such a set of instances is not found then the procedure halts reporting that the initial formula is falsifiable. Otherwise a new falsifying assignment is searched and the whole process iterated.

Before presenting `FOLTAUT` in detail it is worth emphasizing that neither `FOLTAUT` nor anyone of the previously described procedures require the input formula to be in a particular normal form. Besides complexity considerations, the translation in any normal form often obscures the form of the original formula and this is particularly bad in an interactive theorem proving setting.

---

[2] We assume that a preliminary step of skolemization has been already carried out.

4   Case Study: the FOLTAUT Procedure

Hereinafter we assume that $\exists x_1, \ldots, x_m.\beta(x_1, \ldots, x_m)$ denotes the closed formula to be proven, where $\beta(x_1, \ldots, x_m)$ is a quantifier-free formula without function symbols. We define D_β to be the set of constants in $\beta(x_1, \ldots, x_m)$ (if there are none, we pick out a newly introduced constant c). By a *substitution* $\sigma = \{x_1/t_1, \ldots, x_m/t_m\}$ we mean a map from the variables of $\beta(x_1, \ldots, x_m)$ to terms such that each t_i is either x_i or an element in D_β. By an *instance* of $\beta(x_1, \ldots, x_m)$ we mean a formula $\beta(t_1, \ldots, t_m) = \beta(x_1, \ldots, x_m)\sigma$ where $\sigma = \{x_1/t_1, \ldots, x_m/t_m\}$ (and $\beta(x_1, \ldots, x_m)\sigma$ is defined in the usual way). We say that an instance is *ground* if and only if it does not contain free variables. For the sake of brevity, we write $\beta(\vec{x})$ for $\beta(x_1, \ldots, x_m)$, $\beta(\vec{t_i})$ for $\beta(t_{i_1}, \ldots, t_{i_m})$ (*i.e.* for the instance $\beta(x_1, \ldots, x_m)\sigma$ where $\sigma = \{x_1/t_{i_1}, \ldots, x_m/t_{i_m}\}$) and $\overline{\beta} = \{\beta(\vec{t_0}), \ldots, \beta(\vec{t_n})\}$ for an arbitrary set of instances of $\beta(\vec{x})$ such that $\beta(\vec{x}) \in \overline{\beta}$.

Let A_β be the set of the atomic formulas occurring in some instance of β. By a *truth value assignment* (in brief an assignment) μ we mean a partial map from A_β to boolean values (*i.e.* T or F). Given an assignment μ and a quantifier-free formula α, we define the evaluation of α under μ (denoted by $\mu(\alpha)$) in the standard way. Notice that since μ is a partial map, $\mu(\alpha)$ can be undefined.

Given a set of instances $\overline{\beta}$, it is a trivial consequence of Herbrand's Theorem that, if the disjunction of the instances in $\overline{\beta}$ is a tautology, then the input formula $\exists \vec{x}.\beta(\vec{x})$ is a valid formula. This fact is formally stated by the following theorem.

Theorem 1. *If there is no truth value assignment μ such that $\mu(\bigvee_{\beta' \in \overline{\beta}} \beta') = F$ then $\models \exists \vec{x}\beta(\vec{x})$.*

If such an assignment does exist, then we are not entitled to conclude that the input formula is not valid, unless $\overline{\beta}$ contains the set of all the ground instances. However, Jeroslow [Jer88] provides a sufficient condition for determining whether the input formula is not valid even in such cases. Intuitively the main idea is to consider each instance $\beta_i \in \overline{\beta}$ as the representative of a set of instances, called the set of instances "directly covered" by β_i. Let us suppose that we find an assignment μ falsifying the disjunction of the instances in $\overline{\beta}$. We say that μ is "not blocked", if to each occurrence of an atomic formula in an instance β_j of $\beta(\vec{x})$ (*not* necessarily in $\overline{\beta}$) we can assign the same truth value of the corresponding (in the construction trees of the two formulas) atomic formula in β_i, where $\beta_i \in \overline{\beta}$ and β_i directly covers β_j. If this is the case then we can conclude that $\exists \vec{x}.\beta(\vec{x})$ is not provable. This is ensured by the fact that the union of the set of the instances directly covered by the instances in $\overline{\beta}$, is the set of all the instances (and hence it contains the set of all the ground instances) of $\beta(\vec{x})$. In order to state precisely this result, we need to refine the notions of directly covered instance and blocked assignment. Let $\leq$ be the binary relation on the set of instances of $\beta(\vec{x})$ such that $\beta(\vec{x})\sigma_i \leq \beta(\vec{x})\sigma_j$ if and only if there exists a substitution σ_k such that $\sigma_i = \sigma_j\sigma_k$ (where composition of substitutions is defined in the usual way).

Definition 2. (Directly covered instance) An instance $\beta(\vec{t_i}) \in \overline{\beta}$ *directly covers* an instance $\beta(\vec{t})$ if and only if $\beta(\vec{t}) \leq \beta(\vec{t_i})$ and there is no $\beta(\vec{t_j}) \in \overline{\beta}$ (with $i \neq j$) such that $\beta(\vec{t}) \leq \beta(\vec{t_j}) \leq \beta(\vec{t_i})$.

From definition 2, it is evident that (since $\beta(\vec{x}) \in \overline{\beta}$) the union of the set of instances directly covered by the instances in $\overline{\beta}$ is the set of *all* the instances. Furthermore, it is also apparent that the set of instances directly covered by an instance $\beta' \in \overline{\beta}$, strictly depends on the set of instances $\overline{\beta}$ under consideration. Supposing $\overline{\beta} = \{\beta(\vec{x})\}$, then $\beta(\vec{x})$ *directly covers* the set of all the instances. As soon as we consider a new instance $\beta(\vec{x})\sigma_0$ (*i.e.* $\overline{\beta} = \{\beta(\vec{x}), \beta(\vec{x})\sigma_0\}$), $\beta(\vec{x})$ no longer directly covers the whole set of instances, but only the instances which are not directly covered by $\beta(\vec{x})\sigma_0$. On the other hand $\beta(\vec{x})\sigma_0$ directly covers all the instances $\beta(\vec{x})\sigma_0\sigma_1$ for any substitution σ_1.

Example 1. Consider $\beta(x, y) = (P(a) \rightarrow (P(x) \wedge P(y)))$. If we take $\overline{\beta} = \{\beta(x, y)\}$, then the set of instances directly covered by $\beta(x, y)$ is the set of all the instances, *i.e.* $\{\beta(x, y), \beta(x, a), \beta(a, y), \beta(a, a)\}$. Let now $\overline{\beta} = \{\beta(x, y), \beta(a, y)\}$ then the set of instances directly covered by $\beta(a, y)$ is $\{\beta(a, y), \beta(a, a)\}$ and $\beta(x, y)$ directly covers the set of the remaining instances (*i.e.* $\{\beta(x, y), \beta(x, a)\}$).

Definition 3. (Blocked assignment) An assignment μ is *blocked* w.r.t. $\overline{\beta}$ if and only if there exist two atomic formulas P_1 and P_2 (occurring in $\beta_{i_1} \in \overline{\beta}$ and $\beta_{i_2} \in \overline{\beta}$ respectively) and two substitutions σ_1 and σ_2 (*blocking substitutions*) such that:

1. μ is defined both on P_1 and on P_2 and $\mu(P_1) \neq \mu(P_2)$,
2. $P_1\sigma_1 = P_2\sigma_2$,
3. β_{i_j} directly covers $\beta_{i_j}\sigma_j$ $(j = 1, 2)$.

By a *blockage* (w.r.t. μ and $\overline{\beta}$) we mean a 6-tuple $\langle P_1, P_2, \sigma_1, \sigma_2, \beta_{i_1}, \beta_{i_2} \rangle$ satisfying clauses 1-3 of the previous definition. Whether an assignment μ is blocked or not depends on the set of instances considered.

Example 2. Continuing the previous example, if $\beta(\vec{x}) = (P(a) \rightarrow (P(x) \wedge P(y)))$ and $\overline{\beta} = \{\beta(\vec{x})\}$ then the assignment $\mu = \{P(a) \leftarrow T, P(x) \leftarrow F\}$ is blocked. The same assignment is not blocked if we consider the set of instances $\overline{\beta} = \{\beta(x, y), \beta(a, y)\}$. Notice that in the first case, μ falsifies the disjunction of the instances in $\overline{\beta}$, but this is no longer true in the second case. There are further assignments that falsify the disjunction of $\beta(x, y)$ and $\beta(a, y)$, but they are blocked w.r.t. $\{\beta(x, y), \beta(a, y)\}$. For example the assignment $\mu = \{P(a) \leftarrow T, P(x) \leftarrow T, P(y) \leftarrow F\}$ is blocked w.r.t. $\{\beta(x, y), \beta(a, y)\}$ with blocking substitution $\sigma = \{x/x, y/a\}$.

The following result allows to conclude that the input formula is not valid as soon as an unblocked falsifying assignment is found.

Theorem 4. *If there is a truth value assignment v such that $v(\bigvee_{\beta' \in \overline{\beta}} \beta') = F$ and v is not blocked w.r.t. $\overline{\beta}$ then $\not\models \exists \vec{x} \beta(\vec{x})$.*

The operation of *unblocking* a blocked assignment consists in adding suitable instances to those so far generated. The new instances must be such that to directly cover the instances responsible of the blockage.

Example 3. Let $\beta(x,y) = ((Q(a,y) \vee Q(x,b)) \rightarrow Q(x,y))$. If we take $\overline{\beta} = \{\beta(x,y)\}$, then $\mu = \{Q(a,y) \leftarrow T, Q(x,y) \leftarrow F\}$ is blocked. It is easy to verify that extending $\overline{\beta}$ with the instance $\beta(a,y) = ((Q(a,y) \vee Q(a,b)) \rightarrow Q(a,y))$ then μ is no longer blocked.

Let us make this informal discussion more precise by defining the notion of *unblocking function*. Let μ be an assignment blocked w.r.t. $\overline{\beta}$. We define $Bl_\mu^{\overline{\beta}}$ to be the set of blockages w.r.t. μ and $\overline{\beta}$, *i.e.* the set of 6-tuples $\langle P_1, P_2, \sigma_1, \sigma_2, \beta_{i_1}, \beta_{i_2} \rangle$ satisfying clauses 1-3 in definition 3.

Definition 5. (Unblocking function) Let f be a function defined from assignments and sets of instances of $\beta(\vec{x})$ to sets of instances of $\beta(\vec{x})$. We say that f is an *unblocking function* if and only if when μ is blocked w.r.t. $\overline{\beta}$ and $f(\mu, \overline{\beta}) = \overline{\beta'}$, then $Bl_\mu^{\overline{\beta}} \cap Bl_\mu^{\overline{\beta} \cup \overline{\beta'}} \subset Bl_\mu^{\overline{\beta}}$.

Informally speaking an unblocking function reduces the number of "old" blockages, and it possibly introduces "new" ones.

Example 4. A simple example of unblocking function can be sketched as follows. Let μ be blocked w.r.t. $\overline{\beta}$, we choose a blockage $\langle P_1, P_2, \sigma_1, \sigma_2, \beta_{i_1}, \beta i_2 \rangle \in Bl_\mu^{\overline{\beta}}$ and define $f(\mu, \overline{\beta}) = \{\beta_{i_1} \sigma_1, \beta_{i_2} \sigma_2\}$. Let us do this for any μ and $\overline{\beta}$ (if μ is not blocked we may define $f(\mu, \overline{\beta}) = \emptyset$). It can be easily verified that f is an unblocking function, since $\langle P_1, P_2, \sigma_1, \sigma_2, \beta_{i_1}, \beta i_2 \rangle \notin Bl_\mu^{\overline{\beta} \cup f(\mu, \overline{\beta})}$. Notice that we do not make any commitment on the particular choice of the element in $Bl_\mu^{\overline{\beta}}$.

The algorithmic structure of FOLTAUT is showed below.

```
1: FOLTAUT(β⁺, α, β̄)
2: if there is no assignment falsifying (α → β⁺)
3:    then return TRUE
4:    else let μ be an assignment falsifying (α → β⁺)
5:        if μ is not blocked w.r.t. β̄
6:            then return FALSE
7:            else let β̄' = unblock(μ, β̄)
8:                return (FOLTAUT(⋁_{β'∈β̄'} β', μ*, β̄ ∪ β̄') and
9:                        FOLTAUT(β⁺, ¬μ* ∧ α, β̄))
```

The arguments of the algorithm have the following meaning: $\overline{\beta}$ is the set of instances generated so far (initially set to $\{\beta(\vec{x})\}$), β^+ is the disjunction of a non empty subset of $\overline{\beta}$ (initially set to $\beta(\vec{x})$) and α is a propositional formula embodying the search state (initially set to the sentential constant $True$). The algorithm determines whether there exists an enumeration $\beta_1, \ldots, \beta_n$ of instances of $\beta(\vec{x})$ such that $(\alpha \rightarrow \bigvee_{i=1}^{n} \beta_i)$ is a tautology. It is immediate to verify that in the initial case (i.e. when $\overline{\beta} = \{\beta(\vec{x})\}$, $\beta^+ = \beta(\vec{x})$ and $\alpha = True$) this amounts to determine the existence of an enumeration $\beta_1, \ldots, \beta_n$ of instances of $\beta(\vec{x})$ such that $\bigvee_{i=1}^{n} \beta_i$ is a tautology. By theorem 1, this guarantees that the existential closure of $\beta(\vec{x})$ is valid.

Let us analyze in detail the main steps of the procedure. In line 2 a truth value assignment falsifying $(\alpha \rightarrow \beta^+)$ is sought (this activity can be carried out by PTAUT). If such an assignment does not exist, then the algorithm halts returning a positive answer (we have determined the enumeration $\beta_1, \ldots, \beta_n$ of instances of β such that $(\alpha \rightarrow \bigvee_{i=1}^{n} \beta_i)$ is a tautology). If such an assignment (say μ) does exist, then (in line 5) FOLTAUT checks whether μ is blocked. If it is not blocked, the algorithm halts (in line 6) and returns a negative answer (i.e. it asserts that the formula is not provable). This step is justified by theorem 4. If it is blocked, then in general many blockages may exist relative to a given blocked assignment. The unblocking strategy (implemented by unblock) chooses one or more blockages and then generates new instances according to the chosen blockages (line 7).

The two recursive calls of the algorithm (lines 8 and 9) implement a depth-first search for an assignment falsifying the disjunction of the instances in $\overline{\beta}$ (but a breadth-first search strategy can be realized simply by swapping the two recursive calls). By μ^* we mean the formula obtained from the conjunction of the literals in the set

$$\{P : P \in A_\beta, \mu(P) = T\} \cup \{\neg P : P \in A_\beta, \mu(P) = F\}.$$

For example, if μ is such that $\mu(P(x)) = T$, $\mu(P(a)) = F$ and μ is undefined elsewhere, then $\mu^* = (P(x) \wedge \neg P(a))$. Let us now discuss in detail the two recursive calls.

1. First recursive call (line 8), i.e. FOLTAUT($\bigvee_{\beta' \in \overline{\beta'}} \beta', \mu^*, \overline{\beta} \cup \overline{\beta'}$). The first argument is given by the disjunction of the new instances generated by unblock. There is no need to include the previous disjunct (namely β^+) since it is falsified under the current assignment (encoded in μ^*). Notice that in the execution of such a recursive call, the formula to be falsified at line 2 is $\gamma = (\mu^* \rightarrow \bigvee_{\beta' \in \overline{\beta'}} \beta')$. Falsifying γ requires to make μ^* true and therefore any possible falsifying assignment for γ must be necessarily an extension of μ. For this reason, before applying a decider for discovering a falsifying assignment, $\bigvee_{\beta' \in \overline{\beta'}} \beta'$ can be simplified w.r.t. μ.

2. Second recursive call (line 9), i.e. FOLTAUT($\beta^+, \neg\mu^* \wedge \alpha, \overline{\beta}$). It continues the search by looking for falsifying assignments that are extensions of α, but are different from μ (this fact is encoded in the second argument, i.e. $\neg\mu^* \wedge \alpha$). Hence during the execution of the recursive call, the formula to be falsified

(at line 2) is $\gamma = ((\neg\mu^* \wedge\ \alpha) \rightarrow \bigvee_{\beta' \in \overline{\beta}} \beta')$. Notice that the new generated instances (*i.e.* $\overline{\beta'}$) are not included in the third argument of the procedure. This approach avoids cluttering the latest calls with possibly useless instances (but it has the drawback that the same instance might be generated several times in different branches of the search).

It is easy to prove that at any recursive call, for any (partial) assignment satisfying α, there exists an enumeration $\beta_1 \ldots \beta_n$ of instances of $\beta(\vec{x})$ such that $((\mu^*\wedge\alpha) \rightarrow \bigvee_{i=1}^{n} \beta_i)$ and $((\neg\mu^*\wedge\alpha) \rightarrow \bigvee_{i=1}^{n} \beta_i)$ are tautologies, if and only if there exists an enumeration $\beta_1' \ldots \beta_n'$ of instances of $\beta(\vec{x})$ such that $(\alpha \rightarrow \bigvee_{i=1}^{n} \beta_i')$ is a tautology. Intuitively, this guarantees the correctness and completeness of the FOLTAUT algorithm.

Theorem 6. FOLTAUT$(\beta(\vec{x}), True, \{\beta(\vec{x})\})$ = TRUE *if and only if* $\models \exists\vec{x}.\beta(\vec{x})$.

Formally, the proofs of both directions of the double implication are by well-founded induction with well-founded relation $\prec$ given by the following definition:

$$\langle \beta, \alpha, \overline{\beta} \rangle \prec \langle \beta', \alpha', \overline{\beta}' \rangle \equiv (\overline{\beta}' \subset \overline{\beta} \vee (\overline{\beta}' = \overline{\beta} \wedge models(\alpha) \subset models(\alpha')))$$

where $models(\alpha)$ is the set of assignments v such that $v(\alpha) = T$.

We do not include the formal proofs for lack of space.

The correctness and the completeness of FOLTAUT do not depend on the strategy used to find blockages. On the other hand, it is clear that this strategy greatly affects the performance of the procedure. However, this issue is out of the scope of this paper. It is worth stressing that variants and optimizations to the basic procedure we have described can be proposed. Each modification, if suitably implemented, could make the procedure effective on particular classes of formulas. Notice also that FOLTAUT has the claimed modularity. It does not depend on the particular propositional decider used to determine the falsifying assignment. Furthermore, the extension to treat equality in a special way can be accomplished by using PTAUTEQ instead of PTAUT and suitably modifying the definition of blocked assignment.

5 Final Remarks

Considering FOLTAUT per se as a decision procedure, there are three issues we have to discuss: comparison with Jeroslow's procedure (presented in [Jer88]), applicability, and effectiveness (compared with present, state-of-the-art decision procedures).

FOLTAUT is considerably more effective than the procedure presented in [Jer88] since FOLTAUT applies the propositional decider only to the newly generated instances, while the procedure presented in [Jer88] is applied each time to the whole set of instances so far generated. Moreover, it allows the integration of any decision/proof procedure for testing the validity of the evaluated formula. In other words, any of the decision procedure presented in section 2, or any proof strategy developed by the user can be invoked instead of **FOLTAUT** in the body of the algorithm.

The existential fragment of first order logic is particularly interesting since many important theories can be expressed in it (*e.g.* partial order, congruence relations). Furthermore, the Bernays-Schönfinkel class, which represents one of the widest classes known to be decidable [DG79], can be easily reduced to it via skolemization. As far as real applications are concerned, a decision procedure for the Bernays-Schönfinkel class can be used for query formation and answering in relational databases (but see [Jer88] for more details on this topic). In [AG93] it is shown that a very wide class of formulas can be reduced to the Bernays-Schönfinkel class and hence to the existential class, through finitely many applications of truthful preserving rewriting rules. Other important classes of formulas can be reduced to the existential fragment via the **reduce** procedure (*e.g.* the monadic calculus, see section 2). Finally, notice that the existential fragment is a significant testbed for the analysis and development of proof procedures for first order logic. This consideration contrasts with the frequent practice of analyzing the effectiveness of proof procedures for first order logic on the propositional fragment only. In fact the complexity of the full first order case often makes impractical the task of evaluating the computational effectiveness of the procedures.

It is obvious that **FOLTAUT** performance strictly relies on the performance of the propositional decider employed. With this respect it is worth recalling that **PTAUT** is a generalization of DPL to deal with non clausal formulas which retains all the optimizations of the original procedure. Recent comparative studies on different propositional deciders working on clausal formulas [LP90, BB92] confirm that DPL is to date one of the most efficient. The generalization to directly manage any input formula provides many advantages w.r.t. the deciders requiring the input formula to be translated into some normal form (either clausal form or negative normal form).

Future work will be focussed on carrying out experimental comparisons of the effects of different unblocking functions on the performance of the procedure and on adapting the general strategy presented in section 4 to effectively deal with specific theories. The extension of **FOLTAUT** to deal with equality by using **PTAUTEQ** will be the first step in such a direction.

References

[AG93]   A. Armando and E. Giunchiglia. Embedding Complex Decision Procedures inside an Interactive Theorem Prover. *Annals of Mathematics and Artificial Intelligence*, 8(3–4):475–502, 1993.

[And81] P.B. Andrews. Theorem Proving via General Matings. *Journal of the ACM*, 28(2):193–214, 1981.

[BB92]   M. Buro and H. Kleine Büning. Report on a SAT competition. Technical Report Nr. 110, FB 17 – Mathematik/Informatik Universität Paderborn, Nov. 1992.

[Bib82] W. Bibel. *Automated Theorem Proving*. Vieweg, Braunschweig, 1982.

186

[BM88]   R.S. Boyer and J.S. More. Integrating decision procedures into heuristic theorem provers: A case study of linear arithmetic. *Machine Intelligence*, 11:83–124, 1988.

[DG79]   B. Dreben and W.D. Goldfarb. *The Decision problem - Solvable classes of quantificational formulas*. Addison-Wesley Publishing Company Inc., 1979.

[DP60]   M. Davis and H. Putnam. A computing procedure for quantification theory. *Journal of the ACM*, 7:201–215, 1960.

[Gil60]   P.C. Gilmore. A proof Method for Quantification Theory: its Justification and Realization. *IBM Journal on Research and Development*, 4:28–35, 1960.

[Giu92]   F. Giunchiglia. The GETFOL Manual - GETFOL version 1. Technical Report 9204-01, DIST - University of Genova, Genoa, Italy, 1992.

[Jer88]   R.G. Jeroslow. Computation-Oriented Reduction of Predicate to Propositional Logic. *Decision Support System*, 4:183–197, 1988.

[Joy76]   W.H. Joyner. Resolution strategies as decision procedures. *Journal of the ACM*, 23(3):398–417, 1976.

[LP90]   S.J. Lee and D.A. Plaisted. Eliminating Duplication with the Hyper-Linking Strategy. Technical Report TR90-032, The University of North Carolina - Dept. of Computer Science, Aug. 1990.

[NO78]   G. Nelson and D.C. Oppen. Simplification by Cooperating Decision Procedures. *ACM Transactions on Programming Languages and Systems*, 1(2), Oct. 1979.

[Pra60]   D. Prawitz. An improved proof procedure. *Theoria*, 26:102–139, 1960.

[Sti85]   M. Stickel. Automated Deduction by Theory Resolution. *Journal of Automated Reasoning*, 4:333–356, 1985.

Knowledge Representation, Exemplification, and the Gupta-Belnap Theory of Circular Definitions[1]

Francesco Orilia

Università di Cagliari, Facoltà di Lettere e Filosofia
Piazza D'armi
09123 Cagliari
Italy
orilia@iei.pi.cnr.it

Abstract. Gupta's and Belnap's revision theory of circular definitions (RTD) provides a general technique for specifying circular definitions in a way that at worst gives rise to some "vacuous" uses of definienda, but never to contradiction. This is a first step in applying RTD to the problem of constructing a type-free theory of properties, relations and propositions (in short, *PRP's*). To this end, exemplification is viewed as a circular concept analyzed in terms of RTD. This yields a formal semantics system, **P***, wherein the generality of lambda-conversion is circumscribed so as to avoid, e.g., Russell's paradox. The construction of **P*** is motivated by showing how it can provide a foundation for a knowledge representation system capable of dealing with belief (or more generally intensional) contexts and with inferences involving PRP's in subject position.

1 Introduction

According to Gupta and Belnap [8], many fundamental notions of our ordinary conceptual background are inherently circular and thus cannot be fully understood as long as one remains within the confines of the standard theory of definitions. As an alternative, they develop a *revision theory of definitions* (RTD), which allows definitions to be circular, without this giving rise to contradiction, but at worst only to "vacuous" uses of definienda. The crucial idea is that behind the use of the predicates expressing circular concepts is not *a rule of application* that fixes their extension in a definite way, but rather a *rule of revision*, i.e., a rule that enables one to gradually improve on any *hypothetical* extension, on the basis of the information concerning the extension of the primitive predicates, once this is assumed to be known.

Gupta's and Belnap's main goal is to present old[2] and new formulations of the revision theory of truth as applications of RTD. This amounts to viewing truth as a circular concept. Gupta and Belnap also suggest that exemplification can naturally be viewed as a circular concept in order to apply RTD to the goal of constructing a type-free property theory along the lines of [20]. In sects. 3 and 4 below I present a first

---

[1] I wish to thank Anil Gupta, Achille Varzi and an anonymous referee for some useful comments. The first paragraph of this work is drawn from a forthcoming review of [8] by this author and Achille Varzi.
[2] Cf. [2], [7], [11], etc.

step in this direction. Sect. 2 will motivate this enterprise, by illustrating the relevance of type-free property theory for the task of providing a sound logical foundation for sophisticated AI knowledge representation systems, capable of dealing with intensional contexts and of reasoning with properties.

2   Data and Desiderata

In ordinary language we speak of properties, relations and propositions (in short, *PRP's*) both as individuals which are subjects of predication and as items that can be predicated of individuals, as the following examples witness:

(1)   Socrates is wise.
(2)   Wisdom is a a nice property.
(3)   John is taller than Mary.
(4)   Being taller is an asymmetrical relation.
(5)   Dolphins are fish.
(6)   That dolphins are fish is not true.

The fact that PRP's have this double role is essentially what makes arguments such as the following intuitively valid (cf. [1]):

        John is wise.
(7)   Socrates is wise.
        ∴ There is a property shared by John and Socrates.

Moreover, ordinary language suggests that in principle, out of any sentence, we can construct complex predicates intuitively corresponding to "conceptually complex" PRP's. For example,

(8)   Tom is not wise, but he is nice

suggests that there exists a complex PRP, being both nice and not wise, such that

(8') Tom exemplifies being both nice and not wise

is logically equivalent to (8).

A type-free property theory is a formal system that takes these data at face value, (i) by allowing for terms that are meant to express PRP's and that can in some appropriate sense occurr in both subject and predicate position, so as to validate arguments such as (7); and (ii) by allowing these terms to be complex roughly in the sense in which molecular sentences are complex.

Point (ii) can be met in a formal language with Church's variable binding *lambda operator*, "λ," by means of a grammar rule that tells us that if A is a wff then $[\lambda x_1 \dots x_n A]$ is a singular term (that I shall also call a *lambda-term*). Point (i) can be met either in a second order (cf. [4], etc.) or in a first order setting (cf. [1], [20], etc.). Here I shall pursue the latter alternative. Consider lambda-terms as singular terms that cannot stand in predicate position and allow quantifiers to bind only subject positions. To compensate for these limitations, let us introduce, for any n, an n-adic *exemplification* relation p^n that intuitively (in light, e.g., of the intuitive equivalence of (8) and (8')) should obey this version of *lambda-conversion*:[3]

(λ-conv) $p^{n+1}([\lambda x_1 \ldots x_n\, A], t_1, \ldots, t_n) \leftrightarrow A(x_1/t_1, \ldots, x_n/t_n).$

Ideally, we would like to add (λ-conv) to standard axioms and rules for first-order logic. Clearly, a formal system around these lines can provide a foundation for a knowledge representation system that tries to simulate the human capacity to reason with PRP's.

Moreover, such a knowledge representation system would be able to deal in a systematic way with issues that have since long been recognized as central in many AI applications, namely intensional contexts and more specifically belief contexts (cf. [5], [9], [10], [12], [14], [16], etc.).

To illustrate,[4] consider once more the following Fregean triad:

(9)   the morning star is the evening star.
(10) x believes that the morning star is bright.
(11) x believes that the evening star is bright.

Prima facie, we would like to take the "is" of (9) to mean identity. But then by the substitutivity rule for identity (11) should follow from (9) and (10). Yet, it may well be the case that (9) and (10) are true and (11) is false.

This problem can be solved naturally with a type-free property theory available. Drawing on [13], we can represent singular terms such as "the morning star" with "$[\lambda z\ \exists x(\forall y(p^2([\lambda z\ p^2[\lambda w\ \mathrm{MORNING\_STAR}(w)], z], y) \leftrightarrow x = y) \wedge p^2(z, x))]$"[5] and predicates such as "bright" with "$[\lambda x\ p^2(x, [\lambda z\ \mathrm{BRIGHT}(z)])]$."

---

[3] In this sect. I implicitly rely on a first order language such as L^+, formally introduced in the next section. A close relative of it, to be called "L," will also be needed. With reference to L or L^+, as the case may be, "A," "B," "C," "A_1," "A_2," etc. will range over wff's, and "s," "t," "t_1," "t_2," etc. over singular terms, i.e., as far as we are concerned here, individual variables and lambda-terms. Further, "u," "w," "x," "y," "z," "x_1," "x_2," etc. will be used both as object language individual variables and metavariables ranging over them (the context should allow one to disambiguate, when necessary). $A(x_1/t_1, \ldots, x_n/t_n)$ will be understood to be the wff resulting from simultaneously substituting in A each x_i with t_i (for $1 \le i \le n$), provided t_i is free for x_i in A. Standard notions of *wff*, *term*, *closed wff* (*term*), a term being *free in* a wff, and *free for* another term *in* a wff will be assumed.

[4] For additional details on the topics of this sect. and for an essentially analogous account (albeit in a second-order setting) see [14] and references therein.

[5] This representation (rather than the simpler "$[\lambda z\ \exists x(\forall y(p^2([\lambda w\ \mathrm{MORNING\_STAR}(w)], y) \leftrightarrow x = y) \wedge p^2(z, x))]$" or "$[\lambda z\ \exists x(\forall y(\mathrm{MORNING\_STAR}(y) \leftrightarrow x = y) \wedge p^2(z, x))]$") is here suggested for reasons (cf. [15]) having to do with both Montague-style compositionality and an appropriate treatment of Meinongian "predication" (see below). Of course, in AI applications where these reasons are not relevant the above simpler representations may be preferred.

(For simplicity's sake, I shall from now on abbreviate terms of the form "$[\lambda z$ $\exists x (\forall y (p^2([\lambda w\, p^2(t_1, w) \wedge ... \wedge p^2(t_n, w)], y) \leftrightarrow x = y) \wedge p^2(z, x))]$" as "$[\text{THE } t_1 \wedge ...$ $\wedge t_n]$." Thus, "$[\text{THE } [\lambda u\, \text{MORNING\_STAR}(u)]]$" is short for "$[\lambda z\, \exists x(\forall y(p^2([\lambda w$ $p^2([\lambda u\, \text{MORNING\_STAR}(u)], w)], y) \leftrightarrow x = y) \wedge p^2(z, x))]$." Let us agree that these terms stand for *individualizing intensions*.)

The subordinate clause in (10) is then represented as

(12) $p^2([\lambda x\, p^2(x, [\lambda z\, \text{BRIGHT}(z)])], [\text{THE } [\lambda z\, \text{MORNING\_STAR}(z)]])$.

Given (λ-conv), (12) is equivalent to the "Russellian" (cf. [17])

(12a) $\exists x(\forall y(\text{MORNING\_STAR}(y) \leftrightarrow x = y) \wedge \text{BRIGHT}(x))$,

which insures that (12) is adequate to provide the intended informative content of its English counterpart.

Similarly, (9) is to be represented as

(9a) $p^3([\lambda zw\, p^2\, (z, [\lambda x\, p^2\, (w, [\lambda y\, (x = y)])])]$, $[\text{THE } [\lambda z$ $\text{MORNING\_STAR}(z)]]$, $[\text{THE } [\lambda z\, \text{EVENING\_STAR}(z)]])$,[6]

which, given (λ-conv), is equivalent to the Russellian

(9b) $\exists x(\forall y(\text{MORNING\_STAR}(y) \leftrightarrow x = y) \wedge \exists z(\forall y(\text{EVENING\_STAR}(y) \leftrightarrow z = y) \wedge x = z))$.

Furthermore, we can represent propositions, denoted by that-clauses, by means of vacuous lambda-terms. Thus, if A is a sentence we can read "$[\lambda\, A]$" as "that A." Hence, (10) and (11) are to be represented, respectively, as follows:

(10a) $\text{BELIEVE}(x, [\lambda\, p^2([\lambda x\, p^2(x, [\lambda z\, \text{BRIGHT}(z)]], [\text{THE } [\lambda z$ $\text{MORNING\_STAR}(z)]])])$.
(11a) $\text{BELIEVE}(x, [\lambda\, p^2([\lambda x\, p^2(x, [\lambda z\, \text{BRIGHT}(z)]], [\text{THE } [\lambda z$ $\text{EVENING\_STAR}(z)]])])$.

Note that we cannot appeal to the identity substitutivity law to deduce (11a) from (9a) and (10a).

In a type-free property theory we can naturally capture the intuition behind the so called *Meinongian predication*. Consider

(13)   the round square is round.

There is a clear sense in which (13) is true even though there can exist no round square. It has thus been proposed (i) that the "is" of (13) should be taken to express a special form of predication (*Meinongian predication*) that does not entail the (physical) existence of the subject of predication, and (ii) that a definite description can express a *Meinongian object* "constituted" in some sense exactly by the properties

---

[6] Cf. [13].

expressed by the predicates involved in the definite description in question. Thus, the round square would only have, Meinongianly speaking, the properties of roundness and squareness (cf. [3], etc.). These ideas have been used in AI as a foundation for the SNePS knowledge representation system (cf. [18]).

The AI applications addressed by the SNePS system can be approached from a different, ontologically more economical, perspective, if a type-free property theory is available. In fact, we can take the "is" of (13) to express a relation, that I shall call $*\in$,[7] holding exclusively of a PRP and an individualizing intension, and obeying the following principle:

(MEIN) $t *\in [\text{THE } t_1 \wedge ... \wedge t_n] \leftrightarrow t = t_1 \vee ... \vee t = t_n.$

We can thus interpret (13) as

(13a) $[\lambda z \text{ ROUND}(z)] *\in [\text{THE } [\lambda z \text{ ROUND}(z)] \wedge [\lambda z \text{ SQUARE}(z)]].$

Given (MEIN), (13a) is analytically true and yet does not commit one to the existence of any round square in that it does not entail

(14) $\exists x(\text{ROUND}(x) \wedge \text{SQUARE}(x)).$

Meinongian predication allows us to give an appropriate formal representation of *Geach sentences* (cf. [6]). An example of a Geach sentence is

(14) x believes that a ghost inhabits Manor Castle and y fears that it will appear tomorrow.

This sentence does not necessarily commit the speaker to the existence of ghosts and yet it forces us to give the quantifier phrase "a ghost" wide scope with respect to the intensional verbs "believes" and "fears." These two requirements appear to be irreconcilible within the standard resources of first-order logic. These resources often provide the formal background in AI research, even when AI deals with intensional contexts (see, e.g., [12]). The importance of appropriately representing Geach sentences in AI knowledge representation systems is illustrated in [14].

With type-free property theory a sentence such as (14) can be represented, by relying on (MEIN), as follows:

(14a) $\exists z ([\lambda u \text{ GHOST}(u)] *\in z \wedge \text{ BELIEVE}(x, [\lambda \ p^2([\lambda w \ p^2(w, [\lambda u \text{ INHABIT\_MANOR\_CASTLE}(u)])], z)])) \wedge \text{FEAR}(y, [\lambda \ p^2([\lambda w \ p^2(w, [\lambda u \text{ WILL\_APPEAR\_TOMORROW}(u)])], z)]))).$

Unfortunately, type-free property theory, as outlined above, is inconsistent. Let "RP" stand for the property $[\lambda x \ \neg p^2(x, x)]$. This version of Russell's paradox is then an immediate instance of (λ-conv):

(RP) $p^2(\text{RP}, \text{RP}) \leftrightarrow \neg p^2(\text{RP}, \text{RP}).$

---

[7] This symbol is meant to be remindful of set membership and I shall thus use the infix notation for it.

To capture as much as possible of the above data, while avoiding inconsistency, we can impose constraints that limit in a systematic way the generality of (λ-conv). In principle, these constraints should not be *ad hoc* but motivated by a general, intuitively appealing theory. I think that this role can be played by RTD.

The basic strategy is this. The intuitions that we have taken to motivate (λ-conv) should rather be seen as suggesting a definitional schema along the lines of

(λ-def) $p^{n+1}([\lambda x_1 \ldots x_n A], y_1, \ldots, y_n) =_{df} A(x_1/y_1, \ldots, x_n/y_n)$.

whereas "$=_{df}$" should be understood in terms of RTD. This will give rise to a formal semantics that does not license all instances of (λ-conv), although, as we shall see, it grants instances that can support the applications outlined in this section.

3   The System P*

Enter the first order language L^+. It is based on standard punctuation signs, the connectives "$\neg$," and "$\wedge$," the quantifier "$\forall$," the abstraction operator "λ," a denumerable set $\mathcal{V}$ of individual variables, and a countable set $\mathcal{P}^+$ of predicate constants including the identity sign "$=$," the dyadic predicate "$*\in$," and, for any $n > 0$, the predicate constants p^n, that are meant to express exemplification. The sets of wff's and singular terms of L^+ are defined inductively in the standard way.[8] For clarity's sake, I however point out the crucial clause for lambda-terms:

(LT)   If A is a wff and $x_1, \ldots, x_n$ individual variables in $\mathcal{V}$, then $[\lambda x_1 \ldots x_n A]$ is a *singular term* (also called *n-adic lambda-term*).

The *base* language L is the language that contains exactly the same singular terms as L^+,[9] but does not have the definienda, i.e., the exemplification predicates of the form p^n in the set, call it $\mathcal{P}$, of its primitive predicate constants.

Let us say that an occurrence o of an exemplification predicate is *active* in a wff A iff o is not within the scope of any occurrence of the lambda operator in A. Otherwise, o is *disactivated*. Note that in L the exemplification predicates always occur as disactivated. The possibility of disactivated occurrences of exemplification predicates in L allows us to specify a realm of PRP's as subjects of predication, but does not yet allow us, so to speak, to actually predicate such PRP's of other individuals. For this we need active occurrences of the exemplification predicates. Intuitively, L^+ extends L in that it also grants such active occurrences. As we shall see, the exemplification predicates, as so used in L^+, are to be understood as circularly defined on the basis of L's predicates (i.e., the members of $\mathcal{P}$).

---

[8] With "$=$" and "$*\in$," the infix notation will be used. Further, I shall assume that the connectives "$\leftrightarrow$," "$\vee$," "$\rightarrow$," and the quantifier "$\exists$" are defined as usual.

[9] Such terms should be considered as given in formulating explicitly the grammar of L.

In order to apply RTD to truth, Gupta and Belnap allow circular definitions to be *partial* (cf. [8], p. 197). A partial definition permits one to specify the conditions under which a certain n-adic definiendum applies to a given n-tuple of a model's domain *only if* singular terms denoting the elements of such n-tuple are available in the base language that does not contain the definiendum in question. It is convenient for our purposes not to burden our base language L with this requirement. I shall thus present the models for L and L^+ in a way reminiscent of Raymond Smullyan's [19] elegant characterization of the models for standard first-order logic. Toward this goal, a few preliminary notions will have to be defined.

From now on "D" will be used as ranging on any set disjoint from the set P of closed lambda terms of L^+. Any set $D \cup P$ will be called a DL^+-*set*. Intuitively, these sets will provide the domains of the models of L and L^+, whereas the members of D represent the individuals that are not PRP's and the closed lambda terms directly represent the PRP's that are meant to signify.

Further, we need the following inductive definitions, relative to a set D, of "DL^+-lambda-term" and "DL^+-wff:"

(D1)   If $d_1, ..., d_n$ are either members of D or $\mathcal{V}$, or DL-lambda terms, and R is an *n*-adic predicate constant in P^+, then $R(d_1, ..., d_n)$ is a DL^+-*(atomic) wff*.

(D2)   If x is an individual variable in $\mathcal{V}$, and A and B are DL^+-wff's, then $\neg A$, $(A \wedge B)$ and $(\forall x)A$ are DL^+-*wff's*.

(D3)   If A is a DL^+-wff and $x_1, ..., x_n$ individual variables in $\mathcal{V}$, then $[\lambda x_1, ..., x_n A]$ is an *n-adic DL^+-lambda-term*.

(D4)   Nothing else is a DL^+-sentence or a DL^+-lambda term.

We then define a DL^+-*sentence* to be a closed DL^+-wff. Intuitively, a DL^+-sentence (closed DL^+-lambda term) is like a wff (lambda-term) of L^+, except that it has elements of D, to be called *D-terms*, where the latter has free variables.[10]

The set of *DL-wff's (sentences)* is given by the set of DL^+-wff's (sentences) minus the set of DL^+-wff's (sentences) in which there are active occurrences of exemplification predicates.

Let the set of *truth values* be $\{t, f\}$. In the following I shall use "**x**," and "**y**," as ranging over such set. Let *DV* be the set of *valuation* functions v from atomic DL-sentences onto the set of truth values such that v obeys the following constraints:

(C1)   if A and B are alphabetic variants[11] of each other, then $v(A) = v(B)$.

----

[10] In the following I shall use "d," "d_1," "d_2," etc. (possibly primed) as ranging over DL^+-terms (where some fixed domain D is presupposed). The metavariables "s," "t," "t_1," "t_2," etc. will still be used as ranging exclusively over the singular terms of L and L^+. With this in mind, it can be assumed that, *mutatis mutandis*, the metalinguistic conventions of note 3 above apply in this context as well, with the understanding that D-terms are to be viewed as primitive individual constants.

[11] This notion is understood as usual. Roughly, two wff's or terms are alphabetic variants of each other iff they differ at most for the choice of their variables. Note that a D-term is to be considered an alphabetic variant of itself.

(C2)   If A is a sentence of the form $d = d'$, then $v(A) = t$ iff d and d' are alphabetic variants of each other.

(C3)   If A is a sentence of the form $d * \in d'$, then $v(A) = t$ iff d is of the form [THE $d_1 \wedge ... \wedge d_n$] (where $d_1, ..., d_n$ are closed monadic DL$^+$-lambda-terms) and d is an alphabetic variant of at least one d_i, for $1 \leq i \leq n$.

In specifying the models for L and L$^+$, clause (C1) and (C2) allow us to grant the standard identity laws. Moreover, (C2) induces very fine-grained identity conditions for PRP's. (These conditions could in principle be relaxed; cf. [1], [10], [14], etc..) Finally, Clause (C3) is meant to take care of Meinongian "predication" and in particular allows us to make (MEIN) valid.

The *set of hypotheses* DH is the set of all functions h from atomic DL$^+$-sentences of the form $p^{n+1}(d, d_1, ..., d_n)$ into $\{t, f\}$ that complies with clause (C1) above.

We are now in a position to characterize the models of L. A *model* of L is a structure $<D \cup P, I_v>$ where v is a fixed member of DV and I_v is an *interpretation* function that maps the sets of DL-sentences (and hence the set of sentences of L) onto $\{t, f\}$ as follows:

(M1)   If A is an atomic DL-sentence then $I_v(A) = v(A)$.

(M2)   If A is $\neg B$, then $I_v(A) = t$ iff $I_v(B) = f$.

(M3)   If A is $B \wedge C$, then $I_v(A) = t$ iff $I_v(B) = t$ and $I_v(C) = t$.

(M4)   If A is $(\forall x)B$, then $I_v(A) = t$ iff for every DL-sentence $B(x/d)$, $I_v(B(x/d)) = t$.

Similarly, a *model* M of L$^+$ is a structure $<D \cup P, I_v+h>$, where h is a fixed member of DH and I_v+h is an interpretation function that obeys clauses (M2)-(M4) above,[12] as well as the following clause (replacing (M1)):

(M1')   If A is an atomic DL$^+$-sentence then $I(A) = v \cup h(A)$.

If M $= <D \cup P, I_v>$ is a model of L and h a hypothesis in DH, we understand M+h to be the model $<D, I_v+h>$ of L$^+$. Under these assumptions, h will be called a hypothesis *relative to* M. Intuitively, a model M+h of L$^+$ interprets each sentence of L$^+$ that is also a sentence of L (i.e., that contains no active occurrence of an exemplification predicate) just as M interprets it. Moreover, M+h interprets the sentences of L$^+$ with active occurrences of an exemplification predicate on the basis of the hypothesis h (that assigns a truth value to any such atomic sentence).

In general, given a model M and a sentence A, we take $[A]_M$ to be the truth value that the interpretation function I of M assigns to A.[13] Further, we say that M $\models$

---

[12] With the understanding that in (M4) "DL$^+$-sentence" should replace "DL-sentence" and that the metavariables "A," "B," and "C" now range over DL$^+$-sentences.

[13] From now on, in talking about models of L and L$^+$ I shall drop the reference to a valuation function v and to a hypothesis h, unless the context requires it.

A (A is *true in* M) iff $[A]_M$ is **t**. If A is a sentence of L (L$^+$), we say that $\models A$ (A is *valid*) iff A is true in all models of L (L$^+$).

Given a model M of L, consider those sequences S of hypotheses relative to M, whose length *lh(S)* is either a limit ordinal or the class *On* of all ordinals. Let us call them *revision sequences for* M. Let "S_α" designate the αth member of S, where "α," "β," etc. range over ordinals.

The following definitions are crucial. A DL$^+$-sentence A is *stably x* in a revision sequence S for a model M = <D ∪ P, I> of L iff there is an ordinal β < lh(S) such that, for all ordinals γ, if $\beta \leq \gamma$ < lh(S), then $[A]_{M+S\gamma}$ = **x**. A sentence A of L$^+$ is *stable* (*unstable*) in a revision sequence S for M iff it is stably **x**, for some **x** (stably **x**, for no **x**).

If M = <D ∪ P, I> is a model of L, we take $\mathcal{D}_D$ to be the smallest set containing all the items of the form

(DF1) $p^{n+1}([\lambda x_1 \ldots x_n A], d_1, \ldots, d_n) =_{df} A(x_1/d_1, \ldots, x_n/d_n)$

and

(DF2) $p^{n+1}(d, d_1, \ldots, d_n) =_{df} \bot$,

where $[\lambda x_1 \ldots x_n A]$, $d, d_1, \ldots, d_n$ are DL$^+$-(closed) terms, d is not an n-adic DL$^+$-lambda-term, and "$\bot$" is some contradictory sentence of L.

We can call each such member of $\mathcal{D}_D$ a *partial definition* of an exemplification predicate p^n (relative to the model of L in question) in that, intuitively, each member of the form (DF1) provides an instance, with respect to a model, of the general schema (λ-def), whereas each member of the form (DF2) specifies, roughly, that the exemplification predicates can be truly applied only to PRP's of the appropriate adicity. Such partial definitions may be circular in that exemplification predicates may occur as active predicates in a definiens.

For any model M = <D ∪ P, I> of L, a *revision rule* $\rho_M^{\mathcal{D}}$ is an operation relative to the model M that, given a hypothesis h, yields a new hypothesis h' on the basis of the set of partial definitions $\mathcal{D}_D$. More specifically, for any hypothesis h relative to M, any definiendum A and the corresponding definiens B in $\mathcal{D}_D$, $\rho_M^{\mathcal{D}}$ (h)(A) = $[B]_{M+h}$.

We shall now restrict our attention to M*-revision sequences. An *M*-revision sequence* S is a revision sequence for a model M = <D ∪ P, I> of L such that:

(a) S_0 is any hypothesis relative to M.
(b)   if α+1 is a successor ordinal, $S_{\alpha+1} = \rho_M^{\mathcal{D}} (S_\alpha)$.
(c)   if α is a limit ordinal, then, for every definiendum A in the domain of the hypotheses DH, if A is stably **x** in the revision sequence S' for M resulting from restricting S to its first α members, then $S_\alpha(A) =$ **x** (i.e., $[A]_{M+S\alpha} =$ **x**).

Clause (c) grants that at any limit ordinal, all the "verdicts" on the interpretation of definienda reached in the preceding stages are preserved.

If M = <D ∪ P, I> is a model of L and A is a DL$^+$-sentence, we define " $\models_{P*}$ " (*P*-validity in* a model M of L) thus: M $\models_{P*}$ A iff A is stably **t** in all On-long M*-revision sequences.

We can now define what it is for a sentence A of L$^+$ to be **P***-valid (in symbols " $\models_{P*} A$ ") as follows: $\models_{P*} A$ iff for all models M of L, M $\models_{P*} A$.

Finally, we take the system **P*** to be {A: $\models_{P*} A$ }, i.e., the set of **P***-valid sentences of L$^+$. It will also be convenient, for any model M of L, to define $\mathbf{P}^*_M$ to be {A: M $\models_{P*} A$ }.

4   Properties of P*

The system **P*** is based on a *vacuous choice policy* (cf. [2]) in the sense that clause (c) above leaves the assignment of truth values to unstable sentences at limit ordinals completely arbitrary. **P*** can then be considered in a fundamental sense a special case of **S***, the general system for circular definitions based on the vacuous choice policy, studied in great detail by Gupta and Belnap. It can then be claimed that **P***($\mathbf{P}^*_M$) inherits from **S*** the following properties[14] (cf. [8], p.192 and p. 219):

(P1)   **P*** is *strongly conservative*, i.e., if A is a sentence of L, then M $\models_{P*} A$ only if M $\models A$. (This insures that the definitions for the exemplification predicates, though possibly circular, are *non-creative*, i.e., so to speak, they do not "generate" new facts.)

(P2)   For any M, $\mathbf{P}^*_M$ is *consistent*, i.e., there is no sentence A of L$^+$ such that $A \in \mathbf{P}^*_M$ and $\neg A \in \mathbf{P}^*_M$.[15]

(P3)   **P*** *sustains classical logic*, i.e., if A is a classical validity, then $\models_{P*} A$. More generally, if $\models A$ then $\models_{P*} A$.

(P4) $\mathbf{P}^*_M$ is *closed under classical logical consequence*, i.e., if M $\models_{P*} A$ and M $\models_{P*} A \rightarrow B$, then M $\models_{P*} B$.

(P5)   M $\models_{P*} A$ iff M $\models_{P*} p^{n+1}([\lambda x_1 ... x_n A(d_1/x_1, ..., d_n/x_n)], d_1, ..., d_n)$.

The following definitions are needed to state (P6) and (P7) below. For reasons of space, proofs for these propositions must be left for an extended version of this paper.

If A is any wff of L or L$^+$, we indicate by UC(A) its universal closure.

If A is a wff of L$^+$, lambda-conversion *holds* for A iff $\models_{P*}$ UC($p^{n+1}([\lambda x_1 ... x_n A(t_1/x_1, ..., t_n/x_n)](t_1, ..., t_n) \leftrightarrow A$).

---

[14] In the rest of this section "M" always ranges over models of L.

[15] From this it immediately follows that **P*** is consistent in the sense that for no sentence A of L$^+$, $A \in$ **P*** and $\neg A \in$ **P***. Note that the consistency of **P*** in the weaker sense that not all wff's of L$^+$ are in **P*** already follows from strong conservativeness.

A wff A of L^+ comes from a wff B of L^+ by *lambda-substitution* iff A results from B by substituting a sub-wff C of B with $p^{n+1}([\lambda x_1 \ldots x_n \, C(t_1/x_1, \ldots, t_n/x_n)], t_1,$ $\ldots, t_n)$. A wff A of L^+ is *L-based$_n$* iff it comes from a wff of L by a finite sequence of n lambda-substitutions.

(P6)   If $\models UC(A)$, then lambda-conversion holds for A.

(P7)   If A is an L-based$_n$ wff, then lambda conversion holds for A.

(P1)-(P7) are important for the potential applications of the framework outlined here. In particular, (P6) and (P7) grant a rich set of instances of (λ-conv) capable of supporting many interesting applications meeting the desiderata outlined in sect. 2.

5   Concluding remarks

Other instances of (λ-conv) can be established, and other interesting property-theoretic systems, based on non-vacuous choice policies, can be constructed. This must be left for a future occasion.

References

1.   Bealer G., *Quality and Concept*, London:Oxford University press, 1982.
2.   Belnap N., "Gupta's Rule of Revision Theory of Truth," *Journal of Philosophical Logic* 11 (1982), pp. 103-116.
3.   Castañeda H.-N., "Thinking and The Structure of the World", *Philosophia* 4 (1974), pp. 3-40.
4.   Cocchiarella N., "Frege, Russell, and Logicism: a Logical Reconstruction," in Haaparanta L. and Hintikka J. (eds.), *Frege Synthesized*, Dordrecht, The Netherlands: Reidel, 1986.
5.   Fagin R. and Halpern J. Y., "Belief, Awareness, and Limited Reasoning," *Artificial Intelligence* 34 (1988), pp. 39-76.
6.   Geach P. T., "Intentional Identity," *The Journal of Philosophy* 20 (1967), pp. 627-632.
7.   Gupta A., "Truth and Paradox," *Journal of Philosophical Logic* 11 (1982), pp. 1-60.
8.   Gupta A. and Belnap N., *The Revision Theory of Truth*, Cambridge, Mass.: The MIT Press, 1993.
9.   Haas A. R., "Sentential Semantics for Propositional Attitudes," *Computational Linguistics* 16 (1990), pp. 213-233.
10.   Hadley R. F., "A Sense-Based, Process Model of Belief," *Minds and Machines* 1 (1991), pp. 279-320.
11.   Herzberger H. G., "Notes on Naive Semantics," *Journal of Philosophical Logic* 11 (1982), pp. 61-102.
12.   Konolige K., *A Deduction Model of Belief*, London: Pitman, 1986.

13. Montague R., *Formal Philosophy* (Thomason R., ed.), New Haven, CN: Yale University Press, 1974.

14. Orilia F., "Belief representation in a Type-free Doxastic Logic," *Minds and Machines* 4 (1994), pp. 163-203.

15. Orilia F., "Guise Theory, Property Theory, and Castañeda's philosophical Methodology," forthcoming.

16. Rapaport W., "Logical Foundations for Belief representation," *Cognitive Science* 10 (1986), pp. 371-422.

17. Russell B., "On Denoting," *Mind* 59 (1905), pp. 479-493.

18. Shapiro S. and Rapaport W., "SNePS considered as a Fully Intensional Propositional Semantic Network," in Cercone N. and McCall G. (eds.), *The Knowledge Frontier*, Berlin: Springer Verlag, 1987, pp. 262-315.

19. Smullyan R., *First-Order Logic*, Berlin: Springer-Verlag, 1968.

20. Turner R., "A Theory of Properties," *Journal of Symbolic Logic* 52 (1987), pp. 455-472.

$\mathcal{TRDL}$: a language for conceptual modelling in Information Systems Engineering

Giovanni Rumolo [1] and Ernesto Compatangelo [2]

1 - Dipartimento di Informatica e Sistemistica,
Università di Roma "La Sapienza"
via Salaria, 113 - 00198 ROMA (Italy)
e-mail rumolo@assi.dis.uniroma1.it

2 - Istituto di Informatica della Facoltà di Ingegneria, Università di Ancona
via Brecce Bianche, 30 - 60125 ANCONA (Italy)
e-mail compatan@anvax1.unian.it

Abstract: This paper presents $\mathcal{TRDL}$, a new logic-based language for conceptual modelling in Information Systems Engineering. $\mathcal{TRDL}$ is a formal analyst-oriented Terminological Requirements Description Language allowing an integrated representation of both structural and behavioural requirements concepts. Its semantics is based on a new enhanced terminological language called $\mathcal{ERP}$, which is an extension of terminological languages introduced in order to capture process concepts. The expressive power of TRDL-based schemes is shown expressing them in terms of the $\mathcal{ERP}$ language. The correspondence with $\mathcal{ERP}$ characterises the overall reasoning properties of the $\mathcal{TRDL}$ model: completeness, soundness and EXPTIME complexity. $\mathcal{TRDL}$ is explicitly tailored for Requirements Modelling & Analysis performed during the early stage of Information Systems development. It is regarded as a formal kernel for the development of a new generation of CASE tools endowed with deductive capabilities.

1 Introduction

Conceptual Modelling in Information Systems Engineering (ISE), better known as Requirements Modelling, is currently considered as a critical, error-prone phase in this area [28, 15, 12, 23]. Four main classes of approaches to Conceptual Modelling, namely the Semantic, the Object-Oriented, the Deductive and the Knowledge-Based ones have been proposed so far in order to cope with the Requirements Modelling & Analysis (RM&A) stage in ISE. Each approach has been based on a different description scheme implicitly influencing the corresponding analysis results.

Semantic Modelling includes the Entity-Relationship (ER, [6]) and Structured Data Flow (SDF, [30]) semiformal approaches, which are complementary between them and separately used. Object-Oriented Modelling includes semiformal approaches which are generally considered as extensions of object-oriented programming and design paradigms to the requirements analysis phase (OOA, [7]). No deductive capability is possible using most of them, although a formal scheme overcoming these limitations has been recently proposed [27]. Deductive Conceptual Modelling is a completely formal, declarative approach to RM&A [22]. Knowledge-based Modelling [29, 20] encompasses a wide spectrum of approaches extending semantic models with the introduction of a knowledge representation method dealing with a temporal dimension or with a particular semantics.

Empirical findings about the state of the practice in this field [24] show that inadequacy of the description scheme (and thus inadequacy of the corresponding conceptual model) of an Information System (IS) generally leads to major misunderstandings about its purposes. These findings thus remark the importance of basing RM&A on a formal description scheme supporting automatic reasoning about a requirements model. In this way, hidden IS properties can be derived and inconsistencies can be detected, thus providing more effective modelling and analysis results.

This paper introduces the $\mathcal{TRDL}$ analyst-oriented Terminological Requirements Description Language as an attempt to cope with problems arising during the RM&A phase. The presentation is organised as follows: Section two outlines the characteristics of the ontological and methodological framework underlining $\mathcal{TRDL}$. Section three introduces the main syntactical features of the language. Section four describes $\mathcal{TRDL}$ semantics focusing on its expressive capability. Finally, section five outlines some major conceptual results as well as still-to-be-done work.

2 Conceptual Modelling in Information Systems Engineering: a framework for $\mathcal{TRDL}$

Requirements Modelling and Analysis (RM&A), i.e. Conceptual Modelling in ISE, is a knowledge-intensive phase in which knowledge elicitation and representation are performed at two distinct ontological and methodological levels [8]. In fact IS requirements, i.e. relevant knowledge about the problem represented by the IS itself, are constraints imposed over the corresponding Application Domain. Knowledge about the latter should be thus captured and analysed before defining the corresponding IS requirements. Two major analysis items are perceived as fundamental within the IS requirements phase: (i) a problem-oriented optative one, known as the prescriptive IS requirements level and (ii) a situation-oriented indicative one, known as the descriptive IS domain level. Both are concerned with implementation-independent, description-oriented modelling and analysis (the "what"). Other IS development phases are concerned with implementation-dependent, solution-oriented IS modelling (the "how"). However, being outside the scope of conceptual modelling, the latter phases are not considered in this paper.

2.1 Description structures in Conceptual Modelling

Two distinct analysis activities are identified in this work, namely:

- The analysis of Domain-independent concepts. Generic concepts defined in this phase can be used in representing different kinds of knowledge common to distinct application areas;

- The analysis of Domain-dependent concepts. Specific concepts defined in this phase can be used in representing a particular kind of knowledge within a definite application area.

Moreover, two distinct description structures can be introduced in order to characterise analysis activities within every ISE paradigm, namely:

- A Terminological, domain-independent and analysis-independent internal description structure which is based on a syntactically and semantically well-founded set of concept constructors belonging to the family of description logics [26]. This concept language naturally supports automatic reasoning. The terminological level is considered by the authors as the internal logical basis for investigating decidability, computational complexity and feasibility problems.

- An Epistemological, analysis-dependent external description structure which is based on a set of concept constructors strongly bound to the specific nature of the analysis activity. Each epistemological concept is expressed using an analyst-oriented syntax which can be understood at the same time by IS users. Each syntactical declaration of a given concept constructor in the epistemological description structure is mapped into a corresponding finite set of declarations in the underlining terminological structure.

2.2 Knowledge Representation & Reasoning in Conceptual Modelling

Knowledge representation and reasoning [18] is a wide area of Artificial Intelligence (AI) whose contributions are becoming of considerable importance in Information Systems Engineering [4] as well as in Requirements Modelling and Analysis [3, 20]. Considerable attention has been paid by the ISE/RM&A communities to the first structured knowledge representation techniques used in Artificial Intelligence, i.e. semantic networks and frame systems [19]. The KL-ONE family of languages and Knowledge Representation Systems [5, 29] was later introduced in AI in order to give more expressive power and an unambiguous semantics to the former structured approaches. The KL-ONE approach led to the development of the so-called terminological (i.e. concept-based) representations of knowledge allowing automatic classification and concept subsumption. This approach was chosen by the authors as the KR&R framework for conceptual modelling in Information Systems Engineering.

3 The Terminological Requirements Description Language

$\mathcal{TRDL}$ is based on three fundamental assumptions: the first one says that the Universe of Discourse (UoD) should be divided in two parts: the structural and the behavioural ones. The second assumption says that the definition of indicative assertions about the UoD should be considered as the main goal of any analysis activity. In other words, *the analyst should deal with the intensional outlook of reality*. The third assumption says that any analysis activity should be focused on the description of UoD concepts as well as on assertions about them.

$\mathcal{TRDL}$ gives the analyst three different linguistic categories in order to get a description of the UoD, namely: *class concepts, relationship concepts and process concepts* (see Appendix A). Each class represents an abstraction of some autonomous individual populating the UoD. Each relationship represents an abstraction of some class aggregation while each process is an abstraction of some transformation between classes or between relationships. A relationship is characterised by a minimum of two role assertions. A role defines a link between a relationship and a class of individuals. Assertions describe, for each role, class elements playing that role.

3.1 The Description of the structural part of the UoD

Each individual in a class is characterised by a set of structural properties, called attributes, and by a set of behavioural properties, called activities. Each attribute can be limited in the number of its values (the default is one). Each activity is a process, i.e. *a transformation from the class we are defining the activity for, to another class*. Every process can be either a basic or a derived one. The transformation is given in the *indicative mood* [16], so it represents a map from set to set. Any further process specification as a function from a domain element to a specific element of the codomain is intentionally left to the design activity. For instance, the `Notebook` class is characterised by an `owner`, a set of `appointments` and two special activities: `owner_?`, returning information about the owner and `view_all`, displaying all the appointments in the notebook:

```
Class Notebook
Attributes owner : Person
           appointments : Appointment
Activities owner_? : Person
           view_all : Appointement
end
```

Each class may belong to an ISA generalisation; declaring that Class C_2 is C_1 means that class C_2 is a subset of class C_1. Monotonic inheritance let analysts verify by consistency check whether an attribute of a parent class is not correctly redefined for some subclasses. Moreover, each relationship can belong to an ISA generalisation, but all ISA members must have the same set of roles. $\mathcal{TRDL}$ has a rich set of operators used in class and relationship expressions, including conjunction, disjunction and negation. Furthermore, existential, universal quantification and number restriction are allowed in class definitions. Using $\mathcal{TRDL}$, it is sufficient to say that Class C is C_1 or C_2 or ... C_k in order to assert the closure of a class C over its k subclasses. A $\mathcal{TRDL}$ relationship specifying roles, restrictions and structures of each class component can be used in the definition of an assembly structure which is analogous to the one used in Object Oriented Analysis [7].

3.2 The Description of the behavioural part of the UoD

Each process is characterised by at least one type declaration. Furthermore, the behaviour of a process may be defined in terms of a process expression. For every type declaration only one behavioural expression is possible; however, every process can be overloaded. The $\mathcal{TRDL}$ set of operators used in process expressions is very rich and includes sequential process, parallel process and conditional selection. For instance, let us consider a process *PMS* (Patient Monitoring System) receiving physiological data about a patient. Whenever these data enter into a dangerous range, an alarm process is activated.

The $\mathcal{TRDL}$ description of the *PMS* process can be expressed as:

```
Process   SendAlarm : DangerousData → Alarm
Process   PMS : PatientData → Alarm
   begin
      if ( PatientData and DangerousData )
      then SendAlarm
   end
```

In $\mathcal{TRDL}$, `SendAlarm` is a basic process described by its signature only (i.e. `DangerousData → Alarm`). *PMS* is a derived process described by its signature (i.e. `PatientData → Alarm`) as well as by its behaviour (i.e. `if ( PatientData and DangerousData ) then SendAlarm`).

3.3   The Description of global scheme assertions about the UoD

In $\mathcal{TRDL}$, the analysis of the structural part leads to a description of the corresponding concepts in terms of a set of assertions about UoD elements which define the set of all possible valid states. The analysis of the behavioural part leads to a description of behavioural concepts identifying transformations between structural concepts. These transformations define the desired transition between possible states. Moreover, set containment is used as a general rule for assertions about entities, relations and roles. Processes are used as transitions between concepts already introduced in the structural part of the UoD in order to describe behaviours. Process type and composition are both defined as assertions about the behavioural part, constrained by structural assertions.

4   The semantics of $\mathcal{TRDL}$: an outline

The $\mathcal{TRDL}$ semantics can be satisfactorily characterised using the $\mathcal{ERP}$ language [25], which is an extension of terminological languages [11, 21] introduced in order to capture process concepts. With respect to the previously described twofold classification introducing the terminological and the epistemological description levels, the $\mathcal{TRDL}$ language can be regarded as the epistemological level, while the $\mathcal{ERP}$ language can be regarded as the terminological level. This classification reflects different research perspectives: the first one, represented by $\mathcal{TRDL}$, studies how the proposed approach can be used in both industrial and teaching environments. The second perspective, represented by the $\mathcal{ERP}$ language, is used as a theoretical tool in the investigation of both expressive power and computational properties of the language itself. The most important characteristic of the $\mathcal{ERP}$ language is its correspondence with Propositional Dynamic Logic (PDL) [26, 25, 9]. PDL is a kind of propositional modal logic [14] originally developed in Theoretical Computer Science in order to reason about program schemes. PDL has been extensively used in Artificial Intelligence in order to establish decidability and computational complexity results. For instance, PDL was used in investigating Description Logic [26, 10], Feature Logic [1] and Common Knowledge [13]. The correspondence with PDL thus characterises the general reasoning properties of the $\mathcal{ERP}$ model: completeness, soundness and EXPTIME complexity. The formal semantics of each $\mathcal{TRDL}$ statement is obtained trough its translations into a finite set of $\mathcal{ERP}$ expressions. The overall $\mathcal{ERP}$ semantics is shown in appendix B.

4.1 The Description of the structural part of the UoD through examples

The previously described `Notebook` declaration is translated as in table 1. Each attribute has two fixed roles: Object and Value. *The element playing the role* Object *is the same one we are defining the attribute for. The element playing the role* Value *is the attribute value domain.* $\mathcal{TRDL}$ identifies a class as that set of elements playing the role Object in all attribute relationships defined for that class. This grants that any class description defines the set of elements characterised by their attribute properties. The final result of the above translation is a set of terminological assertions which can be used in verifying concept coherence as well as in deriving some entailed properties of the scheme. The meaning of the `Notebook` class is the set of all UoD elements verifying the following properties:

- `Notebook` instances always play the `Object` role in the `owner` relationship connecting them to a `Person`; they are specified by one and only one instance of the `owner` relationship

- `Notebook` instances always play the `appointments` role in the `owner` relationship connecting them to an `Appointment`; they are specified by one and only one instance of the `owner` relationship.

Source ($\mathcal{TRDL}$)	Rule	Target ($\mathcal{ERP}$)

Class `Notebook`
`Attributes`
    `owner:Person`
    `appointments:`
        `Appointment`
`Activities`
    `owner_?:Person`
    `view_all:`
        `Appointment`
`end`
	Final
	Result
		$Person \sqsubseteq T_e$
		$Appointment \sqsubseteq T_e$
		$Notebook \sqsubseteq T_e$
		$Notebook \sqsubseteq$
		$\forall owner[Object].Value:Person \sqcap$
		    $\sqcap (\leq 1\ owner[Object]) \sqcap$
		    $\sqcap \neg (\leq 0\ owner[Object])$
		$Notebook \sqsubseteq$
		$\forall appointments[Object].$
		    $Value:Appointment \sqcap$
		        $\sqcap (\leq 1\ appointments[Object]) \sqcap$
		        $\sqcap \neg (\leq 0\ appointments[Object])$
		$owner\_?:Notebook \rightarrow Person$
		$view\_all:Notebook \rightarrow Appointement$

Tab. 1: Translation of a $\mathcal{TRDL}$ class declaration into the corresponding set of $\mathcal{ERP}$ assertions

The two `Person` and `Appointment` classes are considered as primitive ones. Two transformations are specified in the above domain in addition to the `Person`, `Notebook` and `Appointment` classes. The type only is known about these transformations. Such a scheme will be considered as consistent if $\mathcal{ERP}$ assertions are satisfiable.

4.2 The Description of the behavioural part of the UoD through examples

The previously described *PMS* declaration is translated as in table 2. The meaning of $\mathcal{ERP}$ assertions defines an UoD with three primitive classes, namely `Patient-Data`, `Alarm`, `DangerousData` and two transformations, namely `SendAlarm` and `PMS`. The latter activates `SendAlarm` if the two `PatientData` and `DangerousData` intersect. Therefore, `PMS` will be a valid transformation if, for instance, it is possible to say that `PatientData` is a subclass of `DangerousData` by looking at the UoD. A basic process must only satisfy its signature, while a derived process must satisfy both its signature and its definition.

Source ($\mathcal{TRDL}$)	Rule	Target ($\mathcal{ERP}$)

`Process SendAlarm:`
 `DangerousData →`
 `Alarm`
`Process PMS:`
`PatientData → Alarm`
`begin`
 `if(PatientData and`
 `DangerousData)`
 `then SendAlarm`
`end`
	Final Result	$DangerousData \sqsubseteq T_e$
		$Alarm \sqsubseteq T_e$
		$PatientData \sqsubseteq T_e$
		$SendAlarm: DangerousData \rightarrow Alarm$
		$PMS: PatientData \rightarrow Alarm$
		$PMS: PatientData =$
		 $if(PatientData \sqcap DangerousData,$
		 $SendAlarm)$

Tab. 2: Translation of a $\mathcal{TRDL}$ process declaration into the corresponding set of $\mathcal{ERP}$ assertions

A process type declaration $\beta:I \rightarrow O$ defines a map β such that the activation using an I element returns at least one O element. Let us consider a modal temporal logic where an operator M expresses obligation and its dual L expresses possibility, an operator $[\beta]$ has the meaning "...must be true after β", while its dual $<\beta>$ has the meaning "...is possible after β". In such a logic the exact meaning of a $\mathcal{TRDL}$ process β can be written as $M(I \wedge \neg[\beta] O) \equiv L(I \rightarrow <\beta> O)$. A process is valid if it can be represented by a non empty map. Process operators include parallel activation in way which is better suited for requirements analysis than for computational description. For instance, a process P declared as: `Process P:InData →` `OutRelationship begin` $(P_1 \parallel P_2 ... \parallel P_k)$ `end` defines a transformation from a common domain (i.e. `InData`) to a k-ary relationship with a role for each process (i.e. `OutRelationship`). According to the semantics of `OutRelationship`, there exists at least one element of the specified class for each role.

4.3 Expressivity vs. decidability and computational complexity

During requirements analysis, several checks on the scheme being developed are often performed. $\mathcal{TRDL}$ is suitable in order to reason about all the meaningful aspects of the intentional level of a problem. A statement in the scheme is valid if the corresponding PDL formulas are satisfiable, otherwise it is not valid. The translation of $\mathcal{ERP}$ expressions into the corresponding set of PDL formulas gives rise to the conjunction of three subformulas (see also [25]). The first one, namely α, represents valid static as well as dynamic terms. The second one, namely β, represents actions ought to be true in every reachable state. The last formula, namely γ, represents the statement to be checked. The β formula expresses the condition that all scheme assertions are valid in every reachable state. Information System evolution is described by a collection of both states and accessibility relations among states. The type of relations and the internal structure of states differ from system to system. The goal of RM&A is a full description of both states and accessibility relations. The $\mathcal{TRDL}$ proposal allows the analyst to reach this goal within a decidable logic framework. The inference problem can be thus solved, although worst case analysis shows that it belongs to the EXPTIME problem class.

5 Conclusions

The comparison between $\mathcal{TRDL}$ and other widely diffused semiformal analysis schemes like E-R, SADT or Coad's OOA, shows that: (i) semiformal approaches are neither sound nor complete. Soundness and completeness are not considered even in many formal approaches; (ii) $\mathcal{TRDL}$ subsumes most modelling concepts proposed in semiformal models. Moreover, a comparison with others recent proposals like COMIC [17] and E/S [2] shows that: (i) both proposals do not express process meaning at a conceptual level; (ii) most ontological principles of COMIC are shared by $\mathcal{TRDL}$, although the latter uses a precise set theoretic semantics in concept definitions, thus leading to a formal study of model properties; (iii) E/S has a different ontological representation of the Relationship concept (called Situation in E/S) which is not considered by us as an epistemologically well founded one.

The proposal described in this paper is an attempt to investigate the conceptual kernel of the analysis activity, looking for those basic concepts supporting RM&A as perceived by analysts. This purpose is accomplished on the basis of the theoretical framework underlying Terminological Languages. As most existing analysis models already try to capture the overall characteristics of IS requirements, at first sight one more model might seem unnecessary. However, the ultimate goal of this proposal is the development of a CASE tool that may support RM&A activities using the deductive power of logic. The proposed model is endowed with enough expressive power, but without loss of decidability and completeness with respect to a fully logic-based framework. Comparisons with other proposals show a widely shared need for a sound, complete and decidable modelling language. The authors are trying to accommodate the need for a mathematical foundation in RM&A with pragmatical needs in the analysis phase of Information Systems Engineering. Knowledge Representation and Reasoning based on a terminological approach is a suitable framework for accomplishing this goal. The $\mathcal{TRDL}$ approach may lead to the development of a powerful automated assistant helping the analyst during the continuous revision process of a requirements specification. Future work will deal with the effectiveness of the proposed framework in building a CASE tool embedding the ontological and methodological assumptions contained in the approach described in this paper.

207

References

[1]   P. Blackburn, E. Spaan. *A modal perspective on computational complexity of attribute value grammar.* Journal of Logic, Language and Computation. n° 2, 1993, pp. 129-169

[2]   S. Bergamaschi, et. al. *The E/S Knowledge Representation System.* Data & Knowledge Engineering, vol. 14, 1994, pp. 81-115

[3]   A. Borgida, et al. *Knowledge Representation as the basis for Requirements Specification.* IEEE Computer, Apr. 1985, pp. 82-91

[4]   A. Borgida, M.Jarke, eds. *Special Issue on KR&R in Software Engineering.* IEEE Transactions on Software Engineering, vol. 18, n° 6, 1992

[5]   R.J. Brachman, J.G. Schmolze. *An overview of the KL-ONE Knowledge Representation System.* Cognitive Science, vol. 9, n° 2, 1985, pp. 171-216

[6]   P.P. Chen. *The Entity-Relationship Model: towards a unified view of data.* ACM Trans. on Database Systems, vol. 1,n° 1, Mar 1976, pp. 9-36

[7]   P. Coad, E. Yourdon. *Object-Oriented Analysis, 2nd ed.* Prentice-Hall, 1991

[8]   E. Compatangelo, G. Rumolo. *Terminological Requirements Modelling & Analysis in Information Systems Engineering.* To be published in AICA'95, Proceedingsof the annual conference of the AICA, Cagliari, 1995

[9]   G. De Giacomo, M. Lenzerini. *Boosting the correspondence between description logic and propositional dynamic logics.* In Proceeding of the 12th National Conference on Artificial Intelligence, 1994, pp. 205-212

[10]   G. De Giacomo, M. Lenzerini. *Description Logic with inverse roles, functional restriction, and n-ary relations.* In Proc. of the 4th Europ. W.shop on Logics in A.I., Lecture Notes in AI, vol. 838. Springer, 1994, pp. 332-346

[11]   F.M. Donini, et al. *The complexity of Concept Languages.* In Proc. of the 2nd Int. Conf. on the Princ. of KR&R . Morgan Kaufmann, 1991, pp. 151-162

[12]   S. Greenspan, et al. *On Formal Requirements Modeling Languages: RML Revisited.* In Proc. of the 16th Int. Conf. on Sw. Eng. (ICSE-16), 1994

[13]   Y. Halpern, J.Y. Moses. *A guide to completeness and complexity for modal logics of knowledge and belief.* Art. Int., vol. 54, 1992, pp.319-379

[14]   D. Harel, *Dynamic Logic.* In Handbook of Phil. Logic, 1984, pp. 497-603

[15]   ICRE'94. Int. Conf. on Req. Eng., Colorado-Springs (USA), Apr., 1994

[16]   M.A. Jackson, P. Zave. *Domain Descriptions.* In [28], pp. 56-64

[17]   H. Kangassalo. *COMIC: A system and methodology for conceptual modelling and information construction.* Data & Knowledge Engineering, vol. 9, 1992/93, pp. 287-319

[18]   R.J. Brachman, H. Levesque, eds. *Readings in Knowledge Representation.* Morgan Kaufmann, 1985

[19]   F. Lehmann, *Semantic Networks*, Computer & Mathematics with Applications, vol. 23, n° 2-5, 1992, pp.1-50

[20]   J. Mylopoulos, et al. *Telos: Representing Knowledge About Information Systems.* ACM Trans. on Inf. Systems, vol. 8, n° 4, Oct. 1990, pp. 325-362

[21] B. Nebel. *Reasoning and revisions in hybrid representation systems*. In Lecture Notes in Artificial Intelligence, Springer Verlag, 1990

[22] A. Olivè. *On the design and Implementation of Information Systems from Deductive Conceptual Model*. In 15th Int. Conf. on very large DB, 1989

[23] K. Pohl. *The three dimensions of Requirements Engineering: a framework and its applications*. Inform. Systems vol. 19, n° 3, Apr. 1994, pp. 243-258

[24] C. Potts. *Software Engineering Research Revised*. IEEE Software, Sept. 93, pp. 19-28

[25] G. Rumolo, M. Lenzerini. *Information Systems Analysis: a formal model for the specification of behavioural and structural class properties*. In Proc. of the 4th Int. Conf. on Inform. Sys. Development (ISD94), 1994, pp. 63-72

[26] K. Schild. *A correspondence theory for terminological logics: preliminary report*. In Proc. of the 12th Int. Conf. on A.I. (IJCAI91), 1991, pp.486-471

[27] A. Sernadas, R. Li. *Reasoning about Objects using a tableaux method*. Journal of Logic and Computation, vol. 1, n° 5, 1991, pp.575-611

[28] RE93. *Proc. of the 1st IEEE Int. Symp. on Req. Eng.* IEEE, 1993

[29] W.A. Woods, J. G. Schmolze. *The KL-ONE Family*. Computers & Mathematics with Applications, vol. 23, ns. 2-9, 1992, pp. 1-50

[30] E. Yourdon. *Modern Structured Analysis*. Prentice Hall, 1989

Appendix A: $\mathcal{TRDL}$ Syntax

\<RequirementsSpecification\>	::=	\<DescriptionOfConcepts\> [\<ConceptAssertions\>]
\<DescriptionOfConcepts\>	::=	\<DescriptionOfClasses\> \<DescriptionOfRelationships\> [\<DescriptionOfProcesses\>]
\<ConceptAssertions\>	::=	[\<ClassAssertions\>] [\<RelationshipAssertions\>]
\<DescriptionOfClasses\>	::=	(Class \<C-Name\> [is \<ClassList\>] [\<ClassBody\>] end)$^+$
\<DescriptionOfRelationships\>	::=	(Relationship \<R-Name\> [is \<RelationshipList\>] [\<RelationshipBody\>] end)$^+$
\<DescriptionOfProcesses\>	::=	(Process \<P-Name\> : \<ProcessType\> [\<ProcessBody\>] end)$^+$
\<ClassAssertions \>	::=	(Class \<C-Name\> is \<ClassList\>)$^+$
\<RelationshipAssertions \>	::=	(Relationship \<R-Name\> is\<RelationshipList\>)$^+$
\<ClassList\>	::=	\<ClassExpression\> (, \<ClassExpression\>) *
\<ClassExpression\>	::=	\<C-Name\>|aClass|not in \<ClassExpression\>| \<ClassExpression\> and \<ClassExpression\>| \<ClassExpression\> or \<ClassExpression\>| All in \<R-Name\> with \<U-Name\> SuchThat \<Condition\> holds| Some in \<R-Name\> with \<U-Name\> Where \<Condition\> holds| Those in \<R-Name\> with \<U-Name\> RestrictedTo (\<min\> , \<max\>)

Appendix A: $\mathcal{TRDL}$ Syntax (continued)

<Condition>	::=	<C-Name> in <ClassExpression> [<ConjuntiveCondition>]
<ConjuntiveCondition>	::=	(and <C-Name> in <ClassExpression>)$^+$ [and <U-Name> RestrictedTo (<min>,<max>)]

<RelationshipList>	::=	<RelationshipExpression> (,<RelationshipExpression>)*
<RelationshipExpression>	::=	<R-Name>|aRelationship| not in <RelationshipExpression>| <RelationshipExpression> and <RelationshipExpression>| <RelationshipExpression> or <RelationshipExpression>

<ClassBody>	::=	[<DescriptionOfAttributes>] [<DescriptionOfActivities>]
<DescriptionOfAttributes>	::=	Attributes (<AttributeDefinition>)$^+$
<AttributeDefinition>	::=	<A-Name>:<ClassExpression> [RestrictedTo (<min>,<max>)]
<DescriptionOfActivities>	::=	Activities <ActivityDefinition>$^+$
<ActivityDefinition>	::=	<P-Name> : <ClassExpression> [<ProcessBody>]

<RelationshipBody>	::=	(<ClassExpression> has role <U-Name>)$_2^+$
<ProcessType>	::=	<ClassExpression> $\rightarrow$ <ClassExpression> | <RelationshipExpression> $\rightarrow$ <RelationshipExpression>
<ProcessBody>	::=	begin <ProcessExpression> end
<ProcessExpression>	::=	<P-Name>|select <num>| (<ProcessExpression>)| <ProcessExpression> ; <ProcessExpression>| <ProcessExpression> || <ProcessExpression>| if <StructuralExpression> then <ProcessExpression> [else <ProcessExpression>]
<StructuralExpression>	::=	<ClassExpression>|<RelationshipExpression>

<min>	::= <num>|m	<R-Name>	::=	"Relationship Name"
<max>	::= <num>|M	<U-Name>	::=	"Role Name"
<num>	::= 0|1|...	<P-Name>	::=	"Process Name"
<C-Name>	::= "Class Name"	<A-Name>	::=	"Attribute Name"

Appendix B: The $\mathcal{ERP}$ Language

Constructor Name	Syntax	Semantics
Class Name	C, D	$C^I, D^I \subseteq \mathcal{E}^I$
Role Name	U	$U^I \subseteq \mathcal{R}^I \to \mathcal{E}^I$
Relationship Name	R, P	$R^I, P^I \subseteq \mathcal{R}^I$
Process Name	m, α	$m^I, \alpha^I \subseteq (2^{\mathcal{E}^I} \to 2^{\mathcal{E}^I}) \cup (2^{\mathcal{R}^I} \to 2^{\mathcal{R}^I})$
Projector Name	π_j	$\pi_j^I \subseteq (2^{\mathcal{R}^I} \to 2^{\mathcal{E}^I})$
Top Class	T_e	$\mathcal{E}^I$
Top Relationship	T_r	$\mathcal{R}^I$
Class Conjunction	$C \sqcap D$	$C^I \cap D^I$
Class Negation	$\neg C$	$\{e \in \mathcal{E}^I \mid e \notin C^I\}$
Universal Quantification	$\forall R[U].T_1{:}C_1 \,..T_n{:}C_n$	$\{e \in \mathcal{E}^I \mid \forall r \in \mathcal{R}^I$ $r[U]{=}e \to (r[T_1] \in C^I_1 \wedge .. \wedge r[T_n] \in C^I_n)\}$
Existential Quantification	$\exists R[U].T_1{:}C_1\,..T_n{:}C_n$	$\{e \in \mathcal{E}^I \mid \exists r \in \mathcal{R}^I$ $r[U]{=}e \wedge (r[T_1] \in C^I_1 \wedge .. \wedge r[T_n] \in C^I_n)\}$
Number Restriction	$(\leq n\,R[U])$	$\{e \in \mathcal{E}^I \mid \#\{r \in \mathcal{R}^I \mid r[U]{=}e\} \leq n\}$
Relationship Conjunction	$R \sqcap P$	$R^I \cap P^I$
Relationship Negation	$\neg P$	$\{e \in \mathcal{R}^I \mid e \notin P^I\}$
Process if	$if(C, def)$	$\{(u, t) \mid u \in C^I \wedge (u, t) \in \|def\|^P\}$
Process ife	$ife(C, def_t, def_e)$	$\{(u, t) \mid u \in C^I \wedge (u, t) \in \|def_t\|^P\} \cup \cup \{(u, t) \mid u \notin C^I \wedge (u, t) \in \|def_e\|^P\}$
Process Sequence	$\alpha; def$	$\{(u,t) \mid \exists w\,(u, w) \in \|\alpha\|^P \wedge (w,t) \in \|def\|^P\}$
Process Parallel	$def_1 \|..\| def_n$	$\{(u, t) \mid \exists w_1 .. w_n\, t$ $(\wedge^n_{\iota=1}((u, w_i) \in \|def_i\|^P \wedge t[U_i] = w_i) \wedge$ $\wedge\,(t \in \mathcal{R}^I))\}$

Tab. B1: Syntax and Semantics for the $\mathcal{ERP}$ language

Assertion	Syntax	Semantics
Class Assertion	$C \sqsubseteq D$	$C^I \subseteq D^I$
Relationship Assertion	$R \sqsubseteq P$	$R^I \subseteq P^I$
Process Assertion: Type	$m{:}I_1 \to O_1, .., m{:}I_n \to O_n$	$\{(u, t) \mid u \in \cup^n_{\iota=1} I^I \wedge t \in \cup^n_{\iota=1} O^I \wedge$ $\wedge\,\forall^n_{\iota=1}\exists(u, t)\,(u \in I^I \wedge t \in O^I)\}$
Process Assertion: Behaviour	$m{:}I_1 = def_1, .., m{:}I_n = def_n$	$\{(u, t) \mid u \in \cup^n_{\iota=1} I^I \wedge t \in \cup^n_{\iota=1} O^I \wedge$ $\wedge\,\forall^n_{\iota=1}\forall u \in I^I \to (u, t) \in \|def_i\|^P\}$

Tab. B2: Syntax and Semantics for $\mathcal{ERP}$ assertions

The Different Roles of Abstraction in Abductive Reasoning

Daniele Theseider Dupré and Mauro Rossotto*

Dipartimento di Informatica – Università di Torino
Corso Svizzera 185 – 10149 Torino, Italy – E-mail: dtd@di.unito.it

Abstract. The use of knowledge at different levels of abstraction can be proposed to make automated abduction more flexible. This paper analyzes several declarative and computational ways of exploiting abstractions in abduction, including the definition and implementation of preference criteria for explanations based on abstraction, and the use of abstractions to focus the explanation process.

1 Introduction

An important challenge in knowledge representation and reasoning is the reproduction, at least to some extent, of the human capability of exploiting abstractions, i.e. of being able to deal with information at different levels of abstraction, and to shift from one level to another when necessary. The goal of this paper is to analyze the use of abstractions in abductive reasoning (i.e. reasoning from observations to their possible explanations) and, in particular:

- pointing out that there are different ways of exploiting a representation language for abductive reasoning with abstractions both from a declarative and a computational point of view, depending on the scenario in which the abductive system is expected to operate;
- discussing how and how much the declarative and computational goals can be achieved in logic-based abductive reasoning.

2 Explanatory hierarchies

A simple propositional language is introduced in [2] (based on the one in [4]) as a minimal one for introducing abstractions in abduction. The language distinguishes two orthogonal dimensions: the common one in abductive reasoning, providing links between hypotheses and possible observations, and a second one providing abstraction links (which could also be seen as inheritance links) between entities (in particular, hypotheses and observations) and their specializations. This language does not include all of the ways abstraction can be used or has been used in AI [3, 5] but is sufficient for the goals of this paper.

---

* Currently with the Artificial Intelligence Research Unit, CSELT, Torino, Italy.

Definition 1. An **explanatory hierarchy** is a pair $\langle T_E, T_A \rangle$ where:

- T_E, the set of **explanatory axioms**, is a set of definite clauses $P_1 \wedge ... \wedge P_n \rightarrow Q$ where $P_1 \wedge ... \wedge P_n$ is intended as a direct explanation of Q.
- T_A, the set of **abstraction axioms**, is a set of definite clauses $P \rightarrow Q$ where P is intended as a specialization of Q (Q is an abstraction of P).
- There is a distinguished set of symbols, the **abducible atoms** or **assumptions**, that can be accepted in explanations and are the ones that do not appear in the consequent of any explanatory axiom.
- There are no cyclic dependencies in $T_E \cup T_A$.

The following definition of abductive explanation (a variation on definitions used in the literature) can be adopted if the two dimensions of explanatory hierarchies are disregarded, i.e. if the set $T_E \cup T_A$ is considered in the same way as a "flat" domain theory. The same definition will be used as a reference in the following for analyzing the role of abstractions in abduction.

Definition 2. Given an explanatory hierarchy $\langle T_E, T_A \rangle$, an **explanation** of a set of literals OBS is a set E of abducible atoms such that $T_E \cup T_A \cup E \vdash O$ for each positive literal O in OBS and $T_E \cup T_A \cup E \not\vdash O$ for each negative literal $\neg O$ in OBS.

3 Avoiding unnecessarily detailed explanations

A first main goal in defining abduction in the presence of abstractions is the introduction of *preference criteria based on abstraction*: explanations that are as abstract as possible could be preferred, according to a form of parsimony that generalizes the preference for minimal explanations: unnecessarily detailed assumptions should be avoided, in the same way as unnecessary assumptions. A good declarative characterization for this preference is the notion of least presumptive explanation introduced in [6], where however the computational counterpart is not addressed: avoiding the computation of non-preferred explanations would be much better than discarding them a-posteriori.

The task discussed here is relevant if the observations can be explained by "abstract" assumptions whose refinement is not necessarily required; i.e. the goal of the user (either a human which uses the system for consultation, or some other software module, e.g. a planning system), at least in a first step, is *just* to have explanations of the observations, no more and no less. In this task the role of abstraction is relevant at least for allowing a natural and economic representation of a domain, where *inheritance* is used to avoid repeating common consequences of a class of hypotheses, and for being flexible enough to deal with observations and assumptions at different levels of abstraction.

Figure 1 is an explanatory hierarchy adapted from [4] (the task consists in recognizing the dish - or menu - an agent is preparing by observing his/her actions). Thick grey arrows correspond to abstraction axioms while thin black arrows correspond to explanatory axioms; abducible symbols are in boldface.

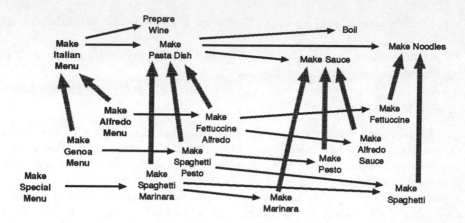

Fig. 1. A cooking hierarchy.

If $MakeNoodles$ is observed, the explanation $E_1 = \{MakeItalianMenu\}$ can be preferred to $E_2 = \{MakeGenoaMenu\}$ and $E_3 = \{MakeAlfredoMenu\}$ since they are unnecessarily specific. This can be formalized as in the definition of **least presumptive explanation** [6]: since each of E_2 and E_3 implies E_1, given T_A, they are considered *more presumptive* than E_1, which is a *least presumptive* explanation. However, $E_4 = \{MakeSpecialMenu\}$ is not more presumptive than other explanations (it does not imply other ones). In this case the abstraction is *incomplete* since there is no counterpart, at the abstract level, for knowledge about $MakeSpecialMenu$; therefore, not all of the least presumptive explanations of $MakeNoodles$ can be found using just explanatory axioms. The problem is how to constrain an explanation algorithm based on backward search in such a way that explanations such as E_2 and E_3 are *not found*, rather than found and discarded, while explanations such as E_4, if any, are not disregarded.

There are several possible answers to this problem. One is to require abstractions to be complete, disallowing hierarchies like the given one. This would require duplicating at abstract levels knowledge that cannot be significantly abstracted. A different answer is the approach in [2], which, however, does not necessarily find all the least presumptive explanations. A way to ensure that all such explanations are found (described in more detail in [7]) relies on a preprocessing phase to identify the incomplete abstractions, so that when explaining observations at some level, only those parts of lower levels that have no correspondent in the current level could be taken into account. In the example this means identifying that $MakeSpecialMenu$ is an explanation of $MakePastaDish$ that is not represented in $MakeItalianMenu$ (the only explanation of $MakePastaDish$ that uses explanatory axioms only). There are several ways to implement this form of preprocessing, based on the following definitions.

Definition 3. Given an explanatory hierarchy $\langle T_E, T_A \rangle$:

- A set D of atoms is **represented** in a set D' of atoms if D is more presumptive than D'.

- A **flat** explanation of an atom O is a set E of abducible atoms such that $T_E \cup E \vdash O$.
- An abstraction axiom $Q \to P$ is **complete** if every explanation of Q is represented in a flat explanation of P.
- An explanatory hierarchy $\langle T_E, T_A \rangle$ is **complete** if every abstraction axiom in it is complete.

Completeness ensures that, given an abstraction axiom $Q \to P$, the use of Q to explain P in a backward search algorithm can be avoided without loosing any least presumptive explanation. However, verifying completeness is in general expensive since it may require computing explanations for all the atoms in the explanatory hierarchy that are involved in abstraction axioms. A solution relies on a local version of completeness that only refers to the direct explanations (in the sense of definition 1) of P and Q. This notion, which provides an approximation of completeness, only requires a linear time preprocessing phase, and still leads to algorithms that compute all the least presumptive explanations without exhaustive search in the hierarchy (details are given in [7]).

4 Top-down abduction

The second main goal for introducing abstractions in abduction is the *use of abstractions to focus the explanation process*. This is relevant in scenarios where detailed observations are available from the beginning, and is a purely computational goal: speeding up the computation of explanations satisfying definition 2. The idea is to explain an abstraction of the detailed observations, possibly discriminating among alternative abstract explanation, and to use the abstract explanation(s) in order to (hopefully) focus the explanation of detailed observations. Explanation could also be limited to the abstract level in case the (human or automated) user does not need the refinement (or if there is no knowledge to explain the actual observations; see [2, 7] for a discussion).

There are essentially two ways of exploiting the fact that high-level explanations have already been found:

- backward chaining from detailed observations and accepting only those solutions that are refinements (under some appropriate definition) of high-level explanations (**backward chaining refinement**);
- generating all the refinements (according to an appropriate definition) of high-level explanations and testing such refinements (by forward chaining), in order to check whether they actually explain low-level observations (**forward chaining refinement**). This is similar to [5] (but see section 5).

In order to adopt one of these two approaches rather than the "flat" one which directly explains low-level observations, a number of subtleties have to be taken into account even under the simplifying assumption that the hierarchy is made of different layers, each one containing an abstract or refined version of the same knowledge (there is no incompleteness), as in figure 2.

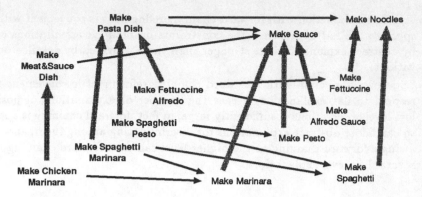

Fig. 2. Another explanatory hierarchy in the cooking world.

Problem 1: refining minimal abstract explanations does not suffice.
More precisely, search cannot be limited to explanations that can be obtained
from *minimal* high-level explanations, substituting every assumption P with a
Q such that $Q \rightarrow P \in T_A$. Consider in fact figure 2 and suppose that $OBS = \{MakeMarinara, MakeSpaghetti\}$. The abstract observations are $OBS' = \{MakeSauce, MakeNoodles\}$, having $E_1 = \{MakePastaDish\}$ as a minimal
explanation. The minimal explanations of OBS are $\{MakeSpaghettiMarinara\}$
and $\{MakeChickenMarinara, MakeSpaghettiPesto\}$; the latter is not a refinement of E_1 in the sense defined above.

Problem 2: singleton refinements do not suffice, i.e. an abstract assumption P cannot be just refined into *one* Q such that $Q \rightarrow P \in T_A$. Suppose in fact that $OBS = \{MakeFettuccine, MakeSpaghetti\}$. The corresponding abstract set of observations is $OBS' = \{MakeNoodles\}$ with explanation
$E = \{MakePastaDish\}$, but there is no singleton refinement of E which explains OBS: two specific pasta dishes have to be assumed.

Problem 3: abstraction may unfocus. This problem is even more fundamental than problems 1 and 2. Suppose that in figure 2 $MakePesto$ is observed.
There is only one explanation at the detailed level, $MakeSpaghettiPesto$; but
at the abstract level, $MakeSauce$ has two explanations, $MakePastaDish$ and
$MakeMeat\&SauceDish$. There is no need for trying to discriminate among
these two explanations; abstraction causes a loss of information.

Due to problems 1 and 2, the generation of refinements in the forward chaining refinement approach has to be much less constrained than one would expect
(even if it is not necessary to consider all non-minimal abstract explanations,
and to refine each assumption with an unlimited number of its specializations
[7]). Even in cases where problems 1 and 2 do not arise, the convenience of the
two top-down approaches with respect to the flat approach can be questioned.
Problem 3 is an extreme case; in general, the following consideration can be
made (some experimental results are reported in [7]):

- Top-down abduction with forward-chaining refinement is convenient with respect to the flat approach if the constraints on detailed assumptions given by abstract explanations are stronger than those provided by detailed observations.

- Top-down abduction with backward chaining refinement is convenient with respect to flat explanation in case the number of explanations of positive low-level observations is sufficiently large; in fact, forward chaining is applied to candidate abstract explanations for discriminating among them, and then a single forward chaining at the higher level can save forward chaining from several low-level explanations.

5 Concluding remarks

While the use of descriptions at different levels of abstraction is appealing, the discussion in this paper shows that obtaining the desired flexibility in an automated abductive reasoner is not trivial.

The use of abstractions for focusing model-based diagnosis is proposed in [5]; the results in that paper are positive since it deals with models where backward reasoning is too expensive; therefore the top-down approach (with forward-chaining refinement) is seen as an improvement of a naive generate-and-test approach. This is not in contrast with the discussion in section 4.

The use of abstractions in the set-covering approach to diagnosis is proposed in [1]. In that paper there is no explicit evaluation of the advantages, if any, of using abstractions if the ultimate goal of the user is to discriminate between specific assumptions that explain initial observations, and no way of generating refined explanations relying in some way on abstract explanations is proposed.

References

1. B. Chu and J. Reggia. Modeling diagnosis at multiple levels of abstraction I and II. *International Journal of Intelligent Systems*, 6(6):617–671, 1991.

2. L. Console and D. Theseider Dupré. Abductive reasoning with abstraction axioms. In *Foundations of Knowledge Representation and Reasoning*, pages 98–112. Lecture Notes in Computer Science 810, Springer Verlag, 1994.

3. F. Giunchiglia and T. Walsh. A theory of abstraction. *Artificial Intelligence*, 57:323–389, 1992.

4. H. Kautz. A formal theory of plan recognition and its implementation. In J. Allen, H. Kautz, R. Pelavin and J. Tenenberg, *Reasoning about Plans*, Morgan Kaufmann, 1991.

5. I. Mozetic. Hierarchical model-based diagnosis. *Int. J. of Man-Machine Studies*, 35(3):329–362, 1991.

6. D. Poole. Explanation and prediction: An architecture for default and abductive reasoning. *Computational Intelligence*, 5(2):97–110, 1989.

7. D. Theseider Dupré. *Characterizing and Mechanizing Abductive Reasoning*. PhD Thesis, Dip. Informatica, Università di Torino, 1994.

A Cognitive Model of Causal Reasoning about the Physical World

Antonella Carassa[1], Alessandra Valpiani[2],
Giuliano Geminiani[2], Stefania Bandini[3]

[1] Dipartimento di Psicologia Generale, Università di Padova
via C. Battisti 3, 35139 Padova
tel 049/8751886 fax 049/8763226
email carassa@psych.unito.it
[2] Centro di Scienza Cognitiva, Università di Torino
via Lagrange 3, 10123 Torino
tel 011/549475 fax 011/549653
email valpiani@psych.unito.it
[3] Dipartimento di Scienze della Informazione, Università di Milano
via Comelico, 39 20135 Milano
tel 02/55006269 fax 02/55006276
email bandini@hermes.mc.dsi.unimi.it

Abstract. The aim of this paper is to present a cognitive model and a related computational system for representing and simulating the causal reasoning about the physical world. The cognitive model of causal reasoning is based on two main assumptions, the assumption of reasoning by examples and the assumption of causality by contact. The computational model has been developed using an Extended version of the Qualitative Processes Theory (EQPT); the use of the EQPT as a qualitative simulator allows to represent and treat the various commonsense physical domains. The modular and flexible architecture of the implemented system allows it to be used as an automated support for psychological experimentations.

1 Introduction

A recent and increasingly important topic in Artificial Intelligence (AI) concerns the investigation of *qualitative* and *commonsense reasoning models* of everyday physical situations (Qualitative Reasoning – QR) [Weld et al., 1993]. The main reasons of this research effort arose from the following considerations:

- traditional analytical models show limitations in the description and computation of real life physical situations;
- humans interact with the surrounding physical environment using a wide variety of studied [Bozzi,1992] and yet undiscovered cognitive models;
- qualitative and commonsense models are often employed and managed also by experts while solving formalized problems (e.g. [Yip, 1993]).

Within the general framework of a cognitive approach to QR, the study of the role that *causal models* play in qualitative reasoning about physical world is crucial, as it is in other more traditional approaches (e.g. physics itself or diagnostics). Causal models have been created and studied throughout several specific subfields of QR, and the related literature show results and approaches (both "theoretical" and computational) charcterizing this research activity.

A *cognitive approach* in the investigation of causal models used by humans while reasoning about and interacting with the everyday physical world comprises classical theories and experimental results created and tested during the last 50 years. Models and results coming from a cognitive perspective would increase both the knowledge of the inner working of mental models in humans and the possibility of designing computational models and tools supporting computer systems that tackle problems not easily solvable with more traditional approaches.

The aim of this paper is to present a cognitive model and a related computer system for the representation and simulation of causal reasoning activities about circumscribed physical situations usually well handled by humans. From a cognitive perspective, the main features which characterize our model derive from the two following basic assumptions.

– *Assumption of reasoning by examples*
  In the general framework of dynamical mental models [Johnson–Laird, 1983] reasoning processes are a matching of a "target" situation with a "model" of it. It is required to build and test a sequence of examples as a sequence of refined models of physical processes.
– *Assumption of causality by contact*
  The physical contact between two objects (an *agent* and a *target*) is the necessary condition for the realization of a causal link between two events.

The creation of a computational model which allows for the representation and the simulation of a cognitive model to be performed requires, on its own turn, some assumptions and restrictions:

– a qualitative model of the involved physical processes;
– the explicit representation of all the individual components occurring in the cognitive model and their relationships;
– the possibility of switching from some condition to some other by means of explicit *actions* activated in the simulation.

The computational model used is an Extension of the Qualitative Process Theory (QPT) [Forbus, 1984] presented in [Bandini et al., 1988] and here applied in the cognitive modeling framework[4]. EQPT introduces the explicit representation and management of actions.

---

[4] QPT has been used in the same framework in its original version too [Gentner et al., 1983]

In Sections (2) and (3) the general cognitive model of causal reasoning about physical circumscribed situation and the general architecture of the related computer simulation system will be presented. Section (4) will illustrate an example of the simulation results obtained using backward inference. Finally, some concluding remarks will be drawn.

2 A Theoretical Framework of Causal Reasoning about the Physical World

2.1 What to Represent

It has been experimentally demonstrated that humans and most of the superior mammals [Sperber et al., 1995] perceive causality when they are observing objects that come into direct contact. The term *perception* denotes that no cognitive process is required. Infants (4–5 months old) have the same interpretation of causal sequences as adults. This kind of perception is automatic, obliged and innate ([Leslie, 1984], [Leslie et al., 1987], [Michotte, 1946]).

Carassa et al. [Carassa et al., 1993] maintain that contact between objects is the crucial aspect of physical causality, not only in perception, but also at the cognitive level of causal analysis. When human subjects are reasoning about two events that they judge to be causally linked, they try to represent a physical interaction between objects. The very concern is in assigning causal roles to two specific objects (AGENT and TARGET) and in envisaging how they come into *contact*. Contact is seen as the necessary condition for the realization of the causal link between events at a more abstract level.

At a first level, the aim of the reasoning process is to establish a cause-effect link between two events (causal attribution). At a second level, the concern is in analysing the linked events in term of the objects which play the role of the AGENT and the TARGET and their relationship. The causal roles can be derived from perception, or given by information or hypothesized by the subject on the basis of general or domain knowledge. The cause and the effect are in temporal sequence, and the former is characterized by the fact that an AGENT and a TARGET are not yet in contact as they will necessarily be in the latter. At a third level, there is the analysis of the dynamics of the causal process.

We deal either with the problem of how people postulate causal links between events (causal attribution) nor of how they assign causal roles to objects. Our interest is in exploring how people model the physical process that results in the contact between the AGENT and the TARGET. In order to reason about the dynamics of the causal process it is necessary to postulate the presence of a MEDIUM, an object or a set of objects that allows the AGENT to act on the TARGET in spite of their spatial not-contiguity. As with the AGENT and the TARGET, the MEDIUM also has physical features that are relevant for the dynamic evolution of the process. The causal process is the process that temporally precedes and allows the realization of the contact between the AGENT and the TARGET. As an example, it is possible to think that a solid object (AGENT) is transported by a fluid (MEDIUM) so as to reach another solid object (TARGET). Or alternatively, a fluid can move through the air so as to reach a solid object causing a physical modification of the last. As discussed in Carassa et al. [Carassa et al., 1993] each kind of interaction strictly depends on the physical features of the two objects, in the first place on the cynematic aspects, which is the relative movement of the two objects: as an example the AGENT moves into the MEDIUM, otherwise the AGENT is still in a moving MEDIUM and so on. In the following we will name "elementary physical phenomena" the AGENT-MEDIUM interactions. It is stressed that the knowledge regarding the elementary phenomena is knowledge that develops as a consequence of direct experience of the world. In this sense, reasoning processes on complex phenomena always refer to a more basic knowledge shared by all individuals. As an example, you can reason about a poisoning process (complex phenomenon) applying the knowledge about the interaction between a fluid, the poison, and another fluid, the blood flowing in the circulatory system (elementary process).

2.2 The Model Representation

Causal reasoning is based on the manipulation of mental models, an analogical representational structure originally proposed by Johnson–Laird [Johnson–Laird, 1983]. If based on mental models, reasoning processes are always relying on examples; a mental model is in fact a representation of a specific situation. To verify the general validity of a reasoning process based on the analysis of particular cases, it is necessary to generate a finite set of significative examples using "falsify" procedures on mental models [Johnson–Laird, 1983]. A causal model represents the AGENT, the MEDIUM, the TARGET and sometimes also the MODIFIERS, that are objects interfering with the "natural" evolution of the process. Causal models comprehend:

- a structural component that represents the objects, their physical behavior and relations between objects;
- a modifiable component that represents the quantitative aspects of the objects.

To specify the quantitative aspects corresponds to the construction of a specific model. A reasoning process starts with the construction of a BASE MODEL, the simplest model representing the process without MODIFIERS and with standard values of the quantitative aspects taken as a reference system for all other models. Alternative models can be constructed by variating the quantitative aspects of the BASE MODEL or by introducing MODIFIERS. It is important to note that a causal model is a dynamic model that simulates the temporal evolution of the physical process.

2.3 Reasoning Processes

The architecture of the inferential system is domain general as the procedures for manipulating and revising mental models are the same in any domain of physical causality. This implies that some general principles guide the reasoning processes in any domain. In the following, to be clearer, we will refer to a specific example where the causal process is the poisoning of a person and the elementary physical phenomenon is that of a fluid carried by another fluid flowing in an elastic duct. The poison (AGENT) is represented as an aggregate of particles carried by the blood flowing in the circulatory system (MEDIUM) towards the heart (TARGET). Let us consider the reasoning processes based on linguistic premises. Two kind of inferences are drawn by the system: in forward inferences the event-cause (the bite of a snake) and some enabling conditions (i.e. the injection of an antidote) are given and the aim is to draw the event-effect (death or survival); in backward inferences the event-cause and the event-effect are both given and the aim is to define some enabling conditions that corroborate the causal link. We postulate two kinds of general procedures, construction procedures and control procedures.

– **Construction procedures**
  Models of causal processes are constructed, making use of data drawn from the premises and from knowledge of physical phenomena and causal links. Two models are always constructed, a first standard model of the causal process, BASE MODEL, and a MODIFIED MODEL, based on the contents of the premises. These models temporally develop simulating how different factors reciprocally interact. Every simulation results in a final state of the process. The final state regards the conditions of the TARGET: the contact with the AGENT could have been fulfilled or not and in case of contact the quantitative aspects of the contact itself are specified.
– **Control procedures**
  The control procedures allow to draw a plausible conclusion by comparing two dynamic models. As an example, given the premises:
  Albert was bitten by a snake
  Albert was applied a string
  two models are generated:
  1. a model "without the string" (BASE MODEL)
  2. a model "with the string" (MODIFIED MODEL)
  The conclusion is drawn by comparing the final states of the two models. In both models:
  Albert died
  but in the MODIFIED MODEL the temporal interval between the bite of the snake and the death is longer.

3   The Computational Model

The inferential system consists of two modules, corresponding to the construction and the control procedures. A first implementation of the inferential system, SNAKE [Valpiani et al., 1994], has been developed in the past. In this paper we present a computational model based on an Extended version of the Qualitative

Process Theory, called EQPT. We have chosen to adopt QPT for representing mental models and simulating their dynamic aspects, in order to preserve the character of generality of the inferential system. QPT interpreter allows the simulation of all physical phenomena provided that the physical phenomenon is represented in QPT language. The EQPT is a remarkable extension of the QPT for the following reasons:

- it allows an accurate representation of the quantities of the objects and of the functional dependencies between these quantities;
- when conflicting influences impinge on a single quantity, it is able to determine the resulting direction of change for the quantity;
- it allows the introduction of actions and new objects during the simulation of a process. In this new version, the inferential system has been developed in Prolog language, at the Expert Systems Lab at the Department of Computer Science (University of Milan). A testing of the system is being currently carried out at the Cognitive Science Center (University of Turin).

3.1 The SYNTACTIC - SEMANTIC ANALYZER

The module of the system devoted to the syntactic and semantic analysis of the crucial terms representing quantities in a qualitative way allows the introduction of natural language sentences. They give information about the victim and the circumstances about the poisoning caused by the bite of a snake. The processing of natural language sentences consists of two phases:

1. *analysis phase* – includes a text correctness check, both syntactic and semantic. Correct sentences are expressed as lists:

   `[predicate, subject(attribute), direct object(attibute)]`

   As an example, given the premise:
   Albert was bitten by a big snake
   the following list is produced:

   `[bite, subject, snake(big), object, albert]`

2. *synthesis phase* – consists of two processes:
   (a) the first one generates facts from the premises for the construction of a model of the specific poisoning process.
   (b) the second process translates quantitative aspects from natural language into qualitative values using fuzzy sets theory.
   For example, given the list

   `[bite, subject, snake(big), object, albert]`

   the following facts are inferred[5]:

   `fact(snakebite) = true`
   `snake_size has_value highpos`

---

[5] The quantitative aspects of the objects are represented by qualitative variables; `highpos` is a qualitative variable that represents the value 'big'.

3.2 The CONSTRUCTION MODULE

In the general architecture of the system, the module devoted to the construction of the model consists of:

- **Activation procedures**
  They activate the knowledge concerning the structural component of the model, namely the objects with their physical behavior. They lead to the construction of a pre-model.
- **Quantification procedures**
  They specify the quantitative aspects of the objects. The values of the quantitative aspects of the BASE MODEL are the reference system for all the successively generated models. This means that in a reasoning process the absolute value of a quantity is not relevant per se, but only with reference to another model where this quantity is increased or reduced. The values of the quantitative aspects of the components of the MODIFIED MODELS, if not specified in the premises, are assigned by default. These procedures lead to the construction of a physical model.
- **Simulation procedures**
  They simulate the temporal evolution of the model by activating the knowledge about an elementary physical phenomenon and about the effect of the MODIFIERS; they lead to the construction of a dynamic model. The MODIFIERS can be introduced since the beginning on the basis of the content of the premises and/or added during the revision phase by the CONTROL MODULE.

We used an Extended version of QP theory [Bandini et al., 1988] to represent and simulate the temporal evolution of the involved physical processes.

EQPT LANGUAGE QPT [Forbus, 1984] identifies the fundamental components of a physical phenomenon to be the objects involved, the relevant quantities describing the interesting parameters of the objects, and the processes operating on or between the objects. A causal model of a physical phenomenon formalized in EQPT language consists of:

- **Objects** – In the poisoning process there are poison, heart, circulatory system and MODIFIERS as antidote, cardiotonic and so on. The quantitative aspects of the objects are represented by qualitative variables, which take values in the totally ordered set of symbols [EQPT]:

  { infneg, highneg, highmedneg, medneg, lowmedneg, lowneg, zero, lowpos, lowmedpos, medpos, highmedpos, highpos, infpos }

  This set is called *Quantity Space* (QS), where every value represents an interval of real numbers except zero which is a number. This is another remarkable extension of the QPT, because it allows to be more accurate in the representation of the quantities.

– **Processes** –

Processes act on objects by changing their quantitative aspects. In our example, they are the flow of the poison towards the heart and the action of the MODIFIERS on this flow. A source of ambiguity in QPT in the original version is caused by the lack of detailed information about the functional relationships between quantities. When conflicting influences impinge on a single quantity, QPT is unable to determine the resulting direction of change for the quantity ([D'Ambrosio, 1989a], [D'Ambrosio, 1989b]).To obviate this difficulty, EQPT proposes to represent the influences using this syntactic construct:

`type_influence (intensity, quantity)`

where `intensity` takes values in the totally ordered set of symbols:

$$\{\text{very\_weak, weak, normal, strong, very\_strong}\}$$

During a poisoning process, for instance, the lethal threshold can be influenced by both the injection of a cardiotonic and by the general condition of health of the victim. The EQPT influences allow to determine how the threshold is modified by these two joint factors.

– **Dependencies** –

These qualitatively describe the functional dependencies between quantities. In EQPT they are represented with greater accuracy by the construct:

`q_prop (direction, type, quantity1, quantity2)`

where `direction` indicates the direct or inverse direction of the dependency, and `type` indicates the type of the dependency between `quantity1` and `quantity2`. Type takes values in the totally ordered set of symbols :

$$\{\text{log, rad, lin, poli, exp}\}$$

For instance, the force of constriction exerted by an hemostatic string linearly reduces the velocity of the flow of the blood.

– **Actions** –

They describe the instantaneous changes which can occur during a process. The mechanism which allows the actions to be handled, and the related operational semantics in EQPT have been illustrated in [Bandini et al., 1988]. In the poisoning process actions allow MODIFIER to be introduced. The effects of an action persist during all the simulation or until a new action is introduced, restoring the previous state.

EQPT INTERPRETER The INTERPRETER of the EQPT language is devoted to generate models of causal processes. It always generates two models, a BASE MODEL as a first model, and then a MODIFIED MODEL based on the contents of the premises. Following the instructions of the CONTROL MODULE, in the revision phase, it constructs new MODIFIED MODELS. It simulates how the different factors reciprocally interact. Simulations stop in a final state of the process. The interpreter follows these steps (for more details, see [Corcione, 1994]).

- **Activation of starting conditions.** Objects (poison, heart, circulatory system) are activated and a value of the Quantity Space is assigned to each of their quantitative aspects. Then the starting processes (flow of the blood) are activated.
- **Modification of the quantitative aspects.** Until a steady state, the following steps are executed (the steady state corresponds to the exhaustion of the particles of poison or to the reaching of the deadly threshold):

  1. **Control of Activity.**
     The interpreter checks if an action must be activated (an action corresponds to the introduction of a new object, a MODIFIER, or to the exhaustion of the particles of poison or to the reaching of the deadly threshold). Then it controls if active elements (individual views or processes) must be disactivated or if disactive elements activated.
  2. **Determination and resolution of influences.**
     The interpreter looks for the influences in the active processes : these will contribute to the evolution from the present state to the next by changing the quantitative values of the objects on which the processes act. As an example, the flowing of the blood contains two influences, the first decreases the amount of the poison in the wound and the second increases the amount of the poison in the heart.
  3. **Propagation of influence.**
     When a change occurs in a quantity, all the quantities linked to it by a functional dependency are consequently changed.

3.3 The CONTROL MODULE

The Control Module is composed of *matching procedures* and *revising procedures*. The matching procedures work on the two dynamic models generated by the CONSTRUCTION MODULE, the BASE MODEL and a first MODIFIED MODEL initially, or two MODIFIED MODELS during the revision phase. They find out how the two dynamic models differ in their quantitative aspects and in their final states. In backward inferences, if the final state of the MODIFIED MODEL corresponds to the effect-event mentioned in the premises, the conclusion consists in a description of the model. In particular, the quantitative aspects of the model are made explicit. If the correspondence is not fulfilled, the revising procedures lead to the construction of alternative models. The two following alternative strategies can be applied.

1. New objects (MODIFIERS) are introduced. They can be progressively added to the initial model, so to originate more and more complex models. As an example, in a model where the person dies, the effect of a cut in the wound is simulated, and different values of its quantitative aspects are explored

(depth and moment of the cut) until a model is reached, whose final state corresponds to the event-effect of the premises.

2. Quantitative aspects of the already represented objects are systematically changed. As an example, in a model where a person dies in spite of the injection of an antidote, the amount of the antidote is changed until a model is produced where the quantity of antidote is insufficient to act against the poison. In both cases no explicit rules prescribe how to modify a model so as to advance nearer to a fixed conclusion. Revision proceeds by trials. These trials are evaluated on the basis of a comparison of couples of model successively generated. So doing, the revising procedures select those modifications that get the final state of a MODIFIED MODEL nearer to the prescribed final state, while rejecting the other models.

4 An example of backward inference

Given the premises

Albert was bitten by a snake
Albert was injected a big dose of antidote
Albert died

the following facts are drawn by the SYNTACTIC-SEMANTIC ANALYZER:

```
fact(snakebite) = true
fact(died) = true
antidote_quantity has_value highpos
```

These facts are given to the CONSTRUCTION MODULE. First, the CONSTRUCTION MODULE constructs the BASE MODEL by applying the activation and the quantification procedures. The quantitative aspects of the BASE MODEL become the reference system for all the successively generated models; these aspects assigned by default take the value **medpos** in the QS. The initial values of the BASE MODEL are:

```
Initial values BASE MODEL
amount_poison(heart) = zero
amount_poison(vein) = medpos
diameter(vein) = medpos
lenght(vein) = medpos
threshold(heart) = medpos
blood_velocity(vein) = medpos
```

Then, on the basis of the premises, the CONSTRUCTION MODULE generates the MODIFIED MODEL 1. The quantification procedures specify the quantitative aspects of the MODIFIED MODEL 1 by integrating the qualitative values (**medpos**) of the BASE MODEL with the qualitative values drawn by the premises. The quantitative procedures use the relations:

```
amount_poison(vein) depends_on bite_depth & snake_size
lenght(vein) depends_on bite_position & height
threshold(heart) depends_on health & age
blood_velocity(vein) depends_on agitation
```

As an example, given the premise *the bite of the snake was deep* the quantification procedures apply the rule:

```
q_prop (direction, lin, bite_depth, amount_poison (wound))
```

where direction can be **increasing** or **decreasing** and generate a model where

```
amount_poison(vein) = highmedpos
```

where

```
highmedpos = medpos + lowpos
```

The unspecified quantitative aspects are assigned by default to **medpos**. The poisoning process starts when the following conditions are verified:

```
amount_poison(heart) = zero AND amount_poison(vein) > zero
```

The initial values of the MODIFIED MODEL 1 are:

```
Initial values MODIFIED MODEL 1
amount_poison(heart) = zero
amount_poison(vein) = medpos
diameter(vein) = medpos
lenght(vein) = medpos
threshold(heart) = medpos
blood_velocity(vein) = medpos
```

The antidote is not yet present as it is injected a MEDIUM time after the bite. The temporal evolution of the models is simulated by the simulation procedures. Let us consider the quantities in the two models at an intermediate instant:

```
Intermediate values BASE MODEL        Intermediate values MODIFIED MODEL
amount_poison(heart) = lowmedpos      amount_poison(heart) = lowpos
amount_poison(vein) = lowmedpos ...   amount_poison(vein) = lowmedpos ...
after 8 steps                         after 8 steps
```

The time of the simulation is measured by the number of the time-steps. The number of time-steps in the BASE MODEL is the reference for all other models. The final state of the simulation is reached when:

```
amount_poison(heart) >= threshold(heart) OR amount_poison(vein) = zero
```

The final values result:

Final values BASE MODEL   Final values MODIFIED MODEL 1
```
amount_poison(heart) = medpos    amount_poison(heart) = lowmedpos
amount_poison(vein) = lowpos ... amount_poison(vein) = zero ...
after 15 steps                   after 18 steps
```
The CONTROL MODULE considers the final state of the MODIFIED MODEL 1 and according to the following rules:

```
amount_poison(heart)<threshold(heart) ==> fact(alive)
```

produces a conclusion:

```
alive is true
died is false
```

If, as in our example, the final state of the MODIFIED MODEL does not corresponds to the event-effect mentioned in the premises, the CONTROL MODULE by applying the revising procedures leads to the construction of an alternative model by modifying the MODIFIED MODEL. No explicit rules prescribe how to modify a model of a poisoning process in order to move toward a fixed conclusion, but explicit rules prescribe how to modify whichever causal model. New objects (MODIFIERS) can be introduced or quantitative aspects of the already represented objects can be sistematically changed. Therefore, the revising procedures casually choose the new objects to introduce or the quantitative aspects to modify. The revising procedures randomly choose the modification:

```
    modification: the antidote was injected after a short time
```

It corresponds to

```
antidote_time has_value lowmedpos
```

From the MODEL 1, a MODIFIED MODEL 2 is constructed, where the antidote is injected a short time after the bite. So the final values result:
Final values MODIFIED MODEL 1 Final values MODIFIED MODEL 2
```
amount_poison(heart)=lowmedpos amount_poison(heart)=lowpos
amount_poison(vein)=zero ...    amount_poison(vein)=zero ...
after 18 steps                  after 20 steps
```

The CONTROL MODULE produces the conclusion:

```
alive is true
died is false
```

The CONTROL MODULE through the matching procedures evaluates the effect of the modification by comparing the two successively generated models: the amount of poison accumulated in the heart, the time requested for this amount and so on are considered. The CONTROL MODULE verifies that in the MODIFIED MODEL 2

```
amount_poison(heart)=lowpos
```

whereas in the MODIFIED MODEL 1

```
amount_poison(heart)=lowmedpos
```

So, by matching these values with the value of the lethal threshold

```
threshold(heart)=medpos
```

the CONTROL MODULE finds that the final state of the MODIFIED MODEL 2 is farther than the one of the MODIFIED MODEL 1 to the final state prescribed by the premises. Therefore the MODIFIED MODEL 2 is rejected. Now the CONTROL MODULE finds out that the quantity of poison in the heart depends on the time of inoculation of the antidote. Hence it chooses the modification:

```
modification: the antidote was injected after a long time
```

It corresponds to:

```
antidote_time has_value highmedpos
```

Starting from the MODEL 1, the CONSTRUCTION MODULE constructs a MODIFIED MODEL 3. The novel aspect is that the antidote is injected after a long time. So the final values result

```
Final values MODIFIED MODEL 1     Final values MODIFIED MODEL 3
amount_poison(heart)=lowmedpos    amount_poison(heart)=medpos
amount_poison(vein)=zero ...      amount_poison(vein)=lowpos ...
after 18 steps                    after 16 steps
```

Now the conclusion is compatible with the facts expressed in the premises:

```
alive is false
died is true
```

The matching procedures find out which parameters the MODEL 3 and the MODEL 1 differ in. The goal is to find the differences that justify the conclusion (Albert died). The significant parameter is:

```
the antidote was injected after a long time
```

5   Conclusions

In this paper we have presented a cognitive model of causal reasoning about the physical world based on the reasoning by examples and the causality by contact assumptions. The adoption of an Extended version of the Qualitative Processes Theory allowed the implementation of a computational model for building and testing models of physical situations and verification of it on an experienced example. The general architecture of the realized system shows many advantages:

1. the choice of the QPT model supports the qualitative approach to the representation of quantities in mental models;
2. the use of the EQPT as a qualitative simulator allows to represent and treat the various commonsense physical domains;
3. the modular and flexible architecture allows the implemented system to be used as an automated support for psychological experimentations.

References

[Bandini et al., 1988] Bandini, S., M. Bruschi, M. G. Filippini, A. Molesini, An Interpretation of QPT Computational Model according to Logic Programming, W.N. of Second Workshop on Qualitative Physics, IBM Research Center, Parigi, 1988; also in . Martelli, A., G. Valle (eds.), "Computational Intelligence", Noth Holland, Amsterdam, 1988.

[Bozzi,1992] Bozzi, P., La Fisica Ingenua, Garzanti, Milano, 1992.

[Carassa et al., 1993] Carassa A, G. Geminiani, B. G. Bara, Causalità per Contatto: un Modello Computazionale di Ragionamento Quotidiano, Sistemi Intelligenti, 5(3), Il Mulino, Bologna, 1993.

[Corcione, 1994] Corcione D., Un Sistema per la Simulazione di Modelli Cognitivi, Tesi di Laurea, Scienze dell'Informazione, A. A. 1993/94.

[D'Ambrosio, 1989a] D'Ambrosio B., Extending the Mathematics in QPT, International Journal of Intelligent Systems, 4, 1989

[D'Ambrosio, 1989b] D'Ambrosio B., Qualitative Process Theory Using Linguistic Variables, Symbolic Computation, Artificial Intelligence, Springer-Verlag, 1989.

[Forbus, 1984] Forbus, K.D., Qualitative Process Theory, Artificial Intelligence, 24, 1984.

[Gentner et al., 1983] Gentner, D., A. L. Stevens, Mental Models, Lawrence Erlbaum Ass., NJ, 1983.

[Johnson–Laird, 1983] Johnson–Laird, P. N., Mental Models, Cambridge University Press, Cambridge, UK, 1983.

[Leslie, 1984] Leslie A. M., Spatiotemporal Continuity and the Perception of Causality in Infants, Perception, 13, 1984.

[Leslie et al., 1987] Leslie A. M., Keeble S., Do Six-month-old Infants Perceive Causality?, Cognition, 25, 1987.

[Michotte, 1946] Michotte A., La Perception de la Causalité , Louvain, Ed. de l'Institut Superieur de Philosophie (Etudes de Psychologie), VIII, 1946, (Trad. "The Perception of Causality", Methuen, London, 1963).

[Sperber et al., 1995] Sperber D., D. Premack, A. J. Premack, Causal Cognition. A Multidisciplinary Debate, Clarendon Press, Oxford, 1995.

[Valpiani et al., 1994] Valpiani, A., A. Carassa, G. Geminiani, Un Sistema di Ragio namento Causale basato sui Modelli Mentali, Atti del Congresso Annuale dell'Associazione Italiana per l'Informatica ed il Calcolo Automatico, Palermo, 1994.

[Weld et al., 1993] Weld, D., J. De Kleer, Readings on Qualitative Physics, Morgan Kaufmann, 1993.

[Yip, 1993] Yip, K. M. - K., Understanding Complex Dynamics by Visual and Symbolic Reasoning, Artificial Intelligence, 51,1991.

[Zadeh, 1978] Zadeh L., The Concept of Linguistic Variable and its Application to Approximate Reasoning, Fuzzy Set and Systems, 1, 1978.

A Generalized Approach to Consistency Based Belief Revision

Aldo Franco Dragoni, Francesca Mascaretti, Paolo Puliti

Computer Sciences Institute
University of Ancona
Via Brecce Bianche
Ancona,Italy 60131
E-mail dragon@anvax2.cineca.it

Abstract: This paper presents the basic ideas of a consistency-based approach to Belief Revision that allows the rejection of the newcoming information. This choice is justified for some application domains and leads to the definition of two distinct sets of formulas: the "Belief Base", which is the eventually inconsistent collection of all the available pieces of information, and the "Reasoning Base" which is the consistent outcome of the revision process. The selection of the Reasoning Base, among the many possible maximally consistent subsets of the Belief Base, is induced by an ordering on the sentences that does not reflect necessarily the chronological order of the arrivals of the information.

1   Introduction

Every kind of knowledge is doomed to evolve, hence any intelligent agent has to be able to change its opinion about a certain circumstance when new information contradict some of its beliefs. For this reason, knowledge revision is a crucial and discussed argument in the Artificial Intelligence community. There are lots of works about this subject [2-5,9,10,12,13,14-17]; most of them refer to the theory of Alchourrón, Gärdenfors and Makinson [1] [11]. This theory is placed in a logical setting and knowledge is represented by a deductively closed set of formulas called "belief-set". This is the aspect of the theory that has been criticized because the deductive closure is very costly to compute (generally intractable) and it has been noticed that the asserted beliefs are more important than the derived ones; some authors, like Nebel [15,16], have studied the revision of "belief-bases", namely finite sets of formulas.

However both kinds of revision are based on the next principles.

1) Consistency: any revision should yield a consistent belief-sets/bases.

2) Minimal change: as few pieces of knowledge as possible should be altered.

3) Priority to the incoming information: newcoming information is always part of the rearranged belief-sets/bases.

However, while this third rule is certainly justified when keeping up to date the representation of an evolving world, it seems not completely acceptable when revising the representation of a static world by a contradictory or uncertain incoming information. In general, the chronological order of the arrives of the pieces of knowledge has nothing to do with their credibility. Especially when revising knowledge coming from a multi-agent environment [6], it is absolutely unjustified giving priority to the incoming information. This paper proposes the basic ideas of a consistency-based approach to Belief Revision that doesn't impose the last principle. We compare our approach with the one presented in [2].

2 Inconsistency Management and the "Store and Recover Principle"

In this section we present a new approach to Belief Revision relying on a new principle that replaces the "Priority of Incoming Information" one. We start by summarizing an interesting paper [2], that we'll use for a camparison. Let L be a propositional language. A *belief base* S is a non-empty set of formulas of L that is neither deductively closed nor necessarily consistent. Moreover the formulas of S are ranked by a complete pre-ordering $\leq$, or equivalently, S consists in a collection $(S_1, ...,S_n)$ of belief bases, where S_i is a class of priority and S_1 contains the formulas of the highest one. The aim is that of defining a non-trivial inference from an inconsistent knowledge base of the form "S entails β if β can be classically inferred in all the preferred consistent subbases of S". The selection of preferred subbases of S is made easier if the pre-ordering $\leq$ is extended into a preference relation $\langle\langle$ on 2^S to compare sets of formulas. Let $A=A_1\cup...\cup A_n$, $B=B_1\cup...\cup B_n$ two consistent subsets of S (where $A=A_i\cap S_i$ e $B_i=B\cap S_i$).

The *Inclusion based ordering* is the strict ordering defined by $A\langle\langle_S^{inc} B$ iff $\exists i$ such that $A_i\subset B_i$ and for any $j<i$ $A_j=B_j$.

The maximal consistent elements of $\langle\langle_S^{inc}$ are of the form $A=A_1\cup...\cup A_n$ such that

i) A_1 is a maximal consistent subbase of S_1

ii) $A_1\cup...\cup A_i$ is a maximal consistent subbase of $S_1\cup...\cup S_i$ for i=1...n.

Definition 1 A subbase A of S is $\langle\langle_S^{inc}$ maximal α-consistent iff $A\cup\{\alpha\}$ is consistent and A is maximal with respect to $\langle\langle_S^{inc}$ among the α-consistent subbases of S.

Definition 2 Let α be a formula. $Add(\alpha,S)=(S_0=\{\alpha\},S_1...S_n)$.

Definition 3 $\alpha \mid\sim_S^{inc} \beta$ iff for any $\langle\langle_S^{inc}$ maximal α-consistent subbase A of S $A\cup\{\alpha\} \vdash\beta$.

Proposition $\alpha \mid\sim_S^{inc} \beta$ iff $\mid\sim_{Add(\alpha,S)}^{inc}\beta$ with $\alpha \neq\perp$.

As every knowledge revision model that is suggested in the literature (A.G.M. theory [1,11-13], Nebel theory [15,16], probabilistic and possibilistic theories [9] et al.), even this approach relies on the unconditioned acceptance of the incoming information. This means that any cognitive state has to be modified so that the incoming information can be taken into account. From a cognitive point of view, this choice is justified when updating the representation of an evolving world, but it is rather questionable when revising knowledge about a static world, especially in fields where there are multiple and varied sources of information like inquiries [8] and distributed environments [7]. In fact when someone has a collection of beliefs about a certain circumstance, he can decide to reject a new uncertain information contradicting the already available knowledge. For example, during a detective inquiry, there is no reason for the "a priori" acceptance of a recently given testimony if it contradicts other already available evidences. Hence our aim is to present an approach that deals with the possibility that the newcoming information can be rejected. We consider Belief Revision from a *normative* point of view, rather than from a *descriptive* one. To take advantage of the potentially unlimited computer's capacity to store information, we impose that the eventually rejected information has to be stored somewhere to permit its recovery after further evidences that support it or contribute to contradict the previously accepted knowledge. So we replace the "priority to the incoming information" principle with the following one:

3) *Store and recover principle*: every incoming information has to be stored to be eventually recovered by a revision process whenever it will be possible.

Let the "belief-base" KB be the set of the received information, that is a finite set of formulas of L. On the arrival of a new piece of information α, it has to be added to KB. If KB is inconsistent (as normally it might be) it cannot be used to make inferences. For this reason we define the "reasoning-base" B as a maximally consistent subset of KB.

Let's start with the case that KB is consistent so that B=KB. Let KB' be $KB \cup \{\alpha\}$. If KB' is consistent then no revision must be done and B is simply expanded by α. If KB' is inconsistent then there are two possibilities:

i) α is rejected so that the outcome of the revision is the consistent set B=KB.

ii) α is accepted so that a classical revision must take place. Following Nebel [15,16] we choose as outcome the set B which is the union of α and a maximally consistent subset of KB that fails to imply $\sim\alpha$.

These two operations can be collapsed into the following revision rule: select one of the maximally consistent subsets of $KB \cup \{\alpha\}$. In fact the next theorem is valid:

Theorem 1

Let A be a finite and consistent set of sentences and β a sentence such that $A \cup \{\beta\}$ is inconsistent. Let $A \downarrow \sim\beta$ be the set of maximal subsets of A that fail to imply $\sim\beta$. Let $H=\{C \cup \{\beta\} \mid C \in A \downarrow \sim\beta\}$. Let F be the set of maximally consistent subsets of $A \cup \{\beta\}$. The set H is the set $F \setminus \{A\}$.

Proof

If A is a finite and consistent set of sentences and $A \cup \{\beta\}$ is inconsistent, then the only maximally consistent subset of $A \cup \{\beta\}$ that doesn't contain β is A. Let $D \neq A$ be an element of F. Then β belongs to D. Let $D=D' \cup \{\beta\}$. $\sim\beta$ is inferred from D' iff $D' \cup \{\beta\}$ is unsatisfiable. D is satisfiable, so $\sim\beta$ cannot be inferred from D'. Hence $D \neq A \in F$ iff $D' \in A \downarrow \sim\beta$ so that $D \in H$. Hence $F=H \cup \{A\}$. ∎

Let's now consider the normal case that KB is inconsistent. Let β be the new information. Generalizing the above behaviour and following the theorem 1, the

revision is performed by selecting one of the maximally consistent subsets of $KB \cup \{\beta\}$. This decision problem can be decomposed into two steps:
1. define an ordering of credibility on the sentences in KB,
2. extend this ordering into another one on the maximally consistent subsets of KB
Credibility does not necessarily respect a semantical meaning (as the epistemic entrenchment does) because it applies to sentences that, although eventually derivable from each other, are not derived but assumed. Furthermore, it isn't static since it can be changed by the newcoming information. The second step can be performed in various ways. Many possible strategies are based on the following procedure: let `stack` contain all the sentences in KB sorted from the least (on the bottom) to the most credible one (on the top).

> **begin**
> $S := \{C \subseteq KB \cup \{\beta\} \mid C \nvdash \perp, \forall C' : C \subset C' \subseteq KB \cup \{\beta\} \Rightarrow C' \vdash \perp)\}$;
> > **repeat**
> > $\phi := pop(\text{stack})$;
> > **if** $S' = \{C \in S \mid \phi \in C\} \neq \emptyset$
> > > **then** $S := S'$
> > **until** $S = \{C_0\}$;
> > **return** C_0;
> **end.**

The remaining maximally consistent subset C_0 is the preferred one and is also one of the subbases maximal with respect to the inclusion-based ordering.
If C_0 contains β then it is the outcome of classical revision too. If C_0 doesn't contain β then β is rejected. The revision process applies not to the consistent reasoning-base B, but to the overall inconsistent belief-base KB. There are two advantages in doing so:
1. this permits the recovery of previously rejected formulas (sentences belonging to KB, but not to B)
2. the whole knowledge base KB can be reviewed in the light of the new information and vice-versa.
If we allow that the newcoming information β might alter the credibility ordering of the sentences in KB, then β can lead to a revision (the new reasoning-base B' can be different from $B \cup \beta$) even if it doesn't contradict the current reasoning-base B.
Consider the case that KB is consistent and a newcoming information α is such that $KB' = KB \cup \{\alpha\}$ is inconsistent. Let β be a new information so that the belief base becomes $KB'' = KB' \cup \{\beta\}$.
The revision's outcome B can have one of the following structures:
1. It contains neither α nor β and B=KB. Both the pieces of information are rejected.
2. It contains α, but not β. The new information β is rejected. If the outcome of the previous revision by α was a set that didn't contain α, then this is an example of recovering of an information.
3. It contains β, but not α. The new information is accepted. If the outcome of the previous revision by α was a set containing α, then this is an example of how an information can be rejected anytime after the reception of a new piece of evidence.
4. It contains both sentences. This can occour only if β is consistent with α.

3   Conclusions

Our consistency-based model for Belief Revision is close to the one reported in [2]. Both of them are, substantially, methods to escape from the inconsistency of KB minimizing the changes. Both of them sort the subsets of KB with respect to a pre-ordering between the sentences of KB.

The most important difference is the possibility to reject an incoming information. The model in [2] puts the newcoming information in the lowest layer (the most important one) so that it surely belongs to the preferred subbases.

We firstly generalize this approach in a natural way by simply putting the newcoming information in the layer correspondent to its degree of credibility (which is not necessarily the most important one) and selecting as the preferred subbase one that is maximal with respect to the inclusion-based ordering. Depending on the level of the layer in which it has been put, the newcoming information might not appear in the new reasoning base. However, no sentence will ever be removed from the belief base so that, if the newcoming information is inconsistent with the current reasoning base and its credibility is sufficiently high, then the new reasoning base can contain previously discarded pieces of information.

We can ulteriorly generalize the mechanism by allowing that the newcoming information alter the credibilities of all the sentences in the belief base. In this case, we can still recover previously discarded pieces of information even if the newcoming information is consistent with the current reasoning base.

Another difference is that in our model only one subset of KB is selected so that the following rule of no-trivial inference can be defined: "KB entails β if β can be classically inferred in the preferred maximal consistent subset of KB".

Having shown how the principle of priority to the incoming information can be a constriction for some kinds of application domains, this paper presents the basic ideas of a consistency-based model of Belief Revision that overcomes this restriction. However this is a research in progress since, to be complete, such a model should also clarify, at least, how a degree of credibility can be attached to a piece of information and how such "credibilities" can be revised after the newcoming information. We are still examining which of the various approaches to uncertainty management available in the AI community is the most appropriate in this context (if any). The aim is that of merging symbolic and numerical approaches toward an uncertainty-driven consistency-based model for Belief Revision.

References

[1] C.E.Alchourrón, P.Gärdenfors and D.Makinson, "On the logic of Theory change: partial meet contraction and revision functions", The Journal of Symbolic Logic, vol. 50, 510-530, (1985).

[2] S.Benferhat, C.Cairol, D.Dubois, J.Lang and H.Prade, "Inconsistency management and prioritized syntax-based entailment", Proc. of the 13th Inter. Joint Conf. on Artificial Intelligence (IJCAI' 93), 640-645.

[3] G.Brewka, "Preferred subtheories: An extended logical framework for default reasoning", Proc. of the 11th Inter. Joint Conf. on Artificial Intelligence (IJCAI' 89), 1043-1048.

[4] M.Dalal, "Investigations into a theory of knowledge base revision: preliminary report", (AAAI' 88), 475-479.

[5] S.Dixon and N.Foo, "Connections between the ATMS and AGM belief revision", (IJCAI' 93), 534-539.

[6] A.F.Dragoni, "A Model for Belief Revision in a Multi-Agent Environment", E. Werner & Y. Demazeau (Eds.), Decentralized A. I., 3. NH Elsevier Science Publisher, 1992.

[7] A.F.Dragoni, P.Puliti and P.Giorgini, "Distributed belief revision versus distributed truth maintenance", Proc. of the 6th IEEE Inter. Conf. on Tools with Artificial Intelligence, New Orleans, 6-9 November 1994.

[8] A.F.Dragoni, M.Di Manzo, "Supporting Complex Inquiries", accepted for publication by International Journal of Intelligent Systems, John Wiley & Sons (Eds.), 1995.

[9] D.Dubois and H.Prade, "A survey of belief revision and updating in various uncertainty models", International Journal of Artificial Intelligent Systems, vol. 9, 61-100, (1994).

[10] J.R.Galliers, "Modelling Autonomous Belief Revision in Dialogue", Tech Rep. Cambridge University Comp. Lab., Cambridge (England), 1989.

[11] P.Gärdenfors, "Knowledge in Flux: Modeling the Dynamic of Epistemic States", The MIT Press, Cambridge, MA, 1988.

[12] Léa Sombé, "A glance at revision and updating in knowledge bases", International Journal of Artificial Intelligent Systems, vol 9, 1-27, (1994).

[13] F.Lévy, "A survey of belief revision and updating in classical logic", International Journal of Artificial Intelligent Systems, vol 9, 29-59, (1994).

[14] J.P.Martins, S.C.Shapiro, "A Model for Belief Revision", Artificial Intelligence, 35 (1), 25-79, 1988.

[15] B.Nebel, "A knowledge level analysis of belief revision", R.J. Brechman H.J. Levasque and R. Reiter (Eds.), Proc. of the Inter. Conf. of Principles in Knowledge Representation and Reasoning (KR' 89), 301-311.

[16] B.Nebel, "Base revision operations and schemes: semantics, representation and complexity", (ECAI' 94), 341-345.

[17] L.Willard and Y.Y.Li, "The revised Gärdenfors postulates and update semantics", Proc. of the 3th Inter. Conf.on Database Theory (ICDT' 90), Lectures Notes in Computers Sciences, vol 470, Springer-Verlag, Berlin.

A Framework for Dealing with Belief-Goal Dynamics

Cristiano Castelfranchi[1], Daniela D'Aloisi[2] * and Fabrizio Giacomelli[1]

[1] IP-CNR, National Research Council of Italy
Viale Marx 15, I-00137 Rome, Italy
cris@pscs2.irmkant.rm.cnr.it
fabrizio@pscs2.irmkant.rm.cnr.it
[2] Fondazione Ugo Bordoni
Via B. Castiglione 59, I-00142 Rome, Italy
dany@fub.it

Abstract. This paper illustrates the Goal Dynamics theory, a proposal for dealing with some crucial aspects of "goal revision", bas belief revision, one of the most fundamental aspects in a cognitive agent architecture. The theory concerns the relationships between beliefs, goals and intention; moreover it shows the different forms that goals and intentions can assume according to the status of their supporting beliefs. Since beliefs support goals and intentions in the various phases of their processing, it is possible demonstrate how the acquisition or the elimination of beliefs brings to goal activation—and then to actuate the intention—or their suspension or withdrawal.

1 Introduction

An autonomous agent is an entity able to solve some categories of problems in its environment without any external intervention. In literature there exist several proposals of how to model such an agent and each of them reflects some issue that the designers reckoned relevant. In our opinion an agent's architecture should include not only the capacity of planning and then re-planning but also the possibility of changing completely its goals. That could lead to a real adaptivity of the agent to its environment and this adaptivity cannot be shown if the agent is not able to review its preferences in relation to external dynamic constraints. A means to reach this result is to stress the relationships between a goal and the beliefs that support it, that is to analyze how the status of a goal changes following the changes of its supporting beliefs.

The detailed analysis of the belief-goal relationship has brought us to develop a specific theory of the *goal dynamics* that supplies a classification of goals with respect to the kind of beliefs supporting them. This theory has been embedded in an agent architecture called DYNGO (DYNamic GOal), whose behavior reflects the theory. DYNGO is a system written in Lisp and based on SNePS (Semantic

---

* Work carried out in the framework of the agreement between Italian PT Administration and the FUB.

Networks Processing System) [5], a knowledge representation system based on the propositional semantic networks' approach. Our agent model is built in a perspective of a multi-agent environment although the current implementation refers to a single agent world.

2 The Goal Dynamics Theory: Preliminary Remarks

The Goal Dynamics (GD) theory concerns the interactions between some kinds of attitudes that form an agent model, in particular between goals and intentions and beliefs. As a matter of fact, our starting point are the BDI architectures ([1, 2, 3, 4]), for which an agent consists of three kinds of attitudes: Beliefs, Desires (or goals) and Intentions. Generally, and that is true for our approach, these attitudes are represented as propositions that express states of the world. A belief is a state the agent thinks true; a goal is a state the agent would like to reach; an intention is a state the agent is committed to achieve.

In our theory, a goal can be characterized by several states, and it can belong to two main classes, the idle goal class and the active goal class. A goal is an idle goal if some condition for its achievement lacks, e.g., it is a sort of *concern*; when all conditions hold, it becomes an active goal. In the case of some additional beliefs become true, it enters in the class of intentions. This path can also be covered on the contrary: for example an intention can enter the class of the idle goals if one of the condition supporting it suddenly drops.

The problems we want to face with have been neglected in many of the previous models of agents. The two main issues that our theory deals with are: why, when and how to drop a goal; why, when and how to activate a goal. These two aspects are relevant also in the DAI and concern respectively how an agent can get another agent to give up or to adopt a goal. In our opinion, these two problems cannot be solved if one does not analyze organically the relationship between goals (intentions) and beliefs. On the ground of these considerations, a simple definition of agent can be introduced.

Definition 1 *An agent is an autonomous and cognitive entity consisting of a set of beliefs, a set of goals and a set of intentions. It grounds its decisions and actions on its beliefs.*

Given the link between what an agent believes in and how an agent is willing to act, it is possible to introduce the Postulate of the *Cognitive Autonomous Agent*.

Postulate 1 *It is not possible to directly modify the goals of a cognitive autonomous agent. In order to influence it, and hence to change its goals, it is necessary to interfere in the beliefs supporting the goals.*

The GD theory shows the dependence between beliefs and respectively goals and intentions. The main point is that each goal (intention) has a set of beliefs that supports it—and hence it is called the *supporting set*—and that supplies the conditions so that the goal can be pursued. Each modification in the supporting set causes a change in the goal (intention) status.

3   The Supporting Set

Each goal has a set of beliefs that expresses the conditions that allow it to be pursued: there exists a specific structure that maintains a goal in a certain status.

Definition 2 (Supporting Set) *The Supporting Set of a goal (intention) is the set of beliefs that support it in the sense that all the beliefs in the set must hold so that the goal (intention) holds. In the case of even only one belief in the Supporting Set is not true, the goal (intention) changes its status.*

From this definition, it derives that the revision of a goal (intention) requests the revision of its supporting beliefs.

The number of beliefs in the supporting set increases with the change of status of the entity connected to it. Given a idle goal g_i that becomes an active goal g_a that becomes an intention i_{ia}, the supporting set of i_{ia} is larger than the supporting set of g_a that is larger than the supporting set of g_i. As the status of a proposition becomes *more stable*, the number of beliefs that support it grows. The beliefs forming the supporting set belong to specific categories that can be outlined as follows:

- *explicit beliefs*: they concern the status of the goal or of the plan to achieve it, e.g., the agent believes of having the plan to achieve the goal. These beliefs are represented by assertions;
- *implicit beliefs*: they concern the achievement of the goal, e.g., the agent believes that the goal can be accomplished only if a certain state of the world holds. These beliefs are represented in a procedural way;
- *evaluative beliefs*: they concern evaluation measures about the goal, e.g., the agent assigns a cost or an utility function to the goal. These beliefs can be represented both assertionally and procedurally. This kind of beliefs are not all implemented yet.

Some of these beliefs are actually meta-beliefs since they are beliefs on the goal and not on the state of the world. The following list outlines some of supporting beliefs (or meta-beliefs) that are present in the current model: the agent believes that

- the goal is internally consistent, i.e., the goal is not absurd;
- the goal is achievable, i.e., the circumstances necessary to reach the goal hold true;
- there exists a plan sufficient to achieve the goal;
- it is able to perform the actions necessary for the goal;
- its action is necessary;
- the conditions for the goal hold true. This is the case of the so-called conditional goals (see Section 4);
- it is the time for the goal to be achieved. This is the case of periodic goals (see Section 4);
- two goals are compatible;

– it is better to accomplish the higher number of goals. This is an example of evaluative belief.

A supporting set consists of some of these beliefs depending on the type of the goal or intention: they can also appear in boolean combination or in a negated form.

4 A Classification for the Goals

In many of the agent architectures, a goal can simply hold or not hold; our theory considers several levels in which the goal can be before being dropped.

Definition 3 *A goal is in the class of the active goals when all the beliefs in its supporting set hold, i.e., they are true. A goal is in the class of the idle goals when at least one of the beliefs in its supporting set does not hold, i.e., at least one belief is not true.*

Besides these two classes, there is also another type of goal, the *reactive goal* or *reflex*. A reactive goal does not have any supporting set: the agent does not need to take any kind of decision but it reacts *physiologically* to a stimulus.

An *idle goal* is in a watchful status waiting for the change of its supporting set, and its further classification depends on the type of its supporting beliefs. As the beliefs become true, the goal *tends towards activation* and becomes a member of the class of the active goals when all the beliefs are true. At the moment of its being preferred and chosen, the goal changes its status and becomes *intention*. An intention maintains the supporting set of the goal but beliefs that regard its specific status are added: however, it can be dropped if something in the world changes before its accomplishment. The class of idle goal is in turn divided in several subclasses. At the first level there are the *sleeping goals* and the *suspended goals*. Goals whose supporting set is incomplete—the truth value of some belief is undefined or false—belong to the first class, while the second class consists of goal that were active—even intentions—but changes in the world made some belief in their supporting sets false.

The *sleeping goals*, that are in turn partitioned in *conditional goals* and *periodic goals*, are characterized by two parts, the goal itself and a trigger part. The *trigger part* is a condition that must be satisfied so that the goal can become active. The trigger part is called *condition part* for the conditional goals and *time part* for the periodic goals. The *goal part* is simply the goal, i.e., the proposition representing the goal, to be activated if the trigger part matches: it is called the *token goal*. The *condition part* is a specific belief that pushes the goal towards activation. The *time part* is a temporal trigger: the goal tends towards activation periodically, following a specific temporal period. In this case it is not a new belief that awakes the goal, but it is a structural condition.

Also the reactive goals have a structure similar to that of sleeping goals: their trigger part is called *stimulus part*. As a matter of fact, a conditional goal is like a high level reactive goal or cognitive reactive goal. The reactive goals and the sleeping goals are also called *type-goals*.

Also the *suspended goals* are partitioned in subclasses, the self, planless and actionless classes. A *self goal* is a goal for which the agent believes that its action is not necessary because it will be eventually true without its intervention. A *planless goal* is a goal the agent believes not to have a plan to satisfy it. An *actionless goal* is a goal the agent believes not to know how to execute the plan for it. It does not know how to perform some action in the plan, i.e., it lacks for ability or resource.

5 From Active Goals to Intentions: the Dyngo's Model

The GD theory has been tested and implemented in a system called DYNGO (DYNamic GOal). The three attitudes' classes are described by specific structures (the belief structure, the goal structure and the intention structure) each of which consists of one or more SNePS context: a context allows us to organize the propositions in logically-linked set where all the classic set operators are available.

The *belief structure* is divided in two contexts: the world belief context, that contains beliefs about the world, and the AUX belief context, that contains beliefs about internal objects, i.e., goals and intentions. The *goal structure*, reflecting the theory of goal dynamics, is articulated in a more complex taxonomy. The *intention structure* is a simple structure built on a single context. It contains the agenda of intentions. At the present, an operator simulates the influence of the external world and the other agents.

The agent continuously executes a loop whose first step is to verify the presence of new beliefs in the belief structure, then it carries out the activations and de-activations of goals and intentions that the new beliefs concern. The goals in the active goal context are submitted to an algorithm that produces an agenda containing the intentions to execute. In each cycle the agent completes an intention of this agenda. At the next loop, if there are not new beliefs, the agent executes the next intention until their depletion or until a new belief changes the state of affair by producing a new agenda. Between two loops the operator can input new beliefs again. It is to be remembered that periodic and reactive goals exhibit a particular behavior since they are activated not by a belief.

The agent performs specific actions to transform the set of active goals into a particular sequence of intentions to be carried out and hence into a particular sequence of actions to be executed on the world. The most important feature to consider is that the active goal set is not necessarily consistent. To solve possible conflicts, two procedures are performed on the set: partitioning and ordering. The aim of partitioning is to divide the active goal set in consistent sub-sets. The subsets represent the potential agendas. These procedures hide two procedural beliefs that enter in the supporting set of the intention. The first regards the belief compatibility; the second beliefs is an evaluative belief deriving from the belief the agent has on the utility of achieving as many goals as possible. The goals in the agendas must be cohestensive with respect to original set of active goals, i.e., all the elements of that set must be at least in an agenda. Then each agenda must be maximal, namely it must contain all goals which are reciprocally compatible. Then the agent operates a selection by choosing the agenda containing the higher number of goals. Only after this phase the agent disposes of the final sequence of the intentions.

It is important now to put in evidence a particular feature of our theory. It is possible that an active goal might not be chosen to be pursued: in fact, if its agenda is lighter than others, it will be not preferred although the goals in it remains valid and active. That reflects a fundamental characteristic of the goal dynamics theory: a goal, intended in a wide sense, has different activation phases and for each of them specific supporting beliefs are needed, which permit a multi-level and multi-state management of goals and therefore a true preference dynamic for them.

6 Conclusions and Future Developments

In this paper the theory of the Goal Dynamics has been illustrated and several issues have been pointed out. One of the relevant aspect of our model is that its reactivity is not merely in its reactions and reflexes, but there is a *higher level* reactivity notion, namely cognitive reactivity, in which goals are activated and deactivated by beliefs. Moreover there is a multiplicity of types of goals and intentions supported by specific types of beliefs. In our model, the possibility of revision is enlarged to intentions. Since our aim was to implement a real dynamics of the preferences, it is possible that a goal—having all the necessary characteristics to be chosen as intention and to be pursued—is not preferred. The system could prefer another goal and maintain the first with all the supporting beliefs. Currently, Dyngo is only a limited experimental system, but it confirms our view that it is possible to practice important aspects of the cognitive revision of goals.

References

1. Georgeff, M.P and Rao, A.S., Decision Making in an Embedded Reasoning System. In Proceedings of the 11th IJCAI, Detroit (MI), 972-978, 1989.
2. Cohen, P.R and H.J.Levesque, H.J., Persistence, Intention and Commitment. SRI Technical Note 415, February 1987.
3. Castelfranchi, C., Guarantees for Autonomy in Cognitive Agent Architecture. In M. Wooldrige, N.R., Jennings (eds.), *Intelligent Agents*, Proceedings of the 1994 ECAI Workshop on Agent Theories, Architectures and Languages, Springer-Verlag, 56-70, 1994.
4. Kumar, D., Rational Engines for BDI Architectures. In Proceedings of the 1993 AAAI Spring Symposium on Automated Planning.
5. Shapiro, S.C. and The SNePS Implementation Group, SNePS 2.1 User's Manual. Technical Report, State University of New York at Buffalo, September 1993, SUNY.

Evolving non-Trivial Behaviors on Real Robots: an Autonomous Robot that Picks up Objects

Stefano Nolfi   Domenico Parisi

Institute of Psychology, National Research Council
15, Viale Marx - 00187 - Rome - Italy
voice: 0039-6-86090231
stefano@kant.irmkant.rm.cnr.it
domenico@kant.irmkant.rm.cnr.it

Abstract

Recently, a new approach that involves a form of simulated evolution has been proposed for the building of autonomous robots. However, it is still not clear if this approach may be adequate to face real life problems. In this paper we will show how control systems that perform a non-trivial sequence of behaviors can be obtained with this methodology by carefully designing the conditions in which the evolutionary process operates. In the experiment described in the paper, a mobile robot is trained to locate, recognize, and grasp a target object. The controller of the robot has been evolved in simulation and then downloaded and tested on the real robot.

1 Introduction

Work in *Artificial Life* (see Langton, 1989) has introduced new techniques for developing creatures living and behaving in a variety of environments. More recently, there have been several attempts to apply Artificial Life techniques to the design of mobile robots. This type of approaches, identified as *Evolutionary Robotics* because they try to develop autonomous robots through an automatic design process involving artificial evolution, have attracted the interest of researchers of both the Artificial Life and the Robotics communities (Brooks, 1992; Cliff, Husband and Harvey, 1993; Nolfi, Floreano, Miglino, and Mondada, 1994; Steels, 1994; and others).

Evolutionary Robotics approaches are based on the genetic algorithm technique (Holland, 1975). An initial population of different "genotypes" each codifying the control system (and possibly the morphology) of a robot are created randomly. Each robot is evaluated in the environment and to each robot is assigned a score ("fitness") corresponding to the ability of the robot to perform some desired task. Then, the robots that have obtained the highest fitness are allowed to reproduce (sexually or agamically) by generating copies of their genotypes with the addition of random changes ("mutations"). The process is repeated for a certain number of generations until, hopefully, desired performances are achieved (for methodological information see Nolfi, Floreano, Miglino and Mondada, 1994).

2 Related Work

Different types of artificial systems that perform various behaviors have been obtained through artificial evolution. However, the majority of these systems have been obtained and tested in simulations without being validated on real robots. Although these simulated models can be useful for exploring many theoretical and practical questions, care must be taken in using them to draw conclusions about behavior in real world.

Only recently the evolutionary approach has produced results that have been validated on real robots. Lewis, Fagg and Sodium (1992) evolved a motor controller for a six-legged robot called Rodney that was able to walk forward and backward. Colombetti and Dorigo (1992) have evolved a the control system for a robot called Autonomouse to perform a light approaching and following behavior. Floreano and Mondada (1994) and Nolfi, Floreano, Miglino, and Mondada (1994) have evolved control systems for the miniature mobile robot called Khepera (see below) that should perform an obstacle avoidance task. Miglino, Nafasi, and Taylor (in press) evolved a controller for a mobile Lego robot that should explore an open arena. Yamauchi and Beer (1994) describe an experiment in which dynamical neural networks were evolved to solve a landmark recognition task using a sonar. They tested the network on a Nomad 200 robot with a built in wall-following behavior. Harvey, Husband, and Cliff (1994) evolved a system able to approach a visual target (in the most complex experiment the system was successfully trained to approach a triangle target and to distinguish it from a rectangular one). The system was not implemented on a standard autonomous robot but on a specially designed robotic equipment in which the robot is suspended from a platform which allows translational movements in the X and Y directions.

In some of these experiments the evolutionary process was conducted in simulation and then the obtained control system was downloaded and tested on the robot (Colombetti and Dorigo, 1992; Miglino, Nafasi, and Taylor, in press; Yamauchi and Beer, 1994). In other cases the evolutionary process was conducted entirely on the real robot (Lewis, Fagg, and Sodium, 1992; Floreano and Mondada, 1994, Harvey, Husband, and Cliff, 1994). In still other cases evolution took place in part in simulation and then it was continued on the real robot (Nolfi, Floreano, Miglino, and Mondada, 1994). When the evolutionary process was conducted partially or totally on the real robot in some cases the evaluation process was conducted automatically, i.e., without requiring an external support (Floreano and Mondada, 1994; Nolfi, Floreano, Miglino, and Mondada, 1994) while in other cases performance were evaluated by human observers (Lewis, Fagg and Sodium, 1992). In all of the work described neural networks were used in order to implement the controller with the exception of Colombetti and Dorigo (Colombetti and Dorigo, 1992) who used a classifier system.

This work clearly shows that evolutionary robotics is a very active and promising new field of research. However, it is also clear that real life problems require system able to produce behaviors significantly more complex than those described above. In this paper we will show how control systems that perform a more complex sequence of behaviors can be obtained with this methodology by carefully designing the conditions in which the evolutionary process operate. In doing so we will also discuss several methodological issues.

Fig.1. The Khepera robot.

3 Our Framework

Having at our disposal a Khepera robot with the gripper module (see next section) we decided to try to develop a control system for a robot that, when placed in an arena surrounded by walls is able to recognize target objects, to grasp them, and to carry them outside the arena. Given our prevous experience with Khepera and the difficulties of evolving a behavior of this type in the real robot we decided to conduct the evolutionary process in simulation by using an extended version of our Khepera simulator (described in Nolfi, Floreano, Miglino, and Mondada, 1994). The obtained control system was then downloaded on the robot and tested in the real environment. In this section we will describe the robot, the environment of the robot, and the simulator. In section 4 we will describe the architecture of the controller and the type of genetic algorithm and fitness formula used. In section 5 we will describe the results obtained in the simulations and on the real robot.

3.1 The Robot

The robot was Khepera (Figure 1), a miniature mobile robot developed at E.P.F.L. in Lausanne, Switzerland (Mondada, Franzi, and Ienne, 1993). It has a circular shape with a diameter of 55 mm, a height of 30 mm, and a weight of 70g. It is supported by two wheels and two small teflon balls. The wheels are controlled by two DC motors with an incremental encoder (10 pulses per mm of advancement of the robot), and they can move in both directions. In addition, the robot is provided with a gripper module with two degrees of freedom. The arm of the gripper can move any angle from vertical to hotizontal while the gripper can assume only the open or closed position. The robot is provided with eight infra-red proximity sensors (six sensors are positioned on the front of the robot, the remaining two on the back), a speed of rotation sensor for each motor, an optical barrier sensor on the gripper able to detect the presence of an object in the gripper, and an electrical resistivity sensor also on the gripper.

A Motorola 68331 controller with 256 Kbytes of RAM and 512 Kbytes ROM manages all the input-output routines and can communicate via a serial port with a host computer. Khepera was attached to the host by means of a lightweight aerial cable and specially designed rotating contacts. This configuration makes it possible to trace and record all important variables by exploiting the storage capabilities of the host computer and at the same time it provides electrical power without using time-consuming homing algorithms or large heavy-duty batteries.

3.2 The Environment

We built a rectangular environment of 60x35 cm organized as an arena surrounded by walls. The walls are 3 cm in height, are made of wood, and are covered with white paper. The target object is a cilinder with a diameter of 2.3 cm and a height of 3 cm. It is made of cardboard and is covered with white paper. The target is positioned in a random position inside the arena.

3.3 The Simulator

To evolve the controller of the robot in the computer the simulator described in Nolfi, Floreano, Miglino, and Mondada (1994) was extended in order to take into account the gripper module of Khepera.

A sampling procedure is been used to calculate values for the infra-red sensors. The walls and the target object were sampled by placing the physical Khepera in front of them, letting it turn 360°, and at the same time recording the sensory activations at different distances with respect to objects. The activation level of each of the eight infra-red sensors was recorded for 180 different orientations and for 20 different distances. In this way two different matrix of activations where obtained for the two types of objects (walls and target). These matrices were then used by the simulator to set the activation state of the simulated sensors depending of the relative position of Khepera and of the objects in the simulated environment. (When more than one object is within the range of activation of the sensors, the resulting activation was computed by summing the activation contribution of each object). This sampling procedure may result time consuming in the case of very unstructured environments because it requires to sample each different type of objects present in the environment. However, it has the advantage of taking into account the fact that different sensors, even if identical from the electronic point of view, do respond differently. Sampling the environment throught the real sensors of the robot allowed us, by taking into account the characteristics of each individual sensor, to develop a simulator shaped by the actual physical characteristics of the individual robot we have.

The effects of the two motors were sampled similarly by measuring how Khepera moved and turned for a subset of the 20x20 possible states of the two motors. At the end of this process a matrix was obtained that was then used by the simulator in order to compute the displacements of the robot in the simulated environment.

The physical shape of Khepera (including the arm and the gripper), the environment structure, and the actual position of the robot were accurately reproduced in the simulator with floating point precision. Motor actions that may produce a crashing of the robot into the walls are not executed in the simulated environment. Therefore, the robot may get stuck into the walls if it is unable to avoid them. On the contrary, crashes between the arm and the target object are simulated by re-positioning the target object in a new randomly selected position inside the arena.

4 Evolving the Controller

Like the majority of people who use evolutionary methods to obtain control systems for autonomous robot we decided to implement the controller with a neural network. This was motivated by several reasons:

- Neural networks are resistant to noise that is massively present in robot/environment interactions.
- We agree with Cliff, Harvey, and Husband (1993) that the primitives manipulated by the evolutionary process should be at the lowest possible level in order to avoid undesiderable choices made by the human designer. Synaptic weights and nodes are low level primitives.
- Neural networks can easily exploit various form of learning during life-time and this learning process may help and speed up the evolutionary process (Ackley and Litmann, 1991; Nolfi, Elman and Parisi; 1994).

In the following sections we will describe the architecture, the fitness formula, and the form of genetic algorithm used.

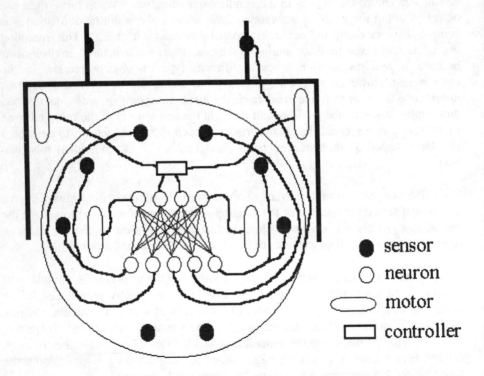

● sensor
○ neuron
⬭ motor
▭ controller

Fig. 2. The control system of the robot. The 5 sensory neurons are directly connected to the 6 frontal sensors of the robot located on the body of Khepera and to the light barrier sensor located on the gripper. Two motor neurons are directly connected with the two wheels of Khepera while the other two neurons are connected with the two motors that control the arm and the gripper.

4.1 The Neural Controller

We tried several different network architectures (we will come back to this point in the discussion) and we found that the best architecture was a very simple one, a feedforward network with 5 sensory neurons, 4 motor neurons, and no internal neurons. The first 4 sensory neurons were used to encode the activation level of the two frontal sensors of Khepera and the average activation of the two left and right lateral sensors (see Figure 2). The fifth sensory neuron was used to encode the barrier light sensor on the gripper. On the motor side, the first 2 neurons were used to encode the movement of the two wheels, the third neuron was used to trigger the object pick-up procedure, and the last neuron was used to trigger the object release procedure.

The activation of the sensors and the state of the motors are encoded each 100 milliseconds. However, when the activation level of the object pick-up neuron or of the object release neuron reach a given treshold a sequence of action occurs that may require one or two seconds to complete (e.g. move a little bit back, close the gripper, move the arm up, for the object pick-up procedure; move the arm down, open the gripper, and move the arm up again, for the object release procedure). This implies that in order to accomplish the task the weights of the neural network should be set in a way that allows Khepera to perform the following sequence of behaviors:

- explore the environment avoiding the walls
- recognize the target object
- place the body in a relative position with respect to the target that makes it possibile to grasp the object
- pick-up the target object
- move toward the walls without avoiding them
- place the body in a relative position with respect to the wall that makes it possible to drop the object out of the arena when released
- release the object

4.2 The Genetic Algorithm

To evolve neural controllers able to perform the task described above we used a form of genetic algorithm. We begin with 100 randomly generated genotypes each representing a network with a different set of connection weights assigned randomly. This is Generation 0 (G0). G0 networks are allowed to "live" for 5 epochs, with an epoch consisting of 500 actions (about 5 seconds in the simulated environment using an IBM RISK/6000 computer or about 250 seconds in the real environment). At the beginning of each epoch the robot and the target object are randomly positioned in the arena and during each epoch the object is re-positioned randomly when the robot releases the object after having picked it up. At the end of life the robots have the possibility to reproduce. However, only the 20 individuals which have accumulated the most fitness in the course of their life reproduce (agamically) by generating 5 copies of their neural networks. These 20x5=100 new robots constitute the next generation (G1). Random mutations are introduced in the copying process resulting in possible changes of the connection weights. The process is repeated for 300 generations.

The genetic encoding scheme was a direct one-to-one mapping. The encoding scheme is the way in which the phenotype (in this case the connection weights of the neural network) is encoded in the genotype (the representation on which the genetic algorithm operates). The one-to-one mapping is the simplest encoding scheme in which to each phenotypical character corresponds one and only one 'gene'. In our case to each connection weights corresponds a sequence of 8 bits in the genotype which has a total length of 192 bits. (For more complex encoding schemes that allow the evolution of the neural architecture, see Cliff, Harvey and Husband, 1993; Nolfi, Miglino, and Parisi, 1994).

4.3 The Fitness Formula

The fitness formula is the way in which individuals are evaluated in order to decide which individuals are allowed to reproduce. To help the evolutionary process we decided to use a fitness formula with 5 components in order to score individuals not only for their ability to perform the complete sequence of correct behaviors but also for their ability to perform only portions of the complete sequence. In particular, we increased the fitness of an individual in the following cases:

- if the individual is close to the target object
- if the target object is in front of the robot
- if the robot tries to pick-up the object
- if the robot has the object in the gripper
- if the robot release the object outside the arena

It is important to note that, despite the complexity of the fitness formula, several behaviors that are necessary in order to accomplish the task are not directly rewarded. For example, the ability to avoid the walls, the ability to explore the environment efficiently in order to find the target object, and the ability to distinguish between the walls and the target object, are not directly rewarded. Similarly, there is no direct reward for correct or incorrect behaviors after the object has been grasped. For example, if the robot decides to stay still or to move makes no difference for the obtained fitness. Only if the robot performs the entire sequence of correct behaviors ((a) moving in the direction of a wall, (b) approaching the wall instead of avoiding it as before grasping the object, (c) releasing the object, it is rewarded.

5 Results

We run 10 simulations starting with populations of 100 networks with randomly assigned connection weights. Each simulation lasted 300 generations (about 3 hours using a standard IBM RISC/6000). In all 10 simulations individuals able to perform the task rather well evolved.

We tested the best individual of the last generation for each simulation. On average, in the simulated evironment, individuals were able to perform the complete sequence of behaviors 6.6 times (i.e., in the 500x5 cycles of their life they were able to find, recognize, pick up, transport, and correctly release outside the arena 6.6 target objects on average). Incorrect behaviors (such as crashing into the walls) were generated by the evolved individuals very unfrequently. In fact, individuals never tried to grasp a wall, failed to grasp the object only 2% of the times along 500x5 cycles, and released the object in an incorrect position (i.e., inside the arena) only 10% of the times.

We then downloaded the 10 evolved networks into the physical robot and we tested them in the real environment. The performance of the 10 best individuals resulted less good, on average, in the real than in the simulated environment. However, all individuals were able to perform the entire sequence of actions correctly at least 2 times. The best individual, out of the ten, was able to correctly pick-up and deposit outside the arena 6 target objects, it never crashed into the walls, it never failed to grasp the objects, and it never tried to incorrectly grasp the walls. Given this successful performance it did not seemed necessary to continue the evolutionary process in the real environment in order to allow individuals to adapt to the differences between the simulated and the real environment, as we did in our previous work (see Nolfi, Floreano, Miglino, and Mondada, 1994).

6 Discussion

We were able to evolve neural controllers for a Khepera robot that can perform a relatively complex task. Hence, one first conclusion we can draw from this work it that the evolutionary robotics approach appears to be adequate to face real life problems in simple environments.

The present work can also help us to find an answer to the question: In what conditions is is possible to evolve robots that are able to perform complex behaviors?

We think the key point is to view robots and their environments "as agent-environment systems whose interaction dinamics have to be got right" instead of "thinking of robots as information processing systems and of sensors as measuring device" (Smithers, 1994; see also Nolfi, Floreano, Miglino, and Mondada, 1994). In other words, what is important is to reduce the complexity of the interaction between each component of the system (body, controller, sensory and motor system) and the given environment. And this should be accomplished by designing each component by taking into account all the others, i.e., by adapting each component to each others, instead of trying to design very smart and complex components that are general purpose.

The type of neural controllers we evolved and the hardware we used are very simple. The evolved controllers, in fact, are implemented on neural networks with an extremely simple architecture and with only 22 free parameters to optimize (20 weights values and 2 biases). On the body side, the infrared sensors used are both very imprecise and very noisy devices. In addition we found that by increasing the complexity of the system on the control side (by using more complex neural architecture, such as architectures with internal or recurrent units) or on the body side (by allowing the neural network to rely on more sensors) makes the task harder rather than easier to evolve and does not produce better performances.

To design by hand each component of the system by taking into account all the others is certainly difficult. For this reason an auto-organization process such as evolution that spontaneously allows co-adaptation of the sub-components of the systems appears a good solution to develop simple robots that perform complex tasks. In this work, in order to reduce the number of parameters to be optimized, we applied the evolutionary process only to the weights of the neural controller and we tried to carefully design the neural architecture and the sensory-motor system. However, the auro-organization process can be extended to the neural architecture and the sensory system and this may be a better solution in principle and a necessary one in complex cases.

A final remark concerns the fitness formula we used. As we noted in section 4.3, not all required sub-behaviors necessary to accomplish the task were directly rewarded by the fitness formula. However, some of the intermediate states prior to the final goal state were directly rewarded. It is clear that to reward only the desired final state (the object is out of the arena) instead of also some of the intermediate states would eliminate constraints, on the evolutionary process, that have been introduced by hand and that therefore may result inadequate. We decide to reward some of the intermediate states because it appeared necessary given the difficulty of the task. However, it is not clear if there are other ways to solve this type of problem. We are presently trying to determine if and to what extent it is necessary to impose this type of constraints in the case of the task desrcibed in this paper.

Acknowledgments

This research has been supported by P.F. "ROBOTICA", National Research Council, Italy.

References

Ackley, D. H., M. L. Littman, 1991. Interactions between learning and evolution. In *Artificial Life II*, edited by C. G. Langton, J. D. Farmer, S. Rasmussen, C. E. Taylor. Reading, Mass., Addison-Wesley.

Brooks, R. A. 1992. Artificial life and real robots. *In Toward a Practice of Autonomous Systems: Proceedings of the First European Conference on Artificial Life,* edited by F. J. Varela, P. Bourgine. Cambridge, Mass, MIT Press/Bradford Books.

Cliff D. T., I. Harvey, P. Husbands. 1993. Explorations in Evolutionary Robotics. *Adaptive Behavior* **2**: 73-110.

Colombetti M., Dorigo M. 1992. Learning to control an autonomous robot by distributed genetic algorithms. In J. A. Meyer, H. L. Roitblat, and S. W. Wilson, (eds), *From Animals to Animats 2*, Proceedings of 2rt International Conference on Simulation of Adaptive Behavior, MIT Press.

Floreano D., F. Mondada. 1994. Automatic Creation of an Autonomous Agent: Genetic Evolution of a Neural-Network Driven Robot. In *From Animals to Animats 3: Proceedings of Third Conference on Simulation of Adaptive Behavior,* edited by D. Cliff, P. Husbands, J. Meyer, S. W. Wilson. Cambridge, Mass, MIT Press/Bradford Books.

Harvey I., Husband I., Cliff, D. 1994. Seeing the light: artificial evolution, real vision. In D. Cliff, P. Husband, J-A Meyer, and S. Wilson, (eds), *From Animals to Animats 3*, Proceedings of 3rt International Conference on Simulation of Adaptive Behavior, MIT Press/Bradford Books.

Holland J. H. 1975. *Adaptation in Natural and Artificial Systems*. Ann Arbor, Mich., University of Michigan Press.

Langton, C. G. 1989. *Proceedings of Artificial Life*. C.G. Langton (ed.), Addison-Wesley.

Lewis, M.A., Fagg, A.H., Sodium, A. 1992. Genetic programming approach to the contruction of a neural network for control of a walking robot. In *Proceedings of the IEEE International Conference on Robotics and Automation*, Nice, France.

Miglino O., K. Nafasi, C. Taylor. in press. Selection for Wandering Behavior in a Small Robot. *Artificial Life*.

Mondada F., E. Franzi, P. Ienne. 1993. Mobile Robot miniaturisation: A tool for investigation in control algorithms. In: *Proceedings of the Third International Symposium on Experimental Robotics*, Kyoto, Japan.

Nolfi, S., Miglino, O., Parisi, 1994. Phenotypic Plasticity in Evolving Neural Networks. In: D. P. Gaussier and J-D. Nicoud (Eds.) Proceedings of the Intl. Conf. From Perception to Action, Los Alamitos, CA: IEEE Press

Nolfi, S., Florano D., Miglino, O., Mondada, F. 1994. *How to evolve autonomous robots: different approaches in evolutionary robotics*. Proceedings of fourth International Conference on Artificial Life, Cambridge MA, MIT Press.

Nolfi, S., Elman, J.L., Parisi, D. 1994. Learning and Evolution in Neural Networks. *Adaptive Behavior*,vol. 3, **1**, pp.5-28.

Smithers T. 1994. On why better robots make it harder. In D. Cliff, P. Husband, J-A Meyer, and S. Wilson, (eds), *From Animals to Animats 3*, Proceedings of 3rt International Conference on Simulation of Adaptive Behavior, MIT Press/Bradford Books.

Steels L. 1994. *Emergent functionality in robotic agents throught on-line evolution*. Proceedings of fourth International Conference on Artificial Life, MIT Press, Cambridge MA.

Yamauchi B., Beer R. 1994. Integrating reactive, sequential, and learning behavior using dinamical neural networks. In D. Cliff, P. Husband, J-A Meyer, and S. Wilson, (eds), *From Animals to Animats 3*, Proceedings of 3rt International Conference on Simulation of Adaptive Behavior, MIT Press/Bradford Books.

A Formal Domain Description Language for a Temporal Planner

Amedeo Cesta[1] and Angelo Oddi[2]

[1] IP-CNR, National Research Council of Italy, Viale Marx 15, I-00137 Rome, Italy,
amedeo@pscs2.irmkant.rm.cnr.it
[2] Dipartimento di Informatica e Sistemistica, Università di Roma "La Sapienza"
Via Salaria 113, 00198 Rome, Italy
oddi@assi.dis.uniroma1.it

Abstract. The Domain Description Language (DDL) is the basic knowledge representation service in any problem solving architecture. This paper introduces DDL.1 a DDL for a planning and scheduling architecture that adopts basic features from control theory and extends them to the specification of constraints. A general overview of the language is given, its syntax and semantics described. Finally, the problem of temporal planning by using such a language is briefly addressed.

1 Introduction

A Domain Description Language (DDL) is a specialized knowledge representation language used in problem solving architectures to specify the basic components of a domain, to associate a description to those components, and to specify the constraints and mutual relationships among them. Classical planners usually refer to description languages derived from STRIPS ([3, 8]); various approaches were devoted to add an explicit treatment of time in those languages (e.g., Allen's work [1]); usually, application oriented planners are endowed with their own peculiar DDLs (e.g., the *Task Formalism* in O-Plan [4]).

A general problem with the current approaches is the lack of a methodology that guides the user in the description of the relevant domain features for a planning application. The problem of knowledge acquisition has been generally neglected and only recently is being considered (e.g., see [9]). Planning research has mainly produced problem solving techniques. To achieve actual applicability it should also create tools that assist the user during the description of an application domain. To this purpose, a needed requirement is a description language that suggest ways to decompose the representation task and whose semantics is sufficiently clear to allow the development of tools for checking consistency of user definitions. In planning literature formal analysis has mainly concerned classical planner, while application oriented systems generally miss such an investigation. The present paper is far from solving the problem but in the short space available gives a contribution in the devised direction. In particular, it presents a DDL named DDL.1 that is a subset of the domain description language used in the HSTS planning and scheduling practical architecture ([6, 7]).

DDL.1 from one side suggests the user a methodology, drawn from control theory ([5]), for describing a domain and its relevant constraints, from another is endowed with a clear semantics that enables the creation of verification mechanisms for the user domain specification. Although DDL.1 is a restricted version of HSTS-DDL it maintains the relevant features of the HSTS ontology that has been successfully used in practical applications (see [6, 7]).

The paper is organized as follows: Section 2 presents the various aspects of the DDL.1 language and its syntax; Section 3 presents the semantics of the language, while Section 4 concisely introduces the connection between DDL.1 and a temporal planner. For lack of space the paper does not include a presentation of a temporal planner that uses DDL.1, the interested reader may refer to [2].

2 The DDL.1 Domain Description Language

DDL.1 uses a representation that adopts basic features from control theory and extends them to the specification of constraints. The behavior of a given domain is seen as the continuous interaction among different components. The domain components are represented using state variables, each state variable (SV) represents a key feature of the component. DDL.1 definition primitives allow the intensional description of plausible temporal evolutions of state variables. For each SV the set of values it may assume can be defined. In DDL.1 state variables' values are restricted to a discrete set. The values are instances of predicates of the form $P(x_1, \ldots, x_m)$. More formally, given a state variable SV_i, a set $D_{P_{SV_i}}$ of the value-predicates $P(x_1, \ldots, x_m)$ is defined; for each variable x_j appearing in the value-predicated the domain D_{V_j} of its possible values is determined. The set D_{SV_i} is the domain of the state-variables SV_i values. D_{SV_i} is the set of the ground terms obtained by substituting the variables in $D_{P_{SV_i}}$ with the domain values D_{V_j}. A state variable SV_i is defined as the set Σ_i of all the functions $s : T \to D_{SV_i}$ where T is the discrete set of time instants. Given the definition of each SV, the set Δ of the *domain* evolutions may be defined as: $\Delta = \Sigma_1 \times \Sigma_2 \times \ldots \times \Sigma_n$.

To exemplify what we are talking about we use a simple example taken from Allen [1] concerning the door of the CS Building in Rochester. That door requires two hands to be opened, because there is a spring lock that must be held open with a hand while the door is pulled open with the other hand. In DDL.1, such a domain may be represented by using two state variables: one describing the door, the second describing the spring lock. The possible values for the state variable door are $D_{P_{DOOR}} = \{CLOSED, OPENING(x), OPEN, CLOSING(x)\}$. $CLOSED$ and $OPEN$ represent two stable door states, while $OPENING(x)$ and $CLOSING(x)$ represent the status transitions in which an agent x is moving the door to open or close it. Similarly, the spring lock may assume the values $D_{P_{SPRING-LOCK}} = \{BLOCKED, FREE(y)\}$. When $BLOCKED$ the latch is closed, when $FREE(y)$ it is being hold open by agent y. DDL.1 allows also to represent constraints on the legal sequences of values that a state variable may assume over time. A given value may be constrained either by different values on the same state variable, and/or by values on different state variables. Those further constraints express the *domain theory*, namely the description of the domain laws in terms of compatibility, synchronization, and dependency relations among the values. Such constraints are specified associating to each state variable a set of *compatibility* constraints that for each value specify the constraints it should satisfy in order to be legally assumed by the SV. A generic compatibility c constrains the situations in which a given value may be assumed and then represents a restriction of the possible evolutions of the domain Δ. A compatibility asserts an intensional constraint on the behavior of a state variable. Such constraint has two components: a) a *causal component* that defines a causal relation between two values: a *reference value* and a *constraining value*; b) a *temporal component* that specifies a temporal constraint on the causal component. The temporal relation may specify both a qualitative and a quantitative constraint. For the sake of simplification, DDL.1 uses a restricted number of the qualitative temporal relations usually defined in the literature [1] (only the MEET, MET-BY and DURING are allowed). The MEET and MET-BY relations constrain two value belonging to the same state variable to appear in strict sequence in any legal behavior of the SV (namely, MET-BY (MEET) states that the start-time (end-time) of the reference value coincide with the end time (start-time) of the constraining value). The DURING relation is used to constrain two values belonging to different state-variables. It is used to express synchronization constraints between the state variables' behaviors (more specifically DURING states that the start-time of the constraining value precedes the start-time of the reference, and its end-time follows the end-time of the reference).

To sum up, a domain description that can be built by a DDL.1 specification contains state-variables, state-variable values, and compatibilities. Table 1 shows the whole specification of the language. To clarify the compatibility specification we can consider again the example of the Rochester door and write just one compatibility down following the syntax in Table 1.

```
(COMP (DOOR (OPENING (x : agent)) (d₁(x)D₁(x)))
      (MET-BY (DOOR (CLOSED) (0 ∞)))
      (MEET (DOOR (OPEN) (0 ∞)))
      (DURING (SPRING-LOCK (FREE (x : agent) (0 ∞)) (0 ∞) (0 ∞))))
```

According to the syntax a value is a 3-ple: the state variable the value belongs to, the value predicate, the minimal and maximal bounds on the value duration. The example refers to the reference value $OPENING(x)$ of the SV_{DOOR} whose duration should be in the $[d_1(x), D_1(x)]$ interval. Furthermore, MEET and MET-BY constraints are useful to describe legal value transitions on the SV_{DOOR}. In particular the $OPENING(x)$ may happen after $CLOSE$ and before $OPEN$ (the duration of these other two values is unspecified (see $[0, \infty]$)). A DURING constraint is used to specify values synchronization between SV_{DOOR} and $SV_{SPRING-LOCK}$, namely it is possible to execute a door $OPENING$ only if the spring lock is hold $FREE$ by the agent.

Table 1. BNF Specification of DDL.1

$< DomainDefinition >$ ::= (DOMAIN $< DomainName >$ {$< StateVariable >$})
$< DomainName >$ ::= a constant symbol
$< StateVariable >$ ::= (SV $< StateVariableName >$
$\qquad\qquad\qquad\qquad < DomainValues >$ {$< Compatibility >$})
$< StateVariableName >$ ::= a constant symbol
$< DomainValues >$ ::= $< StateVarValName >$, {$< StateVarValName >$}
$< StateVarValName >$ ::= a constant symbol
$< Compatibility >$ ::= (OR-COMP {$< AndComp >$}) | $< AndComp >$
$< AndComp >$ ::= (COMP $< RefValue >$ (MEET $< ConstrValue >$)
$\qquad\qquad\qquad\qquad$ (MET-BY $< ConstrValue >$)
$\qquad\qquad\qquad\qquad$ {(DURING $< ConstrValue >$
$\qquad\qquad\qquad\qquad\qquad\qquad < DurationInt >< DurationInt >$) })
$< RefValue >$ ::= $< Value >$
$< ConstrValue >$ ::= $< Value >$
$< Value >$ ::= ($< StateVariableName >$
$\qquad\qquad\qquad\qquad$ ($< StateVarValName > < VarList >$) $< DurationInt >$)
$< VarList >$ ::= { ($< VarName >$:$< VarDomain >$) }
$< VarName >$ ::= a constant symbol
$< VarDomain >$ ::= application dependent
$< DurationInt >$ ::= ($< TemporalExpr >< TemporalExpr >$)
$< TemporalExpr >$ ::= ($< FunctionName >< VariableList >$) | $< TimeConstant >$
$< TimeConstant >$ ::= 0|1|2|..
$< FunctionName >$ ::= a constant symbol

3 A Semantics for DDL.1

The constraints stated by compatibility specification bound the number of evolutions of the represented domain (the set Δ previously introduced). The semantics
of any language sentence is defined as the set of the evolutions compatible with
the given constraints. To obtain a formal shape for such an intuitive idea some
preliminary definitions are needed.

Considering the syntax in Table 1, v_j denotes an element belonging to the
syntactic category $< Value >$ of the state variable SV_i. We designate with e_k
a ground element of a temporal evolution of the state variable SV_i. It is worth
noting that e_k is a 3-ple: $e_k =< SV_i, p, [t_s, t_e] >$, where $p \in D_{SVi}$ and $t_s, t_e \in T$
with $t_s \leq t_e$.

Given a function: $s_i : T \to D_{SVi}$, an element of evolution e_k is contained in
$s_i(t)$ (denoted by $e_k \sqsubseteq s_i(t)$), if the function $s_i(t)$ assumes the value $p \in D_{SVi}$ in
the interval $[t_s, t_e]$. Furthermore an element of evolution $e_k =< SV_i, p, [t_s, t_e] >$
is contained in a value $v_j =< SV_i, p(x_1 \ldots x_m), [d(x_1 \ldots x_m), D(x_1 \ldots x_m)] >$
(denoted by $e_k \subseteq v_j$) if exist a ground instance $v_j^q =< SV_i, p, [d, D] >$ of v_j such
that $d \leq t_s - t_e \leq D$.

The DDL.1 semantics is defined by using the function: $\mathcal{E} : \mathcal{L}_{DDL.1} \to 2^\Delta$
where $\mathcal{L}_{DDL.1}$ represents the set of sentences allowed by the DDL.1 grammar
and 2^Δ is the power-set of Δ.

As said above, the semantics of a given domain description is a subset of Δ.
The subset can be obtained by the intersection of the sets of temporal evolution
allowed by each constraint of the language (that is, by each compatibility). The

further step to define the DDL.1 semantics involves the definition of a function $\mathcal{T}$ that given a compatibility c computes the subset of admissible evolutions contained in Δ.

The function $\mathcal{T}$ is a function of the kind: $\mathcal{T} : \Delta \times C_{DDL.1} \rightarrow 2^{\Delta}$ where $C_{DDL.1}$ is the set of compatibility that can be defined using DDL.1. $\mathcal{T}$ can be defined as follows (where s_{SV_e} represents the temporal evolution s of the SV in which the ground element e is assumed) :

$$\mathcal{T}(\Delta, (OR\text{-}COMP\ (AndComp_1)\ldots(AndComp_n)) = \bigcup_{i=1}^{n} \mathcal{T}(\Delta, AndComp_i)$$

$$\mathcal{T}(\Delta,\ (COMP\ v_{ref}(MEET\ v_{meet})\ (MET\text{-}BY\ v_{met\text{-}by})$$
$$(DURING\ v_{during_1}\ int_{i_1}\ int_{f_1})\ldots(DURING\ v_{during_k}\ int_{i_k}\ int_{f_k})) =$$
$$\{< s_{SV_1}(t)\ldots s_{SV_n}(t) >\in \Delta\ |$$
$$(\exists e_{ref})\ (\exists e_{meet})\ (\exists e_{met\text{-}by})\ (\exists e_{during_1})\ldots(\exists e_{during_k})$$
$$(e_{ref} \sqsubseteq s_{SV_{e_{ref}}})\wedge (e_{ref} \subseteq v_{ref}) \supset$$
$$(e_{meet} \sqsubseteq s_{SV_{e_{meet}}})\wedge (e_{meet} \subseteq v_{meet}) \wedge P_{MEET}(e_{ref}, e_{meet})\wedge$$
$$(e_{met\text{-}by} \sqsubseteq s_{SV_{e_{met\text{-}by}}})\wedge (e_{met\text{-}by} \subseteq v_{met\text{-}by}) \wedge P_{MET\text{-}BY}(e_{ref}, e_{met\text{-}by})\wedge$$
$$(e_{during_1} \sqsubseteq s_{SV_{e_{during_1}}})\wedge (e_{during_1} \subseteq v_{during_1})\wedge P_{DURING}(e_{ref}, e_{during_1}, int_{i_1}, int_{f_1})$$
$$\wedge\ldots\wedge$$
$$(e_{during_k} \sqsubseteq s_{SV_{e_{during_k}}})\wedge (e_{during_k} \subseteq v_{during_k})\wedge P_{DURING}(e_{ref}, e_{during_k}, int_{i_k}, int_{f_k})\}$$

To complete the definition of $\mathcal{T}$, a definition for the temporal predicates P_{MEET}, $P_{MET\text{-}BY}$ e P_{DURING} is needed. Given any couple of elements $e_1 = < SV_1, p_1, [t_{s1}, t_{e1}] >$, and $e_2 = < SV_2, p_2, [t_{s2}, t_{e2}] >$, and two intervals $int_i = [d_i, D_i]$ and $int_f = [d_f, D_f]$ those predicates are defined as follows:

$$P_{MEET}(e_1, e_2) = (t_{s1} \leq t_{e1})\wedge (t_{s2} \leq t_{e2})\wedge (t_{e1} = t_{s2})$$
$$P_{MET\text{-}BY}(e_1, e_2) = (t_{s1} \leq t_{e1})\wedge (t_{s2} \leq t_{e2})\wedge (t_{e2} = t_{s1})$$
$$P_{DURING}(e_1, e_2, int_i, int_f) = (t_{s1} \leq t_{e1})\wedge (t_{s2} \leq t_{e2})\wedge$$
$$(d_i \leq t_{s1}-t_{s2} \leq D_i)\wedge (d_f \leq t_{e2}-t_{e1} \leq D_f)$$

Finally the formal semantics $\mathcal{E}$ can be inductively defined as:

1. $\mathcal{E}((DOMAIN\ldots(SV\ldots)_1\ldots(SV\ldots)_n)) =$
   $$\bigcap_{i=1}^{n} \mathcal{E}(SV\ldots(Compatibility_1\ldots Compatibility_p))_i)$$
2. $\mathcal{E}((SV\ldots(Compatibility_1\ldots Compatibility_p))) = \bigcap_{i=1}^{p} \mathcal{E}(Compatibility_i)$
3. $\mathcal{E}(Compatibility_i) = \mathcal{T}(\Delta, Compatibility_i)$

4 Temporal Planning with DDL.1

DDL.1 is a formal DDL able to describe the set of the functions $s_i(t)$ possible temporal evolution of the state variable SV_i. In order to satisfy some given goals a planner for such a specification language should decide a possible temporal evolution for each state variable. The usual notion of *goal* in planning systems becomes the specification of a (set of) constraint(s) stating that a state variable should assume a certain value in a given time interval (an example of goal may be $< DOOR, (OPENING\ Agent_1), [20, 40] >$ that require to open the Rochester door by $Agent_1$ for an interval of at least 20 seconds and no more than 40). A planner for DDL.1 solves problems searching in the space Δ a behavior of the whole domain that satisfy the goal. The planner search is driven by compatibility constraints. In fact it should come out with a behavior of the state variables that supports the goal in the requested interval. Supporting the goals means that the constraints specified in the *domain theory* are completely satisfied. Broadly speaking, for each goal the planner inserts a ground element in the state variable behavior, then unifies the corresponding compatibility reference value with the goal, and generates a sub-goal for each constraining value. It recursively tries to satisfy the sub-goals until it finds out a behavior consistent with any involved compatibility constraint. A temporal planner for DDL.1 is described in [2].

5 Conclusions

This paper formally describes a language for the description of physical domains. Such a language (DDL.1) is intended to be used to specify planning problems as problems of controlling the domain temporal behavior. The paper, after presenting a BNF specification of the syntax, introduces a model theoretic semantics for DDL.1 and shortly discusses the possible connections between DDL.1 and a planner. Although preliminary this work suggests a methodology for domain description in complex planning application and introduces a DDL semantic account that represents a step towards the creation of tools for automated verification of domain specifications.

Acknowledgments. The first author would like to thank Nicola Muscettola and Stephen F. Smith that allowed him to work at the HSTS Project during 1990. Several discussions with Nicola were in particular useful to get acquainted with the HSTS representation ontology. Both authors are indebted to Francesco M. Donini for useful discussions on formal semantics for representation languages. The authors are of course the only responsible for any mistake still in the paper. This research is partially supported by Esprit III BRWG project No.8319 "ModelAge", CNR Special Project on Planning, CNR Committee 04 on Biology and Medicine.

References

1. Allen, J.F., Temporal Reasoning and Planning. In: Allen, J.F., Kautz, H.A., Pelavin, R.N., Tenenberg, J.D., Reasoning about Plans. Morgan Kaufmann Pub.Inc., 1991.
2. Cesta, A., Oddi, A., Using a Formal Domain Description Language in a Partial Order Temporal Planner, unpublished document, 1995.
3. Chapman, D., Planning for Conjunctive Goals. Artificial Intelligence, 32, 1987.
4. Currie, K., Tate, A., O-Plan: the open planning architecture. Artificial Intelligence, 52, 1991.
5. Kalman, R.E., Falb, P.L., Arbib, M.A., Topics in Mathematical System Theory, McGraw-Hill, New York, 1969.
6. Muscettola, N., Smith, S.F., Cesta, A., D'Aloisi, D., Coordinating Space Telescope Operations in an Integrated Planning and Scheduling Architecture, IEEE Control Systems, Vol.12, N.1, February 1992.
7. Muscettola, N., HSTS: Integrating Planning and Scheduling, in M.Zweben, M.S.Fox (Eds), Intelligent Scheduling, Morgan Kaufmann, 1994.
8. Pednault, E.P.D., ADL: Exploring the Middle Ground between STRIPS and the Situation Calculus. Proceedings of the 1st Conference on Principles of Knowledge Representation and Reasoning, 1989.
9. Valente, A., Knowledge-Level Analysis of Planning Systems, Sigart Bullettin, Special Section on Planning Agents, Vol.6, N.1, 1995.

A Method for Solving
Multiple Autonomous Robots Collisions Problem
Using Space and Time Representation

Carlo Ferrari[§], Enrico Pagello[§][*], Jun Ota[°] and Tamio Arai[°]

(§) Department of Electronics and Informatics, Faculty of Engineering,
The University of Padua (Italy)
(*) Institute of System Sciences and Bioengineering, National Research Council,
(LADSEB-CNR), Padova (Italy)
(°) Department of Precision Machinery Engineering, Faculty of Engineering,
The University of Tokyo (Japan)

Abstract. The problem of planning the motion of multiple autonomous robots, is approached by a decoupled analysis in the space and time domains. Proper representations are given for both, with a particular emphasis on the definition of some performance indexes to weight the goodness of a path with respect to motion and time. Sublinear algorithms are used for planning in space. Reasoning in the temporal domain is based on a proper subdivision of the time axis that leads to a polynomial algorithm.

1 Introduction

Planning the motion of several robots that act simultaneously in the same environment cannot be solved using the usual techniques developed for the single robot path planning problem. Many meaningful parameters used in static domains (like the shortest distance path criterium) are no longer valid in dynamic environments. In this paper, we address the problem of planning the motion scheduling and timing of each robot, that has to reach its goal position under the given spatial and temporal constraints. The basic idea is to use an appropriate and simple space representation together with the time representation and to associate some performance indexes to weight the goodness of a path with respect to motion and time. The solution of multiple robots motion planning problem has a great importance and a strong practical impact, being applied both to factory automation at the shopfloor level and in outdoor environment for traffic control.

A survey on motion planning of multiple mobile robot systems can be found in [1]. Different papers in the literature has dealt both with some theoretical and practical aspects of the problem [2],[3],[4],[5],[6]. Among the various approaches, Kant and Zucker's Velocity Tuning method [7], looks very powerful, because it allows to separate conveniently space information from time information, by splitting the problem of avoiding the obstacles into two subproblems, i.e. the problem of Path Planning among stationary obstacles (Path Planning Problem - PPP) and the problem of Velocity Planning along a fixed path (Velocity Planning Problem - VPP). In [8], Kant and Zucker's approach has been made more effective, by using sublinear collision detection algorithm for computing the free trajectories of the X-Y Space (in the PPP), and the free trajectories of the Path-Time Space (in the VPP), in the case of planning the motion of a single robot. In [9], that method has been extended to deal with multiple robots. In this paper, we focus on the use of performance indexes to get a suitable timing for each robot.

Both robots and fixed and movable obstacles are modelled by convex polygons. Moving obstacles are modeled as moving objects whose path and velocity is known, but it cannot be modified. They have the same shape of moving robots and move only along straight lines with constant velocity, while the robots can vary their speed. Moving robots must choose their path and velocity profile to avoid any collision among them and with any kind of obstacles. It is not possible for a robot to hit or move any object to clear its path. The robots move at their maximum allowable speed along the path segments where it is guaranteed that no collisions will occur.

A short description of the Path Planning algorithm proposed in [8] and [9], is given in the next paragraph. The Velocity Planning algorithm, regarding all robots paths simultaneously, weighting their goodness by some performance indexes, is described in section 3. In particular, in this paper we evaluate paths according some minimum time criteria, and the maximum allowable motion error. The proposed method has a strong practical impact (although it is not optimal) because its complexity is polynomial in the number of robots. Finally we would note that robot tasks are independent, i.e. each robot can reach its goal configuration without waiting for others robot to be in their goal position. Hence, in the worst case the solution can be to move a single robot at a time.

2 The Path Planning Problem

The proposed method for solving the path planning problem relies on sublinear algorithms to check for collisions between convex elements [10], [11]. These algorithms form a small core of elementary 2D and 3D geometric problem solvers that can be combined to approach more complex problem. The PPP is solved considering successive refinement of obstacles representations. With this approach it is not necessary to completely compute the Configuration Space [12], but only a detailed local description is computed just when needed, by a two step growing and refinement process. The basic idea is to grow the obstacle in order to obtain a box enclosing it. Then, when two boxes overlap, a refinement process is activate to check if also the two related obstacles overlap [13]. Then, by systematically discovering a reasonable number of free trajectories, a connectivity graph is built to look for a family of possible paths from the start point to the target point.

3 The Timing Planning Problem

The output of the path planning phase is a sequence of different paths for each robot, connecting its starting position to its goal position. Each path is composed by a few linear segments. The time planning problem is devoted to give each robot some velocity profile to avoid collision at intersections.

Given r robots in the environment (and each of them can choose one among k different paths towards its goal), there are k^r different way the robots can reach their goals. Searching for the best solution leads to a polynomial problem in the number of paths, but an exponential one in the number of robots. To reduce the complexity of the problem, it is possible to carry on the timing analysis considering all the k paths for each robot simultaneously, and to associate some performance measure to each of them. This measure can be obtained using one or more performance indexes.These indexes can give a measure of how good a path is with respect to the time constraints and robustness to motion errors. They can be modified during the time analysis of robot motion and allow to reject those paths that do not meet some minimum criteria. Hence any robot r of the original problem is substituted by a family of k robots each running along one of the different paths connecting the starting position and the goal position of r . While planning considering this new version of the problem, the intra-family robot collisions are ignored.

Two robots will collide if some segments of their paths intersect and they are running on them at the same time. In order to reduce the number of comparison of all the path segments, we will perform a time analysis first, and check for spatial path segments collision when two path segments temporally overlap. When a collision occurs one of the two robots is delayed (or stopped) until the other has cleared the path. If a collision between a robot and a moving obstacle will occur, the robot is stopped until the obstacle has cleared the way.

As a performance indexes, we associate to a path the *running time* (RT), that is the minimum time a robot should need for reaching the goal using that path and the *motion error* (ME), that can measure how a robot can move away from its path without colliding with obstacles or other robots. The RT index can be used to choose which robot has to be delayed and which is the path to be considered for each robot. Any time some robot is stopped this index is recomputed. The ME index is computed during the PPP phase and gives a measure of how a robot can move away from its path without any risk of collision. The ME is computed considering the distance between the sides of the obstacles and the sides of their bounding boxes.

This planning algorithm can be divided into three basic steps: a preprocessing step whose goal is to divide the time axis into basic time intervals and to associate to them those segments in use in that interval, a collision checking step that determines if two robots running on intersecting segment will collide and a delaying step that decides which is the robot to stop (or delay) and recompute the basic time scheduling for each robot.

Each path is made up of some segments and hence the first step is to (pre)-compute (for each robot) the time intervals that correspond to each segment in its path. In this phase we compute T^i_j, that is the minimum amount of time the i-th robot spends on the j-th segment of its path. The total running time for each robot is obtained summing up the T^i_j, where $1 < j < s$. This total time is the minimum amount of time required to reach the goal and it is the initial value for the RT performance index. Then the time axis must be divided into smaller intervals B_l whose extrema correspond to those instants when at least one robot move from one path segment to the next one in the corresponding path. These intervals are naturally ordered and do not overlap, except for the extrema. The set P_k of all path segments that are in use by any robot during B_k is also determined and associated to B_k.

Discovery collisions in space+time means checking spatial intersection over segments that are in use in the same basic time interval (i.e. that temporally overlap). The search for intersection can start considering all the segments in P_1 related to the first basic time interval B_1. Each couple of segments is tested. If an intersection exists, the schedule of the related robots along the intersecting segments is verified. If a collision exists, the delaying phase is activated. If no collision exists then the second interval is considered. This method is iterated over all the interval B_1. Each time a new interval B_k is considered it is not necessary to test all the couples of segments in P_k. In fact at time $t=t_k$ new path segments start to be in use while others are released. Then, it is enough to test each new path segment with those in use both in B_{k-1} and B_k. The computational complexity of this phase is quadratic in the number of robots and paths. The worst case number of comparison between pair of path segments is r'^2, $(r' = k\,r)$. Hence collisions can be discovered in $O(k^2 r^2)$ time.

If two segments intersect, and the related robots collide, the two robots must be synchronised. Collision will involve a spatial region around the intersection point of the two segments (critical region). The critical region shape can be computed starting from the robots' shape. The simplest way to guarantee no collision will occur is to stop the robot with the lower value of RT just before it enters the critical region, waiting for the other robot to clear the region and then to resume the stopped robot motion. The time intervals associated to the path segments of the stopped robot are recomputed and the time axis is again divided into basic time intervals. The process then continues by looking for collision in space+time starting from the current time interval and using the updated time subdivision.

5   A Planning Example

We now illustrate the proposed method applied to a real situation involving two robots R and S, that has to reach respectively G and H, and a moving obstacle O (see fig. 1). The PPP phase gives two possible paths for each robot, and a ME value for them. These ME value for R on path 1 and S on path 1 are 0,01 and for R on path 2 and S on path 2 are 0.05. The initial value of the RT index for R on path 1 is 37.2, for R on path 2 is 35.4, for S on path 1 is 27.2 and for S on path 2 is 29.5.

The first potential collision could occur during the interval $[t_3,t_4]$, involving S running on n and O on t. Collision analysis confirms that there would be a collision. Because O cannot be stopped, S is properly delayed, and a new timing diagram from t_3 is recomputed. The new RT index for the path1 of S becomes 28.8. The timing analysis will continue considering the intervals that follow t_4. Three collisions could occur in $[t_7,t_8]$, the first one involving R on b and O on t, the second one involving R on h and S on n, and the latter one involving R on h and O on t. From the timing diagram it comes up that R will not collide with the moving obstacle, because the critical region related to the intersection points has been already cleared by O, when R arrives. Instead there will be a collision between R on h and S on n. Because the RT index for R is greater then the RT index for S (and the ME index is the same), it is S that stops. The new RT index for the path1 of S becomes 31.8. In the interval $[t_9,t_{10}]$ again there is a temporal overlap of S on s and O on t. But again O will clear the critical region of the intersection point before the arrival of S. In the interval $[t_{11},t_{12}]$ the intersection involves two segments of paths related to the same robot, and hence it is not necessary to further check for spatial collision. Finally, a path can be chosen for each robot simply by looking to the lowest RT index in the set of paths related to the robot. In the example, R will run along path2 (RT equals to 35.4) and S will run along path2 (RT equals to 31.2).

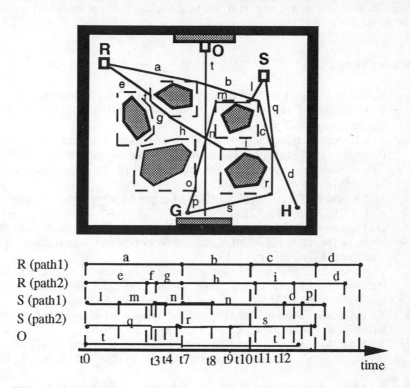

Fig. 1. An example of planning at the shopfloor level

6 Conclusions

We have presented a technique for planning the motions of several robots that share the same environment cluttered by both fixed and moving obstacles. The planning process recomputes the time intervals of the Path-Time Space any time a possible collision is discovered. This process is iterated until all path segments are considered. When the collision involves a moving obstacle, the robot will stop until the obstacle has cleared the path. Moving robots may stop and go also to avoid collisions with other robots. The number of segment path intersection tests is greatly reduced, and the correct timing of a robot along one path is provided. All paths are weighted by some performance indexes, according some minimum time criteria and robustness to motion error, improving the performance of the system. The proposed method may have a strong practical impact (although it is not optimal) because its complexity is polynomial in the number of robots. The Planning Algorithm presented in this paper is under implementation and testing on a SUN-4, at the Institute LADSEB of CNR.

Acknowledgements

This research is being pursued in cooperation between the Department of Electronics and Informatics (DEI) of the University of Padova, from the Italian side, and the Department of Precision Machinery Engineering of the University of Tokyo, from the Japanese side. Grants have been provided by the Italian National Research Council and by the Italian Ministry of Education.

References

1. T.Arai & J.Ota: "Motion Planning of Multiple Mobile Robots", Proc. of the 1992 IEEE/RSJ Int. Conf. on Intelligent Robots and Systems (IROS'92), Raleigh, July 1992 pp. 1761-1768.
2. J.E. Hopcroft, J.T. Schwartz & M. Sharir: "On the Complexity of Motion Planning for Multiple Independent Objects; PSPACE Hardness of 'Warehouseman's Problem'". The Int. Journal of Robotics Research, Vol. 3, No. 4, Winter 1984, pp. 76-88.
3. M. Erdman & T. Lozano-Pérez: "On Multiple Moving Objects". Algorithmica, Vol. 2, 1987, pp. 477-521.
4. D. Parsons & J. Canny: "A Motion Planner for Multiple Mobile Robots". Proc. of the 1990 IEEE Int. Conf. on Robotics and Automation (ICRA90), Cincinnati May 1990, pp. 8-13.
5. P. Fiorini & Z. Shiller: "Motion Planning in Dynamic Environment using the Relative Velocity Paradigm", Proc. of the 1993 IEEE Int. Conf. on Robotics and Automation (ICRA93), Atlanta 1993, pp. 560-565.
6. K. Fujimura: "Motion Planning amidst Transient Obstacles", Int. Journal of Robotics Research", vol 13, n. 5, Oct 1994, pp. 395-407.
7. K. Kant & S.W. Zucker: "Towards Efficient Planning: the Path-velocity decomposition". Int. Journal of Robotics Research, Vol. 5, No. 2, 1986, pp. 72-89.
8. E.Modolo & E.Pagello: "Collision Avoidance Detection In Space and Time Planning for Autonomous Robots". Proc. of the Int. Conf. on Autonomous Sistem (IAS-3). Pittsburgh 1993, pp. 216-225.
9. C. Ferrari, E. Pagello, J.Ota, T. Arai "Planning Miltiple Autonomous Robots Motion in Space and TIme", to be presented at the Int. Conf. on Intelligent Robots and Systems '95 (IROS'95), Pittsbourgh (USA), August 1995.
10. C. Mirolo & E. Pagello: "A Solid Modelling System for Robot Action Planning". IEEE Computer Graphics and Applications, Vol. 9, No.1, Jan. 1989, pp. 11-19.
11. C. Mirolo & E. Pagello: "Geometric Modeling for Robot Task Planning". To appear in G.W. Zobrist & C.V. Ho Eds., Progress in Robotics Volume 6, Ablex Publ. Co.
12. T. Lozano-Pérez: "Spatial Planning: A Configuration Space Approach", IEEE Trans. on Computers, Vol. C-32, No. 2, Feb. 1983, pp. 108-120.
13. C. Mirolo & E. Pagello: "Local Geometric Issues for Spatial Reasoning in Robot Motion Planning". Proc. of the IEEE/RSJ Int. Workshop on Intelligent Robots and Systems '91 (IROS'91). Osaka 1991, pp. 569-574.

Mapping Symbolic Knowledge into Locally Receptive Field Networks

Enrico Blanzieri[1] and Attilio Giordana[2]

[1] Centro di Scienza Cognitiva, Università di Torino,
Via Lagrange 3, 10100 Torino, Italy
e-mail: blanzier@psych.unito.it
[2] Dipartimento di Informatica, Università di Torino,
C.so Svizzera 185, 10149 Torino, Italy
e-mail: attilio@di.unito.it

Abstract. This paper investigates Locally Receptive Field Networks, a broad class of neural networks including Probabilistic Neural Networks and Radial Basis Function Networks, which naturally exhibit symbolic properties. Moreover, specific attention is given to the sub-class of Factorizable Radial Basis Function Networks whose architecture can be directly translated into a propositional theory and viceversa. Exploiting this characteristics, symbolic and numeric algorithms can be easely integrated for automating network synthesis. Several methods including classification and regression trees, and statistical clustering are evaluated on a classification task in a difficult medical domain. The obtained results show that the considered network class is able to achieve a high accuracy, while conserving a symbolic readability.

1 Introduction

The problem of converting a body of symbolic knowledge into a neural network and viceversa has been already investigated by several authors. A major contribution comes by Towell and Shavlik [15, 14] which tackled this problem among the firsts. The claimed benefits deriving from this form of integration of symbolic and subsymbolic knowledge, are first of all, a speed up in neural network training and a general improvement of the performances. Second, the possibility of mapping back a neural network into symbolic knowledge [13] offers a good interface toward the end user which frequently refuses to trust a "black box".

However, the seminal works of Towel and Shavlik, mostly relates to backpropagation networks based on Multilayer Perceptron. A step towards the integration between this architecture and symbolic algorithms is made in the work of Sethi [11]. In this paper, we will show that the Locally Receptive Field Networks (LRFN), a broad family including Probabilistic Neural Networks [12], Radial Basis Function Networks [10, 9], Fuzzy Controllers [1] and some others, naturally exhibits the same symbolic properties obtained by Shawlik without requiring sophisticated translation algorithms.

Insertion, refinement and extraction of rule-based knowledge in a Basis Function Network was proposed by Tresp *et al.* [16]. The symbolic proprieties of Fuzzy

Controllers are straightforward and prior knowledge is widely used for their synthesis. Giordana *et al.* [5] already shown how to exploit their symbolic readability for integrating symbolic learning methods and rule-based knowledge insertion. In the following we will show how symbolic learning algorithms such as SMART+, CART and C4.5 can be used to synthesize a LRFN which can be still refined by performing the error gradient descent reaching performances comparable (or better) to the ones obtainable using classical backpropagation networks.

Alternatively, we will show how clustering algorithms such as *k-means* can be used to synthesize a F-RBFN which can be converted into a propositional classification theory. The methods are evaluated on a non trivial domain and compared with multi-layer perceptron and multivariate statistical analysis.

The paper is organized as follows. The next section investigates LRFNs and defines a reference network architecture, based on a variant of the F-RBFNs, which is suitable both for classification and for regression tasks. Section 3 describes several learning methods for synthesising a F-RBFN from examples and a domain theory, and Section 4 presents an experimental evaluation. Finally, the approach is compared to the one of Shavlik [15] in Section 5.

2   Locally Receptive Field Networks

In the following of this paper we will restrict our interest to the problem of learning a function (called the *target function* in the following) from an n-dimensional continuous domain $D \subset R^n$ to a co-domain $Y \subset R$, being n the number of input features. Boolean input and boolean outputs can be represented as threshold functions on continuous spaces. Therefore, we will restrict our attention to networks with an arbitrary set of inputs, but a single output, as it is usually done for RBFNs.

As it has been proven in [6], a universal function approximator can be constructed using at least three layers of nodes (input, hidden and output), provided the activation function in the hidden layer be non-linear. In the backpropagation network family, derived from the Multi-Layer Perceptron (MLP), the most frequently used activation function is the sigmoid. On the contrary, LRFN family, while similar in the topological structure, makes use of activation functions having axial symmetry. For instance, multidimensional Gaussian functions are used in Probabilistic Neural Networks (PNN) [12] and in Radial Basis Function Networks (RBFNs) [10], pyramidal or trapezoidal functions are used for fuzzy controllers, and cylindric functions in the Restricted Coulomb Energy model [4]. As a consequence, MLP and LRFNs encode the target function in a totally different way.

Considering the sigmoidal activation function $O_i = \sigma(\sum_{j=1}^{N} w_{ij} I_j)$ of the MLP's hidden units, we see that each neuron, apart from a narrow region where the sigmoid transient occurs, splits the input domain into two semi-spaces where its output is significantly close to 1 or to 0. The whole semispace where the output is close to 1 contributes to the value of the target function. On the contrary, in a LRFN, each hidden neuron is associated to a convex closed region in the input domain (*activation area*), where its response is significantly greater than zero, and dominates over every other neuron. The greatest contribution of a neuron to the output value Y comes essentially from this region.

From a mathematical point of view, Poggio and Girosi [10] have shown that LRFNs (more specifically RBFNs) tend to reproduce a serial development of the target function in terms of Green's functions.

However, LRFNs exhibit properties substantially different with respect to both the learning algorithms and the semantic interpretation. In order to understand the different behaviors of the two network types, suppose to modify a weight between two nodes in the MLP, as it is done by the backpropagation updating rule during the training phase. The effect involves an *infinite* region of the input space and can affect large part of the co-domain of the target function. On the contrary, changing the amplitude of the region of the input space, in which the activation function of a neuron in an LRFN fires, or shifting its position will have an effect *local* to the region dominated by that neuron. More in general, this *locality property* of the LRFN allows the network layout to be incrementally constructed (see for instance [8]) adjusting the existing neurons and/or adding new ones. As every change has a local effect, the knowledge encoded in the other parts of the network is not lost; so, it will not be necessary to go through a global revision process.

A second important property of the LRFNs is the possibility of giving an immediate, symbolic interpretation of the hidden neuron semantics. In fact, the closed regions corresponding to neuron activation areas can be labeled with a symbol and interpreted as elementary concepts. In the following we will define a more precise network architecture which has straightforward interpretation in term of propositional logics.

2.1 An F-RBFN Architecture

The specific network architecture we will investigate in this paper is a hybrid between the Factorized Radial Basis Function Networks (F-RBFNs), mentioned in [10] and the fuzzy/neural networks introduced by Berenji [1] for implementing fuzzy controllers capable of learning from a reinforcement signal. It is similar to the architecture proposed by Tresp *et al.* [16]. Figure 1 describes the basic network topology.

The activation function used in an F-RBFN with n input units is defined as the product of n unidimensional radial functions, each one associated to one of the input features. Therefore a F-RBFN can be described as a network with two hidden layers. The neurons in the first hidden layer are feature detectors, each associated to a single unidimensional activation function and are connected to a single input only. Assuming to use Gaussian functions, the neuron r_{ij} (the i-th component of the j-th activation area) computes the output:

$$\mu_{ij} = e^{-\left(\frac{I_i - C_{ij}}{\sigma_{ij}}\right)^2}$$

(1)

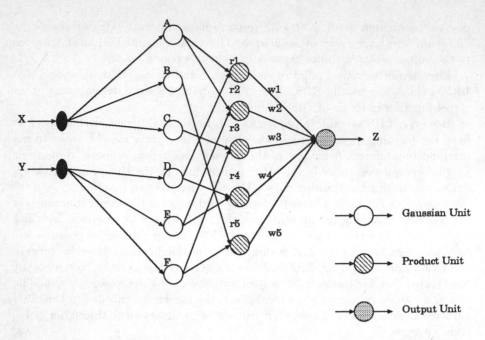

Fig. 1. Reference LRFN architecture. The first layer hidden units have a unidimensional Gaussian activation function. The second layer hidden units compose the input values using arithmetic product. An average sum unit performs the weighted sum of the activation values received from the product units.

The neurons in the second hidden layer simply compute a product and construct multi-dimensional radial functions:

$$r_j = \prod_i \mu_{ij} \tag{2}$$

Finally, the output neuron combine the contributes of the composite functions computed in the second hidden layer. In our architecture, a choice among four different activation functions is possible for the output neuron, in order to adapt the network to different needs. The output function, normally adopted for RBFNs, is a weighted sum

$$Y = \sum_j w_j r_j \tag{3}$$

The same function can be followed by a sigmoid, realizing so a perceptron, when the network is used for a classification task. Using this function the network tends to produce an output value close to '0' everywhere the input vector I falls in a point of the domain which is far from every activation area. The consequence is under-generalization in the classification tasks.

This problem can be avoided by introducing a normalization term in the output activation function:

$$\hat{Y} = \frac{\sum_j w_j r_j}{\sum_j r_j} \qquad (4)$$

This function is frequently used for fuzzy controller architectures [1]. In this case, one obtains a network biased toward over-generalization in a similar way as it happen for the multi-layer perceptron. Depending on the application, under-generalization or over-generalization can be preferable. The results reported in this paper refer to networks based on function (4).

2.2 Associating a Symbolic Interpretation to a LRFN

Factorized RFBNs have an immediate symbolic interpretation. In fact, defining the activation area A_j of a neuron r_j as the region in the input domain where the output of r_j is greater than a given threshold T, we obtain an ellipse with the axis parallel to the input features. Moreover, A_j is inscribed into a rectangle R_j having the edges parallel to the input features (see Figure 2).

Then, every edge r_{ij} of R_j can be seen as a pair of conditions on the input I_i and then the whole rectangle can be read as a conjunctive condition on the input. A variant of this symbolic interpretation could be to assign a symbol to every edge, interpreted as an atomic proposition. In this way, the unidimensional activation functions can be seen as a "fuzzy" semantics of the atomic propositions.

Finally, links from the second hidden layer to to output neuron can be seen as implication rule of the type:

$$R_j \rightarrow w_j \qquad (5)$$

being R_j the logical description of the rectangle R_j. In other words, the meaning of (5) is: "if conditions R_j hold then the value of the output is w_j". Then, the activation function associated to the output neuron implements a kind of *evidential reasoning* taking into account the different piece of evidence coming from the rules encoded in the network.

In any case we must be conscious that this symbolic interpretation has to be considered only as a heuristic approximation of the knowledge encoded in the network and so we cannot expect a full logical equivalence. Moreover, this logical interpretation is plausible when the activation areas are not too overlapped in the input space.

2.3 Mapping a Propositional Theory into a LRFN

Given an n-dimensional continuous domain D, a classification theory in propositional calculus defined on D can always be reduced to a set of one step implication rules of the type: $C_1 \wedge C_2 \wedge ... \wedge C_n \rightarrow H$ with $C_1, C_2, ..., C_n$ representing conditions (thresholds) on the dimensions of D. Moreover, we observe that real

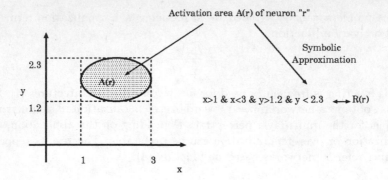

Fig. 2. The closed region where LRF-Function is dominant can be roughly approximated using a conjunctive logical assertion.

continuous domains always have finite boundaries (defined by the range of the input sensors); then, the precondition of every classification rule always defines a rectangle in the space D.

Therefore, mapping such a theory into the network structure of Figure 1, is immediate according to the discussion we made in the previous section. The antecedent of a rule R_i will be represented by a proper set of neurons in the first hidden layer and by a single neuron in the second one connected to the output neuron representing class H. The weight on the link will be set to the numeric value (say 1) representing the concept of "true", if the rule is a positive one (implies H) or to the numeric value representing the "false" (say 0 or -1) if the rule is a negative one (i.e implies $\neg H$).

In order to preserve the theory's semantics, the activation function in the first hidden layer, should be rectangular. In fact, using Gaussian functions or other kinds of continuous functions, the logical conditions of the classification theory will become blurred and then, the performance will degrade owing to the translation into the network. On the other hand, the use of continuous activation functions allows to refine the network by performing the error gradient descent, as it will be described later on; then, the initial performance decay can be recovered in a few learning steps and in general the final performances can go far beyond the ones of the initial logical theory.

In our experiments, we will use Gaussian functions having width (at half height) coincident with the length of the rectangle edges.

Using activation functions having a non-null value on all the domain D, such as Gaussians do, the choice of function (3) or (4) for the output neuron is not so obvious and deserves some more discussion. In logics, it is quite common to have .the Closed World Assumption (CWA) so that, anything is not explicitly asserted is assumed false. Under this assumption, a classification theory can contains only positive rules, because the negation of a class follows from the CWA.

If function (3) is used, the CWA can be automatically embedded in the network semantics by using a threshold function (a sigmoid in our case) in order to split the output co-domain into two regions: one, above the threshold where the output value is high and the target *class* is asserted, and another, below the threshold, where the output value is low and the *class* is negated. As a consequence we can model in the network only positive rules.

On the contrary, using function (4) the output value tend to be always "1", if the theory contains only positive rules, because of the normalization factor. Then, the CWA doesn't hold anymore and negative rules must be explicitly inserted in the network in order to cover the whole domain D either with a positive or with a negative rule.

The considered F-RBFN architecture is able to approximate continuous functions as well as classification functions and, also in this case, it is possible to give them a *qualitative* symbolic interpretation, as it is done for fuzzy controllers. In this case, both function (3) or (4) can be used for the output neuron.

When the function (4) is used, our network is similar to one of the networks described by the general architecture proposed by Tresp *et al.*. The main difference is that we use factorizable activation functions whereas Tresp uses directly Basis Functions. In this way we can connect a first hidden layer neuron that has an unidimensional activation function with different product units. That leads to a more compact networks and, from a symbolic point of view, permits to handle unidimensional conditions that may appear in more than one rule.

3 Supervised Learning Algorithms for F-RBFNs

Given the peculiar properties they exhibit, F-RBFNs are suitable for exploiting and integrating both symbolic and numeric learning algorithms. In particular, it is possible to exploit the methods for Radial Basis Function synthesis, the ones for learning classification theories, both deductive and inductive, and the error gradient descent typical of the backpropagation networks. Moreover, it is also possible to directly implant in the network the knowledge of a human expert as it is usually made for fuzzy controllers.

In the following we will briefly overview several of this methods, which will be experimentally evaluated in Section 4.

3.1 Statistical Clustering

The usual methods for learning from examples Radial Basis Function networks [10] are based on a two step learning procedure. First a statistical clustering algorithm, such as *k-Means* is used to determine the centers and the amplitude of the activation functions. Then, the weights on the links to the output neuron are determined by computing the coefficients of the pseudo-inverse matrix [10]. The method is usually faster than gradient descent. On the other hand, this last is sometime preferable, because it is more simple to implement and because it is suitable for on-line learning. In this paper we will show results only for the gradient descent.

3.2   Symbolic Algorithms

Most symbolic algorithms for concept learning in propositional calculus produce, directly or indirectly, a classification theory described in form of implication rules. Then, they can be used for automatically constructing the layout of a F-RBFN. In the present case we focused on two specific algorithms, not because they are considered the best for this specific purpose, but because they where immediately available to the authors.

The first algorithm is the well known CART [3] which can work both for classification and for regression. In both cases the trees produced by CART can be simply translated into rules and then used to construct a network.

The second algorithm is SMART+ [2] which has the peculiarity of combining inductive and deductive techniques. In this way it is possible to force the system to exploit a domain theory even when it is imperfect. Afterwards, the rules learned by CART or SMART+ are translated into a F-RBFN which is finely tuned by performing the error gradient descent by means of the Δ-Rule.

Gradient Descent As we adopted continuous activation functions, which are derivable in the whole domain, it is immediate to apply the classical error gradient descent technique in order to finely tune the weights and the parameters in the activation functions. More specifically, let E be the quadratic error evaluated on the learning set and let, moreover, λ_k indicate a generic parameter in the network, such as, a weight w on a link, the width σ or the center c of a Gauss activation function, or the threshold of the sigmoid in the output neuron. We are able to compute all the necessary derivatives, and the learning rule takes the form:

$$\Delta\lambda_i = -\eta\frac{\partial E}{\partial \lambda_k} \tag{6}$$

A problem which can arise is that the Δ-Rule tends to move the position of the activation areas trying to minimize the error. Then, it may happen that the areas overlap, so that the original symbolic structure is no more preserved. However, it is not difficult to modify the gradient descent procedure so that the centers of the radial functions cannot come too close each other. In fact it is easy to control the overlap by means of direct monitoring and freeezing of the centers. Alternatively, it is possible to adopt one the strategy proposed by Tresp *et al.* [16] in order to preserve the knowledge inserted in the network.

4   Experimental Evaluation

In the following we will test the learning methods described in the previous section on a classification task in a real medical domain using data collected from the Italian National Research Council.

What emerges from the experiments is that excellent F-RBFNs can be learned from examples while preserving the symbolic readability, especially when they are synthesized using the symbolic approaches based on CART.

4.1   Medical Prognosis Test Case

The problem is to estimate the risk of death for patients in intensive care units, starting from a a set of physiological variables (see Table 1) measured on a patient at its arrival in the hospital.

The state-of-the-art method currently used for predicting the outcome, from this physiological variables, is based on the Simplified Acute Physiology Score (SAPS-II) [7], a statistical method for evaluating the severity of the patient status. SAPS-II has developed and validated using logistic regression analysis on more then 8,000 patients and it can be converted to a probability of death.

The problem presents itself as a classification task and it is well suited for our present purposes. In fact a-priori knowledge is available from domain experts (not used here in the learning process) and learned rules can be interesting to them. We used a database collected in the context of an epidemiological study on infection diseases in a group of intensive care units in hospitals.

The dataset available up to now consists of 2,020 patient records for which the outcome is known. In order to compare the results, only the variables that are involved in the SAPS-II computation were used in the experimentation described in the following. Two missing variables have been substituted by others with the same informative content not affecting the SAPS-II evaluation. The variables (attributes) actually used for learning are shown in Table 1.

Parameter	Meaning	Type
AGE	Age	continuos
HR	Heart rate	continuos
SBP	Systolic blood pressure	continuos
TEMP	Body temperature	continuos
V-ROFS	Ventilation, Respiratory Organ Failure Score*	discrete
URO	Urinary flow	continuos
N	Serum urea nitrogen level	continuos
WBC	White Blood Corpuscles count	continuos
NA	Serum sodium level	continuos
K	Serum potassium level	continuos
HCO3	Serum bicarbonate level	continuos
GCS	Glascow Coma Score	continuos
HOFS	Hepatic Organ Failure Score*	discrete
ADM	Type of admission	discrete
CD	Chronic diseases	discrete
OUT	Outcome	discrete (target)

Table 1. Attributes used in the medical prognosis problem. (*) Parameters that differs from the ones originally used for SAPS-II computation

The dataset (2020 records) was randomly split in a learning set (1020 records) and in a validation set (1000 records) and all the data were normalized.

Method	N of rules	$Err_{initial}$	Epochs	Err_{final}
KM+GD	15	24.90	100	23.30
KM+GD	18	26.10	100	22.70
KM+GD	20	24.00	100	22.30
KM+GD	22	24.70	100	24.20
KM+GD	25	24.70	100	25.70
KM+GD	35	24.80	100	24.60
CART+GD	13	22.70	300	22.60
CART+GD	18	22.70	200	22.60
CART+GD	24	22.70	200	22.10
CART+GD	31	24.70	200	21.40
CART+GD	46	24.09	100	22.30
CART+GD	52	24.30	100	21.00
CART+GD	60	25.60	200	22.60
MLP	7	—	6000	21.60
MLP	10	—	2000	21.20
MLP	5+5	—	2000	20.60
SAPS-II	–	—	—	19.30

Table 2. Comparative results on the Medical Prognosis Problem. The third column reports the error before performing the gradient descent. In the case of *k-Means* (KM) it corresponds to the untrained network error whereas in the case of CART, it corresponds to the error of the classification tree itself. The fifth column reports the final error after training.

Two groups of experiments have been performed. In the first group a F-RBFN was constructed using the *k-Means* algorithm trying with different numbers of clusters. In the second group, a version of CART (developed by the authors) was used. Several alternative rules sets have been obtained by running CART with different accuracy requirements (minimum impurity in a leaf). A pruning set of 300 examples was selected from the learning set.

The major difference between the two methods is in the feature selection operated by CART, which systematically leads to more compact and general rules. The best results reached are summarized in Table 2, where a comparison with the well known Multilayer Perceptron and with SAPS-II method is also presented. However, SAPS-II clearly emerges from the results as the best, with an advantage of around 1% over the best result obtained with the neural networks. However, we must take into account that it has been developed using a database much larger and with a low degree of noise. So, its good performance is not surprising. On the other hand MLP and F-RBFN performances are very comparable in terms of accuracy. The MLP, that shows the best performance, has two hidden layers with a feedforward fully connected topology.

Considering the results for F-RBFNs, it is evident that the synthesis procedure based on CART is better than the one based on /em k-Means. Moreover, it is interesting to see how the gradient descent can still significantly increase the performances of the classification theories produced by CART, in a relatively small number of epochs. We see that, even very small set of rules (13 rules) can still reach reasonable performances, thank to the continuous valued semantics and the evidential reasoning performed by the network architecture. However, we wondered whether the gradient descent did blur or not the original symbolic structure. Therefore we tried map back the networks into rules which have been tested again on the data. The result was that, in general, the rules extracted from the network were better than the original ones. For instance, referring to the rule set of 52 rules (12th row in Table 2) the extracted rules set had an error rate of 22.60 original 24.30 a rule generated by CART with the corresponding one extracted from the network after refinement.

$$R12(Before Refinement) : SBP > 127.5 \wedge V - ROFS > 1.00 \wedge 27.09 < HCO3$$
$$\wedge HCO3 < 29.96 \wedge 4.50 < GCS \wedge GCS < 9.00$$
$$\wedge ADM < 3.00 \rightarrow OUT = 0$$

$$R12(After Refinement) : SBP > 130.9 \wedge V - ROFS > 0.97 \wedge 26.90 < HCO3$$
$$\wedge HCO3 < 29.47 \wedge 4.58 < GCS \wedge GCS < 8.65$$
$$\wedge ADM < 3.04 \rightarrow OUT = 0$$

5 Conclusions

In this paper, we investigated a class of neural networks, called Locally Receptive Field Networks, which is particularly suitable for integrating the symbolic and connectionist paradigms, in the line of Shavlik and Towell [15, 13].

More specifically, we shows how classical symbolic learning algorithms can be used in order to synthesize a network which can still be refined by performing the gradient descent. After refinement, the network tends to conserve its symbolic readability. However, here we still didn't exploit all the potential of this network architecture. For instance, we didn't take advantage of a priori knowledge in order to improve the network accuracy, and, we didn't exploit the incremental property which makes them particularly attractive for many practical applications where it is required to learn on-line.

Moreover, we restricted our analysis to simple networks with a single output and capable of encoding only one step classification rules. Even if it is not essential to go beyond this model because a propositional theory can always be reduced to this form, it could be interesting to extend the model in order to account for hierarchies and more complex logical constructs.

Finally, in our opinion an important point of this paper is the unifying view we proposed for comparing and integrating different approaches, such as RBFNs, Probabilistic Neural Networks, Fuzzy Logics and Instance Based Learning, which seem to share many properties which up to know have been little recognized.

6 Acknowledgements

The authors wish to thank M. Musicco and his staff (CNR-Milan) who furnished the data of the Medical Prognosis Problem and S. Selva Cirio and F. Sola who extracted the database, computed the SAPS-II and performed the experimentation with the Multilayer Perceptron.

References

1. H.R. Berenji. Fuzzy logic controllers. In R.R. Yager and L.A. Zadeh, editors, *An Introduction to Fuzzy Logic Applications in Intelligent Systems*. Kluver Academic Publishers, 1992.
2. M. Botta and A. Giordana. SMART+: A multi-strategy learning tool. In *IJCAI-93, Proceedings of the Thirteenth International Joint Conference on Artificial Intelligence*, volume 2, Chambéry, France, 1993.
3. L. Breiman, J.H. Friedman, R.A. Ohlsen, and C.J. Stone. *Classification And Regression Trees*. Wadsworth & Brooks, Pacific Grove, CA, 1984.
4. L.N. Cooper D.L. Reilly and C. Elbaum. A neural model for category learning. *Biological Cybernatics*, 45:35–41, 1982.
5. A. Giordana, M. Kaiser, and M. Nuttin. Robot controller synthesis: How to reduce costs. In *Proceedings of the Workshop on Learning Robots*, Torino, October 1993.
6. K. Hornik, M. Stinchcombe, and H. White. Multilayer feed-forward networks are universal approximators. *Neural Networks*, 2:359–366, 1989.
7. F. Saulnier J.R. Le Gall, S. Lemeshow. A new simplified acute physiology score (saps ii) based on a european/north american multicenter study. *JAMA*, 270(24):2957–2963, 1993.
8. J.R. Millán. Learning efficient reactive behavioral sequences from basic reflexes in a goal-directed autonomous robot. In *Proceedings of the third International Conference on Simulation of Adaptive Behavior*, 1994.
9. J. Park and W. Sandberg. Universal approximation using radial-basis functions. *Neural Computation*, 3:246–257, 1991.
10. T. Poggio and F. Girosi. Networks for approximation and learning. *Proceedings of the IEEE*, 78(9):1481–1497, September 1990.
11. I.K. Sethi. Entropy nets: From decison trees to neural networks. *Proceedings of the IEEE*, 78(10):1605–1613, October 1990.
12. D.F. Specht. Probabilistic neural networks. *Neural Networks*, 3:109–118, 1990.
13. G. Towell and J.W. Shavlik. Extracting refined rules from knowledge-based neural networks. *Machine Learning*, 13(1):71–101, 1993.
14. G. Towell and J.W. Shavlik. Knowledge based artificial neural networks. *Artficial Intelligence*, 70(4):119–166, 1994.
15. G.G. Towell, J.W. Shavlik, and M.O. Noordwier. Refinement of approximate domain theories by knowledge-based neural networks. In *Proceedings of the 8th National Conference on Artificial Intelligence AAAI'90*, pages 861–866, 1990.
16. V. Tresp, J. Hollatz, and S. Ahmad. Network structuring and training using rule-based knowledge. In *Advances in Neural Information Processing Systems 5 (NIPS-5)*. Morgan Kaufmann, 1993.

Knowledge Representation for Robotic Vision Based on Conceptual Spaces and Attentive Mechanisms

A. Chella, M. Frixione*, S. Gaglio

Dipartimento di Ingegneria Elettrica
Universita' di Palermo - Viale delle Scienze - 90128 Palermo Italy

*Istituto Internazionale per gli Alti Studi Scientifici
Via Pellegino, 19 - 84019 Vietri sul Mare (Salerno) Italy

Abstract

A new cognitive architecture for artificial vision is proposed. The architecture is aimed for an autonomous intelligent system, as several cognitive hypotheses have been postulated as guidelines for its design. The design is based on a conceptual representation level between the subsymbolic level processing the sensory data, and the linguistic level describing scenes by means of a high-level language. The architecture is also based on the active role of a focus of attention mechanism in the link between the conceptual and the linguistic level. The link between the conceptual level and the linguistic level is modelled as a time-delay attractor neural network.

1 Introduction

In classical symbolic reasoning systems, the symbols are related to abstract entities according to model theoretic semantics. This turns out to be completely unsatisfactory for an autonomous agent, that needs to find the meaning for its symbols within its internal representation and in its interaction with the external world, overcoming in some way the well known symbol grounding problem [Chella 1994].

This paper presents a cognitive architecture for an artificial vision system, in which an effective internal representation of the environment is built by means of processes defined over a suitable intermediate level that acts as an intermediary between the sensory data and the symbolic level.

We hypothesise three representation levels as the basis of our architectural design: the subsymbolic level, in which the information is strictly related to the sensory data; the linguistic level, in which information is expressed by a symbolic language; and an intermediate, "prelinguistic" conceptual level. At this level the information is characterised in terms of a metric space defined by a certain number of "cognitive" dimensions, independent from any specific language [Gärdenfors 1992]. The aim of this level is to generate the very internal representation of the agent's external environment and to provide a precise interpretation for the linguistic level.

The interpretation of linguistic level categories is implemented by a mapping between the conceptual and the linguistic levels in terms of a connectionist device. Neural networks allow to avoid an exhaustive description of conceptual categories at the symbolic level. Moreover, the measure of similarity between a prototype and a given object is implicit in the behaviour of the network and is determined during the learning phases.

A correlated cognitive aspect of the proposed architecture is the role of attentive processes in the link between the linguistic and the conceptual level. In fact, a finite agent with bounded resources cannot carry out a one shot, exhaustive, and uniform analysis of a perceived scene within reasonable time constraints. Furthermore, some aspects of a scene are more relevant then others, and it would be irrational to waste time and computational resources to detect true but useless details. These problems can be faced by hypothesising a sequential attentive mechanism, that scans the internal representation of the scene.

The focus of attention is hypothesised to be driven on the basis of the knowledge, the hypotheses, the purposes and the expectations of the system, in order to detect the relevant aspects in the perceived scene. Hence, it is a task of the higher level components to use the information acquired through the perceptual system to create expectations or to form contexts in which hypotheses may be verified and, if it is necessary, adjusted.

Three focus of attention modalities are hypothesised at the basis of the proposed architecture: a reactive modality, in which the attention is driven only by the characteristics of scene, a linguistic modality in which the attention is driven by simple inferences at the linguistic level, and an associative modality in which the attention is driven by free associations among concepts.

2 The design of the architecture

The cognitive assumptions introduced in the previous section are the guidelines for the design and implementation of the proposed architecture for artificial vision.

Fig. 1 shows the overall architecture in which the previously described three levels of representations are evidentiated. The block A is the kernel of the subsymbolic level: it receives one or more input pictorial digitised images acquired by a camera and, by means of shape from shading and/or stereo vision algorithms, gives as an output the depth images. The depth images are input to the block B, which builds a scene description in terms of a combination of 3D geometric primitives.

The computer vision literature proposes several possible implementations of the blocks A and B; the current implementation of both blocks in the proposed architecture is outlined in Sect. 8.

The block C implements the associative mapping between the conceptual level and the symbolic level; the aims of this block is to recognise the objects and situations. The input to the block C is a vector configuration in the conceptual space, its output is sent to the linguistic level to produce a sentential description of the scene.

The symbolic knowledge base represents the kernel of the linguistic level. The aim of this block is twofold: it describes in a high-level language the perceived scene by interpreting the input coming from the block C, and it generates, by means of its inferences capabilities, the linguistic "expectations" that drive the focus of attention mechanism.

The block D is the block responsible for the linguistic modality of the focus of attention mechanism. It receives as input the instances of concepts from the knowledge base and it suitably drives the focus of attention, in order to seek for the corresponding objects and situations in the acquired scene.

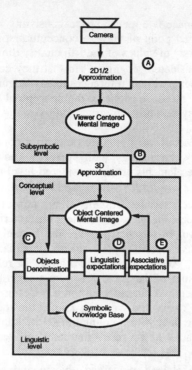

Fig. 1. The proposed architecture. The three levels of representation are evidentiated.

The block E is the block responsible for the associative modality of the focus of attention. Its operation is similar to block D, but it drives the focus of attention looking for the objects in the scene which can be freely associated to the input instances.

The reactive modality of the focus of attention is implemented as an internal mechanism of block D: when the block does not receive any expectations as input, it generates some generic expectations in order to start the operations of the system.

3 The three levels of representation

Gärdenfors [Gärdenfors 1992] proposes three levels of information representation: a linguistic level, a conceptual level and a subsymbolic level. At the linguistic level the information is described in terms of a symbolic language, e.g. first order logic; at the subsymbolic level information is characterised directly in terms of the perceptual inputs of the system. Between these two levels, a third level is hypothesised: the conceptual level, in which information is described by means of a conceptual space.

In fig. 1, the three big blocks correspond to Gärdenfors' levels of representation. The first level can be seen also as a visual, viewer centered, mental image. The central level embeds an object centered mental image. The upper level consists of a propositional, linguistic, knowledge representation.

A conceptual space is a metric space consisting of a number of quality dimensions. From a formal point of view, a conceptual space is an n-dimensional space CS where X_i is the set of values of the i-th quality dimension ($1 \leq i \leq n$). The dimensions should be considered "cognitive" in that they correspond to qualities of the represented environment, without references to any linguistic descriptions. In the case of visual perception, the dimensions of the conceptual space correspond to the parameters of a suitable system of geometric primitives, e.g. superquadrics [Pentland 1986].

We define the *knoxel* as a generic point in a conceptual space (the term "knoxel" is suggested by the analogy with "pixel"); knoxels therefore represent epistemological primitive elements at the considered level of analysis. Formally a knoxel is a vector $k = < x_1, x_2,, x_n >$ where $x_i \in X_i$ ($1 \leq i \leq n$); each component corresponds to a parameter describing a quality dimension of the domain of interest. In the case of visual perception, these parameters characterise geometric primitives of the kind quoted above. In this perspective, the knoxels correspond to simple geometric building blocks, while complex objects or situations are represented as suitable sets of knoxels. Accordingly, each knoxel is related to measurements, obtained via suitable sensors, of the geometric parameters of "simple basic" objects in the external environment. A metric function d is defined in CS, which may be considered as a measure of similarity among knoxels in the conceptual space. For the sake of simplicity we deal with a countable set of knoxels by discretizing the axes of the conceptual space CS. As result the set of all perceivable knoxels k_i is the countable set $KS = \{k_1, k_2, ...\}$.

As previously explained, perceived objects and situations correspond to suitable sets of knoxels; we define a perception cluster $pc = \{k_1, k_2, ..., k_l\}$ on a finite set of knoxels corresponding to an object or a situation in KS. The set PC of all the perception clusters in KS is defined as:

$$PC = \{\{k_1, k_2, ..., k_l\} | l \in N, k_i \in KS \text{ for } 1 \leq i \leq l\} \tag{1}$$

The conceptual level is independent from any linguistic characterisation. On the contrary, the semantics of the symbols at the linguistic level is based on the conceptual level; since symbols are interpreted on configurations at the conceptual level, as described in Sect. 5.

4 The linguistic level

The role of the linguistic level in the proposed architecture is to provide a rough and concise description of the perceived scene in terms of a high-level logical language, suitable for symbolic knowledge-based reasoning.

In order to describe the symbolic knowledge base we adopt a hybrid representation formalism, in the sense of Nebel [Nebel 1990]. According to this point of view, a hybrid formalism is constituted by two different modules: a terminological component and an assertional component. In our model, the terminological component contains the descriptions of the concepts relevant for the represented domain (e.g., types of objects and of situations to be perceived). The assertional component stores the assertions describing the specific perceived scenes. As an example, consider in fig. 2 a simple fragment of the terminological knowledge base, concerning the description of objects. In the figure, the network notation developed by Brachman for the KL-ONE system [Brachman 1985] has been adopted. The assertional component is based on a first order predicate language, in which the concepts of the terminological component correspond to one argument predicates, and the roles (e.g., *hammer-head* or *hammer-handle*) correspond to two argument relations.

Concerning situations, they are also represented as concepts in the terminological formalism. In other words, we assume that situations are reified, i.e., we assume that to every specific situation correspond an individual in the domain [Davidson 1967]. Fig. 3 shows the network description of the *Situation* concept, and of two particular types of situation, *On* and *Sided*.

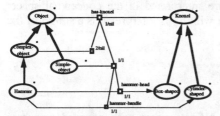

Fig. 2. A fragment of the terminological knowledge base.   Fig. 3. Network description of the *Situation* concept.

5 The mapping between the conceptual and linguistic levels

The mapping between the conceptual and the linguistic level defines an internal, cognitive oriented, semantic interpretation for the symbols at the linguistic level. The interpretation function associates a perception cluster to any individual constant representing an object or a situation at the linguistic level a perception cluster. Therefore, if C is the set of assertional constants representing objects and situations, the interpretation function φ has the following type:

$$\varphi : C \to PC \tag{2}$$

where PC represents the set of all perception clusters as defined in eq.1.

The assertional language can also treat assertional constants, representing more specific features of objects and situations, like, for instance, the main axis of an object or its shape. The set C' of such assertional constants is mapped by the interpretation function to the specific structures of the conceptual space:

$$\varphi : C \to X \tag{3}$$

where $X = \bigcup_{i=1}^{n} X_i$ is the set of all the values of the quality dimensions of the conceptual space.

The compositional aspects of the interpretation of symbolic structures at the linguistic level can be defined according to the usual model theoretic semantics of terminological languages [Nebel 1990]. The main difference between the proposed internal semantics and the usual model theoretic semantics is that the extensions of predicates are uniquely defined at the conceptual level and, therefore, the truth of atomic assertions in which primitive concepts are involved can be easily determined by specific relations among the conceptual entities.

Consider for example a *participant* role. Given the assertion *participant(i,j)*, in a purely extensional model theoretic semantics its truth is justified exclusively by the fact that the pair of the extensions of *i* and *j* belongs to the extension of *participant*.:

$$< \varphi[i], \varphi[j] >\in \varphi[participant]$$ (4)

In the internal semantics, the truth of *participant(i,j)* can be determined by examining the entities on which *i* and *j* are interpreted in the conceptual space: *participant(i,j)* is true if the set of knoxels on which *j* is interpreted is a subset of the set of knoxels on which *i* is interpreted:

$$\varphi[j]\subseteq \varphi[i]$$ (5)

6 The focus of attention process

As sketched in the introduction, a finite agent with bounded resources cannot carry out a one shot, exhaustive, and uniform analysis of a perceived scene within reasonable time constraints. In our architecture, the conceptual level described in the previous section acts as a "buffer interface" between subsymbolic and linguistic processing. The information coming up from the subsymbolic level has the effect of contemporary activating an (eventually very large) set of knoxels in the conceptual space. It is the focus of attention mechanism that imposes a sequential order in the conceptual space according to which the linguistic expressions can be given their interpretation.

In order to model the focus of attention mechanism, we define a *perception act p* as a generic sequence of knoxels in the conceptual space:

$$p \in KS*$$ (6)

where $KS*$ is the set of all sequences of knoxels in KS.

With reference to a perception cluster *pc*, we say that a perception act *p* is associated to the perception cluster *pc* if $p \in pc*$, where $pc*$ is the set of all sequences of knoxels belonging to *pc*. The perception act associated to a perception cluster therefore corresponds to a specific way of perceiving an object or situation described by the perception cluster.

In this context we introduce the denotation function ϑ mapping a perception act to the corresponding assertional constant:

$$\vartheta: KS* \to C$$ (7)

$\vartheta(p)$ is therefore the assertional constant perceived by the perception act *p*. The block C in fig. 1 implement the denotation function by means of a suitable neural network, as described in the next Sect.

The description of complex elements in terms of sequences of knoxels seems to be a natural extension of Gärdenfors' notion of conceptual space. It should be noted that the perception act assumption avoids the necessity to augment the dimensions of the space in order to describe complex objects or situations made up by several blocks: they are described by perception acts of several length.

In order to individuate the grouping paths among knoxels and generate the most meaningful perception acts, it is necessary to suitable orient the focus of attention. In the proposed architecture the focus of attention is determined by three concurrent modalities: the reactive, the associative and the linguistic modality. The "reactive" modality is the simpler one: the grouping paths among knoxels are determined only by the characteristics of the visual stimulus, e.g. the volumetric extension of the forms, or the aggregation density of the perceived objects.

In the associative modality, the grouping paths are determined by an associative, purely Hebbian mechanism determining the attention on the basis of free associations between concepts. Whenever two objects in the same scene are perceived, the weight of the associative connection between the corresponding concepts is increased.

In the linguistic modality, the focus of attention is driven by the symbolic information explicitly represented at the linguistic level. Consider the hammer example: at the linguistic level (see fig. 2) a hammer is described as composed by a handle and a head. If an object similar to an hammer handle has been recognised, the linguistic level hypothesise that an hammer may be present in the scene. The focus of attention is directed to try to identify its parts, in particular its handle and its head, in order to confirm the presence of such an hammer in the scene. This corresponds to find the suitable fillers for the role parts of the object, i.e. a filler for the *hammer-head* role and a filler for the *hammer-handle* role. Therefore, whenever a hammer handle is recognised, the focus of attention tries to identify a hammer by identifying suitable fillers for its head and its handle.

The focus of attention mechanism may be modelled as an expectation function ψ linking the linguistic to the conceptual level; the function has its domain in the set C of assertional constants representing the expected objects or situation and its range in the set of perception acts belonging to the corresponding perception clusters. In other worlds, the focus of attention looks for specific perception acts belonging to the perception clusters corresponding to the "expected" assertional constant in the perceived scene. The function ψ has the following type:

$$\psi^i : C \to KS^* \quad i = 1, 2 \tag{8}$$

where KS^* is the set of all perception acts; i indicates the attentive modality: 1 stands for the linguistic modality and 2 stands for the associative modality.

7 The neural network implementation of the mapping between the conceptual and the linguistic levels

This section only sketches the neural network implementation of the mapping between conceptual and linguistic level. A perception cluster, as described in sect. 3, is a set of knoxels associated to a perceived object or situation: $pc = \{k_1, k_2, ..., k_n\}$. Each knoxel k_i may be viewed as a point attractor of a suitable energy function associated to the perception cluster. A set of fixed point attractors is a good candidate as the model for a perception cluster: starting from an initial state representing a knoxel imposed, for instance, from the external input, the system state trajectory is attracted to the nearest stored knoxel of the perception cluster. Therefore the implementation of perception clusters by means of an attractor neural networks [Hopfield 1982] appears to be natural. Following this approach the implementation of the perception acts associated to a perception cluster is built by introducing time delayed connections storing the corresponding temporal sequences of knoxels.

In order to describe the dynamics in the conceptual space an adiabatically varying energy landscape E is defined. The energy E is the superimposition of three energies (eq. 9): E_1 represents the fast dynamics for period of duration τ and it models the point attractors for the single knoxels belonging to the perception clusters; E_2 represents the slow dynamics for period of duration $t \gg \tau$ due to time-delayed connections and it models the perceptions acts; E_3 model the global external input to the network.

The global energy function of the time delayed synapses attractor neural network is [Kleinfeld 1986]:

$$E\ (t) = E_1\ (t) + \lambda E_2(t) + \varepsilon E_3(t) \tag{9}$$

where E_1, E_2, E_3, are the previously described energy terms; λ and ε are the weighting parameters respectively of the time delayed synapses and the external input synapses.

The expectation functions ψ^i describing blocks D and E of our architecture are implemented by setting of parameters of the energy function E to $\lambda > 1$ and $\varepsilon = 0$. In fact, the task of these blocks is the generation of suitable knoxel sequences representing the expected perception acts. This choice of parameters allows the transitions occurs "spontaneously" with no external input. Referring to eq. 9, an attractor is stable for a time period significantly long due to the E_1 term. As $\lambda > 1$, the term λE_2 is able to destabilize the attractor and to carry the state of the network toward the successive attractor of the sequence representing the successive knoxel of the stored perception act. The neural network therefore visits in a sequence all the knoxels of the stored perception acts.

The denotation function ϑ describing the block C of our architecture of fig. 1 is implemented by setting of parameters of the energy function E to $\lambda < 1$ and $\varepsilon > 0$. The task of the block C is the recognition of input knoxel sequences representing the input perception acts. In order to accomplish this task it is necessary to consider the input term of the energy in order to make the transitions among knoxels happen as driven from the external input. When $\lambda < 1$ the term λE_2 is not be able to drive itself the state transition among the knoxels of the perception act, but when the term εE_3 is added, the contribution of both terms will make the transition happen. The neural network therefore recognises the input perception act as it "resonates" with one of the perception acts previously stored.

8 Experimental results

In this section some experimental results obtained by the implementation of the described architecture are presented. The considered framework consists in static scenes made up by objects like hammers, tennis balls, computer mouse and telephones; all the object are situated on a black table. Sensory data are 2-D images acquired by a video camera (two-dimensional arrays of pixels) representing one or more views of the observed scene. Fig. 4a shows a sample scene representing a hammer, a computer mouse and a tennis ball.

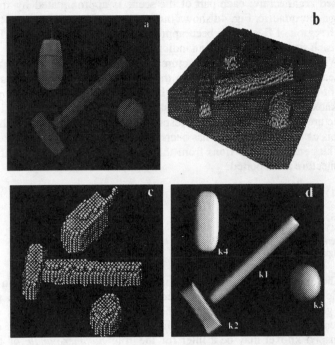

Fig. 4. Results obtained by operations of the blocks A and B of the architecture.

As described in Sect. 2, the operation of block A of fig. 1 is the extraction of the depth map from the acquired image. In the current implementation the operation is performed by a simple shape from shading algorithm. Fig. 4b shows the depth map obtained by the shape from shading algorithm from the acquired image.

In order to extract the knoxels representing the 3D primitives from the image, a segmentation step is performed by edge detection and region growing processes on the recovered surface. Each region will give rise in block B to a knoxel.

Both the depth map and the information about the segmented regions are feed as input to block B of fig.1. The first operation of this block is the volumetric representation of the input depth map by a spatial array. The result is a discrete representation of the spatial occupancy of the objects present in the scene in terms of "voxels". Fig. 4c shows the voxels representation of the acquired scene.

This rich set of raw and unstructured data does not permit a straightforward interpretation in terms of knoxels. A direct mapping between this level and the linguistic level would be therefore hard to be obtained. On the contrary, a geometric model of the scene, i.e. an analytically coded representation of the data would allow a compression and grouping of information present at this level.

From this point of view the representation system proposed by Pentland [Pentland 1986] is well suited in order to describe both natural and man-made forms. The representation primitives, i.e. the "parts" or building blocks of complicated objects, are modelled by using a parameterized family of mathematical shapes known as *superquadrics* . The superquadrics represents the knoxels of the conceptual level of the proposed architecture: each part of the scene is approximated by means of the best fitting superquadric. Fig. 4d shows the results of this operation on the acquired scene: each region of fig. 4a has been approximated by a superquadric. For the sake of clarity, each superquadric has been indicated by a tag.

When the described architecture is in "reactive" modality the focus of attention searches for generic objects in the scene. In the case of the current scene, the focus of attentions is directed to the hammer handle, corresponding to knoxel *#k1*. The knoxels related to this perception act are sent to the denomination block of the architecture in order to find the corresponding linguistic constant at the linguistic level. In this case the knoxel *#k1* has been recognised as a *Cylinder_shaped* knoxel.

The generated assertions from the linguistic level describing the operation of the architecture are reported:

```
Knoxel (#k1)
Knoxel (#k2)
Knoxel (#k3)
Knoxel (#k4)
Input_sequence (#k1)
Cylinder_shaped (#k1)
```

The expectation functions suitably drive the focus of attention in order to find the relevant perception acts in the scene. The linguistic expectation function, in particular, generates hypotheses by inferences at the linguistic level. As an example with reference to the previous scene, the linguistic level hypothesises that the cylinder shaped knoxel may be a filler for the role *hammer-handle* of the concept *Hammer*. Therefore the architecture hypothesises the presence of an hammer in the scene; the linguistic expectation block generates perceptions act hypotheses for the fillers of the role part *hammer-head* and for the filler of the role part *hammer-handle*.

The time-delayed neural networks implementing the linguistic expectation block of the architecture generates the expected perception acts for the hammer-head filler and the hammer-handle filler. When some of these expected knoxels are satisfied by some corresponding knoxels in the scene, the perception act made up by the so found knoxels is sent to the denomination function in order to recognise the hammer. The corresponding assertions generated at the linguistic level are reported:

```
Linguistic_expectation (Cylinder_shaped, Hammer)
Expected (Hammer, Hammer_head_filler)
Expected (Hammer, Hammer_handle_filler)
Satisfied_by (Hammer_head_filler, #k2)
Satisfied_by (Hammer_handle_filler, #k1)
Hammer (#k1, #k2)
```

The task of the associative expectation function in block E is to suitably drive the focus of attention in order to explore the scene by free associations among concepts. As an example, referring to the previous scene, the concept *Hammer* is associated by a Hebbian mechanism to the concepts of *Ball* and *Mouse,* due to a previous learning phase of the architecture.

As in the linguistic modality, when some of these expected knoxels are satisfied by some corresponding knoxels in the scene, the perception act made up by the so found knoxels is sent to the denomination function. The corresponding generated assertion by the linguistic level are:

```
Associative_expectation (Hammer, Ball)
Associative_expectation (Hammer, Mouse)
Expected (Hammer, Ball)
Expected (Hammer, Mouse)
Satisfied_by (Ball, #k3)
Satisfied_by (Mouse, #k4)
Ball (#k3)
Mouse (#k4)
```

The recognition task of perception acts related to spatial relation is similar to the recognition task of objects; the generated assertions related to spatial relations referred to the previous scene are reported. Fig. 5 shows the resulting perception act of the architecture after the previously described operations of the focus of attention.

```
Up (Hammer, Ball)
Sided (Ball, Mouse)
```

Fig. 6a shows a complex scene made up by a hammer, a cordless telephone, a wood block and a mouse. Fig. 6b shows the superquadric reconstruction of the same scene along with the focus of attention movements through the scene exploration. It should be noted that the focus of attention follows two sequences: a sequence in which the attention is focused on the hammer, the block and the mouse, and another sequence in which the attention is focused on the body and the antenna of the telephone.

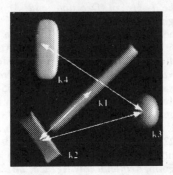

Fig. 5. The resulting perception act related to previous scene when the focus of attentions is driven by the linguistic and associative expectations.

290

The scene is therefore analysed as a concatenation of these two sequences. The focus of attention mechanism allows in fact the creation of "attentional contexts" in which an object is analysed: during the analysis of the first sequence, the telephone has been ignored, because the object does not belongs to the current attentional context. The telephone has been examined during the second sequence. The system is able to find out the relevant paths, to aggregate the information, in order to generate only the linguistic descriptions "useful" and "interesting" for the system in the current attentional context.

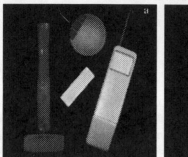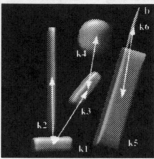

Fig. 6. A complex scene made up by a hammer, a cordless telephone, a wood block and a mouse.

References

[Brachman 1985] R.J. Brachman, J.C. Schmoltze: An Overview of the KL-ONE Knowledge Representation System, *Cognitive Science*, **9**, 2, 171-216, 1985.

[Chella 1994] A. Chella, M. Frixione, S. Gaglio: A Hybrid Model for Visual Perception Based on Dynamic Conceptual Space, *Proc. ECAI-94 Workshop on Combining Symbolic and Connectionist Processing*, 123-132, Amsterdam, The Netherlands, 1994.

[Davidson 1967] D. Davidson: The Logical Form of Action Sentences, in: N. Rescher (ed.): *The Logic of Decision and Action*, 81-95, University of Pittsburgh Press, Pittsburgh, Pa. 1967.

[Gärdenfors 1992] P. Gärdenfors: Three Levels of Inductive Interence, Lund University Cognitive Studies 9, Tech. Rep. LUHFDA/HFKO-5006-SE, 1992.

[Hopfield 1982] J.J. Hopfield: Neural Networks and Physical Systems with Emergent Collective Computational Abilities, *Proceedings of the National Academy of Sciences, USA*, **79**, 2554-2558, 1982.

[Kleinfeld 1986] D. Kleinfeld: Sequential State Generation by Model Neural Networks, *Proc. Nat. Acad. Sci. USA* **83**, 9469-9473, 1986.

[Nebel 1990] B. Nebel: *Reasoning and Revision in Hybrid Representation Systems*, LNAI 422, Springer-Verlag, Berlin, 1990.

[Pentland 1986] A.P. Pentland: Perceptual Organization and the Representation of Natural Form, *Artificial Intelligence*, **28**, 293-331, 1986.

A Weakest Precondition Semantics for Conditional Planning

M. Baioletti, S. Marcugini, A. Milani *

Dipartimento di Matematica
Università di Perugia
Via Vanvitelli, 1
06100 Perugia, Italia

Abstract. In this paper we show an approach to conditional planning which is based on a particular three valued logic. Assignments and conditional formulae (built by means of the alternate operator as introduced in [7]) are used to represent uncertain situations. A model for actions in a conditional framework is defined by giving an execution function, which returns the updated situation after the execution, and an executability predicate. We also define a weakest precondition semantics in order to determine the least alternative situation in which a plan is executable and, after the execution, a required formula holds. The tools we introduced allow us to compile a plan in a macroaction, which is an abstraction of a plan, neglecting its internal decomposition. It is possible to prove that the use of macroactions is correct in a more complex plan.

1   Introduction

A formal definition of conditional planning model is introduced within the framework of three-valued logic. Basing on the operator "alternate" as introduced in [7], we define the notion of conditional formula that denote the set of states to represent uncertain situations.

The operator "alternate" denotes situations which cannot be described by the usual disjunction. A multiple situation, in which, for istance, "either" *head* "or" *no head* is true cannot be described by a disjunctive two-valued logic formula: in fact in this framework such a formula reduces to a tautological sentence. In the paragraph 2 we introduce the model based on conditional formulae and operators in order to manage them.

The planning model, in paragraph 3, gives the semantics of execution of conditional actions (i.e. action with conditional preconditions and effects) in an uncertain situation (i.e. situations which are denoted by a conditional formula). Conditional nonlinear plans are built by composing actions by the usual precedence operators (sequence, anyorder), and by a special conditional construct.

---

* This work has been partially supported by Progetto Speciale "Pianificazione Automatica" under contract n. 93.006.27.CT07 of Italian National Research Council - C.N.R. and by 40% project "Algoritmi, Modelli di Calcolo e Strutture Informative" of M.U.R.S.T.

The semantics of plans is given in term of a weakest precondition model similar to the axiomatic semantics of programming languages.

A remarkable result of this paper is that actions and plans can be seen in a homogeneous framework. The weakest precondition semantics of plans, the semantics of plans execution and the notion of conditional formula allow us to define plans as macroaction with their own preconditions and effects. We can abstract or compile libraries of solved plans by building new sets of operators which can be used exactly as actions. An interesting property is the "decomposition correctness": if we compile a plan in its corresponding macroaction and if the obtained macroplan is correct, then the detailed plan, obtained by substituting the macroactions with their detailed internal structure, is still correct.

Note that the problem of the compilation of a plan into a macroaction requires conditional formula even if you limit the original planning model to nonlinear planning (i.e. conditional are not allowed in the plan to compile).

2 Three Valued Logic

We shall use a three valued logic which is an extension of the classical Boolean logic. The third truth value, U, represents the state of lack of knowledge about a certain fact.

We can assign to every proposition p a truth value $t(p)$: $t(p) = 1$ means that p is known to be true, 0 means that p is known to be false and U means that we have no information about p.

With a construction similar to classical domain theory we define a partial order relation on truth values $\{0, U, 1\}$, $\sqsubseteq$:

- $U \sqsubseteq U, U \sqsubseteq 0, U \sqsubseteq 1,$
- $0 \sqsubseteq 0,$
- $1 \sqsubseteq 1.$

$x \sqsubseteq y$ means that either y is consistent with x or is more determined than x.

Definition 1. The greatest lower bound operator $\sqcup$ with respect to $\sqsubseteq$ is defined as follows:

$$x \sqcup y = \begin{cases} x & \text{if } y \sqsubseteq x \\ y & \text{if } x \sqsubseteq y \\ \text{not defined} & \text{if } x \text{ and } y \text{ are incomparable} \end{cases}$$

$\sqcup$	0	U	1
0	0	0	-
U	0	U	1
1	-	1	1

It is easy to show that

Proposition 2. ⊔ *is commutative, associative and U is its unit.*

A new operator, which will be useful for the planning model, is now introduced:

Definition 3. The operator ▷ (to be read "after") is defined as:

$$ x \triangleright y = \begin{cases} y & \text{if } y \neq U \\ x & \text{otherwise.} \end{cases} $$

$x \triangleright y$ represents the state obtained when x is updated by y.

Proposition 4. *Operator ▷ is left and right distributive with respect to ⊔, that is*

$$ (x \sqcup y) \triangleright z = (x \triangleright z) \sqcup (y \triangleright z), z \triangleright (x \sqcup y) = (z \triangleright x) \sqcup (z \triangleright y) $$

when there are no unconsistencies.

3 Assignments

Any general description of world can involve several propositions, here called atoms, each of them can be true, false or unknown.

Definition 5. A three valued assignment a on the atoms A is any map $a : A \rightarrow \{U, 0, 1\}$.

If x is an atom we denote with $a(x)$ the truth value of x in assignment a. For instance, in the block world, the state of knowledge "I know that a and b are one the table, but I do not know if c is on" can be formulated by the assignment a from the atoms {on(a,table),on(b,table), on(c,table)} to {0, U, 1} which is defined as: a(on(a,table)) = 1, a(on(b,table)) = 1 and a(on(c,table)) = U.

Definition 6. For each literal λ (either an atom or its negation) the basic assignment δ_λ is the assignment giving 1 (or 0, respectively) to that atom and U to any other atom.

It is possible to extend the operators and the order relation ⊑ to assignments:

Definition 7. If a and b are three-valued assignments then

1. $a \sqsubseteq b$ if and only if for each atom x, $a(x) \sqsubseteq b(x)$,
2. $c = a \sqcup b$ if and only if for each atom x, $c(x) = a(x) \sqcup b(x)$ is defined, otherwise c is undefined,
3. $c = a \triangleright b$ if and only if for each atom x, $c(x) = a(x) \triangleright b(x)$.

Note that $c = a \sqcup b$ represents the state in which both a and b are joined; when a and b are incompatible we obtain the unconsistent state (denoted by ϕ); we point out that it is different from the state of total ignorance (denoted by the assignment $u(x) = U$ for each atom x).

4 Alternative States

A more complex state of uncertain knowledge can be represented by several different assignments which are mutually exclusive.

For istance (this example is due to [4]) knowing that "either the door or the window is open" means that one of these following five situations is possible:

1. d and w are both true
2. w is true and d is false
3. d is true and w is false
4. d is true and w is unknown
5. w is true and d is unknown

where the atoms d and w obviously mean "the door is open" and "the window is open".

Situations 1-5 correspond to five different assignments a_1, a_2, a_3, a_4, a_5 to the atoms d and w, namely:

$$a_1(d) = 1, a_1(w) = 1$$
$$a_2(d) = 0, a_2(w) = 1$$
$$a_3(d) = 1, a_3(w) = 0$$
$$a_4(d) = 1, a_4(w) = U.$$
$$a_5(d) = U, a_5(w) = 1.$$

Hence any description of partial knowledge can be viewed as a set of different three valued assignments.

4.1 Conditional Formulae

A concise way to denote a set of assignments is obtained by means of conditional formulae (formulae for short). Formulae are built by composing literals with the operator &, which means "and", and with the operator |, which means "alternate". The special simbols ϕ and Ω denote the empty assignment and the total ignorance assignment respectively.

We provide a BNF syntax for formulae:

Formula ::= ϕ | Ω | Literal | Formula & Formula | Formula "|" Formula

Each formula F denotes a set of assignments $[F]$ according to the following definitions. We say that two formulae are equivalent if they denote the same set of assignments.

Definition 8. 1. $[\phi] = \emptyset$;
2. $[\Omega] = \{u\}$;
3. for each literal λ, $[\lambda] = \{\delta_\lambda\}$;
4. $[F|G] = [F] \cup [G]$;

5. $[F\&G] = \{f \sqcup g : f \in [F], g \in [G] \text{ and } f \sqcup g \text{ is defined}\}.$

The alternative formula $F|G$ represents all the states of knowledge belonging either to F or to G (or to both). Its behaviour is similar to the disjunction but it allows us to represent "tautological" situations explicitly . Note that | is isomorphic to the operator "alt" as defined in [7].

The conjunctive formula $F\&G$ represents all the possible states of knowledge which is composed by any alternative of F joined to any alternative of G, when these are compatible with each other. When any assignment in $[F]$ is incompatible with any assignment in $[G]$ we set by definition that $F\&G = \phi$. Note that & is similar to the operator "and" as defined in [7]. It reduces to the usual conjunction when F and G do not contain alternatives.

It is easy to state that

Proposition 9. | *is commutative, associative and ϕ is its unit.*

Proposition 10. & *is commutative, associative and distribuitive with respect to* |. *Moreover Ω is its unit and ϕ is its absorbing element.*

Note that any assignment a can be denoted by a unique conjunctive clause which is composed only by those literals whose corresponding atoms are given a non-unknown value by a: for example if a maps x, y, z, t to respectively $U, 1, 0, U$, then it can be written as $y\&\neg z$.

Therefore we can prove the main property about formulae:

Proposition 11. *For any set of assignments S there exists a formula F such that $[F] = S$.*

It is easy to show that a normal disjunctive form exists for formulae:

Proposition 12. *For any formula F there exists an equivalent formula $F_1|F_2|\ldots|F_k$ where the F_i's are conjunctive clauses.*

For instance the formula $a\&(a\&c|d) \mid b\&(c|b\&d)$ can be written in the normal form as $a\&c|a\&d|b\&c|b\&d$.

We generally want to avoid the normal disjunctive form because it explicitly represents all the assignments embedded in a formula. Using distributive and associative laws we can find a parsimonious way to express the same set of assignments: the previous example reduces to the equivalent formula $(a|b)\&(c|d)$.

4.2 Disjunctions

Note that the meaning of the operator | is not equivalent to the boolean disjunction since $a|b$ means that the two following situations are possible: either we know that a is true, but b is unknown, or vice-versa we know that b is true, but a is unknown.

Definition 13. We denote by $< F >$ (to be read "don't care about F") the formula denoting the set of the assignments which give all the possible truth values to the atoms involved in the formula F, and which give the truth value U to any other atom.

For instance $< a\&b >$ is $a\&b|a\&\neg b|\neg a\&b|\neg a\&\neg b|a|b|\neg a|\neg b|\Omega$. The same result could be obtained if we compute $< a|b >$ since the atoms which are involved in this formula are the same as before.

$F \vee G$ should be true in all the alternatives in which F is true and G does not matter and similarly in all the other alternatives in which G is true and F does not matter. Hence we define

Definition 14. Given two formulae F and G their disjunction is

$$F \vee G = (F\& < G >)|(G\& < F >)$$

For instance we have $a \vee b = (a\& < b >)|(b\& < a >) = a\&b|a\&\neg b|\neg a\&b|a|b$.

Proposition 15. $\vee$ *is associative, commutative and distributive with respect to* $\&$.

The operator $\vee$ allows us to write some formulae in a very concise way, for instance $a \vee b \vee c$ is composed by 19 assignments.

We can also extend the operators "after" to formulae in the following way:

Definition 16. Given two formulae F and G,

$$[F \rhd G] := \{p \rhd q : p \in [F] \text{ and } q \in [G]\}.$$

It is easy to show that

Proposition 17. $\rhd$ *is associative and distributive with respect to* $\&$ *and* $|$.

We shall point out that $\rhd$ is not distributive with respect to disjunction $\vee$, that is

$$(F \vee G) \rhd R = (F \rhd R) \vee (G \rhd R)$$

does not hold in general.

5 Necessary Consequences and Minimality

The concept of formula necessarily true in a situation is extended to conditional formulae.

Definition 18. Given two formulae P and Q, we say that Q is necessarily true in P (or is a necessary consequence of P) and we write $P \models Q$ if and only if for each assignment $p \in [P]$ there exists an assignment $q \in [Q]$ such that $q \sqsubseteq p$.

Some useful properties are here described:

Proposition 19. *Let* P, Q, P_1, P_2, Q_1, Q_2 *be formulae, then*

1. $P \models P$;
2. *if* $P \models Q$ *and* $Q \models R$ *then* $P \models R$;
3. $P \models P|Q$ *and* $P\&Q \models P$;
4. *if* $P_1 \models Q_1$ *and* $P_2 \models Q_2$ *then* $P_1|P_2 \models Q_1|Q_2$;
5. *if* $P_1 \models Q_1$ *and* $P_2 \models Q_2$ *then* $P_1\&P_2 \models Q_1\&Q_2$;
6. *if* $P \models Q_1|Q_2$ *then there exist* P_1 *and* P_2 *such that* $P = P_1|P_2$ *and* $P_1 \models Q_1$ *and* $P_2 \models Q_2$

Definition 20. A set of assignments S is said to be minimal if it does not contain two assignments which are comparable, that is for each $p, q \in S$ $p \sqsubseteq q$ if and only if $p = q$. A formula P is minimal if $[P]$ is minimal.

For instance $p|p\&q|q$ is not minimal, while $p|q$ is minimal.

Definition 21. Given a formula P, its minimalization $\mu(P)$ is a formula denoting the greatest minimal subset of assignments of $[P]$:

$$[\mu(P)] = \{p \in [P] : \forall q \in [P] \ q \sqsubseteq p \Rightarrow p = q\}$$

Given a formula P there is a simple algorithm to find its minimalization: in fact it suffices to remove from $[P]$ all the assignments p such that there exists another assignment $q \in [P]$ such that $q \sqsubseteq p$.
The following properties of the minimalization hold:

Proposition 22. *1.* $\mu(P) \models P$ *and* $P \models \mu(P)$;
2. $\forall Q \ P \models Q$ *if and only if* $\mu(P) \models Q$;
3. *if* P *and* Q *are minimal then* $P \models Q$ *and* $Q \models P$ *if and only if* $P = Q$;
4. $P \models Q$ *and* $Q \models P$ *if and only if* $\mu(P) = \mu(Q)$;

6 A Model for Conditional Planning

Our model of conditional planning is based on the notions of set of assignments and conditional formulae that we previously introduced. We denote by $\mathcal{F}$ the set of all the formulae on all the existing atoms.

Definition 23. An elementary action A is a triple $(\mathcal{V}, \mathcal{P}, \mathcal{E})$ where $\mathcal{V}$ is the set of its parameters, $\mathcal{P}$ and $\mathcal{E}$ are the parametric families of formulae denoting preconditions and effects respectively.

For instance for the action *puton* we obtain
$\mathcal{V} = (x, y, z)$, $\mathcal{P} = cl(x)\&cl(y)\&on(x, z)$ and $\mathcal{E} = \neg cl(y)\&on(x, y)\&\neg on(x, z)$.

Definition 24. An instance I of A is a couple (P_I, E_I) where P_I and E_I are obtained from $\mathcal{P}$ and $\mathcal{E}$ by replacing every parameter with a constant value.

For example, an instance of *puton* can be obtained by replacing x, y, z with *block_1, block_2, place_1* respectively.

Definition 25. An instance $I = (P_I, E_I)$ of an action A is executable in a situation F if $F \models P_I$.
The situation after the execution of I is $F \triangleright E_I$.

P_I and E_I being formulae, this definition allows us to define conditional preconditions, effects and execution in an uncertain framework which may be not totally defined.

Example 1. Consider again the former example about the *door and window problem*
Initial situation $S_0 = w \vee d$
Action instance: CD
$$\mathcal{P} = \Omega$$
$$\mathcal{E} = \neg d$$

If we execute CD in S_0 then we obtain $(w \vee d) \triangleright \neg d = (w\& < d > |d\& < w >) \triangleright \neg d = (w\& < d >) \triangleright \neg d | (d\& < w >) \triangleright \neg d = w\&\neg d|\neg d\& < w >= \neg d\& < w >$

6.1 Conditional Plans

Conditional nonlinear plans are built by composing actions by means of the precedence operator ";", which denotes an ordered sequence, by means of the operator "||", which means that any order is allowed, and by means of the conditional construct IF-THEN-ELSE. The syntax of plans is:

Plan ::= Instance_Elementary_Action | Plan;Plan | (Plan) | Plan || Plan | IF Literal THEN Plan ELSE Plan

The semantics of the plan execution is described by an execution function $X : \mathcal{F} \rightarrow [\text{Plans} \rightarrow \mathcal{F}]$. Given a plan and a conditional formula denoting a situation the function X computes the situation after the plan execution. We denote by $X(\Pi)_S$ the formula describing the situation after the execution of plan Π in situation S.

In order to give X we also need the notion of executable plan, we denote this condition by the boolean predicate $R(\Pi)_S$ whose value is true if the plan Π is executable in situation S, it is false otherwise.

We give the semantics for plan construction by describing X and R for each production.

By convention if either $S = \phi$ or $R(\Pi)_S$ is false then $X(\Pi)_S = \phi$.

Definition 26. If Π is a plan formed by a single instance $I = (P_I, E_I)$ of elementary action then
$$R(\Pi)_S \equiv S \models P_I$$

and

$$X(\Pi)_S = \begin{cases} S \triangleright E_I & \text{if } S \models P_I \\ \phi & \text{otherwise} \end{cases}.$$

Definition 27. Let $\Pi = \Pi_1; \Pi_2$ be an ordered sequence. Define $R(\Pi)_S \equiv R(\Pi_1)_S \wedge R(\Pi_2)_{X(\Pi_1)_S}$ and $X(\Pi)_S = X(\Pi_2)_{X(\Pi_1)_S}$.

Definition 28. Let $\Pi = \Pi_1 \| \Pi_2$ be an unordered sequence. Define $R(\Pi)_S \equiv R(\Pi_1; \Pi_2)_S \vee R(\Pi_2; \Pi_1)_S$ and $X(\Pi)_S = X(\Pi_1; \Pi_2)_S | X(\Pi_2; \Pi_1)_S$.

Definition 29. Let $\Pi = $ IF c THEN Π_1 ELSE Π_2 be a conditional action. Define $R(\Pi)_S = (c \wedge R(\Pi_1)_S) \vee (\neg c \wedge R(\Pi_2)_S)$ and $X(\Pi)_S = X(\Pi_1)_{S\&c} | X(\Pi_2)_{S\&\neg c}$.

6.2 Observing Actions

Note that before executing a conditional action it is required to know whether c is true or false.

In some case we do not know c, that is c could have the value U in some assignment of our situation F, and therefore we cannot execute the conditional action because its effects would be undefined.

A way to solve this kind of uncertainty about a proposition c could be the execution of an action, like "to look at", "to hear" or "to ask someone", whose only effect is $c | \neg c$. This kind of actions adds knowledge in a situation. Note that the opposite is unattainable, that is it is impossible to express an action as "forget something" or "hide something", simply because $\triangleright$ never adds uncertainty to the world.

It is worth noting that such a kind of action is similar to conditional action in CNLP [2].

7 The Weakest Preconditions: an Axiomatic Semantics for Conditional Planning

Given the actions in a plan we define a notion that is equivalent to the weakest preconditions for the instruction in a programming language.

Given a plan Π and a formula K $W(\Pi)_K$ is (in some way) the "least" situation in which Π is executable and, after its execution, K holds. Our choice for the meaning of "least" is the following:

Definition 30. We denote by $W(\Pi)_K$ the minimal formula such that for each formula S: $S \models W(\Pi)_K$ if and only if $R(\Pi)_S$ and $X(\Pi)_S \models K$.

There are cases in which no such formula can be found: for instance when K requires an atom x to be true, but the effects of Π denies it. In these cases $W(\Pi)_K = \phi$, by convention .

if such a formula exists, it is unique modulo the equivalence relation we have introduced. If, ab absurdo, two non equivalent formulae W and W' both satisfy the previous definition, we will have $R(\Pi)_W \wedge X(\Pi)_W \models K \Rightarrow W \models W'$. Similarly we have $R(\Pi)_{W'} \wedge X(\Pi)_{W'} \models K \Rightarrow W' \models W$. By the minimality, W and W' should be equivalent, contradicting the assumption.

It can be easily shown that

Proposition 31. *for each instance* $I = (P_I, A_I)$ *of an elementary action*

$$W(I)_K = \mu(P_I \& W(I')_K)$$

where I' *is the instance of an action whose preconditions are empty* $(P_{I'} = \Omega)$ *and effects are the same as* I.

Henceforth we can always handle with actions with empty preconditions. We denote by $K \lhd E_I$, $W(I')_K$.

At this point a question comes out naturally: how is it possible to determine $K \lhd E$ for any formula K and E?

It is clear that $\lhd$ is in some way an inverse of the operator $\rhd$.

We describe now an effective way to calculate $K \lhd E$, proceeding by induction.

Suppose first that K and E are conjunctive formula, that is they contain only one assignment, namely k and e.

Then we have that

Proposition 32. $K \lhd E$ *is defined if and only if for each atom* x *the truth values* $k(x)$ *and* $e(x)$ *are comparable and in this case* $K \lhd E$ *is a formula denoting the single assignment*

$$\forall x \, (k \lhd e)(x) = \begin{cases} k(x) & \text{if } e(x) = U \\ U & \text{otherwise} \end{cases}$$

In the second step we allow K to be alternative, thus we have:

Proposition 33. *if* $K = K_1 | K_2$, *where* K_1 *and* K_2 *are formulae, then* $(K_1 | K_2) \lhd e = \mu(K_1 \lhd e | K_2 \lhd e)$

In the final step we allow both E and K to be alternative, therefore we have:

Proposition 34. *if* $E = E_1 | E_2$, *where* E_1 *and* E_2 *are formulae, then* $K \lhd (E_1 | E_2) = \mu(K \lhd E_1 \& K \lhd E_2)$

Finally using the previous propositions we can complete the weakest preconditions for plans:

Proposition 35. *Weakest precondition of an ordered sequence*

$$W(\Pi_1; \Pi_2)_K = W(\Pi_1)_{W(\Pi_2)_K}.$$

Proposition 36. *Weakest precondition of an unordered sequence*

$$W(\Pi_1 \| \Pi_2)_K = W(\Pi_1; \Pi_2)_K \& W(\Pi_2; \Pi_1)_K.$$

Proposition 37. *Weakest precondition of a conditional action*

$$W(IF \, p \, THEN \, \Pi_1 \, ELSE \, \Pi_2)_K = (p \& W(\Pi_1)_K) | (\neg p \& W(\Pi_2)_K).$$

7.1 Compile Plans into Macroaction

It is worth noting that the use of the weakest precondition model and the execution function X could give a method to compile plans into macroactions. To compile a conditional plan into a conditional (macro) action means to generate a conditional action description whose preconditions and effects are equivalent to preconditions and effects of the plan.

Definition 38. A macroaction M_Π derived from plan Π can be easily obtained by defining

$$PRE(M_\Pi) = W(\Pi)_\Omega$$

and

$$EFF(M_\Pi) = X(\Pi)_{EFF(M_\Pi)}$$

The advantages of using macroactions in planning are apparent: libraries of solved plans can be handled with the same mechanisms used for elementary actions. The given conditional planning semantics guarantees that if a plan built by macroaction obtains a goal G, then the detailed plan, which is obtained by substituting each macroaction with the detailed elementary actions, is still correct.

As we noted in the introduction, we point out that the conditional model (with conditional formulae and operator |) is necessary to compile a plan into action even if the plan that is to be compiled does not use conditional actions but it is nonlinear (suppose for example that the plan use only deterministic Strips-like actions, with no alternatives in preconditions and effects). The reason is that when a nonlinear plan Π is compiled into a macroaction M_Π, $PRE(M_\Pi)$ and $EFF(M_\Pi)$ must contain all the information needed to compute the precondition of the execution of Π and the effects of the execution of Π. The internal structure of Π is not known at this level but Π may contain two unordered actions, A' and A''. Since the order of the execution of A' and A'' will be known only at the execution time, the effect of $A'\|A''$ could be different in different executions. A conditional formula is required to express the effects of nonlinearly ordered actions at the planning time as the effects of a macroaction which contains them.

References

1. M.J. Schoppers, "Universal Plans for Reactive Robots in Unpredictable Domains", Proc. IJCAI-87, 1039 (1987)
2. M.A.Peot, D.E.Smith, "Conditional Nonlinear Planning", Proc.of the 1st Int. Conf. on A.I.Planning Systems, AIPS92, J.Hendler Ed., Morgan Kaufmann, 189 (1992)
3. D.H.D. Warren, "Generating Conditional Plans and Programs" Proc. of AISB-76 Summer Conference, Edinburgh, 277 (1976)
4. G.Brewka, J.Hertzberg: How To Do Things with Worlds: "On Formalizing Actions and Plans", Tasso-report n.11, GMD, (1990)
5. M.L.Ginsberg, D.E.Smith, "Reasoning About Action I: A Possible Worlds Approach" Art.Int., n. 35 , 165 (1988)

6. R.G. Sani, S. Steel "Recursive Plans", in Proceedings of the 1st European Workshop on Planning EWSP 1991, Sankt Augustin, Germany, Lecture Notes in Artificial Intelligence 522, Springer Verlag, 53 (1991)

7. A. Milani "A Representation for Multiple Situations in Conditional Planning", in Current Trends in AI Planning, EWSP'93 - 2nd European WorkShop on Planning, IOS Press (1994)

8. G. Antognoni, A.Milani, S.Marcugini "Extending a Conditional Planning Model with Multiple Situations Management", Tech.Rep. n.12 January 1993, Dipartimento di Matematica, Università di Perugia, Perugia, Italy (1993)

9. G. Antognoni, "Pianificazione di Azioni con Effetti Alternativi: un Modello di Rappresentazione", Tesi di Laurea, Dipartimento di Matematica, Università di Perugia, Perugia, Italy (1992)

10. R.E.Fikes, N.J.Nillson "STRIPS: A New Approach to the Application of Theorem Proving to Problem Solving", Artific. Intell. n.2, 189 (1971)

11. D.Chapman "Planning for conjunctive goal", Artific. Intell. n.32 (1987)

12. S.Hanks, "Pratical Temporal Projection", Proc. AAAI-90, (1990)

13. V.Liftschiz "On the semantics of STRIPS", Proc. 1986 Workshop Reasoning About Actions and Plans, Timberline, OR, Morgan Kaufmann, 1, (1987)

14. L.P.Kaelbling, "An Architecture for Intelligent Reactive Systems", Proc. 1986 Workshop Reasoning About Actions and Plans, Timberline, OR, Morgan Kaufmann, 1, (1987)

15. D.H.D. Warren, "Warplan: A System for Generating Plans" in Readings in Planning; J. Allen, J.Hendler, A. Tate ed., Morgan Kaufmann (1990)

16. M.Winslett, "Reasoning about Action Using a Possible Models Approach", Proc. AAAI-88, 89 (1988)

17. T.Bylander, "Complexity Results for Planning", Proc. of IJCAI- 91, 274 (1991)

18. L.Morgensten, "Knowledge Preconditions for Actions and Plans" in Proceeding of IJCAI-87 (1987)

A Cognitive Hybrid Model for Autonomous Navigation

Marcello Frixione[†], Maurizio Piaggio, Gianni Vercelli, Renato Zaccaria

DIST - University of Genova, via Opera Pia 13, Genova, Italy
† also with *IIASS, Vietri sul Mare, Salerno, Italy*

e-mail: {frix, piaggio, gianni, renato}@dist.unige.it

ABSTRACT. Action representation and planning is one among the most important research fields in which it has been experienced the failure of single paradigms in isolation to solve real, complex problems. The goal of this paper is to present a system for action representation and reasoning in complex, real-world, and real time scenarios, characterised by the integration of different representation paradigms: symbolic, diagrammatic, and procedural. In this sense the system is called "hybrid". The paper focuses on the cognitive model and on the representation and reasoning system. A realistic navigation system for the guidance and control of autonomous mobile robots is used as an example to describe the potentiality of the system in solving real complex problems and it is currently being tested in an indoor environment.

1. Introduction

In this paper we propose a hybrid framework for the integration of different paradigms for action representation and planning in advanced robotics (for similar approaches see for example Ferguson 1992; Slack 1993). We consider the problem of moving a robot in a complex and partially unknown real world environment, managing different types of knowledge and data, from low-level time-varying signals coming from sensors and sent to actuators, to topological and geometrical knowledge of the environment (e.g., pictorial and diagrammatic representations reconstructed by the system from the sensor data), to high-level abstract entities useful to plan future movements (e.g., by means of a traditional symbolic apparatus).

We distinguish two main types of knowledge: a declarative explicit representation of tasks and of (parts of) the environment, and a procedural, partially reactive, component to cope the unpredictable occurrences and variations of the real world. In fig. 1, the general structure of our model is depicted. The *symbolic component* contains the declarative representations that constitute the "high level" knowledge of the system. It is responsible for plan selection and adaptation. It is structured in two blocks. The LTM (Long Term Memory) is the permanent, "encyclopaedic" storage of general knowledge. The STM (Short Term Memory) is the explicit, symbolic representation of the actual "context", or "reasoning horizon", regarding the state of the affairs of the world and the problems actually faced. Arrows LTM<>STM indicate the information flow that keeps the model updated. While the horizon of the action evolves, new long term information is instantiated to build a local short term description of the state of the affairs. This description is used to update and drive the procedural component evolution.

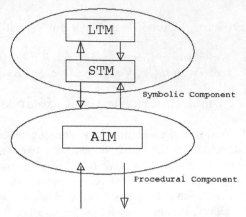

Fig. 1. Cognitive Model Structure

The general structure of the *procedural component* is shown in fig. 2. The procedural component encompasses both the execution of reactive behaviours and the processing of iconic, analogical, representations (Steels 1990) in the tradition of mental imagery (Kosslyn 1980). We consider these representations *sub-symbolic* in a wide sense. The procedural component is organised as a set of concurrent procedures called *experts*. In fig. 2, different types of experts are represented as ellipses. Ellipses labelled with A are actuators, ellipses labelled with R are recognisers. The iconic representations are managed by the AIM (Active Isomorphic Memory), which is an analogical, image based, representation of the environment. Representations in the AIM are "snapshots" of the world, which are "interpolated" by suitable internal generative processes. This concerns a second main characteristic of the AIM: it is a dynamic representation, an evolving image of the environment, similar, in a certain sense, to a "mental cartoon". Some experts (labelled *a* in fig. 2) determine the dynamic evolution of the AIM. The AIM can drive external actions in the real world, or carry out simulations in an imagined model. In the former case, experts *b* and *c* connect the AIM with the external world. Experts *b* keep aligned the AIM with the sensor data. Expert *c* control the robot effectors. Simulations in the AIM can have a corresponding symbolic representation in the symbolic component. AIM evolution can be triggered by the contents of the symbolic memory (experts *d*), and, in turn, can generate new symbolic information in the STM describing the AIM contents (experts *e*). Experts *f* correspond to purely reactive behaviours, directly connecting sensing to acting. Other experts (*g* and *h*) can possibly directly connect sensing or acting with the symbolic component. Some type of experts not specifically connected to the symbolic component can possibly cause, as a side effect, the generation of new symbolic information (dotted arrows). In literature, mental models and diagrammatic representations are usually timeless models. The implicit dynamic behaviour of the AIM that we called generative process cannot be simply *added* to a static model. Choosing and developing the proper mathematical model is part of the ongoing research activity.

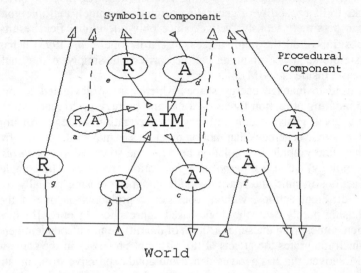

Fig. 2. Procedural Component. A - Actuator R - Recogniser: a (determine dynamic evolution of AIM), b-c (connect AIM to real-world), d-e (connect AIM to symbolic component, f (purely reactive), g-h (connect sensing and acting directly to symbolic)

We conjecture that several approaches can be considered and are, under certain assumptions, interchangeable or, at least, "compatible"; in the sense that every approach better fits certain domains with respect to others. Examples could be *self organising neural networks* and *cellular automata*. These models have in common two typical features: they are highly parallel and they are complex dynamic systems. We suppose that parallelism and dynamic complexity are key points for the AIM component, to support the desired characteristics of being analogical and capable of problem solving activity. We are currently investigating a model based on artificial potential fields in the domain of robotic motion planning for manipulation and navigation. This approach shares with those previously mentioned, in a simpler way, the complex dynamics and parallelism features. Potential fields were originally introduced by Khatib (1986) for motion control, and successively widely used in robot navigation (Latombe 1991). They have an associated energy function, and their dynamics depend on the different ways the robot can navigate through the field towards some global minimum, while avoiding "obstacles" characterised by regions with a high energy value. Although naturally suited for navigation, of which it is an intuitive metaphor, this approach can also cope with multi-dimensional problems, like the C-space in Robotics (Lozano-Perez 1983), or some higher level planning problems that have been faced by (Steels 1990; Zaccaria *et al.* 1994; Ardizzone *et al.* 1993), or solving ill-posed problems, for example, in inverting the redundant kinematics of complex robotic structures, e.g., a human-like arm manipulating a compliant object (Mussa Ivaldi *et al.* 1988). The artificial potential field model for the AIM uses, as generative law, a "navigation function" that interpolates from one icon to another, exhibiting a dynamic behaviour in time. Goals are "absolutely attracting icons"; constraints are "repelling icons" (in particular, an obstacle is avoided thanks to its capability of generating a repulsive force); multiple goals and constraints can be simultaneously "active" since only one global field results from the superimposition of all the field sources. In (Ardizzone *et al.* 1993) it has been shown how simple sequence planning can be carried out simply at the analogical level (in our case, inside the AIM).

The AIM is used to manage energy shapes which can be navigated by means of algorithms simulating attraction forces on a moving point, e.g., to reach a minimum of energy or a given goal position with a given navigation strategy. An important advantage of an iconic scheme is that motion processes (which "interpolate" from one icon to another, like graphic interpolation between the so called *key postures* in the cartoons terminology) can use *superposable* generation processes. The complexity of superposing actions in time and space (by adding, superimposing partially or totally the effects of different actions, without consistency problems) is one of the weak points when using purely symbolic, logic-based approaches. In our AIM model the resulting action comes from the superposition of the different, independent generation processes, which integrates the effects of the different processes in the same way the world does. Moreover, this has good evidence and good expressive strength: an action can be captured, at any instant, as a set of active icons to be reached, and a set of repulsive situations to keep away from.

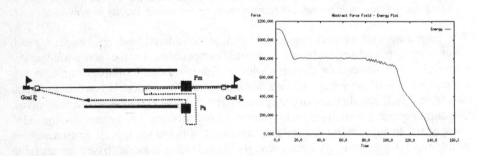

Fig. 3. (a) Two robots in a corridor **(b)** Energy evolution during navigation

An example of task involving sequence and navigation planning is shown in fig. 3a, in which the trajectories of two robots crossing the same narrow passage in opposite directions are depicted; the solution comprehends mutual avoidance and trajectory formation. This was achieved by pure navigation in a 4-dimensions space in the AIM. Fig. 3b shows the energy evolution during the task. In this paper these generative aspects are not further discussed; we focus on the capabilities about reasoning on sub-symbolic representations, on reactive behaviour, and on analogical/symbolic interaction in a specific domain.

2. The Symbolic Component

The formalism we adopted for the symbolic component is a hybrid system (in the sense of Nebel 1990), combining a terminological and an assertional language. The LTM includes both terminological and assertional information. The terminological component of the LTM is a KL-ONE like network, describing the concepts and the relations concerning the navigation domain. Assertional long term knowledge includes factual generalisations and long term knowledge concerning specific objects of the domain.

A portion of the net is depicted in fig. 4 (double arrows represent *IS-A relations* between concepts; single arrows represent *roles*). For sake of semplicity, the general ontology (including *action*, *situation*, and time representation based on intervals) is not represented (Ardizzone *et al.* 1993). The concepts describing *action*s are situated on the lower right, *situation*s on the lower left, environment description on the upper left and finally path description on the upper right.

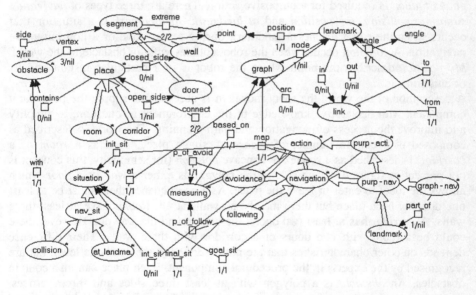

Fig. 4. Terminological component

*Action*s, and *navigation* in particular, can be either purposive or non-purposive. *Non-purposive navigation* are simply reactive robot behaviours that have no goal. Obstacle *avoidance* and feature *following* are an example. Both of them analyse sensorial data to explore the world the robot moves in. *Avoidance* and *following* generate intermediate situations that correspond to a series of *landmark*s that describe the local particular characteristics of the place where the robot is in that specific instant. Each landmark has a *position* in the world, relative to a common frame, and the *orientation* the robot has when the landmark is generated. Landmarks are connected using *link*s to form a *graph*. When a landmark is visited more than once, and has more than two links, it can have more orientations. The graph represent possible paths for the robot, and is used in planning purposive navigations. When performing a purposive navigation, an initial series of connected landmarks represented in the STM is used to plan a possible path that moves the robot to the goal position. The easiest case in *purposive navigation* is the movement between two landmarks. A more complex case can be seen as an iteration of navigation between two nodes together with a suitable path planning. There can be different possible paths that accomplish the same goal because a landmark can have more than one link. This allows the system to backtrack and find alternative solutions to the navigation problem in case the first, preferable solution (shortest path, easiest path..), fails. The graph is updated during the process of navigation if additional world measuring is carried out by the *avoidance* or *following* action. The newly formed landmarks are then inserted in the existing graph. *Safe navigation* is a compound action that carries out landmark navigation and obstacle avoidance at the same time.

Actions begin and end in situations. *Intermediate situations* are also possible and a *goal situation* is required for a purposive action. There are three types of *navigation situation*: *collision*, *my position* and *at landmark*. *At landmark* is a situation that occurs when the robot reaches a landmark during a purposive or a non purposive navigation. A *collision* occurs when the robot collides with an obstacle in the world. *My position* describes the point where the robot is in a particular instant and its orientation.

A description of the world the robot moves in is necessary to supply the procedural component with declarative knowledge of the environment in question, to simplify and improve the process of navigation and path planning. The world is described as composed of a certain number of *places*. A single place, such as a *room* or a *corridor*, is described as a convex or concave *polygon* (for semplicity, this concept is not present in figure 4). Each side of the polygon is either a *wall* or a *door* which allows the robot to enter or leave the place. As a consequence there must be at least one door for each place but there may be no walls at all. *Rooms* have at least three walls. A *corridor* has at least two doors: the way in and the way out. However there could be a room with two doors or a corridor with three walls. Their difference depends on other characteristics that are not described at the symbolic level, but are recognised by the experts in the procedural component. Each place can also contain obstacles. An *obstacle* is a polygon with at least three sides and three vertices. Obviously a complete taxonomy of possible obstacles is possible. It has been omitted to allow a better understanding of the general structure of the net.

The STM language is purely assertional. A STM knowledge base consists of grounded first order formulas describing the evolution of the actual context. Such assertions describe specific instances of the network concepts. Some simple example will be given in the next section.

3. A Procedural Component for Robot Navigation

Here follows a brief sketch of the procedural component for robot navigation. As mentioned in section 1, it is a network of *experts* (concurrent procedures with simple structure). Experts can be recognisers or actuators; the former ones work on the incoming data flow (sensors, or internal sub-symbolic representations of the world) towards the higher levels, to aggregate information inside the AIM, and/or to generate symbols (assertions). The latter ones generate actuator commands on the basis of sensor information and/or assertions. Experts are autonomous, and the whole structure resembles a behaviour-based architecture like subsumption architecture (Brooks 1990). However, the AIM structure is dynamic, in the sense that it is expected to change when new tasks are required; a certain AIM structure is determined by higher level inferential processes. These structural changes will not occur frequently; the low level sensing-acting loop is, on the contrary, operating in real time: the AIM has hence a reactive behaviour. In a sense, the AIM is a network of experts, each one behaviour-based, in which the knowledge about a specific task is *compiled*. Experts share a common, general structure; that can be sketched as follows:

```
expert E
when a do
    loop
            when c do
                    { input physical data  |
                      input internal data  |
                      read assertions }
                    <code>
                    { output physical data  |
                      output internal data  |
                      write assertions }
        end loop
exception:
    when killing-assertion do
                    <code>
                    write assertion
    when completion
                    <code>
                    write assertion
    end expert
```

An expert is an agent defined in procedural terms. It has an initial activation which depends only upon an assertion, or a formula, in the STM. The expert's body is a sense-react loop which ends only in two cases: when the expert itself ceases to be, or when a killing assertion is generated at the symbolic level. In the reactive loop, the expert has access to three kinds of input data: "physically" external; part of an internal sub-symbolic representation; or assertions. Similarly happens for output data. For sake of briefness, we do not include here a description about the allocation/deallocation mechanisms, related to the underlying software architecture. Note that an expert is expected to seldom generate assertions during its behaviour.

The network of experts assumes (a set of) sub-symbolic representations (in the literature, often referred to as *analogical*) stored in the AIM. In the navigation problem, these are pixelmaps or bitmaps of parts of the environment, of the objects and obstacles involved, road maps and more abstract (but still analogical) entities like graphs of landmarks, "forbidden places" and so on. These representations are generated and updated by experts of type recogniser; higher level recognisers generate assertions of type situation basing on them. For example, "being at a door" (a saddle in the potential field) is recognised by an expert (of type *e* in fig. 2) and a landmark assertion at time t is generated by it. Several experts, which act concurrently on a metaphorical representation of reality based on potential fields, are involved in the navigation problem (the navigation algorithm is summarised in appendix). Here we describe only the fundamentals of few of them.

Localisers (type *b, a, e* in fig. 2). They carry out data fusion among different sensors and localisation methods. Odometry, inertial systems, beacons-based methods are performed by type *b* experts. Data fusion is performed by a type *a* expert. Heuristics are managed by type *e*. An instance of *I am here* concept is generated by the emerging behaviour of several such experts under the form

> *I am here (sit$_k$)*
> *location (sit$_k$, [x,y])*
> *orientation (sit$_k$, theta)*
> *begin(sit$_k$, t$_h$)*
> ....

(being at (x,y) point with orientation theta at time t$_h$). The *begin* assertion comes from a temporal role defined in the general ontology. The localisation algorithms used in the experiment are based on fusion between odometry, active beacons and heuristics, described in (Giuffrida *et al.* 1995).

At landmark expert (type *e* in fig. 2). When the robot reaches some relevant points in the AIM (saddles, meet points or leave points in the energy landscape, obstacle collisions, and so on), the expert generates a new instance of *at landmark* situation in the STM, and causes the insertion of the corresponding landmark in the graph of visited landmarks. Examples of the assertions generated by the expert could be:

> *at_landmark(sit$_n$)*
> *landmark(lk$_n$)*
> *at(sit$_n$, lk$_n$)*
> *position(lk$_n$, [x,y])*
> *node (g$_h$, lk$_n$)*
> ....

Collision avoider (experts of type *a, b, f, c* in fig. 2). These experts perform a non-purposive navigation, keeping away from obstacles. This behaviour correspond to the rule 4 in the appendix. It can be accomplished both by a purely reactive expert (type *f*), and by a set of experts of type *b, c* and *a*, cooperating on the potential field represented in the AIM. The execution of a collision avoidance in the AIM can cause, as a side effect, the assertion of an *avoidance* instance in the STM.

Landmark navigation (experts of type *a, c* in fig. 2). They perform a purposive navigation in the AIM, connecting a starting landmark with a goal landmark, taking into account the robot orientation at the starting point and at the goal (but without taking into account the possible presence of obstacles). This behaviour corresponds to rules 1, 2, 3 in the appendix. The execution of a landmark navigation in the AIM can cause, as a side effect, the assertion of a *landmark navigation* instance in the STM.

Safe navigation (experts of type *a, b, c, f* in fig. 2). They perform a purposive navigation connecting two landmarks in the AIM, taking into account at the same time the possibility of obstacles. This correspond to the combination of obstacle avoidance and landmark navigation experts (see the appendix). The execution of safe navigation in the AIM can cause, as a side effect, the assertion of a *safe navigation* instance in the STM. Figs. 5a-b show an example of navigation in a potential field in the AIM generated by a concave obstacle.

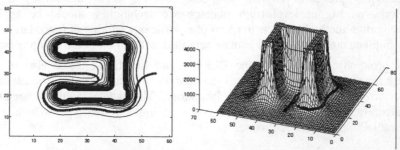

Fig. 5. (a) Equipotential curves and trajectory
(b) Potential Field of a concave obstacle

Graph navigation is the complex task of finding a route inside an existing graph of landmarks, also when the graph is dynamically updated by the generation of new landmarks discovered by the at *landmark expert*. This latter can typically happen when exploring an unknown environment. Graph navigation, not discussed in this paper, involves both symbolic processes and procedural reasoning in the AIM (experts of type *a, e, d*, plus the experts involved in safe navigation).

4. Conclusions

The current state of the research has lead to some preliminary results, both in simulation and in a real set-up. However, there are still open problems only taken into account or partially solved. The most important is probably the treatment of inconsistent or contradictory information and incoherence between the different levels of representation. Inconsistent information for an autonomous vehicle concerns bitmap construction and robot localisation. In the first case the bitmap model of the world is built using of temporal non-linear filter to remove spurious pixels

Fig. 6. Example of reactive navigation
(multiple exposures)

or to distinguish fixed objects from moving ones. In the second case different data sources are fused using DLPS© (a novel localisation and communication device developed at DIST-Laboratorium). The problem of incoherence occurs when explicit symbolic representations are used in real-time. This is partially intrinsically solved by the AIM for reactive behaviours. Some considered but yet to be resolved aspects remain in the STM-AIM interface: the symbolic information is generated asyncronously and in real-time, thus a mechanism to keep the on-going symbolic reasoning processes aligned with the evolving STM description is required. Moreover, higher level truth maintenance techniques should be applied. The navigation method (the reactive part plus some other forms of procedural reasoning) is implemented on a TRC Labmate equipped with an on-board 486 processor, a belt of proximity sensors, and the DLPS©, and has being tested also in industrial environments. Fig. 6 shows a navigation trajectory with obstacle avoidance performed by the robot in our laboratory. The whole cognitive architecture is currently under development, basing on a preliminary prototype, written in C++ and SicstusProlog, called X-Procne.

Appendix: The Navigation Strategy.

The *Wild Rover Algorithm (WRA)* (Vercelli and Zaccaria 1995) is a navigation method defined by a set of asynchronous rules which fuses three cognitive components: trajectory formation, path planning, and exploration. *Trajectory formation*, including obstacle avoidance (Cox and Wilfong 1990) copes with generating control laws for actuators. *Path planning* (Latombe 1991) copes with discovering free paths towards a goal basing on pure spatial reasoning. *Exploration methods* cope with integration of a priori knowledge about the environment and sensor data. It is well known how none of these, by itself, can solve the navigation problem in a real world.

Rules for Trajectory formation. A control law is the kernel of WRA, derived from (Vercelli *et al.* 1991). It is a heuristic, non linear law which reactively generates *speed* (v) and *jog* (ω) commands basing on *i)* an estimate of the actual position and the target position, and *ii)* on a local measure of proximity of obstacles.

rule 1 (trajectory formation towards goal): **when** in the free space, **then** v is an independent variable
rule 2 (trajectory formation towards goal): **when** not in the free space, **then** v is decreased as non linear monotonic function of the field U (see rules 4 and 6)
rule 3 (trajectory formation towards goal): **when** an angle $\theta > 0$ exists between the orientation of the robot and the orientation of the goal position, **then** three angles are computed:

> θ': an angle such that, if the robot would be rotated of θ', it could reach the goal by *pure circular* motion
> θ'': the angular misalignment between the robot and the goal
> φ: a non linear composition of θ' and θ'' such that θ' is "dominant" (to privilege smooth circular motion):

$$\Delta\varphi = \Delta\theta' + \Delta\theta'' \cdot e^{-\frac{\Delta\theta'^2}{2\sigma^2}},$$

and an ω_{goal} is generated with the law

$$\omega = \frac{\Delta\varphi}{\Delta r} \cdot v$$

where Δr is the target distance.

These rules generate a realistic smooth motion law, in terms of v and ω, that keeps the steer velocity reasonably bounded.

rule 4 (obstacle avoidance): **when** the robot is at distance r from an obstacle, **then** a *potential field U* is computed (Khatib 1986) with expression

$$U = \frac{1}{2}\left(\frac{1}{r} - \frac{1}{r_0}\right)^2$$

and an *avoiding target* A is generated at a point along the tangent of the equipotential line passing at the actual position of the robot (this local target is used to circumnavigate the obstacle), and $\omega_{avoidance}$ is generated with the same rule 3 using A as target

rule 5 (obstacle avoidance): **when** the robot is at distance r from an obstacle, **then** v and ω generated by rules 3 and 4 are composed so that the former decreases as much as the robot approaches the obstacle, and the latter increases at the same time; at a limit distance r_l (where $U = U_l$) only the "avoidance" target has effect:

$$v = v_{min} + v_{max} \cdot \left(1 - \frac{U}{U_l}\right)$$

$$\omega = \left(1 - \frac{U}{U_l}\right) \cdot \omega_{t\arg et} + \frac{U}{U_l} \cdot \omega_{avoidance}$$

Path planning. It is conjectured, even if not formally proved, that this navigation strategy always succeeds, since it is free from *local minima*, unlike classical potential field navigation (Vercelli and Zaccaria 1995). Simulative results never showed failures. Path planning is obtained by symbolic interactive construction of path graphs of *landmarks*. Landmarks are small circular regions defined by the following rules:

rule 6: starting and target points are landmarks
rule 7: a *saddle point* is a landmark
rule 8: a *hit point* (when an obstacle is encountered) is a landmark
rule 9: a *leave point* (when an obstacle is left away) is a landmark.

Exploration is carried out by the trajectory formation rules themselves. Non-linearity highly increases the exploration capabilities during motion.

References

E.Ardizzone, A.Camurri, M.Frixione, and R.Zaccaria (1993), A hybrid scheme for action representation, *International Journal of Intelligent Systems*, 8 (3), 371-403.

R. Brooks (1990), Elephants don't play chess, in (Maes 1990).

I.J. Cox and G.T. Wilfong (eds.) (1990), *Autonomous Robot Vehicles*, Springer, New York and Berlin.

I.A. Ferguson (1992), *TouringMachines: Autonomous Agents with Attitudes*, Compuer Laboratory, University of Cambridge, Cambridge, UK, 1992. Technical Report 250.

F. Giuffrida, C. Massucco, P. Morasso, G. Vercelli, and R. Zaccaria (1995), Multi-level navigation using an active localisation system, *Proc. Intl. Conf. on Intelligent Robots and Systems - IROS'95*, Pittsburg (PA), USA.

O. Khatib (1986), Real time obsatcle avoidance for manipulators and mobile robots, *Int. J. Robotics Res.*, 5 (1), 90-99.

S. Kosslyn (1980), *Image and Mind*, Harvard University Press.

J.-C. Latombe (1991), *Robot Motion Planning*, Kluwer Academic Publishers, Boston.

T. Lozano-Perez (1983), Spatial planning: a configuration space approache, *IEEE Trans. on Computers*, 32, 108-120.

P. Maes (ed.) (1990), *Designing Autonomous Agents*, MIT Press, Cambridge (Ma).

F.A.Mussa Ivaldi, P.Morasso, and R.Zaccaria (1988), Kinematic networks - a distributed model for representing and regularizing motor redundancy, *Biological Cybernetics,* 60, 1-16.

B. Nebel (1990), *Reasoning and Revision in Hybrid Representation Systems*. Spriger Verlag, Berlin.

V. Sanguineti, T. Tsuji, and P. Morasso (1993), A dynamical model for the generation of curved trajectories, in S. Gielen and B. Kappen (eds.), *Artificial Neural Networks*, London, 115-118, Springer.

M.G. Slack (1993), Navigation templates: mediating qualitative guidance and quantitative control in mobile robots, *IEEE Transactions on Systems, Man, and Cybernetics*, 23 (2).

L. Steels (1990). Exploitong analogical representations, in (Maes 1990).

G. Vercelli and R. Zaccaria (1995), Reactive motion planning and navigation based on artificial potential fields, *DIST Technical Report*, University of Genova.

G. Vercelli, R. Zaccaria, and P. Morasso (1991), A theory of sensor-based robot navigation using local information, in E. Ardizzone, S. Gaglio, and F. Sorbello (eds.), *Trends in Artificial Intelligence, Proc. of the 2nd Congress of AI*IA*, Springer, Berlin, 342-351.

R.Zaccaria, G.Vercelli, A.Camurri, and P.Morasso (1994), From tasks to knowledge: a theory for knowledge-based robots, *DIST Technical Report*, University of Genoa.

Using a Chemical Metaphor to Implement Autonomous Systems

Antonio D'Angelo
Laboratorio di Intelligenza Artificiale
Dipartimento di Matematica e Informatica
email : antonio@dimi.uniud.it
Università di Udine

Abstract. The aim of this paper is to outline a planning system architecture which allows robots to exhibit varying degrees of autonomous behaviour. While several systems have been developed to cope with specific classes of robot tasks, a litte effort has been made towards the autonomy itself. Looking at the behaviour of animals from the ethological point of view we can suppose that even robots need to exibit a wide variety of specific behaviours. Starting from Brooks and Rosenschein's approach we can think of an autonomous system as a vertical composition of its basic behaviours, or *instincts* , to produce the overall *emergent activity*. The key point, however, is how to really obtain it considering that robot actions require to be planned in some way to complete their mission. In this paper we propose an analternative way to design and build an autonomous system introducing the metaphor of a chemical machine. We th ink of the whole system as a set of behaviours, each implementing a specific response to incoming environmental stimuli, equipped with appropriate receptors which can be inhibited if a behaviour is not currently requested. Such an inhibitor schema is directly driven by the system itself using sensor data and the knowledge it has about its state. The advantage of this robot design lies in its ability to make explicit the adaptive capabilities of the system during its implementation.

1 Introduction

Robotics, dealing with mechanical devices that operate in the physical world, needs to design systems which respond to the world changes reflecting that they usually know a little about the environment they move around. As well, such systems require to be autonomous, because they must take decisions about situations unpredictable in advance. Moreover, the environment could be adverse, so they need to monitor it using sensors to recognise environmental changes which, affecting the system, could compromise their normal way of operation. So the computational complexity of algorithms, which handle their sensors and actuators, could impose severe limitations to their performance.

Thus, if we want an autonomous system to respond to a stimulus in real time, we should provide it with a suitable planning system that drives it appropriately in the environment to achieve its goals. This means that the architecture of an autonomous system should be able to handle reactively sensor data flow. The term **reactive** was first introduced by Brooks [1, 2] to implement a new generation of robot architecture, denoting the ability of such systems to respond in real time to stimuli incoming from the environment.

2 Robot planning

Robots are machines whose main goal is to solve sensorimotor tasks in a way they can bring the world about a desired state of affairs. So they are conceived as systems which are capable to generate a suitable sequence of actions according to the constraints imposed by the environment. To this aim, they need to be equipped with appropriate control programs which plan their actions to avoid both inefficiencies and disasters and their implementation should be modelled taking into account how systems behave in the environment.

But robot programs present a number of pecularities. First, they must be time bound to environment modifications and this response must be based on a model of how it reacts to the system. Second, they need to be parallel in nature because robot sensors and effectors, needing intermittent attention, can be driven concurrently. Third, the properties of some objects manipulated by the program must be acquired by their identification outside the robot. Adopting the following definition of plan we can meet all our requirements.

A plan is a structure of three component: a set of actions, a partial ordered relation over them and a set of assertions such that $\{p\}\alpha\{q\}$ denotes the applicability of the action α when the preconditions $\mathbf{p}$ are verified and yields the effects described by the postcondition $\mathbf{q}$.

Analogous methods have been advocated by Hoare [8] for program correctness, Sacerdoti [11] and Nilsson [10] for rapresenting plan generation in STRIPS even if preconditions, in this case, are all assumed to be inside the planner and, moreover, actions are executed sequentially. On the contrary, autonomous systems should execute actions concurrently and the validity of preconditions can depend upon properties which need to be observed outside the system. Separating all its components, we can rewrite action selection as follow

$$\{p\&q\&B_i\&e_j\} \ \alpha_k \ \{p\&B_k\}$$

where e_j is the *event* perceived in the environment using some sensor and it is implemented as a **boolean function** which verifies if the event has happened. On the other hand, *actions* are defined as **procedures**. Notice that some parameters can refer to objects in the world.

Looking at the preconditions in more detail, we can identify the following assertions:

- interference $\mathbf{p}$, defining which constraints must be satisfied when actions are executed concurrently,
- persistency $\mathbf{q}$, stating which conditions need when the action is repeatedly applied,
- consistency $\mathbf{B}_i$, $\mathbf{B}_k$ designating the features of the selected action using the knowledge the system has about it,
- sensitivity e_j, naming properties which can be observed in the environment as events.

It should be even noticed that each set of sequentially executed actions can be obtained exploiting the usual tools of structured sequential programming.

We shall see in the follow that some subsequences of actions are organized as a behavioural unit with the schema advocated by Brooks and Rosenschein. To make it esplicit, let us consider the rules, appearing in the follow, to compose total ordered set of actions to which we add two structural rules with the obvoius rule of inference which allows us to build arbitrarily complex set of actions with their related pre and postconditions.

- **sequencing**

$$\frac{\{p\} \ \alpha_1 \ \{q\} \qquad \{q\} \ \alpha_2 \ \{r\}}{\{p\} \ \alpha_1; \ \alpha_2 \ \{r\}}$$

- **case**

$$\frac{\{p \ \& \ e_i\} \ \alpha_i \ \{q\} \quad \neg[e_i \ \& \ e_j] \quad e_1 \lor ... \lor e_n}{\{p\} \ \mathbf{case} \ s \ \mathbf{of} \ S_1: \ \alpha_1; ...; S_n: \ \alpha_n \ \mathbf{end}\{q\}}$$

- **selection**

$$\frac{\{p \ \& \ \neg e\} \ \alpha \ \{q\} \qquad \{p \ \& \ e \supset q\}}{\{p\} \ \mathbf{if} \ \neg e \ \mathbf{then} \ \alpha \ \{q\}}$$

$$\frac{\{p \ \& \ e\} \ \alpha_1 \ \{q\} \qquad \{p \ \& \ \neg e\} \ \alpha_2 \ \{q\}}{\{p\} \ \mathbf{if} \ e \ \mathbf{then} \ \alpha_1 \ \mathbf{else} \ \alpha_2 \ \{q\}}$$

- **loop**

$$\frac{\{p \ \& \ e\} \ \alpha \ \{p\}}{\{p\} \ \mathbf{while} \ e \ \mathbf{do} \ \alpha \ \{p \ \& \ \neg e\}}$$

$$\frac{\{p \ \& \ e\} \ \alpha \ \{p\}}{\{p \ \& \ e\} \ \mathbf{repeat} \ \alpha \ \mathbf{until} \ \neg e \ \{p \ \& \ \neg e\}}$$

- **weakening**

$$\frac{\{p\} \ \alpha \ \{q\} \qquad q \supset r}{\{p\} \ \alpha \ \{r\}}$$

- **enforcement**

$$\frac{p \supset q \qquad \{q\} \ \alpha \ \{r\}}{\{p\} \ \alpha \ \{r\}}$$

Thinking about effectors in isolation, the primary actions a robot can execute are bound in number and simple in type. On the other hand, conceiving a robot as a whole it is convenient to group its actions so that we can referred to as easily identifiable situations. So, the first level of abstraction considers actions to be grouped into **tactics** which identify activities with the same preconditions except the component for the event type detectable by robot sensors. Thus, we make the definition

$$\tau_i \equiv \text{if } e_i \text{ then } \alpha_j \text{ else}... \quad \{p \;\&\; q \;\&\; B_i\} \;\; \tau_i \;\; \{p\}$$

with the corresponding representation in terms of pre and postconditions as it can be easily verified using selection and structural rules.

If, now, we group all tactics which differ one another only for their consistency conditions, we obtain a **schema**, formally defined with

$$\beta \equiv \text{case } s \text{ of } S_1 : \tau_1; \; ... \;; S_n : \tau_n \text{ end} \quad \{p \;\&\; q\} \;\; \beta \;\; \{p\}$$

where $S_1, ..., S_n$ are labels which are attached to each consistency condition. It should be noticed that preconditions involve only assertions referring to a possible interaction with other schemas.

The repeated application of a schema, until it is possible, gives rise to a **behaviour** and it is formally defined with the expression

$$\beta^* \equiv \text{repeat } \beta \text{ until } \neg q \quad \{p \;\&\; q\} \; \beta^* \; \{p \;\&\; \neg q\}$$

It also should be noticed how the whole planning process can be split in a number of sequential planning components, each identifying a behaviour in Brooks' approach. Morever, it is possible that single actions, related to different behaviours, can combine temporally so that the system executes the compound action $\alpha \equiv \alpha_1 \mid \alpha_2 \mid ... \mid \alpha_n \quad \alpha_i \in \beta_i^*$ which is obtained by the concurrent execution of its component actions.

3   Reactive planning

We have already observed that a behaviour of an autonomous systems works as an idealized robot that operates inside an environment whose objects have the properties that behaviour is referring to. Thus, if we consider the behaviour of avoiding obstacles the only property of interest is the impenetrability of solids. The whole robot behaviour is brought about by the interaction among basic ones so that system control needs to find out what component behaviours should be supplied with the necessary input data.

Every behaviour is implemented as a finite state automaton defined by the following state transition function

$$\phi(S_i, e_j) = S_k \quad \chi(S_k) = \alpha_k$$

to which we couple the corresponding output function. The state S_i is a label which identifies the condition to apply action α_k according to the preceding section. It should also be noticed the distinction between *event* and *action*, the former used to denote a changing of the environment caused from an agent different from the robot itself, the latter identifying what robot is doing. The advantage of finite state automata is to find out in real time the most appropriate action to issue within a behaviour as a response to external stimulus. The motivation is related to the aptitude of such systems to store permanently information as labelled states.

Let us consider the task of avoiding obstacles for a robot, moving along a trajectory, which uses a sensor providing a repulsive force whose magnitude depends on object proximity and direction tells robot the best way to run away. Omitting the conditions of interference and persistency of actions, the mechanism of avoiding an obstacle can be implemented as shown in fig. 1 where $\mathbf{f}$ denotes a repulsive force, $\mathbf{f}_0$ the threshold of intervention.

As it can be easily noticed, the behaviour that allows the robot to run away an obstacle is made up of two actions, the former having no effect, while the intrinsic conditions of

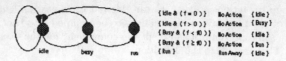

{ Idle & (f = 0)}	No Action	{ Idle }
{ Idle & (f > 0)}	No Action	{ Busy }
{ Busy & (f < 10)}	No Action	{ Idle }
{ Busy & (f ≥ 10)}	No Action	{ Run }
{ Run }	Run Away	{ Idle }

Fig. 1. runaway behaviour

applicability are related to different states of robot attention with the respect of the obstacles placed along its trajectory. Obviously, every state of attention corresponds to a state of the related automaton as shown in fig. 1 where the only transition which issues an action is that linking the states labelled busy and run.

The part of planner which implements individual reactive behaviours has been already discussed in literature [2], [9], [6] so that it is not yet considered.

4 Behavioural planning

The definition of behaviour given in the preceding section assume that the conditions of applicability depend upon both the interference $\mathbf{p}$ and the persistency $\mathbf{q}$ of its component actions. Thus, a behaviour β^* is identified by a description in terms of pre/postconditions $\{p\&q\}\ \beta^*\ \{p\&\neg q\}$ where the set of conditions $\mathbf{p}$ plays the same role as the invariants for the while and repeat loops appearing in sequential structured programming. So, the inhibition of a behaviour β^* can be achieved falsifying either $\mathbf{p}$ or $\mathbf{q}$ which yields, in the former case, the blocking of an action issued by β^* and, in the latter, the suppression of sensor activity.

Without loss of generality, let us assume that the precondition $\mathbf{q}$ of persistency be always true, so it can be ignored. Moreover, we can think of $\mathbf{p}$ as the denial of inhibitory conditions, expressed with a prenex conjunctive form. So, we have

$$p \quad \equiv \neg(r_1\&g_1 \ \vee ... \vee r_n\&g_n) \quad \equiv \quad (r_1 \supset \neg g_1)\&...\&(r_n \supset \neg g_n)$$

where each $\mathbf{g}_i$ denotes a conjunction of terms taken from the closed set G of global states $G \equiv \{G_1, G_2, G_3, ...\}$ and whose purpose is to capture the meaning of external condition for the application of an action α_k related to its behaviour β.

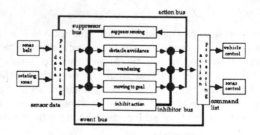

Fig. 2. behaviour arbitration

Now, we shall characterize in more detail the kind of information appearing as precondition $\mathbf{p}$. Thus, because a planning system is based upon states and actions we shall introduce a language including two disjoint sets, the former R consisting of *primitive actions* and the latter G of *global states*, to represent each $r_i \supset \neg g_i$. We shall suppose that each $\mathbf{r}_i$ is expressible as a conjunction of terms built on the set $R \equiv \{R_1, R_2, R_3, ...\}$ where every R_i defines a primitive action which competes to determine the system activities.

To block an action α_k, belonging to the behaviour β^*, it is sufficient that some conditional form $r_i \supset \neg g_i$ be not valid, namely, $r_i \& g_i$ be satisfiable. So, if we suppose $\mathbf{r}_i$ satisfiable, we need $\mathbf{g}_i$ valid

$$| \sim r_i, \; \models g_i \implies \; | \sim r_i \& g_i$$

making this schema fundamental for the mechanism which verifies the applicability of actions. We called such schemas *receptors* because they behave as selection mechanism of an inhibition/activation structure. It should be noticed that such a schema works even if we take $\mathbf{p}$ in the following form

$$r_1 \& r_2 \& ... \& r_n \supset \neg (g_1 \vee g_2 ... \vee g_n)$$

The use of the term **receptor** shall be elucidated in the next section where we shall acquaint a chemical metaphor to implement a control mechanism where behaviour maintenance is triggered by a verification that no inhibitor can combine with any of receptors related to that behaviour.

Such an inhibitory mechanism suggests the design of a control system like that appearing in fig.2 where we have highlighted sensor and effector processing units as well as inhibitor and suppressor ones with their related buses. Sensor data enter event bus and, then, they are dispatched to those behavioural units which require them. The suppressor bus operates as triggering unit which eventually block input data for some behaviour so that no transition is generated by the corresponding automaton.

A signal, generated by some sensor, is processed using information incoming from the *action bus* and referring to actions in course of execution. So, it gives rise to an abstract representation of sensor data and supplies input for behavioural units. The **inhibitor unit**, driven by events present on the event bus, can generate signals towards the *inhibitor bus* so that some action doesn't generate the related command for the effector driver.

5 The chemical machine

As opposite to reactive planning, based upon finite state automaton to grant a real time stimuli response, behavioural planning has less severe temporal constraints because it must only schedule those units that are recognized to remain active, inhibiting any other. To this aim we have devised a general schema to maintain information about both the state of the world and the internal functioning of robot whose global state is recognized using a represention schema based on a chemical machine [7].

The system which controls the robot behaviour is realized by the *suppress sensing* and *inhibit action* modules which, notifying either input suppression or output inhibition to selected behaviours, give rise to the **emergent activity** of the robot. So, we need to establish which kind of information must be considered to trigger adequately the execution of each behavioural unit.

To this aim we shall consider the biological metaphor built upon the abstract chemical machine introduced by Boudol [7]. All data, exchanged among behaviour modules along with inhibitor bus, are treated as *moleculas* which are built using the following operators:

- **parallel**, $p \mid q$
- **prefix**, $a.p$
- **restriction**, $p \setminus a$
- **signature**, $\overline{p}$
- **airlocking**, $p \lhd q$
- **membrane**, $\ll p \gg$

The whole state of an autonomous system is represented by a **chemical solution** where floating moleculas can interact each other according to suitable **reaction rules**. Their implementation corresponds to Brownian motion in chemistry and characterizes the solution transformation process.

Moleculas react inside the solution but not to their internal structure, in according to the following two rules

- parallel
  $$p \mid q \; \rightleftharpoons \; p, q \qquad (R1)$$
- reaction
  $$a \cdot p, \; \overline{a} \cdot q \; \rightarrow \; p, q \qquad (R2)$$
- inaction cleanup
  $$\emptyset \; \rightarrow \qquad (R3)$$
- restriction ion
  $$(\alpha \cdot p) \setminus a \; \rightleftharpoons \; \alpha \cdot (p \setminus a) \;\; (R4)$$

- restriction membrane
  $$p \setminus a \; \rightleftharpoons \; \ll p \gg \setminus a \qquad (R5)$$
- airlock
  $$\ll p, q_1, ..., q_m \gg \; \rightleftharpoons \; p \triangleleft \ll q_1, ..., q_m \gg \; (R6)$$
- heavyion
  $$(\alpha \cdot p) \triangleleft q \; \rightleftharpoons \; \alpha \cdot (p \triangleleft q) \qquad (R7)$$

First rule is reversible and states that a molecula of type $a \mid b$ can always be heated up to decompose into its component parts and, vice versa, every pair of moleculas can be cooled down to rebuild the molecula having the pair as components. To deal with the null action, denoted by $\emptyset$, we need the rule R3 which establishes that, heating up the solution, it vanishes so that it cannot be ever considered.

The rule R2 always involves moleculas with opposite prefix, called their **valence**, realising their body into the solution. This rule also applies if a molecula takes the form $a \setminus p$ provided that its former part has some prefix allowing the valence to be exported outside. But, if p is compound it should perform internal reactions and to also react with other ions floating in the main solution, using its own ions of unrestricted valences. To this aim we have the rule R5 where the local solution obeys the same rules as the global one.

However, if we want some ion in the local solution to react with its complementary in the global solution, we need to make membranes *porous* to valences. So, using the airlock mechanism we extract a selected molecula from the solution, putting the rest of the solution within a membrane and isolating the extracted molecula (rule R6) within an airlock attached to the membrane. Then, we build an heavy ion from any one appearing within the airlock construct using the rule R7. In this way we guarantee reversibility by preserving the attachment between α and p. Also notice that a restriction molecula can propose several valences in succession to its environment until a reaction takes place.

Within this chemical methaphor, we shall suppose that the receptor structure, attached to each behaviour, is a membrane containing a molecula whose component parts correspond to the receptor schema devised in the preceding section

$$\ll (\overline{g_1}.\overline{r_1}.s_1) \mid ... \mid (\overline{g_n}.\overline{r_n}.s_n) \gg$$

where the signature, allowing ion reaction, implements the receptor structure. It shoud be noticed that each molecula $\overline{g_i}.\overline{r_i}.s_i$ has a term built over the finite set $S \equiv \{S_1, S_2, S_3, ...\}$ whose elements work as inhibitor mechanism blocking the behaviour where the receptor is installed. If we assume that the receptor is built upon a simple molecula, we have the following chain of reactions

$$(g_i.\emptyset), \; \ll \overline{g_i}.\overline{r_i}.s_i, \; r_i.\emptyset \gg \qquad R6 \qquad \rightarrow (g_i.\emptyset), \; (\overline{g_i}.\overline{r_i}.s_i) \triangleleft \; \ll r_i.\emptyset \gg \; R7$$
$$\rightarrow (g_i.\emptyset), \; \overline{g_i}.((\overline{r_i}.s_i) \triangleleft \; \ll r_i.\emptyset \gg) \; R2, R3 \rightarrow (\overline{r_i}.s_i) \triangleleft \; \ll r_i.\emptyset \gg \qquad R6$$
$$\rightarrow \; \ll \overline{r_i}.s_i, r_i.\emptyset \gg \qquad R2, R3 \rightarrow \; \ll s_i \gg$$

The enzyme $r_i.\emptyset$, appearing inside the membrane and working as **activator** $\overline{r_i}.s_i$, is generated during action executions and establishes a selection mechanism between receptors and the **inhibitor hormones** s_i in order to block the execution of the action α_k, issued by the behaviour β_i^*.

So the validity of the precondition of interference **p**, specifying each behaviour, depends on a set of terms we have called its global states, which play the role of firing elements which activate a reaction chain to produce a molecula s_i whose detection gives rise to the inhibition of the corresponding behaviour.

6 A robot example

The inhibitor schema proposed in the preceding section is adequate to cause the set of a robot basic behaviours to actively cooperate. As an example we shall consider the robot Allen built by Brooks [2] to illustrate the subsumption architecture principles within minimalism. We recall that Allen moves within a well-structured environment where there are several obstacles which it can detect using sonar. Odometry is used to localise itself and generate the goal behaviour trying to reach some fixed position.

This simple example shows that robot *survival* is normally obtained by avoiding obstacles and stopping if one of these is too near to try any corrective moving without crashing. The *goal behaviour* is generated as a linear trajectory connecting the current with the goal position. To avoid the robot moving into a dead area, it is endowed with an *auxiliar behaviour* of wandering. So, putting Allen in some place, it will try to complete its mission using the behaviours: **runaway** from an obstacle, eventually, **halting** in front of an obstacle, **wander** and **follow** the glimmer with *runaway* always active and *halt* inhibited unless the case of unavoidable obstacle.

With some detail we can consider navigation as a task controlled by two different drivers, the former causes the robot to move ahead with the action **go** whereas the latter is responsible of its rotation using the action **turn**. The Allen whole movement is given by a repeated action *go* with a fixed displacement parameter together an appropriate rotation angle for the turn *action*.

Thus, Allen can be characterized by two global states - panic and desire - and four primitive actions - move, tend, stop and float - denoted, for simplicity, with their initial

$$G \equiv \{p, d\} \quad R \equiv \{m, t, s, f\}$$

where tend and float are the rotations caused by the following and wandering modules, respectively, and move is the rotation related to runaway. Thus, if we consider that the following propositional theorems are valid

$$
\begin{aligned}
\neg(\neg p \& s) &\quad \supset (s \supset p) \\
\neg(p \& m) &\quad \supset (m \supset \neg p) \\
\neg(p \& m) \& \neg(d \& f) &\quad \supset (m \& f \supset \neg(p \vee d)) \\
\neg(p \& m) \& \neg(\neg d \& t) &\quad \supset (m \& t \supset \neg(p \vee \neg d))
\end{aligned}
$$

we can take their consequent as preconditions to verify for the maintainace of the corresponding behaviour. Now, if we define the inhibitor hormones $S \equiv \{S_1, S_2, S_3, S_4\}$ and put the indicated moleculas into their membranes, we obtain the following receptor structures

halt	$(s \supset p)$	$\ll p.\overline{s}.S_1 \gg$
runaway	$(m \supset \neg p)$	$\ll \overline{p}.\overline{m}.S_2 \gg$
wander	$(m \& f \supset \neg(p \vee d))$	$\ll (\overline{p}.\overline{m}.S_3) \mid (\overline{d}.\overline{f}.S_3) \gg$
follow	$(m \& t \supset \neg(p \vee \neg d))$	$\ll (\overline{p}.\overline{m}.S_4) \mid (\overline{d}.\overline{f}.S_4) \gg$

which give a complete specification for the robot Allen. Thus, the presence of a molecula like either $p.\emptyset$, $d.\emptyset$, etc..., produces immediately the inhibition of the behaviour β_i if the molecula S_i can freely float inside its related membrane. Also, notice how panic discriminates between *move* and *stop* whereas desire distinguishes *float* from *tend*.

7 Conclusions

In this paper we have presented an architecture for autonomous systems based upon a chemical machine whose model of computation is suitable to implement an inhibitor mechanism of the behaviours the system is equipped with. Moreover, each of these is defined as a reactive module in the same sense it is used by Brooks.

Considering we have made the simplified assumption that a behaviour cannot be stopped when it is switched on, the inhibitor schema seems general enough to implement a wide variety of system operations. Moreover, sensor data handling has been implemented within a reactive paradigm to get the best response to incoming stimuli in terms of temporal constraints.

We expect that such an inhibitor schema can be more natural and flexible in dealing with more complex architectural choices, including learning and further sophisticated adaptive behaviours.

Acknowledgement

The present work has been realized within the Progetto Finalizzato di Robotica of C.N.R. MANUEL particularly referring to the control architecture for the robot RAP, built on the vehicle Labmate and equipped with sonars and camera. I would thank Claudio Sossai, Nino Trainito and Gaetano Chemello for discussions and suggestions during the development of the chemical machine.

References

1. R. A. Brooks. A robust layered control system for a mobile robot. *IEEE J. Robotics and Automation*, RA-2:14–23, 1986.
2. R. A. Brooks. Elephants don't play chess. *Robotics and Autonomous Systems*, 6:3–15, 1990.
3. A. D'Angelo. Automatic and reactive planning: a perspective of integration. In *Workshop Italiano sulla Pianificazione Automatica*, Roma (I), 1993.
4. A. D'Angelo. Un sistema di navigazione reattiva per un robot mobile. Technical Report UDMI/15/93/RR, Dipartimento di Matematica e Informatica, Universitá di Udine (I), 1993.
5. A. D'Angelo. Behaviour-based distributed systems. In *Workshop Italiano sull'Intelligenza Artificiale*, Parma (I), 1994.
6. D. Chapman E. Agre. What are plans for? *Robotics and Autonomous Systems*, 6:17–34, 1990.
7. G. Boudol G. Berry. The chemical abstract machine. In *International Conference on Principles of Programming Languages*, pages 81–93, 1990.
8. C. A. R. Hoare. An axiomatic basis for computer programming. *Comm. of ACM*, 12:576–583, 1969.
9. S. J. Rosenschein L. P. Kaelbing. Action and planning in embedded agents. *Robotics and Autonomous Systems*, 6:35–48, 1990.
10. N. Nilsson R. Fikes. Strips: A new approach to the application of theorem proving to problem solving. *Artificial Intelligence*, 2:189–208, 1972.
11. E. Sacerdoti. *A Structure for Plans and Behaviour*. Elsevier-North-Holland, New York, 1977.

Modeling Process Diagnostic Knowledge
Through Causal Networks

Paolo Pogliano and Luisella Riccardi

CISE - Tecnologie Innovative
P.O. Box 12081, 20134 Milan, Italy
[paolo I luisella]@sia.cise.it

Abstract. Diagnosis in process industry is a complex task which can be effectively supported by knowledge based system technology. The majority of applications in this field have focused on rule-based implementations of the heuristic classification approach. In this paper we argue for the exploitation of a causal model based approach to knowledge representation and diagnostic reasoning which can overcome some of the problems manifested by first generation expert systems. The proposed approach can be more viable than other model-based approaches requiring a complete qualitative or quantitative modeling of correct behavior.

The paper presents the causal representation formalism, a definition through a logical framework of the process diagnosis problem considered and the reasoning process which has been defined to solve it. Examples concerning both representation and reasoning issues are taken from DIOGENE, a system devoted to support on-line diagnosis of steam generation process in thermal power plants.

Keywords. Knowledge Representation, Causal Models, Diagnostic Reasoning, Knowledge-Based Systems.

1.   Introduction

The use of causal models for diagnosis can be traced back to the pioneering work of Patil [PAT 81] in the ABEL system. Since then, many systems adopted a similar approach in different application areas to overcome the limitations of rule-based expert systems (such as, for instance, [NEL 82], [SAC 86] and [HAK 91] in the field of process diagnosis). Systems based on causal models were characterized both by a shift in the implementation level knowledge representation formalism and in the kind of knowledge exploited. In this latter respect, the so called "knowledge level" [NEW 82] characterization of KBS, the attention shifted from subjective experience knowledge to more sound structural and functional knowledge which could be effectively represented through causal networks.

The causal modeling approach to process diagnosis is based on a representation of the behavior of the physical system in terms of causal relationships between events, where an event can be either a variation in the value of a continuous variable representing a physical quantity or of a discrete variable representing the state of a component. These models can concern either the correct functioning of the physical system [STE 85] or the evolution of malfunctions [PAT 81].

In the specific domain of process diagnosis, several applications exist adopting different forms of causal modeling, such as fault trees, signed digraphs, event digraphs and unsigned digraphs weighted with fault propagation probabilities and times. The approach of causal modeling of faulty behavior seems to suit particularly well to this domain for several reasons:

- *Epistemological adequacy*. The representation language allows the designer to easily express most of the knowledge relevant to the task. That means that it allows one to express different kinds of knowledge (mainly structural and functional) relevant to the task of diagnosing complex processes.
- *Uniformity*. The diagnostic knowledge is represented through a unique formalism and can be handled by a single interpreter.
- *Economy*. A qualitative faulty causal model allows the expression of knowledge in a simple way and is amenable to efficient computation. In this respect the approach revealed to be more viable than equational model approaches, as the causal model must only represent the diagnostically relevant knowledge describing the qualitative evolution of known malfunctions and not a complete model of the artifact in terms of basic components. In the domain of process diagnosis of complex systems, a sufficiently detailed model (either causal or equational) of correct behavior is seldom available or computationally and practically usable for diagnostic purposes.
- *Cognitive correspondence*. Last but not least, the representation can be very easily mapped to a causal conceptual model, minimizing the effort to overcome the gap between knowledge acquisition and knowledge representation at the implementation level [TOU 94].

On the other hand, the main limitation in adopting a faulty causal modeling approach is that expertise concerning faults must be available and has to be extensively acquired. Moreover, the causal formalism by itself does not force the exploitation of a specific knowledge type; on the contrary, it leaves many degrees of freedom to the designer in choosing the entities and the relationships to be represented, so that even heuristic knowledge could be easily included in causal models. An accurate knowledge-level analysis is thus required to define what kind of knowledge must be conceptualized and represented in order to develop sound and maintainable applications.

Besides this epistemological remark, the adoption of a causal modeling approach forces the application designer to consider other fundamental matters, such as the level of abstraction of the causal model which the system relies on, the identification of uncertainties and incompleteness of the model and how they must be dealt with, the definition of the diagnostic reasoning and the definition of the solution(s) to the diagnostic problem.

In this paper we present a causal representation formalism and a diagnostic interpretation process which could be adopted in the development of knowledge based applications in the domain of process diagnosis. In order to address the above mentioned critical points of faulty causal modeling, we will take advantage of a logical formalization of the representation formalism, the diagnostic problem and its solutions, following the approach proposed by L. Console and P. Torasso (see, for instance, [CON 89] and [TOR 89]).

The paper is organized as follows: chapter 2 presents the causal representation formalism in terms of modeled entities and relationships; chapter 3 gives a formal definition of the diagnostic problem and tackles reasoning issues; chapter 4 contains some concluding remarks and presents future research issues that could lead to interesting extensions of the formalism. The exposition will take advantage of example models from DIOGENE (DIagnosis Of steam GENErator), an application system devoted to support on-line diagnosis of steam generation process in thermal power plants.

2.   Knowledge Representation Formalism

A generic causal model can be defined as a directed acyclic graph whose nodes represent states, events or variables and whose directed arcs represent a direct cause-effect relationship between two nodes (the starting node being the cause and the ending node the effect of the relationship).

We enriched this basic structure through the introduction of several other kinds of nodes and relationships, described in the following paragraphs. The formalism will be exemplified through models taken from DIOGENE, the application system which allowed us to test, refine and evaluate the ideas presented in this paper. The diagnostic activity of DIOGENE is based on the following main steps:

- DIOGENE acquires plant measures from the power plant supervisory system.
- By means of local checks mainly based on numeric thresholds, the sensors' reliability is evaluated. Further considerations based on measure consistency verification lead to further prune malfunctioning sensors.
- The plant measures are checked against their reference values in order to identify the malfunction symptoms. The symptoms are then used to determine the causal networks, each describing a different malfunction of the steam generation process, that can be satisfied thus leading to a diagnosis identification.

DIOGENE is currently under laboratory testing and will be installed and field tested on the power plant of Santa Gilla (CA, Sardinia).

In fig. 1 we present the graphical notation adopted for entities and relationships, while in fig. 2 some examples of DIOGENE causal models are provided.

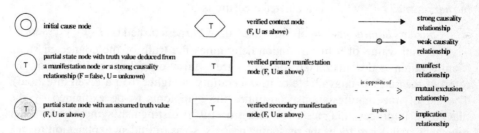

Fig. 1 Graphical notation for entities and relationships in causal networks.

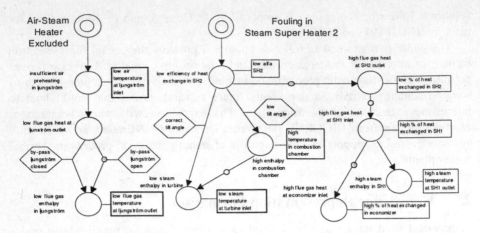

Fig. 2 Examples of causal networks in the DIOGENE knowledge base.

2.1. Entities

The kind of nodes used in the causal models are the following:

Partial state nodes. These nodes model anomalous situations of the physical system by specifying a propositional condition on the value of a single state variable which characterizes the state itself, usually involving a qualitative evaluation of a plant parameter (e.g., *"high enthalpy in combustion chamber"* in fig. 2). They represent "partial" states as they are partial definitions of the modeled system "global" state, which can be defined by specifying the values of the complete set of state variables.

Initial cause nodes. This kind of nodes represents the malfunctions which are to be considered by the diagnostic process (that is, the diagnostic hypotheses which could be included in the diagnoses). They are named "initial causes" as the causal model does not include any incoming causal arc for them.

Initial causes are not epistemologically different from partial states: they can represent both an anomalous variable value (e.g., *"high excess of air"*), or, more often than ordinary partial states, a component malfunction (as *"air-steam heater excluded"* in fig. 2).

Manifestation nodes. A manifestation node represents a logical condition on one or more basic measures acquired from the physical system or calculated from them. Examples of basic measures in DIOGENE are *"oil flow rate"*, *"oil pressure"*, *"n. of burners turned on"*, while a calculated measure is:

$$\textit{"burners admittance"} = \text{oil flow rate* n. of burners turned on} / \sqrt{\text{oil pressure}}$$

The truth value of a manifestation determines the truth of the connected state. Manifestation nodes may take the value true, false or unknown (if one of the referred measures is unavailable or its uncertainty is higher than a given threshold). The set of true manifestations constitutes the symptoms to be explained by the diagnosis. In process diagnosis it is often useful to distinguish symptoms by their relevance in order to focus the reasoning process, so as to find an explanation for the most significant ones first. For this reason, our causal formalism allows one to partition the manifestation nodes in primary (e.g., "*low steam temperature at turbine inlet*") and secondary nodes (e.g., "*high % of heat exchanged in economizer*"), whose significance in the diagnostic process will be cleared up in chapter 3.

Context nodes. A context node represent a propositional condition on the modeled system which is to be verified in order to allow a particular causal evolution. The purpose of context nodes is to represent the structural and operating conditions of the modeled system which contribute in determining the effects of malfunctions. An example of contextual information in fig. 2 is "b*y-pass ljungström closed*". Unlike manifestation nodes, the truth value of context nodes may be derived either from the supervisory system or from operator input, as its variability in time is usually lower and its availability is fundamental for the diagnostic reasoning.

2.2. Relationships

The relationships allowed by the representation formalism are the following:

Strong causality relationship. A strong causal arc connects a partial state or an initial cause (cause) to a partial state (effect). As we stated above, a causal arc can also be connected to a context node restricting its applicability (see context "*by-pass ljungström closed*" in fig. 2). The following is a logical formalization of the semantic of this relation:

cause [∧ context] ⇒ effect

where *cause*, *context* and *effect* are atomic formulas.

Weak causality relationship. This causal relationship differs from the previous one in that the cause *may* produce the effect, but not necessarily. Similarly to strong relationships, weak ones can be connected to context nodes which restrict their validity (e.g., "*by-pass ljungström open*" in fig. 2). The logical semantic of this relation is the following:

cause ∧ assumption [∧ context] ⇒ effect

where *assumption* is a non-modeled condition which has been abstracted.

Thanks to weak causality relationships, malfunction models can explicitly represent the lack of knowledge on certain processes or the lack of observable manifestations concerning preconditions which have to be verified in order to enable the cause-effect relationship. Moreover, the usefulness of explicitly representing uncertain cause-effect relationships stems from the fact that the reasoning process can take advantage of uncertain information to provide a better evaluation of alternative diagnoses and a more comprehensive explanation of symptoms.

Manifest relationship. A manifest arc connects a partial state to a manifestation node. A manifest relationship is itself a kind of causal relationship from the partial state to the manifestation node, as a manifestation Ψ_i can be considered an effect of the physical system state ps_i which it is connected to:

$$ps_i \Rightarrow \Psi_i$$

Mutual exclusion relationship. A mutual exclusion arc connects two partial states which cannot be simultaneously true. The two nodes involved in this relationship are named *opposite*. The logical definition of this relationship is:

$$ps_i \Rightarrow \neg ps_j \wedge ps_j \Rightarrow \neg ps_i$$

where ps_i and ps_j are the opposite partial states.

Implication relationship. An implication arc connects a partial state (the "implying node") to another one (the "implied" node) and means that the truth of the first one entails the truth of the latter one, too. In the logical formalism:

$$ps_i \Rightarrow ps_j$$

where ps_i is the implying partial state and ps_j is the implied partial state.

It is important to point out the difference between causality and implication relationships. Although they share the same logical interpretation, implication relationship does not model a causal evolution of the physical system, but, as well as mutual exclusion, a consistency constraint among partial states associated to the same state variable (e.g., "*low flue gas enthalpy at chimney outlet*" and "*high flue gas enthalpy at chimney outlet*" in fig. 3) or to closely related state variables (e.g., "*excessive air flow rate*" and "*high oxygen concentration in flue gas*" in fig. 3).

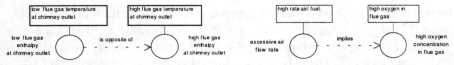

Fig. 3. Examples of mutual exclusion and implication relationships.

3. Diagnostic Reasoning

In this chapter we will deal with the diagnostic reasoning defined to exploit the causal formalism previously described. The basic assumptions we made concerning the diagnostic process are the following:

1. At diagnosis time, the malfunction evolution has completed, that is, every consequence of initial causes has already manifested itself.
2. Several malfunctions may have occurred at the time of diagnosis.
3. The measures which are referred in manifestation nodes may be unavailable but, when they are actually available, they are assumed to be correct. This assumption is acceptable if the measure validation is assured by other means before the diagnostic process takes place. In DIOGENE, measures validation is carried out by means of an equational model exploited by ODS [CER 94], a diagnostic system realized in the frame of the Esprit Project ARTIST (P5143).
4. The system must not question the user to discriminate among diagnoses.
5. The causal model can be incomplete or inconsistent. However, the following weaker assumption of knowledge base completeness ("partial completeness") has been done in DIOGENE: if a partial state connected to a primary symptom is true, at least one of its modeled causes must be true. This assumption is justified by the consideration that all the mostly relevant diagnostic knowledge related to primary symptoms has been acquired and modeled.

Under these assumptions, the diagnostic reasoning aims at finding a minimal (according to certain criteria) set of initial causes that explain all of the symptoms and only these ones. More formally, we can define our diagnostic problem P as a 4-tuple:

$$P \equiv \, < CN, IC, CTX^+, \Psi^+ >$$

where CN is the causal network model, IC is the set of initial causes in CN, $CTX^+ \subseteq CTX$ is the subset of contextual conditions CTX of CN which are verified and $\Psi^+ \subseteq \Psi$ is the set of symptoms, that is, the set of verified manifestations to be covered by the diagnosis.

Assuming the logical interpretation given in the previous chapter to causal relationships, a solution (diagnosis) of a diagnostic problem can be defined as any subset D of IC such that:

$$D \wedge CN \wedge CTX^+ \wedge A \vdash \Psi^+ \quad \text{and} \quad D \wedge CN \wedge CTX^+ \dashv\!\!\vdash \Psi^-,$$

where A is a set of assumptions (non-modeled conditions) and $\Psi^- = \Psi - \Psi^+$ is the set of non-observed (false) manifestations.

The description of the diagnostic process requires us some more definitions:

Manifestations covered (explained) by an initial cause. We define the set *man* (IC_i) of manifestations covered by the initial cause IC_i in the diagnostic problem P as:

$$\text{man } (IC_i) = \{\Psi_i^+ \mid IC_i \wedge CN_i \wedge CTX^+ \wedge A \vdash \Psi_i^+\}$$

where CN_i is the subnetwork spawning from IC_i.

Partial states derivable from an initial cause. We define the set of partial states $ps(IC_i)$ which can be derived in a given problem P by assuming the occurrence of the initial cause IC_i as:

$$\text{ps } (IC_i) = \{ps_i \mid IC_i \wedge CN_i \wedge CTX^+ \vdash ps_i\}$$

where ps_i is any partial state belonging to CN_i. Note that this definition only includes partial states whose truth must necessarily follow from the truth assumption of the initial cause.

Consistent initial cause. A consistent initial cause is an initial cause IC_i such that its associated subnetwork contains at least one primary symptom $\Psi_{P_i}^+$, that is:

$$\exists \, \Psi_{P_i}^+ \in \text{man } (IC_i)$$

and all the manifestations contained in the subnetwork have a truth value consistent with the assumption of truth of the initial cause, that is:

$$\neg \exists \, ps_i \in \text{ps } (IC_i) \mid ps_i \Rightarrow \Psi_i^-$$

Only consistent initial causes are taken into account in order to define possible diagnoses to be evaluated.

Candidate Diagnosis. A candidate diagnosis is a set of consistent initial causes such that no conflicting truth values of partial states can be deduced from assuming their truth. Conflicting truth values rise from propagating truth values whenever:

- opposite truth values are derived for the same partial state, i.e.:
  $$\exists \, ps_i, IC_i, IC_j \mid ps_i \in \text{ps } (IC_i) \wedge \neg ps_i \in \text{ps } (IC_j).$$
- opposite truth values are derived for a state and one of its implied states, i.e.:
  $$\exists \, ps_i, ps_j, IC_i, IC_j \mid ps_i \in \text{ps } (IC_i) \wedge \neg ps_j \in \text{ps } (IC_j) \wedge ps_i \Rightarrow ps_j,$$
  where $ps_i \Rightarrow ps_j$ means that ps_j is an implied partial state of ps_i.
- the truth of a state and of one of its opposite states are derived, i.e.:
  $$\exists \, ps_i, ps_j, IC_i, IC_j \mid ps_i \in \text{ps } (IC_i) \wedge ps_j \in \text{ps } (IC_j) \wedge ps_i \Rightarrow \neg ps_j,$$
  where $ps_i \Rightarrow \neg ps_j$ means that ps_j is an opposite partial state of ps_i.

The definition of consistent initial causes entails that initial causes explaining secondary symptoms only can never be included in candidate diagnoses.

Manifestations covered (explained) by a candidate diagnosis. We define the set *man* (D_i) of manifestations covered by the diagnosis D_i as the union of the manifestations covered by its initial causes IC_j, i.e.:

$$man\ (D_i) = \cup_{IC_j \in D_i} man\ (IC_j).$$

Minimal diagnosis. A minimal diagnosis is a candidate diagnosis whose initial causes *explain* all primary and secondary symptoms, where explain means that the initial causes are able to generate all the symptoms while a subset of these causes would not. A formal definition of explanation based on the set covering model can be derived from [REG 83]:

D_m is a minimal diagnosis if

$$(\Psi_P^+ \cup \Psi_S^+) \subseteq man\ (D_m)\quad and\quad \forall D_{m'} \subseteq D_m, (\Psi_P^+ \cup \Psi_S^+) \neg\subseteq man\ (D_{m'})$$

where Ψ_S^+ is the set of secondary symptoms and $D_{m'} \subseteq D_m$ means that the set of initial causes composing $D_{m'}$ is a subset of those composing D_m.

The above definition includes two parsimony criteria [PEN 86], i.e. *relevancy* (causal association among initial causes and symptoms) and *irredundancy* (no proper subset of initial causes is itself a minimal diagnosis). Another parsimony criterion has been considered in order to evaluate alternative minimal diagnosis, i.e. *minimality*: rank higher the minimal diagnoses including a lower number of initial causes, so that truth assumptions on initial causes get minimized.

Sub-optimal diagnosis. A sub-optimal diagnosis is a partial solution to the diagnostic problem as it covers only a subset of the manifested symptoms. It is defined as a candidate diagnosis whose initial causes explain at least all primary symptoms, while a subset of these causes would not:

D_{so} is a sub-optimal diagnosis if

$$\Psi_P^+ \subseteq man\ (D_{so})\quad and\quad \forall D_{so'} \subseteq D_{so}, \Psi_P^+ \neg\subseteq man\ (D_{so'})$$

Two parsimony criteria are used in order to sort sub-optimal diagnoses, i.e. a *covering* criterion on secondary symptoms and a *minimality* criterion on assumptions.

Incomplete diagnosis. An incomplete diagnosis is a partial solution to the diagnostic problem covering only a subset of primary symptoms which cannot be explained by a proper subset of its initial causes, i.e.:

D_p is an incomplete diagnosis if

$$\Psi_P^+ \cap man\ (D_p) = \Psi_{D_p} \neq \Phi\quad and\quad \forall D_{p'} \subseteq D_p, \Psi_{D_p} \neg\subseteq man\ (D_{p'})$$

Three parsimony criteria are used in order to sort incomplete diagnoses, i.e. a *covering* criterion on primary symptoms, a *minimality* criterion on initial causes and another *covering* criterion on secondary symptoms.

Starting from the above set of definitions, the rest of the chapter will be devoted to describe the reasoning process. For clarity of representation, the diagnostic reasoning assumes to work separately on subsets of the causal model and then to combine the partial results obtained. In particular, the network has been partitioned into as many subnetworks as initial causes, where each subnetwork includes all the nodes and arcs reachable from its initial cause. Under this assumption, the reasoning process can be described as follows:

1. *Analysis of symptoms*: if at least one primary symptom is present, the diagnostic algorithm is activated, else the system halts.
2. *Computation of consistent initial causes*: for each causal subnetwork including at least one primary symptom, the consistence of the associated initial cause is assessed through network navigation. If no consistent initial cause exists, the process comes to a halt and a notification informs the user that no diagnosis has been reached because of inconsistencies or incompleteness of the causal model. Otherwise proceed to step 3.
3. *Computation of candidate diagnoses*: consistent initial causes are grouped in order to build minimal, sub-optimal and incomplete diagnoses. Here a consistency check is performed to prevent conflicting truth values of partial states in candidate diagnoses.
4. *Evaluation of diagnoses*: candidate diagnoses are sorted according to the following classification: first of all minimal diagnoses, then sub-optimal diagnoses and at last incomplete diagnoses. Diagnoses belonging to the same class are ranked according to the parsimony criteria defined above and a suitable subset of them (to be defined for each specific application) is presented to the user with the causal explanation of covered symptoms and needed assumptions.

Step 2 will be further detailed in § 3.1 and an example of network navigation from DIOGENE will be reported in § 3.2.

3.1. Computation of Consistent Initial Causes

Computation of consistent initial causes is accomplished through causal network navigation. The strategy we followed for network evaluation is basically depth first with the addition of backward propagation of truth values in particular situations. The diagnostic process begins assuming the truth of the initial cause and then deduces all its consequences according to modeled causal relationships. In order to assess the consistency of an initial cause, the system analyses the accordance of the truth value of each consequent partial state with the observed manifestations.

A partial state reached by the interpretation algorithm may take one of the following values:

- True, either because it is connected to a symptom or as a consequence of back-propagation of a true value (allowed by the assumption of partial completeness of the knowledge base) or because it is an effect of a causal link. In the last case, a distinction is made as follows:
  - ⟩ the state is *deduced* true if the causal link is strong and no assumptions have already been made to reach it;
  - ⟩ otherwise, it is *assumed* true and, if the link is weak, the state is added to the already existing assumptions.
- False, either because it is connected to an unobserved manifestation or as a consequence of back-propagation of a false value (allowed by the definition of strong causal relationship).

The consistency of a partial state depends on the kind of causal relationship with the cause which has been considered and on the value of the state itself:

- When the causal relationship is strong, the state is consistent only if it is true (either deduced or assumed). If it is false, an inconsistency condition is identified and, if a strong causal path exists from a partial state with a connected symptom and the current state, the system can warn the user that an inconsistency has been detected in the model.
- When the causal relationship is weak, a partial state is consistent independently from its value. If the state is assumed true, the initial cause will be considered able to explain the symptoms following the weak link, under the assumption that the state effect actually occurs. The assumption can be removed if a back-propagation of a true or false value takes place.

In both kinds of relationship, when a state is false the analysis, for efficiency reasons, will be stopped and a false value will be back-propagated to its causes. The consistency of a network is established when no more partial states need to be visited, and no inconsistency conditions have appeared.

3.2. Example of Network Interpretation

In fig. 4 an example of navigation in a causal subnetwork is given. The initial cause *"Fouling in Steam Super Heater 2"* is recognized as consistent as follows:

1. Assuming the truth of the initial cause *"Fouling in Steam Super Heater 2"*, the strong causality relationship is followed and the partial state *"low efficiency of heat exchange in SH2"* is recognized as consistent, being connected to an unknown manifestation. Therefore a true value is assumed for the state.
2. As the context *"correct tilt angle"* is verified, the strong causality relationship is followed and the partial state *"low steam enthalpy in turbine"* is recognized as consistent, being connected to a symptom. The other strong causality relationship stemming from *"low efficiency of heat exchange in SH2"* is not followed, because the connected context is false.
3. The true value can be back-propagated because *"low efficiency of heat exchange in SH2"* is the only possible cause of *"low steam enthalpy in turbine"*, connected to a primary symptom; the assumption for *"low efficiency of heat exchange in SH2"* is consequently removed.
4. Following the weak causality relationship to *"low flue gas heat at SH2 outlet"*, the truth of the state, connected to a symptom, is recognized and the network navigation follows the weak causality relationship to *"high flue gas heat at SH1 inlet"*.
5. The state *"high flue gas heat at SH1 inlet"* is assumed as true, being connected to an unknown manifestation, and it is added to the set of assumptions for the current initial cause.
6. As *"high flue gas heat at economizer inlet"* is connected through a weak causality relationship, the falsity of the state, connected to an unverified manifestation, does not affect the consistency of the subnetwork.

7. Following the strong causality relationship to "*high steam enthalpy in SH1*", the falsity of the state, connected to an unverified manifestation, is recognized; the assumption for "*high flue gas heat at SH1 inlet*" is removed after the back-propagation of value false from "*high steam enthalpy in SH1*".

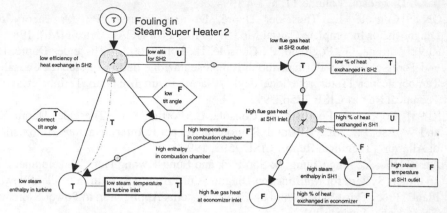

Fig. 4. An example of navigation in a causal subnetwork.

4. Conclusions

The causal formalism presented in this paper aims at representing the faulty behavioral knowledge of a physical system for the purpose of process diagnosis. The causal formalism, and the diagnostic process defined above it, have been successfully tested in DIOGENE, an application system devoted to support on-line diagnosis of steam generation process in thermal power plants. Due to its generality, we believe the approach could be adopted also for more demanding tasks, such as real-time monitoring and diagnosis or alarm handling, provided that it be significantly extended both on representation and reasoning capabilities. In particular, we identified the need of the following main extensions:

- the modeling of time delays in causal relationships, in order to further constrain the consistency evaluation of causal evolutions and to allow the performance of the diagnostic process while the effects of a malfunction are still evolving;
- the modeling of actions that operators may carry out on the physical system in order to avoid malfunction consequences, both to recognize their effects on malfunction evolutions and to use them as suggested remedial actions.

A preliminary study concerning these extensions has already been carried out in the domain of alarm handling in power plants [CRI 92] [CRI 93], but a thorough definition of an effective reasoning process on the extended models still requires further research efforts.

Acknowledgments

The work described in this paper has been funded by the Thermal Research Center (CRT) of the Italian Electricity Board (ENEL).

References

[CER 94] Cermignani, S. and Tornielli, G.: "Model-based diagnosis of continuous static systems". Annals of Mathematics and Artificial Intelligence on Model-based Diagnosis, Volume 11, n. 1-4 1994.

[CON 89] Console, L., Theseider Dupré, D. and Torasso, P.: "A Theory of Diagnosis for Incomplete Causal Models". Proc. 11th IJCAI, Detroit (Mi), 1989.

[CRI 92] Crippa, G., Pogliano, P., Console, L., Portinale, L., Theseider Dupré, D. and Torasso, P.: "Un Formalismo di Rappresentazione della Conoscenza Causale-Temporale per l'Interpretazione degli Allarmi in un Impianto Termoelettrico". Technical Report CISE 7256, 1992.

[CRI 93] Crippa, G., Pogliano, P., Console, L., Portinale, L., Theseider Dupré, D. and Torasso, P.: "Meccanismi di Ragionamento per la Interpretazione Automatica di Allarmi". Technical Report CISE 7592, 1993.

[HAK 91] Hak-Yeoung Chung, Ik-Soo Park and Sung-Kwang Hur: "Development of an Expert System for Malfunction Diagnosis of Primary System in Nuclear Power Plant". Proc. Third Symposium on Expert Systems Application to Power Systems, Tokio-Kobe, Japan, 1991.

[NEL 82] Nelson, W. R.: "REACTOR: an Expert System for Diagnosis and Treatment of Nuclear Reactor Accidents". Proc. Second International Conference on Artificial Intelligence, Los Altos, California, 1982.

[NEW 82] Newell, A.: "The Knowledge Level". Artificial Intelligence, Vol. 18, 1982, pp. 87-127.

[PAT 81] Patil, R.: "Causal Representation of Patient Illness for Electrolyte and Acid-Based Diagnosis". MIT/LCS/TR-267, Cambridge, MA, 1981.

[PEN 86] Peng, Y. and Reggia, J. A.: "Plausibility of Diagnostic Hypotheses". Proc. of National Conference on Artificial Intelligence, AAAI, 1986.

[REG 83] Reggia, J. A., Nau, D. S. and Wang, P. J.: "Diagnostic expert systems based on a set covering model". International Journal on Man-Machine Studies, Vol. 19, 1981, pp. 437-460.

[SAC 86] Sachs, P. A., Paterson, A. M. and Turner, M. H. M.: "ESCORT - An Expert System for Complex Operations in Real Time". Expert Systems, Vol. 3, No. 1, Jan 1986, pp. 22-29.

[STE 85] Steels, L. and Van de Velde, W.: "Learning in Second Generation Expert Systems". In Knowledge-based Problem Solving, Kowalik ed., Prentice Hall, 1985.

[TOR 89] Torasso, P. and Console, L.: "Diagnostic Problem Solving: Combining Heuristic Approximate and Causal Reasoning". Van Nostrand Reinhold, 1989.

[TOU 94] Tourtier, P. A. and Boyera, S.: "Validating at Early Stages With a Causal Simulation Tool". Proc. European Knowledge Acquisition Workshop, EKAW'94, Berlin, Germany, 1994.

Formalizing Reasoning About Change: A Temporal Diagnosis Approach

Johann Gamper and Wolfgang Nejdl

Universität Hannover
Institut für Rechnergestützte Wissensverarbeitung
Lange Laube 3, 30159 Hannover, Germany
{gamper,nejdl}@kbs.uni-hannover.de

Abstract. In this paper we describe a framework for reasoning about temporal explanation problems, which is based on our previous work on model-based diagnosis of dynamic systems. We use an explicit representation of qualitative temporal information which provides a simpler and more natural representation than the situation calculus. We show how to generate more specific explanations by instantiating explanations and assuming an Open World Assumption. We argue that a framework for reasoning about action should be able to deal with concurrent and durative actions and show how they can be represented in our system.

1 Introduction

Reasoning about action has been a very active topic since Hanks and McDermott showed surprising weaknesses of conventional non-monotonic reasoning formalisms to handle simple problems like the Yale Shooting Problem. The last years have seen formalizations of various complexities, which often seemed intuitive, only to be contradicted by simple extensions of the same examples they handled. It can be argued, that finally formalizations have been found for these examples, but difficulties and uncertainties remain even in the latest papers.

Different styles of reasoning can be distinguished. Given some observations about an initial situation, what might be true in some later situation? This style of forward reasoning in time is called *temporal prediction*. The opposite direction is reasoning backward in time and is called *temporal explanation*. Given some observation we are interested in what happened in previous situations.

In this paper, which extends our work in [5], we focus on the problem of temporal explanation in reasoning about action examples, and discuss an approach strongly related to our recent formalism for doing temporal diagnosis in a model-based reasoning system [12]. In particular, we tackle the following issues: what do we want to explain, how do we want it to be explained (what are the abducibles), how can we formalize persistence of fluents, how can we generate more specific explanations, and how can we represent concurrent actions. Our formalism is based on a interval-based temporal logic which we argue is a more suitable representation than conventional situation calculus based formalisms.

2 Introductory Example

One of the most important representational frameworks for reasoning about action and change is the *Situation Calculus* [11]. A situation s is considered to represent a snapshot of the world. The function $Result(a, s)$ represents the situation resulting from performing action a in situation s. The predicate $Holds(p, s)$ asserts that fluent (property) p holds in situation s.

Example 1 (The Stolen Car Problem). The most famous temporal explanation problem is Kautz's Stolen Car Problem (SCP) [7]. In the initial situation, $S0$, a car is not stolen. After waiting two times, $S2$, the car is stolen. What happened?

$$\neg Holds(Stolen, S0), \tag{1}$$

$$S2 = Result(Wait, Result(Wait, S0)), \tag{2}$$

$$Holds(Stolen, S2) \tag{3}$$

The intended model is that the car has been stolen during either of the two waiting phases, there is no reason to prefer one over the other. □

Recently, Shanahan [13] described an interesting approach to formalize temporal explanation within the situation calculus using the SCP as an example. The key point in Shanahan's work is that the axioms (1), (2) and (3) do not constitute a good representation for the SCP. In particular, axiom (2) states that $S2$ is the situation after waiting two times in $S0$, nothing else. As waiting actions have no effects and we assume persistence of properties, the car should still be parked in $S2$ contradicting the observation (axiom 3). The point is that we do not know exactly what actions occured between $S0$ and $S2$. Shanahan's alternative representation states only that $S2$ follows $S0$ and that there must be a sequence of actions leading from $S0$ to $S2$. The task is to find this sequence of actions, which represents an explanation for the observation in $S2$. Shanahan studied a deductive and an abductive approach for temporal explanation using the standard and the alternative representation.

The situation calculus is a simple framework and rather expressive. However, several problems and counterexamples have been identified. The aim of this paper is to show how temporal explanation problems can be formalized in our model-based diagnosis framework for dynamic systems and that this formalization yields clearer and more intuitive results. We will use the SCP and the extensions introduced in [13] as examples throughout the paper.

3 The Basic Temporal Diagnosis Approach

In this section we develop the basic framework for temporal explanation problems by extending our temporal diagnosis approach [12], which is based on explicit representation of qualitative temporal information.

Basic relation	Inverse relation	Meaning
I_1 before I_2	I_2 after I_1	
I_1 meets I_2	I_2 met I_1	
I_1 overlaps I_2	I_2 overlapped I_1	
I_1 starts I_2	I_2 started I_1	
I_1 during I_2	I_2 contains I_1	
I_1 finishes I_2	I_2 finished I_1	
I_1 equal I_2	I_2 equal I_1	

Table 1. The 13 basic relations that hold between two intervals.

3.1 Temporal Framework

We use a subset of the interval-based temporal logic described by Allen and Hayes in [1]. The basic temporal primitives are *time intervals* with a positive duration. *Time points* are introduced as unique meeting places of intervals having zero duration. Based on these primitives the following mutually exclusive *qualitative temporal relations* are defined: 13 relations between two intervals (see table 1), 5 relations between a point (an interval) and an interval (a point), {*before, starts, during, finishes, after*} ({*before, finished, contains, started, after*}) , and 3 relations between two points, {*before, equal, after*}. Indefinite knowledge is expressed as disjunction of basic relations.

Properties are used to denote that something is true over a time period. We do not allow for properties to hold at time points. An important characteristic of properties is homogeneity: a homogeneous property holds during a time interval I iff it holds during each subinterval of I. Intuitively, the notion of properties captures the static behavior of the world.

Events are classified as durative and instantaneous. *Durative* events occur during time intervals and are intended to take time. *Instantaneous* events occur at time points and are durationless. Intuitively, they can be considered as causing transitions of properties, and thus represent the dynamic behavior of the world. The most important type of events in this paper are actions.

3.2 Formalizing the Domain Theory

We use a sorted First Order Language and a Prolog-like notation: Variables begin with an upper case letter, constants and predicates with a lower case letter. Unless stated otherwise, time intervals are denoted by I (i) (possibly indexed), time points by P (p) (possibly indexed). Qualitative temporal relations are represented by 2-ary predicates with the obvious meaning.

Definition 1. An *Action Model* for an action α is defined as a first order formula, $\alpha \wedge \beta \rightarrow \gamma$, where β represents the preconditions and γ the effect of α.

To describe the *temporal behavior* of an action, both preconditions β and the effect γ may contain qualitative temporal relations.

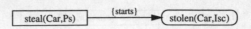

Fig. 1. Temporal behavior of the steal action.

Example 2. Following Shanahan's alternative representation of the SCP we have an action *steal* (axiom (AR5) in [13]) represented by the action model

$$\forall Car \forall P_s \exists I_{sc}\ steal(Car, P_s) \rightarrow stolen(Car, I_{sc}) \land starts(P_s, I_{sc})$$

Stealing a car *Car* at time point P_s starts an interval, I_s, during which the car is stolen. This action has no preconditions. □

We use a graphical representation for the temporal behavior of an action model. The nodes represent the temporal extent of the actions and properties. The arcs are labeled with the qualitative temporal relation between them and are denoted as a set of basic relations. The temporal behavior of the steal action is shown in figure 1. For clarity, the nodes are denoted by the whole action (property) expression rather than by the corresponding temporal extent, rectangular boxes represent time points, and rounded boxes represent time intervals. We follow this convention through the rest of the paper.

The steal action in the above example is an instantaneous action with an immediate effect. In general, we allow for durative actions as well as more complex, possibly indefinite temporal relationships between the action and its effects. Sometimes the effect of an action is delayed which is easily represented in our framework, e.g. *overlaps*. The representation of delayed effects in the situation calculus is not straightforward, as it requires the representation of time and the assumption of an additional action taking place after the real action which would lead to the situation where the effect holds [6]. In the event calculus [8] the effects of events take place immediately corresponding to the *starts*-relation.

3.3 Observations and Abstract Observations

Observations describe what we know about the actual behavior of the world and are usually given in terms of properties at time points. This is difficult to imagine from a cognitive point of view, as time points are durationless entities. A more intuitive interpretation of observations in dynamic systems is to interpret them over time periods "around" the observation time point. This is captured by the concept of an abstract observation, which represents the assumption that there exists a time interval during which a property holds. Usually, we neither determine exactly the extent of an abstract observation nor its location on the real time line, rather we only constrain it using qualitative temporal relations.

Definition 2. An *Abstract Observation* is defined as a formula $\exists I\ o(I) \land \rho(I)$, where o is a predicate which states that a property holds during a time interval I, and the *(temporal) anchor* ρ is a conjunction of qualitative temporal relations constraining I relative to the real time line and/or other abstract observations.

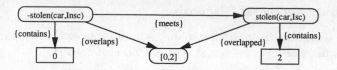

Fig. 2. Abstract observations in the SCP.

Example 3. The two observations, the car is not stolen in $S0$ (axiom (1)) and the car is stolen in $S2$ (axiom (3)), are represented by the abstract observations $\exists I_{nsc} \neg stolen(car, I_{nsc}) \wedge contains(I_{nsc}, 0)$ and $\exists I_{sc} stolen(car, I_{sc}) \wedge contains(I_{sc}, 2)$, stating that the time period over which the car is not stolen (stolen) contains time 0 (2). We represent time by the real numbers and assume the ordering axioms of real numbers. This avoids to state explicitly that $S2$ follows $S0$, as through axiom (2), or in [13] through axiom (AR3). $\square$

Exclusiveness of abstract observations. The temporal constraints in the above example do not prevent I_{nsc} from including time 2, which contradicts the second observation. From the homogeneity assumption of properties it follows that two intervals I_1 and I_2 during which a property and its negation hold are exclusive. This can be expressed as $before(I_1, I_2) \vee meets(I_1, I_2) \vee met(I_1, I_2) \vee after(I_1, I_2)$. In particular, in the above example we get $before(I_{nsc}, I_{sc}) \vee meets(I_{nsc}, I_{sc})$.

Maximality of abstract observations. An abstract observation is *maximal* iff it persists as long as possible in both direction of time, into the past and the future. From this assumption follows that consecutive maximal abstract observations which represent that a property holds and that it does not hold, are constrained by the relation *meets*. Maximal abstract observations capture the persistence assumption of properties: properties persist unless there is some reason to assume otherwise. We make this assumption throughout most of the paper. This concept of maximal abstract observations is different from chronological minimization [14], which assumes persistence of properties only forward in time, and in the SCP would conclude that the car has been stolen during the second waiting action.

Example 4. Given that we use homogeneous properties and maximal abstract observations, we get the final set of abstract observations in the SCP

$$AOBS = \{ \exists I_{nsc} \neg stolen(car, I_{nsc}) \wedge contains(I_{nsc}, 0) \wedge meets(I_{nsc}, I_{sc}),$$
$$\exists I_{sc} stolen(car, I_{sc}) \wedge contains(I_{sc}, 2) \wedge met(I_{sc}, I_{nsc}) \}$$

A graphical representation of $AOBS$ is shown in figure 2. To make the temporal relationships clearer we added the interval $[0, 2]$. $\square$

The concept of abstract observations allows also to represent exact knowledge about the temporal extent of properties. For instance, we represent the fact that property f holds during the time interval $[0, 2]$ as $\exists I f(I) \wedge equal(I, [0, 2])$.

3.4   Abstract Temporal Diagnosis

The aim of temporal diagnostic reasoning is to find an explanation in terms of abducible expressions for the actual abstract observations [12].

Abducible Expressions. Intuitively, an abducible expression is one for which no further explanation can be generated. This is the case for the truth-value *true*, as well as for all expressions occuring only on the left-hand side of action models, in particular actions itself. To get a temporal diagnosis additionally the qualitative temporal relations must be abducible even if they appear also in the right-hand side of action models. Later we will discuss the need for additional abducible expressions if one assumes an Open World Assumption.

Similar to [4] we use a combination of abductive and consistency-based diagnosis: a diagnosis must abductively explain a "subset" of abstract observations, $AOBS^+$, while being consistent with the set of all abstract observations, $AOBS$.

Definition 3. A set D of abducible expressions is an *Abstract Temporal Diagnosis* for a theory T and a set of abstract observations $AOBS$ iff

- D covers $AOBS^+$, i.e. $T \cup D \models AOBS^+$.
- D is consistent with $AOBS$, i.e. $T \cup D \cup AOBS$ is consistent.

The set $AOBS^+$ consists basically of the *abnormal* abstract observations. Assuming persistence of properties, each change of a property without known cause is abnormal. In general we cannot entail the temporal extent of abstract observations and their temporal location on the real time line. We define $AOBS^+$ to consist of the abnormal abstract observations without their temporal anchors relative to the real time line and relative to normal abstract observations. This gives an explicit notion about what to include in $AOBS^+$, in contrast to the vague characterization in [13].

The basic procedure to compute an abstract temporal diagnosis is a backward-chaining procedure. Starting from the initial set $AOBS^+$ we choose an action model which predicts a non-empty set of abstract observations in $AOBS^+$ not yet explained. In first order logic we would unify the explained observations with the effects predicted by the chosen action model. In our temporal logic, we instead cover them by adding an equal relationship between the explained observations and the predicted effects, which leads to an instantiation of variables and connects the temporal networks of the chosen action model with $AOBS^+$. The left-hand side of the instantiated action model represents the abductive hypothesis. The connection of networks leads to additional temporal relationships between action model, abstract observations and hypothesis. Similar to first order logic, where the unified literals are dropped, we can also drop the covered literals and the corresponding temporal relations, though we need additional assumptions to avoid losing information in this step. Specifically, we have to assume maximal persistence of properties[1]. An action with preconditions can

---

[1] This is similar to the assumption of maximal abstract observations.

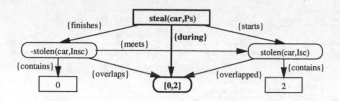

Fig. 3. Explanation (in boldface) and $AOBS$ in the SCP.

give rise to new abnormal property changes, in which case we extend $AOBS^+$ accordingly (see example 5). If all abstract observations in $AOBS^+$ are covered, the conjunction of the generated hypotheses represents an abstract temporal diagnosis.

Example 5. The theory T for the SCP contains the action model for steal, $\forall Car \forall P_s \exists I_{sc}\ steal(Car, P_s) \rightarrow stolen(Car, I_{sc}) \wedge starts(P_s, I_{sc})$. The set of abstract observations, $AOBS$, is calculated as in example 4. Initially the car is not stolen and due to the persistence assumption we should be able to conclude that it is still not stolen at time 2. However, we observe the contrary, indicating an abnormal property change which needs an abductive explanation, so $AOBS^+ = \{\exists I_{sc}\ stolen(car, I_{sc})\}^2$. We cover this abstract observation with the effect $stolen(Car, I_{sc})$ of the steal action, which instantiates the variable Car to car and unifies the interval variables from action model and observation giving $stolen(car, I_{sc})$. In the consistency based step, which includes the temporal anchors of $AOBS$, we then get the additional temporal relation $during(P_s, [0, 2])$. We can now drop $stolen(car, I_{sc})$. All abstract observations in $AOBS^+$ are covered and we get the abstract temporal diagnosis (see figure 3)

$$\exists P_s\ steal(car, P_s) \wedge during(P_s, [0, 2])$$

This is the intended explanation and corresponds to Shanahan's one. □

Even if the above explanation is the intended one and it is not very probable that the car has been brought back and stolen again, we should at least not be forced to exclude it. If we do not use maximal abstract observations, i.e. constrain the two abstract observations by *before* ∨ *meets* instead of *meets*, we can consistently assume several steal actions between time 0 and 2. To explain the abstract observations abductively one steal action still suffices.

4 Extending the Basic Approach

Additional problems in reasoning about action and change arise, when preconditions for actions are introduced. Following Shanahan [13] we extend the SCP.

---

² $meets(I_{nsc}, I_{sc})$ is a relation to a normal abstract observation, $overlapped(I_{sc}, [0, 2])$ is a relation to the real time line. Both of them are excluded from $AOBS^+$.

342

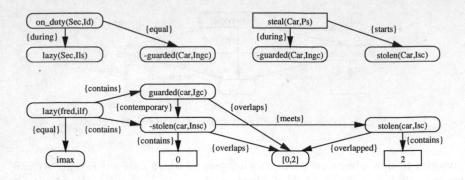

Fig. 4. Action models and abstract observations in the extended SCP.

Example 6 (Axioms AR7 through AR10 in [13]). In order for a steal action to be successful, the car must be unguarded. This action has a precondition and is represented by the action model $\forall Car \forall P_s \forall I_{ngc} \exists I_{sc}\, steal(Car, P_s) \wedge \neg guarded(Car, I_{ngc}) \wedge during(P_s, I_{ngc}) \rightarrow stolen(Car, I_{sc}) \wedge starts(P_s, I_{sc})$. A second action is introduced for a security guard to be on duty. If a lazy security guard comes on duty, he immediately falls asleep, and the car will be unguarded for the time he is on duty. Initially the car is guarded, and Fred is known to be a lazy security guard. The actions and the abstract observations of the extended SCP are shown in figure 4 (*contemporary* is an abbreviation for the disjunction of the basic relations *overlaps*, *starts*, *during*, *finishes*, *equal* and their inverses). Properties which are always true, such as Fred being lazy, are represented by abstract observations, whose temporal extent is equal to a maximal interval i_{max}.

Turning to the generation of an explanation, we start with the same set $AOBS^+$ as before and hypothesize $\exists I_{ngc} \exists P_s \neg guarded(car, I_{ngc}) \wedge steal(car, P_s) \wedge during(P_s, I_{ngc})$. Testing consistency with $AOBS$ yields $during(P_s, [0, 2])$ and $during(I_{ngc}, [0, 2]) \vee finishes(I_{ngc}, [0, 2]) \vee overlapped(I_{ngc}, [0, 2])$. This hypothesis contains the non-abducible $\neg guarded(car, I_{ngc})$ representing an abnormal property change violating the persistence assumption. We add $\exists I_{ngc} \neg guarded(car, I_{ngc})$ to $AOBS^+$ and continue the diagnostic process. The action *on_duty* predicts the desired property, and we cover the effect $\neg guarded(Car, I_{ngc})$. From this and the *equal*-relation in the action model we get $contains(I_d, P_s)$, which we include in the final explanation, and drop $\neg guarded(Car, I_{ngc})$ and the corresponding temporal relationships

$$D = \exists Sec \exists I_d \exists I_{ls} \exists P_s\, on\_duty(Sec, I_d) \wedge lazy(Sec, I_{ls}) \wedge steal(car, P_s) \wedge$$
$$during(I_d, I_{ls}) \wedge contains(I_d, P_s)$$

— while a lazy security was on duty the car has been stolen. In this and the following examples we leave out constraints stating that all this happens between time 0 and 2. This explanation corresponds to Shanahan's one in his deductive approach. □

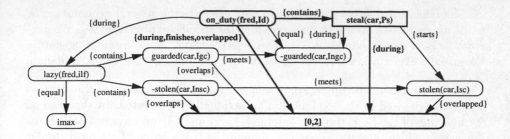

Fig. 5. Explanation D_1 — while Fred was on duty the car has been stolen.

4.1 Specifying Explanations

The explanation in the last example is not satisfactory as it does not exploit the fact that Fred is a lazy security guard, and it contains the non-abducible expression $lazy(Sec, I_{ls})$.

Instantiating Explanations. As we know that Fred is a lazy security guard, we want to specify the explanation and instantiate the variable Sec to *fred*. To formalize this we represent a fact f as a formula $true \rightarrow f$, and extend the abduction policy by instantiating variables and eliminating non-abducibles in an explanation by using known facts, i.e. abstract observations not in $AOBS^+$.

Example 7. Fred is a lazy security guard is represented as $true \rightarrow lazy(fred, i_{lf})$ $\wedge\ equal(i_{lf}, i_{max})$. Using this rule we instantiate the variable Sec in D to *fred*, eliminate the non-abducible $lazy(Sec, I_{ls})$ and get the first intended explanation

$$D_1 = \exists I_d \exists P_s\ on\_duty(fred, I_d) \wedge steal(car, P_s) \wedge contains(I_d, P_s)$$

— while Fred was on duty the car has been stolen (see also figure 5) □

Open World Assumption. The Open World Assumption (OWA) admits the existence of objects not currently known. This allows us to generate explanations on the existence assumption of such objects rather than on known facts. Using the OWA we must extend the set of abducible expressions accordingly.

Example 8. We hypothesize the existence of a lazy security guard other than Fred by adding the rule $\exists Sec \exists I_{ls}\ lazy(Sec, I_{ls}) \wedge Sec \neq fred \rightarrow lazy(Sec, I_{ls})$ to the theory. We add the left-hand side of this rule to the set of abducible expressions and generate the second intended explanation

$$D_2 = \exists Sec \exists I_d \exists I_{ls} \exists P_s\ on\_duty(Sec, I_d) \wedge lazy(Sec, I_{ls}) \wedge Sec \neq fred\ \wedge$$
$$steal(car, P_s) \wedge during(I_d, I_{ls}) \wedge contains(I_d, P_s)$$

— while a lazy security guard other than Fred was on duty the car has been stolen. □

Shanahan's deductive approach can only generate the general explanation D, while his abductive approach only provides the specific explanation D_1. We generate in each case explanation D_1. If we use the OWA we additionally generate the specific explanation D_2. Hence, we always are more specific than Shanahan.

Unknown Actions. One might argue that our approach just encodes the solution as all actions used in the explanation are explicitly represented. In the original formulation of the SCP through axioms (1), (2) and (3) we have only the waiting action which, however, does not change the truth value of stolen. In order to get a model we have to introduce unknown changes which in [9] are called miracles. While it is arguable, if we should include the steal action in our theory or not, miracles seem to be too abstract. We know at least, that some action has taken place which results in our car to be stolen, and we should include this knowledge in our theory. We exploit once again the OWA and hypothesize the existence of an unknown action. We use a slightly modified representation of actions, and represent the steal action as $\forall Car \forall P_s \exists I_{sc}\ action(steal, Car, P_s)$ $\rightarrow stolen(Car, I_{sc}) \land starts(P_s, I_{sc})$. Then the unknown action U is represented as $\forall Car \forall P_u \exists I_{sc} \exists U\ action(U, Car, P_u) \land U \neq steal \rightarrow stolen(Car, I_{sc})$ $\land starts(P_u, I_{sc})$ and leads to an additional explanation — an unknown action other than the steal action caused the car to be stolen. If we do not use the steal action at all we remove the precondition $U \neq steal$, and we get exactly one explanation — an unknown action caused the car to be stolen.

4.2 Concurrent and Durative Actions

Shanahan's approach is based on the observation that $S2$ cannot be the situation from just waiting two times in $S0$. He goes on to assume a sequence of actions between $S0$ and $S2$, and only states that $S2$ follows $S0$. Now he cannot express anymore that we already know an action sequence characterizing the interval between $S0$ and $S2$ (while not sufficient to explain the changed properties).

Example 9. We extend the story again. The owner of the car, after parking the car at time 0, goes to lunch. He comes back at time 2 and the car is stolen. The new action *lunch* is durative and takes place from time 0 to time 2, i.e. $\exists I_{lo}\ lunch(owner, I_{lo}) \land equal(I_{lo}, [0, 2])$. As going to lunch hardly affects the properties used so far, this is consistent with all our explanations and we can conclude, for example, that the theft of his car occured during lunch. □

Now Shanahan can assume some other action between $S0$ and $S2$ without affecting the explanation, which however has to be instantaneous and not concurrent with another action. Because of this restriction caused by the situation calculus, Shanahan has to say that the owner went to lunch between $S0$ and $S2$, either before or after the steal action. This is one of the major drawbacks of the situation calculus that concurrent actions as well as durative actions cannot be represented without introducing major extensions [6, 10] leading to quite complex formalisms. Aside from really concurrent actions we can represent various other complex temporal relationships between actions in a very natural fashion.

5 Discussion

Even if the situation calculus is rather simple and expressive, the underlying ontology is problematic for many problems. The notion of a situation representing an instantaneous snapshots of the world, which is originally defined as a sequence of actions, has been criticized by several authors. Shanahan [13] proposed an alternative representation for temporal explanation within the situation calculus and studied in detail a deductive and an abductive approach. Even if his alternative representation improves the standard approach, we have shown that our temporal diagnosis approach leads to better results. In particular, by instantiating explanations and allowing to use an Open World Assumption we can always give more specific explanations. Moreover, we have shown the need for concurrent and durative actions, which cannot be represented in the situation calculus without major extensions [6].

An alternative framework to deal with action and change is the event calculus [8]. The basic primitives are events which start or finish a time period, while in our framework the primitives are time intervals and time points derived from intervals [1]. In the event calculus properties persist until they are clipped by some contradicting event. This behavior is realized in our approach by the concept of maximal abstract observations. If we do not use maximal abstract observations, properties can cease to hold earlier, for example depending on quantitative temporal information. While we allow arbitrarily complex temporal relationships between actions and their effects, events in the event calculus have immediate effects corresponding to the *meets*-relation in our framework.

6 Conclusion

In this paper we propose a framework for temporal explanation based on our model-based temporal diagnosis approach. We focus mainly on the expressive power of our framework and on the natural and easy representation of temporal knowledge in reasoning about change. We use an explicit representation of qualitative temporal relations between properties holding during time intervals and actions occuring at time points or during time intervals. This provides a powerful language for modeling actions with preconditions and effects. The concept of maximal abstract observations capture the persistence assumption of properties and can easily be extended to various forms of persistence assumptions. Temporal explanations are generated by using abduction and testing additional consistency constraints. We give a concise characterization of what needs to be explained and what can be used in an explanation. We show how our framework deals with an open world assumption and how this leads to additional, more specific explanations. Finally, we argue that concurrent and durative actions are useful in reasoning about action and change, and can be handled in a very natural way in our framework.

Current and future work include an exact formalization of our approach in First Order Logic as well as detailed complexity analysis and a detailed comparison to abductive reasoning in first order logic, such as worked out for example in

[3, 2]. We are also investigating which kind of temporal knowledge is required to abductively explain various temporal relations. Another important topic is how to exploit temporal knowledge in order to reduce the computational complexity inherently in abductive reasoning. Finally we consider various forms of persistence assumptions for different properties, such as adding quantitative temporal information.

References

1. James F. Allen and Patrick J. Hayes. Moments and points in an interval-based temporal logic. *Computational Intelligence*, 5:225–238, 1989.
2. Tom Bylander, Dean Allemang, Michael C. Tanner, and John R. Josephson. The computational complexity of abduction. *Artificial Intelligence*, 49:25–60, 1991.
3. Luca Console, Daniele Theseider Dupré, and Pietro Torasso. On the relationship between abduction and deduction. *Journal of Logic and Computation*, 1(5):661–690, 1991.
4. Luca Console and Pietro Torasso. A spectrum of logical definitions of model-based diagnosis. *Computational Intelligence*, 7(3):133–141, 1991.
5. Johann Gamper and Wolfgang Nejdl. Formalizing reasoning about change: A temporal diagnosis approach. In *Proceedings of the 2nd Dutch/German Workshop on Non-Monotonic Reasoning*, pages 60–66, Utrecht, The Netherlands, March 1995.
6. M. Gelfond, V. Lifschitz, and A. Rabinov. What are the limitations of the situation calculus? In R. Boyer, editor, *Automated Reasoning: essays in honor of Woods Bledsoe*, pages 167–179. Kluwer Academic, 1991.
7. Henry A. Kautz. The logic of persistence. In *Proceedings of the National Conference on Artificial Intelligence (AAAI)*, pages 401–405, Philadelphia, Pennsylvania, 1986. Morgan Kaufmann Publishers, Inc.
8. Robert Kowalski and Marek Sergot. A logic-based calculus of events. *New Generation Computing*, 4(1):67–95, 1986.
9. Vladimir Lifschitz and Arkady Rabinov. Miracles in formal theories of action. *Artificial Intelligence*, 38(2):225–237, March 1989.
10. Fangzhen Lin and Yoav Shoham. Concurrent actions in the situation calculus. In *Proceedings of the National Conference on Artificial Intelligence (AAAI)*, pages 590–595, San Jose, California, July 1992. MIT Press.
11. J. McCarthy and P. J. Hayes. Some philosophical problems from the standpoint of artificial intelligence. *Machine Intelligence*, 4, 1969.
12. Wolfgang Nejdl and Johann Gamper. Harnessing the power of temporal abstractions in modelbased diagnosis of dynamic systems. In *Proceedings of the 11th European Conference on Artificial Intelligence*, pages 667–671, Amsterdam, The Netherlands, August 1994. John Wiley & Sons.
13. Murray Shanahan. Explanation in the situation calculus. In *Proceedings of the International Joint Conference on Artificial Intelligence*, pages 160–165, Chambéry, France, August 1993. Morgan Kaufmann Publishers, Inc.
14. Yoav Shoham. Chronological ignorance: Experiments in nonmonotonic temporal reasoning. *Artificial Intelligence*, 36:279–331, 1988.

Preventive Diagnosis: Definition and Logical Model

Giovanni Guida and Marina Zanella
Dipartimento di Elettronica per l'Automazione - Via Branze, 38
Università degli Studi di Brescia, I-25123 Brescia, Italy

Abstract

Preventive diagnosis is aimed at foreseeing likely future faults in a physical system before they actually occur. Although this task is extremely important in several practical application domains, there is currently no general theory of preventive diagnosis. This paper is an attempt to set up a foundation of such a theory. First, a definition of preventive diagnosis is proposed, and an abstract model that contains the main assumptions underlying this concept is developed. Later, a logical model of the preventive diagnosis task which outlines a problem-solving process, called Check-up And Foresee, is described. Attention is then focused on the appropriateness of the knowledge-based technology as a way for implementing the Check-up And Foresee approach. Finally, a high-level analysis of the fundamental knowledge sources involved in the task of preventive diagnosis is performed.

1 Defining Preventive Diagnosis

Preventive diagnosis is a research topic that, unlike symptomatic diagnosis [Reiter 1987] and operator diagnosis [Chittaro et al. 1993], has not been tackled yet by the AI community. All diagnostic tasks deal with *physical systems*, i.e. systems submitted to physical laws: they may be either engineering artifacts or natural systems.

Reference variables are the measurable variables which describe the system operation at a given level of abstraction and detail.

Operational conditions gathers all the conditions that, applied from the outside, affect the system operation, that is:

– *input variables*, which are the variables the system manipulates in order to perform its function (and achieve the goals it was designed for); their set is disjoint from that of reference variables;

– *system settings*, which are system attributes whose values can be set by the user/operator (for instance, by choosing the position of a switch);

– *environmental conditions*, which are the conditions of the surrounding environment.

Operational requirements specify the admissible ranges of input variables, system settings, and environmental conditions, along with the acceptable combinations of all the three classes of values. They enable to distinguish all the physically possible operational conditions into *correct operational conditions* and *incorrect operational conditions*, depending on whether the conditions comply with the operational requirements or not.

Technical requirements specify the constraints to be fulfilled in order not to overcome the constructive limits of the system during its operation. They typically involve further variables besides operational conditions. For instance, a technical requirement (which involves time as an extra variable) may state that a correct operational condition can be applied uninterruptedly to the physical system only for a limited time interval, lest the system may be irreversibly damaged.

Given a physical system, each *operating mode* specifies the values of reference variables corresponding to stated values of operational conditions when the health state of the system is perfect. *Normal operating modes* and *abnormal operating modes* specify the values of reference variables corresponding to given correct and incorrect operational conditions, respectively.

The *actual operating mode* exhibited by the physical system at a given instant is described by the values of the operational conditions applied to the system at that instant, and by the actual values of reference variables as they are measured at the same instant. At a precise instant *the physical system is well-functioning* if its actual operating mode is a normal operating mode, otherwise *the physical system is ill-functioning*.

Given an ill-functioning physical system, *operator diagnosis* is the task of finding out possible incorrect operational conditions, and *symptomatic diagnosis* is the task of identifying possible *faults*, i.e. changes occurred in the structure of the system and/or in its internal physical-chemical composition.

Given a well-functioning physical system, *preventive diagnosis (PD)* is the task of foreseeing the occurrence of possible faults within the system itself in a given time interval.

2 An Abstract Model of Physical Systems

Further concepts as to physical systems and their evolution over time are introduced in this section.

2.1 The Wear State of a Physical System

We call *wear state* of a physical system at a certain time instant the values of the totality of its (structural, physical, chemical) properties at that instant. The wear state reflects the internal situation of the physical system, which may be either faulty or not. The wear state at instant t is represented as WS(t).

In the course of its active life, the system incessantly passes from one current wear state to another. At any moment, there are several possible next states and, therefore, several potential transitions: each sample system has its own evolution path.

2.2 The History of a Physical System

The record of 1) normal operation, 2) abnormal operation, 3) accidents, 4) repair and maintenance actions, in a time interval ranging from t_1 to t_2 is called *system history* in the given interval, and is represented as $H[t_1,t_2]$.

The separate effects on the wear and tear of the system produced by each one of the four kinds of causes above are called 1) aging, 2) stress, 3) shocks, and 4) reparations, respectively. *Aging* collectively represents the effects of age, together with the effects of the total amount of working hours in normal operating modes accomplished by the system. *Stress* is the effect of working in abnormal operating modes and/or in violation of the technical requirements of the system. *Shocks* are the consequences of accidental (thermal, mechanical, electrical, ..) events occurred to the system. *Reparations* represent the effects of fixing or replacing actions and/or of invasive diagnostic activities.

2.3 Basic Assumptions

The abstract model is completed by two assumptions as to the natural evolution of physical systems:

Assumption N. 1: $\{WS(t_k), H[t_k, t_{k+1}]\}$ *causes_1* $WS(t_{k+1})$,

Assumption N. 2: $\{WS(t_k), H[t_k, t_{k+1}]\}$ *causes_2* faults$[t_k, t_{k+1}]$,

where

• faults$[t_k, t_{k+1}]$ represents the set of all the faults that occur, instant by instant, in the interval $[t_k, t_{k+1}]$. If a fault that occurs in interval $[t_k, t_{k+1}]$ terminates within the same interval, both the instant when it begins and the instant when it comes to an end are specified;

• *causes_1* and *causes_2* are two distinct binary relations, dependent on the particular physical system at hand, such that X *causes_1/2* Y denotes the existence of a causal link between X and Y, where X is a cause and Y an effect. Relations *causes_1* and *causes_2* embody all the rules that, in the natural life of the physical system, preside over the evolution of the wear state and the generation of faults, respectively.

The above axiomatic assumptions mean that, given a physical system and a generic time interval, the faults that occurred or will occur to the physical system in this interval and its final wear state are both caused by the initial wear state along with the history of the system throughout the interval.

3 A Logical Model of the Preventive Diagnosis Task

3.1 Check-up And Foresee: a Decomposition Approach to Preventive Diagnosis

A valid instance of Assumption N. 2 is the following

$\{WS(t_1), H[t_1, t_2]\}$ *causes_2* faults$[t_1, t_2]$,

where t_1 is the current instant and t_2 is a future instant. This instance shows that the occurrence of faults within a physical system in the next future (i.e. from the current instant t_1 till instant t_2) is affected by the current wear state - $WS(t_1)$ - and by the history of the system in the considered interval - $H[t_1, t_2]$. Then, to determine future faults, a causal relation which mimics *causes_2* can be exploited; this implies that the past history has to be recorded and the current wear state has to be evaluated. On the basis of the previous instance of Assumption N. 2, we have decomposed the problem of PD into two subproblems, computing the wear state and foreseeing system faults, which are tackled by two distinct sequential phases of a problem-solving process, called *Check-up And Foresee*.

3.2 The Check-up Phase

The first phase of the Check-up And Foresee process, namely Check-up, is aimed at computing the wear state of the physical system at hand at the current instant. The concept of wear state given in the abstract model is here restricted to a bound set of properties which are meaningful for the system at hand at the selected level of abstraction and detail, so that to make the wear state computable. The Check-up phase is in turn split into two distinct steps, namely assigning the values of variables and estimating the wear state.

Estimating the Wear State

By instancing Assumption N. 1 so that to have the current wear state on the RHS, we obtain:

$\{WS(t_0), H[t_0, t_1]\}$ *causes_1* $WS(t_1)$,

where t_1 is the current instant and t_0 is a generic past instant.

To estimate the current wear state of a given physical system, a relation which mimics as best as possible the relation *causes_1* which exists in nature can be used. Of course,

350

it is very difficult to build a good computable relation *causes_1*. In fact, it requires to know specifically what are aging, stress, shocks and reparations for the system of interest and what are the rules for accurately combining them into one resulting state, $WS(t_1)$, taking into account an initial wear state, $WS(t_0)$, and the temporal sequence according to which normal operation, abnormal operation, accidents, repair and maintenance actions occurred in interval $[t_0,t_1]$.

The use of the above expression for computing the wear state recursively requires that the result of the computation of a previous wear state is available. Even if every newly computed wear state is saved, as we assume, at the end of the recursive chain, one computation at least of an early wear state is needed. Therefore, an additional method for estimating the wear state is necessary all the same: a cognitively plausible method is described below, after some more concepts about physical systems are introduced. According to the logical model of PD we are envisaging, this method has to be used also for corroborating the results produced by *causes_1*.

First of all, a further set of variables, called *state variables*, is introduced. They are physical variables, disjoint from reference variables, whose values (measurable or not) are considered relevant in order to define and assess the wear state of the physical system. Roughly speaking, they are the cues of the wear state of the system, useful for getting an insight into its health, much as the results of clinical tests are useful to the physician in order to assess the health of a patient.

Given a physical system, each *state mode* represents the values of state variables under assigned values of operational conditions when the health state of the system is perfect. *Normal state modes* and *abnormal state modes* describe the expected values of state variables corresponding to correct and incorrect operational conditions, respectively.

The *actual state mode* exhibited by the system at a certain time instant is described by the values of the operational conditions applied to the system at that instant, and by the values of state variables as they are measured or estimated at the same instant.

Coming back to the additional method for computing the wear state, it is expressed by means of the following equality:
$$WS(t_1) = E(RVact(t_1), RVnorm(t_1), SVact(t_1), SVnorm(t_1)),$$
where
- E is a multi-dimensional function dependent on the particular physical system at hand;
- RVact(t1) are the values of reference variables (one value for each variable), as they are measured at instant t1;
- RVnorm(t1) are the values of reference variables defined by normal operating modes under the operational conditions holding at instant t1; normal operating modes usually do not impose a single fixed value on each reference variable;
- SVact(t1) are the actual values of state variables at instant t1;
- SVnorm(t1) are the values of state variables defined by normal state modes under the operational conditions holding at instant t1; normal state modes usually do not impose a single fixed value on each state variable.

Of course, it is very difficult to build a good computable function E: it needs being able, first, of defining a multi-dimensional space for wear states, and, second, of computing the value of each dimension based on the actual and normal values of both reference and state variables.

Assigning the Values of Variables

In order to compute the wear state of a physical system by means of function E, it is necessary that the actual values of both reference and state variables are available. Reference variables are all measurable while state variables are partly measurable and partly non-measurable. In order to estimate the values of the non-measurable state variables it is necessary to use one or more available statistical/deterministic models of the system itself. These models may be generic (i.e. describing the whole class of physical systems the system of interest belongs to) and/or specific (i.e. describing the single system under analysis).

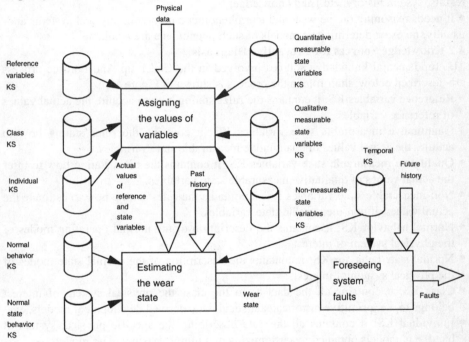

Figure 1

3.3 The Foresee Phase

As we said in section 3.1, to foresee the possible faults that will occur to the physical system in the next future, we refer to the following instance of Assumption N. 2:

$$\{WS(t_1), H[t_1,t_2]\} \; causes\_2 \; faults[t_1,t_2].$$

A relation which mimics as best as possible the relation *causes_2* existing in nature can be used for foreseeing faults[t_1,t_2]. It is not worth saying that it is very difficult to build a good computable relation *causes_2*: it requires to know specifically the rules according to which normal and abnormal operation, accidents, repair and maintenance actions give raise to faults, depending on the temporal order in which they occur.

The prevision of future faults is uncertain in nature, since H[t_1,t_2] necessarily represents only the predictable information as to the system operation and maintenance in the future interval $[t_1, t_2]$ along with the accidents that, with uncertainty, will occur in the same interval.

4 Preventive Diagnosis as a Knowledge-Based Task

4.1 Why Knowledge-Based Technology?

There are several facts that make the task of PD as solved by means of the Check-up And Foresee approach suitable for the knowledge-based technology; in fact:

• it involves two important subtasks which are among the most typical performed by knowledge-based systems, namely data interpretation (in the Check-up phase) and envisioning (in the Foresee phase);

• it must be able to manage uncertainty in information (measurement values, test results, system history, etc.) and knowledge;

• it needs reasoning on the wear and tear phenomena involving physical systems and, usually, no exact deterministic models of such phenomena are available.

4.2 Knowledge Sources for Preventive Diagnosis

The fundamental knowledge sources involved in the Check-up And Foresee process are described below; their role in the process is shown in Figure 1.

• Reference variables KS: it contains the rules stating how to acquire the actual values of reference variables.

• Quantitative measurable state variables KS: it contains the rules stating how to acquire the actual values of quantitative measurable state variables.

• Qualitative measurable state variables KS: it contains the rules stating how to infer the actual values of qualitative measurable state variables.

• Non-measurable state variables KS: it contains the rules stating how to estimate the actual values of non-measurable state variables.

• Normal behavior KS: it contains the description of the normal operating modes of the physical system of interest.

• Normal state behavior KS: it contains the description of the normal state modes of the physical system of interest.

• Class KS: it contains all the data as to the class the physical system of interest belongs to, i.e. primitive historical/statistical data, derived development models, etc.

• Individual KS: it contains all the data describing the specific physical system at hand, e.g. models obtained by customizing and tuning existing class models.

• Temporal KS: it contains the knowledge needed in order to reason about the evolution of the physical system at hand over time, e.g. the description of the physical rules that produce the transitions between wear states, that preside over the generation of faults, etc.

References

[Chittaro et al. 1993] L. Chittaro, G. Guida, C. Tasso and E. Toppano, Functional and teleological knowledge in the multi-modeling approach for reasoning about physical systems: a case study in diagnosis, *IEEE Transactions on Systems, Man and Cybernetics*, Vol. 23, No. 6, 1993, 1718-1751

[Reiter 1987] R. Reiter, A theory of diagnosis from first principles, *Artificial Intelligence*, 32, 1987, 57-95

Learning Programs in Different Paradigms using Genetic Programming

Man Leung Wong   Kwong Sak Leung

Department of Computer Science
The Chinese University of Hong Kong
Hong Kong
Fax: 852-26035024

wong045@cs.cuhk.hk   ksleung@cs.cuhk.hk

Abstract

Genetic Programming (GP) is a method of automatically inducing programs by representing them as parse trees. In theory, programs in any computer languages can be translated to parse trees. Hence, GP should be able to handle them as well. In practice, the syntax of Lisp is so simple and uniform that the translation process can be achieved easily, programs evolved by GP are usually expressed in Lisp. This paper presents a flexible framework that programs in various programming languages can be acquired. This framework is based on a formalism of logic grammars. To implement the framework, a system called LOGENPRO (The LOgic grammar based GENetic PROgramming system) has been developed. An experiment that employs LOGENPRO to induce a S-expression for calculating dot product has been performed. This experiment illustrates that LOGENPRO, when used with knowledge of data types, accelerates the learning of programs. Other experiments have been done to illustrate the ability of LOGENPRO in inducing programs in difference programming languages including Prolog and C. These experiments prove that LOGENPRO is very flexible.

1 Introduction

Genetic Programming (GP) is a method of automatically inducing programs by representing them as parse trees. In theory, programs in any computer languages such as Prolog, C, and Fortran can be represented as parse trees. Hence, GP should be able to handle them as well. In fact, the process of translating a program in some languages to the corresponding parse tree is not trivial. Since the syntax of Lisp is so simple and uniform that the translation process can be achieved easily, programs evolved by GP are usually expressed in Lisp.

This paper presents a flexible framework that programs in various programming languages can be acquired. This framework is based on a formalism of logic grammars and a system called LOGENPRO (The LOgic grammar based GENetic PROgramming system) is developed. The formalism is also powerful enough to represent context-sensitive information and domain-dependent knowledge. This knowledge can be used to accelerate the learning speed and/or improve the quality of the programs induced.

We present the formalism of logic grammars and the details of LOGENPRO in section two. Section three demonstrates the application of LOGENPRO in learning

S-expressions in Lisp. The subsequent two sections further illustrate the flexibility of the framework in inducing programs in Prolog and C. Section six is the conclusion.

2 The Logic Grammars Based Genetic Programming System (LOGENPRO)

LOGENPRO can induce programs in various programming languages such as Lisp, Prolog, and C. Thus, it must be able to accept grammars of different languages and produce programs in these languages. Most modern programming languages are specified in the notation of context-free grammar (CFG). However, logic grammars are used in LOGENPRO because they are much more powerful than that of CFG, but equally amenable to efficient execution. In this paper, the notation of definite clause grammars (DCG) is used (Pereira and Warren 1980).

A logic grammar differs from a CFG in that the logic grammar symbols, whether terminal or non-terminal, may include arguments (Table 1). The arguments can be any term in the grammar. A term is either a logical variable, a function or a constant. A variable is represented by a question mark ? followed by a string of letters and/or digits. A function is a grammar symbol followed by a bracketed n-tuple of terms and a constant is simply a 0-arity function. Arguments can be used in a logic grammar to enforce context-dependency or to construct representation "meaning" in the course of parsing.

1:	start	->	[(*)], exp(X), exp(X), [)].
2:	start	->	{member(?x,[X, Y])}, [(*], exp-1(?x), exp-1(?x), [)].
3:	start	->	{member(?x,[X, Y])}, [(/], exp-1(?x), exp-1(?x), [)].
4:	exp(?x)	->	[(+ ?x 0)].
5:	exp-1(?x)	->	{random(0,1,?y)}, [(+ ?x ?y)].
6:	exp-1(?x)	->	{random(0,1,?y)}, [(- ?x ?y)].
7:	exp-1(?x)	->	[(+ (- X 11) 12)].

Table 1. A logic grammar

The terminal symbols, which are enclosed in square brackets, correspond to the set of words of the language specified. For example, the terminal [(+ ?x ?y)] creates the constituent (+ 1.0 2.0) of a program if ?x and ?y are instantiated respectively to 1.0 and 2.0. Non-terminal symbols are similar to literals in Prolog, exp-1(?x) in figure 1 is an example of non-terminal symbol. Commas denote concatenation and each grammar rule ends with a full stop.

The right-hand side of a grammar rule may contain logic goals and grammar symbols. The goals are pure logical predicates for which logical definitions have been given. They specify the conditions that must be satisfied before the rule can be applied. For example, the goal member(?x, [X, Y]) in figure 1 instantiates the variable ?x to either X or Y if ?x has not been instantiated, otherwise it checks whether the value of ?x is either X or Y. The special non-terminal start corresponds to a program of the language. The number before each rule is a label for later discussions. It is not part of the grammar.

In LOGENPRO, populations of programs are genetically bred (Goldberg 1989) using the Darwinian principle of survival and reproduction of the fittest along with genetic operations appropriate for processing programs. LOGENPRO starts with an initial population of programs generated randomly, induced by other learning systems, or provided by the user. Logic grammars provide declarative descriptions of the valid programs that can appear in the initial population. A high-level algorithm of LOGENPRO is presented in table 2.

1.	Generate an initial population of programs.
2.	Execute each program in the current population and assign it a fitness value according to the fitness function
3.	If the termination criterion is satisfied, terminate the algorithm. The best program found in the run of the algorithm is designated as the result.
4.	Create a new population of programs from the current population by applying the reproduction, crossover, and mutation operations. These operations are applied to programs selected by fitness proportionate or tournament selections.
5.	Rename the new population to the current population.
6.	Proceed to the next generation by branching back to the step 2.

Table 2. A high level algorithm of Logenpro

3 Learning Functional Programs

In this section, we describe how to use LOGENPRO to emulate Koza's GP (Koza 1992; 1994). Koza's GP has a limitation that all the variables, constants, arguments for functions, and values returned from functions must be of the same data type. This limitation leads to the difficulty of inducing even some rather simple and straightforward functional programs. For example, one of these programs calculates the dot product of two given numeric vectors of the same size. Let X and Y be the two input vectors, then the dot product is obtained by the following S-expression:

```
(apply (function +) (mapcar (function *) X Y))
```

Let us use this example for illustrative comparison below. To induce a functional program using LOGENPRO, we have to determine the logic grammar, fitness cases, fitness functions and termination criterion. The logic grammar for learning functional programs is given in table 3. In this grammar, we employ the argument of the grammar symbol s-expr to designate the data type of the result returned by the S-expression generated from the grammar symbol. For example,

```
(mapcar (function +) X
        (mapcar (function *) X Y))
```

is generated from the grammar symbol s-expr([list, number, n]) because it returns a numeric vector of size n. Similarly, the symbol s-expr(number) can produce (apply (function *) X) that returns a number.

The terminal symbols +, −, and * represent functions that perform ordinary addition, subtraction and multiplication respectively. The symbol % represents function that normally returns the quotient. However, if division by zero is attempted, the function returns 1.0. The symbol protected-log is a function that calculates the logarithm of the input argument x if x is larger than zero, otherwise it returns 1.0. The logic goal random(-10, 10, ?a) generates a random floating point number between -10 and 10 and instantiates ?a to the random number generated

Ten random fitness cases are used for training. Each case is a 3-tuples $\langle X_i, Y_i, Z_i \rangle$, where $1 \leq i \leq 10$, X_i and Y_i are vectors of size 3, and Z_i is the corresponding dot product. The fitness function calculates the sum, taken over the ten fitness cases, of the absolute values of the difference between Z_i and the value returned by the S-expression for X_i and Y_i. A fitness case is said to be covered by an S-expression if the value returned by it is within 0.01 of the desired value. A S-expression that covers all training cases is further evaluated on a testing set containing 1000 random fitness cases. LOGENPRO will stop if the maximum number of generations of 100 is reached or a S-expression that covers all testing fitness cases is found.

```
start                           ->    s-expr(number).
s-expr([list, number, ?n])      ->    [(mapcar (function ], op2, [)],
                                      s-expr([list, number, ?n]),
                                      s-expr([list, number, ?n]),[)].
s-expr([list, number, ?n])      ->    [(mapcar (function ], op1, [)],
                                      s-expr([list, number, ?n]),[)].
s-expr([list, number, ?n])      ->    term([list, number, ?n]).
s-expr(number)                  ->    term(number).
s-expr(number)                  ->    [(apply (function ], op2, [)],
                                      s-expr([list, number, ?n]),[)].
s-expr(number) ->                     [(], op2, s-expr(number),
                                      s-expr(number), [)].
s-expr(number) ->                     [(], op1, s-expr(number), [)].
op2                             ->    [ + ].
op2                             ->    [ - ].
op2                             ->    [ * ].
op2                             ->    [ % ].
op1                             ->    [ protected-log ].
term( [list, number, n] )       ->    [X].
term( [list, number, n] )       ->    [Y].
term( number )                  ->    { random(-10, 10, ?a) },  [?a].
```

Table 3. A logic grammar for the Dot Product problem

For Koza's GP framework, the terminal set T is {X, Y, ℝ} where ℝ is the ephemeral random floating point constant. ℝ takes on a different random floating point value between -10.0 and 10.0 whenever it appears in an individual program in the initial population. The function set F is {protected+, protected-, protected*, protected%, protected-log, vector+, vector-, vector*, vector%, vector-log, apply+, apply-, apply*, apply%}, taking 2, 2, 2, 2, 1, 2, 2, 2, 2, 1, 1, 1, 1 and 1 arguments respectively.

The primitive functions protected+, protected- and protected* respectively perform addition, subtraction and multiplication if the two input arguments X and Y are both numbers. Otherwise, they return 0. The function protected% returns the quotient. However, if division by zero is attempted or the two arguments are not numbers, protected% returns 1.0. The function protected-log finds the logarithm of the argument X if X is a number larger than zero. Otherwise, protected-log returns 1.0.

The functions vector+, vector-, vector* and vector% respectively perform vector addition, subtract, multiplication and division if the two input arguments X and Y are numeric vectors with the same size, otherwise they return zero. The primitive function vector-log performs the S-expression:

```
(mapcar (function protected-log) X)
```

if the input argument X is a numeric vector, otherwise it returns zero. The functions apply+, apply-, apply* and apply% respectively perform the following S-expressions if the input argument X is a numeric vector:

```
(apply (function protected+) X),
(apply (function protected-) X),
(apply (function protected*) X) and
(apply (function protected%) X),
```

otherwise they return zero.

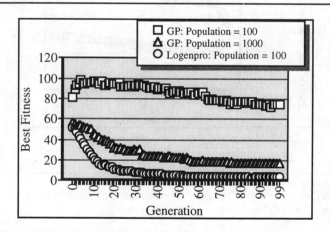

Figure 1. Fitness curves showing best fitness for the Dot Product problem

The fitness cases, the fitness function and the termination criterion are the same as those used by LOGENPRO. Three experiments are performed. The first one evaluates the performance of LOGENPRO using a population of 100 programs. The other two experiments evaluate the performance of Koza's GP using respectively populations of 100 and 1000 programs. In each experiment, over sixty trials are attempted and the results are summarized in figures 1 and 2. From the curves in figures 1, LOGENPRO has superior performance than that of GP.

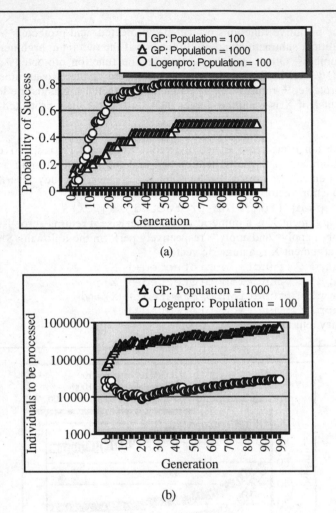

(a)

(b)

Figure 2. Performance curves showing (a) cumulative probability of success P(M, i) and (b) I(M, i, z) for the Dot Product problem

The curves in figure 2a show the experimentally observed cumulative probability of success, P(M, i), of solving the problem by generation i using a population of M programs. The curves in figure 2b show the number of programs I(M, i, z) that must be processed to produce a solution by generation i with a probability z (Koza 1992; 1994). Throughout this paper, the probability z is set to 0.99. The curve for GP with a population of 100 programs is not depicted because the values is extremely large. For the LOGENPRO curve, I(M, i, z) reaches a minimum value of 8800 at generation 21. On the other hand, the minimum value of I(M, i, z) for GP with population size of 1000 is 66000 at generation 1. LOGENPRO can find a solution much faster than GP and the computation (i.e. I(M, i, z)) required by LOGENPRO is much smaller than that of GP.

The idea of applying knowledge of data type to accelerate learning has been investigated independently by Montana (1993) in his Strongly Typed Genetic Programming (STGP). He presents three examples involving vector and matrix manipulation to illustrate the operation of STGP. However, he has not compare the performance between traditional GP and STGP. Although it is commonly believed that knowledge can accelerate the speed of learning, Pazzani and Kibler (1992) shows that inappropriate and/or redundant knowledge can sometimes degrade the performance of a learning system. One advantage of LOGENPRO is that it can emulate the effect of STGP effortlessly.

4 Learning Logic Programs

In this section, we describe how to use LOGENPRO to induce logic programs. To induce a target logic program, we have to determine the logic grammar, the fitness function and other major parameters such as the population size, the maximum number of generations, and the probabilities of applying various genetic operations.

For concept learning (DeJong et al. 1993, Janikow 1993), each individual logic program in the population can be evaluated in terms of how well it covers positive examples and excludes negative examples. Thus, the fitness functions for concept learning problems calculate this measurement. Typically, each logic program is run over a number of training examples so that its fitness is measured as the total number of misclassified positive and negative examples. Sometimes, if the distribution of positive and negative examples is extremely uneven, this method of estimating fitness is not good enough to focus the search. For example, assume that there are 2 positive and 10000 negative examples, if the number of misclassified examples is used as the fitness value, a logic program that deduces everything are negative will have very good fitness. Thus, in this case, the fitness function should find a weighted sum of the total numbers of misclassified positive and negative examples.

The modified Quinlan's network reachability problem is used as a demonstration. The problem is originally proposed by Quinlan (Quinlan 1990), the domain involves a directional network such as the one depicted as follows:

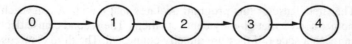

The structural information of the network is the literal linked-to(A, B) denoting that node A is directly linked to node B. The extension of linked-to(A, B) is {<0, 1>, <1, 2>, <2, 3>, <3, 4>}. Here, the learning task is to induce a logic program that determines whether a node A can reach another node B. This problem can also be formulated as finding the intensional definition of the relation can-reach(A, B) given its extension. Its extensional definition is

{<0, 1>, <0, 2>, <0, 3>, <0, 4>, <1, 2>, <1, 3>, <1, 4>, <2, 3>, <2, 4>, <3, 4>}. The tuples of this relation are the positive training examples and {<0, 0>, <1, 0>, <1, 1>, <2, 0>, <2, 1>, <2, 2>, <3, 0>, <3, 1>, <3, 2>, <3, 3>, <4, 0>, <4, 1>, <4, 2>, <4, 3>, <4, 4>} are the negative examples.

```
start               ->      clauses.
clauses             ->      clauses, clauses.
clauses             ->      clause.
clause              ->      consq, [:-], antes, [.].
consq               ->      [can-reach(A, B)].
antes               ->      antes, [,], antes.
antes               ->      ante.
ante                ->      {member(?x,[A, B, C])},
                            {member(?y,[A, B, C])}
                            {not-equal(?x, ?y)},
                            literal(?x, ?y).
literal(?x, ?y)     ->      [linked-to(?x, ?y)].
literal(?x, ?y)     ->      [can-reach(?x, ?y)].
```

Table 4. The logic grammar for the modified Quinlan's network reachability problem

The logic grammar for this experiment is shown in table 4. In this experiment, the population size is 1000. The standardized fitness is the total number of misclassified training examples. The maximum number of generations is 50. Five runs are performed and LOGENPRO can find a perfect program that covers all positive examples while excludes all negative ones within a few generations. One program found is:

```
can-reach(A, B) :- linked-to(C, B),linked-to(A, C).
can-reach(A, B) :- linked-to(A, B),linked-to(A, C).
can-reach(A, B) :- can-reach(A, C),can-reach(C, B).
```

This program can be simplified to

```
can-reach(A, B) :- linked-to(A, C),linked-to(C, B).
can-reach(A, B) :- linked-to(A, B).
can-reach(A, B) :- can-reach(A, C),can-reach(C, B).
```

The first clause of this program declares that a node A can reach node B if there is another node C that directly connects them. The second clause declares that a node A can reach a node B if they are directly connected. The third clause is recursive, it expresses that a node A can reach a node B if there is another node C, such that C is reachable from A and B is reachable from C. In fact, this program is semantically equivalent to the standard solution

```
can-reach(A, B) :- linked-to(A, B).
can-reach(A, B) :- linked-to(A, C),can-reach(C, B).
```

This experiment demonstrates that LOGENPRO can learn recursive program naturally and effectively. Recursive functions are difficult to learn in Koza's GP (Koza 1992; 1994), this experiment shows the advantage of LOGENPRO over GP. Figure 3 depicts the best, average and worst standardized fitnesses for increasing generations. These fitnesses curves are obtained by averaging the corresponding fitness values obtained from five different runs.

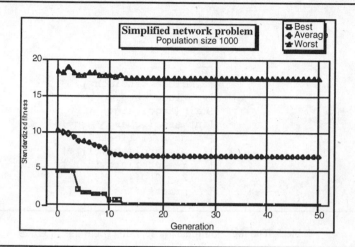

Figure 3. Fitness curves for the modified network reachability problem

5 Learning Programs in C

The target program calculates the function value $f(X, Y)$ for the two input arguments and outputs the result. The function $f(X, Y)$ is $((X+Y)^2-Y)$ and the population size used in this experiment is 500. The ten fitness cases are 3-tuples $<X_i, Y_i, f(X_i, Y_i)>$, where $1 \leq i \leq 10$ and X_i, Y_i are random integer between 0 and 10. The fitness function calculates the sum, taken over the ten fitness cases, of the absolute values of the difference between $f(X_i, Y_i)$ and the value returned by the generated C program using X_i and Y_i as the inputs. A fitness case is said to be covered by a program if the value returned by it is within 0.01 of the desired value. LOGENPRO terminates if the maximum number of generations, which is 50, is reached or a C program that covers all fitness cases is found.

The logic grammar for this problem is shown in table 5. In this grammar, only simple assignment statement can be generated. This restriction is enforced only to limit the size of the search space for the problem so that solutions can be found using the available computational resources. In fact, the search space will be extremely large if the complete grammar for the C programming language is used. In this grammar, the symbol preamble produces statements that declare and initialize variables used in the program. On the other hand, the symbol outputs creates statement that prints the final result of the program.

```
start              ->      preamble, statements, outputs.
statements         ->      statements, statements.
statements         ->      statement.
statement          ->      id, [=], expression, [;].
expression         ->      [(], expression, op, expression, [)].
expression         ->      id.
op                 ->      [+].
op                 ->      [-].
op                 ->      [*].
id                 ->      [X].
id                 ->      [Y].
id                 ->      [Z].
preamble           ->      [#include <stdio.h>],
                           [#include <stdlib.h>],
                           [main(argc, argv)],
                           [int argc; char **argv;],
                           [{ int X Y; float Z;],
                           [   X = atoi(argv[1]);],
                           [   Y = atoi(argv[2]);],
                           [   Z = 0.0;].
outputs            ->      [   printf("\n%f", Z)].
```

Table 5. The logic grammar for learning programs in C

In one successful run of **LOGENPRO**, the following correct C program is found in generation 4:

```
#include <stdio.h>
#include <stdlib.h>
main(argc, argv)
int argc; char **argv;
{ int X, Y; float Z;
  X = atoi(argv[1]);
  Y = atoi(argv[2]);
  Z = 0.0;
  Z = (((X-Z)*X)+((Y*Y)+(((X+X)*Y)-Y)));
  printf("\n%f", Z);}
```

The program is correct because the assignment statement $Z = (((X - Z) * X) + ((Y * Y) + (((X + X) * Y) - Y)))$ can be simplified to $Z = X^2 + Y^2 + 2XY - Y$ as the variable Z is initialized to 0.0. The statement can be further simplified to $Z = (X + Y)^2 - Y$ which is the desire statement. It should be emphasized that the goal of this section is to demonstrate the possibility of learning programs in some imperative languages. The symbolic regression problem is deliberately constructed as simple as possible so as to illustrate the point clearly.

Twenty trials are attempted using different random number seeds and fitness cases. The results are summarized in figures 4 and 5. Figure 4 shows, by generation, the fitness of the best program in a population. Figure 5 shows the performance curves when the population size M is 500 and the probability z is 0.99. The value of $I(M, i, z)$ reaches a minimum value of 21000 at generation 5.

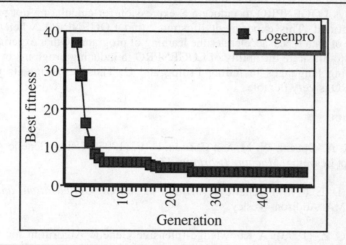

Figure 4. Fitness curve for the problem of inducing a C program

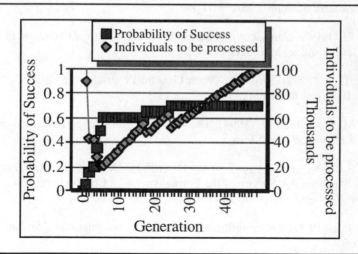

Figure 5. Performance curves for the problem of inducing programs in C

6 Conclusion

We have proposed a flexible framework that programs in various programming languages can be acquired. This framework is based on a formalism of logic grammars. To implement the framework, a system called LOGENPRO (The LOgic grammar based GENetic PROgramming system) has been developed. An experiment that employs LOGENPRO to induce a S-expression for calculating dot product has been performed. This experiment illustrates that LOGENPRO, when used with knowledge of data types, accelerates the learning of programs. Other experiments have been done to illustrate the ability of LOGENPRO in inducing programs in difference programming languages including Prolog and C. These experiments prove that LOGENPRO is very flexible.

Reference

DeJong, K. A., Spears, W. M. and Gordon, D. F. (1993). Using Genetic Algorithms for Concept Learning, *Machine Learning*, **13**, 161-188.

Goldberg, D. E. (1989) *Genetic Algorithms in Search, Optimization, and Machine Learning*. MA: Addison-Wesley.

Janikow, C. Z. (1993). A Knowledge-Intensive Genetic Algorithm for Supervised Learning, *Machine Learning*, **13**, 189-228.

Koza, J. R. (1992). *Genetic Programming: on the Programming of Computers by Means of Natural Selection*. MA: MIT Press.

Koza, J. R. (1994). *Genetic Programming II: Automatic Discovery of Reusable Programs*. Cambridge, MA: MIT Press.

Montana, D. J. (1993). Strongly Typed Genetic Programming. Bolt, Beranek, and Newman Technical Report no. 7866.

Pazzani, M. and Kibler, D. (1992). The Utility of Knowledge in Inductive learning. *Machine Learning*, **9**, pp. 57-94.

Pereira, F. C. N. and Warren, D. H. D. (1980). Definite Clause Grammars for Language Analysis - A Survey of the Formalism and a Comparison with Augmented Transition Networks. *Artificial Intelligence*; **13**, pp. 231-278.

Quinlan, J. R. (1990). Learning logical definitions from relations. *Machine Learning*, **5**, 239-266.

Revision of Logical Theories

Giovanni Semeraro, Floriana Esposito, Nicola Fanizzi, and Donato Malerba

Dipartimento di Informatica - Università degli Studi di Bari
Via E. Orabona 4 - 70126 Bari, Italy

Abstract. This paper presents a system for revising hierarchical first-order logical theories, called INCR/H. It incorporates two refinement operators, one for generalizing clauses which do not cover positive examples, and the other one for specializing the inconsistent hypotheses inductively generated by any system that learns logical theories from positive and negative examples. The generalizing operator is inspired from Hayes-Roth and McDermott's Interference matching, while the specializing operator is completely novel. Both of them perform a search in the space of logical clauses and take advantage of the structure of this set. The main characteristic of the system consists of the capability of autonomously performing a representation change, that allows INCR/H to extend the search to the space of clauses with negated literals in the body (program clauses) when no correct theories exist in the space of definite clauses. Experimental results in the area of electronic document classification show that INCR/H is able to cope effectively and efficiently with this real-world learning task.

1 Introduction

A logical theory can be viewed as a set of conditions, expressed in a logical language, that are necessary and sufficient to explain a number of observations in a given environment. In addition to the capability of explaining past events, the usefulness of a theory relies on its ability of predicting future situations in the same environment. If we assume that the only source of knowledge available is represented by a set of previously classified observations and no prior knowledge can be exploited, the process of formulating a new theory is bound to be progressive. Starting from contingent observations, it is not possible to define concepts that are universally regarded as true. The validity of the theory itself extends to the available knowledge. Conversely, new observations can point out the inadequacies in the current formulation of the concepts. In such a case, a process of theory revision should be activated.

Formulating logical theories from facts is the ultimate objective of concept learning. In this area, a *theory* consists of a set of hypotheses, a *hypothesis* is a concept definition and observations are called *examples*. An example that should be explained by a theory is called positive, an example that should be refuted is called negative.

Initially, the research efforts in this area centred on the analysis and development of learning systems that induce a logical theory in a *batch* way. These systems start from an empty theory and stop the learning process when the current set of hypotheses is able to explain all the available examples. When new evidence contradicts the learned theory, the whole learning process must be repeated, taking no advantage of the previous version of the hypotheses. Such a drawback can be overcome by means of incremental learning systems. These systems are able to revise and refine a theory in an *incremental* way, thus the previously generated hypotheses are not completely rejected, but they are taken as the starting point of a search process whose goal consists of a new theory that explains both old and new observations.

This paper presents a new incremental learning system, called INCR/H, that learns theories, expressed as sets of first-order logical clauses, from positive and negative examples. It adopts a full memory storage strategy [18] (i.e. it retains all the available examples, thus the learned theories are guaranteed to be valid on the whole set of known examples) and it incorporates two refinement operators, one for generalizing hypotheses that refute positive examples, and the other for specializing hypotheses that explain negative examples. Both the operators, when applied, change the *answer set* of the theory (by answer set, we mean the set of examples that are satisfied by the theory). Therefore, INCR/H is a system for theory revision rather than for *theory restructuring*, if we agree on the definition of theory restructuring as a process that does not change the answer set of a theory [27].

In the next section, we present the architecture of INCR/H. In section 3, the logical language used to represent both the learned theory and the examples used by INCR/H is introduced. Sections 4 and 5 describe the incremental operators used by INCR/H to refine incorrect theories. The validity of these incremental operators is empirically evaluated on the task of document classification, that is a typical problem in the area of electronic document processing.

2 The Architecture of INCR/H

Incremental learning is necessary when either incomplete information is available at the time of initial theory generation or the nature of the concepts evolves dynamically. The latter situation is the most difficult to handle since time evolution needs to be considered. In any case, it is useful to consider learning as a *closed loop* process, where feedback about performance is used to activate the theory revision phase [1].

INCR/H is a classical closed loop learning system implemented in C language. The process of hypothesis refinement consists of a number of functions related to each other by a closed loop information flow. The architecture of INCR/H is shown in Figure 1. INCR/H takes from the *Expert/Environment* a set of examples of the concepts to be learned. This set can be subdivided into three subsets, namely *training*, *tuning*, and *test examples*, according to the way in which examples are exploited during the learning process. Specifically, training examples, previously classified by the Expert, are exploited by the *Rule Generator* in a batch mode in order to generate a first version of a theory that is able to explain the provided examples. Our Rule Generator embodies a *model-driven* inductive learning system, called INDUBI/H [7]. Subsequently, the theory is used by the *Rule Interpreter* in order to verify that rules continue to be valid also when new examples become available. The Rule Interpreter takes in input the set of rules (inductive hypotheses) and a tuning/test example and produces a decision. The *Critic/Performance Evaluator*, that may be a human expert or a computer program, compares the decision produced by the Rule Interpreter to the correct one and decides whether firing the rule refinement process or simply communicating the decision. Besides this, the Critic takes care of locating

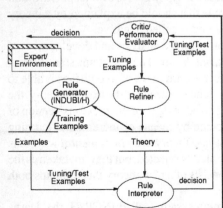

Fig. 1. The architecture of INCR/H.

the cause of the wrong decision and choosing the proper kind of correction. In such a case, tuning examples are exploited incrementally by the *Rule Refiner* to modify incorrect rules according to a *data-driven* strategy. The Rule Refiner consists of two distinct modules, a *Rule Specializer* and a *Rule Generalizer*, which attempt to correct respectively, too week and too strong hypotheses. Test examples are exploited to put to the proof the predictive capabilities of the theory, intended as the behaviour of the theory on previously unclassified observations.

3 The Representation Language

Henceforth, we refer to [13] for what concerns the basic definitions of a *substitution*, *positive* and *negative literal*, *clause*, *definite* and *program clause*, and *normal program*. We will indifferently use the set notation and the Prolog notation for clauses. Given a first-order clause ϕ, $vars(\phi)$, $consts(\phi)$ and $|\phi|$ denote respectively the set of the variables, the set of the constants and the number of literals occurring in ϕ. By *logical theory* we mean a set of *hypotheses*, by *hypothesis* we mean a set of program clauses with the same head. In the paper, we are concerned exclusively with logical theories expressed as *hierarchical programs*, that is, as programs for which it is possible to find a *level mapping* [13] such that, in every program clause $P(t_1, t_2,...,t_n) \leftarrow L_1, L_2,...,L_m$, the level of every predicate symbol occurring in the body is less than the level of P. Another constraint on the representation language is that, whenever we write about clauses, we mean *Datalog* (i.e., function-free) *linked* clauses. A definition of linked clause can be found in [12]. An instance of a linked clause is $C = P(x) \leftarrow Q(x,y), Q(y,z), \neg R(x,v)$. Conversely, the clauses $D = C - \{Q(x,y)\}$ and $F = C \cup \{\neg R(v, w)\}$ are not linked.

The differences existing between examples and hypotheses are the following.
- Each example is represented by one *ground* clause with a unique literal in the head.
- Each hypothesis is a set of program clauses with the same *head*.

An *example E* is *positive* for a hypothesis *H* if its head has the same predicate letter and sign as the head of the clauses in *H*. The example *E* is *negative* for *H* if its head has the same predicate, but opposite sign. Thus, more precisely, a negative example is a *generally Horn clause* [10].

Subsequently, we define a quasi-ordering $\leq_{ol}$ on the set **LP** of the Datalog linked program clauses.

Definition 1 (θ_{ol}-subsumption ordering) Let C, D be two elements of **LP**. We say that D θ-subsumes C under object identity (D θ_{ol}-subsumes C) if and only if (iff) there exists a substitution σ such that $D.\sigma \subseteq C$ and σ is a one-to-one mapping. In such a case, we say that D is more general than or equal to C (D is a generalization of C and C is a specialization of D) under object identity and we write $C \leq_{ol} D$. We write $C <_{ol} D$ when $C \leq_{ol} D$ and $not(D \leq_{ol} C)$ and we say that D is more general than C or C is more specific than D.

This ordering is inspired from the notion of θ-*subsumption* [17] and makes the assumption that variables with different names denote distinct objects (*object identity*). Object identity can be interpreted as an extension of the *unique-names assumption* [19] to any kind of term, including variables. For instance, the following clause $P(x) \leftarrow Q(x, y), R(y, a)$ denotes the clause $P(x) \leftarrow Q(x, y), R(y, a), [x{\neq}y], [x{\neq}a], [y{\neq}a]$, under the object identity assumption. θ_{ol}-subsumption is a strictly weaker order relation than θ-subsumption. A thorough analysis of θ_{ol}-subsumption as a generalization model can be found in [22]. Furthermore, we adopt the *negation-as-failure* rule [4] to define the meaning of a negated literal in the body of a program clause.

Generally, the canonical inductive paradigm requires the fulfilment of the properties of completeness and consistency for the learned rules. More formally, we introduce the following definitions.

Definition 2 (Inconsistency) A *theory T* is *inconsistent* iff at least one of its hypotheses is inconsistent with respect to (wrt) some negative example. A *hypothesis* is *inconsistent* wrt a negative example *N* iff at least one of its clauses is inconsistent wrt *N*. A *clause C* is *inconsistent* wrt *N* iff there exists a one-to-one substitution σ such that the following conditions are satisfied:

$$1) \; body(C).\sigma \subseteq body(N), \qquad\qquad 2) \neg \, head(C).\sigma = head(N)$$

where $body(\varphi)$ and $head(\varphi)$ denote the *body* and the *head* of a clause φ, respectively. If at least one of the two conditions above is not met, we say that *C* is *consistent* wrt *N*.

Definition 3 (Incompleteness) A *theory T* is *incomplete* iff at least one of its hypotheses is incomplete wrt some positive example. A *hypothesis* is *incomplete* wrt a positive example *P* iff each of its clauses does not θ_{OI}-subsume *P*. Otherwise it is *complete* wrt *P*.

With these definitions, we can formally define the notions of commission and omission error.

Definition 4 (Commission/Omission error) Given a theory *T* and an example *E*, *T* makes a *commission error* if there exists at least a clause *C* in a hypothesis in *T* that is inconsistent wrt *E*. *T* makes an *omission error* if there exists a hypothesis in *T* that is incomplete wrt *E*.

When a commission error occurs, it becomes necessary to specialize the inconsistent clause *C* so that the new clause *C'* restores the consistency property of the theory. When an omission error occurs, it becomes necessary to generalize the incomplete hypothesis *H* so that the new hypothesis *H'* restores the completeness property of the theory.

4 The Generalizing Operator

The generalizing operator is inspired from the Interference Matching proposed by Hayes-Roth and McDermott [11]. Differently from the original operator, our algorithm works on clauses rather than on Parameterized Structural Representations (PSR's). Therefore, it extends the notion of *maximal abstraction* to the concept of *least general generalizations* (lgg) under θ_{OI}-subsumption.[1] The basic idea of the algorithm consists in searching for all the possible *intersections* between the clauses to be generalized.

The generalizing process starts by choosing a literal in one of the two clauses and goes on by searching in the other clause for a literal that unifies through a one-to-one mapping. Such a pair of literals, if any, is used to produce a new literal, which is the kernel of one of the output generalizations. The new literal is the least general generalization of the literals in the pair and is stored, together with the detected variable bindings, for future processing. After this step, further pairs of literals are generated and the corresponding

---

1. A least general generalization of two clauses under θ_{OI}-subsumption is a generalization which is not more general than any other such generalization, that is, it is either more specific than or not comparable to any other such generalization. Formally, given $C_1, C_2 \in$ **LP**:

$$lgg(C_1, C_2) = \{ \, C \mid C \leq_{OI} C_i, \, i=1,2 \text{ and } \forall D \text{ such that } C_i \leq_{OI} D, \, i=1,2 : not(\, D <_{OI} C \,) \, \}$$

least general generalizations are added to the existing kernel. When a one-to-one variable binding for a new pair of literals is not consistent with the current bindings, a new kernel for an alternative generalization is created. This causes multiple lgg's to be built in parallel. Evaluation criteria are exploited to rank the current generalizations. In addition to this, our implementation of the operator adds the lgg of a pair of literals to each generalization kernel whose variable bindings are consistent with the current bindings, even though in the original formulation of the algorithm it is not clear whether it should be added only to the current generalization kernel or to each generalization whose bindings are consistent with the current ones.

The implemented algorithm consists of five steps:

1) Given a clause C that does not θ_{oi}-subsume a positive example P, the literals in C are decomposed into two subsets, C^1 and C^2, where C^1 meets the following condition: $C^1 \subseteq C$, $vars(C^1) = vars(C)$ and $|C^1| = \max\{|D| \mid D \subseteq C$ and $vars(D) = vars(C)\}$ and C^2 is made up of the remaining literals, that is $C^2 = C - C^1$.

2) All the one-to-one most general unifiers of each literal in C^1 with literals in P are computed and the corresponding variable bindings are stored.

3) All the one-to-one substitutions σ such that $C^1.\sigma \subseteq P$ are produced by properly combining the most general unifiers found in the previous step, one for each literal in C^1, in all the possible ways.

4) For each one-to-one substitution produced by step 3), a distinct generalization is built by computing the lgg of each pair of literals that are unified by the substitution. In these generalizations, at least one literal in C^2 has been dropped.

5) The set of all the generalizations produced by the previous step is pruned in order to remove inconsistent clauses, and that maximizing an evaluation function is chosen. Such a generalization is a clause that is guaranteed to θ_{oi}-subsume the positive example P.

If the previous process does not produce a consistent clause, a new clause is added to the theory. Such a clause is obtained by properly turning constants in the positive example P into variables.

The generalization produced by such operator complies with the language bias of linkedness. In addition, the application of the generalizing operator proposed in this section needs to keep a record of the only negative examples.

5 The Specializing Operator

Differently from the generalizing operator, the specializing operator proposed in this paper is completely novel. Essentially, it relies on the addition of a non-redundant literal to a clause that turns out to be inconsistent wrt a negative example, in order to restore the consistency property of the clause. The space in which such a literal should be searched for is potentially infinite and, in any case, its size is so large that an exhaustive search is unfeasible. The novelty of the operator consists in focusing the search into the portion of the space that contains the solution. This peculiarity is the result of an analysis of the structure of the search space.

The search is firstly performed in the space of positive literals. This space contains information coming from the positive examples used to train and tune the learning system, but not yet exploited by the current theory. When the search in this space fails, the algorithm autonomously performs a representation change that allows the system to learn hypotheses made up of *program* clauses rather than definite ones. In other words, the search is performed into a space of negative literals, built by taking into account the negative example that caused the commission error.

First of all, given a hypothesis H which is inconsistent wrt a negative example N, the Performance Evaluator locates the clause C of H that caused the inconsistency. Let us suppose that the subset of the positive examples θ_{OI}-subsumed by C were $\{P_1, P_2, ..., P_n\}$. The search process aims at finding one of the *most general specializations (mgs) under object identity* of C against N given $P_1, P_2, ..., P_n$, denoted with $mgs(C, N/P_1, P_2, ..., P_n)$ and formally defined as follows.

$$mgs(C, N/P_1, P_2, ..., P_n) = \{M \in mgs(C, N) \mid P_j \leq_{OI} M, j=1,2,...,n\}$$

where the superset of the *most general specializations under object identity* of C against a negative example N, denoted by $mgs(C, N)$, is formally defined as:

$$mgs(C, N) = \{M \mid M \leq_{OI} C, M \text{ consistent wrt } N,$$
$$\forall D \ D \leq_{OI} C, D \text{ consistent wrt } N : not(M <_{OI} D)\}$$

Throughout this section, we shall denote with C a clause that needs to be specialized, since it is inconsistent wrt an example N. More precisely, the body of C needs to be subjected to a suitable process of specialization in order to restore the consistency property.

Let us consider the problem of finding one of the clauses in the set $mgs(C, N/P_1, P_2, ..., P_n)$. Since the specializations we are looking for satisfy the property of maximal generality, it may happen that the clause C is overly general, even after some refinement steps. This suggests us the possibility of further exploiting the positive examples in order to specialize C. Specifically, if there exists a literal that, when added to the body of C, is able to discriminate from the negative example N that caused the inconsistency of C, then the specializing operator should be able to find it. The resulting specialization should restore the consistency of the clause C, by refining it into a clause C' which still θ_{OI}-subsumes all the positive examples used to train or tune the system.

The process of specializing a clause by means of positive literals can be described as follows. For each $P_i (i=1, 2, ..., n)$, let us suppose that there exist n_i distinct substitutions such that $C \theta_{OI}$-subsumes P_i. Then, let us consider all the possible n-tuples of substitutions obtained by picking one of such substitutions for every positive example. Each of these substitutions is used to produce a distinct *residual*, consisting of all the literals in the positive example that are not involved in the θ_{OI}-subsumption test, after having properly turned their constants into variables. Formally, a residual can be defined as follows.

Definition 5 (Residual) Let C be a clause, E an example, and σ_j a one-to-one substitution such that $body(C).\sigma_j \subseteq body(E)$. A *residual* of E wrt C under the mapping σ_j, denoted by $\Delta_j(E, C)$, is the following set of literals: $\qquad \Delta_j(E, C) = body(E).\underline{\sigma}_j^{-1} - body(C)$

where $\underline{\sigma}_j^{-1}$ is the *extended antisubstitution* (or *inductive substitution*) obtained by inverting the corresponding substitution σ_j. Indeed, an antisubstitution is a mapping from terms into variables [24]. When a clause $C \theta_{OI}$-subsumes an example E through a substitution σ, then it is possible to define a corresponding antisubstitution, σ^{-1}, which is exactly the inverse function of σ. Then, σ^{-1} maps some constants in E to variables in C. Not all constants in E have a corresponding variable according to σ^{-1}. Therefore, in Def. 5, we introduce the extension of σ^{-1}, denoted with $\underline{\sigma}^{-1}$, that is defined on the whole set of constants occurring into E, $consts(E)$, and takes values in the set of the variables of the language:

$$\underline{\sigma}^{-1}(c_n) = \begin{cases} \sigma^{-1}(c_n) & \text{if } c_n \in \text{vars}(C).\sigma \\ \_ & \text{otherwise} \end{cases}$$

Henceforth, variables denoted by _ will be called *new* variables and managed as in Prolog.

The residuals obtained from the positive examples P_i, $i = 1, 2,..., n$, can be exploited to build a *space of complete positive specializations*, denoted with **P**, and formally defined as follows.

$$\mathbf{P} = \bigcup_{\substack{i=1,2,...n \\ j=1,2,...n_i}} \bigcap_{k=1,2,...n} \Delta_{i_k}(P_k, C)$$

where $\Delta_{j_k}(P_k, C)$ denotes one of the n_k residuals of P_k wrt C and $\bigcap_{k=1,2,...,n} \Delta_{j_k}(P_k, C)$, when j_k takes one of the values in $\{1,2,...,n_k\}$, is the set of the literals common to an n-tuple of residuals (one residual for each positive example P_k, $k = 1, 2,..., n$). The definition of the set **P** allows us to achieve the completeness (more precisely the ideality) of the specializing operator (Proof is given in [9]).

Moreover, let us denote with θ_j, $j = 1, 2, ..., m$, all the substitutions which make C inconsistent wrt N. Then, let us define a new set of literals.

$$\mathbf{S} = \bigcup_{j=1,2,...,m} \Delta_j(N, C)$$

Then, the following theorem holds (Proof can be found in [8]).

Theorem. *Given a clause C, that θ_{OI}-subsumes the positive examples $P_1, P_2,..., P_n$ and is inconsistent wrt the negative example N, then any linked clause $C' = C \cup \{l\}$ with $l \in$ P - S, satisfies the following property: C' is in $mgs(C, N \mid P_1, P_2, ..., P_n)$.*

This result states that every specialization built by adding a literal in **P - S** to the inconsistent clause C restores the properties of consistency and completeness of the original hypothesis. Moreover, it is one of the most general specializations of C against N. The Pascal-like function that realizes the search in the space of positive literals **P - S** is described in Figure 2.

```
function specialize_by_positive_literals (C : clause;
                N : example;
                { P₁, P₂, ..., Pₙ} : examples) : clause;
begin
(sigma, nsost) :=
        test_for_θₒᵢsubsumption ( body(C), body(N) );
for i := 1 to nsost do
    R[i] := make_residual (i, sigma, C, N);
S := make_union(R, nsost);
P := make_P (C, { P₁, P₂, ..., Pₙ} );
if (( P - S ) ≠ ∅) then
    begin
    l := choose_best_literal ( P - S );
    C' := C ∪ { l };
    return C'
    end;
return C     (* no spec. found by this operator *)
end;
```

Fig. 2. Pascal-like function that implements the search in the space of the positive literals.

When the space **P - S** does not contain any solution to the problem of specializing an inconsistent clause, the search is automatically extended to the space of negative literals. A detailed description of the specializing operator that searches in the space of negative literals can be found in [6]. The operator implemented in INCR/ H is a straight transposition of such an operator from VL_{21} language to clausal logic.

6 Application to the Problem of Document Classification

Several experiments have been organized in order to compare the performance of hierarchical logical theories learned incrementally to those learned in batch mode. All the experiments have been performed by using INCR/H. The evaluation of the results takes into account both the predictive accuracy of the learned theories and the time spent during the learning process.

Experiments have been carried out in the area of *document classification* [7], which is a crucial task in electronic document processing. Document classification aims at identifying the *membership class* of a document. In fact, wherever paper documents are handled, a primary demand is that of grouping documents into classes, according to criteria that usually differ from an environment to another, such as the common subject or the kind of processing the documents must undergo. In most cases, documents belonging to the same class have a set of relevant and invariant layout characteristics, called *page layout signature*, which allows the document to be recognized. The page layout of a document is reconstructed by a process of layout analysis and is translated into a linked clause. An example of the page layout of a document and the corresponding description in clausal form is given by Figure 3.

In our experiments, we considered a database of 171 single-page documents (faxes, forms and letters), belonging to five document classes from specific firms (*AEG, Olivetti, SIFI, SIMS* and *SOGEA*) and to a further set of nine heterogeneous documents (*Reject*). Each document is a positive example for the class it belongs to and, at the same time, is a negative example for all the other classes. The only exceptions are represented by the nine documents in *Reject*, which are exploited as negative examples for all five classes to be learned. For each class, the two refinement operators have been tested separately. The experiments have been replicated five times for the generalizing operator and ten times for the specializing one, by randomly splitting the database of 171 documents into two subsets, namely a *learning* set and a *test* set. In turn, the learning set has been subdivided into *training* set and *tuning* set (the sizes of these sets for each class are reported in Table 1). The learning set has been exploited in two distinct ways, according to the mode - batch or incremental - adopted to learn the logical theory. For the batch

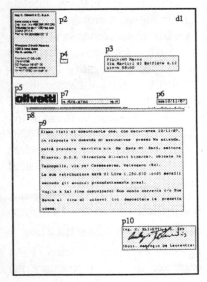

Olivetti(d1) :-
part_of(d1,p2), part_of(d1,p3), part_of(d1,p4), part_of(d1,p5), part_of(d1,p6), part_of(d1,p7), part_of(d1,p8), part_of(d1,p9), part_of(d1,p10),
width-medium(p2), width-medium-large(p3), width-smallest(p4), width-medium(p5), width-medium-small(p6), width-medium-large(p7), width-very-very-large(p8), width-very-very-large(p9), width-medium-large(p10),
height-medium-large(p2), height-small(p3), height-smallest(p4), height-very-small(p5), height-very-very-small(p6), height-very-very-small(p7), height-smallest(p8), height-large(p9), height-medium-small(p10),
type-text(p2), type-text(p3), type-text(p4), type-picture(p5), type-text(p6), type-text(p7), type-text(p8), type-text(p9), type-mixture(p10),
position-top-left(p2), position-top(p3), position-top-left(p4), position-top-left(p5), position-top-right(p6), position-top(p7), position-center(p8), position-center(p9), position-bottom-right(p10), on_top(p5,p8), on_top(p6,p8), on_top(p7,p8), on_top(p9,p10), to_right(p2,p4), to_right(p5,p7),
aligned-both-columns(p2,p5), aligned-only-lower-row(p5,p7), aligned-only-left-col(p4,p7), aligned-both-rows(p7,p6), aligned-only-right-col(p8,p9), aligned-only-upper-row(p4,p3)

Fig. 3. Page layout of an Olivetti letter and its logic description.

Table 1. Sizes of the example sets in the experimentations with (a) the generalizing operator and (b) the specializing one.

	(a)					(b)			
	Training set (batch) #pos+#neg	Training set (incr.) #pos+#neg	Tuning set #pos	Test set #neg		Training set (batch) #pos+#neg	Training set (incr.) #pos+#neg	Tuning set #neg	Test set #neg
AEG	27+74	7+74	20	70	AEG	27+94	27+24	70	50
Olivetti	46+80	20+80	26	65	Olivetti	46+55	46+30	25	70
SIFI	34+67	14+67	20	70	SIFI	34+67	34+37	30	70
SIMS	30+70	10+70	20	71	SIMS	30+71	30+31	40	70
SOGEA	25+70	5+70	20	76	SOGEA	25+86	25+16	70	60

mode, this set has been entirely given to INDUBI/H as its input. For the incremental mode, only the training set has been used by INDUBI/H in order to produce the first version of the theory, while the tuning set has been used by the Rule Refiner to correct both omission and commission errors, if any. It is worth noting that the tuning set is made up of only positive (negative) examples in every replication concerning the generalizing (specializing) operator. As a consequence, only omission (commission) errors may occur when testing the generalizing (specializing) operator. The lower number of replications performed for the generalizing operator is justified by the fact that the positive examples available for each class are largely fewer than the negative ones. The specializing operator has been tested according to three distinct approaches. In the first approach (*positive*), the search for a complete and consistent hypothesis has been performed only in the space of positive literals. In the second approach (*negative*), the search has been restricted to the space of negative literals, whereas both spaces have been explored in the last approach (*integrated*).

Table 2 shows the results concerning the generalizing operator. Specifically, this table compares the theory learned in batch mode with that learned incrementally along two dimensions, namely their predictive accuracy on the test set (*P.A.*) and the computational time taken by the learning system to produce the theory (*Time*). All the reported figures refer to the averages on the five replications. Table 3 illustrates the results of the paired two-tailed t-test for each learned class (each entry contains the t value and the corresponding significance level).

It is worthwhile to note that the batch theory outperforms the incremental one for all the classes, with the exception of *Olivetti*, as regards the predictive accuracy. However, Table 3 states that there is no statistically significant difference between the two theories (the probability of error in rejecting the hypothesis that the two average values are equal is greater than 0.01). On the contrary, there is a statistically significant improvement when learning a theory in incremental mode wrt learning it in batch mode, as regards the computational time.

Generalizing Operator		batch	incremental
AEG	P.A. %	100	91.2
	Time (secs)	490.2	281.2
Olivetti	P.A. %	90.6	93.8
	Time (secs)	580.8	338.2
SIFI	P.A. %	99.8	99.4
	Time (secs)	386.2	254.6
SIMS	P.A. %	96.2	96.0
	Time (secs)	717.2	329.0
SOGEA	P.A. %	98.0	97.2
	Time (secs)	219.2	173.4

Table 2. Comparison of the average predictive accuracies on the test set (*P.A.*) and the average computational times (*Time*) for the generalizing operator.

The results concerning the specializing operator are reported

Table 3. t value and significance value for the paired two-tailed t-test on the results obtained by the generalizing operator.

Generalizing Operator	P.A.		Time	
	t value	significance value	t value	significance value
AEG	2.357	.0779	4.982	.0076
Olivetti	-.382	.07217	6.578	.0028
SIFI	.590	.5870	1.628	.1789
SIMS	.087	.9346	4.874	.0082
SOGEA	1.372	.2420	4.746	.0090

in Table 4. In this case, the theory learned in batch mode is compared with three theories learned incrementally according to the three distinct approaches above mentioned, namely by searching either into the space of positive literals (*pos*), or into the space of negative literals (*neg*) or into both these spaces (*int*). Again, the comparison has been focused on the values of the predictive accuracies on the test set (*P.A.*) and of the computational times (*Time*), averaged on the ten replications.

An analysis of Table 4 leads us to observe that: i) Both the positive incremental approach and the negative one have a lower error rate on three hypotheses out of five; ii) The integrated incremental approach determines an increase in the predictive accuracy of all the hypotheses with the exception of the class *SIMS*; iii) For two hypotheses, namely those concerning *AEG* faxes and *SIFI* letters, each incremental method gives better results than the batch one, as to their predictive accuracy; iv) Each incremental method outperforms the batch one as to the computational times, as expected.

By pairwise comparing the average predictive accuracies and computational times obtained by the different methods by means of the paired two-tailed t-test (Table 5), we can conclude that neither the increases nor the decreases of the predictive accuracies for the theories learned by the three incremental methods are statistically significant, with the exceptions of the results concerning the class *SIFI*. In such a case, for both the positive and the integrated incremental approach the probability of error in rejecting the hypothesis that the two average values are equal is less than the confidence level 0.01. Conversely, the difference in the computational times is statistically significant.

Specializing Operator		batch	Incremental (pos)	Incremental (neg)	Incremental (Int)
AEG	P.A. %	97.8	99.6	98.8	99.6
	Time (secs)	508.4	196.8	198.4	200.5
Olivetti	P.A. %	97.7	97.3	98.1	98.1
	Time (secs)	490.9	330.6	332.6	334.1
SIFI	P.A. %	98.7	99.7	99.1	99.7
	Time (secs)	194.4	143.9	138.0	138.3
SIMS	P.A. %	98.4	97.2	96.3	97.4
	Time (secs)	446.8	257.1	252.3	252.4
SOGEA	P.A. %	98.0	98.6	97.0	98.6
	Time (secs)	194.3	56.3	55.2	54.6

Table 4. Comparison of the average predictive accuracies on the test set (*P.A.*) and the average computational times (*Time*) for the specializing operator.

The overall analysis of the experimental results shows that the differences of the predictive accuracies between the batch method and the incremental ones are not statistically significant in most cases (18 out of 20) and, in the only two cases in which they

Table 5. Specializing operator: statistical results.

Specializing Operator	batch vs. positive				batch vs. negative				batch vs. integrated			
	P.A.		Time		P.A.		Time		P.A.		Time	
	t value	sign. value	t value	sign. value	t value	sign. value	t value	sign. value	t value	sign. value	t value	sign. value
AEG	-3.000	.0150	9.463	.0001	-1.103	.2987	9.380	.0001	-2.212	.0543	9.413	.0001
Olivetti	.368	.7215	6.946	.0001	-.440	.6704	6.835	.0001	-.440	.6704	6.721	.0001
SIFI	-3.354	.0085	11.908	.0001	-.802	.4433	13.006	.0001	-3.354	.0085	12.902	.0001
SIMS	1.230	.2497	14.564	.0001	2.045	.0712	14.075	.0001	1.103	.2987	14.078	.0001
SOGEA	-.745	.4754	16.427	.0001	1.205	.2590	16.479	.0001	-.745	.4754	16.522	.0001

are significant, the incrementally learned theory outperforms the batch one. In addition, by comparing the percentage values of the predictive accuracies, the incremental approach behaves better than the batch one in 11 cases out of 20. As to the computational times, the decrease occurs in all the cases and, in addition, it is statistically significant in 19 cases out of 20.

7 Conclusions and Related Work

Automated revision of first-order logical theories is a complex task. In fact, most systems for theory revision deal with propositional logic, including RTLS [9], DUCE [14], EITHER [16], KBANN [25]. Nevertheless, it is possible to find in the literature of machine learning a number of systems that can revise first-order theories. Some of them, such as MIS [23], CIGOL [15], CLINT [5], strongly rely on the interaction with the user to reduce the search space, while others, such as WHY [21], TRACEY [2] and KBI [3], do not require any interaction with the user during the induction process and adopt sophisticated search strategies or more informative search structures. Other systems for theory revision, such as FORTE [20], and AUDREY [26], do not allow negative literals to be expressed in the body of the clauses. In fact, several systems that learn and revise theories from positive and negative examples do not search in the space of negative literals because of computational complexity considerations. As a consequence, half of the whole search space is not explored during either a batch learning process or an incremental one. This choice has some potential harmful consequences on the learnability of the correct theories in some tasks and on the predictive accuracy of the learned theories in other tasks.

In the paper, we have presented INCR/H, a new system for revising hierarchical first-order logical theories. The main characteristic of the system consists of the capability of autonomously performing a representation change, that allows it to extend the search for a correct theories to the space of clauses with negative literals in the body. This lets INCR/H cope effectively and efficiently with the real-world task of document classification. The results obtained show that an incremental approach to theory revision is able to produce theories that have a predictive accuracy statistically comparable to that of theories learned *from scratch*. Nevertheless, as expected, the computational costs of incremental learning are largely lower than those required by batch learning, and this difference is statistically significant.

Future work will concern the use of a distance measure to face the problems of selecting the *most promising* example when more than one observation contradicts the theory, and of selecting the most promising clause in an incomplete hypothesis.

References

[1] Becker, J.M., *Inductive Learning of Decision Rules with Exceptions: Methodology and Experimentation*, B.S. dissertation, Department of Computer Science, University of Illinois at Urbana-Champaign, Urbana, Illinois, UIUCDCS-F-85-945, August 1985.

[2] Bergadano, F., and Gunetti, D., Learning Clauses by Tracing Derivations, *Proceed. of the 4ᵗʰ Int'l Workshop on Inductive Logic Programming, ILP-94*, S. Wrobel (Ed.), 1-29, 1994.

[3] Botta, M., Learning First Order Theories, in *Methodologies for Intelligent Systems - Proceedings of the 8th International Symposium, ISMIS '94*, Lecture Notes in Artificial Intelligence 869, Z.W. Ras and M. Zemankova (Eds.), Springer-Verlag, 356-365, 1994.

[4] Clark, K.L., Negation as failure, in *Logic and Databases*, H. Gallaire and J. Minker (Eds.), Plenum Press, New York, 1978.

[5] De Raedt, L., *Interactive Theory Revision - An Inductive Logic Programming Approach*, AP, 1992.

[6] Esposito, F., Malerba, D., and Semeraro, G., Negation as a Specializing Operator, in *Advances in Artificial Intelligence - Proceedings of the Third Congress of the Italian Association for Artificial Intelligence AI*IA 93*, Lecture Notes in Artificial Intelligence 728, P. Torasso (Ed.), Springer-Verlag, 166-177, 1993.

[7] Esposito, F., Malerba, D., and Semeraro, G., Multistrategy Learning for Document Recognition, *Applied Artificial Intelligence: An International Journal*, Vol.8, No.1, 33-84, 1994.

[8] Esposito, F., Fanizzi, N., Malerba, D., Semeraro, G., Downward Refinement of Hierarchical Datalog Theories, *Proceedings of the Joint Conference on Declarative Programming, GULP-PRODE'95*, 1995.

[9] Ginsberg, A., Theory Reduction, Theory Revision, and Retranslation, *Proceedings of the 8th National Conference on Artificial Intelligence* (AAAI-90), 777-782, 1990.

[10] Grant, J., & Subrahmanian, V.S., Reasoning in Inconsistent Knowledge Bases, *IEEE Transactions on Knowledge and Data Engineering*, Vol.7, N.1, 177-189, 1995.

[11] Hayes-Roth, F., and McDermott, J., Knowledge acquisition from structural descriptions, *Proceed. of the 5th International Joint Conference on AI*, Cambridge, MA, 356-362, 1977.

[12] Helft, N., Inductive Generalization: A Logical Framework, in *Progress in Machine Learning - Proceedings of EWSL 87: 2nd European Working Session on Learning*, I. Bratko & N. Lavrac (Eds.), Sigma Press, Wilmslow, 149-157, 1987.

[13] Lloyd, J.W., *Foundations of Logic Programming*, Second Edition, Springer-Verlag, New York, 1987.

[14] Muggleton, S., Duce, an Oracle based approach to constructive induction, *Proceedings of the 10th International Joint Conference on Artificial Intelligence*, 287-292, 1987.

[15] Muggleton, S., and Buntine, W., Machine Invention of First-order Predicates by Inverting Resolution, *Proceed. of the 5th International Conference on Machine Learning*, 339-352, 1988.

[16] Ourston, D., and Mooney, R. J., Changing the Rules: A Comprehensive Approach to Theory Refinement, *Proceed. of the 8th National Conference on AI* (AAAI-90), 815-820, 1990.

[17] Plotkin, G.D., A Note on Inductive Generalization, in *Machine Intelligence 5*, B. Meltzer and D. Michie (Eds.), 153 - 163, Edinburgh University Press, 1970.

[18] Reinke, R.E., Michalski, R.S., Incremental Learning of Concept Descriptions: A Method and Experimental Results, *Machine Intelligence 11*, Donald Michie (editor), 1985.

[19] Reiter, R., Equality and domain closure in first order databases, *Journal of ACM*, 27, 235-249, 1980.

[20] Richards, B. L., and Mooney, R. J., First-Order Theory Revision, *Proceedings of the 8th International Workshop on Machine Learning*, 447-451, 1991.

[21] Saitta, L., Botta, M., and Neri, F., Multistrategy Learning and Theory Revision, *Machine Learning 11*, 153-172, 1993.

[22] Semeraro, G., Esposito, F., Malerba, D., Brunk, C., and Pazzani, M., Avoiding Non-Termination when Learning Logic Programs: A Case Study with FOIL and FOCL, in *Logic Program Synthesis and Transformation - Meta-Programming in Logic*, Lecture Notes in Computer Science 883, L. Fribourg and F. Turini (Eds.), Springer-Verlag, 183-198, 1994.

[23] Shapiro, E. Y., *Algorithmic Program Debugging*, MIT Press, 1983.

[24] Siekmann, J. H., An Introduction to Unification Theory, in *Formal Techniques in Artificial Intelligence - A Sourcebook*, R. B. Banerji (Ed.), Elsevier Science Publishers B.V. (North Holland), 1990.

[25] Towell, G. G., Shavlik, J. W., and Noordewier, M. O., Refinement of Approximate Domain Theories by Knowledge-Based Neural Networks, *Proceedings of the 8th National Conference on Artificial Intelligence* (AAAI-90), 861-866, 1990.

[26] Wogulis, J., Revising Relational Domain Theories, *Proceedings of the 8th International Workshop on Machine Learning*, 462-466, 1991.

[27] S. Wrobel (Ed.), *Proceed. of the MLNet Workshop on Theory Revision and Restructuring in Machine Learning*, ECML-94, Catania, Italy, Arbeitspapiere der GMD N.842, 1994.

Reformulation of Examples in Concept Learning of Structural Descriptions

Jean-Daniel Zucker

LAFORIA-IBP, Université Paris 6
4, place Jussieu - Boite 169,
75252 Paris Cedex 05, France
Tel: (33-1) 4427-7119 Fax: (33-1) 4427-7000
zucker@laforia.ibp.fr

Abstract. This paper describes a novel approach to address the task of learning structural descriptions by incremental representation shifts of learning examples. While in attribute-value representations only one mapping is possible between descriptions, in first order logic based representations there are potentially many mappings. To cope with the intractability of exploring all mappings, classical approaches consider all mappings and then define a restricted hypothesis space. Our approach is to select one particular type of mapping at a time and use it as a basis to define a hypothesis space called Matching Space that may be represented using attribute-value pairs. It appears that characterizing a Matching Space is equivalent to shifting the representation of examples. We provide a proof that Matching Spaces are partially ordered by their size and that there exists a set of Matching Spaces which are, as a whole, equivalent to the initial representation space. Experimental results show the benefits of this approach on a well known learning task.

1 Introduction

In supervised learning, there is a known trade-off between representation and complexity in the choice of the representation space used to represent the examples [20]. On one end of the spectrum of choice, there are propositional logic representations where each example is characterized by a set of attribute/value pairs; on the other end of the spectrum there are first order logic representations where each example is represented using predicates [22]. The main justification for using first order logic based representations is the "representational inadequacy" of attribute-value pairs to represent structured objects and relations [1]. However, for representations based on first order logic, the associated hypothesis space, representing the candidate concept descriptions, is not only infinite but basic operations used for learning such as *matching descriptions* are NP-complete. In machine learning, a classical approach to cope with the intractable nature of this operation consists in strongly restraining the hypothesis space. This approach is typically used by Inductive Logic Programming (ILP) systems that learn relations as logic programs [12].

Another approach to address the representation/complexity trade-off consists in *reformulating* the existing representation space to improve the quality of learning [25, 3]. In *deductive* reformulation, improving the quality of learning involves finding *"conceptual transformations leading to formulations that are computationally effective for certain classes of queries"* [26]. Most of the work in this research area is concerned with *abstracting* representations from the initial representation [5, 6, 8]. Our research belongs to the domain of deductive reformulation inasmuch as we aim at reformulating the existing representation in representations that are computationally more effective with respect to the matching problem in learning structural descriptions. Our approach is original in the sense that we are concerned with the very *nature* of the examples used for learning rather than just the relevant information or level of abstraction to describe them [28].

To the best of our knowledge, no work to date has formalized the relation between the domain examples and the nature of the entity used to represent them. In many domains, there are "natural entities" (a "patient" in medicine, an "animal" in zoology, a "molecule" in chemistry, etc.) that impose themselves as the entities to be represented in the examples used for learning. There are cases where it is useful to shift from the representation of these entities in order to achieve a more efficient learning. The purpose of our research is to provide a framework for representing these new entities and to show that incrementally exploring the different representation shifts based on the different entities is an efficient approach to the complex task of learning structural descriptions. This paper is the continuation of earlier work [28].

In section two we give some definitions and present the problem of matching structural descriptions. In the third section we introduce an approach to this problem based on selective mappings. In section four we present our approach to learn structural descriptions based on such selective mappings and prove a useful theorem justifying an incremental reformulation. In section five we present an experiment of the proposed approach using the REMO system.

2 Definitions and problem overview

In essence, one of the basic ideas presented here is related to the impact of the description of examples on the learning task. In machine learning, examples are often identified with their descriptions [10]. For the purpose of our work we shall emphasize the differences between *domain examples* that stands for "facts or things illustrating a given concept" and *learning examples* that are instances of a given representation language. To illustrate these differences, let us consider the artificial task introduced by Michalski [17] that consists in discriminating trains heading west from those heading east. In this task, the *domain examples* were provided as a picture (see Fig. 1) and the original *learning examples* were given as Variable Logic VL_2 expressions [4]. VL_2 is an "extension to first order predicate logic", an ancestor of APC (Annotated Predicate Calculus), introduced by Michalski and Larson [18]. When such a first order logic representation is

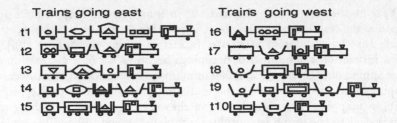

Fig. 1. Domain examples for Michalski's trains

used, it becomes necessary to match structurally the logical descriptions before *generalizing* descriptions [14, 19, 21]. An intuitive perspective on the structural matching of two logical descriptions may be given using their associated graphs G1 and G2. We use Haussler's graphs that he proved to be equivalent to VL_2 conjunctive formulas [10]. A learning example is represented as a complete directed graph called *instance graphe*. Each node, representing an object, is labeled with the observed value of each attribute for that object (e.g. for the first car of train t2: `#wheel=2, location=1, length=long, cshape=engine` and `#load=0`. See Fig 2). A directed edge from the node representing obj1 to the node representing obj2 represents a binary relation between the ordered pair (obj1,obj2). Let us now define the matching of two graphs G1 and G2.

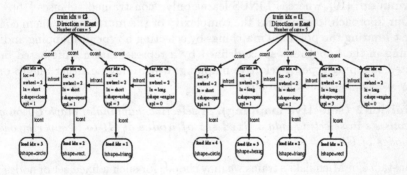

Fig. 2. Two learning examples representing trains t2 and t1 as instance graphs

Definition 1 (graph mapping and graph matching). *A mapping of graph G1 on graph G2 consists in selecting the nodes of G1 to be superimposed on the nodes of G2. If both edges and attributes of the two graphs agree (but not necessarily the values), G1 is said to match G2 under this mapping.*

Two main types of mapping are usually considered: a *one-to-one mapping* where each node of G1 is mapped to a different node of G2, and a mapping called *many-to-one mapping* [11]. In the case of trains t2 and t1 (see Fig. 2), the number of possible mappings of the first graph (with 8 nodes) on the second (10 nodes) is 10!/2! in one-to-one mapping and 10^8 in many-to-one mapping. In practice, to reduce the number of mappings, it is possible to disallow mappings between objects that have different attributes (a sort of typing mechanism [10]). Under such a restriction the number of mappings becomes $1 \times 5! \times 4! = 2880$ in one-to-one mapping and $1 \times 5^4 \times 4^3 = 40000$ in many-to-one mapping. In any case, once mappings have been identified, the matching problem refers to the problem of finding a mapping under which G1 matches G2. This graph matching problem is equivalent to the graph isomorphism problem, known to be NP-complete [13].

3 Selective mapping to address the matching problem in learning structural descriptions

Approaches to the matching problem have so much impact on the tractability of learning algorithms that Dietterich and Michalski have used them as the criterion for comparing computational efficiency between various structural description learning algorithms [4]. In practice, to search for all possible matchings without constraints as in Plotkin's relative least general generalization (rlgg), leads to algorithms that have a complexity which is exponential with the number of examples [21]. In recent ILP systems that learn descriptions of relations as logic programs, strong syntactical restrictions on the hypothesis space have been defined to cope with the computational complexity of the matching problem. For instance, GOLEM learns "determinate" clauses of bounded depth (ij-determinism) [19], whereas LINUS learns only "constrained" clauses [16].

Our approach to cope with the complexity of the matching problem consists in first limiting the potential matchings by selecting a type of mapping and then learning in the hypothesis space defined by a representation shift based on the selected mapping type. A selective mapping, which may be either one-to-one or many-to-one, is defined as follow:

Definition 2 (selective mapping). *A selective mapping of graph G1 on graph G2 consists in selecting only a **fixed set of nodes** of G1 to be superimposed on the nodes of G2.*

For instance in Michalski's trains we may choose for such a fixed set of nodes "one train node and two car nodes". In this case, the number of selective mappings between the trains t2 and t1 is $1 \times 5 \times 4 = 20$ in one-to-one mapping and $1 \times 5^2 = 25$ in many-to-one mapping. In deference to the pioneering work on structural descriptions and partial matching in the field of pattern recognition, we shall call a fixed number of nodes (e.g. "one train node and two car nodes") a *prototype structure* [2, 23].

A somewhat similar approach has been used in INDUCE [4]. Given the VL_2 description of a learning example called *seed*, the system chooses different descriptions of candidate conjunctive generalizations using only *relations* appearing in the seed. Each description is then used to perform a sort of selective mappings with the other examples descriptions. However, one important disadvantage noted by the authors is "the problem of defining plausible descriptions in the space of all relations" [4]. Indeed, the space of all relations is growing exponentially with the number of nodes and relations.

Our main idea is that the different binary relations should not be treated equally. The binary relation *infront* that relates two cars has a different impact on the matching problem than the binary relation *is-part-of* that relates a car and a train. Indeed, the first one will impact on whether or not a given mapping is a matching, while the second does directly impact on the number of possible mappings. We shall now analyze in depth the nature of a particular type of relation, the *part-of* relation, and present how a limited number of plausible prototypes could be defined using such relation.

In knowledge representation, the *part-of* relations, also called *mereological* relations, characterize all the relations that link a whole to its parts [24]. Among the variety of mereological relations, we shall consider the *component/object* relation [27]. This relation is crucial in many real world applications [9] and is also adapted to represent domain examples such as Michalski's trains. A part-of relation is called "component/object" if it is functional (different parts may have different functions), non-homeomerous (parts are not similar to the whole), and separable (parts may be physically or mentally separated from the whole). Let us now introduce the notion of prototype structure based on the component/object relation only. We shall use a neologism, *morion* (from morion, meaning "part" in Greek), to designate such particular prototype structures [28]:

Definition 3 (elementary morion). *Any component/object part of the domain examples shall be called an elementary morion.*

In a logical description, an elementary morion would correspond to a *type* of constant. To illustrate this definition, let us consider some elementary morions that may be defined on the domain examples of trains. An implicit elementary morion is the train itself. Other elementary morions include "one-car", "one-wheel", "one-form" or "one-load". We shall call *morionomy* a taxonomy of elementary morions based on the component/object relation (see examples of morionomies on Fig. 3).

Definition 4 (morionomy). *A directed acyclic tree, where each node represents a different elementary morion and each edge represents a component/object relation, is called a morionomy. An edge of such a tree, between the elementary morions m and sm, is labeled with K_{sm} the greatest numberof occurrences of morions sm in morion m throughout the learning examples.*

Given a morionomy M, we shall call morion μ the *prototype* composed of *exactly* K_{sm} nodes sm for each elementary morion sm of the morionomy M. The morion μ in the morionomy M1 of Fig.3 is a train composed of 5 cars each composed of 1 load. Given a morion μ, let us characterize $L(\mu)$ the set of morions based on μ. A morion x $\in L(\mu)$ iff x is a prototype composed of $k_{sm} \leq K_{sm}$ nodes sm for each elementary morion sm of the morionomy M. For instance, given the morion μ of the morionomy M1 of Fig.3, $L(\mu)$ includes the morions "two-car with one-load" ($k_{car}=2$ and $k_{load}=1$), "one-car with no load" ($k_{car}=1$ and $k_{load}=0$), etc.

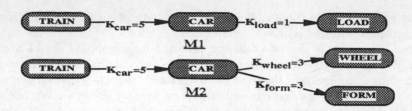

Fig. 3. Two different morionomies M1 and M2 of the domain of trains

A generality relation $\geq_\mu$ between morions of $L(\mu)$ may be easily defined by m1, m2 $\in$ L(μ) m1 $\geq_\mu$ m2 iff L(m2) $\subset$ L(m1). For instance the morion "two-car" is more general than the morion "one-car". This relation provides $L(\mu)$ with a *lattice* structure. Given two morions m1, m2 $\in$ L(μ), let us call m- and m+ respectively their smallest element and greatest element. m+ is obtained by considering the morion $\in$ L(μ) composed of k_{sm}=Max($k1_{sm}, k2_{sm}$) nodes sm for each elementary morion sm of the morionomy M; m- is obtained by considering the morion $\in$ L(μ) composed of k_{sm}=Min($k1_{sm}, k2_{sm}$) nodes sm for each elementary morion sm of the morionomy M. One of the useful properties of the lattice $L(\mu)$ is its limited size. Indeed, the number of morions of $L(\mu)$ is:

$$|L(\mu)| = \prod_{sm \in M} (k_{sm} + 1)$$

For instance, given the morionomy M1 of Fig. 3 (k_{car}=5 and k_{load}=1) there are only $(5 + 1) \times (1 + 1)$=12 different morions in L(μ).

4 Representation shift using morions

Our idea is now to use the set of defined morions to create new learning examples that instead of representing domain examples, represent a particular morion. Let us first introduce the notion of morion instance:

Definition 5 (instance of morion). *The instances of a morion m on a domain example e represent all the different mappings (either one-to-one or many-to-one) of m on the instance graph of e.*

For example, under the one-to-one mapping assumption, there are 20 instances of the morion "two-car" in the first domain example t1. This number represents precisely the number of possible ordered pairs of different cars on the first domain example of Fig.1. Let us use this notion of morion instance to characterize a *representation shift* based on a morion m.

Definition 6 (moriological reformulation). *Using attribute-value pairs for describing all instances of a morion m on all the initial learning examples is called a moriological reformulation based on m.*

383

To illustrate this idea let us present a concrete example of a reformulation in the Michalski's trains problem. Let us consider the prototype "two-car" composed of "one train node, two car nodes and their associated load node". Having defined attributes to describe this prototype structure, the reformulation consists in assigning values to the prototype structure attributes for each mapping of each initial example with the prototype structure (see Table 1). Under the one-to-one mapping assumption this reformulation produces 126 new learning examples of the "two-car" entity described by attribute/value pairs. Using this

new learning exqmples	1 indirect	2 intrain	3 A_infront_B	4 locA	5 locB	....	16 lshapeA	17 lshapeB
ex1	East	t1	true	1	2	....	-	rectangle
ex2	East	t1	false	1	3	....	-	triangle
ex3	East	t1	false	1	4	....	-	hexagon
ex4	East	t1	false	1	5	....	-	circle
ex5	East	t1	false	2	1	....	rectangle	-
..	...	...	...	...	...	....	....	...
ex126	West	t10	false	3	2	....	rectangle	rectangle

Table 1. New learning examples based on a morion two-car

representation along with some knowledge on the tree-structured values of the attributes of the shapes of loads and a propositional learner, we may learn the concept *trains going east* as the following description:

(A_infront_B=true $\wedge$ lshapeA=triangle $\wedge$ lshapeB=polygon) $\Longrightarrow$ in-direct=East

This description may be reformulated in Variable Logic:

$$\exists\ carA,\ carB,\ loadA,\ loadB;\ [infront(carA,carB)]$$
$$[lcont(carA,loadA)]\ [lcont(carB,loadB)]\ [lshape(loadA)=triangle]$$
$$[lshape(loadB)=polygon] \Longrightarrow [direction=East]$$

The representation space defined by the new learning examples shall be called a *Matching Space*. In the case of the above representation shift based on the "two-car" morion (see Table 1), the Matching Space is defined by the 126 learning examples obtained after the moriological reformulation. More formally:

Definition 7 (Matching Space). *A Matching Space, noted MS(m), is the hypothesis space defined by the learning examples obtained after a moriological reformulation based on m.*

Thanks to the inherent structure of MS(m), typical propositional logic-based algorithms may be used to learn in MS(m). Let us now prove that existential conjunctive concepts that can be learned in the initial representation space may be learned in the Matching Spaces.

384

Lemma 8 (Matching Space order). *The Matching Spaces are partially ordered by their associated morion.*

Sketch of Proof: Given a morion μ, let $m1, m2 \in L(\mu)$. If morion $m1$ is more general than morion $m2$ ($m1 \geq_\mu m2$), $L(m2) \subset L(m1)$. Thus any selective mapping based on $m2$ may be obtained as part of a particular selective mapping based on $m1$. Therefore, $MS(m2) \subset MS(m1)$ and the size of $MS(m1) \geq MS(m2)$.

The main interest of this partial ordering is that it provides a partial order on the sizes of the Matching Spaces to search through. Nevertheless, it is only a partial order and for choosing between several morions that cannot be compared, we shall use an estimate measure of their complexity (see table 4). Let us now introduce a theorem that will justify the incremental search within Matching Spaces as an alternative to the search in the initial hypothesis space.

Theorem 9 (equivalence). *Given X a Variable Logic-based representation space, a set of learning examples represented in X, and a morionomy M; searching in X for existential conjunctive concepts is equivalent to searching for the same concepts in all Matching Spaces $MS(m)$ where $m \in L(\mu)$.*

Sketch of Proof. By definition of μ and in virtue of the above lemma, $\forall\ m \in L(\mu)$, $m \leq_\mu \mu$. Therefore, $MS(m) \subset MS(\mu)$ and it follows that

$$\bigcup_{m \in L(\mu)} MS(m) \subset MS(\mu).$$

To prove the theorem it is sufficient to prove that searching in X is equivalent to searching in $MS(\mu)$. For each existential conjunctive expression over X, there exists a canonical form represented as a formula $\exists x_{1,1}, \dots x_{1,k_1}, x_{2,1}, \dots, x_{r,k_r}\ \Phi(x_{1,1}, \dots x_{1,k_1}, x_{2,1}, \dots, x_{r,k_r})$ where $x_{1,1}, \dots x_{1,k_1}, x_{2,1}, \dots, x_{r,k_r}$ are all distinct variables that denote unknown different objects and each k_i is smaller or equal to the maximum number of objects that share the same attributes throughout the learning examples. By definition of μ, the prototype associated to $x_{1,1}, \dots x_{1,k1}, x_{2,1}, \dots x_{r,kr}$ is less general than μ, and Φ may be represented in $MS(\mu)$.

Given a morionomy M, the task of learning structural descriptions from examples may be recast as a problem of repeating two searches: *search in the lattice* $L(\mu)$ for a morion m and then *search in the Matching Space* $MS(m)$ using an efficient algorithm for attribute-value representation. For any given learning task, there are various ways of exploring the lattice $L(\mu)$. We have implemented in a system called REMO an exploration of this lattice from the most specific morion to the most general, i.e. from the smaller Matching Space towards the bigger.

5 An experiment with REMO

We have chosen to experiment the gain from learning in Matching Spaces whose associated morions are of decreasing generality. Given the morionomy $M(\mu)$, we have considered that learning in $MS(\mu)$, where all the possible mappings are performed, was a reference for measuring what could be learning without reformulation. We have used for the experimentation the Michalski's trains learning examples with the morionomy M1 of Fig 3. The experiments consisted in exploring various Matching Spaces of increasing size and comparing the CPU time needed to *find at least one description* that would discriminate the learning examples of trains. The experiments were run using a propositional learner called ENIGME+, an implementation of the CHARADE algorithm [7]. Identical exploration parameters were used in all Matching Spaces. The Matching Spaces explored were automatically generated by REMO for morions of increasing size: "one-car without load", "one-car", "two-car", "three-car " and "four-car". The results are presented in Table 2. For each Matching Space, the CPU time is provided in seconds along with the ratio CPU time (with/without reformulation).

Morion	CPU (sec)	CPU ratio (%)
one-car w/o.load	0,5	0,19
one-car	0,5	0,19
two-car	1,6	0,60
three-car	12,6	4,74
four-car	59,0	22,18
Without Ref.	266,0	100,00

Table 2. CPU time needed to find at least one dicriminant description

The results show that the time required to find a description that covers all learning examples is growing exponentially with the size of the Matching Space. In fact, with a reformulation based on the specific morion "one-car without load", a description that covers all the examples was found almost instantaneously. It is instructive to analyze to which Matching Spaces the rules represented in VL_2 originally given by Michalski and Larson [18] belong. Table 3 provides the definition for each of these rules (we exclude the one based on a constructive induction operator) and indicates the smallest Matching Space required to learn such rules. The complexity of a learning algorithm based on an attribute-value representation depends, amongst other factors, on the number of learning examples N_{Ex}, the number of attributes used in an example description N_{Att} and the number of possible values per attribute. We shall neglect this latter factor in our analysis as it is identical in all Matching Spaces, and use N_{Att} times N_{Ex} as a basic complexity criterion. The complexity ratio is defined as the ratio of the complex-

	Rule description	Smallest Matching Space needed needed to learn such rule
	$[infront(car1, car2)][lcont(car1, load1)]$ $[lcont(car2, load2)][loadshape(load1) = triangle]$ $[loadshape(load2) = polygon] \Longrightarrow [dir = east]$	MS(two-car)
	$[ln(car1) = short][car - shape(car1) = closed - top]$ $\Longrightarrow [dir = east]$	MS(one-car w/o load)
	$[ncar = 3] \vee [car1(carsshape(car1) = jaggedtop]$ $\Longrightarrow [dir = west]$	MS(one-car w/o load)

Table 3. Matching Spaces required to find Michalski's rules

ity criterion for the considered Matching Space by the complexity criterion for $MS(\mu)$. The results obtained in the case of many-to-one mappings are presented in Table 4.

Morion Figures	one-car w/o load	one-car	two-car	three-car
N_Att	9	11	18	26
N_Ex	40	40	166	712
N_{Att} x N_{Ex}	360	440	2988	18512
Ratio	0,06%	0,07%	0,47%	2,90%

Table 4. Estimation of Matching Spaces complexity

This brief complexity analysis shows that in the studied example the Matching Space MS ("two-car"), which has only a small ratio of the complexity of the initial representation (0.47%), supports the learning of all three first rules found by Michalski and Larson. This analysis corroborates the empirical results suggesting that learning with reformulation may improve the computational complexity of the learning task. Nevertheless, the Michalski trains problem is too small and too simple to validate our approach. We are currently working on an evaluation based on a problem involving a few thousands Chinese characters and a comparison of both REMO and INDUCE performances on this task.

6   Conclusion

The problem of matching is crucial in learning structural descriptions from examples because of its impact on the tractability of algorithms. Classical approaches to this problem consider *a priori* all the possible matchings and then define a restricted hypothesis space that limits the number of potential matchings. This paper describes a novel approach to address this problem by incremental representation shifts of learning examples. The structure of the learning examples, represented using a subset of a first order logic language, is modified to produce new learning examples which may be represented using an attribute-value language. These new learning examples define a hypothesis space called Matching Space. We have shown that the Matching Spaces are partially ordered by their size. Moreover, we proved an equivalence between learning in all Matching Spaces and learning in the initial representation space. We have developed a system called REMO that incrementally reformulates its learning base using more and more general morions. Our current work is focused on demonstrating that an exploration of the Matching Spaces similar in principle to that of depth-first iterative-deepening [15] is asymptotically optimal in terms of time among brute-force algorithms. In the long term we shall study carefully how our work may be applied in the context of Inductive Logic Programming algorithms.

References

1. Aha, D. W. (1992). Relating Relational Learning Algorithms. In S. Muggleton (Eds.), Inductive Logic Programming (pp. 233-259). London: Harcourt Brace Jovanovich.
2. Barrow, H. G., Ambler, A. P., and Burstall, R. M. (1972). Some techniques for recognizing structures in pictures. In S. Watanabe (Eds.), Frontiers of Pattern Recognition (pp. 1-29). New York: Academic.
3. Cohen, W. (1990). An analysis of Representation Shift In Concept Learning. In B. Porter and R. Mooney (Ed.), Seventh International Conference on Machine Learning, (pp. 104,112). Austin, Texas.
4. Dietterich, T., and Michalski, R. (1983). A comparative review of selected methods for learning from examples. In Machine Learning: an Artificial Intelligence Approach San Mateo, CA: Morgan Kaufmann.
5. Drastal, G., Czako, G., and Raatz, S. (1989). Induction in an abstraction space: A form of constructive induction. In Proceedings of the twelfth International Jointed Conference in Artificial Intelligence (IJCAI), (pp. 708-712). Detroit, Michigan.
6. Flann, N., and Dietterich, T. (1986). Selecting Appropriate Representations for Learning from Examples. In AAAI, (pp. 460-466). Philadelphia, PA.
7. Ganascia, J.-G. (1987). CHARADE: A rule System Learning System. In Proceedings of the tenth International Jointed Conference in Artificial Intelligence, (pp. 345-347). Milan, Italy.
8. Giordana, A., and Saitta, L. (1990). Abstraction: a general framework for learning. In Working notes of the AAAI Workshop on Automated Generation of Approximations and Abstraction, (pp. 245-256). Boston, MA.
9. Guarino, N., Pribbenow, S., and Vieu, L. (1994). Parts and Wholes: Conceptual Part-Whole Relations and Formal Mereology. In Workshop W2 at the 11th European Conference on Artificial Intelligence, . Amsterdam, The Netherlands.
10. Haussler, D. (1989). Learning Conjunctive Concepts in Structural Domains. Machine Learning, 4, 7-40.
11. Hayes-Roth, F., and McDermott, J. (1978). An interference matching technique for inducing abstractions. Communications of ACM, 21(5), 401-410.

12. Kietz, J.-U., and Wrobel, S. (1992). Controlling the Complexity of Learning in Logic through Syntactic and Task- Oriented Models. In S. Muggleton (Eds.), Inductive Logic Programming (pp. 335-359). London: Harcourt Brace Jovanovich.

13. Köbler, J., Schöning, U., and Torn, J. (1993). The graph-Isomorphism problem : its structural complexity. Boston: Birkhaüser.

14. Kodratoff, Y., and Ganascia, J.-G. (1986). Improving the generalization step in learning. In J. Carbonell and T. Mitchell (Eds.), Machine Learning: an Artificial Intelligence Approach (pp. 215-244). San Mateo, CA: Morgan Kaufmann.

15. Korf, R. E. (1985). Depth-First Iterative-Deepening: An optimal Admissible Tree Search. Artificial Intelligence, 27, 97-109.

16. Lavrac, N., Dzeroski, S., and Grobelnik, M. (1991). Learning Non Recursive Definitions of Relations with Linus. In European Working Session on Learning91, 482 (pp. 265-281).

17. Michalski, R. S. (1980). Pattern recognition as rule-guided inductive inference. IEEE Transaction on Pattern Analysis and Machine Intelligence, 2, 349-361.

18. Michalski, R. S., and Larson, J. B. (1977). Inductive Inference of VL Decision Rules. SIGART Newsletter, ACM(63), 38-44.

19. Muggleton, S., and Feng, C. (1992). Efficient Induction of logic program. In S. Muggleton (Eds.), Inductive Logic Programming (pp. 281-298). London: Harcourt Brace Jovanovich.

20. Neri, F., and Saitta, L. (1994). Knowledge Representation in Machine Learning. In F. Bergadano and L. d. Raedt (Ed.), European Conference on Machine Learning, 784 . Catania, Italy.

21. Plotkin, G. (1971). A further note on inductive generalization. In B. Meltzer & D. Michie (Eds.), Machine Intelligence (pp. 101-124). New York: Elsevier.

22. Quinlan, J.-R. (1990). Learning Logical Definitions from Relations. Machine Learning(5), 239-266.

23. Shapiro, L. G., and Haralick, R. H. (1980). Structural descriptions and inexact matching. IEEE Transaction Pattern Analysis and Machine Intelligence, 3(5), 504-519.

24. Sowa, J. F. (1991). Part I: Issues in Knowledge Representation. In J. F. Sowa (Eds.), Principles of Semantic Networks: Exploration in the Representation of Knowledge San Mateo, California: Morgan Kaufmann.

25. Subramanian, D. (1989). Representational Issues in Machine Learning. In Proceeding of the sixth international Workshop on Machine Learning, (pp. 426-429). California.

26. Subramanian, D. (1990). A Theory of Justified Reformulations. In D. P. Benjamin (Eds.), Change of Representation and Inductive Bias (pp. 147-167). Boston: Kluwer Academic Publishers.

27. Winston, M. E., Chaffin, R., and Hermann, D. J. (1987). A taxonomy of Part-Whole relations. Cognitive Science, 11, 417-444.

28. Zucker, J.-D., and Ganascia, J.-G. (1994). Selective Reformulation of Examples in Concept Learning. In W. Cohen (Ed.), International Conference on Machine Learning, (pp. 352-360). New-Brunswick.

Integrated Model - a Proposal to Handle Noise

João Pedro Guerreiro Neto
e-mail: jpn@fct.unl.pt

Fernando José Gomes Moura Pires
e-mail: fmp@fct.unl.pt

Dept. Informática, FCT-UNL, Quinta da Torre, 2825 Monte de Caparica, Portugal

Abstract: We present the theoretical background of the Integrated Model, a new induction algorithm proposed and implemented by the authors. The algorithm relies on a bottom-up strategy, from particular to general, feature less common that the usual top-down strategy founded in a great number of induction tools. We introduce a method for finding the values of the basic probability assignment according to Theory of Evidence, called probabilistic mass. With this notion, we propose a generalisation of the algorithm capable of handle noisy data.

Keywords: classification rules, decision trees, generalization, induction, machine learning, noise, theory of evidence, uncertainty measures.

Acknowledgements: We thank PRAXIS XXI for the financial support (BM/1525/94) related to the Mh.Thesis. We also acknowledge all support given by UNINOVA and CITIA.

1 Introduction

Induction is the process of inferring from particular to general, *i.e.*, it is a methodology that starts from facts, which are nothing more than empirical propositions, to reach universally valid laws.

Many algorithms use induction to solve classification problems. These can be distinguished by the type of knowledge representation structure they create, like classification rules or decision trees. Many algorithms are based on the idea of starting with a very general structure and then to specialise it with the samples in the training set. In the Integrated Model, IM, we use the inverse process. IM starts with the initial samples, and constructs an independence graph to find descriptions as general as possible. It can create three different structures, incoherent and coherent classification rules, and decision trees [MOURA PIRES 93,95][NETO 95].

2 Probabilistic Mass

In probability theory, the probability function *p* of a specific event, is ideally determined by an unlimited number of results. This theoretical necessity might be a great restriction, specially if the number of samples at our disposal, is so little, that even the Law of Large Numbers cannot be applied.

The main goal of the *probabilistic mass assignment*, see [MOURA-PIRES 93], is to handle sets of samples too small for other measuring processes. This small cardinality brings another kind of uncertainty, the ignorance about the real distribution of sample space.

Let a sample, or description, s, be part of a sample space Ω, ($s \subseteq \Omega$). Consider an urn, where the descriptions are taken with reposition. At the end of some limited number of extractions, we get the set of all samples, S.

Let us denote the pair (s,ω), where ω is the number of times a particular description s was extracted from the urn. The training set, TS, is defined this way,

$$\text{TS} = \{ \, (s,\omega_i) \mid s \in \Omega \wedge (\, \omega_i = \omega \text{ if } s \in S \; \vee \; \omega_i = 0 \text{ if } s \in \neg S \,) \, \} \qquad (1)$$

being N the number of extractions, $N = \sum_{(s,\omega) \in \text{TS}} \omega$.

Let $(s,\omega) \in TS$, the *probabilistic mass assignment*, m, of description s, and the *probabilistic mass assignment of the urn*, $m(\Omega)$, be given by,

$$m(s) = \frac{\omega}{N+|\Omega|} \quad \text{and} \quad m(\Omega) = \frac{|\Omega|}{N+|\Omega|} \tag{2}$$

This means that the probabilistic mass of a description, is proportional to its frequency, during the extraction process. The probabilistic mass function of the urn, is proportional to the cardinality of set Ω. The normalisation factor $N+|\Omega|$, allows the sum of all probabilistic mass is equal to one. As a consequence of this,

$$\lim_{N \to \infty} m(s) - p(s) = 0 \tag{3}$$

If we increase the number of extractions N, the probabilistic mass m tends to values given by the classic probabilistic function p. This happens because of the normalisation factor. If $N \gg |\Omega|$, then $N+|\Omega| \approx N$, and therefore $m(s) = \omega / N$, the value of p. The value $m(\Omega)$, represents the uncertainty level in relation to the sample set, *i.e.*, at what point the sample set is incomplete regarding the urn, Ω. Therefore, when N increases and we have $N \gg |\Omega|$, our ignorance is expected to be reduced towards zero, because we are increasing our understanding of the internal distribution of the urn. In fact, $m(\Omega) = \frac{|\Omega|}{N+|\Omega|} \approx \frac{|\Omega|}{N} \approx 0$, with $N \gg |\Omega|$.

Measures based in Evidence Theory: One way to expand the probabilistic mass concept is to follow the approach of the Theory of Evidence [SHAFER 76]. This can be useful when we need some measures related with set of samples.

Let us denote the set of samples, TS, with N elements, and P a set of samples included in the sample space, Ω ($P \subseteq \Omega$). The *belief* function, *Bel*, and the *plausibility* function, *Pl*, of P, are defined as,

$$Bel(P) = \frac{\sum\limits_{(s,\omega) \in P} \omega}{N + |\Omega|} \quad \text{and} \quad Pl(P) = Bel(P) + m(\Omega) \tag{4}$$

3 Integrated Model

This section presents a summary of the global algorithm presented in [MOURA PIRES 95]. In here, we focus in the analysis of the induction structure made by IM.

- **Representation Space:** Let A be the set of attributes $\{ A_1, A_2, ..., A_{|A|}\}$, in which the attribute A_i has the next set of possible values, $A_i = \{a_{i,1}, ..., a_{i,|A_i|}\}$. A special value '_', meaning "do not care about this particular value" is added to each attribute. We say that an attribute is *defined* if and only if its value is different from '_'. If its value is equal to '_', then the attribute is *not defined*. Therefore, we have a new set of sets of values, $A_i' = A_i \cup \{"\_"\}$. The *representation space* K, of the information processed by the algorithm is the cartesian product of the new set of features, $K = A_1' \times A_2' \times ... \times A_{|A|}'$. A *representation* is a given point $x = (x_1, ..., x_{|A|}) \in K$, that represents a particular set of values for each attribute.

We define the *level n specialization*, of a representation $x \in K(r)$, or $Spe(x,n)$, as the set of all representations that are possible to obtain, when we add n defined values to some undefined attributes of x.

We define the *successor* of a representation x, or $Suc(x)$, as the set of all representations that are possible to obtain, when we add one defined value to some undefined attributes of x. $Suc(x)$ contains all representations that have the same attributes of x, except one of them, where $Suc(x)$ has value '_'. Finally, $Suc(x, A_i)$, is the set of representations contained in $Suc(x)$ with the difference in attribute A_i.

• **Independence Function:** The set of classified samples, together with the set of classes, the set of attributes and its possible values, defines the information managed by the algorithm. This group of samples is the training set, or briefly, TS.

We call a *description*, the pair (representation, class of representation). What any induction algorithm pretends, is an effective extrapolation of the global relation hidden under the problem, by using the subset of possible descriptions given by TS.

In IM, the structure construction is based in the independence of a given value of an attribute, in relation to TS. When a representation x is independent from TS in attribute A_i, we say that relation $Ind(C, x, A_i)$ is true, being C the set of classes. The notion of independence is defined by a specific criterion. We propose in this paper the generalization criterion, see [MOURA-PIRES, 93].

> **Generalization:** Let us denote A_i as one of the defined attributes of representation x. We also have representation y, such as $x = Suc(y, A_i)$, *i.e.*, y is the generalization of x in A_i. If there is no representation z specialization of y, having a different class, then $Ind(C, x, A_i)$ holds.

• **Independence Graph:** A description (x,c), is *representative*, in regard to A_i, of a set of descriptions S, if for each description $(y,c) \in$ S; $y \in Suc(x,A_i)$ and $Ind(C, x, A_i)$ are both true. The set S, is designated by $Rep((x,c),A_i)$.

Each pair (x,c), $(y,c) \in Rep((x,c), A_i)$ defines a simple graph with two nodes, each one representing the descriptions, and an oriented labelled arc connecting the nodes. The arc is oriented in the direction (x,c) to (y,c), *i.e.*, from particular to general. The arc is an *out-arc* relative to (x,c), and an *in-arc* relative to (y,c).

The independence graph, IG, is the set of triples $((x,c), (y,c), A_i)$ respecting the following conditions: $c \in C$; $A_i \in A$; $x, y \in K$, and $y \in Rep((x,c), A_i)$,

$$IG = \{ ((x,c), (y,c), A_i) \mid y \in Rep(\,(x,c), A_i\,) \} \qquad (5)$$

IG is oriented from particular to general, so the most general descriptions are the *terminal nodes* of IG, because they do not have out-arcs. The *initial nodes* are the initial samples given by TS.

• **Prune Process:** Once IG is built, our main goal is to achieve a set of descriptions that can describe all nodes of IG. When all descriptions are found, IM uses them to make the final inductive structure. This is done by a step by step pruning of IG [NETO 95].

4 Noise

In the real world, the gathered information used to construct TS, can be inconsistent. When this happens, we say that the training set has *noise*. To minimise the loss of performance due to this characteristic, we can build some procedures specialised in treating noisy data.

In the first version of IM, there is no concern with this feature, but the structure does not collapse when it meets inconsistent samples. It can resist to most cases, loosing performance in proportion to the noise rate.

To generalise IG to handle noise, we must modify only the independence function. The generalisation function, can only accept one new arc to description d, if and only if, there is no specialization of d with a different class, *i.e.*, it demands no exceptions to d. This can be relaxed, if we accept some rate of exceptions. For instance, if there is a limit of 20% of exceptions, a new arc is made if and only if, the specialisations of d with the same class, are 80% or more of the total specialisations of d founded in the training set (against 100% in the noiseless situation).

This new generalisation function, although very simple, excludes some potential relevant points. This function makes an arc when there aren't many exceptions. But this can be hasty if we do not have many samples at our disposal. An example: IM is deciding on a new node for description d, and d represents 100 descriptions. The algorithm searches all these descriptions in TS, and finds only 4. Three of them with the same class of d. If the exception rate is $\leq 25\%$, node d becomes part of IG. Is this correct, or not? In fact, there are 3 samples against one, and we define that this ratio is negligible. But, we know very little about d (only 4%) to assume that all the other samples must have this class. We must not reach conclusions if we do not have enough facts. So, a good independence function must in first place, calculate how much knowledge it has about the sub-space of descriptions. Only if it has enough information, then we must proceed with the treatment of exceptions.

For this, we can use the notion of probabilistic mass, if we consider the urn Ω has being the sub-space of descriptions defined by d. Let d has n features not defined. Also, S will be the set of samples taken from Ω. Each description $d_i = (s_i, c_i)$, is presented ω_i times, s_i is the set of values for each attribute, and c_i is the class of d_i.

Let N_d be the number of specialisations of level n of description $d = (s_d, c_d)$ that are included in TS. Let $|\Omega_d|$ be the cardinality of the urn, *i.e.*, the number of all distinct specialisations of level n of d. Let P_c, be the set of all samples in TS, that are specialisations of d with the same class of d. Let $P_{\bar{c}}$, be the samples in TS, that are specialisations of d but with different class.

$$P_c = \{ d_i \mid s_i = Spe(s_d, n),\ c_i = c_d,\ d_i \in TS \} \tag{6}$$

$$P_{\bar{c}} = \{ d_i \mid s_i = Spe(s_d, n),\ c_i \neq c_d,\ d_i \in TS \} \tag{7}$$

The probabilistic mass of Ω_d is given by,

$$m(\Omega_d) = \frac{|\Omega_d|}{N_d + |\Omega_d|} \tag{8}$$

Using the belief function, *Bel*, to, P_c e $P_{\bar{c}}$, we obtain,

$$Bel(P_c) = \frac{\sum_{d_i \in P_c} \omega_i}{N_d + |\Omega_d|} \tag{9}$$

and the equivalent expression for *Bel*($P_{\bar{c}}$). We have at this moment, enough data to check if relation *Ind*(C, x, A_i) holds. Let's formulate the first condition C1,

$$P_{\bar{c}} = \varnothing \quad \lor \quad Bel(P_c) + Bel(P_{\bar{c}}) \geq \delta_1 \cdot m(\Omega_d) \tag{10}$$

with $\delta_1 \in [0,1]$. The factor δ_1 gives us the threshold for the minimum level of knowledge that we must know about the urn, to continue with the generalisation process. With $\delta_1 = 0$, we obtain the first case, when there is no restriction about the urn, C1 is always true. With $\delta_1=1$, the algorithm only proceeds if we know at least a number of samples equal to $|\Omega_d|$. In the training sets where $\forall d_i: \omega_i = 1$, this means that we must have all the possible specialisations of d, in TS. If $P_c^- = \varnothing$, C1 is immediately acknowledged.

If C1 is satisfied, we can analyse the relation between the descriptions that satisfy the class demands of d, and the exceptions. Using the values already calculated, we define the second condition C2,

$$Bel(P_c) \geq \delta_2 . [\ Bel(P_c) + Bel(P_c^-) \ ] \tag{11}$$

with $\delta_2 \in [0,1]$. The factor δ_2 represents the maximum exception ratio that is accepted to construct the node with d (*e.g.*, if we can afford having one exception to three samples, we get $\delta_2 = 3/(3+1) = 0.75$).

In conclusion, if for a given description d, conditions C1 and C2 are satisfied, d becomes part of IG.

5 Empirical Evaluations

We implemented IM totally in ANSI-C, and tested it with some known training sets. The program is divided in two, the induction and the classification process. Because there is no discretization mechanism implemented yet, we only use training sets with discrete attributes. C4.5 has been used, with and without pruning. CART has been used treating numeric values as discrete and as continuous. In CN2, we use both ordered and un-ordered algorithms. IM, in Table 1, do not use noise treatment. Each column represents one data set, including a name, the number of attributes, classes and samples (*e.g.*, set Votes: 16 attributes, 3 classes and 435 samples). For more information, see *ftp.ics.uci.edu*. In Votes and Lung-C, we use resubstitution, the others have independent test sets.

	Monks-1 6a/2c/124s	Monks-2 6a/2c/169s	Monks-3 6a/2c/122s	Votes 16a/3c/435s	Hayes 4a/3c/132s	Lung-C 56a/3c/32s
C4.5(no prune)	23.4	34.7	7.4	2.3	21.4	9.4
C4.5 (prune)	25.3	35.0	2.8	2.8	7.1	12.5
CART (cont.)	16.7	36.6	2.8	0.9	13.6	25.0
CART (disc.)	9.3	43.1	0	0.9	12.1	25.0
CN2 (un-ord.)	4.2	24.3	9.3	0.5	28.6	0
CN2 (ordered)	0	26.1	6.7	0	17.9	0
IM (inc. rules)	0	23.6	9.7	0	25.0	0
IM (coe. rules)	0	27.5	13.0	0	21.4	0
IM (tree)	14.8	29.6	9.7	0	21.4	0

Tab. 1. Percentage of error rates.

We see that IM outperforms the other decision tree algorithms in Monks-1 and Monks-2, and is the worst of all in Monks-3. But, this last result is not so bad, if we note that the training set of Monks-3 has 5% of noise, and IM do not use its capacity to handle noisy data, unlike C4.5 and CART. The relative poor result of IM's tree in Monks-1, is due to an unexpected relation hidden in the training set, founded by IM. This relation is only a result of the random choice that builds the set, and therefore does not exist in the complete test set. In Hayes, IM's performance is a little below average. In Votes and Lung-C is perfect, but both have large induction structures.

Next we present a test case, Monks-3, to see the noise capacity of IM. Each error rate is obtained by a specific pair (δ_1, δ_2).

δ_1	no	0			0.25			0.5		
δ_2	noise	0.34	0.51	0.76	0.34	0.51	0.76	0.34	0.51	0.76
inc. rules	9.7	8.6	3.2	6.5	8.6	8.1	8.3	8.6	8.6	7.2
coe. rules	13.0	10.6	3.7	2.8	10.6	10.6	10.2	10.6	10.6	10.2
tree	9.7	9.7	6.0	18.5	9.7	9.3	10.2	9.7	9.7	9.7

Tab. 2. Percentage of error rates for Monks-3.

With some values of (δ_1, δ_2), we obtain good improvements in the error rates (*e.g.*, from 13% to 2.8%). The best results occurs when $\delta_1=0$. What does it mean? Is condition C1 useless? We must not forget that we are dealing with a single case, Monks-3, and this isn't enough to generalise.

C1 has a precise objective: it defines a threshold to what we can relate or not, depending on how much we know about those relations. With $\delta_1=0$, it's easier to "bet" in some relations that don't really exist, and loose even more performance. We must to obtain more results in order to enlarge our knowledge about this problem.

6 Conclusion

Since the presentation of IM [MOURA PIRES 95], we are now learning to cope with noise. Such things as treating continuous unbounded attributes, dealing with unknown values in the data set, holding complex error estimations, like cross-validation, are intended to be implemented for a better approach to the real world.

Right now, the main defect of IM is in the creation of large induction structures. However, IM as it stands, is already a worthy experience in the induction field. If a reliable discretization process would be implemented in IM, perhaps its performances could be maintained when used in continuous problems.

7 References

BREIMAN, L. *et al.* (1984) Classification and Regression Trees. Wadsworth & Brooks / Cole Advanced Books & Software. Pacific Grove, California.

CLARK, P., (1989). Functional Specification of CN and AQ. (Reference: TI/P2154/PC/4/1.2). The Turing Institute.

MOURA PIRES, F., (1993). Aprendizagem por Indução Empírica. Ph.D Thesis in Robotics. FCT-UNL, Lisboa, 1993.

MOURA PIRES, F., NETO, J.P., (1995). Integrated Model - a new algorithm in Empirical Induction. Paper submitted to CAEPIA'95, VI Conference of the Spanish Association for Artificial Intelligence.

NETO, J.P. (1995). Aprendizagem por Indução - Modelo Integrado. Mh. Thesis in Informatics. FCT-UNL, Lisboa, 1995.

QUINLAN, J. R. (1993). C4.5: Programs for Machine Learning. Morgan Kaufman Publishers. San Mateo, California.

SHAFER, G., (1976). A Mathematical Theory of Evidence. Princeton Univ. Press.

Exceptions-Based Synthesis of Boolean Functions as a Core Mechanism to Perform Concept Learning

Giuliano Armano,

Dept. of Electrical and Electronic Engineering,
University of Cagliari, Piazza d'Armi, I-09123 Cagliari, Italy.

Abstract. In this paper, an alternative approach to the synthesis of Boolean functions is presented. Such an approach can be useful in the field of concept learning as well, provided that the semantics of non-specified instances is changed accordingly (i.e., from a *don't-care* to an *unknown* semantics). The underlying framework relies on the concept of *exception*, an exception being, for example, a 0 grouped together with 1's while performing the synthesis. It is shown that an exceptions-based synthesis can be adopted as a core mechanism to perform concept learning in an n-dimensional Boolean space. A learning system is sketched where the decision of re-calculating classification rules can be arbitrarily delayed, as new examples, not consistent with the current hypothesis, can be integrated within the system by temporarily storing them as exceptions.

1. Introduction

The problem of partitioning an n-dimensional space is a fundamental task in several research areas. In the field of *automatic synthesis of Boolean functions*, the problem consists of finding an intensional representation of a given Boolean function, according to some optimality criteria. To this end, a set of instances from the instance space are labelled positive (e.g., they represent a logic 1) or negative (e.g., they represent a logic 0), whereas non-specified instances, if any, are labelled as *don't-care*. Instances labelled as *don't-care* are considered not relevant to the function's behaviour; hence, they can be associated with a logic 1 or 0, according to the choice of the algorithm that performs the synthesis. Boolean expressions are the most common way of representing Boolean functions, even though alternative descriptions are widely used, especially in the fields of test generation, compact testing, and simulation (e.g., Binary Decision Diagrams, [1], [2]). In the field of *concept learning from examples* rules that will accurately predict the class label of future instances from the instance space have to be found. Within such a framework, the most common ways of representing concepts are production rules [3] and decision trees [4], even though alternative descriptions have been given (e.g., decision lists [5]). The task of a learning algorithm is to induce rules that will accurately predict the class label of future instances from the instance space [6]. Here, non-specified (i.e., not *yet* specified) examples are considered as instances whose class label is still *unknown*.

In this paper, an alternative approach to the synthesis of Boolean functions is presented. Such an approach can be useful in the field of concept learning within a Boolean space as well, provided that the semantics of non-specified instances is changed accordingly (i.e., from *don't-care* to *unknown*). The underlying framework relies on the concept of *exception*, an exception being, for example, a 0 grouped together with 1's while performing a synthesis.

2. Boolean Functions Synthesis

2.1. Basic Definitions

The Boolean type and its n-dimensional space are denoted by $B = \{0,1\}$ and $B_n = \{0,1\}^n$, respectively. Thus, a configuration within B_n is represented by an n-tuple (Boolean vector, or simply *vector*), whose components are 0 or 1. Given a letter, say A, its corresponding *literals* are denoted by A and $\overline{A}$. A *minterm* is a string of literals derived from a given vector by replacing each 1 or 0 with the corresponding literal (i.e., with a letter or its negation, respectively). A *term* is a string of literals obtained from a minterm by deleting some [1] of its literals. Given a term t, I say that a vector v *satisfies* t (conversely, t *covers* v) when all literals in t occur in the minterm derived from v. The set of vectors covered by t is denoted by $D(t)$. The *cardinality* of t is the number of vectors it covers, namely $|D(t)|$.

Given a Boolean function $f: B_n \to B$, its domain is denoted by $D(f)$. Each vector $v \in D(f)$ can be thought of as having an associate class label $c \in B$. When f is a partial function (i.e., $D(f) \subset B_n$), everything would go on as if all vectors $v \notin D(f)$ were labelled as *don't-care*. Being t a term and c a class label, the set of vectors covered by t and labelled as c is denoted by $D_f(t,c)$. A vector v is *properly covered* by t, with respect to c, if $v \in D_f(t,c)$; conversely, v is an *exception* of t if $v \in D_f(t,\overline{c})$. The *covering score* $\beta(t,c)$ equates to the number of vectors covered by t and labelled as c, normalized by the cardinality of t. t is said to be *homogeneous*, with respect to c, when $\beta(t,c) > 0$ and $\beta(t,\overline{c}) = 0$, *heterogeneous* when $\beta(t,c) > 0$ and $\beta(t,\overline{c}) > 0$.

2.2. Classical vs exceptions-based synthesis

Basically, a term can be selected as a candidate term for the class label c only if $\beta(t,\overline{c}) \le \beta_e$. Hence, β_e is an upper bound on the relative amount of exceptions that a term is allowed to cover, its range being $0 \le \beta_e < 0.5$ (the reason why $\beta_e < 0.5$ lies in the fact that exceptions should not be allowed to exceed the amount of properly-covered vectors). When $\beta_e = 0$, for any Boolean class to be synthesized, a term can

---

[1] Possibly none; namely, a minterm is a term.

be only homogeneous (*classical* synthesis). On the contrary, when $\beta_e > 0$, a term can be heterogeneous (*exceptions-based* synthesis).

Classical synthesis proceeds by first selecting a set of candidate terms, and then trying to remove redundant terms according to some optimality criteria. Given a class label c, a term can be selected as a candidate only if it is homogeneous with respect to c (i.e., none of the vectors covered by t can be labelled as $\overline{c}$). Finding non-redundant terms while performing a classical synthesis is an NP-hard problem, even though average cases are usually solvable in polynomial time (see, for example, [7]).

Exceptions-based synthesis proceeds by first (i) selecting a set of candidate terms, and then (ii) repeatedly [2] trying to properly cover exceptions, if any. Eventually, (iii) redundant terms are deleted, according to some optimality criteria. Given a class label c, a term can be selected as a candidate only if $\beta(t,\overline{c}) \le \beta_e$, i.e., a limited number of exceptions are allowed. Finding non-redundant terms while performing an exceptions-based synthesis is an NP-hard problem, too.

Let us assume that N is a parameter that controls the maximum number of steps allowed to perform candidates selection during an exceptions-based synthesis. In order to be selected as a candidate, a term must exhibit a $\beta(t,\overline{c}) \le \beta_e$ during the first N-1 steps. If the N-th step is reached, β_e is forced to 0, so that, during the last step, only homogeneous terms will be selected. The easiest way of performing an exceptions-based synthesis is by setting $N = 2$ (*2-steps* synthesis). The first step will take care of generating terms that possibly contain exceptions, whereas the second step, if needed, will generate terms able to properly cover such exceptions, thus inhibiting those terms that otherwise would be erroneously satisfied.

2.3. Interpreting the results of a synthesis (*don't-care* semantics)

The results of a classical synthesis can be represented, without loss of generality, by a set of terms, and can be mapped into a corresponding Boolean formula (e.g., a k-DNF or a k-CNF formula). On the other hand, it could be easily shown that the results of an exceptions-based synthesis can always be represented by a Directed Acyclic Graph (DAG). [3] Hence, the dependencies among terms require a more expressive formalism (such as, for example, Reiter's default logic [8] or Sandewall's *unless* operator [9]) to be suitably translated into a logical form.

Let us assume that the notion of satisfiability, say $\le_s$, is given for a vector with respect to any suitable intensional representation of a Boolean function. A synthesis performed on both class labels gives rise to a pair of intensional representations $H_\Omega(1)$ and $H_\Omega(0)$, whose corresponding Boolean function is defined as:

---

[2]   Step (ii) could be iterated several times, as a term selected to properly cover one or more exceptions may be heterogeneous, too.

[3]   Such a task, anyway, is beyond the scope of this paper.

$$\hat{f}_0(v) = \begin{cases} 0 & v \leq_S H_\Omega(0) \\ 1 & otherwise \end{cases} \qquad \hat{f}_1(v) = \begin{cases} 1 & v \leq_S H_\Omega(1) \\ 0 & otherwise \end{cases}$$

with the obvious constraint that *consistency* must hold, i.e.: $f(v) = c \rightarrow \hat{f}_1(v) \equiv \hat{f}_0(v) = c$. On the other hand: $\hat{f}_1(v) \neq \hat{f}_0(v) \rightarrow f(v) = \bot$. This basically means that only *don't-care* vectors can be arbitrarily assigned to 0 or 1, depending on the choice taken by the algorithm that performed the synthesis.

3. An Example of Exceptions-Based Synthesis

Consider the Boolean function: $f(A,B,C,D) = \sum(0,1,5,7,10,11,15) + \Delta(2,3)$. A classical synthesis leads to the following results:

$$\hat{f}_0(v) = \begin{cases} 0 & v \leq_S A\overline{C} + B\overline{D} \\ 1 & otherwise \end{cases} \qquad \hat{f}_1(v) = \begin{cases} 1 & if\ v \leq_S \overline{A}B + \overline{B}C + \overline{A}D + CD \\ 0 & otherwise \end{cases}$$

An exceptions-based synthesis can be performed on the given function by setting $\beta_e > 0$ and $N > 1$. For example, with $\beta_e = 0.25$ and $N = 2$ (*2-steps* synthesis), the following results are found:

$$\hat{f}_0(v) = \begin{cases} 0 & v \leq_S A\overline{C} + B\overline{D} \\ 1 & otherwise \end{cases} \qquad \hat{f}_1(v) = \begin{cases} 1 & v \leq_S \overline{A}:(B\overline{D}) + C:(B\overline{D}) \\ 0 & otherwise \end{cases}$$

To stress the fact that a term t_1 is inhibited by a term t_2, one can write $t_1:(t_2)$, which is a term, together with a corresponding exception.

4. Learning Classification Rules

4.1. Basic definitions

Given an n-dimensional Boolean space B_n, a *concept* C is a subset of B_n. An element of $v \in C$ is a *positive instance* of the concept, whereas an element of B_n, but not in C, is a *negative instance*. An *example* in B_n may be thought of as an ordered pair $<v,c>$ where $v \in B_n$ and $c \in \{-,+\}$ (or, else, with the same semantics, $c \in \{0,1\}$). A concept may be induced, without loss of generality, by referring to a *sample* (i.e., to a set of examples) of only positive and negative instances. In the standard (*unbalanced*) model of learning from examples, a hypothesis H is a subset of B_n. Let S be a sample of a concept C. Let S_+ be the set of instances in S that are labelled positive, and let S_- be the set of instances that are labelled negative.

According to a classical definition (see, for example, [10]), H is a hypothesis of C *consistent* with S if $S_+ \subseteq H$ and $S_- \cap H = \varnothing$. In this framework, the author prefers to adopt a *balanced* model where a hypothesis is characterized by a pair $< H_+, H_- >$, such that both H_+ and H_- are subsets of B_n, and $H_+ \cup H_- \subseteq B_n$. Given a sample S, the following constraints hold for S_+ and S_-: $S_+ \subseteq H_+$ and $S_- \subseteq H_-$.

4.2. Boolean classifiers

Let us assume that the function f is given as a sequence of pairs of the form $< v, f(v) >$, one pair at a time. After getting k pairs, a *learning set* $LS_k(f)$ holds. [4] $LS_k(f)$ defines a partial function $\tilde{f}_k : B_n \to B$ such that:

$$\tilde{f}_k(v) = \begin{cases} c & if <v,c> \in LS_k(f) \\ \perp & otherwise \end{cases}$$

Hence, any classifier $\hat{f}_k$, derived from $LS_k(f)$, must be *consistent* with respect to the given learning set (i.e., to the corresponding $\tilde{f}_k$). In symbols:

$$\forall v' \in B_n \forall c' \in B : \tilde{f}_k(v') = c' \to \hat{f}_k(v') = c'$$

This basically means that $\hat{f}_k$ preserves every value specified within the current learning set, although some unknown value may be turned into 1 or 0.

It is worth pointing out that, by construction, a total order among the set of functions $\{\tilde{f}_r, r = 1, 2, ...\}$ exists; i.e., both truth and falsity have to be preserved while passing from a $\tilde{f}_h$ to a $\tilde{f}_k$ such that $h < k$. On the other hand, $\hat{f}_k$ is neither truth- nor falsity-preserving, as the only property that must hold is consistency (with respect to $\tilde{f}_k$).

Assuming that the $(k+1)$-th pair is given, the current $\hat{f}_k$, may be consistent or not with such a pair. In the former case, no change is required, and $\hat{f}_{k+1} \equiv \hat{f}_k$. In the latter case, a change is needed in order to preserve consistency (with respect to $\tilde{f}_k$). Such a change can be made either by calculating the function $\hat{f}_{k+1}$ from scratch (i.e., by taking into account the learning set $LS_{k+1}(f)$ as a whole), or by adding an

---

[4] Assume that $< v, b >, < v', \overline{b} > \in LS_k(f) \to v \neq v'$.

exception to $\hat{f}_k$, thus saving computational time. [5] A suitable threshold on the complexity in space of the classifier (i.e., on the intensional representation of the function $\hat{f}_k$) can be used to decide whether or not the function must be calculated again from scratch.

When $\hat{f}_k$ has to be calculated from scratch, any algorithm that performs the synthesis must be able to cope with the different semantics carried out by non-specified instances. Basically, a new parameter β_* (i.e., an upper bound on the relative amount of unknown instances that are allowed to be covered by a given term) is taken into account by the algorithm that performs the synthesis.

4.3. Interpreting the results of a synthesis (*unknown* semantics)

Given a learning set $LS_k(f)$, a classical / exceptions-based *Boolean classifier* is represented by a pair of sets / DAGs $< H_\Omega^{(k)}(0), H_\Omega^{(k)}(1) >$ that implicitly define a partial function $\hat{f}_k : B_n \to B$ as follows:

$$\hat{f}_k(v) = \begin{cases} c & \text{if } v \leq_S H_\Omega^{(k)}(c) \wedge \neg(v \leq_S H_\Omega^{(k)}(\bar{c})) \\ \perp & \text{otherwise} \end{cases}$$

Thus, by definition, $\hat{f}_k$ rules out the case where v satisfies both $H_\Omega^{(k)}(0)$ and $H_\Omega^{(k)}(1)$. On the other hand, for the sake of consistency, only an instance labelled as *unknown* can possibly satisfy both $H_\Omega^{(k)}(0)$ and $H_\Omega^{(k)}(1)$.

5. Conclusions and Future Work

In this paper, an alternative approach to the synthesis of Boolean functions has been presented. Such an approach can be useful in the field of concept learning within a Boolean space as well, provided that the semantics of non-specified values is changed accordingly (i.e., from *don't-care* to *unknown*).

As far as Boolean functions synthesis is concerned, the exceptions-based approach has been described starting from the classical one. It has been shown that the former derives from the latter by relaxing the assumption that candidate terms must cover only vectors labelled according to the current class label. The semantics of *don't-care* instances has been discussed, too.

As far as concept learning is concerned, it has been shown that an exceptions-based synthesis can be adopted as a core mechanism to perform concept learning

---

[5] From a conceptual point of view, exceptions might be dealt with even by a learning system that performs a classical synthesis. Nevertheless, such behaviour is more naturally handled by a learning system where an exceptions-based synthesis is performed.

within a Boolean space, provided that the semantics of non-labelled instances is changed from *don't-care* to *unknown*. A balanced learning model has been proposed, as an alternative to the classical (unbalanced) one. A learning system has been sketched where the decision of re-calculating classification rules can be arbitrarily delayed, as new examples not consistent with the current hypothesis can be integrated within the system by temporarily storing them as exceptions.

As far as future work is concerned, the exceptions-based approach will be studied relaxing the constraints on the number of class labels (i.e., $n > 2$), as well as on the kind of the attributes (i.e., not only Boolean attributes). Furthermore, the possibility of implementing a classifier that gives probabilistic answers will be investigated. All the above goals can be naturally handled within a framework based on exceptions.

References

[1] Akers, S.B., "Binary Decision Diagrams," *IEEE Trans. on Computers*, **27** (6), pp. 509-516, Jun 1978.

[2] Bryant, R.E., "Graph-Based Algorithms for Boolean Function Manipulation," *IEEE Trans. on Computers*, **35** (8), pp. 677-691, Aug 1986.

[3] Michalski, R.S., "On the quasi-minimal solution of the general covering problem," *Proc. 5th Int. Symposium on Information Processing*, Bled, Yugoslavia, pp. 125-128, 1969.

[4] Quinlan, J.R., "Discovering rules from large collections of examples: a case study," in Michie, D. (Ed.) "Expert systems in the microelectronic age," *Edinburgh University Press*, 1979.

[5] Rivest, R., "Learning Decision Lists," *Machine Learning*, **2**, pp. 229-246, 1987.

[6] Carbonell, J., Michalski, R.S., and Mitchell, T.M., "An overview of machine learning," in *Machine Learning: An Artificial Intelligence Approach*, pp. 3-24, Morgan Kaufmann, 1983.

[7] Brayton, R.K., Hachtel, G.D., McMullen C.T., and Sangiovanni-Vincentelli, A.L., "*Logic Minimization Algorithms for VLSI Synthesis*," Kluwer, 1984.

[8] Reiter, R., "A logic for default reasoning," *Artificial Intelligence*, **13**, pp. 81-132, 1980.

[9] Sandewall, E., "An Approach to the Frame Problem and Its Implementation," in *Machine Intelligence*, **7**, B. Meltzer and D. Michie (eds.), Edinburgh Univ. Press, Edinburgh, 1972.

[10] Pagallo, G., and Haussler, D., "Boolean Feature Discovery in Empirical Learning," *Machine Learning*, **5**, pp. 71-79, 1990.

Seeing is Believing
And so are Hearing and Jumping

B. van Linder, W. van der Hoek, J.-J.Ch. Meyer

Utrecht University, Department of Computer Science

Abstract. In this paper a formal framework is proposed in which various informative actions, corresponding to the different ways in which rational agents can acquire information, are combined. In order to solve conflicts that could possibly arise when acquiring information from different sources, we propose a classification of the information that an agent possesses according to credibility. Based on this classification, we formalize what it means for agents to have seen or heard something, or to believe something by default. We present a formalization of observations, communication actions, and the attempted jumps to conclusions that constitute default reasoning. To define the semantics of these informative actions we use a general belief revision action which satisfies the AGM postulates; dependent on the credibility of the incoming information this revision action acts on one or more parts of the classified belief set of an agent.

1 Introduction

The formalization of rational agents is a topic of continuing interest in Artificial Intelligence. Research on this subject has held the limelight ever since the pioneering work of Moore [15] in which knowledge and actions are considered. Over the years important contributions have been made on both *informational* attitudes like knowledge and belief [5], and *motivational* attitudes like commitments and obligations [3]. In our research [6, 7, 9, 10, 11, 12] we defined a *theorist* logic for rational agents, i.e., a logic that is used to *specify*, and to *analyze* the behavior of rational agents. Thus far, we have concentrated on informational attitudes and aspects of action. In the basic framework [6], the *knowledge, belief* and *abilities* of agents, as well as the *opportunities* for, and the *results* of, their actions are formalized. In this framework it can for instance be modelled that an agent knows that some action is *correct* to bring about some state of affairs since it knows that performing the action will lead to the state of affairs, and that it believes that an action is *feasible* in the sense that the agent believes that it is able to perform the action.

The main contribution of this paper is a deeper investigation into the nature of *informative* actions, which correspond to the various ways in which agents can acquire information. We propose a formalization of three different informative actions, viz. *observations*, actions modelling *communication*, and actions that model the jumping to conclusions which is typical for *default reasoning*. We are particularly interested in the various ways in which these different informative actions may interact, and how possible conflicts that may result from this interaction can be solved. To resolve these information conflicts, we propose a classification of the information that an agent possesses according to credibility. Based on this classification, we formalize what it means for agents to have seen or heard something, or to believe something by default. Using the various informational attitudes that we thus introduced, we define the aforementioned informative actions. In the definitions of these actions an important part is played by a general belief revision action which satisfies the AGM postulates. In this paper we concentrate on defining the conditions that determine the opportunity to perform informative actions and the states of affairs that follow execution; the notion of ability for these actions is investigated elsewhere [13]. The various definitions result in a framework in which agents can acquire information from various sources, resolve information conflicts, and attach different degrees of credibility to their beliefs. As such, this framework may be seen as an attempt to formalize intelligent information agents.

The rest of the paper is organized as follows. To sketch the context and the area of application of this research, we start in §2 with the (re)introduction of our basic framework. In §3 we present a classification by credibility of the information of an agent. In §4 we incorporate three informative actions into the basic framework: in 4.1 we formalize observations, in 4.2 communication, and in 4.3 default jumps. In §5 we round off. This paper is an extended abstract; proofs and technical completions are to be found elsewhere [13].

2 Knowledge, belief, abilities, opportunities, and results

We consider both *knowledge and belief* as informational attitudes. Adopting a *Platonic* view, we assume the knowledge of agents to represent the *veridical* information they are born or built with, which neither grows nor shrinks. The beliefs of an agent comprise its knowledge and represent its *working information*. By performing informative actions, this working information may grow, sometimes not justifiedly, in which case it should be possible to retract certain beliefs. Thus beliefs are *defeasible* and *non-veridical*. In representing knowledge and belief we follow both from a syntactical and a semantic point of view, the approach common in epistemic and doxastic logic [5]: the formula $\mathbf{K}_i\varphi$ denotes the fact that agent i knows φ, $\mathbf{B}_i\varphi$ that agent i believes φ, and both are interpreted in a Kripke-style semantics.

Slightly adapting ideas of Von Wright [16], we consider any aspect of the state of the universe following execution of an action to be a *result* of the action. *Ability* and *opportunity* together constitute the preconditions for successful execution of an action: ability comprises mental, physical and moral capacities, and opportunity is best described as circumstantial possibility, i.e., possible by virtue of the circumstances. The abilities of agents are formalized via the $\mathbf{A}_i$ operator; the formula $\mathbf{A}_i\alpha$ denotes the fact that agent i has the ability to do α. When using the definitions of opportunities and results as given above, the framework of (propositional) dynamic logic provides an excellent means to formalize these notions. Using events $\mathrm{do}_i(\alpha)$ to refer to the performance of the action α by the agent i, we consider the formulae $\langle\mathrm{do}_i(\alpha)\rangle\varphi$ and $[\mathrm{do}_i(\alpha)]\varphi$. In our deterministic framework, $\langle\mathrm{do}_i(\alpha)\rangle\varphi$ is the stronger of these formulae; it represents the fact that agent i has the opportunity to do α and that doing α leads to φ. The formula $[\text{do}_i(\alpha)]\varphi$ is noncommittal about the opportunity of the agent to do α but states that if the agent should have the opportunity, only states of affairs satisfying φ would result. As already stated in §1 we will not deal with the ability of agents for informative actions in this paper, but focus on the result of these actions.

Definition 1. Let a finite set $\mathcal{A} = \{1, \ldots, n\}$ of agents, and some denumerable sets Π of propositional symbols and At of atomic actions be given. The language $\mathcal{L}$ and the class Ac of actions are defined by mutual induction as follows: $\mathcal{L}$ is the smallest superset of Π such that:

- if $\varphi, \psi \in \mathcal{L}, i \in \mathcal{A}, \alpha \in Ac$ then $\neg\varphi, \varphi \vee \psi, \mathbf{K}_i\varphi, \mathbf{B}_i\varphi, \langle \text{do}_i(\alpha) \rangle\varphi, \mathbf{A}_i\alpha \in \mathcal{L}$

where Ac is the smallest superset of At such that: if $\varphi \in \mathcal{L}$, $\alpha_1, \alpha_2 \in Ac$ then

- confirm $\varphi \in Ac$ *confirmations*
- $\alpha_1; \alpha_2 \in Ac$ *sequential composition*
- if φ then α_1 else α_2 fi $\in Ac$ *conditional composition*
- while φ do α_1 od $\in Ac$ *repetitive composition*

The purely propositional, non-modal fragment of $\mathcal{L}$ is denoted by $\mathcal{L}_0$. The constructs $\wedge, \rightarrow$ and $\leftrightarrow$ are defined in the usual way; $\text{tt} =^{\text{def}} p \vee \neg p$, for some $p \in \Pi$ denotes a canonical tautology, $[\text{do}_i(\alpha)]\varphi =^{\text{def}} \neg\langle \text{do}_i(\alpha) \rangle\neg\varphi$ denotes the (conditional) result of action α, and $\mathbf{M}_i\varphi =^{\text{def}} \neg\mathbf{K}_i\neg\varphi$ denotes that φ is an epistemic possibility of the agent i, i.e., i considers φ to be possible on the ground of its knowledge. The indexes i and j, possibly marked, always refer to agents.

In the following definition a set $\{0, 1\}$ of truth symbols is assumed to be given. The symbol $\wp$ denotes the power set of a given set.

Definition 2. The class $\mathcal{M}$ of Kripke models contains all tuples $M = \langle S, \pi, R, B, r_0, c_0 \rangle$ such that

- S is a set of possible worlds, or states.
- $\pi : \Pi \times S \rightarrow \{0, 1\}$ assigns a truth value to propositional symbols in states.
- $R : \mathcal{A} \rightarrow \wp(S \times S)$ is a function that yields the epistemic accessibility relations for a given agent. It is demanded that $R(i)$ is an equivalence relation for all i. We define $[s]_{R(i)}$ to be $\{s' \in S \mid (s, s') \in R(i)\}$.
- $B : \mathcal{A} \times S \rightarrow \wp(S)$ is a function that yields the set of doxastic alternatives for a given agent in a given state. This function is such that $B(i, s) = B(i, s')$ if $s' \in [s]_{R(i)}$ and $B(i, s) \subseteq [s]_{R(i)}$ for all $s, s' \in S, i \in \mathcal{A}$.
- $r_0 : \mathcal{A} \times At \rightarrow S \rightarrow \wp(S)$ is such that $r_0(i, a)(s)$ yields the (possibly empty) state transition in s caused by the event $\text{do}_i(a)$. This function is such that for all a it holds that $|r_0(i, a)(s)| \leq 1$ for all i and s, i.e., these events are *deterministic*.
- $c_0 : \mathcal{A} \times At \rightarrow S \rightarrow \{0, 1\}$ is the capability function such that $c_0(i, a)(s)$ indicates whether agent i is capable of performing the action a in s.

Informative actions are interpreted as *model-transformers* rather than the more common *state-transitions*, which is the usual interpretation for actions in dynamic logic. The reason for this is that informative actions do not change the state of the world in which the agent resides, but the *doxastic state* of the agent, which is formalized through its set of doxastic alternatives. Therefore a change in the agent's doxastic state is interpreted as a change in its set of doxastic alternatives, which works out in a change of the model under consideration. To allow these model-transforming actions to occur alongside ordinary, worldly, actions which are interpreted as state-transitions, we generalize the functions r_0 and c_0 to functions r and c, which act on *pairs* consisting of a model and a state. The functions r and c are such that for worldly actions a state-transition interpretation is employed whereas for informative actions a model-transforming interpretation is used.

Definition 3. Let $M = \langle S, \pi, R, B, r_0, c_0 \rangle \in \mathcal{M}$. For φ a propositional symbol, a negation or a disjunction, $M, s \models \varphi$ is inductively defined as usual. For the other clauses it is defined as follows:

$$M, s \models \mathbf{K}_i\varphi \quad\Leftrightarrow \forall s' \in S[(s, s') \in R(i) \Rightarrow M, s' \models \varphi]$$
$$M, s \models \mathbf{B}_i\varphi \quad\Leftrightarrow \forall s' \in S[s' \in B(i, s) \Rightarrow M, s' \models \varphi]$$
$$M, s \models \langle \mathrm{do}_i(\alpha)\rangle\varphi \quad\Leftrightarrow \exists M', s'[M', s' \in r(i, \alpha)(M, s) \,\&\, M', s' \models \varphi]$$
$$M, s \models \mathbf{A}_i\alpha \quad\Leftrightarrow c(i, \alpha)(M, s) = 1$$

where r and c are for $a \in At, \varphi \in \mathcal{L}, \alpha_1, \alpha_2 \in Ac$ defined by:

$$r(i, a)(M, s) \qquad\qquad = M, r_0(i, a)(s)$$
$$r(i, \mathtt{confirm}\,\varphi)(M, s) \quad = M, s \text{ if } M, s \models \varphi \text{ and } \emptyset \text{ otherwise}$$
$$r(i, \alpha_1; \alpha_2)(M, s) \qquad = r(i, \alpha_2)(r(i, \alpha_1)(M, s))$$

where $r(i, \alpha)(\emptyset) \qquad\qquad = \emptyset$

$$c(i, a)(M, s) \qquad\qquad = c_0(i, a)(s)$$
$$c(i, \mathtt{confirm}\,\varphi)(M, s) \quad = 1 \text{ if } M, s \models \varphi \text{ and } 0 \text{ otherwise}$$
$$c(i, \alpha_1; \alpha_2)(M, s) \qquad = c(i, \alpha_1)(M, s) \,\&\, c(i, \alpha_2)(r(i, \alpha_1)(M, s))$$

where $c(i, \alpha)(\emptyset) \qquad\qquad = 1$

Satisfiability and validity are defined as usual.

The definition of $c(i, \mathtt{confirm}\,\varphi)$ expresses that an agent is able to get confirmation for a formula φ iff φ holds. The definitions of $r(i, \mathtt{confirm}\,\varphi)$ and $c(i, \mathtt{confirm}\,\varphi)$ imply that whenever φ holds, agents have both the opportunity and the ability to confirm φ. An agent is capable of performing a sequential composition $\alpha_1; \alpha_2$ iff it is capable of performing α_1 (now), and it is capable of executing α_2 after it has performed α_1. The (abilities for) conditional and repetitive composition are considered elsewhere [13]; for economical reasons they are left out of this abstract.

3 A classification of information

Information acquisition forms an important part of the acts of rational agents; in particular when planning it may be necessary for agents to try and acquire additional information from whatever source possible. Here we consider three possible sources of information for an agent. The first of these is an *exogenous* one and consists of the *observations* that an agent makes about the current world [12]; the second (exogenous) source of information for a rational agent is *communication* with other agents [10]. The third source that we consider is an *endogenous* one: the possibility to *adopt assumptions by default* [11].

In any situation in which information is acquired from different sources, conflicts may arise. Therefore a strategy is needed which prescribes what to do in the case of conflicts between new, incoming information and old, previously acquired information. Castelfranchi [1, 2] proposes that such a strategy should prescribe that an agent sticks to its old beliefs as long as possible, with the proviso that (strictly) more credible information should always be favored over (strictly) less credible information. To define a strategy complying with these ideas, it seems necessary to attach a degree of credibility to each of the beliefs that an agent has in a certain situation. To this end we propose to structure the agent's beliefs into four sets, one encompassing the other. The innermost of these sets contains the *knowledge* of the agent. The set directly encompassing knowledge contains the *observational* beliefs of the agent, which are the beliefs that an agent has on the ground of its knowledge and the observations it has made. The third set contains the *communicational* beliefs of an agent, which are the beliefs that it either knows, or acquired through observations and/or communication. The outermost set contains the *default beliefs*, for which application of a default may have been a necessary condition. Syntactically we account for this structuring of beliefs by tagging the belief modality; for the semantics we propose the use of appropriately nested *belief clusters* [14].

Definition 4. The language $\mathcal{L}$ as given in Def. 1 is thus extended:
- if $\varphi \in \mathcal{L}$ then $\mathbf{B}_i^o \varphi, \mathbf{B}_i^c \varphi, \mathbf{B}_i^d \varphi \in \mathcal{L}$

The formula $\mathbf{B}_i^o \varphi$ states that φ belongs to the observational beliefs of agent i, $\mathbf{B}_i^c \varphi$ states that φ belongs to the communicational beliefs of i, and $\mathbf{B}_i^d$ refers to the default beliefs of agent i. To keep our notation uniform, we sometimes use $\mathbf{B}_i^k$, for *known* beliefs, as a general way of writing $\mathbf{K}_i$.

Definition 5. The models from $\mathcal{M}$ are modified as follows: the function B is replaced by three functions $\mathrm{B}^o : \mathcal{A} \to \wp(\mathrm{S} \times \mathrm{S})$, $\mathrm{B}^c : \mathcal{A} \times \mathrm{S} \to \wp(\mathrm{S})$ and $\mathrm{B}^d : \mathcal{A} \times \mathrm{S} \to \wp(\mathrm{S})$. Defining the set $[s]_{\mathrm{B}^o(i)}$ analogously to $[s]_{\mathrm{R}(i)}$, these functions are such that for all $s, s' \in \mathrm{S}$:
- $\mathrm{B}^o(i)$ is an equivalence relation
- $\mathrm{B}^d(i, s) \neq \emptyset$
- $\mathrm{B}^d(i, s) \subseteq \mathrm{B}^c(i, s) \subseteq [s]_{\mathrm{B}^o(i)} \subseteq [s]_{\mathrm{R}(i)}$
- if $s' \in [s]_{\mathrm{B}^o(i)}$ then $\mathrm{B}^c(i, s') = \mathrm{B}^c(i, s)$ and $\mathrm{B}^d(i, s') = \mathrm{B}^d(i, s)$

Definition 6. For a model M and a state $s \in \mathrm{M}$, $\models$ is thus extended:
- $\mathrm{M}, s \models \mathbf{B}_i^o \varphi \Leftrightarrow \forall s' \in \mathrm{S}[(s, s') \in \mathrm{B}^o(i) \Rightarrow \mathrm{M}, s' \models \varphi]$
- $\mathrm{M}, s \models \mathbf{B}_i^c \varphi \Leftrightarrow \forall s' \in \mathrm{B}^c(i, s)[\mathrm{M}, s' \models \varphi]$
- $\mathrm{M}, s \models \mathbf{B}_i^d \varphi \Leftrightarrow \forall s' \in \mathrm{B}^d(i, s)[\mathrm{M}, s' \models \varphi]$

When interpreting the informational operators as proposed above, we end up with knowledge and observational belief satisfying an S5-axiomatization (corresponding to an equivalence relation denoting the informational alternatives), whereas communicational and default belief validate a KD45-axiomatization (corresponding to a non-empty set of alternatives, or equivalently a transitive, euclidean relation). This means in particular that all informational operators $\mathbf{X}$ validate the axioms of positive ($\mathbf{X}\varphi \to \mathbf{X}\mathbf{X}\varphi$) and negative ($\neg\mathbf{X}\varphi \to \mathbf{X}\neg\mathbf{X}\varphi$) introspection, and the D-axiom ($\neg(\mathbf{X}\varphi \wedge \mathbf{X}\neg\varphi)$). The knowledge and observational belief operator furthermore validate the T-axiom ($\mathbf{X}\varphi \to \varphi$). The definitions given above lead to a credibility ordering — given by the material implication — according to which knowing some formula is the strongest informational attitude, and believing it by default is the weakest one.

Given the four modal operators $\mathbf{B}_i^k, \mathbf{B}_i^o, \mathbf{B}_i^c, \mathbf{B}_i^d$ it is possible to model nine different informational attitudes of a given agent with regard to a given formula. If we define for $x \in \{k, o, c, d\}$, $\mathbf{Ign}_i^x \varphi =^{\mathrm{def}} \neg\mathbf{B}_i^x\varphi \wedge \neg\mathbf{B}_i^x\neg\varphi$ to represent the fact that agent i is *ignorant with regard to* φ *on the level* x — note that $\mathbf{Ign}_i^x\varphi$ is equivalent to $\mathbf{Ign}_i^x\neg\varphi$ — these attitudes are the following:

$\mathbf{B}_i^k\varphi$	i knows φ	$\mathbf{B}_i^k\neg\varphi$	i knows $\neg\varphi$
$\mathbf{Ign}_i^k\varphi \wedge \mathbf{B}_i^o\varphi$	i saw φ	$\mathbf{Ign}_i^k\varphi \wedge \mathbf{B}_i^o\neg\varphi$	i saw $\neg\varphi$
$\mathbf{Ign}_i^o\varphi \wedge \mathbf{B}_i^c\varphi$	i heard φ	$\mathbf{Ign}_i^o\varphi \wedge \mathbf{B}_i^c\neg\varphi$	i heard $\neg\varphi$
$\mathbf{Ign}_i^c\varphi \wedge \mathbf{B}_i^d\varphi$	i jumped to φ	$\mathbf{Ign}_i^c\varphi \wedge \mathbf{B}_i^d\neg\varphi$	i jumped to $\neg\varphi$

Based on these attitudes and their intuitive interpretation, we introduce the following predicates by definitional abbreviation:

- $\mathbf{Saw}_i\varphi =^{\mathrm{def}} \mathbf{Ign}_i^k\varphi \wedge \mathbf{B}_i^o\varphi$
- $\mathbf{Heard}_i\varphi =^{\mathrm{def}} \mathbf{Ign}_i^o\varphi \wedge \mathbf{B}_i^c\varphi$
- $\mathbf{Jumped}_i\varphi =^{\mathrm{def}} \mathbf{Ign}_i^c\varphi \wedge \mathbf{B}_i^d\varphi$

The derived informational operators $\mathbf{Saw}_i, \mathbf{Heard}_i$ and $\mathbf{Jumped}_i$ are used in the definitions of the informative actions. An important remark is that none of these operators is *normal*: although they all validate the K-axiom ($\mathbf{X}(\varphi \to \psi) \to (\mathbf{X}\varphi \to \mathbf{X}\psi)$), none of these operators satisfies the rule of necessitation (if φ is valid then $\mathbf{X}\varphi$ is valid). The reason for this is that as soon as φ is valid, $\mathbf{K}_i\varphi$ is also valid; hence the agent *knows* the formula, and therefore did not observe (hear, jump to) it.

4 Combining informative actions

Having classified the agents' belief, we can now define three kinds of informative actions, which correspond to three kinds of information acquisition. The first action models the observations that agents may make. Through performing an `observe` φ action an agent *observes whether* φ *holds*. The second action formalizes communication. By performing an `inform` (φ, i) action, some *agent j may inform agent i of the fact* φ. The third action corresponds to reasoning by default. By performing `try_jump` φ actions agents *attempt to jump to the default conclusion* φ. To define the semantics of these 'high-level' informative actions, we use special 'low-level' actions that cause the beliefs of an agent to be *revised* in the appropriate manner. The revisions implemented by these low-level actions validate the (in)famous AGM postulates for belief revision [4, 9], which might be taken as a sign for the rationality of these revisions. To deal adequately with the classification of the agent's information, the revision actions are defined to *stretch over* the various belief classes. To emphasize the distinction between the high and the low-level informative actions, we introduce in addition to the set of rational agents a constant e, representing the *external environment*, which is in charge of performing low-level revision actions.

Definition 7. The class of high-level informative actions Ac_I^h and the class of low-level informative actions Ac_I^l are defined by:

- $Ac_I^h = \{\text{observe } \varphi, \text{inform } (\varphi, i), \text{try\_jump } \varphi \mid \varphi \in \mathcal{L}_0, i \in \mathcal{A}\}$
- Ac_I^l is the smallest superset of $\{\text{revise}^x(\varphi, i) \mid x \in \{1, 2, 3, d, c, o\}, i \in \mathcal{A}, \varphi \in \mathcal{L}_0\}$ that is closed under sequential composition.

The class of actions Ac is extended with the class Ac_I^h.

Definition 8. For $M = \langle S, \pi, R, B^o, B^c, B^d, r_0, c_0 \rangle$, $s \in S$, $S' \subseteq S$, and $\varphi \in \mathcal{L}_0$:

- $[\![\varphi]\!] =^{\text{def}} \{s \in S \mid M, s \models \varphi\}$
- $[s]_{B^o(i)}^{\varphi+} =^{\text{def}} [s]_{B^o(i)} \cap [\![\varphi]\!]$
- $[s]_{B^o(i)}^{\varphi-} =^{\text{def}} [s]_{B^o(i)} \cap [\![\neg\varphi]\!] = [s]_{B^o(i)} \setminus [s]_{B^o(i)}^{\varphi+}$
- $\text{Cl}_{\text{eq}}(S') =^{\text{def}} S' \times S'$

The set $[\![\varphi]\!]$ as defined in 8 contains the states in the model M that satisfy the formula φ. The set $[s]_{B^o(i)}^{\varphi+}$ consists of all those states from $[s]_{B^o(i)}$ that satisfy φ, and analogously $[s]_{B^o(i)}^{\varphi-}$ contains the elements of $[s]_{B^o(i)}$ that do not satisfy φ. The function Cl_{eq} yields the cartesian product of a set of states.

Definition 9. For $M = \langle S, \pi, R, B^o, B^c, B^d, r_0, c_0 \rangle$, $s \in S$, and $\varphi \in \mathcal{L}_0$:

- The function r is retyped to $(\mathcal{A} \times Ac) \cup (\{e\} \times Ac_I^l) \to (\mathcal{M} \times S) \to \wp(\mathcal{M} \times S)$.
- $r(e, \text{revise}^1(i, \varphi))(M, s) = M', s$ where $M' = \langle S, \pi, R, B^o, B^c, B^{d'}, r_0, c_0 \rangle$ and $B^{d'}(i', s') = B^d(i', s')$ if $i \neq i'$ or $s' \notin [s]_{B^o(i)}$

$$B^{d'}(i, s') = \begin{cases} B^d(i, s) \cap [\![\varphi]\!] & \text{if } B^d(i, s) \cap [\![\varphi]\!] \neq \emptyset, s' \in [s]_{B^o(i)} \\ B^c(i, s) \cap [\![\varphi]\!] & \text{if } B^d(i, s) \cap [\![\varphi]\!] = \emptyset, s' \in [s]_{B^o(i)} \end{cases}$$

- $r(e, \text{revise}^2(i, \varphi))(M, s) = M', s$ where $M' = \langle S, \pi, R, B^o, B^{c'}, B^d, r_0, c_0 \rangle$ and $B^{c'}(i', s') = B^c(i', s')$ if $i \neq i'$ or $s' \notin [s]_{B^o(i)}$

$$B^{c'}(i, s') = \begin{cases} B^c(i, s) \cap [\![\varphi]\!] & \text{if } B^c(i, s) \cap [\![\varphi]\!] \neq \emptyset, s' \in [s]_{B^o(i)} \\ [s]_{B^o(i)} \cap [\![\varphi]\!] & \text{if } B^c(i, s) \cap [\![\varphi]\!] = \emptyset, s' \in [s]_{B^o(i)} \end{cases}$$

- $r(e, \text{revise}^3(i, \varphi))(M, s) = M', s$ where $M' = \langle S, \pi, R, B^{o'}, B^c, B^d, r_0, c_0 \rangle$ and $B^{o'}(i') = B^o(i')$ if $i' \neq i$

$B^{o'}(i) = (B^o(i) \setminus \text{Cl}_{\text{eq}}([s]_{B^o(i)})) \cup \text{Cl}_{\text{eq}}([s]_{B^o(i)}^{\varphi+}) \cup \text{Cl}_{\text{eq}}([s]_{B^o(i)}^{\varphi-})$

- $r(e, \text{revise}^d(i, \varphi))(M, s) = r(e, \text{revise}^1(i, \varphi))(M, s)$
- $r(e, \text{revise}^c(i, \varphi))(M, s) = r(e, \text{revise}^2(i, \varphi); \text{revise}^1(i, \varphi))(M, s)$
- $r(e, \text{revise}^o(i, \varphi))(M, s) =$
  $r(e, \text{revise}^3(i, \varphi); \text{revise}^2(i, \varphi); \text{revise}^1(i, \varphi))(M, s)$

Proposition 10. *If* M *is a well-defined model with* $s \in M$, *then for all* $\alpha \in Ac_I^h$, M' *such that* $M', s = r(i, \alpha)(M, s)$ *is a well-defined model.*

The idea underlying Definition 9 is that the $\texttt{revise}^x, x = d, c, o$ actions are used to revise the beliefs of the agent at all appropriate levels, whereas the $\texttt{revise}^m, m = 1, 2, 3$ actions are used to perform a revision per level. For example, whenever an agent i observes in a state s that a formula φ holds, the external environment executes the action $\texttt{revise}^o(i, \varphi)$. In the light of the classification of information presented in §3, performing this action should not only revise the agent's observational beliefs with φ, but also its communicational and default beliefs, since the latter belief sets should encompass the former. Corresponding to these three levels of belief revision, three stages can be distinguished in the execution of the $\texttt{revise}^o(i, \varphi)$ action. At the first stage, which consists of execution of the $\texttt{revise}^3(i, \varphi)$ action, the observational doxastic accessibility relation is split in two: one part $(\mathrm{Cl_{eq}}([s]_{\mathrm{B}^o(i)}^{\varphi+}))$ containing all of the observational doxastic alternatives that satisfy φ, the other part $(\mathrm{Cl_{eq}}([s]_{\mathrm{B}^o(i)}^{\varphi-}))$ consisting of the worlds that do not satisfy φ. Thereafter in the second stage, consisting of the execution of the $\texttt{revise}^2(i, \varphi)$ action, it is ensured that the new set of communicational doxastic alternatives of the agent is contained in its observational doxastic alternatives, which ensures that the new set of communicational beliefs encompasses the agent's observational beliefs. In the third and last stage, execution of the $\texttt{revise}^1(i, \varphi)$ action makes sure that the set of default doxastic alternatives is contained in the set of communicational doxastic alternatives.

4.1 Formalizing observations: seeing is believing

Through observations an agent *learns whether* some proposition is true of the state in which it is residing. For artificial agents it seems to be a reasonable assumption to demand that observations are *truthful* [12], i.e., if some observation yields information that φ, then it should indeed be the case that φ. The property of truthfulness implies that all agents see things in the same way, i.e., all agents see things as they are. As such, observations form the most trustworthy way of acquiring information; the formalization that we propose is therefore such that observations overrule any beliefs acquired by other means, thereby possibly causing a belief revision. The truth-value assigned to φ in the current world determines how the (observational) beliefs of the agent are revised: if φ holds, the agent's beliefs are revised with φ, otherwise with $\neg\varphi$.

Definition 11. For all $M \in \mathcal{M}$ with state s, and all $\varphi \in \mathcal{L}_0$ we define:

$$r(i, \texttt{observe}\,\varphi)(M, s) =$$
$$\begin{cases} M, s & \text{if } M, s \models \neg\mathbf{Ign}_i^k\varphi \\ r(e, \texttt{revise}^o(i, \varphi))(M, s) & \text{if } M, s \models \mathbf{Ign}_i^k\varphi \wedge \varphi \\ r(e, \texttt{revise}^o(i, \neg\varphi))(M, s) & \text{if } M, s \models \mathbf{Ign}_i^k\varphi \wedge \neg\varphi \end{cases}$$

Proposition 12. *For all* $\varphi, \psi \in \mathcal{L}_0$, $\chi \in \mathcal{L}$ *we have:*

1. $\models \mathbf{K}_{i'}\psi \leftrightarrow \langle \mathrm{do}_i(\texttt{observe}\,\varphi)\rangle \mathbf{K}_{i'}\psi$
2. $\models \langle \mathrm{do}_i(\texttt{observe}\,\varphi)\rangle\chi \leftrightarrow \langle \mathrm{do}_i(\texttt{observe}\,\neg\varphi)\rangle\chi$
3. $\models \langle \mathrm{do}_i(\texttt{observe}\,\varphi)\rangle\neg\mathbf{Ign}_i^o\varphi$

4. $\models \varphi \rightarrow \langle do_i(\text{observe } \varphi) \rangle \mathbf{B}_i^o \varphi$
5. $\models \neg\varphi \rightarrow \langle do_i(\text{observe } \varphi) \rangle \mathbf{B}_i^o \neg\varphi$
6. $\models \varphi \wedge \mathbf{Ign}_i^k \varphi \rightarrow \langle do_i(\text{observe } \varphi) \rangle \mathbf{Saw}_i \varphi$
7. $\models \neg\varphi \wedge \mathbf{Ign}_i^k \varphi \rightarrow \langle do_i(\text{observe } \varphi) \rangle \mathbf{Saw}_i \neg\varphi$
8. $\models \varphi \wedge (\mathbf{Heard}_i \neg\varphi \vee \mathbf{Jumped}_i \neg\varphi) \rightarrow \langle do_i(\text{observe } \varphi) \rangle \mathbf{Saw}_i \varphi$
9. $\models \varphi \wedge \mathbf{B}_i^c \neg\varphi \rightarrow \langle do_i(\text{observe } \varphi) \rangle ((\mathbf{B}_i^c \chi \leftrightarrow \mathbf{B}_i^o \chi) \wedge (\mathbf{B}_i^d \chi \leftrightarrow \mathbf{B}_i^c \chi))$

Item 1 of Prop. 12 states that the knowledge fluents — the propositional formulae known to be true — of all agents persist under execution of an observe action by one of them. Item 2 states that the observe φ action formalizes 'observing whether': observing whether φ is equivalent to observing whether $\neg\varphi$. Item 3 states that agents always have the opportunity to make observations, and that after observing whether φ, agents are no longer observationally ignorant with respect to φ. Items 4 and 5 follow by a combination of the property of truthfulness with the idea of agents learning whether some proposition is true: if φ is true, agents learn *that* φ, and analogously for $\neg\varphi$. Item 6 and 7 state that for knowledge-ignorant agents observations actually lead to *learning by seeing*. Item 8 states that observations are the most credible source of information. Observations overrule other beliefs acquired through communication or adopted by default, i.e., incorrect communicational or default beliefs are *revised* in favor of observational beliefs. Item 9 sheds some more light on the (rigorous) way in which beliefs are revised: observing something that contradicts communicational beliefs leads to a *reset* of both the latter and the default beliefs of the agent, i.e., after such a revision all beliefs are at least grounded in observations.

4.2 Formalizing communication: hearing is believing

The formalization of communication that we present here is that of super-cooperative, didactic agents, which always have the opportunity to pass on all of their beliefs to every other agent. In our opinion, when modelling communication in multi-agent frameworks, the concept of *trust and dependence relations* between agents deserves considerable attention. These relations are used to model whether some agent is considered to be a credible source on a certain subject by another agent. In communication this notion of credibility is very important: an agent i may or may not accept the information on φ that an agent j sends to it, depending on i's trust in j with respect to φ. We formalize the dependence relations between agents using the *dependent* operator $\mathbf{D}_{i,j}$ [8, 10].

Definition 13. The language $\mathcal{L}$ is extended by:

- if $i, j \in \mathcal{A}$ and $\varphi \in \mathcal{L}$ then $\mathbf{D}_{i,j}\varphi \in \mathcal{L}$

Kripke models are extended with a function $D : \mathcal{A} \times \mathcal{A} \times S \rightarrow \wp(\mathcal{L})$. We define:

- $M, s \models \mathbf{D}_{i,j}\varphi$ iff $\varphi \in D(i, j, s)$

Another factor of importance is *how* the sending agent acquired its information [1]. If the agent itself *observed* the truth of the formula that it is sending, then this formula should be considered more credible than when the agent *heard* the formula, or *adopted it by default*. The formalization that we propose is such that whenever an agent sends its observational beliefs then this will in general lead to a revision of the receiving agent's beliefs. To ensure that communicational beliefs are indeed more credible than default beliefs, the source of these communicational beliefs needs to be credible. Now whenever some agent is sending out formulae that it heard, it is in general not possible to determine the credibility of these formulae, since one lost track of their source. Therefore, beliefs that the sending agent itself acquired through communication lead to a revision of the beliefs of the receiving agent only if this agent is completely ignorant with respect to these formulae. Formulae that the sending agent believes by default are considered to be too weak to be incorporated in the receiving agent's beliefs.

Definition 14. For all $M \in \mathcal{M}$ with state s, and for all $\varphi \in \mathcal{L}_0$ we define:

$$
r(j, \texttt{inform}\,(\varphi, i))(M, s) =
\begin{cases}
\emptyset & \text{if } M, s \models \neg \mathbf{B}_j^d \varphi \\
r(e, \texttt{revise}^c(i, \varphi))(M, s) & \text{if } M, s \models \mathbf{D}_{i,j}\varphi \wedge ((\mathbf{B}_j^o \varphi \wedge \mathbf{Ign}_i^o \varphi) \vee \\
& \qquad (\mathbf{Heard}_j \varphi \wedge \mathbf{Ign}_i^d \varphi)) \\
M, s & \text{otherwise}
\end{cases}
$$

Proposition 15. *For all $\varphi, \psi \in \mathcal{L}_0$, $\chi \in \mathcal{L}$, we have:*

1. $\models \mathbf{B}_{i'}^o \psi \rightarrow [\text{do}_j(\texttt{inform}\,(\varphi, i))] \mathbf{B}_{i'}^o \psi$
2. $\models \mathbf{B}_j^d \varphi \leftrightarrow \langle \text{do}_j(\texttt{inform}\,(\varphi, i)) \rangle \texttt{tt}$
3. $\models \mathbf{B}_j^d \varphi \wedge \neg \mathbf{D}_{i,j}\varphi \rightarrow (\langle \text{do}_j(\texttt{inform}\,(\varphi, i)) \rangle \chi \leftrightarrow \chi)$
4. $\models \mathbf{D}_{i,j}\varphi \wedge \mathbf{B}_j^o \varphi \rightarrow \langle \text{do}_j(\texttt{inform}\,(\varphi, i)) \rangle \mathbf{B}_i^c \varphi$
5. $\models \mathbf{D}_{i,j}\varphi \wedge \mathbf{B}_j^o \varphi \wedge \mathbf{Ign}_i^o \varphi \rightarrow \langle \text{do}_j(\texttt{inform}\,(\varphi, i)) \rangle \mathbf{Heard}_i \varphi$
6. $\models \mathbf{D}_{i,j}\varphi \wedge \mathbf{Heard}_j \varphi \wedge \mathbf{Ign}_i^d \varphi \rightarrow \langle \text{do}_j(\texttt{inform}\,(\varphi, i)) \rangle \mathbf{Heard}_i \varphi$
7. $\models \mathbf{D}_{i,j}\varphi \wedge \mathbf{Heard}_j \varphi \wedge \neg \mathbf{Ign}_i^d \varphi \rightarrow (\langle \text{do}_j(\texttt{inform}\,(\varphi, i)) \rangle \chi \leftrightarrow \chi)$
8. $\models \mathbf{D}_{i,j}\varphi \wedge \mathbf{Jumped}_j \varphi \rightarrow (\langle \text{do}_j(\texttt{inform}\,(\varphi, i)) \rangle \chi \leftrightarrow \chi)$

Item 1 of Prop. 15 states that the observational belief fluents of the agents persist under execution of an `inform` action. Item 2 states that agents have the opportunity to inform other agents of exactly those formulae that they themselves believe. Agents are therefore not allowed to *gossip*, i.e., it is not allowed for an agent to spread around rumours that it itself does not even believe. Item 3 deals with the dependence relation between the agents: if the receiving agent does not trust the sending agent, it lets the information pass and nothing changes. Item 4 states that if some trustworthy agent j tells another agent i some formula that j either knows or observed, this leads to a state of affairs in which the receiving agent believes φ at least with the credibility attached to communicational beliefs; whenever i is *a priori* ignorant with regard to this formula on the level of communicational beliefs, the receiving agent actually *learns* φ (item 5). Items 6 and 7 deal with the situation of *hearsay*: agent j tells i some formula that j itself has heard. In this case the beliefs of the receiving agent are updated only if the agent is ignorant on the default level with respect to the formula. Item 8 states that default beliefs are too weak to be transferred succesfully.

4.3 Formalizing default jumps: jumping is believing

In a previous paper [11] we proposed a dynamic formalization of default reasoning, in which agents attempt to jump to certain plausible formulae, called *defaults*. A noteworthy aspect of this approach is the representation of defaults as *common possibilities*. The idea underlying this representation is that defaults are founded in *common sense*, and in multi-agent systems, *common* sense is related to the knowledge and lack of knowledge of *all* agents.

Definition 16 [11]. For $\varphi \in \mathcal{L}$, the formula $\mathbf{N}\varphi$, for nobody knows not φ, is defined by: $\mathbf{N}\varphi =^{\text{def}} \mathbf{M}_1\varphi \wedge \ldots \wedge \mathbf{M}_n\varphi$.

Definition 16 proposes a novel — and in fact rather controversial — formalization of defaults. For those with serious objections, it is important to remark that one is not *obliged* to formalize defaults in this way: alternative (modal) definitions of defaults are easily incorporated in our framework.

The formalization of attempted jumps to defaults is based on the idea that adopting formulae by default is the last resort: only if no other means of acquiring information is available a jump to a default is attempted. As such, default jumps are effective only for agents that are completely ignorant with respect to the default that is jumped to.

Definition 17. For all $M \in \mathcal{M}$ with state s, and for all $\varphi \in \mathcal{L}_0$ we define:

$$r(i, \mathbf{try\_jump}\ \varphi)(M, s) =$$
$$\begin{cases} \emptyset & \text{if } M, s \not\models \mathbf{N}\varphi \\ r(e, \mathbf{revise}^d(i, \varphi))(M, s) & \text{if } M, s \models \mathbf{N}\varphi \wedge \mathbf{Ign}_i^d\varphi \\ M, s & \text{otherwise} \end{cases}$$

Proposition 18. *For all* $\varphi, \psi \in \mathcal{L}_0$, $\chi \in \mathcal{L}$, *we have:*

1. $\models \mathbf{B}_{i'}^c \psi \rightarrow [\mathbf{do}_i(\mathbf{try\_jump}\ \varphi)]\mathbf{B}_{i'}^c \psi$
2. $\models \mathbf{N}\varphi \leftrightarrow \langle \mathbf{do}_i(\mathbf{try\_jump}\ \varphi)\rangle \mathbf{tt}$
3. $\models \langle \mathbf{do}_i(\mathbf{try\_jump}\ \varphi)\rangle \mathbf{tt} \leftrightarrow \langle \mathbf{do}_i(\mathbf{try\_jump}\ \varphi)\rangle \neg\mathbf{Ign}_i^d\varphi$
4. $\models \mathbf{N}\varphi \wedge \mathbf{Ign}_i^d\varphi \rightarrow \langle \mathbf{do}_i(\mathbf{try\_jump}\ \varphi)\rangle \mathbf{Jumped}_i\varphi$
5. $\models \mathbf{N}\varphi \wedge \neg\mathbf{Ign}_i^d\varphi \rightarrow (\langle \mathbf{do}_i(\mathbf{try\_jump}\ \varphi)\rangle \chi \leftrightarrow \chi)$

Item 1 of Prop. 18 states that the knowledge fluents, the observational belief fluents, and the communicational belief fluents of all agents persist under the attempted jump to a formula by one of them. Item 2 formalizes that attempted jumps to non-defaults are doomed to fail. Item 3 states that default jumps that are possible always result in the agent not being default-ignorant with regard to the formula that is jumped to. Item 4 formalizes the idea that agents that are completely ignorant with respect to some formula φ jump to new default beliefs by applying the $\mathbf{try\_jump}\ \varphi$ action. The last item states that attempted jumps to default conclusions are effective for completely ignorant agents only.

414

5 Discussion

In this paper we formalize various informative actions, which correspond to the different ways in which rational agents can acquire information. To solve conflicts that could possibly arise when acquiring information from different sources, we propose a classification of the information that an agent possesses according to credibility. Based on this classification, we formalize what it means for agents to have seen or heard something, or to believe something by default. A formalization of observations, communication actions, and the attempted jumps to conclusions that constitute default reasoning is proposed. To implement these informative actions we use a general belief revision action which satisfies the AGM postulates; dependent on the credibility of the incoming information this revision action acts on one or more parts of the agents' classified belief set.

Acknowledgements Thanks are due to Cristiano Castelfranchi and the referees for their comments which helped improve this paper. This research is partially supported by Esprit BRWG project No.8319 'ModelAge', Esprit BRA project No.6156 'Drums II' and the Vrije Universiteit Amsterdam; the third author is furthermore partially supported by the Katholieke Universiteit Nijmegen.

References

1. C. Castelfranchi. Private communication. 1994.
2. C. Castelfranchi. Guarantees for autonomy in cognitive agent architecture. In Wooldridge and Jennings, eds., *Intelligent Agents*, LNCS 890:56–70.
3. P. Cohen and H. Levesque. Intention is... *AI* , 42:213–261, 1990.
4. P. Gärdenfors. *Knowledge in Flux*. MIT Press, 1988.
5. J. Halpern and Y. Moses. A guide to completeness and complexity for modal logics of knowledge and belief. *AI*, 54:319–379, 1992.
6. W. van der Hoek, B. van Linder, and J.-J. Meyer. A logic of capabilities. In Nerode and Matiyasevich, eds. , *Procs. of LFCS'94*, LNCS 813:366–378.
7. W. van der Hoek, B. van Linder, and J.-J. Ch. Meyer. Unravelling nondeterminism. In Jorrand and Sgurev, eds., *Procs. of AIMSA'94*:163–172. World Scientific.
8. Z. Huang. Logics for belief dependence. In E. Börger et al., eds., *Procs. of CSL'90*, LNCS 533:274–288.
9. B. van Linder, W. van der Hoek, and J.-J. Meyer. Actions that make you change your mind. To appear in the proceedings of KI-95.
10. B. van Linder, W. van der Hoek, and J.-J. Meyer. Communicating rational agents. In Nebel and Dreschler-Fischer, eds., *Procs. of KI-94*, LNCS 861:202–213.
11. B. van Linder, W. van der Hoek, and J.-J. Meyer. The dynamics of default reasoning. To appear in the proceedings of ECSQARU'95.
12. B. van Linder, W. van der Hoek, and J.-J. Meyer. Tests as epistemic updates. In Cohn, ed., *Procs. of ECAI'94*:331–335. John Wiley & Sons, 1994.
13. B. van Linder, W. van der Hoek, and J.-J.Ch. Meyer. Seeing is believing. Available at http://www.cs.ruu.nl/~bernd/Publications.html.
14. J.-J. Meyer and W. van der Hoek. A modal logic for nonmonotonic reasoning. In van der Hoek et al., eds., *Non-Monotonic Reasoning and Partial Semantics*:37–77. Ellis Horwood, 1992.
15. R. Moore. Reasoning about knowledge and action. TR 191, SRI, 1980.
16. G.H. von Wright. *Norm and Action*. Routledge & Kegan Paul, 1963.

Agents as Reasoners, Observers or Believers*

Enrico Giunchiglia[1] Fausto Giunchiglia[2,3] Luciano Serafini[2]
Mechanized Reasoning Group

[1] DIST - University of Genoa, 16145 Genova, Italy
[2] IRST, 38050 Povo, Trento, Italy
[3] DISA - University of Trento, 38100 Trento, Italy

Abstract. The work described in this paper aims at the definition of a general framework for the formal specification of agents' beliefs in a multiagent environment. The basic idea is to model both agents' beliefs and the view that each agent has of other agents' beliefs as logical theories. The logical theories and the relations among them characterize a *belief system*. Belief systems are naturally presented using *Multi context systems*. We show how some of the modal approaches to the formalization of (non) omniscient belief can be captured within our framework.

1 Introduction

The work described in this paper aims at the definition of a general framework for the formal specification of agents' beliefs in a multiagent environment. The basic idea is to model both agents' beliefs and the view that each agent has of other agents' beliefs as logical theories (here called *reasoners*). For example, an agent a_i's beliefs about another agent a_j's beliefs are modeled introducing two reasoners R_i and R_{ij} modeling respectively a_i's and a_i's about a_j's beliefs. Any sentence has thus different meanings depending on the reasoner it belongs to. For example A in R_i means "a_i believes A" whilst A in R_{ij} means "a_i believes that a_j believes A". That "a_i believes that a_j believes A" is expressed in R_i with the sentence $B^j("A")$. The reasoners R_i, R_{ij} and the predicate B^j used in R_i to express a_i's beliefs about a_j characterize a *basic belief system*. We call it "basic" since it formalizes the "basic" situation of one agent having beliefs about another agent. More complex scenarios are modeled introducing *belief systems*. Belief systems are naturally presented using *Multi context systems* [Giu93, GS94].

Multi context systems allow for a modular, incremental and reasoner oriented design, where the structural characteristics of each reasoner (*e.g.* its language and relations with other reasoners) can be defined *locally* to a theory corresponding to the reasoner. This is not possible in the "traditional" formal approaches (*e.g.* modal logics), where one must impose the properties of each agent's beliefs in a unique theory (see for instance [FH88]). Even more, we show how some of the past proposals for the formalization of non omniscient agent (the logic of general

---

* Alessandro Cimatti and Kurt Konolige have provided very useful feedback and suggestions. The work at IRST has been done as part of the MAIA project.

awareness [FH88, FHMV92] and some types of non normal modal logics [Che80]) can be easily captured in our framework.

In the paper, we address the problem of modeling agents' beliefs starting from the simple case of an agent having beliefs only about the world (section 2), through the case of an agent having beliefs about another agent's beliefs about the world (section 3), up to agents having arbitrary beliefs (section 4). Then, we show how the framework proposed can be specialized to capture some important modal formalizations of belief (section 5). We conclude the paper with some remarks (section 6).

2 Agents as Reasoners

We first consider the case in which we have one agent a_i having beliefs only about the world. At a very abstract level, a_i's beliefs can be modeled by a *reasoner* defined as a pair $\langle L_i, T_i \rangle$: L_i is the *language* of the reasoner and T_i are the *beliefs* of the reasoner (in the following, we abbreviate a reasoner $\langle L_i, T_i \rangle$ with R_i). Both the language L_i and the beliefs T_i of a reasoner can be *extensionally* characterized as sets of formulas satisfying certain conditions (see for instance [Avr87, BS84]). However, R_i can be also *intensionally* characterized by means of an axiomatic formal system (here called context). A *context* is a triple $\langle L_i, \Omega_i, \Delta_i \rangle$ (abbreviated with C_i) where L_i is the *language*, Ω_i are the *axioms* and Δ_i are the *inference rules* of the context. In this simple framework in which we have only one context C_i, the reasoner intensionally characterized by C_i is $\langle L_i, Cl(\Omega_i, \Delta_i) \rangle$, where $Cl(\Omega_i, \Delta_i)$ is the smallest set generated from Ω_i and closed under Δ_i.

Following [GSGF93], we say that a reasoner $R_i = \langle L_i, T_i \rangle$ is *ideal* if T_i is closed under logical consequence. Ideal reasoners are *logically omniscient with respect to their own beliefs i.e.* they believe all the logical consequences of their own beliefs. An ideal reasoner R_i can be finitely presented by a context $\langle L_i, \Omega_i, \Delta_i \rangle$ where Δ_i is the set of Classical Natural Deduction Rules as defined in [Pra65].

The problem is that ideal reasoners are often inadequate for representing the capabilities of real agents (*e.g.* humans and programs). Given them enough knowledge and resources (*e.g.* space, time) humans and programs tend to converge to the behavior of an ideal reasoner but this may never be the case. This situation is modeled by introducing the notion of *real reasoner*, *i.e.* a reasoner $R = \langle L, T \rangle$ such that T is not closed under logical consequence. Real reasoners can be presented "weakening" one or more of the components (the language, the axioms or the inference rules) of a context presenting an ideal reasoner. It is also possible to classify real reasoners according to which component of their finite presentation is the source of the lack of logical omniscience. Such a classification is discussed in detail in [GSGF93].

3   Agents as Observers

We now consider the case in which an agent a_i has beliefs about an agent a_j. We also assume that a_j has only beliefs about the world. This situation is modeled considering three reasoners R_i, R_j and R_{ij} modeling a_i, a_j and a_i's beliefs about a_j respectively. R_{ij} is thus the (mental) representation that a_i has about a_j. A unary predicate B in the signature of R_i is used to express a_i's beliefs about a_j. The proposition "a_i believes that a_j believes A" thus corresponds to the formulas B("A") in R_i and A in R_{ij}. Even though the same proposition can be expressed by two different formulas, the truth of such two formulas should not be independent. In other words, it should be the case that R_i believes B("A") if and only if R_{ij} believes A. This is a strong relation between the two reasoners R_i and R_{ij}. We cannot expect that the same relation shall hold between R_i and R_j (for example a_i may hold incorrect beliefs about a_j).

The relation between the reasoners R_i and R_{ij} (but also between R_i and R_j) is formally characterized introducing basic belief systems. A *basic belief system* is a pair $\langle R_0, R_1 \rangle_B$: R_0 is the *observer*, R_1 is the *observed reasoner* and the parameter B is the *belief predicate* of the basic belief system. Intuitively, a basic belief system $\langle R_0, R_1 \rangle_B$ models the situation in which R_0 has beliefs about R_1 and expresses its beliefs about R_1 using the predicate B (we also say that R_0 B-*observes* R_1).

As for reasoners, a basic belief system $\langle R_0, R_1 \rangle_B$ can be characterized by extensionally defining its components R_0 and R_1. Another possibility is to use multi context systems. A *multi context system* or *MC system* is a pair $\langle \{C_i\}_{i \in I}, BR \rangle$, where $\{C_i\}_{i \in I}$ is a family of contexts and BR is a set of bridge rules, *i.e.* inference rules having premises and conclusion in distinct contexts. For instance, a bridge rule like

$$\frac{\langle B, C' \rangle}{\langle A, C \rangle}$$

allows to derive A in context C (denoted with $\langle A, C \rangle$) just because B has been derived in context C'. Roughly speaking, a deduction in a MC system is a tree of contextual deductions concatenated by one or more applications of bridge rules. Notationally, we write $\Gamma \vdash_{MS} \langle A, C \rangle$ to mean that the formula $\langle A, C \rangle$ is derivable from Γ in the MC system MS [Giu93, GS94].

MC systems provide the proper tools for presenting basic belief systems: each reasoner R_i corresponds to a context C_i. The properties of R_i (*e.g.* the language, the ideality as a reasoner) are mapped in corresponding properties of C_i and the desired relation between R_i and another reasoner R_j can be imposed with bridge rules between C_i and C_j.

Given a basic belief system $\langle R_0, R_1 \rangle_B$, R_0 and R_1 should be related in such a way that B("A") belongs to T_0 if A belongs to T_1 and/or vice versa. We therefore introduce the following formal definition.

Definition 1 $MR_{0,1}^{B-}$. An MC system $\langle \{C_0, C_1\}, BR \rangle$ is an $MR_{0,1}^{B-}$ system if BR is the following set of bridge rules:

$$\frac{\langle A, C_1 \rangle}{\langle B(``A"), C_0 \rangle} \mathcal{R}_{up.1}^{B} \qquad \frac{\langle B(``A"), C_0 \rangle}{\langle A, C_1 \rangle} \mathcal{R}_{dn.1}^{B}$$

and the restrictions for the applicability include:

$\mathcal{R}_{up.1}^{B}$: $\langle A, C_1 \rangle$ does not depend on any assumption in C_1.
$\mathcal{R}_{dn.1}^{B}$: $\langle B(``A"), C_0 \rangle$ does not depend on any assumption in C_0.

We say that an $MR_{0,1}^{B-}$ system $MS = \langle \{C_0, C_1\}, BR \rangle$ *generates* the basic belief system $\langle R_0, R_1 \rangle_B$ if $T_i = \{A \mid \vdash_{MS} \langle A, C_i \rangle\}$ ($i = 0, 1$).

The first bridge rule in Definition 1 is called *reflection up*, the second is called *reflection down*. Reflection up allows to prove $B(``A")$ in C_0 just because A has been proved in C_1 (notice that the restrictions are such that a formula can be reflected up or down only if it does not depend on any assumptions, *i.e.* it is a theorem). Reflection down has the dual effect, *i.e.* it allows to prove A in C_1 just because $B(``A")$ has been proved in C_0.

Reasoners are characterized depending on their ability to reason. Observers can be characterized depending on their ability to observe. Given a basic belief system $\langle R_0, R_1 \rangle_B$, we say that R_0 is an *ideal observer* if $T_1 = \{A \mid B(``A") \in T_0\}$. Ideal observers are *logically omniscient with respect to the observed reasoner's beliefs*, *i.e.* they ascribe to the observed reasoner all and only the beliefs that it actually believes. It is easy to generate ideal observers with MC systems. In fact, for any $MR_{0,1}^{B-}$ system such that

- $L_1 = \{A \mid B(``A") \in L_0\}$, and (condition 1)
- the restrictions on the applicability of reflection up/down are only those listed in Definition 1 (condition 2)

R_0 is ensured to be an ideal observer.

So far, the fact that R_0 be an ideal observer of R_1 does not seem so unrealistic, at least from a proof theoretic perspective. Once a fact A [$B(``A")$, respectively] has been proved in $C_1$ [$C_0$], $C_0$ [$C_1$] can infer $B(``A")$ [A] with one reasoning step, *i.e.* one application of reflection up [down]. Even more, it seems to be cognitively plausible if R_1 is a mental image of R_0, *i.e.* if R_1 is the formalization of the beliefs of an agent according to the agent formalized by R_0.

Nevertheless we cannot in general expect any reasoner be an ideal observer of any other reasoner. For instance, if R_0 and R_1 model agents a_i and a_j respectively, the communication between a_i and a_j may involve using a large and somehow unreliable computer network. This situation is modeled by introducing basic belief systems $\langle R_0, R_1 \rangle_B$ where R_0 is a *real observer i.e.* it is not the case that $B(``A") \in T_0$ iff $A \in T_1$.

An $MR_{0,1}^{B-}$ system generates a real observer only if either condition 1 or condition 2 is false. However, there is no general relation between the falsity of conditions 1 and 2 and the reality of R_0 as an observer or R_1. In other words, the falsity of either or both conditions does not necessarily imply that R_0 is a real observer of R_1.

Finally, notice that a reasoner R_0 being an ideal observer of R_1 does not imply that R_0 is also an ideal reasoner (or vice versa). The two notions are independent. For instance, we may have an ideal observer which is at the same time a real reasoner or a real observer which is at the same time an ideal reasoner. Analogously, there is no a-priori connection between the properties of the observer and those of the observed reasoner. We can have an observer which is an ideal reasoner and an observed reasoner which is a real reasoner, or vice versa.

4 Agents as Believers

We now consider agents with arbitrary beliefs. Suppose we want to model an agent a_i's beliefs about a_j's beliefs about a_k's beliefs. Generalizing what we have done so far, we model a_i's beliefs as a reasoner R_i, a_i's beliefs about a_j as a reasoner R_{ij} and a_i's beliefs about a_j's beliefs about a_k as a reasoner R_{ijk}. R_i observes R_{ij} and R_{ij} observes R_{ijk}. This example can be easily generalized to formalize arbitrary agents' beliefs in a multiagent environment. Thus, any scenario can be simply formalized with a family of reasoners, in which each reasoner is possibly observing other reasoners. Formally, if I is a set of indices (each corresponding to a reasoner), a *belief system* is a pair $\langle \{R_i\}_{i \in I}, \mathbf{B} \rangle$ where $\{R_i\}_{i \in I}$ is a family of reasoners and $\mathbf{B}$ is an n-tuple of binary relations over I. If $\langle i, j \rangle$ is an element of the k-th binary relation then R_i observes R_j and expresses its beliefs about R_j using the B^k predicate (we thus assume that to the k-th binary relation there corresponds the unary predicate B^k). It is easy to check that a basic belief system $\langle R_0, R_1 \rangle_\mathrm{B}$ corresponds to the belief system $\langle \{R_0, R_1\}, \{\langle 0, 1 \rangle\} \rangle$.

As for basic belief systems, we present belief systems using MC systems. The following definition generalizes Definition 1.

Definition 2 $\mathrm{MR}_I^{\mathbf{B}}$ ·. Let I be a set of indexes and $\mathbf{B}$ a n-tuple of binary relations over I. An MC system $\langle \{C_i\}_{i \in I}, BR \rangle$ is an $\mathrm{MR}_I^{\mathbf{B}}$ · system if for each $\langle i, j \rangle$ in the k-th relation in $\mathbf{B}$, BR includes the following bridge rules:

$$\frac{\langle A, C_j \rangle}{\langle \mathrm{B}^k(\text{``}A\text{''}), C_i \rangle} \, \mathcal{R}_{up.}^{\mathrm{B}^k} \qquad \frac{\langle \mathrm{B}^k(\text{``}A\text{''}), C_i \rangle}{\langle A, C_j \rangle} \, \mathcal{R}_{dn.}^{\mathrm{B}^k}$$

and the restrictions for the applicability include:

$\mathcal{R}_{up.}^{\mathrm{B}^k}$: $\langle A, C_j \rangle$ does not depend on any assumption in C_j.
$\mathcal{R}_{dn.}^{\mathrm{B}^k}$: $\langle \mathrm{B}^k(\text{``}A\text{''}), C_i \rangle$ does not depend on any assumption in C_i.

We say that an $\mathrm{MR}_I^{\mathbf{B}}$ · system MS *generates* the belief system $\langle \{R_i\}_{i \in I}, \mathbf{B} \rangle$ if $T_i = \{A \mid \vdash_{\mathrm{MS}} \langle A, C_i \rangle\}$ $(i \in I)$.

It is possible to graphically represent the structure of a belief system as a directed graph, whose nodes are the reasoners and whose edges are the relations. Each edge is also labeled with the unary predicate corresponding to the relation. Thus, for example, the (basic) belief system $\langle \{R_0, R_1\}, \{\langle 0, 1 \rangle\} \rangle$ corresponds to Figure 1.

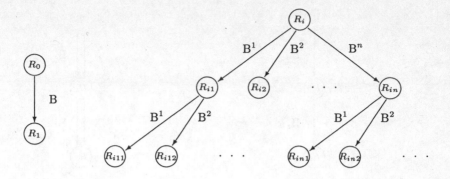

Fig. 1. A basic belief system.   **Fig. 2.** A belief system.

The case in which the belief system corresponds to a tree of reasoners (as the system in Figure 2) is particularly interesting. In Figure 2 each reasoner $R_{i_1,\ldots,i_k,i}$ ($k \geq 0$) models agent a_i from $a_{i_1},\ldots, a_{i_k}$ perspective. Each agent a_i thus corresponds to countably many reasoners $R_{\alpha,i}$ (where α is a string over $\{1,\ldots n\}$), each modeling a_i from different viewpoints. For example, with reference to Figure 2, the two reasoners R_{i12} and R_{in2} (representing a_2's beliefs but from two different perspectives) have in general different properties and/or relations with other reasoners. This is not possible (or at least not so simple to accomplish) in a modal approach where one must characterize the beliefs of all the agents (from whatever perspective) in a single theory.

On the other hand, tree structures of reasoners are not always appropriate. For example, two reasoners may share the same view of a reasoner (the sharing of structures has obvious implementative advantages). Graphically, this amounts to have one node with two fathers. Alternatively, one can have a reasoner R_i B-observing and X-observing another reasoner R_{i+1} ($i \in \omega$) (see Figure 4). R_i may be an ideal B-observer but not an ideal X-observer. In the next section, we will see an MC system — equivalent to Fagin' and Halpern's "logic of general awareness" [FH88, FHMV92] — generating such a belief system.

5   Some Instances

In this section, we compare some instances of our systems with some modal systems proposed in the literature. The equivalence results here presented are to be added to those in [GS94] for the most important normal modal logics (*e.g.* K, T, S4, S5) and in [GSGF93] for Levesque's logic of implicit and explicit beliefs [Lev84]. In order to describe precisely the various modal logics we consider, we introduce the following terminology and definitions.

A *modal system* Σ is a pair $\langle L, T \rangle$ such that L is a full propositional language containing a given set P of propositional letters, $T \subseteq L$ and T is closed under propositional consequence. A formula A is a *theorem* of Σ ($\vdash_\Sigma A$) if $A \in T$ and is *derivable* from a set Γ of formulas ($\Gamma \vdash_\Sigma A$) if $(A_1 \wedge \ldots \wedge A_n) \supset A \in T$ and

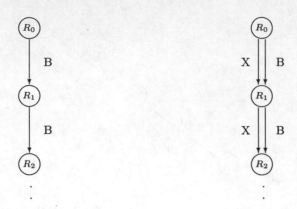

Fig. 3. A chain of reasoners.   **Fig. 4.** A double chain of reasoners.

$\{A_1, \ldots, A_n\} \subseteq \Gamma$. From here on we consider $\mathcal{B}$-modal systems[4], *i.e.* such that $\{\mathcal{B}A \mid A \in L\} \subseteq L$. In such systems, we read a statement like $\mathcal{B}A$ as "agent a believes A". The beliefs ascribed to a in Σ are the formulas A such that $\mathcal{B}A$ is a theorem of Σ.

We also say that a modal system $\Sigma = \langle L, T \rangle$ is

- *n-classical* if $\{(\mathcal{B}A_1 \wedge \ldots \wedge \mathcal{B}A_n) \supset \mathcal{B}A \mid (A_1 \wedge \ldots \wedge A_n) \supset A \in T\} \subseteq T$, $(n \in \{0, 1, 2\})$,
- *normal* if Σ is 0-classical and 2-classical.

In the literature, 1- and 2-classical modal logics are said to be *monotone* and *regular* respectively [Che80].

If A is a formula in a given modal language, by A^* we denote the expression obtained replacing any modal operator $\mathcal{M}$ with a unary predicate M(".") in A. Thus, for example, if A is $\mathcal{B}(P_1 \wedge \mathcal{X}P_2)$, A^* is B("$P_1 \wedge$ X("P_2")"). If Γ is a set of formulas, $\Gamma^* = \{A^* \mid A \in \Gamma\}$.

We start considering $\mathrm{MR}_I^{\mathbf{B}}$- systems corresponding to an infinite chain of reasoners *i.e.* $I = \omega$ and $\mathbf{B} = \{B\} = \{\{\langle i, i+1 \rangle \mid i \in \omega\}\}$. The structure of such belief systems is represented in Figure 3.

We interpret each reasoner in the chain in the following way: R_0 (*i.e.* the reasoner on top of the chain) is a model of agent a's beliefs, R_1 is the mental image that R_0 has of itself, R_2 is the mental image that R_1 has of itself and so on indefinitely. As a first case, we assume that each R_i is both an ideal reasoner and an ideal observer of R_{i+1}. We call MBK$^-$ the subclass of $\mathrm{MR}_\omega^{\mathbf{B}}$ systems generating such belief systems.

Definition 3 MBK$^-$. An MC system $\langle \{C_i\}_{i\in\omega}, BR \rangle$ is an MBK$^-$ system if for each $i \in \omega$ the following conditions are satisfied:

(i) L_i is a full propositional language,

---

[4] We adopt the convention of writing modal operators in calligraphic style.

(ii) Δ_i is the set of Classical Natural Deduction rules,

(iii) $L_{i+1} = \{A \mid B(``A") \in L_i\}$,

(iv) BR consists of the following bridge rules ($i \in \omega$):

$$\frac{\langle A, C_{i+1}\rangle}{\langle B(``A"), C_i\rangle} \; \mathcal{R}^{\mathrm{B}}_{up.i+1} \qquad \frac{\langle B(``A"), C_i\rangle}{\langle A, C_{i+1}\rangle} \; \mathcal{R}^{\mathrm{B}}_{dn.i+1}$$

and the restrictions for the applicability are:

$\mathcal{R}^{\mathrm{B}}_{up.i+1}$: $\langle A, C_{i+1}\rangle$ does not depend on any assumption in C_{i+1}.

$\mathcal{R}^{\mathrm{B}}_{dn.i+1}$: $\langle B(``A"), C_i\rangle$ does not depend on any assumption in C_i.

Trivially, each reasoner R_i generated by an MBK$^-$ system is both an ideal reasoner and an ideal observer of R_{i+1}. One might expect that R_0 be "equivalent" to the smallest normal modal logic $\mathcal{K}$. In fact, the agent a as modeled by R_0 is logically omniscient both with respect to its own beliefs and with respect to the beliefs of own mental image. On the other hand $\mathcal{K}$ is the weakest modal logic in which agent a is said to be "(fully) logical omniscient" (see for example [FH88, FHMV92]). However R_0 and $\mathcal{K}$ are not "equivalent".

Theorem 4. *Let* $\mathcal{K} = \langle L, T\rangle$ *be the smallest normal modal logic and* MBK$^-$ $= \langle\{C_i\}_{i\in\omega}, BR\rangle$ *the smallest* MBK$^-$ *system such that* $L_0 = L^*$.

$$\vdash_{\mathrm{MBK}^-} \langle A^*, C_0\rangle \;\not\Longleftrightarrow\; \vdash_{\mathcal{K}} A.$$

In fact, $\mathcal{K}$ is such that for any set of formulas Γ

$$\Gamma \vdash_{\mathcal{K}} A \;\;\Longrightarrow\;\; \mathcal{B}\Gamma \vdash_{\mathcal{K}} \mathcal{B}A, \tag{1}$$

where $\mathcal{B}\Gamma = \{\mathcal{B}A : A \in \Gamma\}$. This property gives $\mathcal{K}$ a form of omniscience with respect to derivations which is stronger than the form of omniscience possessed by each context C_i with respect to context C_{i+1}, which is only with respect to theorems. Indeed, the left to right implication of Theorem 4 does hold. In order to fill the gap between $\mathcal{K}$ and R_0, we drop the restriction on reflection down in the definition of an MBK$^-$ system.

Definition 5 MBK. An MC system $\langle\{C_i\}_{i\in\omega}, BR\rangle$ is an MBK system if it satisfies all the conditions of Definition 3 except that $\mathcal{R}^{\mathrm{B}}_{dn.i+1}$ ($i \in \omega$) has no restrictions.

The effect of unrestricting reflection down is to obtain the desired correspondence between the consequence relations of contexts C_i and C_{i+1}. For any MBK system MS and set of formulas Γ,

$$\{\langle B, C_{i+1}\rangle \mid B \in \Gamma\} \vdash_{\mathrm{MS}} \langle A, C_{i+1}\rangle \Longrightarrow \{\langle B(``B"), C_i\rangle \mid B \in \Gamma\} \vdash_{\mathrm{MS}} \langle B(``A"), C_i\rangle. \tag{2}$$

Intuitively, the possibility of applying reflection down to a formula which is not a theorem (*e.g.* is an assumption) amounts to imposing, by hypothetical reasoning, a reasoner's new basic belief. This kind of reasoning is very similar to the forms of reasoning formally and/or informally described in [Haa86, Cre79].

Theorem 6 [GS94]. *Let $\mathcal{K} = \langle L, T \rangle$ be the smallest normal modal logic and $MBK = \langle \{C_i\}_{i\in\omega}, BR \rangle$ the smallest MBK system such that $L_0 = L^*$.*

$$\vdash_{\text{MBK}} \langle A^*, C_0 \rangle \Longleftrightarrow \vdash_{\mathcal{K}} A.$$

However, as widely recognized, $\mathcal{K}$ (and thus also MBK) is inappropriate for modeling real agents. Real agents are not (fully) logically omniscient. Starting from an MBK system, various forms of non-logical omniscience can be obtained by weakening the ideality of observing or of reasoning of each reasoner. For example, in [GSGF93] it is showed how it is possible to capture Levesque's logic of implicit and explicit [Lev84] by considering a basic belief system where the observed reasoner is not an ideal reasoner. Here we show how it is possible to capture other non normal modal logics by considering belief systems in which each observer is not ideal.

We start considering the smallest n-classical modal logic $\mathcal{K}_n$ ($n \in \{0,1,2\}$). Since $\mathcal{K}_n$ is n-classical, $A_1, \ldots, A_n \vdash_{\mathcal{K}_n} A$ implies $BA_1, \ldots, BA_n \vdash_{\mathcal{K}_n} BA$. Logical omniscience is hence avoided since equation (1) holds only if Γ consists of exactly n formulas. To capture a n-classical logic we have therefore to ensure that also equation (2) holds if Γ contains exactly n formulas. This can be obtained adding the restriction to reflection up that the premise must depend on exactly n occurrences of atomic formulas.

Definition 7 MBK$_n$. An MBK$_n$ system is obtained from an MBK system adding the restriction to $\mathcal{R}^{\text{B}}_{up.i+1}$ ($i \in \omega$) that the premise depends on exactly n occurrences of atomic formulas.

Obviously, each reasoner R_i in the belief system generated by an MBK$_n$ system is not ensured to be an ideal observer of R_{i+1} unless $n = 0$.

Theorem 8. *Let $\mathcal{K}_n = \langle L, T \rangle$ be the smallest n-classical logic and $MBK_n = \langle \{C_i\}_{i\in\omega}, BR \rangle$ the smallest MBK$_n$ system such that $L_0 = L^*$.*

$$\vdash_{\text{MBK}_n} \langle A^*, C_0 \rangle \Longleftrightarrow \vdash_{\mathcal{K}_n} A.$$

We now consider Fagin and Halpern's logic of general awareness [FH88, FHMV92]. The idea of the logic of general awareness is to distinguish between what an agent *explicitly* believes (modeled via a modal operator $\mathcal{X}$) and what an agent *implicitly* believes (modeled with the modal operator $\mathcal{B}$). Intuitively, an agent's explicit beliefs represents the agent's beliefs, while its implicit beliefs model how the world should be if the agent explicit beliefs were true [Lev84, GSGF93]. In order to characterize what an agent explicitly believes, Fagin and Halpern introduce two other modal operators $\mathcal{A}$ and $\mathcal{X}$: the formulas $\mathcal{A}A$ and $\mathcal{X}A$ mean that the agent is "aware" of A and explicitly believes A, respectively. An agent explicitly believes A if it implicitly believes A and is aware of A. More precisely, a modal system AW= $\langle L_{AW}, T_{AW} \rangle$ is a *system of general awareness* if

– AW is $\{\mathcal{B}, \mathcal{X}, \mathcal{A}\}$-modal and $\mathcal{B}$-normal, and

$- \{\mathcal{X}A \leftrightarrow (\mathcal{B}A \wedge \mathcal{A}A) \mid A \in L_{AW}\} \subseteq T_{AW}.$

To capture the logic of general awareness, we introduce two predicates B and X corresponding to $\mathcal{B}$ and $\mathcal{X}$ respectively. The set of formulas Γ the agent is aware of determines the set of R_{i+1}'s beliefs each reasoner R_i can observe. In other words, if A^* has been derived in the context C_{i+1}, then $X(\text{``}A^*\text{''})$ can be derived in C_i by reflection up only if $A \in \Gamma$.

Definition 9 MAW$_\Gamma$. Let Γ be a set of formulas. An MC system $\langle \{C_i\}_{i \in \omega}, BR \rangle$ is an MAW$_\Gamma$ system if for each $i \in \omega$ the following conditions are satisfied:

(i) L_i is a full propositional language,

(ii) Δ_i is the set of Classical Natural Deduction rules,

(iii) $L_{i+1} = \{A \mid B(\text{``}A\text{''}) \in L_i\} = \{A \mid X(\text{``}A\text{''}) \in L_i\}$,

(iv) BR consists of the following bridge rules $(i \in \omega)$:

$$\frac{\langle A,\ C_{i+1} \rangle}{\langle B(\text{``}A\text{''}),\ C_i \rangle}\ \mathcal{R}^{B}_{up.i+1} \qquad \frac{\langle B(\text{``}A\text{''}),\ C_i \rangle}{\langle A,\ C_{i+1} \rangle}\ \mathcal{R}^{B}_{dn.i+1}$$

$$\frac{\langle A,\ C_{i+1} \rangle}{\langle X(\text{``}A\text{''}),\ C_i \rangle}\ \mathcal{R}^{X}_{up.i+1} \qquad \frac{\langle X(\text{``}A\text{''}),\ C_i \rangle}{\langle A,\ C_{i+1} \rangle}\ \mathcal{R}^{X}_{dn.i+1}$$

and the restrictions for the applicability are:

$\mathcal{R}^{B}_{up.i+1}$: $\langle A,\ C_{i+1} \rangle$ does not depend on any assumption in C_{i+1}.

$\mathcal{R}^{X}_{up.i+1}$: $\langle A,\ C_{i+1} \rangle$ does not depend on any assumption in C_{i+1} and $A \in \Gamma$.

The structure of the belief system generated by an MAW$_\Gamma$ system is given in Figure 4. In the following Theorem, $L_{B,\mathcal{X}}$ denotes the modal language whose only modal operators are $\mathcal{B}$ and $\mathcal{X}$.

Theorem 10. *Let Γ be a subset of $L_{B,\mathcal{X}}$ and $AW_\Gamma = \langle L_{AW}, T_{AW} \rangle$ the smallest logic of general awareness such that $\{\mathcal{A}A \mid A \in \Gamma\} \subseteq T_{AW}$. If $MAW_{\Gamma^*} = \langle \{C_i\}_{i \in \omega}, BR \rangle$ is the smallest MAW_{Γ^*} system such that $L_0 = (L_{B,\mathcal{X}})^*$ then for any formula A not containing the awareness operator $\mathcal{A}$*

$$\vdash_{\mathrm{MAW}_{\Gamma^*}} \langle A^*,\ C_0 \rangle \Longleftrightarrow \vdash_{\mathrm{AW}_\Gamma} A.$$

6   Some Final Remarks

In this paper we have addressed the problem of modeling arbitrary agents' beliefs in a multiagent framework. We have introduced belief systems as a simple framework for the extensional specification of agents' mutual beliefs with reasoners. Two are the capabilities of each reasoner: that of reasoning — *i.e.* of deriving consequences from its own beliefs — and that of observing — *i.e.* of deriving consequences from other reasoners' beliefs. This has led us to the characterization of ideal reasoners (logically omniscient *w.r.t.* their own beliefs) and ideal observers (logically omniscient *w.r.t.* the observed reasoner's beliefs). The two forms of logical omniscience are independent of one another. Each form of (lack of) logical omniscience corresponds to a distinct functionality of a reasoner (a reasoner as such, or as observer). Once one accepts the idea that there are reasoners and observers, our analysis of the logical omniscience problem is exhaustive in the sense that the functionalities considered (of reasoning and observing) are the only ones which is worthwhile considering, still maintaining a natural mapping with the intuitions.

We have also proposed MC systems as a deductive framework for the specification of belief systems. With MC systems, it is possible to define the structural properties of each reasoner as local properties of a corresponding context and to impose the desired relation between reasoners with bridge rules. Once one accepts MC systems as a good tool for the formalization of belief systems, within each form of logical omniscience, it is possible to consider all the sources of lack of such a property. This allows for the construction of very complex forms of belief (which are often needed, in particular, in real world applications) but also the definition of particular instances which are provably equivalent to various modal approaches defined in the literature.

Finally, even though our approach is very different from the current practice in representing agents' beliefs — which usually uses only one propositional or first order theory enriched with modal operators — our work is close to much of the applied work in computational linguistics and AI (see for instance [WB79, McC93, Lan88]), which suggest the use of multiple distinct theories.

References

[Avr87]   A. Avron. Simple consequence relations. LFCS Report Series, Laboratory for the Foundations of Computer Science, Computer Science Department, University of Edinburgh, 1987.

[BS84]   R. Bull and K. Segerberg. Basic Modal Logic. In D. Gabbay and F. Guenthner, editors, *Handbook of Philosophical Logic*, volume III, pages 1–88. D. Reidel Publishing Company, 1984.

[Che80]   B. F. Chellas. *Modal Logic – an Introduction*. Cambridge University Press, 1980.

[Cre79]   L. G. Creary. Propositional Attitudes: Fregean representation and simulative reasoning. In *Proc. of the 6th International Joint Conference on Artificial Intelligence*, pages 176–181, 1979.

[FH88]   R. Fagin and J.Y. Halpern. Belief, awareness, and limited reasoning. *Artificial Intelligence*, 34:39–76, 1988.

[FHMV92]   R. Fagin, J.Y. Halpern, Y. Moses, and M. Y. Vardi. *Reasoning about knowledge*. Stanford Bookstore, 1992.

[Giu93]   F. Giunchiglia. Contextual reasoning. *Epistemologia, special issue on I Linguaggi e le Macchine*, XVI:345–364, 1993. Short version in Proceedings IJCAI'93 Workshop on Using Knowledge in its Context, Chambery, France, 1993, pp. 39–49. Also IRST-Technical Report 9211-20, IRST, Trento, Italy.

[GS94]   F. Giunchiglia and L. Serafini. Multilanguage hierarchical logics (or: how we can do without modal logics). *Artificial Intelligence*, 65:29–70, 1994.

[GSGF93]   F. Giunchiglia, L. Serafini, E. Giunchiglia, and M. Frixione.   Non-
           Omniscient Belief as Context-Based Reasoning. In *Proc. of the 13th Inter-
           national Joint Conference on Artificial Intelligence*, pages 548–554, Cham-
           bery, France, 1993.   Also IRST-Technical Report 9206-03, IRST, Trento,
           Italy.

[Haa86]   A. R. Haas. A Syntactic Theory of Belief and Action. *Artificial Intelligence*,
           28:245–292, 1986.

[Lan88]   A. Lansky.   Localized Event-Based Reasoning for Multiagent Domains.
           Computational Intelligence, 4:319–339, 1988.

[Lev84]   H. Levesque. A logic of implicit and explicit belief. In *AAAI-84*, pages
           198–202, 1984.

[McC93]   J. McCarthy. Notes on Formalizing Context. In *Proc. of the 13th Interna-
           tional Joint Conference on Artificial Intelligence*, pages 555–560, Chambery,
           France, 1993.

[Pra65]   D. Prawitz. *Natural Deduction - A proof theoretical study*. Almquist and
           Wiksell, Stockholm, 1965.

[WB79]   Y. Wilks and J. Biem. Speech acts and multiple environments. In *Proc. of
           the 6th International Joint Conference on Artificial Intelligence*, 1979.

Modelling Interactions in Agent System*

Mauro Gaspari

Dipartimento di Scienze dell'Informazione, University of Bologna
Piazza Porta S. Donato 5, 40127 Bologna, Italy.
E-mail: gaspari@cs.unibo.it

Abstract. We present a study of the interaction properties of multiagent systems where agents communicate by means of speech act based
primitives. We identify a set of basic interaction mechanisms: agent identity, asynchronous message passing, implicit message acceptance, which
are closed to those of the actor model. Then, we define an actor algebra
over actor terms as a basic formalism for multiagent systems. Finally,
we show how it is possible to translate a speech act based language (a
subset of KQML) into the given algebra.

1 Introduction

Over the past few years there has been quite a lot of interest in *multi-agent
systems*. They are the subject of a stream of research within distributed AI,
studying systems made up of multiple heterogeneous intelligent agents where
competition or cooperation is possible between them [12]. This research area
differs from *distributed problem solving* because there is no common global goal
to be solved which is known at design time; on the contrary, it is assumed
that programs of intelligent agents are written by different people, in different
languages, at different times for different purposes.

A central issue is the design of a language to build such systems. This includes
the design of both a *knowledge representation* language (to specify the internal
behaviour of agents) and a *communication* language (to specify the interacts
among agents). Recently, two languages have been proposed for multi-agent systems, which are both based on the *speech act theory* [13], a formal model of
human communication developed by philosophers and linguists. The first one
is the Agent-Oriented Programming (AOP) framework, proposed by Shoham
[14]. AOP specializes object oriented programming by defining the state of an
agent, and restricting the kinds of messages which agents can send or receive.
The second language is Agent Communication Language (ACL) [5], provided
in the context of the ARPA Knowledge Sharing Effort. ACL includes two main
components: (i) a representation language for the contents of messages (called
Knowledge Interchange Format – KIF), which is basically an extension of first-
order logic; and (ii) a communication language KQML (Knowledge Query and

* The author would like to acknowledge discussions with Angela Dalmonte, Roberto
Gorrieri and Gul Agha. This paper has been partially supported by the Italian Ministry of Universities (MURST) and by the ESPRIT BRA Project 9102- Coordination.

Manipulation Language) [8], which consists of a set of communication primitives - called *performatives* - which aim to support cooperation among agents in distributed applications. The KQML performatives enable agents to exchange and request knowledge, and to cooperate during problem solving.

In this paper, we present a first step towards a rigorous approach to the semantics of speech act based languages. In the same way as CCS [9] defines the basic communication mechanisms for synchronous message passing languages in distributed computing, we would like to capture a minimal set of primitives for agent communication languages. First, in Sect. 2, we investigate the basic communication mechanisms of agent communication languages which, we claim, are close to those of the actor model [1]. Then, in Sect. 3, we define an algebra of actors (SAA, for short), which is assumed static (i.e., without dynamic creation) for the sake of simplicity. The actor algebra we are proposing includes many basic communication and synchronization primitives which, apparently, are enough to specify speech act based languages. SAA is equipped with an operational semantics and with a behavioural equivalence (discussed in Sect. 4) which equates actor systems whenever they are to be considered indistinguishable by external observers. Finally, in Sect. 5, we show how a subset of KQML can be translated into SAA. This enable us to import in KQML the theory defined for SAA. For instance, two KQML programs can be defined equivalent if so are their SAA translations. In this way, we provide a rigorous formal base to reason about this language.

2 Agents and Interaction Mechanisms

The multi-agent systems we are considering are systems composed of a set of intelligent software agents, communicating by means of an agent communication language defined according to the speech act theory. That theory, much broader than necessary to our aims, is a general framework to model human communication, which partly influenced the theory of multi-agent systems. The kinds of messages that can be used are rather different. Messages can be classified according to their type (also called *performative*). We introduce here a variation of a classification presented in [8] which distinguishes three classes of performatives, including most of the performatives defined in agent communication languages. A message can be: *assertive*, when it states a fact; *directive*, if it includes a command, a request or a suggestion; *declarative*, when an agent sends to another agents an information on his internal capabilities.

Languages based on speech acts introduce a fixed structure for messages. For instance a KQML message is defined by the following abstract syntax: *Performative(Recipient,Sender,Contents)*. A typical assertive primitive is *tell(B,A,P)* means that the agent A states to B that P is true[2]. A typical instance of a directive primitive is *ask(B,A,P)*, meaning that agent A wants to know from B

---

[2] Note that the notion of true is intended here with respect to a particular agent in this case A believes P to be true.

if P is true, while a typical instance of a declarative primitive is *export(B,A,P)*, meaning that A informs B that he is able to answer queries on P.

Agent Identity. In multi-agent systems there is a notion of *agent-identity* which is similar to the notion of object-identity in object-oriented programming [7]. Identity is that property of an agent which distinguishes each agent from all others. Support for identity in multi-agent systems can be achieved by associating to each agent a unique name; this is the approach followed by KQML. The name of the agent is also used as basic dispatching mechanisms in message passing. This notion of agent-identity based on names has a natural mapping in the Actor model [1]. Actors are named objects with a behaviour which is a function of incoming communications. Each actor has a unique name (mail address) determined at the time of its creation. This name is used to specify the recipient of a message. Conversely, agent-identity is not easily embeddable in formalisms such as CCS [9] or π-calculus [10], where message dispatching is performed by the mean of channels. In fact, in these formalisms the association address-process is not unique a process may have several ports (channels) from which it receives messages and the same channel can be accessed by different processes.

Synchronous vs Asynchronous Message Passing. We distinguish here two versions of message passing: the synchronous version does not allow the buffering of messages, thus a message to be delivered needs a "rendez-vous" between the sending and the receiving agent, this is the mechanism adopted by CCS [9]; the asynchronous version assumes that the buffering of messages is possible, thus it is not required an agreement we the receiving agent to send a message, this is the approach adopted by actors [1] and by asynchronous process algebras [3].

We claim that asynchronous message passing is the most suitable basic interaction mechanism for multi-agent systems. In fact, synchronous communication can be modelled providing adequate synchronization constraints. As an example, an agent performing a send operation, can be programmed in order to wait an acknowledgement from the recipient of the message, before continuing its computation. Vice versa, if we want to model asynchronous message passing with a synchronous language, we need to introduce an extra agent to deal with the buffering of messages. Moreover, according with the thesis presented in [4], asynchronous message passing guarantees a higher-(knowledge)-level programming style.

Explicit vs Implicit Message Acceptance. Given that the basic message passing mechanism is asynchronous, and that the name of an agent is used to specify the recipient of a message, we have still to establish which is the form of receive primitive which is more suitable in multi-agent systems. The receive primitive may be blocking or non-blocking, and may also be explicit or implicit. A blocking receive primitive stops the execution of an agent until a message is available, while a non-blocking receive allows the agent to continue its execution. A receive operation is explicit when it appears in the program, while it is implicit when does not correspond to an operation in the programming language and it is performed implicitly at certain points of the computation: typically in actor systems the receive is implicit and is performed only when the actor is idle, in this case the implicit receive can be only blocking since there is no computation to carry on when the actor is idle.

We think that message acceptance should be implicit in a basic calculus for multi-agent systems. First, the semantics of all the KQML performatives assumes that a certain message is transmitted from a sender agent to a recipient agent and there are no receive performatives. Second, exploiting implicit message acceptance, we can assume that the state of an agent changes only when a message is received. This enable us to model the evolution of the state of an agent and how this is related to interaction.

Staticity vs Dynamicity. An aspect which is not central in the theory of speech act is dynamicity, i.e., the possibility of creating new agents at run time. As an example, KQML does not include performatives to create new agents. Although one may object that any agent which "speaks" KQML will be able to communicate with other agents (KQML is an open system), there is still no way to control how these new created agents will cooperate with the pre-existing ones (for instance, what agent names are known by the new agent).

On the other hand, this issue is central in the current work on the theory of distributed computing [11] and in particular in the recent approaches to the formal description of concurrent object oriented programming languages [2, 16]. For the limited aims of the present paper, however, we restrict our attention to static systems only.

Summary. The actor model captures all the basic interaction mechanisms we have pointed out above providing: support for agent identity, asynchronous message passing, an implicit receive mechanism and support for dynamicity, thus we choose the actor model as a basic model for multi-agent systems[3].

We make the assumption that our set of agents is statically defined and allocated on a set of processors, thus we consider a static variant of the actor model where primitives to create actors are not allowed in programs. We define an associated actor algebra and we study the mapping of a subset of the KQML performatives into this algebra.

3 An Algebra of Actors

In the actor model the behaviour of an object is a function of incoming communications. Actors are self-contained agents that communicate by asynchronous

---

[3] This choice does not weaken the analysis above, which aims to be a strong claim in favour of the actor model as a basic model for agent-oriented programming in particular and object-oriented programming in general.

message passing making use of three basic primitives: *create*, to create new actors; *send*, to send messages to other actors; and *become*, to change the behaviour of an actor [1].

A Static Actor Algebra (SAA) is an algebra which models a *static* actor system, i.e., composed of a fixed set of actors where *create* is not a legal primitive and where actor names (except the name of the sender) are not allowed in messages. Let $\mathcal{A}$ be a finite set of actors names and let $\mathcal{V}$ be a set of values: a, b, c,... will range over $\mathcal{A}$; $true$, $false$, v, v', v'',... will be value constants; and x, y, z, ... range over $\mathcal{V}$. We assume value expressions e built from value variables, value constants, and any operator symbol we wish. $[\![e]\!]$ gives the value of e in $\mathcal{V}$. Also we assume state expressions e^σ built from value expressions including actors names; s, s', s'' will be state variables and $[\![e^\sigma]\!]^\sigma$ gives the value of e^σ. An actor term is defined according to the following syntax:

ActorTerm ::= Actor | Message | ActorTerm || ActorTerm | ActorTerm[f]
       where $L \subset A$ and f is a relabelling function
Actor ::= Idle_Actor | Busy_Actor
Idle_Actor ::= <a, Behaviour>
Busy_Actor ::= <a, Program, Behaviour>
Behaviour ::= $C(a, x, s)$ where $C(a, x, s) \stackrel{def}{=}$ Program | Prog
Program ::= e_1^σ:Prog+e_2^σ:Prog+...+e_n^σ:Prog
Prog ::= *become*(Behaviour).SProg | *send*(**Message**).Prog | $\sqrt{}$
SProg ::= *send*(**Message**).SProg | $\sqrt{}$
Message ::= [a,b,e]

An `ActorTerm` represents a set of actors running in parallel, let Γ be the set of all the actor terms, we assume that A, B, D, E, F, ... range over Γ. || is the parallel composition operator; only actors with different names can be composed, this notion of composable actors will be defined formally below. An actor is *busy*, when it executes a computation, and it is *idle* when is waiting for messages. An idle actor is represented by a pair containing the actor name and the *behaviour* which indicates the program that must be executed when the actor receive a message. A busy actor has a further field representing the continuation *i.e.*, the program which must still be executed. f is a relabelling function defined over actor names following the style of [9], for instance the actor term $A[b/a]$ correspond to the actor term A' where all the occurrences of the actor name a are replaced with b. In the case of actors a relabelling functions may be not adequate, because it is not possible to have two actors with the same name in an actor term, the formal definition of adequate relabelling function is given below. e_1^σ:Prog+e_2^σ:Prog+...+e_n^σ:Prog is a guarded program and $e_1^\sigma, e_2^\sigma, ..., e_n^\sigma$ are conditions on the state of the actor and/or the incoming message. A behaviour defining actor programs ($C(a, x, s)$) takes three arguments which represent respectively: the sender of the incoming message, the contents of the message and the state of the actor. When arguments are not significant they will be omitted, for instance the behaviour which appears in a **become** primitive does usually not specify the first and the second arguments, because they are free variables which will be bound when a message is received; thus *become* has not effect on them.

We assume that P, P', P'',... range over programs and C, C', C'',... range over behaviours. The notation A^a indicates the actor named a in the actor term A, if such an actor does not exist $A^a = NIL$. Given an actor term A the set of actor names $\mathcal{A}$ is partitioned into three subsets $Ext(A)$, $Int(A)$ and $Rest(A)$ as follows: $\forall a \in \mathcal{A}$, if $A^a \neq NIL$ then $a \in Int(A)$; else if if $A^a = NIL$ and a is the recipient of a send primitive of the programs in A, $a \in Ext(A)$; otherwise $a \in Rest(A)$. The notation $Int(a)$ will be an abbreviation of $Int(\{<a, C>\})$. Now we can define formally when two actor terms are composable and when a relabelling function is adequate.

Definition 1. - Composable actor terms. Two actor terms A and B are composable with respect to the parallel composition operator $\|$, if $Int(A) \cap Int(B) = \emptyset$.

Definition 2. - Adequate relabelling. A relabelling function f is adequate with respect to an actor term A if $\forall a \in \mathcal{A}$, $A[f]^a$ has a unique value.

Proposition 3. *Given two composable actor terms A and B then: $Int(A\|B) = Int(A) \cup Int(B)$ and $Ext(A\|B) = (Ext(A) \cup Ext(B)) \setminus ((Int(B) \cap Ext(A)) \cup (Int(A) \cap Ext(B)))$.*

3.1 Operational Semantics

We model the operational semantics of our actor algebra following the approach of Milner [10] which consists in separating the laws which govern the static relation among actors (for instance $A\|B$ is equivalent to $B\|A$) from the laws which rules their interaction. This is achieved defining a static structural congruence relation over syntactic terms and a dynamic reduction relation by means of a labelled transitions system.

Definition 4. - Structural congruence, is the smallest equivalence relation over actor terms ($\equiv$) defined by: (i) $A\|B \equiv B\|A$; (ii) $(A\|B)\|D \equiv A\|(B\|D)$; (iii) $<a, \sqrt{}, C> \equiv <a, C>$; (iv) $A\| <a, \sqrt{}, -> \equiv A$.

Equations (i) and (ii) states that the parallel composition operator ($\|$) is associative and commutative. The Equation (iii) captures the intuitive notion that an actor becomes idle when terminates its computation. The actor term $<a, \sqrt{}, ->$ denotes an actor with an empty behaviour which has terminated its computation, the reason of introducing such an actor term will become clear below.

Definition 5. - Reduction. A transition system modelling reduction in the actor algebra is represented by a triple $(\Gamma, T, \{\xrightarrow{\alpha}: \alpha \in T\})$, T is a set of labels and $\xrightarrow{\alpha}$ is the minimal transition relation satisfying the axioms and rules presented in Table 1.

$$
\begin{array}{ll}
Send & <a, send(b, self, e).P, C> \xrightarrow{send(b,a,[\![e]\!])} <a, P, C> \;\|\; [b, a, [\![e]\!]] \\[2mm]
Bec & \quad\quad <a, become(C').P, C> \xrightarrow{become(a)} <a, P, -> \;\|\; <a, C'> \\[2mm]
Rec & <a, C(d, x)> \;\|\; [a, b, v] \xrightarrow{receive(a,b,v)} <a, P[b/d, v/x], C(d, x)> \; where \; C(d, x) \stackrel{def}{=} P \\[4mm]
Par & \quad\quad \dfrac{A \xrightarrow{\alpha} A'}{A\|B \xrightarrow{\alpha} A'\|B} \qquad\qquad Rel \quad \dfrac{A \xrightarrow{\alpha} A'}{A[f] \xrightarrow{f(\alpha)} A'[f]} \\[6mm]
Sum & \dfrac{[\![e_i^\sigma]\!]^\sigma = true}{<a, e_1^\sigma : P_1 + e_2^\sigma : P_2 + \ldots + e_n^\sigma : P_n, C> \xrightarrow{\alpha} <a, P_i', C>} \quad where \; P_i = \alpha.P_i' \\[6mm]
Con & \quad\quad \dfrac{B \equiv A \quad A \xrightarrow{\alpha} A' \quad A' \equiv B'}{B \xrightarrow{\alpha} B'}
\end{array}
$$

Table 1. Reduction Relation of SAA.

The effect of a send primitive (rule **Send**) is to create an actor term representing a message. The rule **Bec** modifies the behaviour of an actor, a new actor with the same name is created and the rest of the computation is executed by an actor with an empty behaviour, which will be destroyed when terminates its computation (see the structural congruence). The implicit receive (rule **Rec**) is performed only when an actor a is idle (*i.e.*, when an actor ends its computation, see the structural congruence), and there is a message which has a as a target. The rules **Par** describes the behaviour of the parallel composition operator and the rule **Sum** allows to infer guarded commands. Rule **Rel** is the equivalent of the relabelling rule of CCS [9]: $f(\alpha)$ denotes the application of the relabelling function to α.

3.2 An Example: The Contract Net Protocol

We illustrate the expressive power of the language by modelling the *Contract Net Protocol* [15], a protocol which allows an agent to distribute tasks among a set of agents by means of negotiation. We only model a restricted version of the protocol where a single manager agent sends task announcements to a set of workers which evaluate them, bidding only on those of interest. The manager evaluates bids to select the most appropriate worker which will execute the task.

We associate an actor to each agent in the contract net, thus the set of actor names is $\mathcal{A} = \{man, w_1, \ldots, w_n\}$. We also suppose to have a fixed set of values $\mathcal{V} = Bids \cup Tasks \cup \{reject, start\}$ representing possible tasks, bids and protocol keywords, where $Bids = \{bid_1, \ldots, bid_b\}$ and $Tasks = \{task_1, \ldots, task_t\}$. A contract net can be defined by the following actor term: $<man, Do(a, x)> \;\|\; < w_1, WaitTask(a, x)> \;\|\ldots\|\; <w_n, WaitTask(a, x)>$ where the behaviour of the manager agent and of the workers is defined in Fig. 1. The manager agent sends the workers the task to be executed; then it executes a *become* primitive and it starts waiting for bids. The state of the waiting manager is stored in a tuple which contains: the number of agents which have already sent a bid, the list of received bids and the task to perform. The second condition of the behaviour $Do(a, x)$ expresses a synchronization constraint *i.e.*, if the actor receive a message different from start, it send it again to the same address. The fair message delivery assumption in the actor model guarantees that the right message will be eventually executed. The symbol **self** indicates the actor which perform the **send** primitive. Finally, we assume: a set of functions to manage a stack: **push**. **first**, **rest**, **empty**; two functions which operate on bids: **best_bid**, and **other_bids**; and a function (**execute**) which executes tasks.

Manager Agent:
$Do(a, x) \stackrel{def}{=} (x = start) : send(w_1, self, task). \ldots .send(w_n, self, task).$
$$become(WaitBid((0, NIL, task))).\sqrt{+}$$
$$(x \neq start) : send(self, a, x).\sqrt{}$$

$WaitBid(a, x, (m, l, task)) \stackrel{def}{=}$
$\quad (x \in Bids \ and \ m \neq n - 1) : become(WaitBid((m + 1, push((a, x), l), task))).\sqrt{+}$
$\quad (x \in Bids \ and \ m = n - 1) : send(best\_bid(push((a, x), l)), self, task).$
$$become(Broadcast(other\_bids(push((a, x), l)))).$$
$$send(self, self, start).\sqrt{+}$$
$\quad (x \notin Bids) : \qquad\qquad\qquad send(self, a, x).\sqrt{}$

$Broadcast(a, x, s) \stackrel{def}{=}$
$\quad (x = start \ and \ empty(s)) : \qquad become(Do(n)).\sqrt{}$
$\quad (x = start \ and \ not(empty(s))) : send(first(s), self, reject).$
$$become(Broadcast(rest(s))).send(self, self, start).\sqrt{}$$
$\quad (x \neq start) : \qquad\qquad\qquad send(self, self, start).\sqrt{}$

Worker Agents:
$WaitTask(a, x) \stackrel{def}{=}$
$\quad (x \in Tasks) : send(a, self, bid_j).become(WaitAnswer).\sqrt{} +$
$\quad (x \notin Tasks) : send(self, a, x).\sqrt{}$

$WaitAnswer(a, x) \stackrel{def}{=}$
$\quad (x = reject) : become(WaitTask).\sqrt{}$
$\quad (x \in Tasks) : send(x, self, execute(y)).become(WaitTask).\sqrt{}$
$\quad (x \neq reject) \ and \ (x \notin Tasks) : \ send(self, a, x).\sqrt{}$

Fig. 1. The Contract Net Protocol

4 Equivalence of Actor Terms

Intuitively, two actor terms are equivalent if they cannot be distinguished by an external actor term interacting with each of them. Given an actor term A two types of events are observed: when an actor $a \in Int(A)$ receives a message from an actor in $b \in Ext(A)$, and when an actor in $a \in Int(A)$ sends a message to an actor in $b \in Ext(A)$. Since for actors there is arrival-order non-determinism in message delivery, the equivalence does not depends on the order in which send operations are performed. To illustrate these notions we consider an instance of the contract net protocol presented in Sect. 3.2.

Example 1. A contract net including two workers can be defined by the following actor term: $A = <man, Do(a,x)> \parallel <w_1, WaitTask(a,x)> \parallel <w_2, WaitTask(a,x)>$ where the behaviour of the manager is:

$$Do(a,x) \stackrel{def}{=} (x = start) : send(w_1, self, task).send(w_2, self, task).$$
$$become(WaitBid((0, NIL, task))).\surd +$$
$$(x \neq start) : send(self, a, x).\surd$$

If we give an alternative definition of behavior of the manager, as follows:

$$Do'(a,x) \stackrel{def}{=} (x = start) : send(w_2, self, task).send(w_1, self, task).$$
$$become(WaitBid((0, NIL, task))).\surd +$$
$$(x \neq start) : send(self, a, x).\surd$$

we can define a new actor term $B = <man, Do'(a,x)> \parallel <w_1, WaitTask(a,x)> \parallel < w_2, WaitTask(a,x)>$ representing a similar contract net.

The actor terms $<man, Do(a,x)>$ and $<man, Do'(a,x)>$ cannot be distinguished by an external actor term interacting with them. In fact, whenever the external actor sends man a $start$ message, man will send back two messages: one to an actor named d and another to an actor named b[4]. The order in which the send operations are performed is not relevant because the actor model does not guarantee ordered message delivery. As a consequence $<man, Do(a,x)>$ and $<man, Do'(a,x)>$ can be considered equivalent.

$Send'$	$<a, send(b, self, e).P, C> \xrightarrow{send(b,a,[\![e]\!])} <a, P, C> \parallel [b, a, [\![e]\!]]$ if $b \neq a$	
$Send''$	$<a, send(b, self, e).P, C> \xrightarrow{\tau} <a, P, C> \parallel [b, a, [\![e]\!]]$ if $b = a$	
Bec	$<a, become(C').P, C> \xrightarrow{\tau} <a, P, -> \parallel <a, C'>$	
Rec'	$<a, C(d,x)> \xrightarrow{receive(a,b,v)} <a, P[b/d, v/x], C(d,x)>$	$C(d,x) \stackrel{def}{=} P$ $\forall v \in V, \forall b \in Ext(a)\ b \neq a$
Rec''	$<a, C(d,x)> \parallel [a, b, v] \xrightarrow{\tau} <a, P[b/d, v/x], C(d,x)>$	$C(d,x) \stackrel{def}{=} P$
Par'	$\dfrac{A \xrightarrow{\alpha} A'}{A\|B \xrightarrow{\alpha} A'\|B}$ $\alpha \notin \{send(a,b,v), receive(b',a,v)\},\ a \in Int(B)$	
Par''	$\dfrac{A \xrightarrow{\alpha} A'}{A\|B \xrightarrow{\tau} A'\|B}$ $\alpha = send(a,b,v),\ a \in Int(B)$	

Table 2. Observing SAA Computations.

---
[4] Since here we are considering only the manager actor $d, b \in Ext(<man, Do(a,x)>)$.

To give a formal definition of the equivalence described above, we introduce observations in the transition system as presented in Table 2. The transition system includes two instances of rules **Send** and **Rec** which specify when send and receive operations are observed[5]. Rules **Par'**, and **Par''**, define observations with respect to the parallel composition operator. Rules **Rel**, **Sum** and **Con** must be imported from Table 1.

Our observations are different from those made in other asynchronous calculus such as [6, 2], where two extra rules, **out** and **in**, are introduced to model the interaction with the outside world. As an example, in [2] these rules specify when an external actor receives a message from the bag of incoming messages and when an external actor sends a message into the bag. The advantage of our approach with respect to [6, 2] is that the resulting equivalence is more related to the structure of an actor rather than being mediated by the bag of incoming messages. Our definition of observation, which is strongly dependent from the structure of an actor term, is also an innovation: in [2] observations depend on two sets of external and internal (receptionists) actors defined a priori and independently from the structure of an actor term.

Then, we define a new transition relation over actor terms, where the execution of several send primitives collapses into a single execution step. The new label will be a string of labels including all the observable send operations performed.

Given a sequence of labels $t \in T^*$ such that $\forall \alpha \in t,\ \alpha = send(a,b,v) \vee \alpha = \tau$, $t\downarrow$ denotes the string representing the sequence of labels obtained from t by removing the τ labels and ordering alphabetically the remaining $send(a,b,v)$ labels. The new transition relation $\Longrightarrow$ is defined below.

$$\frac{A \overset{t}{\longrightarrow}^* A'}{A \overset{t\downarrow}{\Longrightarrow} A'} \quad where\ \forall \alpha \in t,\ \alpha = send(a,b,v) \vee \alpha = \tau$$

$$\frac{A \overset{receive(a,b,v)}{\longrightarrow} A'}{A \overset{receive(a,b,v)}{\Longrightarrow} A'}$$

We denote the set of labels which appear in $\Longrightarrow$ with $T\downarrow$. Starting from the new transition relation strong bisimulation and strong equivalence can be defined as usual [9].

Definition 6. Strong Bisimulation. A binary relation $S \subseteq \Gamma \times \Gamma$ over actor terms is a strong bisimulation if $(A, B) \in S$ implies, for all $\beta \in T\downarrow$, (1) whenever $A \overset{\beta}{\Longrightarrow} A'$ then, $\exists B', B \overset{\beta}{\Longrightarrow} B'$ and $(A', B') \in S$; (2) whenever $B \overset{\beta}{\Longrightarrow} B'$ then, $\exists A', A \overset{\beta}{\Longrightarrow} A'$ and $(A', B') \in S$.

Definition 7. Strong equivalence - A and B are strongly equivalent $(A \cong B)$ if $(A, B) \in S$ for some strong bisimulation S.

Proposition 8. *Given two actor terms A and B such that $A \cong B$ then $Int(A) = Int(B)$ and $Ext(A) = Ext(B)$.*

---

[5] Remember that $Int(a) = \{a\}$.

This proposition is a direct consequence of the definition of equivalence given above. Intuitively, if two actor terms are strong equivalent, they contain the same set of actor names. Note that the inverse of the above proposition does not hold. Two actor terms may be defined on the same sets of actor names but they result different with respect to an external observer.

Given the definition of strong equivalence, we would like to prove that the given equivalence is a congruence with respect to the parallel composition operator $\|$. Thus, if two actor systems are proved to be equivalent also their compositions with any other composable actor system are equivalent. As an example, if we consider the actor terms A and B defined in the example 1, we would like to prove that if $<man, Do(a, x)> \cong <man, Do'(a, x)>$ then $A \cong B$. This result is established by the following theorem.

Theorem 9. Congruence. *The equivalence relation $\cong$ over actor terms is a congruence with respect to the parallel composition operator.*

Proof. We have to prove that if $(A \cong B)$ then $\forall D \in \Gamma$ such that D is composable with both A and B, we have $A\|D \cong B\|D$. Let $E = A\|D$ and $F = B\|D$, from the Propositions 3 and 8 we can prove that $Int(A) = Int(B)$ and $Ext(A) = Ext(B)$ and thus $Int(E) = Int(F)$ and $Ext(E) = Ext(F)$. This implies that it is always possible to build a bisimulation which equates terms E and F.

5 Translating KQML into SAA

The set of performatives used in KQML is large, as different communication protocols are supported, thus it is not possible to provide a formal account of the whole system in this paper. Therefore we will only consider a subset of the KQML performatives (*insert*, *ask−if*, and *tell*).

Agents communicate by means of the above subset of KQML. Each agent is composed of a name, a set of programs and a *virtual knowledge base* (VKB). We assume to have given a fixed set of agent names $\mathcal{A}_{KQML}$ and let a, b, range over agent names.

Agents react to messages received from other agents and from the outside world. We model only communication actions and we assume that each communication action has associated a contents in a given knowledge representation formalism, we denote with $\mathcal{V}_{KQML}$ the set of all the possible contents and with $k, k', k", \dots$ its elements.

The messages that can be received from an agent named a in our subset of KQML are: insert(a,b,k), the agent a is asked to insert the proposition k into its VKB; ask-if(a,b,k), the agent b wants to know if k is in the VKB of a; and tell(a,b,k), the sentence k is in the VKB of b.

Each agent has an associated *handler function* [8] [6] which maps the received message into a KQML program which executes it. We assume that all the program are associated to constant by means of defining equations ($C \stackrel{def}{=}$

---

[6] This function is called dispatch in [4].

KQMLProgram). Programs specify the way in which agents deal with messages. The syntax of programs is shown below, where the symbol $\sqrt{}$ represents a terminating internal program which does not involve communication actions.

```
KQMLProgram ::= CommAction.KQMLProgram | √
CommAction ::= insert(a,b,k) | tell(a,b,k) | ask-if(a,b,k)
```

An operational semantics for a synchronous and an asynchronous variant of this subset of KQML has been presented in [4]. In this paper we show how the semantics of the asynchronous variant of KQML can be expressed by means of translation into our actor algebra.

As described in above a KQML system consists of a set of agents executing **KQMLPrograms**, each agent has an associated handler function. The state of an agent can be: *busy*, the agent is executing a program; and *idle*, the agent is idle waiting for messages. Agents exploit a non-blocking *ask−if* primitive, thus requests of knowledge do not block the agent executing them; it can continue its current execution. This implies that agents receive answers to *ask−if* questions only when they are idle. Let $Q, Q', \ldots$ be KQML programs, the translation of a KQML system into the actor algebra is defined as follows:

1. Each KQML agent is translated into an actor with the same name, thus $\mathcal{A} = \mathcal{A}_{KQML}$.
2. Each actor a has a initial behavior $C_a(b, x, s) = e_1^{\sigma} : P_1 + e_2^{\sigma} : P_2 + \ldots + e_{n_a}^{\sigma} : P_{n_a}$ encoding the *handler* function where the P_i are actor programs defined below and s is the state of the actor representing the virtual knowledge base.
3. Each KQML program is translated by means of a function Φ which takes as an argument an agent name and a KQML program and returns an actor program. Let ϕ a function that maps $\mathcal{V}_{KQML}$ into $\mathcal{V}$ the set of possible values for actors, Φ is defined inductively on the structure of programs as follows:

$$\Phi(b, ask-if(a, b, k).Q) = send(a, b, (ask-i, \phi(k))).\Phi(b, Q)$$
$$\Phi(b, tell(a, b, k).Q) = send(a, b, (tell, \phi(k))).\Phi(b, Q)$$
$$\Phi(b, insert(a, b, k).Q) = send(a, b, (insert, \phi(k))).\Phi(b, Q)$$
$$\Phi(b, \sqrt{}) = become(C_b(a, d, z)).\sqrt{}$$

Although, we have only modelled a small subset of KQML the straightforward mapping of KQML agents into terms of the actor algebra gives a strong evidence of the expressive power of the algebra.

6 Conclusion

The innovative aspect of the algebra, we have presented, is that it includes only basic interaction mechanisms providing a powerful formalism to study interaction properties of multi-agent systems. On the other hand, the current approaches to the semantic description of actors are quite complex for instance [2] describes the semantics of a functional language which embeds actor based communication primitives.

As a result, our semantics approach is complementary to other approaches to the semantics of KQML, such that the one presented in [8], which is based on the description of the cognitive states of the agents that exploit speech acts. In that report, in fact, the emphasis is not on operational description, rather on logical-based properties that preserved or transformed by program executions.

A issue which will require further research is the study of the dynamic features of agent communication languages. We also developed a dynamic actor algebra with the usual "create" operator of actors, and we are studying an adequate theory of equivalence.

References

1. G. Agha. *Actors: A Model of Concurrent Computation in Distributed Systems.* MIT Press, Cambridge, MA, Cambridge, MA, 1986.
2. G. Agha, I. Mason, S. Smith, and C. Talcott. Towards a Theory of Actor Computation. In *Proc. of CONCUR'92*, volume 630 of *Lecture Notes in Computer Science*, pages 564–579. Springer Verlag, 1992.
3. F. DeBoer, J. Klop, and C. Palamidessi. Asynchronous Communication in Process Algebra. In *Proc. 7th annual IEEE Symposium on Logic in Computer Science*, Santa Crux, California, 1992.
4. M. Gaspari and E. Motta. Symbol-level Requirements for Agent-level Programming. In A. Cohn, editor, *ECAI94 the 11th European Conference on Artificial Intelligence*, pages 364–368. John Wiley and SonsLtd, 1994.
5. M. Genesereth and S. Ketchpel. Software agents. *Artificial Intelligence*, 37(7):49–53, 1994.
6. K. Honda and M. Tokoro. An Object Calculus for Asynchronous Communication. In *The Fifth European Conference on Object-Oriented Programming*, volume 512 of *Lecture Notes in Computer Science*, pages 141–162. Springer-Verlag, Berlin, 1991.
7. S. Khoshafian and G. Copeland. Object Identity. In *Proc. OOPSLA '86*, pages 406–416, September 1986.
8. Y. Labrou and T. Finin. A Semantic Approach for KQML - a general purpose communication language for software agents. In *Proc. Int. Conf. on Information and Knowledge Management*, 1994.
9. R. Milner. *Communication and Concurrency.* Prentice Hall, 1989.
10. R. Milner. Functions as processes. *Mathematical Structures in Computer Science*, 2(2):119–141, 1992.
11. R. Milner. Elements of interaction. *Communications of the ACM*, 36(1):79–89, January 1993.
12. J. Rosenschein and G. Zlotkin. Designing Concensions for Automated Negotiation. *The AI Magazine*, pages 29–46, Fall 1994.
13. J. Searle. *Speech Acts.* Cambridge Univ. Press, 1969.
14. Y. Shoham. Agent-Oriented Programming. *Artificial Intelligence*, 60:51–92, 1993.
15. R. Smith. The Contract Net Protocol: High Level Communication and Control in a Distributed Problem Solver. *IEEE Transactions on Computers*, 29:1104–113, 1980.
16. V. Vasconcelos. Typed Concurrent Objects. In *8th European Conference on Object Oriented Programming*, Lecture Notes in Computer Science. Springer-Verlag, Berlin, 1994.

Agent Coordination and Control
through Logic Theories

Andrea Omicini, Enrico Denti, Antonio Natali

Dipartimento di Elettronica, Informatica e Sistemistica
Università degli Studi di Bologna - Italy
email: {edenti, anatali, aomicini}@deis.unibo.it

Abstract. This work describes an agent interaction model ($\mathcal{ACLT}$, Agent Communicating through Logic Theories) rooted in the concept of logic theory. $\mathcal{ACLT}$ agents and their behaviour are conceived as inferential as well as procedural activities within a multiple theory space. The communication unit (CU) abstraction is exploited, subsuming traditional communication models (both shared memory and message passing) based on explicit and extensional knowledge, while allowing agents to exploit partial/incomplete knowledge through deduction. Agent synchronization is reconducted to the concept of theory evolution, by allowing agents to wait for theory modification until facts can be deduced from a CU. Agent cooperation/competition is re-interpreted in terms of knowledge generation/consumption. A coherent notion of logic consequence in a time-dependent environment is proposed. As a result, the traditional dichotomy between reactive and symbolic systems is here exploited as a feature rather than a problem, leading to an integration of behavioural and planning-based approaches.

1   Introduction

The abstract model of interaction between agents, as well as the balance between high-level agent coordination/management and low-level communication/control, are among the most critical issues in the design and implementation of multiagent systems.

The (high-level) notions of agent and agent coordination cannot be simply reconducted to the (low-level) concepts of process, and process communication/synchronization. Metaphors for communication abstracted from the physical support by which the interaction takes place (like monitors, derived from the idea of using shared memory as a communication device, or message passing, inspired by communication via connection lines) are well suited in the development of machine-level systems, such as operating systems: however, higher-level communication models and abstractions are required to capture the idea of a general-purpose, hardware independent multiagent architecture.

In particular, it is often the case that a multiagent system is designed (or described, once built) as a knowledge-based system where agents interact not simply by exchanging raw information (such as messages or signals), but by sharing and exchanging knowledge. This mainly occurs when the information exchanged by agents can be interpreted as a (partial) model of the world (the application domain), so that agents can exploit that knowledge in order to deduce new facts that are not explicitly generated, exchanged or stored.

In order to promote a knowledge-based approach to agent interaction, new communication abstractions have been proposed, such as the concept of blackboard [1] or the idea of a tuple space as a (generative) communication device [2]. The main benefits of such abstractions are related to the following properties:

- agent interaction can be expressed in a very simple way
- agents can be heterogeneous (the blackboard or the tuple-space acts as a coordination device)
- agent do not need to know each other (agent name independence)
- time uncoupling

However, what these models lack is an effective way to exploit (shared) information as true knowledge, since they provide no means to infer new information from it. This would be useful not only for multiagent systems based on explicit world-modelling and symbolic reasoning, but also for reactive systems, since reactions can take place as a consequence of an inference.

The aim of this work is to show the benefits of endowing a generative communication model with inferential capabilities for designing multiagent systems. The $\mathcal{ACLT}$ (Agents Communicating through Logic Theories) model proposed in this paper is a first-order logic-based approach, rooted in the CPU programming model described in [3]. Its key idea is to take logic theory as an abstract data type which clients can perform three kinds of operations on:

- Linda-like communication operations, based on side-effect,
- logic inferences, based on don't know non-determinism, and
- hybrid operations.

The $\mathcal{ACLT}$ model allows multiagent system designers to obtain a good balance between high-level agent coordination and management and (the cost of) low-level communication/control. In addition, this approach promotes hybrid architectures in which pure reactive behaviours can be naturally integrated with high-level symbolic activities, based on reasoning and planning. In the work we will give examples of these capabilities, by discussing in particular some problems originating from the field of autonomous robot control.

This paper is structured as follows. Section 2 introduces the basics of the $\mathcal{ACLT}$ programming model, as implemented in a multiple theory logic language based on Prolog. Section 3 discusses the implications involved with the coexistence of time-related changes and logic inferences in the $\mathcal{ACLT}$ model, by presenting some $\mathcal{ACLT}$ hybrid primitives. After a short sketch of the actual implementation, given in Section 4, Section 5 is devoted to final remarks and conclusions.

2 The 𝒜𝒞ℒ𝒯 model

2.1 Basic communication primitives

The 𝒜𝒞ℒ𝒯 model for multiagent systems is rooted in the CPU model [3], and is founded on the notion of *logic theory* as a coordination device.

An 𝒜𝒞ℒ𝒯 agent is a process generated by an 𝒜𝒞ℒ𝒯 sequential logic program. However, 𝒜𝒞ℒ𝒯 allows any process able to accomplish the basic communication protocol (𝒜𝒞ℒ𝒯 non-backtrackable Linda-like primitives) to interact with the whole multiagent system. A new 𝒜𝒞ℒ𝒯 agent is started through the `activate/2` primitive: `activate(Theory, Goal)` generates a new agent as a concurrent logic process trying to derive `Goal` from `Theory`.

A multiplicity of 𝒜𝒞ℒ𝒯 agents communicate through a collection of unitary clauses by means of Linda-like operations (*in*, *out*, and *read*). Such primitives work on a clause database used as conventional Linda tuple space, by inserting, removing or accessing *logic tuples* (à la Shared Prolog [4]). Thus, the main features of Linda as a coordination language (time uncoupling, communication orthogonality) and its expressive power can be fully captured in 𝒜𝒞ℒ𝒯.

Following [5], 𝒜𝒞ℒ𝒯 relaxes original Linda constraint of a unique tuple space, by allowing many communication units to be defined and used independently by a collection of agents. An 𝒜𝒞ℒ𝒯 *communication unit* (CU) is a logic theory, denoted by a ground name, to be used as a logic tuple space. The following syntax

```
:- commUnit world.
```

declares that `world` denotes an 𝒜𝒞ℒ𝒯 communication unit, which can be subsequently associated to any 𝒜𝒞ℒ𝒯 communication primitive. Thus,

```
out(p( t̃ ))@world
```

inserts logic tuple p(t̃)(where t̃ is a tuple of terms) into CU `world`. Of course, `in` and `read` primitives can be used the same way:

```
in(p( t̃ ))@world
read(p( t̃ ))@world
```

In addition, 𝒜𝒞ℒ𝒯 provides the full power of *unification* instead of the pure Linda pattern matching. Thus, an agent calling read(p(t̃))@world is suspended until a logic tuple p(t̃') *unifying* with p(t̃) can be found in theory `world`. Then, agent is resumed after unification of p(t̃) and p(t̃'). Analogous considerations can be repeated for `in` primitive, except for the removal of p(t̃') from `world`, occurring between unification and agent resumption.

2.2 Communication units as logic theories

However, the main feature of the logic-based 𝒜𝒞ℒ𝒯 model comes from fully exploiting the twofold interpretation of the CU abstraction. Information shared by agents through CUs can be interpreted as knowledge about the world. In this view, agents do not simply exchange messages through the tuple space, but behave as knowledge sources (such as in a blackboard-based system), each one giving a partial description of the world. Thus, an $\mathcal{ACLT}$ agent can exploit a CU in two distinct ways, (*i*) as a communication device, and (*ii*) as a logic theory describing the application domain.

The main consequence of interpreting the tuple space information as knowledge in a logic framework, is the chance to perform logic inference operations based on CU axioms. $\mathcal{ACLT}$ logic-based model provides primitives such as

$$\text{demo(p(} \tilde{t} \text{))@world}$$

whose intended semantics follows the typical inference mechanism of a logic language based on don't know nondeterminism, like Prolog. In fact, demo(p($\tilde{t}$))@world succeeds iff p($\tilde{t}$) logically follows from logic theory world.

Given that CUs contain only unitary clauses, it might be observed that a very limited notion of logical consequence is used here. However, since the problems of non-deterministic exploration of a knowledge base are basically unaffected by this restriction, this seems not to represent an issue in our framework.

The following simple example shows how Linda-like "standard" primitives and logic-based primitives like *demo* can fruitfully coexist in a multiagent framework.

```
:- unit speedyMouse.
startAt(FX,FY) :-
    read(cheeseAt(TX,TY))@grid,
    in(freeCell(FX,FY))@grid,
    speedyMove(FX,FY,TX,TY,[]),
    out(cheeseFoundAt(TX,TY))@grid.
speedyMove(FX,FY,TX,TY,RPath) :-
    activateDirSensors(FX,FY),
    demoWaitLast(door(FX,FY,Dir))@grid,
    \+ loop([Dir|RPath]),
    nextCell(Dir,FX,FY,X,Y),
    in(freeCell(X,Y))@grid,
    moveTo(X,Y),
    out(freeCell(FX,FY))@grid
    ( X = TX, Y = TY -> true;
      speedyMove(X,Y,TX,TY,[Dir|RPath]) ).
loop([]) :- !, fail.
loop([_]) :- !, fail.
loop([Dir|Path]) :- loop(Path).
loop(Path) :- relMove(Path,(0,0),(0,0)).
relMove([],(X,Y),(X,Y)).
relMove( [Dir|Path], (X,Y), (TX,TY) ) :-
    ( Dir = north -> NY = Y+1, NX = X;
      Dir = south -> NY = Y-1, NX = X;
      Dir = east  -> NX = X+1, NY = Y;
      Dir = west  -> NX = X-1, NY = Y ),
    relMove(Path,(NX,NY),(TX,TY)).
nextCell(west,X,Y,NX,Y) :- NX is X - 1.
nextCell(east,X,Y,NX,Y) :- NX is X + 1.
nextCell(south,X,Y,X,NY) :- NY is Y - 1.
nextCell(north,X,Y,X,NY) :- NY is Y + 1.
...
```

```
:- unit lazyMouse.
startAt(FX,FY,M,N) :-
    freeCells(M,N),
    activateCheeseSensor,
    read(cheeseFoundAt(X,Y))@grid,
    smartMove(FX,FY,TX,TY,0).
smartMove(FX,FY,TX,TY,Dev) :-
    plan(FX,FY,TX,TY,Dev,Path,[])
    -> moveAlong(Path)
    ; NDev is Dev + 1,
      smartMove(FX,FY,TX,TY,NDev).
plan(X,Y,X,Y,_,Path,RPath) :-
    reverse(RPath,Path).
plan(FX,FY,TX,TY,Dev,Path,RPath) :-
    getCellDoors(FX,FY,D),
    ( noDev(D,FX,FY,TX,TY,X,Y)
    -> plan(X,Y,TX,TY,Dev,Path,[D|RPath])
    ; Dev > 0, NDev is Dev - 1
      plan(X,Y,TX,TY,NDev,Path,[D|RPath]) ).
noDev(D,X,Y,TX,TY,NX,NY) :-
    D = west, X > TX -> NX is X - 1, NY = Y;
    D = east, X < TX -> NX is X + 1, NY = Y;
    D = south,Y > TY -> NY is Y - 1, NX = X;
    D = north,Y < TY -> NY is Y + 1, NX = X.
getCellDoors(X,Y,D) :-
    demo(door(X,Y,D))@grid;
    ( D = west  -> NX is X-1, NY=Y, OD = east;
      D = east  -> NX is X+1, NY=Y, OD = west;
      D = south -> NY is Y-1, NX=X, OD = north;
      D = north -> NY is Y+1, NX=X, OD = south ),
    demo(door(NX,NY,OD))@grid.
...
```

Fig. 1. Speedy (a) and lazy (b) mouse code

443

2.3 The Mouse Agents Example

Two sorts of mouse agents (speedy mice and lazy mice) live in a 2-dimensional space, represented by a $m \times n$ grid, whose cells (denoted by a pair of coordinates) are separated by either *doors* or *walls*. Mouse agent's aim is to reach a piece of cheese, located at a given cell of the grid, by moving across the grid. Mice can pass doors, but obviously cannot cross walls.

Each speedy mouse features four sensors, one for each basic direction (north, south, etc.), to tell doors from walls, assuming that there is always at least one door for any cell. Sensor activation is under the explicit agent control through the primitive `activateDirSensors(X,Y)`, which results in storing one to four facts of the form `door(X,Y,Dir)` in the CU `grid`, through an `out` primitive triggered by physical (low-level) sensors. Each `door(X,Y,Dir)` fact denotes the presence of a door allowing agents to move from cell `(X,Y)` in direction `Dir`. Instead, no explicit information is stored about wall positions.

Speedy mouse initially waits for information about cheese location coming from lazy mouse. Thus, it is initially suspended on a `read(cheeseAt(X,Y))` operation on the CU `grid`. When a fact such as `cheeseAt/2` is inserted in `grid` by lazy mouse's cheese sensors, speedy mouse can start its exploration.

Speedy mice cannot occupy the same cell at the same time. These agents wait for a fact `freeCell(X,Y)` (through a `in`) before moving to cell `(X,Y)`, and insert the same fact when stepping out from there. Whenever a new (i.e., never previously visited) cell is entered, a speedy mouse agent activates direction sensors, then chooses where to go according to a simple non-loop strategy. Should two or more directions be possible, one is chosen nondeterministically (while the others are possibly reconsidered on backtracking). When cheese is finally reached, speedy mouse outputs a fact of the form `cheeseFoundAt(X,Y)`, thus triggering lazy mouse agents.

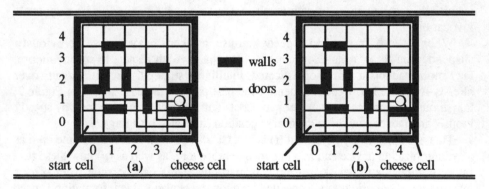

Fig. 2. Speedy (a) and lazy (b) mouse paths in a 5x5 grid

Figures 2 refer to the simple case of two agents (one speedy and one lazy mouse), both starting at the (0,0) cell of a 5×5 grid, and looking for cheese located at (4,1). The following goal leads to the activation of such a 2-agent system.

```
:- commUnit(grid),
   activate(lazyMouse, startAt(0,0,5,5)),
   activate(speedyMouse, startAt(0,0)).
```

It is easy to see how more mice could be started at the same time, even though the trivial protocol used here for free cell detection would be obviously not able to prevent even the simplest case of deadlock.

During its exploration of the grid space, speedy mouse works as a source for information about grid configuration. Such knowledge remains available in the `grid` CU. Figure 3 shows `grid` status after speedy mouse's exploration of Figure 2(a).

```
:- commUnit grid.
freeCell(0,2).     freeCell(3,4).     freeCell(0,0).       freeCell(2,0).
freeCell(0,3).     freeCell(3,5).     door(0,1,south).     door(3,0,east).
freeCell(0,4).     freeCell(4,2).     door(0,1,east).      door(3,0,north).
freeCell(0,5).     freeCell(4,3).     freeCell(0,1).       door(3,0,west).
freeCell(1,0).     freeCell(4,4).     door(1,1,east).      door(4,0,west).
freeCell(1,2).     freeCell(4,5).     door(1,1,north).     freeCell(4,0).
freeCell(1,3).     freeCell(5,0).     door(1,1,west).      freeCell(3,0).
freeCell(1,4).     freeCell(5,1).     freeCell(1,1).       door(3,1,south).
freeCell(1,5).     freeCell(5,2).     door(2,1,south).     door(3,1,east).
freeCell(2,2).     freeCell(5,3).     door(2,1,west).      door(3,1,north).
freeCell(2,3).     freeCell(5,4).     door(2,1,north).     freeCell(3,1).
freeCell(2,4).     freeCell(5,5).     freeCell(2,1).       cheeseFoundAt(4,1).
freeCell(2,5).     cheeseAt(4,1).     door(2,0,east).
freeCell(3,2).     door(0,0,north).   door(2,0,west).
freeCell(3,3).     door(0,0,east).    door(2,0,north).
```

Fig. 3. CU `grid` configuration after speedy mouse exploration

Unlike speedy mice, lazy mouse has no direction sensors. Instead, it is provided with a cheese sensor, which gets it to detect cheese position. In fact, a `cheeseAt(X,Y)` fact is initially inserted in `grid` as a result of `activateCheeseSensor` lazy mouse's invocation.

When cheese is reached, speedy mouse awakens lazy mouse, previously suspended on a `read(cheeseFoundAt(X,Y))@grid`. With respect to speedy mouse, lazy mouse adopts a more sophisticated, intelligent strategy, since it *reasons* over already-available knowledge to identify the best path. In the case shown in Figure 2, lazy mouse recognizes that a better path exists with respect to the one used by speedy mouse, and moves straight to the cheese position (indicated by a flag).

This example clearly points out (*i*) how a CU can be used at the same time both as a synchronization device and as a knowledge repository, as well as (*ii*) how these two interpretations can coexist fruitfully. In particular, this can be seen from sensor information about grid doors: generated by a low-level agent, this information is used first in a reactive fashion by speedy mouse, which waits for sensor input before moving, then as a knowledge base for a planning activity by lazy mouse, inferring the best path to cheese. Moreover, the example highlights how the abstractions defined can be exploited to lift up at the symbolic level some typical, low-level reactive behaviours.

3 Logic consequence and time-related changes

3.1 $\mathcal{ACLT}$ primitives for logic inference

The main problem of using a logic-based language as a coordination language lays in side-effect nature of the communication primitives. While the interpretation of a clause database as communication device is bound to a vision of dynamic, evolving information, the logic theory reading is instead founded over a notion of platonic, universal truth. The main issue of this paper is then how to make the two readings coexist in the same conceptual framework, by pointing out at the same time some benefits of this integration.

The Mouse Agents Example intentionally hides some of the problems connected to the twofold interpretation. Initially, nothing is known about grid doors and walls. Then, information about grid structure grows with speedy mice's exploration, and stops growing when such a task is brought to end. As a result, when lazy mice start moving, CU `grid` contains a (possibly partial) description of the grid space, which will remain unchanged if no other speedy mouse is started. In this case, such a knowledge can be used for reasoning activities with no particular caution: nothing changes in the logic theory during lazy mouse inference operations.

The problem would arise for instance in case the lazy mouse would have started its reasoning while some speedy mouse is still moving. In that case, sequential exploration of a set of axioms under evolution would pose a problem, due its cost in terms of *computational time*: which knowledge have to be considered for the construction of a logic proof in an evolving knowledge space?

In this connection, it is useful to discuss the relation between time-related (such as communication primitives based on side-effect) and time-independent operations (such as logic inference) by defining the class of the *demo* primitives provided by $\mathcal{ACLT}$.

Till now, we only said that `demo(p(t̃))@world` succeeds if `p(t̃)` logically follows from `world`. However, this semantic specification is not satisfactory at all, given that `world` is not a statically defined collection of axioms, but rather a clause database which evolves during the computation. Sequential exploration of an axiom space has a cost in terms of computational time, and the knowledge related to `p` predicate may grow or shrink during the exploration.

However, the notion of logic consequence lays on the assumption of a *fixed* axiom set defining the space of the theorems. Thus, in order to define a coherent notion of logic consequence in a time-dependent environment, we choose to set an instant when to freeze time, so as to perform time-independent activities. As a result, each *demo* operation has to be associated to a given *snapshot* of the involved CU, where to perform safely sequential proofs.

Thus, different semantics for *demo* can be defined according to different definitions of when a communication unit snapshot has to be taken to be associated conceptually to the *demo* operation. Alternatively, different primitives of the *demo* class can be defined by taking the snapshot at different moments.

In particular, $\mathcal{ACLT}$ provides four basic *demo* primitives: `demo`, `demoWait`, `demoLast`, and `demoWaitLast`. If the operation is performed at t, first served at t', and (possibly) fails at t'', then the snapshots associated to the primitives are conceptually taken at t, t', t'', and (again) t'', respectively. In detail, the intuitive semantics of the four primitives can be given conceptually as follows.

When a `demo(p(t̃))@world` operation is performed by an $\mathcal{ACLT}$ agent, a `p(t̃)`-snapshot of `world` (that is, those axioms of `world` unifying with `p(t̃)`) is immediately (at t) taken, and bound to that primitive activation, which is immediately served ($t = t'$). If this snapshot is empty, then the call immediately fails ($t' = t''$). Instead, if some facts unifying with `p(t̃)` exist in `world`, then a logic derivation is performed, using standard Prolog computational rule. If no branch of the derivation succeeds, the computation finally fails ($t' < t''$, where $\Delta t = t'' - t'$ is the non-null computational cost of the exploration of the `p` axioms).

In the Mouse Agents example, for instance, lazy mouse performs several `demo(door(X,Y,Dir))` operations (see Fig. 1) in order to derive the best path from information about grid doors provided by speedy mouse. For instance, when the first call `demo(door(0,0,Dir))@grid` is performed by lazy mouse as an indirect result of `smartMove` in order to step out from the start cell, the snapshot of `grid` associated to that *demo* operation consists of the two facts $\{door(0,0,north),\ door(0,0,east)\}$ (see Figure 2). Any further modification to `grid` theory (for instance, by a third mouse agent) has no effect on `door(0,0,Dir)` demonstration.

Instead, when a `demoWait(p(t̃))@world` operation is performed, the calling agent is suspended until some suitable knowledge is found in. The `p(t̃)`-snapshot of `world` is then taken when the operation is first served (at t'). No suspension takes place iff at t some axioms unifying with `p(t̃)` is already available: in that case, `demo` and `demoWait` semantics perfectly match (since $t = t'$). They differ, instead, when no suitable fact is found in `world` at t, so that the snapshot is taken at $t' > t$. Since `demoWait` is always associated to a theory containing suitable knowledge, the computational cost of its logic proof is never null, so that $t' < t''$ always holds.

Instead, `demoLast(p(t̃))@world` has no suspensive semantics ($t = t'$). It has actually the same behaviour as `demo(p(t̃))@world` in case no facts unifying with `p(t̃)` can be found at t in `world`: it immediately fails ($t' = t''$). However, `world` snapshot is not taken when the operation is performed: instead, `demoLast` try to exploit all the suitable knowledge of `world`, including that one generated *after* the operation was first served (after $t = t'$). Thus, if some suitable axioms exists at t in `world`, they all are taken into account. In addition, since the cost of sequentially exploring them all is not null, further axioms unifying with `p(t̃)` may have been inserted in `world` during the corresponding computation. In that case, this new information too is to be used for logic inference. Such an operation is repeated until all suitable facts in CU `world` have been tried (with failure) and no further facts unifying with `p(t̃)` have been added. Then, and only then, `demoLast(p(t̃))@world` fails. Since failure occurs only when none of the axioms which can be found in `world` at failure time has produced a successful branch, this amounts to say that `p(t̃)`-snapshot of `world` associated to `demoLast` has been taken at t''.

As its name suggests, `demoWaitLast` combines the semantics of `demoLast` and `demoWait`. `demoWaitLast(p(t̃))@world` works like `demoWait` when no suitable knowledge is found in `world`: thus, it never fails immediately, and $t'' > t'$ always

holds. However, when `world` contains some facts unifying with `p( t̄ )`, `demoWaitLast`
behave exactly like `demoLast`, by trying to exploit any suitable knowledge made
available in `world` at any time.

One example of `demoWaitLast` application has been hidden in the Mouse Agents
Example. How can speedy mouse ask for doors, keep itself synchronized waiting for
different knowledge sources (its direction sensors) making information available, and
then exploit it at its best without polling or time-outs? Its suspensive semantics
ensures that the speedy mouse agent waits for at least one sensor response when
performing `demoWaitLast(door(FX,FY,Dir))@grid`. In addition, its delay in taking
the snapshot presumably avoids that only the first `door(FX,FY,Dir)` sensor
information arrived is taken into account. In a situation where we have four distinct
sensors of the same type, having then very similar (even though not identical)
response time, all `door(X,Y,Dir)` facts relative to a cell `(X,Y)` are usually considered
by speedy mouse's `demoWaitLast`. Thus, `demoWaitLast` is actually used as an hybrid
primitive: it first produces a synchronizing behaviour, since it allows speedy mouse to
wait for at least one door to be detected before start moving. But it is then used also
for inference activities since it allows backtracking and possibly exploiting alternative
choices on failure.

3.2   Knowledge classification

However, even though this approach seems to be effective from an operational
viewpoint, it may lead to inconsistencies from a conceptual viewpoint. What happens,
in fact, if some agent withdraws from the tuple space one axiom which belongs to a
demo snapshot currently under execution? Operationally, no problem arises. On the
other hand, it may happen that some agent is pursuing a current line of reasoning
which may be based on assumptions which are no longer valid. This gap between the
model of the world assumed by an agent reasoning, and its current axiomatic
description obviously weakens the meaning of a logic inference.

Since non-monotonic reasoning [14] intentionally falls out of the scope of this
paper, this problem has been faced by adopting a simple classification scheme for the
different sorts of knowledge involved. Take for instance the grid doors information
represented by `door/3` facts in CU `grid` in the Mouse Agent Example. There, a logic
inference would have sense at any time (also during speedy mouse exploration) since
such information is stable, even though partial.[1] On the other hand, if more than one
speedy mouse is activated, they would compete for cell occupation while exploring
the grid. Competition is managed through a simple semaphoric protocol based on
facts of the form `freeCell(X,Y)` to be withdrawn from `grid` before to move to cell
`(X,Y)`, and then re-inserted when leaving it. Any (sequential) logic inference based on
such kind of knowledge should then be avoided.

As a result, the $\mathcal{ACLT}$ model distinguishes between two sorts of knowledge which
may happen to be involved in a communication via a CU:

---

[1]   Here, we obviously lay on the implicit assumption that a faulty sensor does not produce any
information at all. Conversely, we should take into account the case of false believes about the world,
which would call for more complex approaches to non-monotonic reasoning.

- partial, incomplete knowledge
- transient knowledge

The former category refers to those parts of the application domain which are unknown yet, but that can be considered (practically) stable (such as the structure of the grid in the example). The latter refers to that part of the world which evolves during agent life (such as each cell being at a given moment free or occupied), so that they cannot be taken safely as a basis for logic operations.

A possible approach might exploit the multiplicity of "knowledge containers" (CUs) in order to keep transient knowledge separate from incomplete knowledge. In other words, each CU might be defined as containing either one category or the other one, thus forbidding *in* or *demo* class primitives, accordingly.

On the other hand, first-order logic-based languages provide another way to partition knowledge into chunks. In particular, predicate symbols can be thought as a source of a primary form of modularity: given predicate p, the collection of the facts of the form p(t̄) constitutes a unique knowledge chunk. Thus, one could define each predicate symbol as representing either a transient or a partial form of knowledge.

Logic theories (CUs, too) represent objects of the application domain, denoted by elements of the Herbrand Universe (ground terms of a logic language), according to a given interpretation. On the other hand, predicate symbols (which the Herbrand Base of a logic program is built from) define relations over computational objects. Since it seems more reasonable to associate information categories to relations rather than to objects, $\mathcal{ACLT}$ allows each predicate symbol occurring in a CU to be defined (either explicitly, through suitable static declarations, or implicitly, by the primitives dynamically used to access the corresponding axioms) as being either *transient* or *extendible*.

Thus, door/3 predicate in the Mouse Agents Example is implicitly defined as *extendible* with respect to CU grid: any (exploring) agent can add further information about grid doors, and perform logic inference based on this knowledge: however, this knowledge cannot be removed by no one. This corresponds to an idea of the grid structure as being (relatively) non-mutable with respect to the mouse agents computation. Otherwise, it may happen the case of a lazy mouse reasoning on its path toward cheese, trusting some door knowledge, while this knowledge has meanwhile being removed by some other agent, making the assumption inconsistent.

At the same time, a competition between many speedy mouse agents, fighting for cell access, is based on a transient freeCell/2 predicate. Grid structure is fixed, however one given cell being free or occupied by a mouse is an information changing as the multiagent system evolves. As a result, the interaction based on freeCell results in a sequence of *in* and *out* operations performed by different agents, while no agent activates an inferential activity based on sequential exploration and backtracking on freeCell axioms, which is quite reasonable. Thus, no demo(freeCell(X,Y))@grid is conceptually acceptable in the $\mathcal{ACLT}$ categorization.

4 Sketch of the $\mathcal{ACLT}$ implementation

$\mathcal{ACLT}$ has been built starting from a SICStus Prolog [6] system. Since it has been implemented as a library which can be loaded by any SICStus logic process, any SICStus program can easily become an $\mathcal{ACLT}$ agent.

Agents can be spread over a network of machines, each one running an $\mathcal{ACLT}$ daemon. Daemons are in charge of managing communication between $\mathcal{ACLT}$ processes running on the same machine (through UDP connections), as well as on different machines (through TCP connections), ensuring transparency of the communications: no information about physical allocations of agents is needed in order to access to any CU.

The whole $\mathcal{ACLT}$ system (both daemons and agents) is built by exploiting the full power of the CSM programming environment [7]. CSM actually implements upon SICStus Prolog (again, as a SICStus library) a model for declarative object-oriented languages based on first-order logic [8]. Thus, the $\mathcal{ACLT}$ kernel is defined as an open software layer which can be easily specialized by exploiting dynamic inheritance mechanisms. More refined communication protocols can be implemented on top of the $\mathcal{ACLT}$ basic system, by simply adding new layers. In addition, each $\mathcal{ACLT}$ agent can be developed according to an object-oriented design, by exploiting at the same time the full power of a declarative language.

Even though the SICStus programming environment (as well as CSM) is available on most hardware platform (UNIX, PC, Macintosh), current implementation works only on a network of Sun and HP workstations, and on PCs running Linux. Further work will be devoted to extend the number of the different architectures supporting the $\mathcal{ACLT}$ system.

5 Conclusions

Many different models for process communication/synchronization based on logic languages have been proposed in the literature (such as [5,9]). However, the original contribution of $\mathcal{ACLT}$ lays in the twofold interpretation of the communication units as both repositories for message exchange, and logic theories representing evolving models for the objects of the application domain. In fact, $\mathcal{ACLT}$ make such two readings coexist in the same conceptual framework, by clarifying the relationship between time-related tasks and logic inference. By exploiting a simple knowledge classification scheme which distinguishes between partial and transient knowledge, $\mathcal{ACLT}$ provides a set of disciplined primitives for logic inference, allowing multiagent systems to be designed where both single agents, and the system organization as a whole, are able to perform reasoning activities interleaved with reactive behaviours.

On the other hand, despite of some analogies, the $\mathcal{ACLT}$ model cannot be properly classified as a knowedge assimilation framework [12, 13], since the flow of input sentences (knowledge coming from agents) into a theory (CU) is subsantially independent of the logical relation between the theory and the knowledge to be assimilated. Moreover, the $\mathcal{ACLT}$ scheme does not provide direct support for non-monotonic reasoning [14]. Even though it may be argued that $\mathcal{ACLT}$ may somehow be exploited in order to deal with uncertain knowledge, this issue falls far outside the scope of this work.

The starting point for the development of $\mathcal{ACLT}$, rooted in the CPU model [3], has to be found in the experimental work made with CARA [11] (where the Mouse Agents Example comes from), where the need for a unique model integrating reasoning and reaction clearly emerged. Multiagent systems built with CARA were meant to exploit the power of logic programming in advanced application domains such as robotics, where high-level symbolic activities have to coexist with low-level reactive behaviours. Further work will be then devoted to test the effectiveness of both $\mathcal{ACLT}$ model and implementation in real cases, such as the robotics case studies used for CARA testing.

Bibliography

1   R. Englemore, T. Morgan (eds.). *Blackboard Systems*. Addison-Wesley, Reading, Mass., 1988.
2   D. Gelernter. *Generative communication in Linda*. ACM Transactions on Programming Languages and Systems, 7(1), January 1985.
3   P. Mello, A. Natali. *Extending Prolog with Modularity, Concurrency and Metarules*. New Generation Computing, 10(4), August 1992.
4   A. Brogi, P. Ciancarini. *The Concurrent Language, Shared Prolog*. ACM Transactions on Programming Languages and Systems, 13(1), January 1991.
5   D. Gelernter. *Multiple Tuple Spaces in Linda*. Proceedings of PARLE, 1989, LNCS 365.
6   Swedish Institute of Computer Science. *SICStus Prolog User's Manual*. Kista, Sweden, 1994.
7   E. Denti, A. Natali, A. Omicini. *Moving Prolog Toward Objects*. In E. Tick, G. Succi (eds.), Implementations of Logic Programming Systems, Kluwer, Dordrecht (NL) 1994. pp. 89-102.
8   A. Omicini, A. Natali. *Object-Oriented Computations in Logic Programming*. In M. Tokoro, R. Pareschi (eds.), Object-Oriented Programming. LNCS 821. New York, Springer-Verlag 1994, pp. 194-212.
9   P. Ciancarini. *Distributed Programming with Logic Tuple Spaces*. New Generation Computing, 12, 1994.
10 F. Zanichelli, S. Caselli, A. Natali, A. Omicini. *A Multi-Agent Framework and Programming Environment fot Autonomous Robotics*. Proceedings of the International Conference on Robotics and Automation, ICRA '94, S. Diego, May 1994.
11 E. Denti, A. Natali, A. Omicini, F. Zanichelli. *Robot Control Systems as Contextual Logic Programs*. In C. Beierle, L. Plümer (eds.), Logic Programming: Formal Methods and Practical Applications. Elsevier, 1994.
12 R.A. Kowalski. *Logic without Model Theory*. 1993. Found at the following WWW location: http://src.doc.ic.ac.uk/ic.doc.lp/Kowalski/models.ps.gz.
13 R.A. Kowalski. *Logic for Problem Solving*. North Holland Elsevier, 1979.
14 R. Reiter. *Non-monotonic Reasoning*. In Ann. Rev. Computer Science, 1987, 2, pp. 147-186.

Author Index

Springer-Verlag
and the Environment

We at Springer-Verlag firmly believe that an international science publisher has a special obligation to the environment, and our corporate policies consistently reflect this conviction.

We also expect our business partners – paper mills, printers, packaging manufacturers, etc. – to commit themselves to using environmentally friendly materials and production processes.

The paper in this book is made from low- or no-chlorine pulp and is acid free, in conformance with international standards for paper permanency.

Lecture Notes in Artificial Intelligence (LNAI)

Lecture Notes in Computer Science

Vol. 961: K.P. Jantke, S. Lange (Eds.), Algorithmic Learning for Knowledge-Based Systems. X, 511 pages. 1995. (Subseries LNAI).

Vol. 962: I. Lee, S.A. Smolka (Eds.), CONCUR '95: Concurrency Theory. Proceedings, 1995. X, 547 pages. 1995.

Vol. 963: D. Coppersmith (Ed.), Advances in Cryptology - CRYPTO '95. Proceedings, 1995. XII, 467 pages. 1995.

Vol. 964: V. Malyshkin (Ed.), Parallel Computing Technologies. Proceedings, 1995. XII, 497 pages. 1995.

Vol. 965: H. Reichel (Ed.), Fundamentals of Computation Theory. Proceedings, 1995. IX, 433 pages. 1995.

Vol. 966: S. Haridi, K. Ali, P. Magnusson (Eds.), EURO-PAR '95 Parallel Processing. Proceedings, 1995. XV, 734 pages. 1995.

Vol. 967: J.P. Bowen, M.G. Hinchey (Eds.), ZUM '95: The Z Formal Specification Notation. Proceedings, 1995. XI, 571 pages. 1995.

Vol. 968: N. Dershowitz, N. Lindenstrauss (Eds.), Conditional and Typed Rewriting Systems. Proceedings, 1994. VIII, 375 pages. 1995.

Vol. 969: J. Wiedermann, P. Hájek (Eds.), Mathematical Foundations of Computer Science 1995. Proceedings, 1995. XIII, 588 pages. 1995.

Vol. 970: V. Hlaváč, R. Šára (Eds.), Computer Analysis of Images and Patterns. Proceedings, 1995. XVIII, 960 pages. 1995.

Vol. 971: E.T. Schubert, P.J. Windley, J. Alves-Foss (Eds.), Higher Order Logic Theorem Proving and Its Applications. Proceedings, 1995. VIII, 400 pages. 1995.

Vol. 972: J.-M. Hélary, M. Raynal (Eds.), Distributed Algorithms. Proceedings, 1995. XI, 333 pages. 1995.

Vol. 973: H.H. Adelsberger, J. Lažanský, V. Mařík (Eds.), Information Management in Computer Integrated Manufacturing. IX, 665 pages. 1995.

Vol. 974: C. Braccini, L. DeFloriani, G. Vernazza (Eds.), Image Analysis and Processing. Proceedings, 1995. XIX, 757 pages. 1995.

Vol. 975: W. Moore, W. Luk (Eds.), Field-Programmable Logic and Applications. Proceedings, 1995. XI, 448 pages. 1995.

Vol. 976: U. Montanari, F. Rossi (Eds.), Principles and Practice of Constraint Programming — CP '95. Proceedings, 1995. XIII, 651 pages. 1995.

Vol. 977: H. Beilner, F. Bause (Eds.), Quantitative Evaluation of Computing and Communication Systems. Proceedings, 1995. X, 415 pages. 1995.

Vol. 978: N. Revell, A M. Tjoa (Eds.), Database and Expert Systems Applications. Proceedings, 1995. XV, 654 pages. 1995.

Vol. 979: P. Spirakis (Ed.), Algorithms — ESA '95. Proceedings, 1995. XII, 598 pages. 1995.

Vol. 980: A. Ferreira, J. Rolim (Eds.), Parallel Algorithms for Irregularly Structured Problems. Proceedings, 1995. IX, 409 pages. 1995.

Vol. 981: I. Wachsmuth, C.-R. Rollinger, W. Brauer (Eds.), KI-95: Advances in Artificial Intelligence. Proceedings, 1995. XII, 269 pages. (Subseries LNAI).

Vol. 982: S. Doaitse Swierstra, M. Hermenegildo (Eds.), Programming Languages: Implementations, Logics and Programs. Proceedings, 1995. XI, 467 pages. 1995.

Vol. 983: A. Mycroft (Ed.), Static Analysis. Proceedings, 1995. VIII, 423 pages. 1995.

Vol. 984: J.-P. Haton, M. Keane, M. Manago (Eds.), Advances in Case-Based Reasoning. Proceedings, 1994. VIII, 307 pages. 1994. (Subseries LNAI).

Vol. 985: T. Sellis (Ed.), Rules in Database Systems. Proceedings, 1995. VIII, 373 pages. 1995.

Vol. 986: Henry G. Baker (Ed.), Memory Management. Proceedings, 1995. XII, 417 pages. 1995.

Vol. 987: P.E. Camurati, H. Eveking (Eds.), Correct Hardware Design and Verification Methods. Proceedings, 1995. VIII, 342 pages. 1995.

Vol. 988: A.U. Frank, W. Kuhn (Eds.), Spatial Information Theory. Proceedings, 1995. XIII, 571 pages. 1995.

Vol. 989: W. Schäfer, P. Botella (Eds.), Software Engineering — ESEC '95. Proceedings, 1995. XII, 519 pages. 1995.

Vol. 990: C. Pinto-Ferreira, N.J. Mamede (Eds.), Progress in Artificial Intelligence. Proceedings, 1995. XIV, 487 pages. 1995. (Subseries LNAI).

Vol. 991: J. Wainer, A. Carvalho (Eds.), Advances in Artificial Intelligence. Proceedings, 1995. XII, 342 pages. 1995. (Subseries LNAI).

Vol. 992: M. Gori, G. Soda (Eds.), Topics in Artificial Intelligence. Proceedings, 1995. XII, 451 pages. 1995. (Subseries LNAI).

Vol. 993: T.C. Fogarty (Ed.), Evolutionary Computing. Proceedings, 1995. VIII, 264 pages. 1995.

Vol. 994: M. Hebert, J. Ponce, T. Boult, A. Gross (Eds.), Object Representation in Computer Vision. Proceedings, 1994. VIII, 359 pages. 1995.

Vol. 997: K.P. Jantke, T. Shinohara, T. Zeugmann (Eds.), Algorithmic Learning Theory. Proceedings, 1995. XV, 319 pages. 1995. (Subseries LNAI).

Vol. 998: A. Clarke, M. Campolargo, N. Karatzas (Eds.), Bringing Telecommunication Services to the People – IS&N '95. Proceedings, 1995. XII, 510 pages. 1995.

Vol. 999: P. Antsaklis, W. Kohn, A. Nerode, S. Sastry (Eds.), Hybrid Systems II. VIII, 569 pages. 1995.